The Elder Scrolls IV
OBLIVION
OFFICIAL GAME GUIDE

Y0-CAY-586

© 2006 Bethesda Softworks LLC, a ZeniMax Media company, 1370 Piccard Drive, Suite 120, Rockville, Maryland 20850 USA. www.elderscrolls.com.

No part of or image appearing in this publication may be reproduced, stored in retrieval systems, placed on the Internet or world wide web, or transmitted in any form or by any means (electronic, mechanical, photocopying, recording or otherwise) without the prior written permission of Bethesda Softworks LLC. All Rights Reserved.

The Elder Scrolls, Oblivion, Bethesda Game Studios, Bethesda Softworks, ZeniMax and related logos are registered trademarks or trademarks of ZeniMax Media Inc. in the U.S. and/or other countries. Microsoft, Xbox, the Xbox logo, Xbox 360, the Xbox 360 logo, Xbox Live, and the Xbox Live logos are either registered trademarks or trademarks of Microsoft Corporation in the U.S. and/or other countries and used under license from owner.

The game, characters and images presented in this publication and associated trademarks and copyrights are the property of Bethesda Softworks LLC and/or ZeniMax Media Inc.

Prima Games
A Division of Random House. Inc.
3000 Lava Ridge Court, Suite 100
Roseville, CA 95661
1-800-733-3000
www.primagames.com

The Prima Games logo is a registered trademark of Random House, Inc., registered in the United States and other countries. Primagames.com is a registered trademark of Random House, Inc., registered in the United States.

Please be advised that the ESRB Ratings icons, "EC", "E", "E10+", "T", "M", "AO", and "RP" are trademarks owned by the Entertainment Software Association, and may only be used with their permission and authority. For information regarding whether a product has been rated by the ESRB, please visit www.esrb.org. For permission to use the Ratings icons, please contact the ESA at esrblicenseinfo.com.

Important:
Bethesda Softworks has made every effort to determine that the information in this publication is accurate. However, Bethesda Softworks and Prima Games make no warranty, express or implied, as to the accuracy, effectiveness or completeness of this material in this publication, and specifically disclaim any warranties of merchantability or fitness for a particular purpose. Nor do Bethesda Softworks or Prima Games assume any liability for damages, either incidental or consequential, that may result from using the information in this publication. Bethesda Softworks and Prima Games cannot provide information regarding game play, hints and strategies, or problems with hardware or software in this publication. Questions should be directed to the support numbers provided in the game and device manufacturers in their documentation. Some game tricks require precise timing and may require repeated attempts before the desired result is achieved.

ISBN: 0-7615-5276-6
Library of Congress Catalog Card Number: 2005908658
Printed in the United States of America

06 07 08 09 GG 10 9 8 7 6 5 4 3 2 1

TABLE OF CONTENTS

INTRODUCTION

Well, here you are. A prisoner about to be set free.

You owe your freedom to Tamriel's emperor—even as the emperor is losing his own. One last time, Uriel Septim VII has peered into the dark well of destiny—and found a stranger staring back at him.

And that stranger's future is inextricably bound up with the future of a nation.

You're an ordinary person who, whether through the alignment of the stars (as the emperor suggests) or simple dumb luck, is standing at a crossroads in history where great forces converge and push an ordinary person to great deeds.

And who's to say that your ordinary person won't need a little help?

The Elder Scrolls IV: Oblivion finds you traveling within the Tamrielic Empire's "Imperial Province"—otherwise known as Cyrodiil. Named for a dynasty that included three early emperors, it's a great green dogleg that stretches from Anvil on the Abecean Sea in the west, to Cheydinhal in the long shadow of the Valus Mountains in the east, and south down the Niben waterway to Leyawiin and Topal Bay. Roughly at its center, on an island in Lake Rumare, is the Imperial City—a stone wheel

of a city built around the towering Imperial Palace.

Now, trouble has been no stranger to the reign of this emperor, and it is hardly surprising that it should end with trouble as well. In *Arena* and *Daggerfall*, Septim's reign was plagued by treachery and dissension. In *Morrowind*, the rise of Dagoth Ur shook that fiercely independent Dark Elf province to its roots.

And in *Oblivion*, Cyrodiil more and more resembles Rome Before the Fall. The deaths of the emperor and his acknowledged heirs have lowered the natural barriers between Tamriel and the Daedric homeland—a savage parallel plane of existence known as Oblivion—and the armies of Mehrunes

Dagon have embarked on a war to claim Tamriel. You'll soon learn that Kvatch, a city in western Cyrodiil, has already been virtually destroyed by a vast siege machine. Before long, others will be threatened by the appearance of fiery gateways and attendant Daedra near their walls.

These immortal creatures have long been a source of fascination, hope, and sometimes terror to the people of Tamriel. Conjurers summon Daedra as servants and watchdogs. Others seek to court favor by worshipping at shrines to 15 Daedra lords—usually found in the distant wilderness. And every so often a mortal conspires with a Daedric prince to meddle in earthly affairs.

Dagon in particular has a long history of meddling. In *Daggerfall*, he helped Imperial battlemage Jagar Tharn seize power. In *Battlespire*, that training college for battlemages was betrayed to his forces. And in *Oblivion*, he's no longer content with playing the gray eminence behind the throne.

Why? Well, in a manner of speaking, because this god-like entity can't do his nasty thing in his own house. Imagine being the Lord of Destruction and forced to live in a realm where you can't destroy anything in a permanent sense. (Every loose

Daedric soul slips down the cosmic drain and is eventually recycled.) In comparatively fragile Tamriel, Dagon's basest instincts—his only instincts, we suspect—can get a real workout. Here, people die and do not come back. Even emperors can be removed. Cities can be blasted into ruins. A whole civilization potentially laid waste.

The task of plotting the broad strokes of Cyrodiil's response falls to the late emperor's illegitimate son, Martin, and Jauffre, the chief of the Blades, the royal bodyguards. But you are the chief instrument that they wield in the game's central campaign—a desperate struggle whose cost may at length include the lives of friends and allies. Again and again, you'll take the battle into Oblivion in an effort to remove the gates'

anchors and thus the gates themselves from Tamriel.

And yet, however desperate, that story will unfold at a pace you establish. The war takes place across a large, vibrant world, and not everything in that world is bent to the service of that struggle.

For instance, there are five lines of sequential quests. You can be a combatant in the Imperial City's Arena, work your way up the ladder and try to displace the current grand champion. You can join any of four guilds—each of which is having its own crisis. A weakened Fighters Guild is facing competition from a newly formed mercenary outfit. The banning of the black art of necromancy has set off a struggle between the Mages Guild and organized Necromancers. The Thieves Guild is under pressure from a zealous (if overmatched) Imperial Legion captain. And eventually the Dark Brotherhood is going to have some "personnel issues."

You also can perform isolated quests found in your travels—most based in the capital or its satellite cities (the "Miscellaneous" quests) or in small communities that dot the countryside (the "Settlement" quests). You can do the bidding of Daedric princes (though not Dagon himself; he's "out of the office"). An advanced character can perform the "Master Trainer" quests to boost skills to their maximum.

And, off the beaten track, you'll find other things to do, with little or no direction from the game, and other places to go. Some have elements of stories, although many have stories written only in gold, darkness, and blood. Every dark hole in the ground should be considered its own adventure. How you get to those dark holes is up to you.

You won't find public transportation in Cyrodiil. (The one boat ride you'll take is…unexpected.) However, you can buy and ride horses and fast-travel between cities. You won't often have to ask for directions. While on a quest, you'll usually know where you're going thanks to compass and map markers.

And knowing where to go is a help, because *Oblivion* is always in motion. It moves internally—constantly adjusting challenges and rewards to your character's level. And the game world is in motion as well. The non-player characters have their own routines. Many get up and go to work, go out for dinner afterward, and then go home. A number visit neighbors or other cities. Some of them do things that are unexpected. Think of every person as a small mystery. You never know what you'll find.

And away we go.

CHARACTER CLASSES: CHOOSING YOUR RACE, SEX, ABILITIES, SKILLS, AND BIRTHSIGN

In *Oblivion*, you define yourself by race, class, and birthsign. In the introduction, you select a race when you start. Later you get a choice of birthsign and class. Finally, at the end of the introduction, you get a chance to review and revise all the choices made during introductory gameplay.

All archetype classes (that is, the standard classes offered in the game's introduction) have drawbacks. They have skills you can do without, or poor matches of skills with attributes, or poor matches between skills and specializations, or all three.

Therefore, when given the chance at the end of the introduction, make your own custom class. At this time, also revise your selection of a birthsign to best complement your custom class design. Be sure to save your game. This chapter gives you the information and analysis you need to make the right choices in creating your custom class and in choosing your birthsign.

Your Most Important Saved Game

At the end of *Oblivion*'s introduction, just before you leave the sewers, you get an opportunity to revise all your character choices. *Save your game at this point, and make sure you never delete it!*

From this saved game, you can always create a completely new character and start the game over with a new character concept. If you don't preserve this save-game point, you have to go all the way through the introduction again to make a new, different character.

CREATING THE IDEAL CHARACTER FOR YOU

You can optimize your character for efficiency and power, or for role-playing charm and style. First, we show you how to make a character that works well with the system. Later, we tell you to ignore our stuffy, rules-and-mechanics-focused analysis and satisfy your inner barbarian.

This is not breezy doubletalk. Really. The best approach is first to build a system-optimized rough draft, then customize that rough draft with the personal role-playing touches that make a fun character you can love and cherish through many hours of gameplay.

The end of the chapter shows several models of efficient rough drafts that exploit the system's distinctive features. We invite you to take those and accessorize them with bits of role-playing bling to create your ideal character.

The Passing Lane

If you don't care about the details, and you trust our painstakingly constructed recommendations, skip ahead to the "Model Characters" section at the end of the chapter. Pick a model that appeals to you, make your character based on that model, and start playing.

BASIC CONCEPTS OF CHARACTER DESIGN

Read your *Oblivion* manual. Come back here when you understand what "race," "character class," "specialization," "attributes," "skills," "mastery," and "skill perks" are. We'll wait for you…

…Welcome back.

Our most important choices are the seven major skills and the race of our character. The seven major skills we choose start with high scores (25 instead of 5 for a minor skill), and we want them high so we can get to the cool skill perks as fast as possible.

Power-leveling is less important than getting the right skill perks quickly.

Here are the rules for creating a system-optimized custom class. All these rules have important and common exceptions—but you have to understand them in order to break them.

RULES FOR CREATING A SYSTEM-OPTIMIZED CUSTOM CLASS

1. All seven skills should come from one specialization. That is, you must pick one of the three specializations—combat, mage, or stealth—and all seven skills you choose should be the seven skills of that specialization. Why? Because every major skill in your custom class's chosen specialization starts with a +10 bonus (35 instead of 25).

Specialization	Skills
Combat	Armorer, Athletics, Blade, Block, Blunt, Hand-to-Hand, Heavy Armor
Mage	Alchemy, Alteration, Conjuration, Destruction, Illusion, Mysticism, Restoration
Stealth	Acrobatics, Light Armor, Marksman, Mercantile, Security, Sneak, Speechcraft

2. Six of the seven skills should have as their governing attributes the two attributes chosen for your class. And the two attributes chosen should most closely match the governing attributes of skills in your chosen specialization. Why? Because when you use a skill, you contribute to bonuses to that skill's governing attribute when you raise a level. And you want your attribute level-up bonuses in the attributes most useful in your basic character concept—Strength and Endurance for combat, Intelligence and Willpower for spellcasting, and Agility and Speed for sneaking and thieving.

Specialization	Attributes Most Closely Matching Governing Attributes of Skills in that Specialization
Combat	Six of seven combat skills have Strength and Endurance as governing attributes.
Mage	Six of seven mage skills have Intelligence and Willpower as governing attributes.
Stealth	Five of seven stealth skills have Agility and Speed as governing attributes.

Attribute	Skills Governed by the Attribute
Strength	Blade, Blunt, Hand-to-Hand
Intelligence	Alchemy, Conjuration, Mysticism
Willpower	Alteration, Destruction, Restoration
Agility	Block, Marksman, Sneak
Speed	Acrobatics, Athletics, Light Armor
Endurance	Armorer, Block, Heavy Armor
Personality	Illusion, Mercantile, Speechcraft

3. Replace unnecessary skills with other skills you like. The first time you play, concentrate on the most useful and fun skills. Then, when you've played a while and realize you've only scratched the surface of *Oblivion's* profoundly deep gameplay, you can go back and savor these other skills.

You can do without Acrobatics and Athletics. Marksmen can occasionally hop to safe perches and murder enemies in the exterior, but rarely in dungeons where it counts. And Athletics is no help at all in combat. (Exception: If your role-playing concept is a cheerful explorer who loves running around the world, then these skills may be perfect for you.)

Hand-to-Hand is fun, but this skill unfortunately cannot take advantage of the many swell magical weapons found in loot like the other attack skills can. So Hand-to-Hand is second-rate as a primary attack skill. (If you style yourself as a martial arts master, you'll want this skill regardless.)

You can do without Mercantile. Just go clean out a couple of extra dungeons now and then to make up for the cool deals you'll miss.

You can do without Speechcraft. There are relatively few places where Speechcraft challenges are blocking puzzles, and you can get around them with spells, scrolls, bribes, or alternative paths. Or pick an Imperial race character and you can solve virtually all of your Disposition-based quest challenges with the Voice of the Emperor ability.

Illusion is a fun spell college, but you don't get the cool spells until Journeyman level, and practicing lots of less-cool spells to get to the cool spells will dim your enthusiasm for the project. Moreover, since Mercantile, Speechcraft, and Illusion are all governed by Personality, forgoing these three skills together means you never need to spend a class attribute choice on Personality.

If you have Blunt, you don't need Blade. And if you have Blade, you don't need Blunt. Focusing on one melee weapon type is always more efficient.

To Specialize, or Not to Specialize: That Is the Question

In previous *Elder Scrolls* games, the strongest character concepts often depended on two or more specialties. Battlemages and spellswords, for example, were spellcasters with strong melee skills; nightblades were spellcasters with strong stealth skills; and rogues were fighters with strong stealth skills.

Oblivion's design adds greater system incentives for characters focused on combat, spellcasting, or stealth. Characters with multiple specialties may still be the most fun to play in *Oblivion*, but they start significantly weaker than characters focused on a single class of specialized skills.

Pure Combat, Mage, and Stealth Concepts

Those who want characters with a pure mage concept should be happy. This is the only pure character concept that can satisfy all three rules because, by contrast, both combat and stealth have numerous skills you can do without. The only skill you can do without in the mage specialization (Illusion) is actually a good skill that fits well with the concept, but it's also a perfectly reasonable plan to fill this slot with any other combat or stealth skill that fits your fancy.

Those who want characters with a pure melee fighter concept will be less happy. They start with two skills they can definitely do without (Athletics and Hand-to-Hand), and they can also do without either Blade or Blunt. (Their consolation is that they might as well pick some cool mage or stealth skills to round out the concept.)

Those who want characters with a pure stealth concept will also be less happy. They start with three skills they can definitely do without (Acrobatics, Mercantile, and Speechcraft). (Their consolation is that they might as well pick some cool mage or combat skills from to round out the concept.)

SPLIT-SPECIALIZATION CONCEPTS

Since they really haven't much choice, the best melee and stealth concepts tend to pick up skills outside their specialization, thus creating split-specialization characters, like battlemages or spell sneaks. And a pure mage concept, though in theory a very powerful class, is greatly strengthened with at least one attack skill like Blade or Blunt.

Furthermore, split-specialization concepts are more fun because they introduce you to more aspects of *Oblivion* gameplay. Everyone should have fun with stealth and Marksman sneak attacks, or with block-and-counter melee combat, or with magecraft and making poisons. A split-specialization concept may start weaker than a pure specialization one, but the variety of skills and gameplay options makes for a richer experience.

Most of our model characters are split-specialization ones. We offer concept models for each of the three pure specializations, but in the notes, you'll see why we're happy to swap a couple of +10 starting skill bonuses for more interesting and useful skills.

Level Up Fast with Skills You Can Do Without!

It may seem great to level up fast and get more Health and attributes. But since your enemies are *also* leveling up when you level up, this is at best a mixed blessing. In *Oblivion*, it is much cooler to gain a new skill mastery perk than to level up.

However, if you want to power-level, take Athletics and run all the time. And take Acrobatics and hop all the time. Take Destruction and cast a cheap Destruction spell constantly wherever you go. Take Armorer, spend all your cash on repair hammers, and repair every weapon and piece of armor you see, whether you are going to pick it up or not. And repair your weapons and armor after every combat.

Using this strategy with Athletics, Acrobatics, Destruction, Armorer, an armor skill, an attack skill, and Block, you will maximize your skills' uses per unit time ratio and pop through levels like a birthday balloon.

RACE, SEX, AND ATTRIBUTES

The following table summarizes attributes available according to race and sex. Attributes differing according to sex in a race have asterisks to highlight significant choices.

Sadly, only three races offer females with power design advantages. A Wood Elf with a pure thief concept featuring Speechcraft, Mercantile, and Illusion should choose a female, even at the dire cost of desperately needed Health derived from the male's higher Endurance score. A Khajiit thief might flip a coin, male or female, given a choice of trading Strength (carrying capacity and damage-dealing) for Endurance (desperately needed Health). And with the most pronounced sexual dimorphism among Tamriel's races, Argonians designed for spellcasting rather than stealth or combat will definitely be female characters.

In all other cases, to maximize a given race choice for its best-suited character role, pick the male. Where the stats differ between these sexes, the male gets the better benefit from the difference.

ATTRIBUTES ACCORDING TO RACE AND SEX

Attribute	Nord M	Nord F	Redguard M	Redguard F	Breton M	Breton F	Imperial M	Imperial F	Wood Elf M	Wood Elf F	High Elf M	High Elf F	Dark Elf M	Dark Elf F	Khajiit M	Khajiit F	Argonian M	Argonian F	Orc M	Orc F
Strength	50	50	50*	40*	40*	30*	40	40	30	30	30	30	40	40	40*	30*	40	40	45	45
Intelligence	30	30	30	30	50	50	40	40	40	40	50	50	40	40	40	40	40*	50*	30*	40*
Willpower	30*	40*	30	30	50	50	30*	40*	30	30	40	40	30	30	30	30	30*	40*	50*	45*
Agility	40	40	40	40	30	30	30	30	50	50	40	40	40	40	50	50	50*	40*	35	35
Speed	40	40	40	40	30*	40*	40*	30*	50	50	30*	40*	50	50	40	40	50*	40*	30	30
Endurance	50*	40*	50	50	30	30	40	40	40*	30*	40*	30*	40*	30*	30*	40*	30	30	50	50
Luck	50	50	50	50	50	50	50	50	50	50	50	50	50	50	50	50	50	50	50	50
Personality	30	30	30*	40*	40	40	50	50	30*	40*	40	40	30*	40*	40	40	30	30	30*	25*

The following table details the races and their specials and skill bonuses. Notes recommend which races are suitable for certain character concepts and analyze the value of racial specials.

RACES ACCORDING TO SPECIALS AND SKILL BONUSES

Race	Specials	Skill Bonuses	Notes
Argonian	Resist Disease (magnitude 75, constant), Resist Poison (magnitude 100, constant), Water Breathing (constant)	Alchemy +5, Athletics +10, Blade +5, Hand-to-Hand +5, Illusion +5, Mysticism +5, Security +10	Weak skill bonuses and weak specials. Suitable only for lizard-lovers and certain role-playing concepts. Choose a male for a stealth or combat role, a female for a spellcasting role.
Breton	Fortified Maximum Magicka (magnitude 50, constant), Resist Magicka (magnitude 50, constant), Shield (magnitude 50, duration 60 once a day)	Alchemy +5, Alteration +5, Conjuration +10, Illusion +5, Mysticism +10, Restoration +10	Recommended for conservative, defensive spellcasters. Good, balanced package of specials. A Breton has marginally better attributes for a pure spellcaster role than the High Elf, which is slightly better suited for occasional melees.
Dark Elf	Summon Ghost (duration 60 once a day), Resist Fire (magnitude 75, constant)	Athletics +5, Blade +10, Blunt +5, Destruction +10, Light Armor +5, Marksman +5, Mysticism +5	Recommended for battlemage roles. The summoned Ghost is a Level 1 creature, wimpy to start and useless as you raise levels, but the fire resistance is significant against annoyances like Scamps. Well-rounded but unexceptional attributes.
High Elf	Fortified Maximum Magicka (magnitude 100, constant); Weakness to Fire, Frost, and Shock (magnitude 25, constant); Resist Disease (magnitude 75, constant)	Alchemy +5, Alteration +10, Conjuration +5, Destruction +10, Illusion +5, Mysticism +10	Recommended for offensive, go-for-broke spellcasters. Very aggressive and risky to combine with Apprentice birthsign for very high maximum Magicka and very high vulnerability to spellcasting enemies. Choose a High Elf over the Breton for slightly better melee attributes.
Imperial	Absorb Fatigue (magnitude 100, once a day), Charm (magnitude 30, once a day)	Blade +5, Blunt +5, Hand-to-Hand +5, Heavy Armor +5, Mercantile +10, Speechcraft +10	Undistinguished skill bonuses, and Star of the West is useless, but see the sidebar "Voice of the Emperor: Avoiding the Persuasion Mini-Game." Undistinguished attributes unless you love Speechcraft, Mercantile, and Illusion skills.
Khajiit	Demoralize (magnitude 100, once a day), Night-Eye (duration 30, unlimited uses!)	Acrobatics +10, Athletics +5, Blade +5, Hand-to-Hand +10, Light Armor +5, Security +5, Sneak +5	Recommended with reservations for thief concepts. Wood Elf is a better choice for Marksman sneak attacks. Demoralize is occasionally useful, but Night-Eye is ideal for sneaks. Acceptable attributes for a thief role.
Nord	Frost Damage (touch, magnitude 50, once a day), Shield (magnitude 30, duration 60 once a day), Resist Frost (magnitude 50, constant)	Armorer +5, Blade +10, Block +5, Blunt +10, Heavy Armor +10, Restoration +5	Recommended for melee fighters. The Orc has better skill bonuses, while the Nord has exceptional attributes for a pure combat role.
Orc	Berserk (Fortify Health 20, Fortify Fatigue 200, Fortify Strength 50, Drain Agility 100; duration 60; once a day), Resist Magicka (magnitude 25)	Armorer +10, Block +10, Blunt +10, Hand-to-Hand +5, Heavy Armor +10	Recommended for melee fighters. Best skill bonuses, and Berserk is cool. Attributes are significantly inferior to Nord or Redguard for a pure melee role.
Redguard	Adrenaline Rush (Fortify Agility 50, Fortify Speed 50, Fortify Strength 50, Fortify Endurance 50, Fortify Health 25; duration 60), Resist Poison (magnitude 75), Resist Disease (magnitude 75)	Athletics +10, Blade +10, Blunt +10, Light Armor +5, Heavy Armor +5, Mercantile +5	Recommended for melee fighters. Fair skill bonuses, spectacular Adrenaline Rush. Redguard has exceptional attributes for a pure combat role.
Wood Elf	Command Creature (magnitude 20, duration 60, once a day), Resist Disease (magnitude 75)	Acrobatics +5, Alchemy +10, Alteration +5, Light Armor +5, Marksman +10, Sneak +10	Recommended for stealth fighters. Very good skill bonuses; Command Creature is good for problem-solving. Wood Elf has exceptional attributes for stealth roles.

CHARACTER CLASSES: CHOOSING YOUR RACE, SEX, ABILITIES, SKILLS, AND BIRTHSIGN

CHOOSING THE RIGHT RACE

In judging the comparative merits of the races, try to achieve the following objectives for character creation, in order of diminishing priority:

1. Maximize rapid acquisition of desirable Journeyman perks in key major skills.

2. Choose races with high attribute scores to match the governing attributes of skills needed for the character concept. For example, a fighter concept needs an attack skill like Blade, Blunt, and/or Hand-to-Hand. Strength is the governing attribute for these skills, and Nords have base Strength of 50, the highest available. Therefore, Nords are desirable for a character with a fighter concept.

3. Choose racial abilities that suit your character concept.

4. Choose racial abilities that solve specific short- or long-term problems encountered during adventuring.

5. Choose racial abilities that are at least occasionally useful.

6. Avoid races with abilities of limited value.

The Orc alone receives +10 skill bonuses in four skills—Armorer, Block, Blunt, and Heavy Armor—all critical combat skills with desirable skill perks: the best of any race. In particular, the Armorer Journeyman perk of repairing magic weapons and armor lets you repair them as soon as you start finding them in loot (at Level 3).

Both Redguards and Nords have significantly superior attributes for a pure melee role, but the Orc's early access to valuable skill perks both feels cool and adds significant effectiveness to combat. Males of these races are always better suited to the pure melee concept.

The Redguard receives +10 bonuses in three good skills, but, unfortunately, you can only use Blunt *or* Blade at any time, so these skills advance more slowly than the Orc's four combat skills, which may all be practiced at the same time.

When spellcasters reach Journeyman level, they gain access to new spells. The Breton and High Elf receive +10 skill bonuses in three spell colleges. That gives the Breton early access to the very useful Bound Bow, Bound Cuirass, Bound Mace, and Summon Dremora spells in Conjuration. The High Elf gains access to Open Average Lock in Alteration, along with many new Destruction spells, some quite potent and with area effects, like Fireball, Hail Storm, and Shocking Burst. Bretons have better attributes for a pure spellcaster role but are weak on starting Health, whereas High Elves are somewhat tougher in occasional melee situations. Males of these races are always better suited to pure spellcaster concepts.

The Breton's Bound Bow in particular is better than an Elven Bow, weighs nothing, and never suffers from wear. Since you won't begin to see Elven weapons in loot until you reach Level 9, a Bound Bow gives a Marksman specialist a delicious edge at lower levels.

The Wood Elf receives +10 bonuses for Alchemy, Marksman, and Sneak—an excellent combination for a ranged killer. The Journeyman Alchemy perk of identifying three effects of ingredients greatly enhances potion making and, most importantly for a Marksman, poison making. A female is definitely a better choice if Speechcraft, Mercantile, and/or Illusion are desired for a pure thief concept.

This gives us clear best race choices for three common character concepts: Orc for melee fighter, Breton or High Elf for mage, and Wood Elf for stealth fighter. Alas, there is no clear best race choice for another familiar character concept—the thief.

Only one race offers any bonuses at all for the two most important thieving skills—Sneak and Security—and the Khajiit +5 bonuses for each are nothing to cheer about. The Khajiit also lacks any bonuses at all for magic support, while the Wood Elf has bonuses for both Alchemy and Alteration. A Wood Elf is thus a better foundation for a thief, but if you choose the Khajiit, either a male or female will be suitable.

Another popular character concept is the fighter-mage, or battlemage. Only the Dark Elf has +10 bonuses for both a melee skill and a magic skill (Blade and Destruction), and the other skill bonuses are well-suited to a mixed melee and spellcasting role. The Dark Elf has acceptable attributes for the battlemage role, plus excellent Speed for adding Light Armor skill.

> **Voice of the Emperor:**
> **Avoiding the Persuasion Mini-Game**
>
> The Imperial's "Voice of the Emperor" magnitude 30 Charm will solve many Persuasion challenges, and stacked with Alluring Gaze (Novice, magnitude +12 Disposition), a spell any Orc can cast, Voice of the Emperor will solve even the most stubborn Disposition-based challenges. Those few it won't solve can be solved (by wizards) with additional stacking of Seductive Charm (Apprentice, magnitude +24) and Voice of Rapture (Journeyman, magnitude +36) or (by bloated plutocrats) with a judicious application of bribes.

The Zen of Choice: An Eastern Perspective on Choosing a Race

An ancient Chinese philosopher...I forget who... once said, "Fasting at the Feast of Power refreshes the Spirit and Senses." That is, there's more happiness in picking the right race than in picking the most powerful and efficient race.

Pick a race and sex that you'll enjoy looking at each time you open your menus and each time you return from a break in play to see your character displayed in vanity mode. Pick a race and sex that feel right. Be free. Be who you want to be.

Don't sweat the details of picking race, sex, and birthsign for maximum power. We give you the information and analysis so you can make informed choices, but let your heart direct your final decisions. So what if your Redguard sorcerer is a little slower to level or has to work a little harder to defeat an enemy? So what if your High Elf warrior has to scurry and heal a little more than an Orc warrior? There are many ways in *Oblivion* to build and equip your character to face difficult challenges. Thus does your character earn the greater glory. And, best of all, you've done it your way.

BIRTHSIGNS

The following table lists all the birthsigns and features in declining order of desirability. Notes give a quick thumbnail assessment of each birthsign's merits and limitations.

Of course, a birthsign's desirability depends on how it fits your character concept, and sample matchups of races and birthsigns for certain familiar character concepts are given in the "Model Characters" section.

The Mage and Apprentice birthsigns are at the top of the chart because maximum Magicka is the most difficult component of a high-level character to raise to useful levels late in the game. Many players who start with a non-spellcasting character concept decide they'd like to explore the abundant charms of spellcasting gameplay at a later stage in the game, but find themselves permanently crippled by low maximum Magicka scores, which prevent them from casting the most juicy and entertaining spells.

Anyone starting with a combat or stealth specialization who may want to experience the complete glorious spectrum of *Oblivion* gameplay at a later stage in the game is advised to start with the Mage birthsign, regardless of starting character concept, just so he or she can have boatloads of fun casting spells when the character's level is in the late teens and twenties.

BIRTHSIGNS

Birthsign	Features	Notes
Mage	Magicka +50	Spellcaster essential; reliable.
Apprentice	Magicka +100, Weakness to Magicka 100%	Spellcaster essential; aggressive.
Warrior	Strength +10, Endurance +10	Perfect fit for fighters; attribute bonuses are always a safe bet.
Thief	Agility +10, Speed +10, Luck +10	Best fit for general stealth gameplay or for a generalist.
Shadow	Invisibility (duration 60) once a day	Useful for problem-solving; extremely potent for thief and assassin quests; useful often and at all levels.
Lover	Paralyze (touch, duration 10) and lose 120 points of Fatigue once a day	Useful for problem-solving; potent; useful often and at all levels.
Ritual	Restore Health (magnitude 200, instant) once a day, Turn Undead (magnitude 100, duration 30)	Useful for problem-solving; potent; useful often and at all levels.
Tower	Open Average Lock once a day, Reflect Damage (magnitude 5; duration 120)	Useful for problem-solving; potent, but passive and subtle; useful often and at all levels.
Serpent	Four effects, all at once, once a day—Damage Health (touch, magnitude 3, duration 20), Dispel (magnitude 90), Cure Poison, Damage Fatigue (self, magnitude 100)	Useful for problem-solving; weak; rarely useful, but at all levels.
Atronach	Magicka +150, Spell Absorption 50%, no Magicka regeneration	Spellcaster essential; dicey; restoring Magicka is a time-sucking chore.
Lady	Willpower +10, Endurance +10	Attribute bonuses are always a safe bet, but less useful than Warrior unless your character concept mixes many Willpower- and Endurance-based skills.
Steed	Speed +20	Attribute bonuses are always a safe bet, but Speed only governs Acrobatics, Athletics, and Light Armor, and only Light Armor is particularly useful.
Lord	Restore Health (duration 15, magnitude 6), Weakness to Fire 25% all the time	Heal spell is powerful at low levels, remains useful into high levels, but comes with a permanent weakness. Useful for character concept without Restoration.

The first four recommended birthsigns provide attribute bonuses—always a safe bet. Shadow is a rarity: a birthsign with a once-a-day feature for which it is worth forgoing the ever-active effects of attribute bonuses.

Mage: Choose Mage over Apprentice for your spellcaster if you plan to do the Mages Guild faction quests and the Main Quest, and hunt a lot in Necromancer and Conjurer dungeons, because the Apprentice weakness to Magicka will kill you when you're fighting the spellcasting creatures, spellcasters, and their spellcasting summonings in these quests and dungeons.

Apprentice: Choose the Apprentice over the Mage for your spellcaster if you plan a broader campaign, with many Miscellaneous quests and freeform dungeon-looting, where the proportion of spellcasting enemies to non-spellcasting enemies is more favorable to you. And also select the Apprentice if pure power is your lust, because those extra 50 Magicka points make spellcasting a lot more fun…*if* you're willing to put up with the extra prep and hassle when fighting Necromancers, Conjurors, Scamps, Imps, and Dremora.

Warrior: This is the best choice for any melee specialist, and essential if relying on the Heavy Armor skill (heavy armor and great weapons weigh a ton, the best heavy armor and great weapons weigh extra tons, and you'll need lots of strength to carry it all).

Thief: This is the best choice for a stealth specialist. Pick this if you want your birthsign choice to give your Sneak, Marksman, and Security skills added punch in every aspect of your quest and freeform gameplay.

Shadow: This is a good choice for a stealth specialist with particular interest in greasing the most difficult issues in the Thieves Guild and Dark Brotherhood quests. Invisibility is also a more dramatic, entertaining toy than attribute bonuses. However, many players overlook or forget once-a-day powers, so Thief is usually a better bet.

WORTHY ALTERNATIVES

These have the virtue of being active features, fun to play with, while attribute bonuses work quietly and joylessly behind the scenes. But once-a-day abilities get forgotten and overlooked, while attribute bonuses are always working for you.

Lover: Paralyzing enemies is hugely entertaining, a fine equalizer against the occasional super-tough enemy boss. Accidentally passing out when you cast this power with depleted Fatigue is also good for a laugh.

Ritual: Getting 200 points of Health back all at once will solve a lot of ugly boss confrontation problems. But the once-a-day factor is weak.

Tower: Reflect Damage is the rare feature that works against the greatest threat to survival—multiple enemies fighting you all at once. But its effects are subtle and passive, and just not a lot of fun to play with.

Serpent: In theory, it's fun to poison an enemy. But the total effect is modest, and worse yet, it takes too long to get the full benefit.

Atronach: This birthsign has the biggest character creation attribute benefit in the game, but it's saddled with painful liabilities. It's not worth the hassle of forgoing Magicka regeneration for 40 hours of gameplay.

Lady: Attribute bonuses are always worthwhile, but these are useful only if you're specializing in skills from two separate specializations (always weaker than a character that focuses within one specialization). Nonetheless, despite its overall low rating, it's an ideal choice for some unusual character concepts.

Steed: An attribute bonus of +20 is a great benefit, but the attribute governs only one important skill (Light Armor).

Lord: This birthsign has a decent benefit burdened with a permanent weakness. Ritual gives a better Restore Health benefit, with no accompanying weakness, but only once per day. Lord is a good choice for character concepts without a Restoration skill, especially for Dark Elves who are not bothered much by the weakness to fire.

MODEL CHARACTERS

The following model characters combine races and birthsigns into ideal character designs. Use them off the rack or tailor them to your play style and role-playing tastes.

PURE COMBAT WARRIOR WITH MAGIC SUPPORT

Race: Male Orc

Custom Class: Orc Warrior

Specialization: Combat

Class Attributes: Strength, Endurance

Race Bonuses: Berserk, Resist Magicka

Birthsign: Warrior (+10 Strength, +10 Endurance)

ATTRIBUTES

Attribute	Race Base	Class Attributes Bonus	Birthsign Bonus	Start Value
Strength	45	10	10	65
Intelligence	30	0	0	30
Willpower	50	0	0	50
Agility	35	0	0	35
Speed	30	0	0	30
Endurance	50	10	10	70
Luck	50	0	0	50
Personality	30	0	0	30
Health	140	0	0	140
Magicka	60	0	0	60
Fatigue	220	0	0	220

SKILLS

Major Skill	Major Skill Base	Specialization Bonus	Race Bonus	Start Value
Blunt	25	+10	+10	45
Heavy Armor	25	+10	+10	45
Block	25	+10	+10	45
Armorer	25	+10	+10	45
Blade	25	+10	0	35
Restoration	25	0	0	25
Alchemy	25	0	0	25

A conservative and reliable design, this character is close to the warrior ideal. Although you shouldn't take both Blunt and Blade, the decent Blade start value makes Blade magic items you find useful for backup. Warriors get hurt a lot and can use Restoration a lot. Alchemy turns all those ingredients into potions you can sell, and making poisons is fun and useful. Berserk is a useful problem-solver, and the Warrior birthsign's attribute bonuses are blue-chip investments.

COMBAT-STEALTH WARRIOR-AMBUSHER

Race: Male Nord

Custom Class: Skirmisher

Specialization: Combat

Class Attributes: Endurance, Agility

Race Bonuses: Adrenaline Rush, Resist Poison, Resist Disease

Birthsign: Thief (+10 Agility, +10 Speed, Luck +10)

ATTRIBUTES

Attribute	Race Base	Class Attributes Bonus	Birthsign Bonus	Start Value
Strength	50	0	0	50
Intelligence	30	0	0	30
Willpower	30	0	0	30
Agility	40	10	10	60
Speed	40	0	10	50
Endurance	50	10	0	60
Luck	50	0	10	60
Personality	30	0	0	30
Health	120	0	0	120
Magicka	60	0	0	60
Fatigue	200	0	0	200

SKILLS

Major Skill	Major Skill Base	Specialization Bonus	Race Bonus	Start Value
Block	25	+10	+5	40
Armorer	25	+10	+5	40
Heavy Armor	25	+10	+10	45
Blade	25	+10	+10	45
Marksman	25	0	0	25
Sneak	25	0	0	25
Light Armor	25	0	0	30

This split-specialization design has inevitable weaknesses. The attributes are strong, but it will be a long time before the stealth skills reach their valuable Journeyman perks. The skirmisher has the Strength level to carry heavy armor at lower levels, but he'll need to switch to light armor as the weight of heavy armor outpaces his ability to raise his Strength to carry it. Nonetheless, he should be able to sneak-and-shoot and melee effectively. He'll advance levels slowly, however, and his sneak-and-shoot will develop slowly. A Redguard male would have identical attributes but weaker skill bonuses. A Dark Elf would be another possibility in this role, but the +5 Marksman bonus is small potatoes, while the Redguard's Adrenaline Rush is a spectacular once-a-day tool.

PURE MAGE

Race: Male Breton

Custom Class: Wizard

Specialization: Mage

Class Attributes: Intelligence, Willpower

Race Bonuses: Fortified Maximum Magicka, Resist Magicka, Shield

Birthsign: Magicka +100, Weakness to Magicka 100 percent

ATTRIBUTES

Attribute	Race Base	Class Attributes Bonus	Birthsign Bonus	Start Value
Strength	40	0	0	40
Intelligence	50	10	0	60
Willpower	50	10	0	60
Agility	30	0	0	30
Speed	30	0	0	30
Endurance	30	0	0	30
Luck	50	0	0	50
Personality	40	0	0	40
Health	60	0	0	60
Magicka	120	50	100	270
Fatigue	160	0	0	160

SKILLS

Major Skill	Major Skill Base	Specialization Bonus	Race Bonus	Start Value
Alchemy	25	+10	+5	40
Alteration	25	+10	+5	40
Conjuration	25	+10	+10	45
Destruction	25	+10	0	35
Illusion	25	+10	+5	40
Mysticism	25	+10	+10	45
Restoration	25	+10	+10	45

A very strong pure mage, with few weaknesses. The Breton resistance to Magicka compensates partially for the terrible weakness to Magicka for the birthsign. Illusion was chosen over Blade because a start value of 40 is pretty close to getting the Journeyman spells that are so sweet for this skill. The pure mage, however, lacks the attack and armor skills needed to exploit the magical items found in mid-game and late-game loot, and dies when he lets more than one or two enemies get close to him.

PURE WAR WIZARD

Race: Male High Elf

Custom Class: Blade Mage

Specialization: Mage

Class Attributes: Intelligence, Willpower

Race Bonuses: Fortified Maximum Magicka; Weakness to Fire, Frost, and Shock; Resist Disease

Birthsign: Lady (+10 Willpower, +10 Endurance)

ATTRIBUTES

Attribute	Race Base	Class Attributes Bonus	Birthsign Bonus	Start Value
Strength	30	0	0	30
Intelligence	50	10	0	60
Willpower	40	10	10	60
Agility	40	0	0	40
Speed	30	0	0	30
Endurance	40	0	10	50
Luck	50	0	0	50
Personality	40	0	0	40
Health	100	0	0	100
Magicka	120	100	0	220
Fatigue	180	0	0	150

SKILLS

Major Skill	Major Skill Base	Specialization Bonus	Race Bonus	Start Value
Alchemy	25	+10	+5	40
Alteration	25	+10	+10	45
Conjuration	25	+10	+5	40
Destruction	25	+10	+10	45
Illusion	25	+10	+5	40
Mysticism	25	+10	+10	45
Blade	25	0	0	25

This character is a spellcaster with strong Destruction spells who can also survive long enough in melee to finish off enemies with the enchanted blades he'll create, the Bound Blades he'll summon, and the magic blades he finds in loot.

Shifting to Blade gives him time to regenerate Magicka for his next spell attacks. It's a fun, active, risky mage play style.

STEALTH-MAGE-FIGHTER

Race: Male Wood Elf

Custom Class: Bushwhacker

Specialization: Stealth

Class Attributes: Agility, Speed

Race Bonuses: Command Creature, Resist Disease (magnitude 75)

Birthsign: Thief (+10 Agility, +10 Speed, Luck +10)

ATTRIBUTES

Attribute	Race Base	Class Attributes Bonus	Birthsign Bonus	Start Value
Strength	30	0	0	30
Intelligence	40	0	0	40
Willpower	30	0	0	30
Agility	50	10	10	70
Speed	50	10	10	70
Endurance	40	0	0	40
Luck	50	0	10	60
Personality	30	0	0	30
Health	80	0	0	80
Magicka	80	0	0	80
Fatigue	170	0	0	170

SKILLS

Major Skill	Major Skill Base	Specialization Bonus	Race Bonus	Start Value
Marksman	25	+10	+10	45
Sneak	25	+10	+10	45
Light Armor	25	+10	+5	40
Alchemy	25	0	+10	35
Illusion	25	0	0	25
Conjuration	25	0	0	25
Blade	25	0	0	25

This bushwhacker is a hunter and a looter, not a thief. Ranged sneak attacks and one-shot kills are his bread and butter. Alchemy lets him make poisons to add punch to his ranged attacks. With Illusion, he can Frenzy enemies into killing each other and can supplement his stealth skills with Chameleon. Conjuration gives him Bound Blades and especially the Bound Bow, in addition to low-power summonings. When all else fails, he stands and fights with a blade. This is a slow-paced, deliberate predator, without any of the wealth-harvesting abilities of a true thief.

PURE STEALTH THIEF

Race: Female Khajiit

Custom Class: Lootsweeper

Specialization: Stealth

Class Attributes: Agility, Speed

Race Bonuses: Demoralize, Night-Eye

Birthsign: Shadow (Invisibility, duration 60, once a day)

ATTRIBUTES

Attribute	Race Base	Class Attributes Bonus	Birthsign Bonus	Start Value
Strength	30	0	0	30
Intelligence	40	0	0	40
Willpower	30	0	0	30
Agility	50	10	0	60
Speed	40	10	0	50
Endurance	40	0	0	40
Luck	50	0	0	50
Personality	40	0	0	40
Health	80	0	0	80
Magicka	80	0	0	80
Fatigue	150	0	0	150

SKILLS

Major Skill	Major Skill Base	Specialization Bonus	Race Bonus	Start Value
Marksman	25	+10	0	35
Sneak	25	+10	+5	40
Security	25	+10	+5	40
Light Armor	25	+10	+5	40
Mercantile	25	+10	0	35
Speechcraft	25	+10	0	35
Illusion	25	0	0	25

Our lootsweeper is optimized to breeze through the Thieves Guild and Dark Brotherhood quest lines with flying colors, making friends and rich profits in the process. The Shadow birthsign's long-duration Invisibility solves most key quest problems. She won't start any fights she can't finish quickly and quietly, and she'll have to go around rather than through any creature that hasn't got a valuable ingredient drop. We've chosen a female for better starting Health and an easier early game, but we'll miss the Khajiit male's better Strength and higher Encumbrance limits when we need to make double trips to carry all her loot from a dungeon.

MAGE-COMBAT-STEALTH

Race: Male Dark Elf

Custom Class: Lifetaker

Specialization: Mage

Class Attributes: Agility, Intelligence

Race Bonuses: Summon Ghost, Resist Fire

Birthsign: Apprentice (Magicka +100, Weakness to Magicka 100 percent)

ATTRIBUTES

Attribute	Race Base	Class Attributes Bonus	Birthsign Bonus	Start Value
Strength	40	0	0	40
Intelligence	40	10	0	50
Willpower	30	0	0	30
Agility	40	10	0	50
Speed	50	0	0	50
Endurance	40	0	0	40
Luck	50	0	0	50
Personality	30	0	0	30
Health	80	0	0	80
Magicka	100	0	100	100
Fatigue	160	0	0	160

SKILLS

Major Skill	Major Skill Base	Specialization Bonus	Race Bonus	Start Value
Destruction	25	+10	+10	45
Conjuration	25	0	0	25
Illusion	25	0	0	25
Marksman	25	0	5	30
Sneak	25	0	0	25
Blade	25	0	+10	35
Light Armor	25	0	+5	40

The lifetaker is built for the long run, because a mix of skills from all three specialties gets little help from starting skill bonuses or race bonuses. Further, since he's a spellcaster, the birthsign must be reserved to give him the Magicka reservoir to support the high Magicka costs of spells from late-game spell lists. He should advance through the Mages Guild to qualify for access to item enchantment, and he'll need to enchant the Damage Bows, Damage Blades, and the Chameleon rings that will make his sneak attacks first-shot deadly. Alchemy might be a better choice than Conjuration, with potions and poisons, but Conjuration will be a greater comfort in the early game with its handy Skeletons and Zombies and cheap and effective Bound Dagger.

SAMPLE NAMES FOR TAMRIEL'S RACES

Race	Male	Female
Argonian	Bim-Seel, Gold-Heart, Beem-Ja, Raven-Biter, Huleenapa, Putos, Hanei, Beeleez-Ra, Jush-Meeus	Ereek-Wa, Silver-Tail, Amuh-An, Fin-Singer, Chud-Ei, Ten-Tongues, Aleen, Chank-Neeus, Wana, Duh-Ja
Breton	Etienne Rarnis, Claude Ernard, Serge Arcole, Casamir Lirian, Mathias Etienne, Alain Yncan, Arcady Donat, Albert Jerick, Ceasr Branck, Adam Lanier	Eloise Brigette, Elisa Marie, Babette Vien, Arielle Jurard, Veronique Etanne, Yolande Farielle, Alison Derre, Elvira Geline, Anya Herrick, Therese Errard
Dark Elf	Ralas Hlaalu, Baltis Llervu, Sarel Velandas, Galvon Redoran, Endar Telvanni, Neven Hlaram, Arvas Drevan, Taras Verano, Rilen Indoran, Redras Sethran	Llathala Alor, Dravona Ralas, Tilse Areleth, Melisi Daren, Varona Nelas, Voldsea Giryon, Brevasu Heran, Monesa Salen, Davilia Arvel, Aranea Drethan
High Elf	Erandur, Sinderion, Aicantar, Nerien, Valmir, Nelacar, Naarifin, Sanyon, Aicantar, Faramel	Faire, Aste, Nenya, Alanwe, Aranande, Nuralanya, Elenwen, Nirya, Essalma, Fistelle
Imperial	Hastrel Jarol, Gerich Moslin, Wariel Ritch, Jesan Genald, Carody Marillin, Serverus Victrix, Bassus Modius, Octavian Gratus, Curio Avellan, Clemens Vivio	Alessia Armus, Olana Jarich, Ruma Cavain, Jena Trossan, Aliana Lane, Salonia Viria, Narcissa Fausta, Una Armina, Lucia Axia, Cristina Nepia
Khajiit	Ra'zhin-Dar, Ra'jarr, S'rasha, Ra'farruk, Ma'jhad, Ri'zaym, Ra'mathra, Kharjo, S'rasha, Qa-Dar	Hareya, Nisha, Roshira, Tsamusa, Svana, Bashi, Ziniira, Awassi, Shavari, Urijoshi
Nord	Hans Hard-Hands, Rikard the Reader, Vilfred, Henrik the Harrier, Broder the Black, Erich, Mikkel the Wanderer, Peter, Axel, Eric Snowmane	Jonna the Wild, Gertrude Weather-Cock, Britte, Tilde the Fair, Rikke Hearth-Healer, Charlotte, Karoline, Agna Greycloak, Rebekka, Mia the Lean
Orc	Borzol gro-Olug, Burgat gro-Narzul, Sharag gro-Ghash, Kharag gro-Shurkul, Shugak gro-Aruk, Durgub gro-Argumu, Yag gro-Gamul, Shag gro-Ghola, Rogdu gro-Ogrush, Lumbur gro-Marag	Bamug gra-Ghoth, Magdush gra-Snarkum, Morga gra-Nar, Yadbag gra-Grazob, Murga gra-Shag, Snag gra-Oluk, Kharag gra-Namor, Gramat gra-Bolarz, Lurz gra-Shatul, Narzush gra-Uzgak
Redguard	Carlos, Andre, Jaleel, Cyrus, Kurt, Marcus, Amal, Brandon, Tyree, Travis	Nichole, Sierra, Kerah, Rashida, Briana, Angelie, Tasha, Relah, Tamma, Olena
Wood Elf	Eginor, Thrangor, Aranarth, Thoron, Aragorm, Bregor, Aradroth, Gelebor, Amlolas, Edhelas	Carwen, Adanrel, Taragail, Idrolian, Brathel, Celwaen, Elthin, Rilian, Adanael, Iverfin

COMBAT

INTRODUCTION

...Greywyn's blade glinted in the dim greenish light of the Welkynd Stones. The bedraggled assassin was crouched behind a pillar, listening to the footfalls of the Bandits making their way through the main burial chamber. One hand was clutching his short-sword, the other nursing the blood-soaked wound on his side. He had broken the cardinal rule of the assassin by allowing his presence to be discovered. The assault into the Ayleid ruin had been going according to plan. Slaying the first Bandits with his trusty bow was easy for a master of the shadows, and Greywyn had been able to sneak into the second level of the ancient complex with no further resistance.

But then, on a ledge high above the burial chamber, he had missed it: a simple pressure plate hidden in the white-stone rock. Using his uncanny dodging abilities, Greywyn had rolled away from the hail of darts from the long-unused trap, but it was too late; the damage was done. The Bandits that had set up camp here heard the stone plate rumble to life, and his position was compromised. The Bandits loosed a volley of arrows, and one found its mark in Greywyn's side. Pain exploded from the wound, and Greywyn fell two stories to the ground.

Fortunately, he had tumbled as he fell and was on his feet a moment after he had landed, just as his master had taught him so many years ago. The Bandits dropped their bows and drew their blades, looking for the intruder. Using his shadow teachings, Greywyn did the only thing he could—he hid in the darkness and hoped that the Bandits couldn't find him. But now they were drawing closer, and Greywyn knew this was the time to face them. Giving a silent prayer to the Night Mother, he stood and yelled a battle cry as he prepared to face his fate....

Goblin Skirmisher

Combat is a way of life in Cyrodiil. Whether it be against Bandits, Goblins, or even the occasional city guard, sooner or later, combat is inevitable. We give specific tips and tricks for making your combat experience more rewarding as you forge into the depths of the darkest dungeons in *Oblivion*. Depending on how you decide to play, you may wish to incorporate some or all of our tips into your combat repertoire. The beauty of *Oblivion* is that you're not forced into any specific combat style. Whether you favor ranged combat or like to clash with creatures up close and personal, the game allows you to develop your own techniques.

This chapter covers proper methods of equipping oneself, tips for various combat types, and then some general advice. Certain archetypes will not mesh with all of the suggestions we provide, so you have to determine which recommendations best suit your personal style.

EQUIPMENT

Nothing can end a dungeon romp faster than reaching for your pack and finding you forgot to bring some vital component with you. Rushing from dungeon to dungeon is a surefire way of getting yourself killed. It is easy and quick to fast-travel to any city in Cyrodiil and properly equip your character. Taking a few extra steps before your next expedition out into the wild can significantly increase your chance of survival.

- Carrying the proper weapon is your primary concern. Make sure that the weapon you have chosen complements your play style. If you never intend to get into melee, don't bother loading up with an array of blades; all you're doing is weighing yourself down unnecessarily. Conversely, a warrior shouldn't be burdened with hundreds of arrows. Carrying capacity is at a premium in *Oblivion*, so choose wisely.

- Daggers allow you to carry a shield and are extremely fast weapons, but their reach is quite short (barely longer than a punch), which makes stealth kills and power attacks significantly more difficult.

* Most other one-handed weapons allow you to carry a shield; unlike daggers, they generally have reasonable speed and reach, and they deal a decent amount of damage. If you wish to be cautious, this is the best all-around combination.

* Two-handed weapons have numerous benefits but just as many pitfalls. On the plus side, you will have an extremely long reach, making it tough for some opponents to get near you, and allowing you to deal a huge amount of damage. Power attacks from these behemoths are especially devastating. However, these weapons are quite slow, obviously don't allow the use of a shield, and never get the sneak attack bonus for stealth. Because of this, unless you favor maneuvering quite a bit in combat (more on this later), invest in some heavy armor, as you will essentially become a walking target dummy.

• A bow is the thinking player's weapon. You should carefully approach all targets and be in stealth mode for the first shot, and then do your best to stay at long range. Also, always check your arrow supply before you venture out. Consider bringing 50–100 arrows with you at all times.

• Make sure your weapon, shield, and armor are in good repair at all times. Some dungeons barely make a dent in this equipment, but most make you wish you were a full-time blacksmith. Always keep a supply of repair hammers, and hotkey them. This allows easy on-the-fly repair when you are unable to travel back to a town.

• Don't underestimate the power of alchemy. Use the simplest, easy-to-obtain ingredients to make all sorts of potions. Taking a brace of Damage Fatigue potions with you can be invaluable. Just pepper the opponent with arrows or blows with this poison applied, and down they go. A knocked-down opponent is a vulnerable one. Other suggestions include Damage Health, Silence, Burden, and, of course, Paralyze.

 Don't hoard potions. Use them. There are plenty to find in the world, and they're not so difficult to make even if Alchemy isn't a major skill in your character type.

COMBAT STRATEGIES

You must apply different strategies to different opponents to keep yourself alive and to kill your foes as soon as possible. Of course, these strategies are entirely dependent on your play style, so choose whatever advice you feel complements your skills. Combat strategies can be easily broken into two groups: pure melee and marksman.

PURE MELEE

This is the character who likes to run up and whale away at enemies in melee, never afraid of toe-to-toe combat. Every fight is a slugfest ending in simply more damage done to the target than sustained. Be it with a one-hander and a shield or a massive two-hander, the job gets done in brute force fashion.

• When fighting opponents with weak melee attacks (Skeletons, Bandits, or Goblins, for example), try to stand as close to them as you can to maximize your reach. This type of enemy tends to maneuver quite a bit, so make sure you keep them in your sights (third-person mode can help with this). Watch your Fatigue level, especially if you have toggled auto-run. Too much maneuvering with that feature on can drain it alarmingly fast. Reverse the drain with Restore Fatigue potions or even raw ingredients. Never be afraid to block with your shield; the damage dealt from these enemies isn't usually bad enough to wear it down quickly.

• Against opponents with strong melee attacks (Ogres or Trolls, for example), dodge their slower attacks by backing off when they swing, then answer with a few quick strikes. It's easier to anticipate when these enemies are going to strike, so you have a little time to outmaneuver them. In some cases, your shield will allow quite a bit of damage to go through from the powerful blows, putting you in jeopardy, so don't waste too much time trying to block each and every melee attack. The key is to take the foe down quickly, or you will soon succumb to the damage.

• Even though perceived as weak, casters should not be underestimated. These are the most maneuverable of the lot, so keep after them and never let them out of your sight (again, third-person mode may help). Keep the power attacks to a minimum and keep striking them as rapidly as you can. They have less health than non-casters, so you will still do significant damage this way. Taking time to do power attacks and block will just give them the time they need to unleash a nasty spell. If possible, work them into a corner where they cannot easily escape. If you are concerned by their touch spells (some of which do far more damage than ranged ones), make yourself some Silence potions ahead of time and poison your weapon with one (or simply cast it before melee begins if you have it available).

When facing off against an enemy spell-caster who can also summon, completely ignore the summoned creature and go for the caster. If you don't, you'll be fighting an endless supply of them as your Health dwindles.

MARKSMAN

The name of the game is keep-away for this character type. Sharpshooters rarely like to get into melee, instead preferring to turn the enemy into a pincushion of arrows from a safe distance. Usually lightly armored and quick, the marksman can be just as deadly as a pure melee character if played correctly.

- When fighting opponents with weak melee attacks (like Skeletons, Bandits, or Goblins), take your time and open up with a stealth shot if possible. This might be all you need (especially if you've pre-poisoned the shot with Damage Health). Terrain permitting, run at them after you've fired one or two decent shots and engage in melee when they are at about 25 percent Health. Arrows are sometimes scarce in dungeons, and you can carry only a limited number, so there is no reason to waste them on these enemies. If you have plenty of room, however, and you are very lightly armored, attempt to back off and finish them ranged if you wish.

- Against opponents with strong melee attacks (such as Ogres or Trolls), definitely open with a poisoned stealth shot if possible. Do the best you can to back off and keep firing as much as you can. Never be afraid to run away. Use any sort of Chameleon or Invisibility enhancement to do so. Heal up and return to the fight and finish them off. These are probably the most dangerous opponents for your class of fighting. Getting into melee with these can be deadly (as you are likely lightly armored). Keep plenty of healing potions handy (and hotkey them immediately). They are faster to use then Restoration spells.

- Casters are a different kind of animal for marksmen. Opening with a good poisoned stealth shot can mean the difference between a quick and a long battle. Use terrain to your advantage; interpose as much of it as you can between you and the caster while you are reloading. If the caster is a summoner, you can always use the summoned creature itself as cover. Often, the caster will hit the summoned creature in the back when you do this. Try to go for the caster and ignore the summoned creature. A few well-placed shots from a decent sharpshooter will quickly end a caster's life.

TIPS AND TRICKS

You can most likely implement many of the following suggestions during your time in Cyrodiil. Always choose what best complements your character type, and don't be afraid to experiment.

SKILL PERKS

- The Journeyman perk of Hand-to-Hand, Blade, and Blunt skills is Disarm. If you use this perk, make sure you keep several points in mind: React quickly! As soon as you disarm the opponent, pick up that weapon. Make sure you have room in your inventory to pick up a disarmed weapon. Nothing makes you feel more foolish than picking up something that puts you over your weight limit and sticks you in place.

When you're disarming multiple opponents and a few of them die, they tend to drop their weapons, making the Disarm maneuver less useful on the ones that remain. When you grab a disarmed weapon, your victim will simply snatch a fallen comrade's instead, and you wasted time using the Disarm perk for nothing.

- The Expert perk of Hand-to-Hand, Blade, and Blunt skills is Knockdown. Be careful using this perk; it takes split-second timing to execute quickly and successfully. Because it's

COMBAT

essentially a backward power attack, an advantage of the Knockdown is that you'll be less likely to get hit by an enemy's counterattack. If your Knockdown is successful, immediately charge the fallen enemy and swing like crazy. Don't bother with power attacks at this time. Get as many good solid blows in as you can. Knockdown blows to the legs of your opponents tend to knock them higher into the air than torso hits, which can push the enemy farther back. Remember that enemies take the same falling damage as you do, so use Knockdown near the edge of a cliff or on a ledge.

Goblin Skirmisher

- The Master perk of Hand-to-Hand, Blade, and Blunt skills is Paralyze. If you can land the Paralyze maneuver successfully, you've pretty much won the combat. The enemy will freeze and fall down, staying down longer than from a Knockdown. Immediately close and fast-attack as much as possible. As with Knockdowns, don't bother with power attacks. Get as many good, solid blows in as you can. A word of warning: Since Paralyze is executed by a forward power attack, failure to immobilize the enemy leaves you very vulnerable for a few moments. Choose the times for this attack wisely.

- The Journeyman perk of Acrobatics is Dodge. Never discount this highly useful perk. This is a great way to avoid ranged spells and enemy arrows, or even to give you a quick way to get to cover in an emergency (such as when a marksman runs out of arrows or when you need to heal). Yes, it is possible to roll right out of melee and give yourself a chance to put some distance between yourself and your enemy. Some clever sharpshooters can even use it to take a shot, roll behind cover, peek out and take another shot, and so on.

- The Expert perk of Block is Shield Bash. For those that use the "sword and board" method of fighting (a one-hander and a shield), this is a great perk. It is used like a counterattack; after a block you can bash the enemy and cause a stagger. Not quite as effective as a full Knockdown, the stagger still leaves the enemy vulnerable for a moment and spoils a planned attack (especially useful against spell-casters). As with similar combat perks (Knockdown and Paralyze), move in for a few "free" strikes as soon as the bash lands for some major damage.

- Using Sneak allows you access to a "backstabbing" bonus. This administers extra damage if you attack an enemy with a one-handed melee or bow weapon while undetected and sneaking. Technically, this attack doesn't have to come from behind, though you'll naturally have a much better chance of avoiding detection if you remain out of the victim's line of sight. The perks for Sneak vary the amount of damage you do when successful, so this is a favorable skill to build up. The best is the Master perk, which allows a stealth attack as if the opponent isn't wearing armor!

Putting together skill perks can result in devastating "combos." Performing these combos in the correct order deals tremendous damage to your opponent. For example:
- Block, Knockdown, then Paralyze
- Shield Bash, then Paralyze
- Block, Disarm, Knockdown
- Block, Shield Bash, Knockdown

Marauder

RANGED COMBAT

- The key to successful sniping in a dark cave is picking the enemy out from the darkness. Enemies often wander about, making them easier to pick out, so wait patiently to scan a large space for movement when you enter. Learn and use the Night-Eye spell to put dark areas and the enemies in bright, sharp contrast.

- If you need an edge in a bow fight (archer versus archer), keep the Detect Life spell handy. While under cover, you can track an enemy moving to a better firing position.

- When arrows strike, a small cloud of debris and dust on many surfaces marks the point of impact. Use this telltale sign to adjust your aim for those long-distance shots.

- Use animating doors to block incoming arrows during ranged combat. If you stand in a doorway and activate the door just before the enemy fires, you are likely to completely block the shot. This has the added advantage of giving you some free ammunition—simply pluck arrows from the door and send them back to the shooter!

- In a pinch, don't forget that you can block a melee attack with your bow. This will reduce the bow's condition, but it could save you from a potentially fatal blow. This may also give you a moment to switch weapons after the opponent has struck.

- If you can readily cast Invisibility, and stealth is your game, use this simple strategy against tougher opponents: Take a stealth shot for the extra damage, then run back and cast Invisibility. Reposition yourself and follow up with another stealth bow shot. Rinse and repeat as needed.

- Don't forget to poison those arrows! Many useful negative effects can be applied to an arrow to assist you against all types of opponents.

GENERAL

- When fleeing from combat, take the time to close animating doors. This will significantly slow opponents' pursuit.

- Don't underestimate wortcraft (picking up the raw ingredients from the environment). Eating the raw ingredients can mean the difference between life and death. Your key to victory could be underfoot during battle!

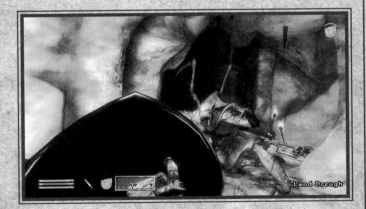

- Conjuring allies while hidden can distract a group of enemies, allowing you to draw them away one by one in the confusion or to sneak by to acquire a better position from which to attack.

- A great time to attack an opponent is right after you successfully block an attack on you and any time you see a foe stagger backward. This moment can afford you one or two quick extra attacks for significant damage.

- Take the time to watch for the enemy's power attacks. If you see your enemy winding up, you'll often have time to dodge the attack and even counter while your foe recovers from the miss.

- Study and learn your enemy's fighting style. Each and every creature has a unique fighting style. If you remember how they tend to fight, you can discover the holes in their strategy. Exploiting an enemy's weakness is the key to victory.

- Arrows make great items for setting off traps. Always carry a small bunch of them to cut a tripwire or activate a Bandit Cave pressure plate.

- Speaking of traps, if you find some untriggered ones in a dungeon, use them to your advantage if they are near the enemy. It isn't tremendously difficult to draw foes into their own traps.

- Enchant your weapons and armor. Even the rudest barbarian can complete the first seven Mages Guild quests and earn access to the Enchantment Maker at Arcane University. (The Enchantment Maker is covered in the "Spellmaking and Enchanting" chapter and in the manual.) Adding any sort of enchantment to weapons and armor can greatly increase so many facets of combat, from adding raw damage to absorbing health to disintegrating armor.

If a fight isn't going your way, don't be afraid to dial back your ambitions by yielding. Granted, authentic bad guys will ignore this action. But friendly and ambiguously disposed opponents will check their Disposition and Aggression levels and, if they wouldn't have started this fight to begin with (which is likely), they may stand down now. (You'll improve your chances if you sheathe your weapon.)

MAGIC

INTRODUCTION

"Sheathe your swords. Lay your shields on the ground. You will need no weapon and no armor, for the Magicka within you will be your guard and your guide from this day forward."
—Raminus Polus, to a group of Mages Guild initiates

Magic is an integral component of the world of Tamriel. To the people of the Imperial province, magic is not a matter of faith but an undeniable truth. Magicka flows through everything and everyone. Most warriors and adventurers wield some form of magic, either from their own essence or through the Magicka of another embedded in their equipment. It will be an essential tool during your time in Tamriel. It will keep you safe from harm, aid you against your enemies, and light your path through the dark corners of Cyrodiil.

The Arcane University

While nearly anyone can cast a simple Flare at a few Rats, a true master of the craft can bring down entire armies with a Flame Tempest. But magic, like any tool, can be difficult to master. The top sorcerers in Tamriel have studied the fundamentals of magic and the universe for decades, and many still struggle to reach the peaks of magical mastery. To add magical might to your arsenal, you must be prepared to study as hard as the great old masters. Your fellow casters will be your allies in your journey—the Mages Guild is an essential resource for all who seek to unlock the massive power that magic can grant. You must search in every corner of Cyrodiil to find the long-forgotten mysteries of magic.

ACQUIRING MAGIC

The Mages Guild retains a centuries-old monopoly on the teaching and advancement of magic. The guild has collected tomes, scrolls, and ancient knowledge of the arcane for hundreds of years, and no library of knowledge can even begin to match the combined learning of the guild. Because there is no better source of magical knowledge in the world, the guild is willing to teach spells to any citizen—in exchange for a sizable fee, of course. Fortunately, Imperial law forbids the guild from restricting access to the spells to guild members only. Any Imperial citizen may seek training at the guild.

The Skingrad Mages Guild

The guild chapters in the cities of Cyrodiil each focus on different schools of magic. Most spells of that school can be found in that individual guild. Although the guild tries to pair mages with similar magical interests together, it is not a hard and fast rule. Although on the whole you will find spells of an individual school in a single guild hall, you may still need to broaden your search for a few of the harder-to-find incantations. In addition to their specialties, all of the guild halls have lower-level spells available for purchase by those who wish to experiment with Novice- and Apprentice-level magic.

GUILD SPECIALIZATIONS

City	Specialization
Cheydinhal	Alteration
Bruma	A sampling of all schools
Bravil	Illusion
Anvil	Restoration
Chorrol	Conjuration
Skingrad	Destruction
Leyawiin	Mysticism

The exceptions to the Mages Guild's control of magical education are the Temples of the Nine Divines. The priests of the temples are trained in the restorative arts and will happily teach adventurers beneficial spells in exchange for a donation to the temple. Seek out the priests of each temple to avail yourself of this service.

ADVANCING

Although the guild can provide anyone with the knowledge to cast spells, the only way to gain magical power is through practice and study. No student of the magical arts ever reaches Master level through talent alone. The surest method to advance your magical ability and gain access to high-level magic is to tap into your own Magicka stores as often as possible. Fortunately for ambitious mages, some tricks can be employed to advance through the ranks faster.

Beware, you will face powerful magic from your enemies.

Rather than the power of a particular spell, it is the frequency with which you use magic that governs your advancement. Frequency of use conveys the knowledge of the workings of magic. Just as a sword fighter gains skill through practice and technique rather than the quality of the sword that is wielded, so too does a mage advance in his or her chosen art.

In addition to practice, magic can only be advanced when it serves a purpose. Lighting trees on fire and healing rocks will never advance your skills, no matter how entertaining it might be. To learn something from the casting, the mage must affect a target. Targets may be enemies or even the caster (in cases where the spells are beneficial).

However, there are reports of mages so desperate to increase their destructive power that they have created low-magnitude Destruction spells that will burn their own flesh. These mages seek greater understanding of the mysteries of Destruction magic by studying its effects firsthand. While a clever mage will combine this practice with a shield against fire damage, not all have access to such magic, and there are twisted casters wandering the world, driven mad from the pain and scars of their dedication to the destructive arts.

Note that while not all mages inflict suffering on their own bodies in the name of learning, the ability to create spells via the Mages Guild is invaluable to any caster wishing to advance quickly through the magical ranks. Low-power spells of any

type can be created, allowing the caster to practice with an individual school of magic easily and often. Traveling is an excellent time to practice. A low-duration life-detecting spell cast continually during a journey on foot will surely raise your knowledge of Mysticism by the time you reach your destination. It is a good idea to create low-cost practice spells for each of the schools of magic that you study.

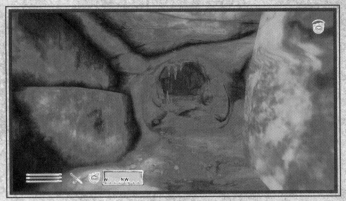

Night-Eye

MAGIC AND COMBAT

An adventurer's life is one of violence and bloodshed. However, with the proper application of your magical skills, you will always triumph over those who wish you harm. The most important thing to remember is that, unlike a brutish warrior who must rely on sword-arm strength, an adventurer with a strong knowledge of magic has options.

This versatility is the mage's greatest asset. Any novice can cast a few Flash Bolts at a Bandit, but when you first cast a Weakness to Fire spell on that Bandit, you give yourself a greater edge. Is a Zombie giving you trouble? Try casting Turn Undead and following up with physical attacks as the fleshbag runs from you. A wise mage uses all available tools.

Burn!

To take advantage of this versatility, an astute caster will make frequent use of the hotkeys to provide fast access to a variety of spells. Switching frequently between spells will help you achieve the maximum effect and give you the edge you need to overcome your opponents. Plan carefully when assigning your hotkeys, and always keep a healing spell handy. Remember that you can also assign potions to hotkeys. This will ensure that you have enough Magicka to last through any combat.

DEFENSIVE COMBAT

The first lesson that is taught to Imperial Battlemage Academy candidates is the vital importance of staying light on one's feet. Because armor limits the effectiveness of your magic, many practitioners of the arcane arts prefer to eschew armor in favor of lighter clothing. This keeps the mage mobile, allowing the spells to be as effective as possible. Unfortunately, this leaves the mage open to attack. For that reason, be sure to avoid direct confrontations with your enemies. While you may be able to unravel the fabric of your enemy's very being, a sword will cleave you all the same if you are caught unaware, so stay alert and keep your distance.

Fortunately, Magicka can be woven into many protective spells to ensure a mage's safety. Even mages that choose to wear armor would do well to make heavy use of the shield spells, as they provide extra protection for both the armored adventurer and the robe-wearing mage. Be sure to cast shield-effect spells whenever you anticipate entering a conflict. Although they can cost you a heavy amount of Magicka, they often last through an entire battle. Keep an eye on your timers; being caught in the fray when the shield spell expires could be very dangerous.

Danger can lurk anywhere.

You must protect yourself not only from physical damage from swords, clubs, and the fangs of creatures, but also from the elemental damage of Daedra, Atronachs, and enemy spellcasters. To keep yourself from being consumed in the fire of an enemy's Heat Blast, you can employ spells to ensure that you will survive an elemental adversary that stands in your path. Like the shield spells, the elemental resistance spells are useful to both armored and unarmored adventurers.

Never underestimate the value of having a companion to fight alongside you. A creature summoned with Conjuration magic can distract enemies, giving you the freedom to maneuver into the best position for an attack. Be warned: Summoned creatures will attack any enemy that they encounter. If you're not careful, following your summoned creature into combat could leave you overwhelmed with enemies.

To defend yourself against enemy casters, use Mysticism to reflect their spells back at them or even to absorb Magicka from spells meant to harm you.

And finally, if the fight becomes too much for you, some spells can help you escape and regroup. Frightening an enemy away with a demoralizing spell or turning an undead opponent can buy you the precious seconds that you need for an escape. An adventurer who is well trained in Illusion magic can even turn invisible.

Magic offers a number of options to keep you alive. Mages and sorcerers throughout Tamriel's history have outlasted and outlived their opponents through clever combinations of spells designed to mitigate damage and keep the fight alive.

ON THE ATTACK

When one thinks of a master mage, the image that comes to mind is of raw power surging in waves through the caster as fire, pain, and death rain down on enemies. Adventurers who choose to concentrate in magic often do so because of the lust for power that rises at the mere thought of the inherent destructive ability in the more violent schools of magic. Imperial battlemages study the school of Destruction more than any other school.

Destruction magic is the most common and most useful of the magical schools when it comes to combat. Because of its ability to inflict raw elemental damage on your enemies, it is the staple of adventurers with a predilection for solving their problems through violence.

Bandits, beware.

Destruction magic can be aimed at a distant target or used for up-close attacks. While many mages and sorcerers prefer to keep their distance from their enemies, spellswords prefer to

MAGIC

use touch attacks to supplement the damage done by their weapons. Because touch spells are a smaller drain on Magicka than targeted spells, they are recommended for melee fighters who may not be blessed with a great amount of intelligence and willpower. No matter the tactic you choose, you must still be able to hit your target. Magic can provide you with might, but you must guide it to its destination. Many who rely on magic as their primary attack form reassign their casting key to replace their primary attack key.

A word of caution regarding Destruction magic—many enemies and monsters have resistance or weaknesses to one or more of the elemental damage types. Carefully watch how much damage your spells are inflicting. If it seems as though you aren't doing as much damage as you should, switch tactics. In the rare event that you encounter an enemy who is resistant to all three of the damage types, you can resort to damaging their health directly. Although it is expensive to cast, the Damage Health effect can be resisted only by magic resistance and can swing the fight with a resistant creature in your favor.

However, if an enemy has no weaknesses to elemental damage, the school of Destruction can inflict those weaknesses on enemies. Weaknesses to elements come in all three elemental damage types and greatly increase the effectiveness of their corresponding damage spells. Definitely increase your enemies' vulnerability to your spells.

Seek out allies.

Magic's ability to benefit a caster during combat goes far beyond the school of Destruction. Even a heavy fighter can benefit from the weightless heavy armor provided by the school of Conjuration. A mage skilled in Illusion can force a crowd of enemies to flee in terror, then deal with them one at a time. Better yet, an illusionist can convince enemies to turn on one another and ignore the mage completely.

SUPPORT

There is the moment before battle in which all conflict is decided. Some say that wars are often decided before the battle begins and that the commander who is the most prepared will inevitably be the victor. Many spells will support you throughout a fight, allowing you to outlast and outlive your opponents. Using these spells can benefit a caster of any type, regardless of preferred style.

The Restoration and Alteration schools both have important spells to fortify your skills and attributes for the coming fight. Boosting your Health so that you can last longer is very important. Even a melee fighter can benefit from an increased Fatigue.

Spells that detect life can be vital to your survival. You can track the movements of the creatures around you, even through walls. This information is priceless when planning an infiltration. Combine the Detect Life effect with Chameleon and you've got a perfect combination for a stealthy approach to any situation, illegal or otherwise.

Mysticism will help you in your adventures.

Light spells bring illumination to the shadows where your enemies hide. Far too many mages have been lost in the underground because they could not see an enemy until it was too late. The light spells last a long time and, unlike a torch, leave both of your hands free to use whatever items you wish.

Finally, Telekinesis can lure enemies into their own traps. Try triggering a tripwire with a remotely controlled item. There is nothing quite as delicious as witnessing the irony of a Bandit undone with his own trap.

STANDARD SPELLS

Many standard spells are available to you. The spells acquired through quests and special events will expand this list, but this section covers the standard spells that have been approved by the Mages Guild for public use.

ALTERATION

Alteration magic can be used to change the fundamentals of physics and biology. It can harden the caster's skin until it is like armor, cause a lock to pop open without a key, or burden an enemy with invisible weight. Alteration magic's greatest strengths are outside of combat; many thieves and assassins make use of this school to benefit their careers.

ALTERATION SPELLS

Name	Skill Level	Range	Effect
Aegis	Master	Self	Gain 50 points of armor for 1 minute
Beast of Burden	Master	Self	Allows the caster to carry 250 additional pounds for 6 minutes
Burdening Touch	Novice	Touch	Increases the target's Encumbrance by 15 for 15 seconds
Defend	Apprentice	Self	Gain 15 points of armor for 30 seconds
Ease Burden	Apprentice	Self	Allows the caster to carry 50 additional pounds for 4 minutes
Electric Shell	Apprentice	Self	Caster gains 10 points of armor and 10% resistance to shock for 30 seconds
Encumbering Touch	Journeyman	Touch	Increases the target's Encumbrance by 50 for 25 seconds
Fire Shield	Expert	Self	Caster gains 30 points of armor and 30% resistance to fire for 30 seconds
Flame Shield	Master	Self	Caster gains 30 points of armor and 30% resistance to fire for 1 minute
Frost Shell	Apprentice	Self	Caster gains 10 points of armor and 10% resistance to frost for 30 seconds
Glacial Wall	Expert	Self	Caster gains 30 points of armor and 30% resistance to frost for 1 minute
Guard	Journeyman	Self	Gain 30 points of armor for 30 seconds
Heat Shell	Apprentice	Self	Caster gains 10 points of armor and 10% resistance to fire for 30 seconds
Hindering Touch	Apprentice	Touch	Increases the target's Encumbrance by 35 for 20 seconds
Ice Shield	Journeyman	Self	Caster gains 30 points of armor and 30% resistance to frost for 30 seconds
Lighten Load	Journeyman	Self	Allows the caster to carry 75 additional pounds for 5 minutes
Lightning Shield	Journeyman	Self	Caster gains 30 points of armor and 30% resistance to shock for 30 seconds
Lightning Wall	Expert	Self	Caster gains 30 points of armor and 30% resistance to shock for 1 minute
Open Average Lock	Journeyman	Target	Automatically opens a lock of average difficulty
Open Easy Lock	Apprentice	Target	Automatically opens a lock of easy difficulty
Open Hard Lock	Expert	Target	Automatically opens a lock of hard difficulty
Open Very Easy Lock	Novice	Target	Automatically opens a lock of very easy difficulty
Oppressing Grasp	Expert	Touch	Increases the target's Encumbrance by 75 for 30 seconds
Pack Mule	Expert	Self	Allows the caster to carry 150 additional pounds for 5 minutes
Protect	Novice	Self	Gain 15 points of armor for 30 seconds
Protect Other	Novice	Touch	Target gains 10 points of armor for 20 seconds
Sea Stride	Apprentice	Self	Walk on water for 30 seconds
Shield	Expert	Self	Gain 40 points of armor for 30 seconds
Water Breathing	Apprentice	Self	Breathe underwater for 30 seconds
Weight of the World	Expert	Target	Increases the target's Encumbrance by 60 for 30 seconds

CONJURATION

Calling on creatures from other worlds and creating items out of Magicka are two of the most beneficial tools a caster has. Because of this, casters of all types make use of the school of Conjuration. Dedicated casters and those dedicated to stealth are helped by having creatures to draw enemy fire, and heavy fighters can enjoy the freedom of movement that conjured armor provides.

CONJURATION SPELLS

Name	Skill Level	Range	Effect
Bound Boots	Novice	Self	Summons and equips a pair of Daedric boots for 20 seconds
Bound Bow	Journeyman	Self	Summons and equips a Daedric bow for 15 seconds
Bound Cuirass	Journeyman	Self	Summons and equips a Daedric cuirass for 60 seconds
Bound Dagger	Novice	Self	Summons and equips a Daedric dagger for 15 seconds
Bound Gauntlets	Novice	Self	Summons and equips a pair of Daedric gauntlets for 60 seconds
Bound Greaves	Apprentice	Self	Summons and equips Daedric greaves for 60 seconds
Bound Helmet	Novice	Self	Summons and equips a Daedric helmet for 20 seconds
Bound Mace	Journeyman	Self	Summons and equips a Daedric mace for 15 seconds
Bound Shield	Expert	Self	Summons and equips a Daedric shield for 120 seconds
Bound Sword	Expert	Self	Summons and equips a Daedric longsword for 15 seconds
Bound War Axe	Apprentice	Self	Summons and equips a Daedric war axe for 15 seconds
Dismiss Undead	Expert	Target	Greatly increases the chance that an undead will flee for 1 minute
Rebuke Undead	Journeyman	Target	Increases the chance that an undead will flee for 30 seconds
Repulse Undead	Apprentice	Target	Moderately increases the chance that an undead will flee for 30 seconds
Summon Clannfear	Expert	Self	Summons a Clannfear to fight for the caster for 45 seconds
Summon Daedroth	Expert	Self	Summons a Daedroth to fight for the caster for 30 seconds
Summon Dremora	Journeyman	Self	Summons a Dremora to fight for the caster for 20 seconds
Summon Dremora Lord	Master	Self	Summons a Dremora Lord to fight for the caster for 35 seconds
Summon Faded Wraith	Expert	Self	Summons a Faded Wraith to fight for the caster for 40 seconds
Summon Flame Atronach	Journeyman	Self	Summons a Flame Atronach to fight for the caster for 30 seconds
Summon Frost Atronach	Expert	Self	Summons a Frost Atronach to fight for the caster for 35 seconds
Summon Ghost	Apprentice	Self	Summons a Ghost to fight for the caster for 25 seconds
Summon Gloom Wraith	Master	Self	Summons a Gloom Wraith to fight for the caster for 25 seconds
Summon Headless Zombie	Journeyman	Self	Summons a Headless Zombie to fight for the caster for 25 seconds
Summon Lich	Master	Self	Summons a Lich to fight for the caster for 20 seconds
Summon Scamp	Apprentice	Self	Summons a Scamp to fight for the caster for 20 seconds

CONJURATION SPELLS CONT.

Name	Skill Level	Range	Effect
Summon Skeleton	Apprentice	Self	Summons a Skeleton to fight for the caster for 40 seconds
Summon Skeleton Champion	Expert	Self	Summons a Skeleton Champion to fight for the caster for 40 seconds
Summon Skeleton Guardian	Journeyman	Self	Summons a Skeleton Guardian to fight for the caster for 50 seconds
Summon Skeleton Hero	Expert	Self	Summons a Skeleton Hero to fight for the caster for 25 seconds
Summon Spider Daedra	Expert	Self	Summons a Spider Daedra to fight for the caster for 20 seconds
Summon Storm Atronach	Master	Self	Summons a Storm Atronach to fight for the caster for 40 seconds
Summon Xivilai	Master	Self	Summons a Xivilai to fight for the caster for 30 seconds
Summon Zombie	Apprentice	Self	Summons a Zombie to fight for the caster for 30 seconds
Turn Undead	Novice	Target	Slightly increases the chance that an undead will flee for 30 seconds

DESTRUCTION

Destruction is by far the most widely used school of magic in all of Tamriel. While most choose to concentrate on dealing out elemental damage, the school of Destruction has a number of useful spells beyond those. A clever caster can hinder an enemy, destroy weapons and armor, and weaken him or her to the point of collapse.

DESTRUCTION SPELLS

Name	Skill Level	Range	Effect
Arctic Blow	Expert	Touch	Deals 80 points of frost damage to a single target
Blazing Spear	Journeyman	Target	Deals 35 points of fire damage to a single target
Blizzard	Master	Target	Deals 75 points of frost damage to all creatures in a 20-foot radius
Burning Touch	Novice	Touch	Deals 10 points of fire damage to a single target
Cold Touch	Novice	Touch	Deals 15 points of frost damage to a single target
Corrode Armor	Apprentice	Touch	Deals 30 points of damage to an enemy's armor
Corrode Weapon	Journeyman	Touch	Deals 60 points of damage to an enemy's weapon
Curse of Weakness	Novice	Touch	Deals 15 points of Fatigue damage to a single target
Damage Attribute: Agility	Novice	Target	Deals 1 point of Agility damage to a single target
Damage Attribute: Endurance	Novice	Target	Deals 1 point of Endurance damage to a single target
Damage Attribute: Intelligence	Journeyman	Target	Deals 5 points of Intelligence damage to a single target
Damage Attribute: Luck	Novice	Target	Deals 1 point of Luck damage to a single target
Damage Attribute: Speed	Apprentice	Target	Deals 3 points of Speed damage to a single target
Damage Attribute: Strength	Journeyman	Target	Deals 5 points of Strength damage to a single target
Damage Attribute: Willpower	Apprentice	Target	Deals 3 points of Willpower damage to a single target
Dire Enervation	Expert	Target	Deals 60 points of temporary Fatigue damage for 30 seconds
Dire Wound	Journeyman	Target	Deals 30 points of temporary Health damage for 10 seconds
Disintegrate Armor	Expert	Touch	Deals 100 points of damage to an enemy's armor
Disintegrate Weapon	Master	Touch	Deals 150 points of damage to an enemy's weapon
Drain Attribute: Agility	Novice	Target	Deals 5 points of temporary Agility damage for 20 seconds
Drain Attribute: Endurance	Novice	Target	Deals 5 points of temporary Endurance damage for 20 seconds
Drain Attribute: Intelligence	Journeyman	Target	Deals 15 points of temporary Intelligence damage for 25 seconds
Drain Attribute: Luck	Novice	Target	Deals 5 points of temporary Luck damage for 20 seconds
Drain Attribute: Speed	Apprentice	Target	Deals 10 points of temporary Speed damage for 20 seconds
Drain Attribute: Willpower	Apprentice	Target	Deals 10 points of temporary Willpower damage for 20 seconds
Drain Skill: Alteration	Journeyman	Target	Reduces Alteration skill by 15 for 25 seconds
Drain Skill: Blade	Expert	Target	Reduces Blade skill by 20 for 45 seconds
Drain Skill: Conjuration	Expert	Target	Reduces Conjuration skill by 20 for 45 seconds
Drain Skill: Destruction	Journeyman	Target	Reduces Destruction skill by 15 for 25 seconds
Drain Skill: Hand-to-Hand	Journeyman	Target	Reduces Hand-to-Hand skill by 15 for 25 seconds
Drain Skill: Heavy Armor	Journeyman	Target	Reduces Heavy Armor skill by 15 for 25 seconds
Drain Skill: Illusion	Apprentice	Target	Reduces Illusion skill by 10 for 20 seconds
Drain Skill: Marksman	Apprentice	Target	Reduces Marksman skill by 10 for 20 seconds
Drain Skill: Restoration	Expert	Target	Reduces Restoration skill by 20 for 45 seconds
Electric Touch	Apprentice	Touch	Deals 25 points of shock damage to a single target
Electrocution	Master	Target	Deals 110 points of shock damage to a single target
Entropic Bolt	Apprentice	Target	Deals 10 points of Health damage to a single target
Entropic Touch	Novice	Touch	Deals 5 points of Health damage to a single target
Fireball	Journeyman	Target	Deals 30 points of fire damage to all targets in a 10-foot radius
Fire Storm	Expert	Target	Deals 50 points of fire damage to all targets in a 15-foot radius
Flame Tempest	Master	Target	Deals 75 points of fire damage to all targets in a 15-foot radius
Flame Touch	Apprentice	Touch	Deals 25 points of fire damage to a single target
Flare	Novice	Target	Deals 6 points of fire damage to a single target
Flash Bolt	Apprentice	Target	Deals 20 points of fire damage to a single target
Frost Bolt	Journeyman	Target	Deals 35 points of frost damage to a single target
Frost Touch	Apprentice	Touch	Deals 25 points of frost damage to a single target
Greater Magicka Drain	Journeyman	Touch	Deals 50 points of temporary Magicka damage for 30 seconds

DESTRUCTION SPELLS CONT.

Name	Skill Level	Range	Effect
Hailstone	Apprentice	Target	Deals 20 points of frost damage to a single target
Hail Storm	Journeyman	Target	Deals 30 points of frost damage to all creatures in a 10-foot radius
Heat Blast	Expert	Target	Deals 70 points of fire damage to a single target
Ice Blast	Master	Target	Deals 110 points of frost damage to a single target
Ice Bolt	Expert	Target	Deals 70 points of frost damage to a single target
Ice Storm	Expert	Target	Deals 50 points of frost damage to all creatures in a 15-foot radius
Immolating Blast	Master	Target	Deals 110 points of fire damage to a single target
Legendary Magicka Drain	Master	Touch	Deals 120 points of temporary Magicka damage for 1 minute
Lightning Ball	Expert	Target	Deals 40 points of shock damage over 2 seconds to all creatures in a 20-foot radius
Lightning Blast	Expert	Target	Deals 70 points of shock damage to a single target
Lightning Bolt	Journeyman	Target	Deals 35 points of shock damage to a single target
Lightning Grasp	Journeyman	Touch	Deals 45 points of shock damage to a single target
Lightning Storm	Master	Target	Deals 60 points of shock damage over 2 seconds to all creatures in a 20-foot radius
Lightning Surge	Expert	Touch	Deals 80 points of shock damage to a single target
Magicka Drain	Apprentice	Touch	Deals 30 points of temporary Magicka damage for 30 seconds
Major Enervation	Apprentice	Target	Deals 30 points of temporary Fatigue damage for 15 seconds
Major Wound	Apprentice	Target	Deals 15 points of temporary Health damage for 10 seconds
Minor Enervation	Novice	Target	Deals 15 points of temporary Fatigue damage for 15 seconds
Minor Wound	Novice	Target	Deals 5 points of temporary Health damage for 10 seconds
Scorching Blow	Expert	Touch	Deals 80 points of fire damage to a single target
Searing Grasp	Journeyman	Touch	Deals 45 points of fire damage to a single target
Sever Magicka	Apprentice	Target	Deals 40 points of Magicka damage to a single target
Shock	Apprentice	Target	Deals 20 points of shock damage to a single target
Shocking Burst	Journeyman	Target	Deals 30 points of shock damage over 2 seconds to all creatures in a 20-foot radius
Shocking Touch	Novice	Touch	Deals 10 points of shock damage to a single target
Snowball	Novice	Target	Deals 10 points of frost damage to a single target
Spark	Novice	Target	Deals 10 points of shock damage to a single target
Superior Magicka Drain	Expert	Touch	Deals 100 points of temporary Magicka damage for 30 seconds
Superior Wound	Expert	Target	Deals 50 points of temporary Health damage for 10 seconds
Weakness to Fire	Apprentice	Target	Target is inflicted with a 25% weakness to fire for 30 seconds
Weakness to Frost	Apprentice	Target	Target is inflicted with a 25% weakness to frost for 30 seconds
Weakness to Magicka	Journeyman	Target	Target is inflicted with a 25% weakness to all Magicka for 30 seconds
Weakness to Poison	Apprentice	Target	Target is inflicted with a 25% weakness to poison effects for 30 seconds
Weakness to Shock	Apprentice	Target	Target is inflicted with a 25% weakness to shock for 30 seconds
Winter's Grasp	Journeyman	Touch	Deals 45 points of frost damage to a single target
Withering Bolt	Expert	Target	Deals 40 points of Health damage to a single target
Withering Touch	Journeyman	Touch	Deals 30 points of Health damage to a single target

ILLUSION

Things are rarely as they seem in Tamriel, and casters who practice the deceptive art of Illusion prefer it that way. Illusion is an excellent talent for a caster who wishes to swindle a merchant, sneak around undetected, or drive a creature into a frenzy to escape in the confusion.

ILLUSION SPELLS

Name	Skill Level	Range	Effect
Alluring Gaze	Novice	Target	Increases the Disposition of a character up to his/her 3rd level for 30 seconds
Beguiling Touch	Novice	Touch	Increases the Disposition of a character up to his/her 3rd level for 30 seconds
Calming Touch	Journeyman	Touch	Reduces aggression of target creature by 30 for 20 seconds
Candlelight	Journeyman	Self	Creates a 40-foot sphere of light around the caster for 3 minutes
Chameleon	Journeyman	Self	Conceals the caster by 25% for 30 seconds
Cloak	Master	Self	Conceals the caster by 75% for 30 seconds
Command Creature	Apprentice	Target	Forces a creature of Level 2 or lower to fight for the caster for 30 seconds
Command Humanoid	Apprentice	Target	Forces a humanoid of Level 2 or lower to fight for the caster for 30 seconds
Commanding Touch	Apprentice	Touch	Forces a creature of Level 3 or lower to fight for the caster for 30 seconds
Daylight	Master	Self	Creates a 60-foot sphere of light around the caster for 8 minutes
Debilitate	Journeyman	Touch	Paralyzes a single target for 3 seconds
Dominate Creature	Expert	Target	Forces a creature of Level 9 or lower to fight for the caster for 30 seconds
Dominate Humanoid	Expert	Target	Forces a humanoid of Level 9 or lower to fight for the caster for 30 seconds
Dominating Touch	Journeyman	Touch	Forces a humanoid of Level 6 or lower to fight for the caster for 30 seconds
Enthralling Presence	Journeyman	Target	Increases the Disposition of all characters up to their 6th level within 20 feet for 30
Eyes of Eventide	Apprentice	Self	Allows the caster to see in the dark for 15 seconds
Eyes of Midnight	Journeyman	Self	Allows the caster to see in the dark for 30 seconds
Fearful Gaze	Expert	Target	Increases the chances of a creature fleeing for 30 seconds
Frenzy	Novice	Target	Increases the aggression of a creature for 30 seconds

ILLUSION SPELLS

Name	Skill Level	Range	Effect
Ghostwalk	Expert	Self	Renders the caster invisible for 1 minute—effect will end if the caster attacks
Grasp of Terror	Master	Touch	Greatly increases the chances of a creature fleeing for 30 seconds
Heroic Touch	Apprentice	Touch	Decreases the chances of an ally fleeing for 60 seconds
Heroism	Apprentice	Touch	Decreases the chances of an ally fleeing for 45 seconds
Hush	Journeyman	Target	Silences a single target for 10 seconds, preventing spellcasting
Illuminate	Novice	Self	Creates a 10-foot sphere of light around a target for 90 seconds
Immobilize	Expert	Touch	Paralyzes a single target for 7 seconds
Inspiration	Novice	Target	Decreases the chances of an ally fleeing for 20 seconds
Inspiring Touch	Novice	Touch	Decreases the chances of an ally fleeing for 30 seconds
Mesmerizing Grasp	Apprentice	Touch	Increases the Disposition of a character up to his/her 6th level for 30 seconds
Moonlight	Apprentice	Self	Creates a 30-foot sphere of light around the caster for 2 minutes
Mute	Expert	Touch	Silences all targets in a 15-foot radius for 15 seconds, preventing spellcasting
Pacification	Apprentice	Target	Slightly reduces the aggression of a single target for 20 seconds
Paralyze	Master	Touch	Paralyzes a single target for 10 seconds
Rage	Apprentice	Target	Increases the aggression of a creature for 40 seconds
Seductive Charm	Apprentice	Target	Increases the Disposition of a character up to his/her 6th level for 30 seconds
Serenity	Novice	Target	Slightly reduces the aggression of a single target for 10 seconds
Shadow	Expert	Self	Conceals the caster by 50% for 30 seconds
Shadow Shape	Journeyman	Self	Renders the caster invisible for 30 seconds—effect will end if the caster attacks
Silence	Master	Target	Silences a single target for 10 seconds, preventing spellcasting
Soothing Touch	Novice	Touch	Slightly reduces the aggression of a single target for 15 seconds
Spectral Form	Master	Self	Renders the caster invisible for 2 minutes—effect will end if the caster attacks
Starlight	Novice	Self	Creates a 20-foot sphere of light around the caster for 1 minute
Terrifying Presence	Master	Target	Greatly increases the chances of a creature fleeing for 30 seconds
Torchlight	Expert	Self	Creates a 50-foot sphere of light around the caster for 4 minutes
Touch of Fear	Apprentice	Touch	Increases the chances of a creature fleeing for 20 seconds
Touch of Frenzy	Novice	Touch	Increases the aggression of a creature for 30 seconds
Touch of Rage	Apprentice	Touch	Increases the aggression of a creature for 30 seconds
Voice of Dread	Journeyman	Target	Increases the chances of a creature fleeing for 20 seconds
Voice of Rapture	Journeyman	Target	Increases the Disposition of a character up to his/her 9th level for 30 seconds

MYSTICISM

The school of Mysticism can unravel the mysteries of the universe if properly applied. It can also tell you what is around the next corner, lying in wait for a hapless adventurer to wander by.

MYSTICISM SPELLS

Name	Skill Level	Range	Effect
Dispel Other	Apprentice	Target	30% chance of dispelling a magical effect on the target
Greater Dispel	Journeyman	Self	75% chance of dispelling a magical effect
Greater Dispel Other	Journeyman	Target	60% chance of dispelling a magical effect on the target
Greater Life Detection	Journeyman	Self	Detects creatures in a 60-foot radius for 1 minute
Greater Soul Trap	Journeyman	Self	Captures a dying creature's soul; lasts 30 seconds
Greater Spell Reflection	Journeyman	Self	15% chance to reflect a spell on the caster for 30 seconds
Legendary Dispel	Master	Self	Dispels any magical effect
Legendary Life Detection	Master	Self	Detects creatures in a 120-foot radius for 2 minutes
Legendary Soul Trap	Master	Self	Captures dying creatures' souls in a 20-foot radius; lasts 1 minute
Legendary Spell Absorption	Master	Self	50% chance to convert a hostile spell into Magicka; lasts 45 seconds
Legendary Spell Reflection	Master	Self	50% chance to reflect a spell on the caster for 45 seconds
Major Dispel	Apprentice	Self	45% chance of dispelling a magical effect
Major Life Detection	Apprentice	Self	Detects creatures in a 60-foot radius for 1 minute
Minor Dispel	Novice	Self	75% chance of dispelling a magical effect
Minor Life Detection	Novice	Self	Detects creatures in a 60-foot radius for 20 seconds
Movement Mastery	Master	Self	Manipulates objects up to 40 feet away for 1 minute
Psychic Motion	Journeyman	Self	Manipulates objects up to 20 feet away for 30 seconds
Remote Manipulation	Apprentice	Self	Manipulates objects up to 10 feet away for 20 seconds
Soul Trap	Apprentice	Self	Captures a dying creature's soul; lasts 20 seconds
Spell Absorption	Journeyman	Self	25% chance to convert a hostile spell into Magicka lasts 20 seconds
Superior Dispel	Expert	Self	Very high chance to dispel any magical effect
Superior Life Detection	Expert	Self	Detects creatures in a 120-foot radius for 2 minutes
Superior Soul Trap	Expert	Self	Captures dying creatures' souls in a 10-foot radius; lasts 40 seconds
Superior Spell Absorption	Expert	Self	35% chance to convert a hostile spell into Magicka; lasts 30 seconds
Superior Spell Reflection	Expert	Self	30% chance to reflect a spell on the caster for 30 seconds
Telekinesis	Expert	Self	Manipulates objects up to 30 feet away for 45 seconds

RESTORATION

Second only to Destruction in popularity, the school of Restoration can keep any adventurer in working order. It can heal physical damage, purge the body of disease, and deal attribute damage from enemy magic.

RESTORATION SPELLS

Name	Skill Level	Range	Effect
Absorb Attribute: Agility	Novice	Touch	Transfers 5 points of Agility from an enemy to the caster for 20 seconds
Absorb Attribute: Endurance	Novice	Touch	Transfers 5 points of Endurance from an enemy to the caster for 20 seconds
Absorb Attribute: Intelligence	Novice	Touch	Transfers 5 points of Intelligence from an enemy to the caster for 20 seconds
Absorb Attribute: Luck	Novice	Touch	Transfers 5 points of Luck from an enemy to the caster for 20 seconds
Absorb Attribute: Speed	Novice	Touch	Transfers 5 points of Speed from an enemy to the caster for 20 seconds
Absorb Attribute: Strength	Novice	Touch	Transfers 5 points of Strength from an enemy to the caster for 20 seconds
Absorb Attribute: Willpower	Novice	Touch	Transfers 5 points of Willpower from an enemy to the caster for 20 seconds
Absorb Fatigue	Novice	Touch	Transfers 10 points of Fatigue from an enemy to the caster
Absorb Health	Novice	Touch	Transfers 5 points of Health from an enemy to the caster
Absorb Magicka	Novice	Touch	Transfers 10 points of Magicka from an enemy to the caster
Absorb Skill: Acrobatics	Novice	Touch	Transfers 5 points of Acrobatics skill from an enemy to the caster for 10 seconds
Absorb Skill: Alteration	Journeyman	Touch	Transfers 15 points of Alteration skill from an enemy to the caster for 10 seconds
Absorb Skill: Athletics	Novice	Touch	Transfers 5 points of Athletics skill from an enemy to the caster for 10 seconds
Absorb Skill: Blade	Expert	Touch	Transfers 25 points of Blade skill from an enemy to the caster for 15 seconds
Absorb Skill: Block	Journeyman	Touch	Transfers 5 points of Acrobatics skill from an enemy to the caster for 10 seconds
Absorb Skill: Blunt	Expert	Touch	Transfers 25 points of Block skill from an enemy to the caster for 15 seconds
Absorb Skill: Conjuration	Journeyman	Touch	Transfers 15 points of Conjuration skill from an enemy to the caster for 10 seconds
Absorb Skill: Destruction	Expert	Touch	Transfers 15 points of Destruction skill from an enemy to the caster for 10 seconds
Absorb Skill: Hand-to-Hand	Apprentice	Touch	Transfers 10 points of Hand-to-Hand skill from an enemy to the caster for 10 seconds
Absorb Skill: Heavy Armor	Journeyman	Touch	Transfers 15 points of Heavy Armor skill from an enemy to the caster for 10 seconds
Absorb Skill: Illusion	Novice	Touch	Transfers 5 points of Illusion skill from an enemy to the caster for 10 seconds
Absorb Skill: Light Armor	Apprentice	Touch	Transfers 10 points of Light Armor skill from an enemy to the caster for 10 seconds
Absorb Skill: Marksman	Journeyman	Touch	Transfers 15 points of Marksman skill from an enemy to the caster for 10 seconds
Absorb Skill: Mercantile	Apprentice	Touch	Transfers 10 points of Mercantile skill from an enemy to the caster for 10 seconds
Absorb Skill: Mysticism	Apprentice	Touch	Transfers 10 points of Mysticism skill from an enemy to the caster for 10 seconds
Absorb Skill: Restoration	Apprentice	Touch	Transfers 10 points of Restoration skill from an enemy to the caster for 10 seconds
Absorb Skill: Security	Novice	Touch	Transfers 5 points of Security skill from an enemy to the caster for 10 seconds
Absorb Skill: Sneak	Expert	Touch	Transfers 25 points of Sneak skill from an enemy to the caster for 15 seconds
Consume Health	Journeyman	Touch	Transfers 20 points of Health from an enemy to the caster
Convalescence	Apprentice	Target	Heals 15 points of Health damage to another creature
Cure Disease	Journeyman	Self	Removes diseases from the caster
Cure Paralysis	Apprentice	Self	Removes paralysis from the caster
Cure Poison	Apprentice	Self	Removes effects caused by poison from the caster
Devour Health	Expert	Touch	Transfers 40 points of Health from an enemy to the caster
Fortify Agility	Apprentice	Self	Increases caster's Agility attribute by 5 for 90 seconds
Fortify Endurance	Apprentice	Self	Increases caster's Endurance attribute by 5 for 90 seconds
Fortify Fatigue	Novice	Self	Increases caster's maximum Fatigue by 25 for 45 seconds
Fortify Health	Apprentice	Self	Increases caster's maximum Health by 30 for 30 seconds
Fortify Intelligence	Apprentice	Self	Increases caster's Intelligence attribute by 5 for 90 seconds
Fortify Luck	Apprentice	Self	Increases caster's Luck attribute by 5 for 90 seconds
Fortify Magicka	Journeyman	Self	Increases caster's maximum Magicka by 30 for 60 seconds
Fortify Personality	Apprentice	Self	Increases caster's Personality attribute by 5 for 90 seconds
Fortify Speed	Apprentice	Self	Increases caster's Speed attribute by 5 for 90 seconds
Fortify Strength	Apprentice	Self	Increases caster's Strength attribute by 5 for 90 seconds
Fortify Willpower	Apprentice	Self	Increases caster's Willpower attribute by 5 for 90 seconds
Greater Convalescence	Journeyman	Target	Heals 40 points of Health damage over 2 seconds to target creature
Greater Fortify Agility	Journeyman	Self	Increases caster's Agility attribute by 10 for 90 seconds
Greater Fortify Endurance	Journeyman	Self	Increases caster's Endurance attribute by 10 for 90 seconds
Greater Fortify Fatigue	Apprentice	Self	Increases caster's maximum Fatigue by 50 for 45 seconds
Greater Fortify Health	Expert	Self	Increases caster's maximum Health by 60 for 30 seconds
Greater Fortify Intelligence	Journeyman	Self	Increases caster's Intelligence attribute by 10 for 90 seconds
Greater Fortify Luck	Journeyman	Self	Increases caster's Luck attribute by 10 for 90 seconds
Greater Fortify Magicka	Expert	Self	Increases caster's maximum Magicka by 60 for 60 seconds
Greater Fortify Personality	Journeyman	Self	Increases caster's Personality attribute by 10 for 90 seconds
Greater Fortify Speed	Journeyman	Self	Increases caster's Speed attribute by 10 for 90 seconds
Greater Fortify Strength	Journeyman	Self	Increases caster's Strength attribute by 10 for 90 seconds
Greater Fortify Willpower	Journeyman	Self	Increases caster's Willpower attribute by 10 for 90 seconds
Heal Greater Wounds	Journeyman	Self	Heals 40 points of Health damage over 2 seconds
Heal Legendary Wounds	Master	Self	Heals 180 points of Health damage over 6 seconds
Heal Major Wounds	Apprentice	Self	Heals 25 points of Health damage

RESTORATION SPELLS CONT.

Name	Skill Level	Range	Effect
Heal Minor Wounds	Novice	Self	Heals 10 points of Health damage
Heal Superior Wounds	Expert	Self	Heals 100 points of Health damage over 4 seconds
Leech Health	Apprentice	Touch	Transfers 10 points of Health from an enemy to the caster
Major Respite	Apprentice	Self	Restores 80 points of Fatigue to the caster
Minor Magic Resistance	Journeyman	Self	Grants 10% Magic Resistance for 15 seconds
Minor Respite	Novice	Self	Restores 15 points of Fatigue to the caster
Restore Agility	Apprentice	Self	Heals 5 points of Agility damage
Restore Endurance	Apprentice	Self	Heals 5 points of Endurance damage
Restore Intelligence	Apprentice	Self	Heals 5 points of Intelligence damage
Restore Luck	Apprentice	Self	Heals 5 points of Luck damage
Restore Personality	Apprentice	Self	Heals 5 points of Personality damage
Restore Speed	Apprentice	Self	Heals 5 points of Speed damage
Restore Strength	Apprentice	Self	Heals 5 points of Strength damage
Restore Willpower	Apprentice	Self	Heals 5 points of Willpower damage
Superior Convalescence	Expert	Target	Heals 80 points of Health damage over 4 seconds to target creature

Stealth

Introduction

Hiding in the shadows, stalking your prey, liberating items from the unworthy. Some call you scoundrel, rogue, thief! But really, is it any more civilized to stomp stridently around in clanking platemail armor, swinging your claymore at anything that crosses your path, or to destroy a person's mind with a spell, or to char someone with a fireball?

It's not that you're lazy or fearful, either, just that you prefer to solve your problems with more elegance and with greater patience and grace than those other types of adventurers. And now you will learn some of the secrets of the trade.

Falanu Hlaalu

Sneaking

The first skill you must master is how to sneak around without others detecting you. Various things come into play here. First is how advanced you are in the Sneak skill, along with how skilled your opponent is. Whether or not someone has line of sight on you determines whether you can be detected. If your foes can't see you, they have only their ears to detect you. Playing in third-person mode with the camera zoomed all the way out lets you see around corners so you can tell if someone is facing toward you or away from you.

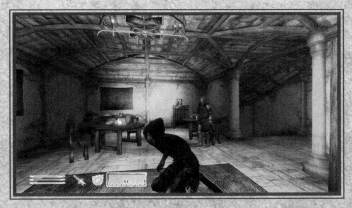

Your success is also based on whether you're moving or standing still. You'll be surprised how often a guard will walk right by you if you aren't moving, but take a single step when one is near and you're caught! The slower you move while sneaking the better; running is a sure way to get caught. If you are in brightly lighted areas you are more likely to get caught, so stay in the shadows!

Lastly, it really doesn't matter what armor you are wearing. You can sneak around in heavy armor just as quietly as in light armor. What does matter is the weight of your boots. So bring along a pair of leather boots or, better yet, go barefoot when you are sneaking around! Bind your boots to a hotkey to quickly put them on and take them off.

THE EYE

When you sneak, your icon turns into an eyeball. If it becomes yellow it means someone is just about to detect you or has already detected you. Note: It only tells you if *something* can detect you, not necessarily that what you are sneaking up on can detect you. A horse could detect you while you're trying to break into his master's house, but he can't call the guards, so who cares!

THE SNEAK ATTACK

If you can score a hit on your opponent while you are sneaking and undetected, you do extra damage! You do more damage the higher your Sneak skill is. You can also sneak attack with a bow and arrow. Add a little poison to the bow before you shoot, and you might be able to drop the target before it can cause trouble for you. This also sometimes works in group battles where your opponent is busy fighting your ally; maneuver for a shot in the back.

 Remember: Once you are in melee combat (after your sneak attack), exit Sneak mode or you will swing really slowly and won't be able to maneuver as easily!

Sneak attack for 6x damage!

INCREASING YOUR SNEAK SKILL

You gain skill in Sneak if you are sneaking undetected near someone who could otherwise detect you. To increase your skill quickly, find a guard who wanders around the city at night. Sneak slowly behind, following your mark around town. Stationary people/creatures on the other side of a wall also work well; walk back and forth gaining Sneak skill. If you can break into a house, sneaking around the bedroom while the owners are sleeping is another easy way to gain skill!

Beware; you aren't the only one gaining skill. Each time you gain a level, all the creatures and people in the world gain increases to their Sneak, too. Granted, most won't be gaining

skill as fast as a dedicated thief, but it will be that much harder for non-stealthy characters to successfully sneak around.

PICKING POCKETS

Sometimes you need just a few more coins, or you must "borrow" a key from someone. Here's how you do it. While sneaking, walk up to and activate your victim (instead of starting a conversation, you will pick the mark's pocket). Your success depends on the same factors that determine successful sneaking.

The value and weight of an item affect the difficulty of stealing it. Trying to take something expensive and heavy is a sure way to get caught! Opening a person's pocket even without taking anything still might be noticed. You can also place objects of zero weight on people when picking pockets.

Even the master thief gets caught sometimes. There is a small chance, no matter how much higher your Sneak skill is than your mark's, that you will be detected. Be ready to run when your target calls for the guards! Each successful pickpocket attempt gets you closer to advancing your Sneak level.

LOCKPICKING

Look in every crate and barrel; you'll be surprised by how many lockpicks you can find lying around. And you'll be glad you have them when it comes time to liberate those lonely items locked away for safekeeping. Every lock has a difficulty

level. Some locks you can't pick open at all—they require a key or are opened elsewhere.

If you have a lockpick and activate a locked door or locked container, the Lockpicking Interface comes up. You can click the Auto Attempt button if you are in a hurry, but you'll break fewer picks and open harder locks if you do it yourself. Move the pick under, then push each tumbler up. The trick is to get it to stick at the right moment. Each time you'll notice the tumbler moves faster or slower. Keep bouncing the tumbler until you see it move up slowly, which signals that it won't fall as quickly, giving you more time to push it into place. On hard locks with fast-moving tumblers, another strategy is to keep the tumbler bouncing repeatedly, feel the rhythm, and click when it hits the top (almost immediately after hitting it with the pick). Finally, use your eyes to see when the tumbler is in place and ignore the sounds of the tumbler; the sound of the tumbler can be distracting to your timing.

The more skilled your character is in Security, the slower tumblers will move and the fewer tumblers that will fall if you break a pick. If you are very skilled at the Lockpicking Interface, you can pick locks that would otherwise be too difficult for your character. With each tumbler you snap into place or pick you break, you get closer to the next skill level in Security.

As your character gains levels, the locks get harder and harder. This means that at higher levels, characters with higher Security skills will be walking out of dungeons with more treasure. Don't neglect your Security skill!

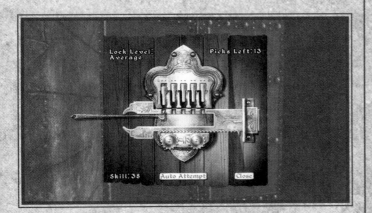

When someone isn't talkative enough (a dialogue topic doesn't gray out after it's discussed), or you want to ply your charms to get a better deal from a merchant, you can use persuasion. This increases the person's Disposition toward you. The Persuasion Interface is covered in the manual, but here's the strategy to use. Spend a moment checking out which are the person's liked and disliked actions. You can tell by the smiling or frowning. Before you start picking wedges, look for a response to each action. If someone likes being intimidated in the first "round," he or she will like being intimidated throughout every round. No matter what, Disposition will go down when you select a wedge for something disliked. Make sure the wedge is tiny so the loss of Disposition is small. The reverse is true: Activate the big wedges for things that are liked. Some things are liked and disliked strongly, and some are liked and disliked a little bit. Choosing a big wedge on something liked a lot will gain more Disposition than choosing a big wedge on something liked a little.

Each round the layout of the wedges changes, so take a brief moment to plan your strategy. For instance, clicking the big wedge all the way around will net you a negative Disposition, so you might need to take a smaller wedge on something that is liked to avoid having to take a big wedge on something disliked. It might be worth taking a medium-sized wedge on the thing disliked a little bit to get a big wedge on something liked greatly. Also, don't bother to wait for the person to stop talking, since you are remembering which things are liked and disliked—keep those wedges spinning! When you have higher Speechcraft skills you gain a "spin" on the wheel. Use this spin to get a better wedge when you need it.

There is a maximum Disposition to which you can persuade someone. It's based on the relative difference between your Speechcraft skill and the other person's. That character's max Disposition is also based on responsibility; a very responsible person will be less inclined to change his or her opinion about you just because you are a fast talker. After you've reached the maximum Disposition available through persuasion, you can turn to bribery for further Disposition increases.

STEALTH

Some people are very responsible and won't ever except bribes from you.

To increase your skill level, make sure you don't get your target to his or her maximum Disposition. You want to lose Disposition sometimes so that you can keep playing the game, thus getting more uses of your Speechcraft skill. If the maximum is reached accidentally, try setting your haggling to be over-aggressive; refusing deals decreases Disposition (see "Mercantile").

MERCANTILE

Although you must use special fences for stolen goods, always try to get the best price for items looted from your foes and dungeons, and work to buy your goods at the lowest prices. The prices you get from merchants are based on their Disposition toward you and the relative difference between each of your Mercantile skill levels.

The Haggle button on the vendor menu lets you set how aggressively you are bartering. Push the prices in your favor by sliding the bar to the right. The higher your Mercantile skill is compared to the merchant's, the farther you can push it. If you push too hard your offer will be rejected, which lowers the merchant's Disposition (and thus the base price gets worse). Always adjust this bar a little bit, because every time you buy or sell an item with this bar bumped, even just a tiny bit, you get points toward raising your Mercantile skill. Also, it doesn't matter what you sell; you get the same Mercantile increase regardless (as long as the bar is moved to the right). So to increase your Mercantile skill, loot dungeons for lots of smaller items rather than a few heavy ones.

ACROBATICS

You can often make your getaway with jumps over, onto, or down from places—jumps that your enemies cannot make. You can then safely shoot arrows and spells or heal yourself while your enemies try to get to your hard-to-reach spot. Acrobatics is the skill for this. You gain skill every time you jump or fall. Until higher skill levels, your Encumbrance affects how far you jump.

LIGHT ARMOR

Sometimes even the best rogue gets into a direct confrontation. Then you will be glad you are wearing your light armor. While offering less protection and able to withstand less punishment than heavy armor, it weighs much less, allowing you to carry more loot (which is why you got into this business in the first place!). Even if you aren't planning on doing much blocking, carry a light armor shield; it adds passively to your armor rating.

Every time you take a hit to a location where you have light armor, you gain skill in Light Armor. You can skill up quickly if you find enemies that don't do lots of damage (like Rats) and let them hit you over and over again.

STEALTH

MARKSMAN

This is a very important skill for those who prefer not to engage in face-to-face conflict. Coupled with the sneak attack and a little poison, the Marksman skill can often cripple, if not outright kill, your opponent before you have to go toe-to-toe. If you kill someone with one arrow shot, your target will die before alerting the guards—however, if the death is due to a poison effect (not straight damage from the arrow), even if it's from only one hit, the dying victim can call for help.

The longer you hold back the bow the more damage you do. Also, the farther away you are, the higher you need to aim to compensate for the arrow falling because of gravity.

You can often pick off targets or "pull" them to you without alerting their comrades. This is a good way to even the odds when you're outnumbered. Rogues are often faster on their feet than their opponents, so you can often kill someone without taking a blow by running away, pulling back the bow while you are running, and then turning around and firing. Rinse and repeat.

Using your Acrobatics skill, set yourself up in out-of-reach areas, excellent places from which to snipe at your enemies. If you run low on arrows and happen to face off against another archer, just sidestep out of the way of the arrows, then collect them after the battle. You'll get more arrows this way than by looting the archer's corpse.

MAGIC

While the best thief needs no magical assistance, it is foolish not to seize every advantage that presents itself. There are certain magical effects that you can learn as spells, make as potions, or have enchanted on your gear that will be especially helpful in your career as a thief.

Chameleon enhancements reduce the effect of the light falling on your character; the Invisibility effect removes the penalty of light altogether (but you lose invisibility if you attack); Paralyze can help you get away; Charm gives you an added boost when getting information and good prices; and Night-Eye is preferable to torches since it does not increase the light falling on your character. As you can see, the school of Illusion is the most useful to the rogue types!

Potato
@1 Ø0.2

Anything that increases the damage potential of your weapons (especially bows and arrows) is greatly appreciated by those who prefer not to be engaged in hand-to-hand fighting. The shield spells are great for boosting your armor rating.

MET YOUR MATCH?

Certain types of enemies are harder to sneak up on, because they too are of a similarly roguish persuasion. Generally speaking, creatures and animals are more difficult to sneak up on than people. Certain types of people, such as Bandits, are also more difficult to sneak around. If you are having trouble, follow all the advice in the "Sneaking" section and try a few spells to help you out. If that doesn't work, you might have met your match. Good thing you brought along some poison and healing potions!

Sneak attack for 6x damage!

Dread Zombie

In your travels across Cyrodiil, at some point, somewhere, your character is bound to commit a crime. When you do, the game distinguishes this act from the law-abiding acts around it, and you may find yourself in trouble with the authorities.

Obviously, not every aggressive act is a crime. Crime only attaches when you're dealing with non-evil characters and factions. Evil characters include Bandits, Conjurers, the Dark Brotherhood, Marauders, the Mythic Dawn, Necromancers, and Vampires.

But even this doesn't always hold true. For instance, the acknowledged Vampires Janus Hassildor and Vicente Valtieri are not wholly evil. You must judge evilness by other, less precise characteristics, such as if a character attacks you unprovoked or what the character's location is. (Apart from Dark Brotherhood and Mythic Dawn members, most evil characters hang out in dungeons.)

THE CRIMES

TRESPASSING

Being where you're not supposed to be is fairly clear-cut. When opening a door would put you on the wrong side of the law, the game tells you so in advance with a red cursor.

There are three types of regions in the game: public areas, which you may enter and wander within freely; private areas, to which you have limited access; and off-limits areas.

In the off-limits areas, like the royal quarters in Castle Anvil, an alarm will go out instantly if you're detected there. (See the "Guards and Alarms" section.)

However, in private areas, you have a grace period of 30 seconds to transact your business and then scoot. An example would be the second-floor Council Chamber in the Arch-Mage's Tower at Arcane University. Outsiders and low-level guild

members are trespassing here, even when they have legitimate business to transact. Advanced guild members are not.

In these areas, you'll be warned by dialogue with NPCs that you've strayed beyond the velvet rope. And after that period elapses, an alarm will go off if you're detected.

Exception: If a non-player character unlocks a door into a private area, this is construed as an invitation to enter, and your presence there is not then considered trespassing. This happens with most homeowners. You are trespassing if you enter through a locked door, but not when the owner unlocks the door, extending an implied invitation.

THEFT

Again, clear-cut, thanks to that red cursor. Many items in the game are owned by other people. Take 'em at your peril.

However, there are different types of ownership, and some are more expansive than others. For instance, when you claim your Mages Guild staff from a cabinet at Arcane University, you'll find the cabinet full of scrolls. The scrolls are not yours personally—they belong to the Mages Guild—but if you're a member of the guild taking them is not a crime. And if you stay at an inn, technically you're in a private area by special sanction, but taking the food in the room isn't a crime. Note that items sold by guild members/merchants will give you the usual red icon.

PICKPOCKETING

This is a form of theft, only you are trying to take the character's possessions. Any possessions that are equipped are safe from your greedy fingers. You can only attempt to pickpocket when you are sneaking. There is a chance of failure, which results in detection and an alarm being sent out. See the "Stealth" chapter for more info on pickpocketing.

ASSAULT

Sometimes you accidentally hit a friend or ally during melee combat. The game understands that accidents happen and makes allowances for it. If the NPC is in combat with someone and you accidentally hit him or her, you'll be forgiven. However, outside of combat you're allowed only a few pot shots before you're considered a threat.

MURDER

You can always defend yourself against an assault, but to kill a character on your own initiative without risking a murder charge, the target must be thoroughly evil. *E-vil*. And there's the rub: Some characters with evil faction affiliations also have non-evil affiliations.

Consider the local Mythic Dawn agents who become active when the Main Quest heats up at the end of the "Dagon Shrine" segment. Perhaps when you read that section, you determined it would be a good move to preemptively remove them. (Indeed, we'll put forward one of them to secure your offer of membership in the Dark Brotherhood.)

Well, that's murder. Because while each is a member of the evil Mythic Dawn cult, each also is an upstanding member of the community. It's only when those characters become hostile and attack that you can kill them freely. In short, killing people after they have attacked you without provocation is never a crime; if you initiate the first blow, you had better be sure they are completely evil or you risk being charged with murder.

If you can accomplish a killing with one blow (and it has to be a blow, not a spell or poison effect), you can prevent the broadcast of an alarm—so long as the murder isn't witnessed by someone else. If it is witnessed, or if the killing turns out to take more than one blow, you've just exchanged one alarm for another.

DETECTION

Let's suppose you're determined to commit a crime. Shame on you. (Unless you're a Thieves Guild or Dark Brotherhood

member, in which case—way to go.) How events proceed from this point depends on whether the crime is detected and, if so, who did the detecting.

Detection is everything. If your crime is undetected, you've gotten away with it—unless you bring the proceeds to the attention of the authorities.

Detection is determined by a formula that includes the possible presence of a witness; the difference between your character's and any witness's Sneak skills; the physical distance and the presence or absence of a line-of-sight between the two people; the amount of light shining on your character; any magic that reduces the visibility of your character; and the level of noise your character is making. See "Sneaking" in the "Stealth" chapter for more details.

When you skulk about a shop or home, the owners will follow you around to keep an eye on you. If you are fast enough you may be able to sprint around the corner and nab something or pick open a lock before they see you.

GUARDS AND ALARMS

What happens after a crime goes down? It depends. Suppose the incident is detected by a character with a high Responsibility stat. This is a another hidden figure, but one that's always high for guards, nobles, and shopkeepers. In that case, the crime is reported immediately and a cash bounty (equivalent to the fine for that offense) immediately is attached to your character.

If the witness is an ordinary person, the crime is not immediately reported, but an alarm is broadcast. An alarm is an order to the nearest guard within about 140 feet to initiate a conversation with you. A guard who hears the alarm will come running—in urban areas, appearing almost immediately—and confront your character.

You'll have real trouble avoiding this meeting. It may not be possible to avoid it at all.

The numbers vary, but guards patrol every city night and day, while others stand guard in fixed positions. Still other guards can be found in the wilderness. Imperial Legion horsemen patrol sections of the province, individual troopers can be found at inns between cities, and Legion "foresters" will abandon their hunting duties to enforce the law.

Moreover, the guards are very persistent in fulfilling their mandate and will pursue the task even if you move to a different region, irrespective of locked doors requiring keys.

If no one responds to the alarm, it means the guards are too far from the scene. The bounty doesn't attach and the crime effectively goes away.

Finally, if no witness sees the crime, it goes undetected and the game closes its eyes to the offense.

Here's another little trick: The guard can't take what you don't have. If you drop the stolen loot before you encounter the guard, you'll still be charged with the crime, but you can come back later and collect the loot rather than undertaking its more difficult extraction from the prison's locked evidence chest. Drop it a little ways off, though. The guards will take anything stolen that is right at your feet.

Note that it's still considered stolen property, so don't let anyone see you pick it up. The only way to strip ownership from an item is to sell it to a fence and then buy it back from the fence. You'll lose money on the deal—the fences are hard bargainers—but you're essentially paying for the privilege of not being hassled by the Man.

ARREST

When confronted by a guard, you'll have two or three options: go to jail, resist arrest, or, if you have ready cash, pay a fine. (Cyrodiil's guards do it all.)

Resisting arrest is just a bad idea. The guards are always 10 levels tougher than you—guard captains 15 levels tougher—and combat with one guard is rewarded by the arrival of more. While combat with guards is doomed to failure, you may be able to run away far enough that they stop pursuing you.

Jail? We don't recommend it. The only comparative advantage is that it keeps you alive without denting your pocket, and if you are a skilled rogue, you may even be able to break out. The term works out to one day for each 100 gold of bounty, with a required minimum term of one day.

However, if you serve out your sentence behind bars, your character stagnates and your skills are almost certain to drop. For each day in the slam, one skill is chosen at random. If the selected skill is any but Security or Sneak, that skill drops one point that day. If it's Security or Sneak, it rises one point. This goes on for a maximum of 10 days. Needless to say, the

counterweight of a less than 10 percent chance in a bump up in two skills doesn't offset the more than 90 percent likelihood of drops in as many as 10 others.

So, most of the time, simply pay the fine (or make a break for it).

FINES FOR CRIMINAL ACTS

Crime	Fine
Trespassing	5
Pickpocketing	25, or value of theft
Attack	40 per level of target
Steal a horse	250
Theft	Value of theft, minimum 10
Murder	1,000

Even this involves some inconvenience. You're transported to a spot outside the local jail.

JAIL

If you can't pay, you won't have much choice: a brief life as a fugitive, suicide by cop, or jail. If you opt for jail, you'll appear in a featureless cell in the local castle or the Imperial City's prison. Your possessions are gone. (If you stole a horse, it will find its way home.) In their place is a prison uniform of plain pants, shirt, and shoes; if you had any lockpicks in your inventory at the time of your arrest, you retain a single lockpick. (We're not sure how the guards failed to find this. Perhaps it's best not to ask.)

You can serve out your sentence, not in real time, but by sleeping on your rough little bed, or escape by picking the lock on the cell door and sneaking out of the jail.

Getting out of your cell is the easy part. You can use your pick, pick the pocket of the passing guard for the master cell key, or cast the appropriate open spell.

However, getting safely out of the jail proper and the surrounding area is likely to be a nasty business. The layout of jails is generally arranged to allow the guards to spot and confront escapees. You'll need a decent Sneak skill, more than a little patience, and ideally a Chameleon spell or one that provides invisibility. The guard makes an initial sweep past your jail cell (giving you an opportunity to pickpocket the key). After that, he randomly wanders the area, occasionally electing to do his sweep patrol again. Sneak slowly, and camp out in dark areas and behind doors. Wait for the guard to make the rounds again, then sneak out.

Prison Cell Door

The time of day you get caught also affects the difficulty. In some jails, off-duty guards come to sleep or eat near the cells. If these guards happen to come in while you are sneaking past the jailor, they will attack you.

Being seen by a guard while escaping is extremely dangerous. If you're spotted by the jailor after you unlock your door, he'll attack and quite possibly kill you. You might be able to run away far enough that he stops chasing you, but he will go to great lengths to capture you.

While you are sneaking or running out you can liberate your gear from the locked evidence chest on your way out.

When you get a certain distance from your cell while escaping, you gain an additional bounty on your head for your jail break. If you have a small bounty to begin with, you will not be attacked on sight by the city guards (if you manage to sneak your way completely out of the jail). However, this additional bounty might put you over the "arrest on sight" threshold of the city guards, which means that even after sneaking out of the jail, you may have to make a run for it.

If you succeed in escaping or evading pursuit (or both), and you belong to the Thieves Guild, rendezvous with Armand Christophe in the Waterfront District in Imperial City or S'krivva in Bravil as soon as possible. Either of these doyens can remove the bounty on your head for half price.

There is a special escape situation set up in the Leyawiin jail. Once a day, after the initial sweep past your cell, the guard sits on a chair. If you have a decent Sneak skill you can sneak around behind him down a short set of stairs, then get your gear from the evidence chest. As you near the chest the guard gets up to get some food; quickly sneak up the set of stairs you came down as the guard comes down the other stairs.

In Skingrad a secret passageway leads out of the jail.

What about your stuff? If you serve out your jail term, you'll get it back automatically (minus any stolen goods) upon your release. If you escape, you can liberate both your own goods and any stolen property from the locked evidence chest in the jail.

Once you serve your term, your debt is paid. The Disposition modifier that made people think less of you when you had a bounty on your head is reset. All is right with the world—until you do it again.

VAMPIRES

INTRODUCTION

There is a darker side to life in Cyrodiil. Few know of it, and even fewer are masters of it. They are the things of nightmares and horror stories. They are Vampires.

In *Oblivion*, it is possible to become a Vampire, opening up an entire new way of playing the game. Depending on how you choose to play, it can be a curse or a blessing. There are great advantages to becoming a creature of the night, but there are significant drawbacks as well. If you are careless, you will be shunned by most characters in the world, prevented from bartering, and you may even burn to death in the sun. If, however, you are careful, you can bypass these effects and use the powers of the Vampire to your great advantage in combat.

BECOMING A VAMPIRE

Vampirism begins its insidious work as a disease, and that disease is contracted the same as any other in Tamriel: being attacked by those who have it. So, to become a Vampire, you must fight Vampires. There's a chance that in each encounter with a Vampire, you will contract porphyric hemophilia, often referred to as the "Vampire disease." The effects of this disease appear mild; you'll notice a very slight drain on your Fatigue, but that's all. If left untreated, however, it will become far more significant than any other disease you may contract.

Once you have the disease, it's time to make a decision. Do you want to become a Vampire? If not, any standard means of curing disease (potion, spell, visit to the local chapel altar) will cure it. No harm, no foul. You may contract it again in the future, so if you don't feel the need to explore this avenue of game play just yet, the opportunity may present itself again.

If you do wish to become a Vampire, simply do nothing. The disease takes three game days to work through your system; after that, the next time you lay down to sleep it takes hold, and vampirism manifests itself.

(There is one alternative to acquiring the disease through combat; a particularly nefarious character in one of the hidden factions will offer to turn you into a Vampire after you complete a quest. Refer to "Faction Quests: The Dark Brotherhood" to learn more.)

You awake from a horrible dream, and you find that things have changed. Your skin is paler and your eyes are a strange red color. More importantly, you're faster and stronger and have a new power at your disposal. There are some things you need to know in order to make the most out of playing as a Vampire.

FINE DINING: FEEDING AS A VAMPIRE

As a Vampire, you have a particular taste for human blood. Your abilities as a Vampire are directly tied to feeding on other characters; in short, for every day you go without feeding, vampirism takes a greater hold on you and turns you into even more of a monster. This means that the benefits you receive from being a Vampire become stronger, but so do the drawbacks. If you reach the end of the cycle without feeding, you're prevented from interacting with most other characters in the world.

Feeding is very simple: Find a sleeping character, and activate him or her. You can either wake the person and converse or feed. (If you're sneaking, you can choose to pickpocket your target.) Choose to feed, and you'll chow down. Don't worry; this doesn't kill your victims, and it won't turn them into Vampires. Each person is a never-ending buffet, so long as you don't wake your target up.

Remember that others won't react well to seeing you feed. It will be treated as a crime, so pick your meals carefully. Since most characters in the world sleep behind closed and locked doors, beggars are a good choice. Find them sleeping on mats outside in towns, and make sure there are no guards around before going to work. Joining a guild, such as the Fighters Guild, Mages Guild, or Dark Brotherhood, gives you access to dozens of sleeping characters. Again, just be sure no one is watching.

Feeding has a direct effect on how much power you have as a Vampire. Below, the various bonuses and weaknesses granted by vampirism are discussed, as are the effects of feeding.

Ungarion

THE GOOD NEWS

At its basic level, vampirism gives you bonuses to several attributes (+5 to Strength, Willpower, and Speed) and skills (+5 to Acrobatics, Athletics, Destruction, Hand-to-Hand, Illusion, Mysticism, and Sneak). You're also granted a resistance to disease and paralysis, and a small resistance to normal weapons. All of these factors combine to make your character a bit tougher than normal.

For every day you go without feeding, your boosted skills and attributes increase by an additional 5. Your resistance to normal weapons increases as well.

THE BAD NEWS

These bonuses come with a price. At the start, you'll only have a weakness to fire. Each day without feeding increases this weakness, and other drawbacks are introduced.

If you've fed within the last 24 hours, you're safe from the sun. Any longer than that, however, and you'll start burning whenever you are exposed to sunlight. Each day that passes without feeding increases the amount of damage the sun does; cloudy or rainy weather will help some, but you're in danger any time you set foot outside.

The worst part of not feeding comes after a full four days without blood. You may notice that for every day you don't feed, your appearance changes. Your face becomes gaunt and pale, your teeth start to look like fangs, and your eyes turn a bright red. Well, you're not the only one who will notice these changes. If it's been long enough since your last feeding, everyone else will recognize you for what you are. Most characters in the game will simply refuse to interact with you, turning you away every time you try to talk to them. This can

make playing the game difficult, as it prevents you from buying and selling, and sometimes prevents you from getting new quests.

VAMPIRE POWERS

For every day you spend as a Vampire without feeding, you are granted a new power. While they may not directly help in combat, each power has a specific use and can be very beneficial.

HUNTER'S SIGHT

The first power you receive as a Vampire, Hunter's Sight, grants you 30 seconds of Night-Eye and 30 seconds of Detect Life over a large area. Useful for carefully exploring dungeons, this power can be used repeatedly for a small Magicka cost.

Vampire Thief

VAMPIRE'S SEDUCTION

The second power received gives you a high-magnitude Charm spell for 20 seconds. While it may not immediately seem useful, this spell has one very important function. Raising a character's Disposition to 100 will allow you to talk to him or her no matter how long you've been a Vampire. This spell helps you to bypass the restriction placed on you for being a full Vampire.

REIGN OF TERROR

Three days as a Vampire gives you the ability to silence and demoralize opponents around you. Particularly useful against fire-wielding opponents, this can be quite an advantage in combat.

EMBRACE OF SHADOWS

A full three minutes of invisibility along with 90 seconds of Night-Eye provides more than enough time to escape any combat situation. Use this one when you're in over your head and need to make a quick getaway.

ADVANCED STRATEGIES

You know the basics. You know how to feed, what powers you have as a Vampire, and when you get them. But how can you make the most of being a Vampire to help you play the game?

Sun damage is one of the biggest drawbacks to being a Vampire. By being careful, and paying attention to the time of day, you can minimize the problems it causes.

- Find someplace to sleep away the daylight hours. An inn or a guild hall works if you're in town, otherwise look for the nearest dungeon and clear yourself a spot to rest in until nightfall.

- Don't fast-travel. The longer the trip, the more time it will take, and the greater the chance you'll arrive during daylight hours.

- Watch the clock. The rest/wait menu and your main character menu both display the current in-game time. Check it before venturing outdoors, especially if you've spent a lot of time in town or in a dungeon.

When you are a full Vampire, many characters in the world won't talk to you. The biggest drawback to this is your inability to buy and sell items, but careful planning can help you get around this.

- Use one vendor for as many transactions as possible. Doing so makes that merchant like you more and makes it easier to keep Disposition as high as possible. Using the Vampire's Seduction power goes a long way toward reaching that target Disposition.

- Remember that shops are only open during daylight hours. Find a nearby building to wait in overnight, so you can sprint to the store in the morning, taking as little sun damage as possible.

- If you're in a guild, use vendors that are in the guild when possible. They'll like you more simply because you're in the same faction and will be more inclined to speak to you even if you're a full Vampire.

- Use all of your options before resorting to feeding. Since feeding puts you back at the lowest level of vampirism, if you've become accustomed to life as a full Vampire you'll want to make sure you've exhausted your possibilities before feeding. Use Charm spells, enchanted items, or whatever other tricks you may pick up along the way to gain favor with characters.

- If you must feed, plan your feedings so that you can take care of as many things in town in a single day. Buy, sell, get quests—do whatever you must in as little time as possible, so you can let your vampirism build back up afterward.

While the attribute and skill boosts you get as a Vampire will assist you in combat, a few additional strategies can give you as much of an edge as possible when dungeon-romping.

- Make use of the Hunter's Sight power whenever possible. The Detect Life effect will allow you to sneak up on your enemies, spotting them before they spot you.

- Watch out for any creatures or characters that regularly use Fire spells. Your weakness to fire means you'll take additional damage from them; use your Reign of Terror power to silence them and beat them down while they're incapable of casting spells.

- Know your limits. The Embrace of Shadows power will get you out of a tight spot at least once a day; don't be afraid to use it if you're outnumbered in combat.

VAMPIRES

CREATURE GUIDE

You can't travel around Cyrodiil long before you run into something (or someone) who tries to kill you. Some of these enemies are nothing more than a nuisance, while others require careful planning if you hope to survive the encounter.

The world adapts to your character, so you generally encounter enemies that are no more powerful than your character at whatever level you are. This is because most enemies you run into are either "leveled" to you or are generated from "leveled lists." In general, most humanoid enemies (Bandits, Vampires, Marauders, Conjurers, Necromancers) are leveled to you—as you increase in level, these enemies increase in strength along with you, so that they always provide a reasonable challenge. Likewise, most creatures are generated from leveled lists—meaning that when you enter a dungeon, the game checks your level and populates the dungeon with enemies appropriate to your level.

You cannot "clear" most dungeons permanently of enemies. If you leave and return after more than three days, the dungeon has been repopulated (and the treasure chests as well). This means that a tomb full of Skeletons and Ghosts that you cleared at Level 4 might be full of Wraiths and Skeleton Champions if you return at Level 20.

HUMANOID ENEMIES

Bandits, Marauders, Vampires, Necromancers, and Conjurers are the main humanoid enemies you will encounter. Instead of having different versions that appear as you increase in level, these enemies simply increase in level along with you. In general, humanoid enemies are 1–4 levels below your current level, while "boss" enemies will be at or slightly above your level.

BANDITS

Bandits favor light armor and blunt weapons. They are also a good source of lockpicks and the occasional poison (if they didn't use it on you first). Dogs guard their camps and lairs, which at lower levels are much better at detecting your approach than their masters. You may also encounter Bandit archers and hedge wizards.

MARAUDERS

Marauders carry heavy armor and bladed weapons. You may find repair hammers on them. Most are melee fighters, but you will also encounter Marauder archers and battlemages in their larger encampments.

VAMPIRES

It is difficult to generalize about Vampires, as they come in a wide variety of classes, from battlemages to pilgrims to crusaders, with the equipment to match. They all have the vampiric power of invisibility, however, as well as the ability to transmit vampirism, so they can be tricky opponents. They often keep Wolves in their lairs as pets and guards.

NECROMANCERS

Necromancers are mages who specialize in the conjuration of undead creatures. Undead servants populate their lairs, and they always summon additional undead to aid them in combat. If you can kill the Necromancers quickly, they can be a good source of potions and scrolls (if they haven't been used on you).

CONJURERS

Conjurers are similar to Necromancers but specialize in Daedra instead of undead.

CREATURES

In general, creatures are *not* leveled to you. If you see an Ancient Ghost, you know that it is Level 9 and has 170 hit points, no matter if you encounter it at Level 9 or at Level 29. Instead, the game provides you with a challenge by pulling creatures from leveled lists—as you rise in level, you will encounter higher-level creatures (although you will continue to see lower-level creatures as well). The exceptions to that rule are the top-level creatures of each creature type, which increase in strength with you to continue to provide a challenge for your high-level character. Quest-specific creatures are also leveled. These are noted in the creature tables with an (L).

Leveled lists are organized by creature type—so you'll always find undead in a tomb, Goblins in a Goblin lair, etc. While there are many exceptions to this rule, the following lists can be used as a guideline as to when you will start encountering creatures in different types of dungeons.

BEAST LAIR

Level	Creature
1	Rat
2	Wolf
6	Timber Wolf
9	Black Bear
12	Mountain Lion
16	Brown Bear

DAEDRA

Level	Creature
1	Stunted Scamp
5	Scamp
5	Clannfear Runt
7	Flame Atronach
11	Clannfear
13	Frost Atronach
14	Daedroth
16	Spider Daedra
17	Storm Atronach
20	Xivilai (L)

DREMORA

Level	Creature
1	Dremora Churl
6	Dremora Caitiff
9	Dremora Kynval
12	Dremora Kynreeve
15	Dremora Kynmarcher
19	Dremora Markynaz
22	Dremora Valkynaz (L)

GOBLINS

Level	Creature
1	Goblin
6	Goblin Skirmisher
8	Goblin Berserker
13	Goblin Shaman (L)
18	Goblin Warlord (L)

MYTHIC ENEMY

Level	Creature
1	Imp
6	Troll
9	Will-o-the-Wisp
10	Spriggan
12	Minotaur
15	Land Dreugh
16	Ogre (L)
18	Minotaur Lord (L)

UNDEAD

Level	Creature
1	Skeleton
1	Zombie
1	Ghost
6	Skeleton Guardian
8	Headless Zombie
9	Ancient Ghost
10	Skeleton Hero
12	Faded Wraith
14	Dread Zombie
15	Skeleton Champion
16	Wraith
17	Nether Lich
21	Gloom Wraith (L)
23	Lich (L)

Most of the statistics listed for the creatures are self-explanatory, but a few attributes might need clarification:

Type: The type of creature is mainly important for certain spell types that are specifically designed to work against creatures, humanoids, or undead.

Level: This is the lowest level the creature will appear in the world; in general, you won't see them commonly until you are two levels above this.

Soul: This is the size of Soul Gem you will need to hold the creature's soul with a soul-trapping spell.

Combat Skill: This value is used any time the creature attempts to do a combat-based skill action such as attacking. Weapon-using creatures will use the perks of the appropriate skill level.

Magic Skill: This value is used any time the creature attempts to do a magic-based skill action such as casting spells.

Attack Damage: This is the damage done by the creature without a weapon. Weapon-using creatures use the weapon damage, unless they are disarmed.

Weapons: Most creatures use leveled lists to generate their weapons, so they may be armed with a variety of weapons. Those listed are the most common used by the creature.

Advantages: Natural or magical abilities that may make the creature more difficult to harm in combat.

Weaknesses: Natural or magical abilities that may make the creature easier to harm.

Ingredient: Some creatures commonly provide an alchemical ingredient when they die.

Ranged Magic: A summary of the damaging ranged magic the creature can use in combat.

Melee Magic: A summary of the damaging touch magic the creature can use in combat.

ANCIENT GHOST

Type: Undead	Combat Skill: 60
Level: 9	Magic Skill: 60
Health: 170	Stealth Skill: 25
Magicka: 120	Attack Damage: Magic attack
Fatigue: 200	only
Soul: Common	Weapons: None

Advantages: Immune to normal weapons, immune to disease, immune to frost, immune to poison
Weaknesses: None
Ingredient: Ectoplasm
Ranged Magic: Icy Blast (damage Fatigue, frost damage)
Melee Magic: Ghostly Touch (drain Fatigue, damage Fatigue, frost damage), Icy Touch (damage Fatigue, frost damage)

Like all noncorporeal undead, the Ancient Ghost can only be harmed by silver or magical weaponry, or destructive magic. It can turn itself invisible and strike from an unexpected direction.

BEAR, BLACK

Type: Creature	Combat Skill: 50
Level: 7	Magic Skill: 5
Health: 150	Stealth Skill: 40
Magicka: 0	Attack Damage: 22
Fatigue: 200	Weapons: None
Soul: Common	

Advantages: Resist frost, disease (Yellow Tick)
Weaknesses: None
Ingredient: Bear pelt
Ranged Magic: None
Melee Magic: None

The smaller of the two Bears native to Cyrodiil, the Black Bear is still a dangerous opponent. It hits hard but is not particularly fast, so it is best dealt with from a distance.

BEAR, BROWN

Type: Creature	Combat Skill: 65
Level: 14	Magic Skill: 0
Health: 330	Stealth Skill: 40
Magicka: 0	Attack Damage: 44
Fatigue: 240	Weapons: None
Soul: Greater	

Advantages: Resist frost, disease (Yellow Tick)
Weaknesses: None
Ingredient: Bear pelt
Ranged Magic: None
Melee Magic: None

This huge Bear can take a tremendous punishment and still stay on its feet. A blow from its paw can stagger the mightiest warrior, so treat this woodland giant with respect.

BOAR

Type: Creature	Combat Skill: 65
Level: 5	Magic Skill: 5
Health: 100	Stealth Skill: 30
Magicka: 0	Attack Damage: 24
Fatigue: 250	Weapons: None
Soul: Lesser	

Advantages: High Agility, resist frost, disease (Chanthrax Blight)
Weaknesses: None
Ingredient: Boar meat
Ranged Magic: None
Melee Magic: None

The woodland Boar's tough hide makes it surprisingly dangerous for its compact size. The Boar can do a great deal of damage if it can land a blow, so staying out of its relatively short reach is advisable.

CLANNFEAR

Type: Daedra	Combat Skill: 60
Level: 11	Magic Skill: 5
Health: 180	Stealth Skill: 15
Magicka: 0	Attack Damage: 36
Fatigue: 250	Weapons: None
Soul: Common	

Advantages: Reflect damage, resist fire
Weaknesses: Weakness to shock
Ingredient: Clannfear claws
Ranged Magic: None
Melee Magic: None

The Clannfear, with its terrifying speed and razor-sharp claws, is one of the most dangerous Daedric beasts. Its heavy strike and damage reflection make it especially deadly to melee fighters. Fight it from a distance if you can, or use magic to bypass its damage reflection.

DAEDROTH

Type: Daedra
Level: 14
Health: 280
Magicka: 20
Fatigue: 500
Soul: Greater

Combat Skill: 100
Magic Skill: 100
Stealth Skill: 25
Attack Damage: 40
Weapons: None

Advantages: Resist fire
Weaknesses: Weakness to shock
Ingredient: Daedroth teeth
Ranged Magic: Fiery Breath
Melee Magic: None

The mighty Daedroth can breathe fire and do terrible damage with its teeth and claws. Its teeth are highly prized by alchemists, but they remain very rare for good reason.

DEER

Type: Creature
Level: 1
Health: 12–23
Magicka: 0
Fatigue: 165
Soul: Petty

Combat Skill: 25
Magic Skill: 50
Stealth Skill: 40
Attack Damage: 4–10
Ingredient: Venison

Advantages: None
Weaknesses: None
Ranged Magic: None
Melee Magic: None

Deer are found throughout the woodlands and fields of Cyrodiil. They are skittish and will flee from danger, but hunters prize their meat. The buck is rather more dangerous when forced to fight.

DOG

Type: Creature
Level: 1
Health: 20
Magicka: 0
Fatigue: 160
Soul: Petty

Combat Skill: 35
Magic Skill: 50
Stealth Skill: 50
Attack Damage: 8
Weapons: None

Advantages: None
Weaknesses: None
Ingredient: None
Ranged Magic: None
Melee Magic: None

These large, fierce canines are often employed as guard dogs by Bandits and Marauders due to their keen sense of smell and excellent eyesight.

DREAD ZOMBIE

Type: Undead
Level: 14
Health: 340
Magicka: 0
Fatigue: 200
Soul: Greater

Combat Skill: 80
Magic Skill: 5
Stealth Skill: 25
Attack Damage: 38
Weapons: None

Advantages: Regenerate Health, immune to disease, resist frost, resist magic, immune to poison, disease
Weaknesses: Weakness to fire
Ingredient: Mort flesh
Ranged Magic: None
Melee Magic: None

The Dread Zombie is easily recognizable by the foul cloud of corruption that it exudes. This cloud may in some way contribute to the Dread Zombie's ability to slowly repair its damaged flesh, which makes it a very dangerous opponent, particularly when attacking in groups. As with all Zombies, fire is the best remedy.

DREMORA CHURL

Type: Humanoid
Level: 3
Health: 44
Magicka: 340
Fatigue: 165
Soul: NPC

Combat Skill: 38
Magic Skill: 37
Stealth Skill: 32
Attack Damage: Weapon
Weapons: Dremora mace

Advantages: Resist magic, resist fire, summon Daedra
Weaknesses: Weakness to shock
Ingredient: Daedra heart
Ranged Magic: Destruction spells
Melee Magic: Destruction spells

Dremora are a class of intelligent, powerful war spirits in the service of the Daedra Lord Mehrunes Dagon. Churls are the lowest rank of Dremora: obsequious to superiors, ferociously cruel to humans and other Daedra. Like all Dremora, they wield both weapons and magic. Dremora mages may summon lesser Daedra to assist them in battle.

DREMORA CAITIFF

Type: Humanoid	Combat Skill: 35
Level: 6	Magic Skill: 48
Health: 74	Stealth Skill: 35
Magicka: 360	Attack Damage: Weapon
Fatigue: 201	Weapons: Dremora mace
Soul: NPC	

Advantages: Resist magic, resist fire
Weaknesses: Weakness to shock
Ingredient: Daedra heart
Ranged Magic: Destruction spells
Melee Magic: Destruction spells

Caitiffs are the second rank of Dremora. They favor a heavy mace and shield in melee combat, and may use magic as well. They often carry potions and scrolls to fortify themselves in battle.

DREMORA KYNVAL

Type: Humanoid	Combat Skill: 47
Level: 9	Magic Skill: 43
Health: 104	Stealth Skill: 38
Magicka: 380	Attack Damage: Weapon
Fatigue: 223	Weapons: Dremora longsword
Soul: NPC	

Advantages: Resist magic, resist fire
Weaknesses: Weakness to shock
Ingredient: Daedra heart
Ranged Magic: Destruction spells
Melee Magic: Destruction spells

The third rank of Dremora are known as Kynval, or knights. They wield longswords and will not hesitate to use magic or potions to gain an advantage in combat.

DREMORA KYNREEVE

Type: Humanoid	Combat Skill: 52
Level: 12	Magic Skill: 46
Health: 124	Stealth Skill: 41
Magicka: 400	Attack Damage: Weapon
Fatigue: 243	Weapons: Dremora longsword
Soul: NPC	

Advantages: Resist magic, resist fire
Weaknesses: Weakness to shock
Ingredient: Daedra heart
Ranged Magic: Destruction spells
Melee Magic: Destruction spells

The Kynreeve is an officer of a Dremora clan battle unit. They are equipped similarly to the Kynval, with the addition of a shield.

DREMORA KYNMARCHER

Type: Humanoid	Combat Skill: 56
Level: 15	Magic Skill: 49
Health: 145	Stealth Skill: 44
Magicka: 424	Attack Damage: Weapon
Fatigue: 267	Weapons: Dremora claymore
Soul: NPC	

Advantages: Resist magic, resist fire
Weaknesses: Weakness to shock
Ingredient: Daedra heart
Ranged Magic: Destruction spells
Melee Magic: Destruction spells

A Kynmarcher is a high officer responsible for a citadel, outpost, or gate, or a commander of a clan battle unit. These dangerous warriors wield heavy claymores, often enchanted, as well as an array of potions and spells.

DREMORA MARKYNAZ

Type: Humanoid	Combat Skill: 62
Level: 19	Magic Skill: 53
Health: 172	Stealth Skill: 48
Magicka: 450	Attack Damage: Weapon
Fatigue: 295	Weapons: Dremora claymore
Soul: NPC	

Advantages: Resist magic, resist fire
Weaknesses: Weakness to shock
Ingredient: Daedra heart
Ranged Magic: Destruction spells
Melee Magic: Destruction spells

The Markynaz, or grand dukes, are members of Mehrunes Dagon's Council of Lords. As such, they are among the most battle-hardened warriors in Dagon's service.

Dremora Valkynaz

Type: Humanoid	Combat Skill: 66+
Level: 22+	Magic Skill: 56+
Health: 192+	Stealth Skill: 51+
Magicka: 470+	Attack Damage: Weapon
Fatigue: 314+	Weapons: Daedric
Soul: NPC	warhammer

Advantages: Resist magic, resist fire
Weaknesses: Weakness to shock
Ingredient: Daedra heart
Ranged Magic: Destruction spells
Melee Magic: Destruction spells

The Valkynaz are Mehrunes Dagon's elite personal guard. They are the most dangerous foes you will encounter within Dagon's realm.

Faded Wraith

Type: Creature	Combat Skill: 75
Level: 12	Magic Skill: 75
Health: 280	Stealth Skill: 30
Magicka: 160	Attack Damage: 24
Fatigue: 255	Weapons: Longsword
Soul: Common	

Advantages: Immune to normal weapons, immune to disease, immune to frost, immune to poison
Weaknesses: None
Ingredient: Ectoplasm
Ranged Magic: Frost Bolt (frost damage), Silence of the Grave (frost damage, silence)
Melee Magic: Winter's Grasp (frost damage)

The Faded Wraith is the weaker version of the Wraith, but it is deadly enough. Spellcasters need to especially beware of its ability to silence its enemies. Not completely incorporeal like the Ghost, the Wraith is even capable of using (all-too-real) weapons.

Flame Atronach

Type: Daedra	Combat Skill: 35
Level: 7	Magic Skill: 50
Health: 150	Stealth Skill: 15
Magicka: 100	Attack Damage: 5
Fatigue: 200	Weapons: None
Soul: Common	

Advantages: Immune to fire, immune to disease, immune to poison, reflect damage
Weaknesses: Weakness to frost
Ingredient: Fire salts
Ranged Magic: Fireball
Melee Magic: Fire Touch

The Flame Atronach is a powerful Daedric summoning associated with elemental fire. Crystalline elemental fire compounds called fire salts may be salvaged from the remains of Flame Atronachs. They prefer to stand off and blast their enemies with fireballs, but they are equally dangerous in melee. Use frost magic to bring them down quickly.

Frost Atronach

Type: Creature	Combat Skill: 90
Level: 13	Magic Skill: 10
Health: 280	Stealth Skill: 20
Magicka: 60	Attack Damage: 40
Fatigue: 165	Weapons: None
Soul: Greater	

Advantages: Immune to frost, immune to disease, immune to poison, reflect damage
Weaknesses: Weakness to fire
Ingredient: Frost salts
Ranged Magic: Frost Bolt (frost damage)
Melee Magic: Freezing Touch (frost damage)

The ponderous Frost Atronach makes up in hitting power what it lacks in speed, so stay out of reach of its huge fists. Its freezing grip can do lasting frost damage, and it can hurl icy chunks of its body great distances.

Ghost

Type: Undead	Combat Skill: 8
Level: 4	Magic Skill: 40
Health: 72	Stealth Skill: 23
Magicka: 100	Attack Damage: Magic attacks
Fatigue: 200	only
Soul: Lesser	Weapons: None

Advantages: Immune to normal weapons, immune to disease, immune to frost, immune to poison
Weaknesses: None
Ingredient: Ectoplasm
Ranged Magic: Frost Damage, Damage Fatigue
Melee Magic: Frost Damage, Drain Fatigue

These restless spirits can only be harmed with silver or enchanted weapons. Beware of their ability to curse your Fatigue.

GLOOM WRAITH

Type: Undead
Level: 21+
Health: 504+
Magicka: 126+
Fatigue: 210+
Soul: Grand

Combat Skill: 50+
Magic Skill: 90+
Stealth Skill: 42+
Attack Damage: 27
Weapons: Longsword

Advantages: Immune to normal weapons, immune to disease, immune to frost, immune to poison
Weaknesses: None
Ingredient: Ectoplasm
Ranged Magic: Ice Bolt (frost damage), Silence of the Grave (frost damage, silence)
Melee Magic: Winter's Grasp (frost damage), Gloom Wraith's Curse (burden, absorb Health)

The strongest version of the Wraith, the Gloom Wraith adds a burden/absorb health curse to the usual deadly combination of weapon, claw, silence, and ranged frost attacks. The Gloom Wraith is leveled to you, so it will continue to increase in strength as your character rises in level.

GOBLIN

Type: Creature
Level: 1
Health: 15
Magicka: 0
Fatigue: 135
Soul: Petty

Combat Skill: 20
Magic Skill: 50
Stealth Skill: 10
Attack Damage: 3
Weapons: Iron shortsword, dagger, mace, or war axe

Advantages: High Agility
Weaknesses: None
Ingredient: None
Ranged Magic: None
Melee Magic: None

The common Goblin is dangerous only in packs. They rarely venture from their underground lairs. Typically armed with iron weapons, they may also carry lockpicks and poisons.

GOBLIN SKIRMISHER

Type: Creature
Level: 4
Health: 75
Magicka: 0
Fatigue: 150
Soul: Lesser

Combat Skill: 70
Magic Skill: 5
Stealth Skill: 15
Attack Damage: Weapon
Weapons: Steel war axe, mace, shortsword, dagger, bow

Advantages: None
Weaknesses: None
Ingredient: None
Ranged Magic: None
Melee Magic: None

The Goblin Skirmisher is stronger than the common Goblin and is often armed with a bow.

GOBLIN BERSERKER

Type: Creature
Level: 8
Health: 170
Magicka: 0
Fatigue: 300
Soul: Common

Combat Skill: 70
Magic Skill: 5
Stealth Skill: 20
Attack Damage: Weapon
Weapons: War axe, mace, shortsword

Advantages: High Agility
Weaknesses: None
Ingredient: None
Ranged Magic: None
Melee Magic: None

The Berserker carries the best weapons of any Goblin and may also carry a shield. Their high Agility makes them formidable melee opponents.

GOBLIN SHAMAN

Type: Creature
Level: 13
Health: 143+
Magicka: 195+
Fatigue: 156+
Soul: Greater

Combat Skill: 60+
Magic Skill: 80+
Stealth Skill: 26+
Attack Damage: 10+
Weapons: Shortsword, staff

Advantages: Spell absorption, high Agility
Weaknesses: None
Ingredient: None
Ranged Magic: Shock Damage
Melee Magic: Paralyze, Frost Damage

The Goblin Shaman is a dangerous spellcasting opponent. Particularly beware of its ability to paralyze you within melee range. The Shaman may carry a staff, but even without it has a range of spells to call on in combat, including summoning a Headless Zombie.

GOBLIN WARLORD

Type: Creature
Level: 18
Health: 540+
Magicka: 0
Fatigue: 288+
Soul: Grand
Advantages: High Agility
Weaknesses: None
Ingredient: None
Ranged Magic: None
Melee Magic: None

Combat Skill: 76+
Magic Skill: 0
Stealth Skill: 56+
Attack Damage: 9
Weapons: War axe, mace, shortsword

The Warlord is the most powerful Goblin, wielding a variety of weapons and a shield. Like the shaman, it will level with you, so it will always provide a challenge even to the highest-level characters.

HEADLESS ZOMBIE

Type: Undead
Level: 8
Health: 175
Magicka: 0
Fatigue: 165
Soul: Common

Combat Skill: 55
Magic Skill: 5
Stealth Skill: 10
Attack Damage: 27
Weapons: None

Advantages: Immune to disease, resist frost, resist magic, poison
Weaknesses: Weakness to fire
Ingredient: Mort flesh
Ranged Magic: None
Melee Magic: None

Headless Zombies are even fiercer than their cranially advantaged fellows, perhaps due to their futile longing to regain their lost brains. As with all Zombies, fire is the preferred method of laying them to rest.

HORSE, BAY

Type: Creature
Level: 1
Health: 250
Magicka: 50
Fatigue: 50
Soul: Lesser

Combat Skill: 30
Magic Skill: 50
Stealth Skill: 30
Attack Damage: 10
Weapons: None
Advantages: None

Weaknesses: None
Ingredient: None
Ranged Magic: None
Melee Magic: None

More expensive than the Paint Horse, the Bay Horse is faster but with lower Health.

HORSE, CHESTNUT

Type: Creature
Level: 1
Health: 200
Magicka: 50
Fatigue: 50
Soul: Lesser
Advantages: None
Weaknesses: None
Ingredient: None
Ranged Magic: None
Melee Magic: None

Combat Skill: 20
Magic Skill: 50
Stealth Skill: 30
Attack Damage: 10
Weapons: None

The Chestnut Horse is faster than the Bay and Paint Horses but has the lowest Health of all the horses.

HORSE, PAINT

Type: Creature
Level: 1
Health: 300
Magicka: 50
Fatigue: 50
Soul: Lesser
Advantages: None
Weaknesses: None
Ingredient: None
Ranged Magic: None
Melee Magic: None

Combat Skill: 40
Magic Skill: 50
Stealth Skill: 30
Attack Damage: 10
Weapons: None

The hardy Paint Horse is a good choice for anyone needing a reliable mount for a reasonable price.

IMP

Type: Creature	Combat Skill: 26
Level: 3	Magic Skill: 66
Health: 45	Stealth Skill: 21
Magicka: 60	Attack Damage: 5
Fatigue: 210	Weapons: None
Soul: Lesser	

Advantages: None
Weaknesses: None
Ingredient: Imp gall
Ranged Magic: Fire, Frost, or Shock
Melee Magic: None

Imps are equally at home in the forests and caves of Cyrodiil. Usually solitary, they possess a mean intelligence that can make them dangerous opponents. Many an unwary traveler has been surprised by a blast of magic from a distant Imp.

LAND DREUGH

Type: Creature	Combat Skill: 75
Level: 15	Magic Skill: 76
Health: 320	Stealth Skill: 30
Magicka: 12	Attack Damage: 30
Fatigue: 250	Weapons: None
Soul: Greater	

Advantages: Resist magic, resist normal weapons
Weaknesses: None
Ingredient: Dreugh wax
Ranged Magic: None
Melee Magic: Shocking Touch (shock damage over time)

The Land Dreugh is one of the odder creatures to infest the wilds of Cyrodiil. Its thick shell is highly resistant to both magical and normal damage, and it has the ability to direct electricity into its prey through its claws. Thankfully it is rather slow-moving, so keeping out of its way is the best way to deal with it.

LICH

Type: Undead	Combat Skill: 68+
Level: 24+	Magic Skill: 95+
Health: 360+	Stealth Skill: 98+
Magicka: 792+	Attack Damage: 32+
Fatigue: 288+	Weapons: Staff
Soul: Grand	

Advantages: Spell reflection, spell absorption, immune to disease, immune to frost, immune to poison, resist magic
Weaknesses: Weakness to fire
Ingredient: Bonemeal
Ranged Magic: None
Melee Magic: None

The Lich is the pinnacle of the Necromancer's art. Particularly dangerous to spellcasters, the lich is difficult to harm with magic and has a wide range of high-level spells to draw upon.

HORSE, WHITE

Type: Creature	Combat Skill: 50
Level: 1	Magic Skill: 50
Health: 400	Stealth Skill: 30
Magicka: 50	Attack Damage: 10
Fatigue: 50	Weapons: None
Soul: Lesser	

Advantages: None
Weaknesses: None
Ingredient: None
Ranged Magic: None
Melee Magic: None

The White Horse is as fast as the Chestnut Horse, but far sturdier.

HORSE, BLACK

Type: Creature	Combat Skill: 60
Level: 1	Magic Skill: 50
Health: 325	Stealth Skill: 30
Magicka: 50	Attack Damage: 10
Fatigue: 50	Weapons: None
Soul: Lesser	

Advantages: None
Weaknesses: None
Ingredient: None
Ranged Magic: None
Melee Magic: None

The Black Horse is the most expensive in addition to being the fastest. With only slightly lower Health than the White Horse, it also has the best combat skill of any of the horses.

MINOTAUR

Type: Creature	Combat Skill: 70
Level: 12	Magic Skill: 26
Health: 300	Stealth Skill: 10
Magicka: 20	Attack Damage: 30
Fatigue: 400	Weapons: Warhammer
Soul: Common	

Advantages: None
Weaknesses: None
Ingredient: Minotaur horn
Ranged Magic: None
Melee Magic: Disintegrate Armor

A fierce fighter with either fists or a warhammer; watch out for the Minotaur's head-butt, which (in addition to doing damage) will heavily damage your armor.

MINOTAUR LORD

Type: Creature	Combat Skill: 66+
Level: 18+	Magic Skill: 60+
Health: 396+	Stealth Skill: 46+
Magicka: 36+	Attack Damage: 33+
Fatigue: 288+	Weapons: Warhammer
Soul: Grand	

Advantages: Resist magic
Weaknesses: None
Ingredient: Minotaur horn
Ranged Magic: None
Melee Magic: Disintegrate Armor

The Minotaur Lord adds magic resistance to the already dangerous capabilities of the normal Minotaur. It is leveled to you, so he will become stronger along with your character.

MOUNTAIN LION

Type: Creature	Combat Skill: 80
Level: 10	Magic Skill: 0
Health: 160	Stealth Skill: 60
Magicka: 0	Attack Damage: 32
Fatigue: 200	Weapons: None
Soul: Common	

Advantages: High Agility, resist frost
Weaknesses: None
Ingredient: Lion pelt
Ranged Magic: None
Melee Magic: None

The Mountain Lion's high Agility and heavy strike make it a very dangerous melee opponent.

MUDCRAB

Type: Creature	Combat Skill: 25
Level: 1	Magic Skill: 90
Health: 10	Stealth Skill: 5
Magicka: 0	Attack Damage: 8
Fatigue: 50	Weapons: None
Soul: Petty	

Advantages: None
Weaknesses: Slow
Ingredient: Crabmeat
Ranged Magic: None
Melee Magic: None

A dangerous nuisance near any body of water, Mudcrabs are interesting only as a source of succulent crabmeat.

NETHER LICH

Type: Undead	Combat Skill: 65
Level: 17	Magic Skill: 80
Health: 225	Stealth Skill: 94
Magicka: 500	Attack Damage: 18
Fatigue: 204	Weapons: Staff
Soul: Greater	

Advantages: Spell absorption, immune to disease, immune to frost, immune to poison, resist magic
Weaknesses: Weakness to fire
Ingredient: Bonemeal
Ranged Magic: None
Melee Magic: None

A weaker version of the Lich, the Nether Lich is still a formidable opponent, with almost all the same dangerous magical abilities.

OGRE

Type: Creature	Combat Skill: 65+
Level: 16	Magic Skill: 0
Health: 416+	Stealth Skill: 0
Magicka: 0	Attack Damage: 30
Fatigue: 520+	Weapons: None
Soul: Greater	

Advantages: None
Weaknesses: Weakness to poison
Ingredient: Ogre's Teeth
Ranged Magic: None
Melee Magic: None

The huge Ogre deals tremendous damage with his fists, if he can get close enough. Despite their great size, Ogres are surprisingly susceptible to poison of all kinds.

RAT

Type: Creature	Combat Skill: 20
Level: 1	Magic Skill: 50
Health: 4	Stealth Skill: 20
Magicka: 0	Attack Damage: 2
Fatigue: 60	Weapons: None
Soul: Petty	

Advantages: Disease (Brain Rot)
Weaknesses: None
Ingredient: Ratmeat
Ranged Magic: None
Melee Magic: None

The Rat is a hardy, abundant hunter-scavenger, found both above- and belowground. A favorite food source of Goblins, although most civilized folk would prefer other fare. Dangerous only in large numbers.

SCAMP

Type: Creature	Combat Skill: 30
Level: 5	Magic Skill: 40
Health: 80	Stealth Skill: 15
Magicka: 50	Attack Damage: 15
Fatigue: 200	Weapons: None
Soul: Lesser	

Advantages: Resist fire, spell reflection
Weaknesses: Weakness to shock
Ingredient: Scamp skin
Ranged Magic: Fireball
Melee Magic: None

The Scamp is a weak, cowardly servant of Mehrunes Dagon. Scamps may be summoned by Conjurers, and their skin is sought by alchemists for its magical properties.

SHEEP

Type: Creature	Combat Skill: 10
Level: 1	Magic Skill: 50
Health: 13	Stealth Skill: 10
Magicka: 0	Attack Damage: 3
Fatigue: 75	Weapons: None
Soul: Petty	

Advantages: None
Weaknesses: None
Ingredient: Mutton
Ranged Magic: None
Melee Magic: None

The common domesticated Sheep is placid and nonaggressive. But tasty.

SKELETON

Type: Undead	Combat Skill: 40
Level: 1	Magic Skill: 5
Health: 20	Stealth Skill: 10
Magicka: 0	Attack Damage: 5
Fatigue: 100	Weapons: Iron or steel war axe
Soul: Petty	

Advantages: Resist frost, immune to disease, immune to paralysis, immune to poison
Weaknesses: None
Ingredient: Bonemeal
Ranged Magic: None
Melee Magic: None

The Skeleton is a revenant that can be found wherever the restless dead are buried. Often the creation of Necromancers pursuing their dark researches, they are capable of using all manner of melee weapons, although the most common Skeleton usually is armed with a war axe.

SKELETON GUARDIAN

Type: Undead
Level: 6
Health: 170
Magicka: 0
Fatigue: 180
Soul: Lesser

Combat Skill: 65
Magic Skill: 5
Stealth Skill: 15
Attack Damage: Weapon
Weapons: Silver mace, bow

Advantages: Resist frost, immune to disease, immune to paralysis, immune to poison
Weaknesses: None
Ingredient: Bonemeal
Ranged Magic: None
Melee Magic: None

The Skeleton Guardian dimly remembers its former life as a warrior and wields mace, shield, and bow with deadly skill.

SKELETON HERO

Type: Undead
Level: 10
Health: 280
Magicka: 0
Fatigue: 300
Soul: Common

Combat Skill: 74
Magic Skill: 5
Stealth Skill: 25
Attack Damage: Weapon
Weapons: Battle axe, bow

Advantages: Resist frost, immune to disease, immune to paralysis, immune to poison
Weaknesses: None
Ingredient: Bonemeal
Ranged Magic: None
Melee Magic: None

The Skeleton Hero's high combat skill makes it a dangerous opponent in melee combat, as it can use a full repertoire of advanced combat moves and is equally adept at blocking.

SKELETON CHAMPION

Type: Creature
Level: 15
Health: 350
Magicka: 50
Fatigue: 245
Soul: Greater

Combat Skill: 99
Magic Skill: 99
Stealth Skill: 30
Attack Damage: Weapon
Weapons: Claymore

Advantages: Resist frost, immune to disease, immune to paralysis, immune to poison
Weaknesses: None
Ingredient: Bonemeal
Ranged Magic: None
Melee Magic: None

The Skeleton Champion has one of the highest combat skills you will encounter, and it will often carry a sword as good as your own.

SLAUGHTERFISH

Type: Creature
Level: 1
Health: 13
Magicka: 0
Fatigue: 185
Soul: Petty

Combat Skill: 50
Magic Skill: 50
Stealth Skill: 40
Attack Damage: 15
Weapons: None

Advantages: None
Weaknesses: None
Ingredient: Scales
Ranged Magic: None
Melee Magic: None

The Slaughterfish is an aggressive predator found in both open waters and subterranean pools.

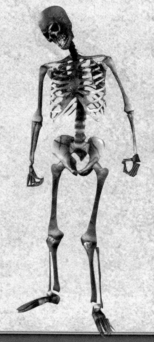

SPIDER DAEDRA

Type: Daedra
Level: 16
Health: 300
Magicka: 150
Fatigue: 285
Soul: Greater

Combat Skill: 80
Magic Skill: 80
Stealth Skill: 50
Attack Damage: 16
Weapons: None

Advantages: Resist fire, immune to paralysis, healing
Weaknesses: Weakness to frost, weakness to shock
Ingredient: Daedra venin, Daedra silk
Ranged Magic: Poison Spit (damage Agility, damage Speed, damage Health), Shock Bolt
Melee Magic: None

The bizarre Spider Daedra can spit poison great distances, but even more deadly is its ability to summon a tiny Spiderling that has a paralyzing bite.

TIMBER WOLF

Type: Creature
Level: 4
Health: 60
Magicka: 0
Fatigue: 250
Soul: Lesser

Combat Skill: 50
Magic Skill: 5
Stealth Skill: 50
Attack Damage: 14
Weapons: None

Advantages: Resist frost, disease (Helljoint)
Weaknesses: None
Ingredient: Wolf pelt
Ranged Magic: None
Melee Magic: None

A larger and fiercer cousin of the Wolf, Timber Wolves can bring down the largest prey when a pack has assembled.

SPRIGGAN

Type: Creature
Level: 11
Health: 175
Magicka: 30
Fatigue: 220
Soul: Common

Combat Skill: 50
Magic Skill: 51
Stealth Skill: 50
Attack Damage: 20
Weapons: None

Advantages: Summon Black Bear, resist shock, heal self x3
Weaknesses: Weakness to fire
Ingredient: Taproot
Ranged Magic: None
Melee Magic: None

The Spriggan is a guardian nature spirit, found both above- and below-ground. She will summon a Black Bear to help her in combat. She also has the ability to heal herself completely three times, so she can be a very difficult opponent unless you can kill her quickly.

STUNTED SCAMP

Type: Daedra
Level: 2
Health: 40
Magicka: 50
Fatigue: 100
Soul: Lesser

Combat Skill: 30
Magic Skill: 25
Stealth Skill: 10
Attack Damage: 10
Weapons: None

Advantages: Fireball, resist fire
Weaknesses: Weakness to shock
Ingredient: None
Ranged Magic: Fireball
Melee Magic: None

A smaller and weaker cousin of the Scamp.

TROLL

Type: Creature
Level: 6
Health: 80
Magicka: 0
Fatigue: 260
Soul: Lesser

Combat Skill: 40
Magic Skill: 0
Stealth Skill: 15
Attack Damage: 12
Weapons: None

Advantages: Regeneration
Weaknesses: Weakness to fire
Ingredient: Troll fat
Ranged Magic: None
Melee Magic: None

The Troll's uncanny ability to regenerate itself makes it a very dangerous opponent. Although the old wives' tale that it can only be killed by fire is false, there is a kernel of truth there. Fire, magical or otherwise, is one of the quickest ways to put an end to a Troll.

STORM ATRONACH

Type: Daedra
Level: 17
Health: 350
Magicka: 30
Fatigue: 165
Soul: Greater

Combat Skill: 50
Magic Skill: 50
Stealth Skill: 25
Attack Damage: 26
Weapons: None

Advantages: Immune to shock, immune to disease, immune to poison, immune to paralysis, reflect damage
Weaknesses: None
Ingredient: None
Ranged Magic: Shock Bolt
Melee Magic: Shock Touch

The Storm Atronach is a powerful Daedric summoning associated with elemental lightning. It can deliver shock damage at range or in melee.

WILL-O-THE-WISP

Type: Creature	Combat Skill: 65
Level: 9	Magic Skill: 100
Health: 220	Stealth Skill: 15
Magicka: 100	Attack Damage: Magic only
Fatigue: 205	Weapons: None
Soul: Common	

Advantages: Immune to normal weapons, immune to disease, immune to paralysis, immune to poison
Weaknesses: None
Ingredient: Glow dust
Ranged Magic: Mind Numb (absorb Health, absorb Magicka, damage Intelligence, damage Willpower)
Melee Magic: Wrack (absorb Health, absorb Magicka)

The Will-o-the-Wisp is unlike any other creature you will encounter. It isn't even clear whether it is a creature or spirit. Its ability to absorb Health and Magicka makes it particularly dangerous to melee fighters. It can also be difficult to hit with ranged weapons, due to its speed and ability to seemingly vanish and reappear in another place.

WRAITH

Type: Undead	Combat Skill: 70
Level: 16	Magic Skill: 75
Health: 400	Stealth Skill: 40
Magicka: 150	Attack Damage: 24
Fatigue: 200	Weapons: Longsword
Soul: Greater	

Advantages: Immune to normal weapons, immune to disease, immune to frost, immune to poison
Weaknesses: None
Ingredient: Ectoplasm
Ranged Magic: Ice Bolt (frost damage), Silence of the Grave (frost damage, silence)
Melee Magic: Arctic Blow (frost damage)

The Wraith can attack with claw, weapon, or magic. Beware of its silence spell, and make sure to bring a magic or silver weapon, because it is immune to normal weapon damage.

WOLF

Type: Creature	Combat Skill: 25
Level: 1	Magic Skill: 5
Health: 20	Stealth Skill: 25
Magicka: 0	Attack Damage: 5
Fatigue: 100	Weapons: None
Soul: Petty	

Advantages: Resist frost, disease (Helljoint)
Weaknesses: None
Ingredient: Wolf pelt
Ranged Magic: None
Melee Magic: None

A common predator throughout Cyrodiil, Wolves can be found both outdoors and in the caves where they make their lairs. Vampires often keep them as guards and companions.

XIVILAI

Type: Daedra	Combat Skill: 85+
Level: 20+	Magic Skill: 85+
Health: 240+	Stealth Skill: 50+
Magicka: 160+	Attack Damage: 25+
Fatigue: 300+	Weapons: Daedric battle axe,
Soul: Grand	warhammer

Advantages: Resist fire, spell absorption
Weaknesses: Weakness to shock, stunted Magicka
Ingredient: Daedra heart
Ranged Magic: Fireball, Summon Clannfear
Melee Magic: Shock Damage

The Xivilai is a powerful, semi-intelligent servant of Mehrunes Dagon. With a balanced combination of high melee skill and spell-casting, the Xivilai is a dangerous opponent for any type of character. Its one weakness is an inability to regenerate Magicka—so be aware that when casting spells at it, you may simply be recharging its Magicka reserves.

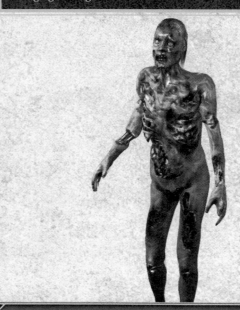

ZOMBIE

Type: Undead	Combat Skill: 40
Level: 2	Magic Skill: 5
Health: 80	Stealth Skill: 5
Magicka: 0	Attack Damage: 10
Fatigue: 165	Weapons: None
Soul: Lesser	

Advantages: Immune to disease, resist frost, resist magic, immune to poison, disease
Weaknesses: Weakness to fire
Ingredient: Mort flesh
Ranged Magic: None
Melee Magic: None

This mindless animated corpse can sustain an impressive amount of damage before being permanently laid to rest. Zombies also carry a wide variety of nasty diseases, so they are best avoided when possible.

Light armor is ideal for speed and stealth. It is a favorite of thieves and wizards. However, it breaks down quickly and doesn't provide as much protection.

Heavy armor provides the maximum protection, but slows down the wearer and makes him easier to detect. It is favored by the warrior classes.

LIGHT ARMOR

Item	Weight	Health	Price	Armor
Fur Helmet	1	50	4	2
Fur Gauntlets	1	50	4	2
Fur Boots	1.5	50	4	2
Fur Greaves	3	75	8	3
Fur Cuirass	5	100	15	5
Fur Shield	2	75	8	6
Leather Helmet	1.5	80	10	2.5
Leather Gauntlets	1.5	80	10	2.5
Leather Boots	2.25	80	10	2.5
Leather Greaves	4.5	120	20	3.75
Leather Cuirass	7.5	160	35	6.25
Leather Shield	3	120	20	7.5
Chainmail Helmet	1.8	135	25	3
Chainmail Gauntlets	1.8	135	25	3
Chainmail Boots	2.7	135	25	3
Chainmail Greaves	5.4	202	45	4.5
Chainmail Cuirass	9	270	90	7.5
Chainmail Shield	3.6	202	45	9
Mithril Helmet	2.2	240	65	3.5
Mithril Gauntlets	2.2	240	65	3.5
Mithril Boots	3.3	240	65	3.5
Mithril Greaves	6.6	360	115	5.25
Mithril Cuirass	11	480	225	8.75
Mithril Shield	4.4	360	115	10.5
Elven Helmet	2.6	440	170	4
Elven Gauntlets	2.6	440	170	4
Elven Boots	3.9	440	170	4
Elven Greaves	7.8	660	315	6
Elven Cuirass	13	880	600	10
Elven Shield	5.2	660	315	12
Glass Helmet	3	675	500	5
Glass Gauntlets	3	675	500	5
Glass Boots	4.5	675	500	5
Glass Greaves	9	1,000	1,000	7.5
Glass Cuirass	15	1,350	1,800	12.5
Glass Shield	6	1,000	1,000	15

HEAVY ARMOR

Item	Weight	Health	Price	Armor
Iron Helmet	6	150	25	4
Iron Gauntlets	6	150	25	4
Iron Boots	9	150	25	4
Iron Greaves	18	225	45	6
Iron Cuirass	30	300	85	10
Iron Shield	12	225	45	12
Steel Helmet	7	250	50	4.5
Steel Gauntlets	7	250	50	4.5
Steel Boots	10.5	250	50	4.5
Steel Greaves	21	375	95	6.75
Steel Cuirass	35	500	180	11.25
Steel Shield	14	375	95	13.5
Dwarven Helmet	8	400	115	5
Dwarven Gauntlets	8	400	115	5
Dwarven Boots	12	400	115	5
Dwarven Greaves	24	600	210	7.5
Dwarven Cuirass	40	800	400	12.5
Dwarven Shield	16	525	600	15
Orcish Helmet	9	600	250	5.5
Orcish Gauntlets	9	600	250	5.5
Orcish Boots	13.5	600	250	5.5
Orcish Greaves	27	900	460	8.25
Orcish Cuirass	45	1,200	940	13.75
Orcish Shield	18	900	460	16.5
Ebony Helmet	10.5	950	550	6
Ebony Gauntlets	10.5	950	550	6
Ebony Boots	15.75	950	550	6
Ebony Greaves	31.5	1,425	1,000	9
Ebony Cuirass	52.5	1,900	1,900	15
Ebony Shield	21	1,425	1,000	18
Daedric Helmet	12	1,350	1,350	7.5
Daedric Gauntlets	12	1,350	1,350	7.5
Daedric Boots	18	1,350	1,350	7.5
Daedric Greaves	36	2,025	2,500	11.25
Daedric Cuirass	60	2,700	4,800	18.75
Daedric Shield	24	1,500	2,025	22.5

ARMOR AVAILABILITY*

Armor	Available at Player Level
Fur/Iron	1
Leather/Steel	3
Chain/Dwarven	6
Mithril/Orcish	10
Elven/Ebony	15
Glass/Daedric	20

* Note: Magic armor and weapons are available two levels higher than their non-magical equivalents.

BLADE WEAPONS

Item	Weight	Value	Health	Speed	Reach	Damage
Iron Dagger	3	6	70	1.4	0.6	5
Iron Dagger, Fine	2.7	12	77	1.4	0.6	6
Iron Shortsword	8	10	98	1.2	0.8	7
Iron Shortsword, Fine	7.2	20	108	1.2	0.8	8
Iron Longsword	20	20	140	1	1	10
Iron Longsword, Fine	18	40	154	1	1	11
Iron Claymore	22	40	168	0.8	1.3	12
Iron Claymore, Fine	19.8	80	185	0.8	1.3	13
Steel Dagger	4	20	112	1.4	0.6	7
Steel Dagger, Fine	3.6	40	123	1.4	0.6	8
Steel Shortsword	10	25	144	1.2	0.8	9
Steel Shortsword, Fine	9	50	158	1.2	0.8	10
Steel Longsword	24	45	192	1	1	12
Steel Longsword, Fine	12.6	90	211	1	1	13
Steel Claymore	26	80	224	0.8	1.3	14
Steel Claymore, Fine	23.4	160	246	0.8	1.3	15
Akaviri Katana	20	120	200	1	1	14
Akaviri Katana, Ancient	18	180	240	1	1	15
Akaviri Dai-Katana	24	150	240	1	1	16
Silver Dagger	5	40	162	1.4	0.6	9
Silver Shortsword	12	50	198	1.2	0.8	11
Silver Longsword	28	80	252	1	1	14
Silver Claymore	32	130	288	0.8	1.3	16
Dwarven Dagger	6	110	220	1.4	0.6	11
Dwarven Shortsword	14	145	260	1.2	0.8	13
Dwarven Longsword	32	200	320	1	1	16
Dwarven Claymore	38	310	360	0.8	1.3	18
Elven Dagger	7	260	286	1.4	0.6	13
Elven Shortsword	16	320	330	1.2	0.8	15
Elven Longsword	36	420	396	1	1	18
Elven Claymore	44	600	440	0.8	1.3	20
Glass Dagger	8	570	360	1.4	0.6	15
Glass Shortsword	18	670	408	1.2	0.8	17
Glass Longsword	40	840	480	1	1	20
Glass Claymore	50	1150	528	0.8	1.3	22
Ebony Dagger	9	1250	442	1.4	0.6	17
Ebony Shortsword	20	1400	494	1.2	0.8	19
Ebony Longsword	44	1700	572	1	1	22
Ebony Claymore	56	2200	624	0.8	1.3	24
Daedric Dagger	10	2700	532	1.4	0.6	19
Daedric Shortsword	22	2900	588	1.2	0.8	21
Daedric Longsword	48	3100	672	1	1	24
Daedric Claymore	62	4000	728	0.8	1.3	26

BLUNT WEAPONS

Item	Weight	Value	Health	Speed	Reach	Damage
Iron War Axe	12	13	112	1.1	0.8	8
Iron War Axe, Fine	10.8	26	123	1.1	0.8	9
Iron Mace	15	17	140	0.9	1	10
Iron Mace, Fine	13.5	34	154	0.9	1	11
Iron Battle Axe	27	35	168	0.8	1.2	12
Iron Battle Axe, Fine	24.3	70	185	0.8	1.2	13
Iron Warhammer	30	60	196	0.7	1.3	14
Iron Warhammer, Fine	27	120	216	0.7	1.3	15
Steel War Axe	16	35	160	1.1	0.8	10
Steel War Axe, Fine	14.4	70	176	1.1	0.8	11
Steel Mace	19	40	192	0.9	1	12
Steel Mace, Fine	17.1	80	211	0.9	1	13
Steel Battle Axe	34	75	224	0.8	1.2	14
Steel Battle Axe, Fine	34	150	246	0.8	1.2	15
Steel Warhammer	39	125	256	0.7	1.3	16
Steel Warhammer, Fine	39	250	282	0.7	1.3	17
Silver War Axe	20	60	216	1.1	0.8	12
Silver Mace	23	70	252	0.9	1	14
Silver Battle Axe	41	125	288	0.8	1.2	16

BLUNT WEAPONS

Item	Weight	Value	Health	Speed	Reach	Damage
Silver Warhammer	48	200	324	0.7	1.3	18
Dwarven War Axe	24	165	280	1.1	0.8	14
Dwarven Mace	27	180	320	0.9	1	16
Dwarven Battle Axe	48	300	360	0.8	1.2	18
Dwarven Warhammer	57	430	400	0.7	1.3	20
Elven War Axe	28	345	352	1.1	0.8	16
Elven Mace	31	380	396	0.9	1	18
Elven Battle Axe	55	580	440	0.8	1.2	20
Elven Warhammer	66	800	484	0.7	1.3	22
Glass War Axe	32	710	432	1.1	0.8	18
Glass Mace	35	750	480	0.9	1	20
Glass Battle Axe	62	1,050	528	0.8	1.2	22
Glass Warhammer	75	1,500	576	0.7	1.3	24
Ebony War Axe	36	1,450	520	1.1	0.8	20
Ebony Mace	39	1,500	572	0.9	1	22
Ebony Battle Axe	69	2,100	624	0.8	1.2	24
Ebony Warhammer	84	2,800	676	0.7	1.3	26
Daedric War Axe	40	3,100	616	1.1	0.8	22
Daedric Mace	43	3200	672	0.9	1	24
Daedric Battle Axe	76	3,800	728	0.8	1.2	26
Daedric Warhammer	93	5,000	784	0.7	1.3	28

BOWS

Item	Weight	Value	Health	Damage
Iron Bow	8	11	112	8
Iron Bow, Fine	7.2	22	123	9
Steel Bow	10	30	144	9
Steel Bow, Fine	9	60	158	10
Silver Bow	12	55	180	10
Dwarven Bow	14	155	240	11
Elven Bow	16	360	308	12
Glass Bow	18	735	384	13
Ebony Bow	20	1,550	468	14
Daedric Bow	22	3,200	560	15

ARROWS

Item	Weight	Value	Damage
Iron Arrow	0.1	1	8
Steel Arrow	0.1	2	9
Silver Arrow	0.1	3	10
Dwarven Arrow	0.1	5	11
Glass Arrow	0.1	8	12
Elven Arrow	0.1	12	13
Ebony Arrow	0.2	20	14
Daedric Arrow	0.25	35	15

WEAPON AVAILABILITY

Weapons	Available at Player Level
Iron	1
Steel	2
Silver	4
Dwarven	6
Elven	9
Glass	12
Ebony	16
Daedric	20

ALCHEMY

Our world is a beautiful and dangerous place, and for those who stop to pick the flowers and taste the poisoned berries, the rewards are enormous. Mastering the Alchemy skill takes a special kind of person, one who takes the more roundabout approach to town, preferring to blaze a new trail rather than sticking to the roads, and who explores the nooks and crannies, finding rare and wondrous things growing right under the noses of those too busy to notice.

Virtually every magical effect can be coaxed into a bottle by extracting and mixing the various life forces flowing through nature. Potions of healing, fortifying attributes, poisons, and debilitating toxins are all produced from the careful art of the alchemist. While it is an art learned through patient scientific experimentation, here is some wisdom harvested from those who have gone before.

INGREDIENTS

Ingredients can be harvested from plants, looted from the corpses of monsters, or purchased from fellow alchemists or shop vendors. Their effects are varied; each ingredient has multiple effects, and the higher your Alchemy skill, the more effects you have available to use in potion-making (one effect is revealed at each skill level: Novice, Apprentice, Journeyman, and Expert). Until you see an effect listed on the ingredient, that effect is unavailable to you. You make potions by mixing ingredients with the same effect. When you have two ingredients with the same effect, your potion gains that effect. Your potions can have multiple effects.

Beware that your recipes may suddenly yield additional and possibly unwanted effects because you have earned additional effects for their ingredients by increasing your Alchemy skill.

By default the view of your ingredients is filtered so that once you start adding ingredients it will only show other ingredients that have one other known effect identical to those already added. Click the View All button if you want to make a potion with two separate effects without needing ingredients with more than one effect in common. For example, two ingredients can share Restore Health and two other unrelated ingredients could share Restore Magicka to make a dual-effect potion without needing to find ingredients with both Restore Health and Restore Magicka effects, but you must click the View All button because there is not a common effect between all four ingredients.

Wortcraft
You can eat an ingredient to gain its first listed effect, but you gain more potent effects and increase your skill faster by making potions than by chewing on raw ingredients.

ALCHEMY APPARATUS

First things first. Before you can make a potion or poison you must have a **mortar and pestle**. The quality of your mortar and pestle affects the base potency of your potions and poisons. The effects of the other apparatus are as follows: A **retort** improves the positive effects of a potion (has no effect on poisons), an **alembic** reduces any negative effects of a potion (has no effect on poisons), and a **calcinator** increases the potency of all the potion's effects. There are higher-grade apparatus that you will find as your character goes up in level; these have the same effect on your potions but to an even greater degree.

Alchemy gear often makes great loot to sell, especially when you consider the weight to value ratio.

The highest-grade apparatus are not sold in stores, so you must find them on your adventures. There's an abundance of alchemy gear in places inhabited by Conjurers.

POTIONS VS. POISONS

Potions are made when the result of alchemy produces a single positive effect (even if it also has negative effects). You drink this potion to gain the positive effect. Any negative effect in the potion is applied to you as well. Potions are pink bottles. Use an alembic to reduce the negative effects of a potion. Keep in mind you can drink a maximum of five potions at once (this number goes up to 10 with the perks gained as you increase your skill in Alchemy).

Poisons are created when the result of alchemy produces only negative results. While it might not seem intuitive, a Fire Damage potion is a poison. Poisons are green bottles. You apply poison to your currently equipped weapon when you activate the poison in your inventory. Poison is applied to bows, not to arrows. Poison gets used up with the next single successful attack with a melee weapon, or the next arrow shot through a bow (poison on arrows that miss their target is wasted). Poison lasts indefinitely until then, so if you have multiple weapons, you can poison them all and then quickly pull them out during combat (you can also apply poison during combat).

For example, you could carry a bunch of daggers and hotkey them to quickly pull them out. Then before every combat, poison them all; after each hit, hotkey the next one into your hand. Magic arrows shot through poisoned bows carry both the poison of the bow and the magic of the arrow for double trouble to the enemy that gets hit with it.

MAKING POTIONS AND POISONS

You might be tempted to become an alchemist to make money selling potions, but making potions is more valuable for increasing your skill and using them, rather than for making money. Note, however, that most potions sell for more as a potion than they do as individual ingredients. Also, the weight of a potion is the average of the weight of the ingredients, so if you are carrying around lots of ingredients you can shave a few points off of your Encumbrance by making potions.

The best way to increase your Alchemy skill is to make potions. Lots of potions! While you are exploring you often find various fruits and vegetables just lying around (or whole crops of them). While the resulting Restore Fatigue potion is hardly something to brag about, even to your non-alchemist friends, making these potions is a great way to increase your skill quickly, since there are so many ingredients for it.

POTIONS TO MAKE AT NOVICE LEVEL

Just getting started can be confusing. So here are some recipes for useful potions you can make at Novice level.

- Restore Magicka (flax seeds, steel blue entoloma)
- Restore Health (cairn bolete cap, lady's smock leaves)
- Damage Health (any two: wisp stalk cap, stinkhorn, nightshade, spiddal stick)

POTIONS TO MAKE AT APPRENTICE LEVEL

When you reach Apprentice level you can really start making worthwhile potions and poisons, some even with multiple effects. Here are some of the more useful ones:

- Feather (flax seeds, venison)
- Cure Disease (mandrake root, Elf cup cap)
- Dispel (bergamot seeds, ectoplasm)

- Restore Health (lady's smock leaves, aloe vera leaves)
- Night-Eye (carrot, viper's bugloss leaves)
- Detect Life (Rat meat, bread loaf)
- Water Breathing (onion, white seed pod [plant: goldenrod]
- Silence (Vampire dust, rice)
- Damage Speed (green stain cup cap, peony seeds)
- Damage Health + Damage Magicka (harrada, spiddal sticks)
- Damage Health + Damage Magicka + Silence (harrada, spiddal sticks, Vampire dust, rice)

POTIONS TO MAKE AT JOURNEYMAN LEVEL

Journeyman level reveals three ingredient effects. Multiple effect combinations are more numerous, and some new potion and poison effects are now possible.

- Water Walking (grapes, tiger lily nectar, stinkhorn)
- Fortify Strength (arrowroot, Elf cup cap)
- Chameleon (radish, bloodgrass)
- Invisibility (tinder polypore, wormwood leaves)
- Reflect Damage (Scamp skin, green stain cup)
- Fire Damage (fire salts, steel blue entoloma)
- Frost Damage (milk thistle, Vampire dust)
- Paralyze (Clannfear claws, Daedra venin)
- Damage Health + Damage Magicka + Silence (harrada, spiddal sticks, rice)
- Damage Health + Damage Magicka + Speed (harrada, spiddal sticks, peony seeds, pear)
- Damage Health + Damage Magicka + Fire Damage (harrada, spiddal sticks, steel blue entoloma)
- Damage Health + Damage Magicka + Fire Damage + Silence (harrada, spiddal sticks, steel blue entoloma, rice)

POTIONS TO MAKE AT EXPERT LEVEL

Expert level reveals all possible ingredient effects. Creating single effect potions/poisons should be easy by now, but here's one brand-new potion and some combination poisons to try:

- Fortify Speed (+ *Damage* Health) (pear, wisp stalk cap)
- Reflect Spell (glow dust, cinnabar polypore cap yellow)
- Fire Damage + Shock Damage + Damage Health (common) (spiddal stick, Imp gall, ectoplasm, fly amanita)

- Fire Damage + Shock Damage + Damage Health (uncommon) (Imp gall, ectoplasm, fire salts, Ogre's teeth)
- Paralyze + Frost Damage (dryad's saddle polypore, milk thistle seeds, fennel seeds)
- Paralyze + Frost Damage + Silence (harrada, milk thistle seeds, Vampire dust)
- Paralyze + Frost Damage + Damage Magicka + Silence (fennel seeds, harrada, milk thistle seeds, Vampire dust)
- Paralyze + Fire Damage + Damage Magicka + Damage Health (steel blue entoloma, Imp gall, harrada, fennel seeds)
- Paralyze + Damage Health + Damage Magicka + Damage Intelligence (fennel seeds, harrada, wisp stalk cap)

INGREDIENTS AND EFFECTS

Below is a table of ingredients and their effects to aid you in making potions. Also listed is an area where that ingredient is to be found in greater abundance than elsewhere. Remember to look in all the sacks, boxes, and barrels you encounter in cities and dungeons, as these often contain alchemy ingredients. Alchemy shops sell ingredients, if you want someone else to do your dirty work for you! The Main Ingredient in the Imperial City even sells rare items taken from the Oblivion realms.

ALCHEMY INGREDIENTS

Ingredient	Plant/Creature Name	Effect 1	Effect 2	Effect 3	Effect 4
Alkanet Flower	Alkanet	Restore Intelligence	Resist Poison	Light	Damage Fatigue
Aloe Vera Leaves	Aloe Vera	Restore Fatigue	Restore Health	Damage Magicka	Invisibility
Apple	—	Restore Fatigue	Damage Luck	Fortify Willpower	Damage Health
Arrowroot	Arrowroot Plant	Restore Agility	Damage Luck	Fortify Strength	Burden
Beef	—	Restore Fatigue	Shield	Fortify Agility	Dispel
Bergamot Seeds	Bergamot	Resist Disease	Dispel	Damage Magicka	Silence
Blackberry	Blackberry Bush	Restore Fatigue	Resist Shock	Fortify Endurance	Restore Magicka
Bloodgrass	Bloodgrass	Chameleon	Resist Paralysis	Burden	Fortify Health
Boar Meat	—	Restore Health	Damage Speed	Fortify Health	Burden
Bog Beacon Asco Cap	Bog Beacon	Restore Magicka	Shield	Damage Personality	Damage Endurance
Bonemeal	Skeletons	Damage Fatigue	Resist Fire	Fortify Luck	Night-Eye
Bread Loaf	—	Restore Fatigue	Detect Life	Damage Agility	Damage Strength
Cairn Bolete Cap	Cairn Bolete	Restore Health	Damage Intelligence	Resist Paralysis	Shock Damage
Carrot	Carrot Plant	Restore Fatigue	Night-Eye	Fortify Intelligence	Damage Endurance
Cheese Wedge	—	Restore Fatigue	Resist Fire	Fire Shield	Damage Agility
Cheese Wheel	—	Restore Fatigue	Resist Paralysis	Damage Luck	Fortify Willpower
Cinnabar Polypore Cap Red	Cinnabar Polypore	Restore Personality	Restore Endurance	Restore Agility	Shield
Cinnabar Polypore Cap Yellow	Cinnabar Polypore	Restore Endurance	Fortify Endurance	Damage Personality	Reflect Spell
Clannfear Claws	Clannfear	Cure Disease	Resist Disease	Paralyze	Damage Health
Clouded Funnel Cap	Clouded Funnel Cap	Restore Intelligence	Fortify Intelligence	Damage Endurance	Damage Magicka
Columbine Root Pulp	Columbine	Restore Personality	Resist Frost	Fortify Magicka	Chameleon
Corn	Corn Stalk	Restore Fatigue	Restore Intelligence	Damage Agility	Lightning Shield
Crabmeat	Mudcrabs	Restore Endurance	Resist Shock	Damage Fatigue	Fire Shield
Daedra Heart	Daedra	Restore Health	Lightning Shield	Damage Magicka	Silence
Daedra Silk	Spider Daedra	Burden	Night-Eye	Chameleon	Damage Endurance
Daedra Venin	Spider Daedra	Paralyze	Restore Fatigue	Damage Health	Reflect Damage
Daedroth Teeth	Daedroth	Night-Eye	Frost Shield	Burden	Light
Dragon's Tongue	Dragon's Tongue Plant	Resist Fire	Damage Health	Restore Health	Fire Shield
Dreugh Wax	Land Dreugh	Damage Fatigue	Resist Poison	Water Breathing	Damage Health
Dryad's Saddle Polypore Cap	Dryad's Saddle Polypore	Restore Luck	Resist Frost	Damage Speed	Frost Damage
Ectoplasm	Ghosts	Shock Damage	Dispel	Fortify Magicka	Damage Health
Elf Cup Cap	Elf Cup	Damage Willpower	Cure Disease	Fortify Strength	Damage Intelligence
Emetic Russula Cap	Emetic Russula	Restore Agility	Shield	Damage Personality	Damage Endurance
Fennel Seeds	Fennel	Restore Fatigue	Damage Intelligence	Damage Magicka	Paralyze
Fire Salts	Flame Atronachs	Fire Damage	Resist Frost	Restore Magicka	Fire Shield
Flax Seeds	Flax	Restore Magicka	Feather	Shield	Damage Health
Flour	—	Restore Fatigue	Damage Personality	Fortify Fatigue	Reflect Damage
Fly Amanita Cap	Fly Amanita	Restore Agility	Burden	Restore Health	Shock Damage
Foxglove Nectar	Foxglove	Resist Poison	Resist Paralysis	Restore Luck	Resist Disease
Frost Salts	Frost Atronachs	Frost Damage	Resist Fire	Silence	Frost Shield
Garlic	Garlic Cluster	Resist Disease	Damage Agility	Frost Shield	Fortify Strength
Ginkgo Leaf	—	Restore Speed	Fortify Magicka	Damage Luck	Shock Damage

ALCHEMY

The ingredients you take from dead creatures are often rare; you will not find these very many other places. Horde these ingredients until they become more useful to you as you unlock their additional effects. And if you manage to become the head of the Mages Guild, you gain access to a device that can replicate ingredients! (See the "Mages Guild" chapter.)

Ingredient: The name of the ingredient.

Plant/Creature Name: The name of the plant or creature from which you harvest the ingredient.

Effect: The effects of the ingredient.

# of Plants: The number of plants found in the world for the ingredient.

Commonly Found in These Places: While most ingredients are spread all over the world, here is where you are more likely to find them.

A Concentration Can Be Found: While there are many places where the ingredient is concentrated, here is one such place to get you started.

Harvest Chance: The chance (by percentage) that you successfully harvest an ingredient from the plant.

# of Plants	Commonly Found in These Places	A Concentration Can Be Found	Harvest Chance
1,305	Between Kvatch and Skingrad (south of road)	East of Miscarcand	80%
137	Gold Coast	South of Gottshaw Inn	80%
—	Food	—	—
223	Gold Coast	South of Hrota Cave	80%
—	Food	—	—
4,211	Great Forest, Nibenay Basin Valley	Southeast of Bloodmayne Cave	80%
140	Between Kvatch and Skingrad	North of Mortal Camp	80%
1,075	Oblivion		50%
—	Food	—	—
444	Nibenay Valley, Blackwood (northeast of Leyawiin)	West of Onyx Caverns	50%
—	Dungeons	—	—
—	Food	—	—
2,390	Caves	—	33%
202	Food	East of Odiil farm	80%
	Food	—	—
	Food	—	—
179	Between Kvatch and Skingrad	Southeast of Sandstone Cavern	50%
	Oblivion	—	—
7,794	Valus Mountains	Northeast of Hame	50%
1,414	West Weald and Heartlands (east of Skingrad and southwest of Imperial City)	Northwest of Shardrock	80%
381	Between Sutch and Kvatch	Whitmond farm	80%
—	Near water	—	—
	Oblivion	—	—
	Oblivion	—	—
	Oblivion	—	—
—	—	—	—
222	Southeast of Bravil, West Weald	South of Bawn	80%
—	—	—	—
48	Colovian Highlands (between Chorrol and Skingrad)	Southwest of Bawn	50%
—	Dungeons	—	—
111	Gold Coast near Anvil, West Weald	South of Arcane University	50%
103	Nibenay Basin Valley	Southwest of Drakelowe	50%
134	Colovian Highlands	West of Niryastare	80%
	Dungeons and Oblivion	—	—
2,489	Anvil (in and around)	Northwest of Fort Istirus	80%
—	Food (look in sacks)	—	—
3,305	Scattered	North of Bedrock Break	50%
2,185	Niberian Valley (eastern—partly on Nibenay Region map, partly on Blackwood map)	East of Bedrock Break	80%
—	Dungeons	—	—
58	Basements and cellars	—	80%
—	—	—	—

ALCHEMY INGREDIENTS

Ingredient	Plant/Creature Name	Effect 1	Effect 2	Effect 3	Effect 4
Ginseng	Ginseng Plant	Damage Luck	Cure Poison	Burden	Fortify Magicka
Glow Dust	Will-o-the-Wisps	Restore Speed	Light	Reflect Spell	Damage Health
Grapes	Grape Vine	Restore Fatigue	Water Walking	Dispel	Damage Health
Green Stain Cup Cap	Green Stain Cup	Restore Fatigue	Damage Speed	Reflect Damage	Damage Health
Green Stain Shelf Cap	Green Stain Shelf	Restore Luck	Fortify Luck	Damage Fatigue	Restore Health
Ham	—	Restore Fatigue	Restore Health	Damage Magicka	Damage Luck
Harrada	Harrada Root	Damage Health	Damage Magicka	Silence	Paralyze
Imp Gall	Imps	Fortify Personality	Cure Paralysis	Damage Health	Fire Damage
Lady's Mantle Leaves	Lady's Mantle	Restore Health	Damage Endurance	Night-Eye	Feather
Lady's Smock Leaves	Lady's Smock	Restore Intelligence	Resist Fire	Damage Fatigue	Fortify Health
Lavender Sprig	Lavender	Restore Personality	Fortify Willpower	Restore Health	Damage Luck
Leek	Leek Plant	Restore Fatigue	Fortify Agility	Damage Personality	Damage Strength
Lettuce	Lettuce Plant	Restore Fatigue	Restore Luck	Fire Shield	Damage Personality
Mandrake Root	Mandrake	Cure Disease	Resist Poison	Damage Agility	Fortify Willpower
Milk Thistle Seeds	Milk Thistle	Light	Frost Damage	Cure Paralysis	Paralyze
Minotaur Horn	Minotaurs	Restore Willpower	Burden	Fortify Endurance	Resist Paralysis
Monkshood Root Pulp	Monkshood	Restore Strength	Damage Intelligence	Fortify Endurance	Burden
Morning Glory Root Pulp	Morning Glory	Burden	Damage Willpower	Frost Shield	Damage Magicka
Mort Flesh	Zombies	Damage Fatigue	Damage Luck	Fortify Health	Silence
Motherwort Sprig	Motherwort	Resist Poison	Damage Fatigue	Silence	Invisibility
Mutton	—	Fortify Health	Damage Fatigue	Dispel	Damage Magicka
Nightshade	Nightshade Plant	Damage Health	Burden	Damage Luck	Fortify Magicka
Ogre's Teeth	Ogres	Damage Intelligence	Resist Paralysis	Shock Damage	Fortify Strength
Onion	—	Restore Fatigue	Water Breathing	Detect Life	Damage Health
Pear	—	Restore Fatigue	Damage Speed	Fortify Speed	Damage Health
Peony Seeds	Peony	Restore Strength	Damage Health	Damage Speed	Restore Fatigue
Potato	Potato Plant	Restore Fatigue	Shield	Burden	Frost Shield
Primrose Leaves	Primrose	Restore Willpower	Restore Personality	Fortify Luck	Damage Strength
Pumpkin	Pumpkin Vine	Restore Fatigue	Damage Agility	Damage Personality	Detect Life
Radish	Radish Plant	Restore Fatigue	Damage Endurance	Chameleon	Burden
Rat Meat	Rats	Damage Fatigue	Detect Life	Damage Magicka	Silence
Redwort Flower	Domica Redwort	Resist Frost	Cure Poison	Damage Health	Invisibility
Rice	—	Restore Fatigue	Silence	Lightning Shield	Damage Agility
Sacred Lotus Seeds	Sacred Lotus	Resist Frost	Damage Health	Feather	Dispel
Scales	Slaughterfish	Damage Willpower	Water Breathing	Damage Health	Water Walking
Scamp Skin	Scamps	Damage Magicka	Resist Shock	Reflect Damage	Damage Health
Somnalius Frond	Somnalius Plant	Restore Speed	Damage Endurance	Fortify Health	Feather
Spiddal Stick	Spiddal Stick	Damage Health	Damage Magicka	Fire Damage	Restore Fatigue
St. Jahn's Wort Nectar	St. Jahn's Wort	Resist Shock	Damage Health	Cure Poison	Chameleon
Steel Blue Entoloma Cap	Steel Blue Entoloma	Restore Magicka	Fire Damage	Resist Frost	Burden
Stinkhorn Cap	Stinkhorn	Damage Health	Restore Magicka	Water Walking	Invisibility
Strawberry	Strawberry Bush	Restore Fatigue	Cure Poison	Damage Health	Reflect Damage
Summer Bolete Cap	Summer Bolete	Restore Personality	Fire Shield	Damage Agility	Night-Eye
Sweetcake	—	Restore Fatigue	Feather	Restore Health	Burden
Sweetroll	—	Restore Fatigue	Resist Disease	Damage Personality	Fortify Health
Taproot	—	Restore Luck	Damage Endurance	Resist Poison	Lightning Shield
Tiger Lily Nectar	Tiger Lily; Lily of the Valley	Restore Endurance	Damage Strength	Water Walking	Damage Willpower
Tinder Polypore Cap	Tinder Polypore	Restore Willpower	Resist Disease	Invisibility	Damage Magicka
Tobacco	Tobacco Plant	Restore Fatigue	Resist Paralysis	Damage Magicka	Dispel
Tomato	Tomato Plant	Restore Fatigue	Detect Life	Burden	Shield
Troll Fat	Trolls	Damage Agility	Fortify Personality	Damage Willpower	Damage Health
Vampire Dust	Vampires	Silence	Resist Disease	Frost Damage	Invisibility
Venison	Deer	Restore Health	Feather	Damage Health	Chameleon
Viper's Bugloss Leaves	Viper's Bugloss	Resist Paralysis	Night-Eye	Burden	Cure Paralysis
Void Salts	Storm Atronachs	Restore Magicka	Damage Health	Fortify Magicka	Dispel
Water Hyacinth Nectar	Water Hyacinth	Damage Luck	Damage Fatigue	Restore Magicka	Fortify Magicka
Watermelon	Watermelon Vine	Restore Fatigue	Light	Burden	Damage Health
Wheat Grain	Wheat Stalk	Restore Fatigue	Damage Magicka	Fortify Health	Damage Personality
White Seed Pod	Goldenrod	Restore Strength	Water Breathing	Silence	Light
Wisp Stalk Caps	Wisp Stalks	Damage Health	Damage Willpower	Damage Intelligence	Fortify Speed
Wormwood Leaves	Wormwood	Fortify Fatigue	Invisibility	Damage Health	Damage Magicka

# of Plants	Commonly Found in These Places	A Concentration Can Be Found	Harvest Chance
255	Colovian Highlands (east of Sutch and northwest of Kvatch)	West of Infested Mine	80%
—	—	—	—
208	Food	South of Grateful Pass Stables	80%
4,311	Blackwood	Southeast of Onyx Caverns	50%
24	Near Leyawiin	South of Onyx Caverns	50%
—	Food	—	—
352	Oblivion	—	50%
—	Dungeons and Oblivion	—	—
134	Gold Coast, Colovian Highlands	Trumbe	80%
1,229	West Weald	East of Fort Black Boot	80%
2,056	Heartlands, West Weald	Sweetwater Camp	80%
54	Scattered	West of Sandstone Cavern	80%
77	A few scattered farms	Whitmond farm; Odiil farm	80%
894	Colovian Highlands	Fort Ontus	80%
1,212	Jerall and Valus Mountains	West of Shardrock	80%
—	Dungeons	—	—
4,692	Nibenay Basin and Valley	Southwest of Wenyandawik	80%
444	West of Imperial City	East of Fort Nikel	80%
—	Dungeons	—	—
4,158	Northwest of Imperial City, West of Skingrad to Colovian Highlands	Dragonclaw Rock	80%
—	Food	—	—
1,600	West Weald	Southwest of Miscarcand	80%
—	Dungeons	—	—
—	Food	—	—
—	Food	—	—
545	West Weald	East of Cursed Mine	80%
130	A few scattered farms	Whitmond farm	80%
310	Southeast of Kvatch	West of Sinkhole Cave	80%
26	Food	West of Sandstone Cavern	80%
86	Food	East of Odiil farm	80%
—	Dungeons and wilderness	—	—
279	Blackwood (northern)	Morahame	80%
—	Common food item (look in sacks)	—	—
598	Pools in the Imperial City, lakes in wilderness areas	—	80%
—	Water	—	—
—	Dungeons and Oblivion	—	—
562	South of Chorrol and east of Colovian Highlands	North of Elenglynn	80%
292	Oblivion Planes	—	50%
619	East and south of Chorrol	West of Brindle Home	80%
2,640	Great Forest	North of Fort Coldcorn	50%
224	Blackwood (swamps)	East of Fieldhouse Cave	50%
102	Between Kvatch and Skingrad	Drakelowe	80%
1,610	Nibenay Basin (southeastern)	East of Peryite's shrine	50%
—	Food	—	—
—	Food	—	—
—	Spriggans	—	—
729	Great Forest	Blankenmarch	80%
1,134	scattered (check on tree trunks)	Hame	50%
43	A few crops spread around	Bleak Mine; Whitmond farm	80%
155	A few crops spread around	North of Skingrad—East Gate	80%
—	Dungeons and wilderness	—	—
—	Dungeons	—	—
—	Wilderness	—	—
4,281	Great Forest	Weatherleah	80%
—	Dungeons	—	—
314	Between West Weald and Heartlands, Gold Coast	West of Fort Roebeck	80%
10	Food	South of Aleswell; east of Odiil farm	80%
16	Rare crops spread around	Brina Cross Inn	80%
136	Gold Coast	Fort Wariel	80%
2,738	Caves	—	33%
243	Jerall Valus Mountains	Toadstool Hollow	80%

SPELLMAKING AND ENCHANTING

INTRODUCTION

While Imperial law requires that the Mages Guild teach any willing student the commonly known incantations of magic, it makes no such provisions for the crafting of magical items or access to the components necessary for the creation of new magical spells. To access the spellmaking and enchanting services of the guild, a citizen must be a member in good standing with access to the Arcane University. (For information on accessing the Arcane University see the chapter "Faction Quests: The Mages Guild"). It is not uncommon for individuals to join the Mages Guild for the sole purpose of gaining access to the Arcane University. Fortunately, when it comes to this practice, the guild looks the other way so long as the member remains in good standing.

SPELL EFFECTS

The core of spellmaking and enchantment is the application of spell effects in new and creative ways. In many cases, you can combine these effects into new and more powerful spells and weapons to create the most powerful weapon or spell that works for you.

The Mages Guild can provide you with any basic spell that you may need. These spells represent the basic uses of magic at varying levels of power. Before you can create your own spell or enchant an item, you must have access to the basic spell effect. You gain access to spell effects by learning spells. For instance, the Flare spell you have from character creation gives you access to the Fire Damage effect.

If your intent is to buy a spell simply to have access to its effect in the spellmaker or enchanter, be sure to seek out the lowest level spell you can find. It will save you money, as spells tend to greatly increase in cost as they increase in power.

Spell components

Note that some spell effects have different options. It is necessary to learn only one version of the spell to access the effect. For instance, learning Greater Fortify Speed will grant you knowledge of the Fortify Attribute effect. You can then create or apply a Fortify Strength effect as well. This holds true for many effects.

The "Spell Effects" table lists all the effects that can be used in the spellmaker and enchantment menus (the Altar of Enchanting). The list shows the effect name, if the effect is available in the spellmaking menu or the enchantment menu, the best use for the effect as an enchantment, and a brief description of the effect.

SPELL EFFECTS

Effect Name	Spellmaking	Enchanting	Enchanting Use	Effect Description
Absorb Attribute	X	X	Weapon	Transfer attribute from target to caster
Absorb Fatigue	X	X	Weapon	Transfer Fatigue from target to caster
Absorb Health	X	X	Weapon	Transfer Health from target to caster
Absorb Magicka	X	X	Weapon	Transfer Magicka from target to caster
Absorb Skill	X	X	Weapon	Transfer skill from target to caster
Bound Axe	X	—	—	Summons Daedric axe
Bound Boots	X	—	—	Summons Daedric boots
Bound Bow	X	—	—	Summons Daedric bow
Bound Cuirass	X	—	—	Summons Daedric cuirass
Bound Dagger	X	—	—	Summons Daedric dagger
Bound Gauntlets	X	—	—	Summons Daedric gauntlets
Bound Greaves	X	—	—	Summons Daedric greaves
Bound Helmet	X	—	—	Summons Daedric helmet
Bound Mace	X	—	—	Summons Daedric mace
Bound Shield	X	—	—	Summons Daedric shield
Bound Sword	X	—	—	Summons Daedric sword
Burden	X	X	Weapon	Increases Encumbrance of target
Calm	X	—		Reduces aggression of target
Chameleon	X	X	Apparel	Conceals target
Charm	X	—		Increases Disposition of target
Command Creature	X	X	Weapon	Forces target to fight to protect the caster

SPELL EFFECTS CONT.

Effect Name	Spellmaking	Enchanting	Enchanting Use	Effect Description
Command Humanoid	X	X	Weapon	Forces target to fight to protect the caster
Cure Disease	X	—	—	Removes disease effects
Cure Paralysis	X	—	—	Removes paralysis effects
Cure Poison	X	—	—	Removes poison effects
Damage Attribute	X	X	Weapon	Causes attribute damage
Damage Fatigue	X	X	Weapon	Causes Fatigue damage
Damage Health	X	X	Weapon	Causes Health damage
Damage Magicka	X	X	Weapon	Causes Magicka damage
Demoralize Creature	X	X	Weapon	Decreases confidence of target
Detect Life	X	X	Apparel	Detects creatures
Disintegrate Armor	X	X	Weapon	Damages target's equipped armor
Disintegrate Weapon	X	X	Weapon	Damages target's equipped weapon
Dispel	X	X	Weapon	Dispels magical effects
Drain Attribute	X	X	Weapon	Causes temporary attribute damage
Drain Fatigue	X	X	Weapon	Causes temporary Fatigue damage
Drain Health	X	X	Weapon	Causes temporary Health damage
Drain Magicka	X	X	Weapon	Causes temporary Magicka damage
Drain Skill	X	X	Weapon	Causes temporary skill damage
Feather	X	X	Apparel	Increases carrying capacity
Fire Damage	X	X	Weapon	Causes fire damage to target
Fire Shield	X	X	Apparel	Provides armor bonus and fire resistance
Fortify Attribute	X	X	Apparel	Temporarily increases selected attribute
Fortify Fatigue	X	X	Apparel	Temporarily increases maximum Fatigue
Fortify Health	X	X	Apparel	Temporarily increases maximum Health
Fortify Magicka	X	X	Apparel	Temporarily increases maximum Magicka
Fortify Skill	X	X	Apparel	Temporarily increases selected skill
Frenzy Creature	X	X	Weapon	Increases target's aggression
Frost Damage	X	X	Weapon	Causes frost damage to target
Frost Shield	X	X	Apparel	Provides armor bonus and frost resistance
Invisibility	X	—	—	Makes the caster undetectable
Light	X	X	Apparel	Creates a sphere of light
Night-Eye	X	X	Apparel	Allows caster to see in the dark
Open	X	X	Weapon	Opens locked doors and containers
Paralyze	X	—	—	Stops target from moving
Rally Creature	X	X	Weapon	Increases confidence of target
Reflect Spell	X	—	—	Gives potential to reflect spells effects back to caster
Resist Disease	X	X	Apparel	Increases resistance to disease
Resist Fire	X	X	Apparel	Increases resistance to fire damage
Resist Frost	X	X	Apparel	Increases resistance to frost damage
Resist Magic	X	—	—	Increases resistance to all magic
Resist Paralysis	X	X	Apparel	Increases resistance to paralysis
Resist Poison	X	X	Apparel	Increases resistance to poison
Resist Shock	X	X	Apparel	Increases resistance to shock damage
Restore Attribute	X	—	—	Heals attribute damage
Restore Fatigue	X	—	—	Heals Fatigue damage
Restore Health	X	—	—	Heals Health damage
Restore Magicka	X	—	—	Heals Magicka damage
Shield	X	X	Apparel	Increases armor rating
Shock Damage	X	X	Weapon	Causes shock damage to target
Shock Shield	X	X	Apparel	Provides armor bonus and shock resistance
Silence	X	X	Weapon	Prevents spellcasting
Soul Trap	X	X	Weapon	Transfers target's soul to empty Soul Gem
Spell Absorption	X	—	—	Gives potential to cancel spell effects and heal Magicka
Telekinesis	X	—	—	Manipulates distant objects
Turn Undead	X	X	Weapon	Causes undead to flee
Water Breathing	X	X	Apparel	Breathe underwater
Water Walking	X	X	Apparel	Walk on the surface of water
Weakness to Disease	X	X	Weapon	Increases target's weakness to disease
Weakness to Fire	X	X	Weapon	Increases target's weakness to fire damage
Weakness to Frost	X	X	Weapon	Increases target's weakness to frost damage
Weakness to Magic	X	X	Weapon	Increases target's weakness to magic
Weakness to Normal Weapons	X	X	Weapon	Increases target's weakness to unenchanted weapons
Weakness to Poison	X	X	Weapon	Increases target's weakness to poison effects
Weakness to Shock	X	X	Weapon	Increases target's weakness to shock damage

SPELLMAKING

The true strength of the spellmaker is the ability to combine two or more of these basic spell effects to create a spell tailored to your individual play style. Think about how you play the game, and then consider how best to combine effects to benefit you. Do you cast a lot of elemental spells? Create a spell that combines a weakness to fire with fire damage. You'll get the advantage of the double effect without wasting precious combat time switching back and forth between spells. Do you always make sure to fortify your Health, Endurance, and Strength before a fight? Combine the three effects and be sure to keep the spell at the ready. This way, you'll be prepared even when a group of Bandits manages to trigger an unexpected ambush.

Spellmaking menu

In spell creation, most effects have three options that can be combined: magnitude, duration, and area. Some have all three, but a few have only one depending on the effect. Magnitude increases the power of the spell. Duration increases the time that a spell lasts. Area increases the area of effect of a spell in a radius around the target. Increasing any of these effects increases both the power and the cost of the spell. Clever manipulation of these three options will help you to create a spell that delivers the most effect for the lowest cost.

Altar of Spellmaking

In addition to these options, most effects have three range options: touch, target, and self. Touch applies the effect to another creature or character within close range. Target casts the spell on a creature or character at a distance. Creating a spell with the range of self applies the spell's effects to you, the caster. Be cautious when creating ranged spells. While touch and self spells have a standard cost, targeted spells increase the cost of the spell by 50 percent.

The total cost of the spell is very important. Though you can see the total Magicka required to cast the spell (which is dictated by your current skill level), that number in itself doesn't determine everything. You're still limited by your skill level when creating a new spell, even if you have the raw Magicka needed to cast that spell. Look for the total skill level needed to create and cast the spell at the bottom of the spell-making menu.

SPELL LEVEL THRESHOLDS

Level	Base Cost
Novice	0–25
Apprentice	26–62
Journeyman	63–149
Expert	150–399
Master	400+

ENCHANTING

Weaving focused Magicka into material objects has long been a practice of mages throughout Tamriel's history. By joining a material object with the essence of a creature captured inside a Soul Gem, you can create powerful magical aids to keep you alive throughout your adventures. Like spellmaking, enchantment requires access to the Arcane University. In Cyrodiil, the Arcane University is the only location that has the materials necessary to infuse Magicka into items.

Enchantment menu

However, even once you have access to the university, you must provide the items for enchantment, the Soul Gems, and the gold required to carry out the enchantment. Any item that can be worn and any weapon that can be wielded can be enchanted. Choose carefully when enchanting items in order to maximize effects.

SOUL GEMS

Soul Gems are vital to the enchantment process. Without them, the Magicka cannot be bound to the item. Soul Gems come in five types, each greater in power: petty, lesser, common, greater, and grand. The type of Soul Gem dictates how much Magicka can be transferred to the item being enchanted. Management of Soul Gems is very important because Soul Gems affect weapon and apparel enchantments very differently.

WEAPONS

The creation of magical weapons is very similar to creating new spells. The same options are presented: magnitude, area, and duration. As with spellmaking, it is important to create a weapon that is tailor-made to your play style. Explore combinations of effects and power levels to suit your needs.

Altar of Enchanting

The most important thing to keep track of when creating a new magical item is the number of uses that your enchantment will get before you need to use a Soul Gem to recharge the item's magical stores. The more powerful the enchantment, the fewer uses you will get out of it. The size of the Soul Gem that you use to create the weapon dictates the total maximum magical power of any item. The more powerful the Soul Gem, the greater the enchantment that it can support.

SOUL GEM ENCHANTMENT POINTS

Soul Gem	Charge
Petty	150
Lesser	300
Common	800
Greater	1,200
Grand	1,600

APPAREL

Unlike weapons, enchanted worn items do not use enchantment points over time, nor do they need to be recharged. Their effects are applied continuously so long as the item is equipped. This makes it simple to specialize in any single enchantment. You can focus all of your enchanted slots on being immune to fire, having a high armor rating, or being able to detect all creatures around you. However, worn enchantments are much more effective when spread out, using a number of different effects to benefit you.

Because of this, enchanting a worn item works differently than creating an enchanted weapon. The Soul Gem used dictates the magnitude of the enchantment and cannot be changed. Only a single effect can be applied to a worn item. The most useful magical effects for worn items are listed below with the magnitude that will be created with each Soul Gem and the cost to create each item.

WORN ENCHANTMENTS

	Magnitude of Enchantment					Cost to Enchant Item				
	Petty	Lesser	Common	Greater	Grand	Petty	Lesser	Common	Greater	Grand
Chameleon	8	11	14	17	20	520	715	910	1,105	1,300
Detect Life	8	11	14	17	20	120	165	210	255	300
Feather	14	23	32	41	50	350	575	800	1,025	1,250
Fire Shield	6	6	7	8	9	900	900	1,050	1,200	1,350
Fortify Attribute	6	7	8	9	10	600	700	800	900	1000
Fortify Fatigue	9	13	17	21	25	225	325	425	525	625
Fortify Health	6	7	8	9	11	900	1,050	1,200	1,350	1,650
Fortify Magicka	6	7	8	9	10	600	700	800	900	1,000
Fortify Skill	6	7	8	9	10	600	700	800	900	1,000
Frost Shield	6	6	7	8	9	900	900	1,050	1,200	1,350
Light	12	19	26	33	40	150	238	325	413	500
Night-Eye	5	5	5	5	5	100	100	100	100	100
Reflect Damage	6	6	7	8	8	2,400	2,400	2,800	3,200	3,200
Reflect Spell	6	6	7	8	8	2,400	2,400	2,800	3,200	3,200
Resist Disease	10	15	20	25	30	150	225	300	375	450
Resist Fire	10	15	20	25	30	500	750	1,000	1,250	1,500
Resist Frost	10	15	20	25	30	500	750	1,000	1,250	1,500
Resist Paralysis	10	15	20	25	30	300	450	600	750	900
Resist Poison	14	23	32	41	50	210	345	480	615	750
Resist Shock	10	15	20	25	30	500	750	1,000	1,250	1,500
Shield	6	7	8	9	10	600	700	800	900	1,000
Shock Shield	7	10	12	15	17	700	1,000	1,200	1,500	1,700
Spell Absorption	5	6	6	7	7	2,000	2,400	2,400	2,800	2,800
Water Breathing	5	5	5	5	5	2,000	2,000	2,000	2,000	2,000
Water Walking	5	5	5	5	5	2,000	2,000	2,000	2,000	2,000

THE MAIN QUEST

ESCAPE THE PRISON

A prison escape? Actually, it's more like a last-minute pardon. Only, you're not the one in the hot seat.

CHARACTER GENERATION

Start by telling the game something about who you are in the world of *Oblivion*.

The default character is a young Imperial male. If you just want to get into the game, simply choose a name and select "Done" when his guileless face appears onscreen. He will serve you as well as any character in this "starter" dungeon. Don't worry; you're not stuck with him. You can revise this choice—and other choices still to come—before you step out into the wide world. Here, you pick your character's name, gender, appearance, and most importantly, race. For help on creating your character, see the "Character Gen" chapter.

THE IMPERIAL PRISON

After you click on "Done," you find yourself in a stony cell. Explore a bit. Approach the cell door to experience the gentle humor of Valen Dreth, who occupies the cell across the hall.

The Imperial Prison

Just for kicks, you can create several quickie characters so you can experience the grand panorama of Dreth's undiscriminating nastiness. (He has unique taunts for each of the game's 10 races, and for each gender as well.)

He stops taunting when visitors appear on the stairs. Dreth makes it sound as though they're coming for you.

They're not. They just need to use your cell.

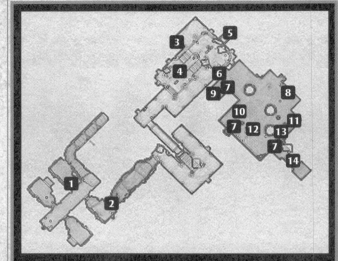

1. **Valen Dreth:** Your Dark Elf neighbor in the prison taunts you mercilessly. In the Dark Brotherhood quest "Scheduled for Execution," you'll take your revenge.

2. **Secret door:** This is opened by Captain Renault near the start of the game.

3. Four Mythic Dawn assassins lie in wait offstage here. They'll hit the royal party around…

4. …here! The emperor survives the Mythic Dawn assault, but Renault doesn't. Take her sword and torch. (The rest of her equipment is unavailable.) Look for potions on the bodies of the assassins.

5. **Imperial Subterrane:** The royal party passes through this door, but not you. See #11.

6. Collapsed section of wall and your way out. When you return in the Dark Brotherhood quest "Scheduled for Execution," the hole is boarded up and impassable.

7. Rats! The northern Rat is right on top of a chest, too. It contains a club, four torches, and two lockpicks.

8. The skeleton of a thief, with an iron dagger, leather cuirass and boots, 28 iron arrows, six lockpicks, and a torch. Nearby, you'll find a leather shield, iron bow, and a locked chest (one tumbler) containing a sapphire and 10 gold. Also a sack. There's a 15 percent chance it contains a bit of gold, a lockpick, common ingredients, and a grab bag ranging from animal pelts and silver items to jewelry, silver nuggets, and arrows.

9. Unlocked chest containing a rusty war axe and six gold.

10. Crate containing a club, four torches, and two lockpicks.

11. Barrel holding a club, an iron dagger, 12 arrows, and two lockpicks.

THE MAIN QUEST

12. Ruined well. Show that bucket who's boss!

13. Dead Goblin Shaman with a club, Fire Damage and Chameleon scrolls, a Restore Magicka potion, three lockpicks, and an iron key that opens the door at #14.

14. Imperial Substructure: The lock can be picked—it has just one tumbler—or unlocked with the key from the dead Goblin (#13).

AN OLD EMPEROR IN A HURRY

The visitors are Emperor Uriel Septim VII and three members of the Blades: Glenroy, Captain Renault, and Baurus. Listen carefully to the dialogue as they approach. It sets up the story for this first stage of the game.

Uriel Septim VII, Emperor of Tamriel

The emperor's sons reportedly have been attacked by assassins—killed, the emperor supposes—and the Blades are trying to spirit the emperor away via an emergency exit before Septim joins his sons in death. (You see only two Blades until the party enters your cell. The third, Baurus, is up the stairs locking the prison door.)

Talk to Glenroy and the emperor through the door. The emperor is as pleasant as someone who has just learned his children are dead can be, but an urgency lurks behind his words.

Glenroy is dismissive. He just wants you out of the way. At this stage, you are merely an administrative inconvenience. This cell was supposed to be empty.

Glenroy of the Blades

For the game to progress, you must satisfy his demand that you stand down; do so now. You can either stand under the high window in the east wall (which allows you a better view of the proceedings) or sit on the stool beside the table. Either way, you're temporarily pinned in place; the cell door opens and the royal party enters.

Captain Renault moves to the northeast corner. Baurus watches the door. Glenroy looks at you with the eyes of a hungry dog. Renault presses a big stone in the seventh row up from the floor. Your alleged bed sinks grindingly into the floor. The north wall opens to reveal a dark, descending passage.

You're free. At least, you're free to explore this large "starter" dungeon. In the Imperial Prison, Imperial Substructure, Natural Caverns, Imperial Subterrane, and the Sanctum, you will find weapons and armor. You use the weapons to kill Rats, a Zombie, and perhaps not a few Goblins. You learn how to cast a spell and pick a lock. You may sneak past a Goblin and deal with a Goblin trap. Perhaps you even spring a trap of your own.

You also witness a defining event in the history of the Tamrielic Empire.

In addition to the advice given to you by the tutorial, here are a few extra things you should know as you make your way through these dark passages.

You don't have to remain with the Blades, but you have no reason to linger in your cell. The cell door was locked again behind the royal party, and Dreth seems to have shot his bolt. And if you do keep up, you can talk to your new friend, the emperor, who offers unique commentary at certain points along the way. In the second large room, the royal party reaches the midpoint between two sets of stairs, and four hooded assassins cascade from a raised area to the west.

You are unarmored and virtually unarmed, so steer clear of the fray, ideally by retreating back down the passage. The Blades can handle the attackers. If you attract the assassins' attention, they try to kill you, and they may well succeed.

Besides, you can't materially influence the key events in this dungeon. In the company of the emperor, you are mostly a spectator. When the battle ends, you learn from an exchange between the Blades and Septim that one of those killed was Captain Renault. She led the royal party down the passage and seems to have borne the brunt of the assassins' attack.

You can claim two items she was holding: a torch and a sword. By searching around you can also find an Akaviri Katana that she dropped when she was killed. Take them all. The torch is a decided comfort in this deep and dark place, and you can hold it in one hand while you hold the sword in the other.

Captain Renault, slain defending the Emperor

A word about taking stuff: It is basic to your existence in Oblivion. You'll buy things at the many stores, of course, but you live and die off loot. Fortunately, there's a lot of it about. Each of the assassins has a Mythic Dawn robe and hood—their weapons have vanished because they were bound items—and some may carry potions or other useful items. Leave the robes and hoods—they will quickly be superseded by more valuable items—but take any potions.

Right now, you're nowhere near the limit of what you can carry, so take anything that has potential value as a weapon, armor, or magic or has significant value. If an item has a value in gold listed in your inventory, you can sell it when you get out of here and buy something more useful. (Gold is weightless.)

However, you'll eventually reach your limit of what you can carry and have to decide what to dump and what to keep. Find a convenient location to leave items that don't contribute directly to your mission but that you're uncomfortable leaving behind. We scout several such locations in the Imperial City area in the "Freeform Quests" chapter. That same chapter we discuss what's involved in buying a house.

As for "Mythic Dawn," the game doesn't make anything of the reference at this point, but this is your first clue.

The royal party passes through the locked gate and the door beyond—and you're on your own. Perhaps it's because the Blades (who don't trust you) are running the show. Speak to the emperor before he disappears. He says he knows you'll meet up with the party later. But first you have to pass through the Imperial Substructure and the Natural Caverns—after finding a way out of the Imperial Prison.

IMPERIAL SUBSTRUCTURE

A section of wall crumbles to the southeast. Two Rats advance through the gap; a third waits beyond it. Kill them and then search this new area for loot. Among other things, you'll come up with a bow, armor, and lockpicks. Use the picks to master the simple lock on the door to the southeast, or use the key on the Goblin's shaman's body.

The opening in the wall

This the Imperial Substructure. In this new area, you'll find a zombie, some odds and ends of loot (including ingredients), and a whole *lot* of rats. (It's a good thing the rats are weak and suicidal.) And, near the door down into the Natural Caverns, you'll find your path semi-blocked by a goblin early-warning system made by hanging skulls. Clever, those goblins. In the next section of dungeon, you'll have a chance to outwit them.

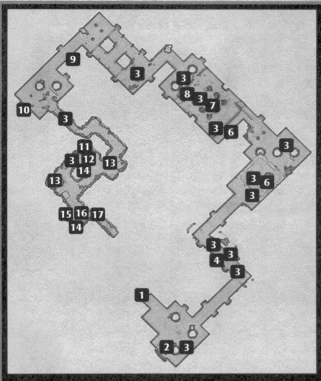

14. Cairn bolete mushrooms: Yields ingredient cairn bolete caps 33 percent of the time. First effect: Restore Health.

15. Stinkhorn: Yields ingredient stinkhorn cap 50 percent of the time. First effect: Damage Health.

16. Goblin alarm system.

17. Natural Caverns.

THE NATURAL CAVERNS

Up to this point, none of your battles should have been intimidating—unless you did something foolish, like deliberately attacking the Blades or the emperor. However, unlike the giant Rats, the Goblins (who occupy the Natural Caverns in force) are quite another matter.

These foes can block and dodge your blows, and their own blows can inflict significant damage. And, if you allow them to gang up on you, you're in real trouble.

Fighting in *Oblivion*

The watchword is caution. You want to hit without being hit. Move slowly, use cover, and sneak when on uncertain ground. Be aware of what's around you. Watch your opponents' movements and look for opportunities for ambush. Don't make a habit of fighting two or more enemies at a time. If possible, take them on individually or if you're not up to it, not at all.

This whole section of the dungeon can be seen as a series of not-at-alls. The first Goblin in the Natural Caverns is watching a Rat roasting over an open fire when you appear on the scene. You can ignore him, but leaving live enemies in the darkness behind you isn't always intelligent. Sneak up on him and put a blade in him.

You can sometimes use your enemies' traps against them. North and east of the campfire is a chamber guarded by a single Goblin. A tripwire stretches across the floor just east of the entrance. Run northeast through the entrance—right through the tripwire, deliberately triggering the trap—and one of the three spiked logs pinned to the ceiling takes the guard out for you.

You also sometimes want to attract the attention of as many enemies as possible. Right at the end of the Natural Caverns is a large Goblin encampment. Two of the ugly little monsters guard the entrance, and the remainder are scattered around the camp. Some of these are tough hombres—notably the spell-casting shaman on the far side of the camp.

1. Imperial Prison

2. Chest: Better armor (an iron cuirass and greaves), 24 arrows, five lockpicks, three torches, a healing potion, and another iron bow and rusty war axe.

3. Rats! (And lots of 'em.)

4. Zombie. Also, the ceiling collapses here, and you'll have a peek at Imperial Prison-style architecture above. (No, you can't get up there.)

5. Chest: Restore Magicka and Restore Fatigue potions and two lockpicks.

6. Chest: Tough lock (for the starter dungeon), with three tumblers. Twenty gold, three lockpicks, and two torches within.

7. Loose loot, including an iron warhammer, shield, and helmet and a bit of food: lettuce, two wedges of cheese, and a tomato. (The first effect of each of these ingredients is Restore Fatigue.)

8. Chest: Rusty war axe and six gold.

9. Sack containing a healing potion and three lockpicks.

10. Barrel: Four portions of ale, semi-concealed inside the wall. (It's a potion that restores Fatigue at the expense of the Intelligence and Willpower attributes.)

11. Chest: Restore Magicka potion and two healing potions.

12. Skeleton with two lockpicks and leveled loot.

13. Wisp stalk plant: Yields ingredient wisp stalk caps 33 percent of the time. (You'll find another wedge of cheese near the southwestern cluster.) First effect: Damage Health.

The goblin encampment

stack and wipe out two of the guards below. But why settle for two weaker Goblins when you can kill all of them? A brisk run through the camp will result in you slamming back up the entry slope with a small army of Goblins on your tail. If you have a lead on them, activate the stack, and now you're overseeing a bloodbath. Afterwards, mop up any Goblins who didn't play Follow the Leader.

You can fight the guards one at a time: engage one in battle, run away to heal, then come back to fight the other one. However, each fight will be tough, will take a while, and taking out the guards in this way isn't really necessary.

Instead, look around. The Goblins have left a large pile of logs just up the slope from the entrance. You can activate the

This maneuver has its hazards—not the least of which is slipping into the pit at the center of the camp, having the Goblins pile in after you, and then being roasted over an open fire. So save your game first and again after you succeed.

Once the mopping-up is complete, you have control of an enormous haul. (To be sure, there's a lot of junk mixed in with the good stuff. Goblins seem to have a deep appreciation for junk.) Mixed in with the junk are lots of usable odds and ends. Once you're done, make your way out the exit to the Imperial Subterrane.

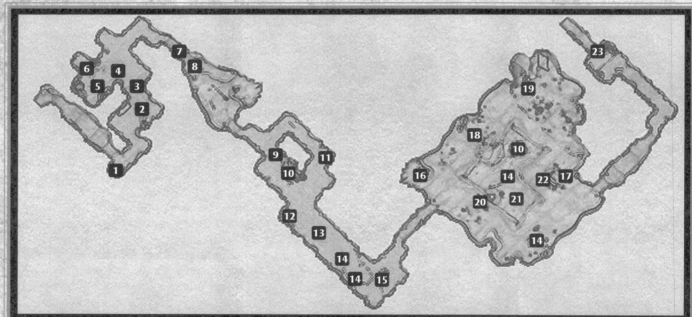

1. Junk

2. Five cairn bolete mushrooms and one stinkhorn plant.

3. Goblin: This fine fellow, who's on patrol, can be avoided or ambushed by sneaking.

4. A crate that's being used as a table. You'll find your first piece of alchemy equipment—a mortar and pestle—along with the ingredients wisp stalk cap and stinkhorn cap, and a Damage Health potion. You can use the mortar and pestle to create Damage Health potion like the one here.

5. If you're sneaking you may be able to take the Goblin by surprise with a backstabbing attack. He carries two lockpicks on him and there are three Rat meat portions on the Rat roasting over the fire.

6. Chest: The lock has one tumbler. Twenty gold, three lockpicks, and two torches.

7. Tripwire: Sets off a swinging-mace trap. Rush through the wire and the three maces hanging above will punt the unfortunate Goblin attendant (#8) into the Fourth Era.

8. The unfortunate Goblin attendant.

9. Dead Rat

10. Bonfire

11. One-tumbler chest containing 26–34 iron arrows and two or three lockpicks. Beside the chest is a dagger and a single gold piece.

12. Two apples. (The first effect of apples is Restore Fatigue.)

13. Rolling-log trap. Activate it to wipe out the two Goblins at the bottom of the slope—or make the four Goblins in the camp beyond chase you, then spring the trap on all of them. Make sure to loot their bodies—especially the Goblin Witch who runs the camp, who has a magical shaman staff, a flawed ruby, and a petty Soul Gem.

14. Goblin

15. A pair of chests. One is identical in contents (and lock) to the one at #11. The other contains three healing and one Restore Fatigue potion.

16. Goblin Berserker

17. Goblin Witch

18. Another yummy roasted Rat.

19. Storage area: In the chest, you'll find an iron longsword, three lockpicks, and a repair hammer you can use to fix up your armor. The barrel holds four ales, and the crate has eight portions of Rat meat.

20. Pull cord that opens the gate to the Rat pen in the pit below.

21. Rat pen: Three rats await the fate of their brother (#16).

22. Treasure chest: Contains 18 gold, two flawed gems, a gold nugget, a repair hammer, and a silver vase. One-tumbler lock.

23. Imperial Subterrane

THE IMPERIAL SUBTERRANE

The emperor and his escorts vanished into the Imperial Subterrane at the bottom of the Imperial Prison.

Now they're just a hop away.

A short corridor leads west to a broken section of wall. Here, peer down into a chamber like the one where you parted ways with the royal party, watch the emperor and Blades appear out of the southern tunnel, and listen to Glenroy and Baurus quarrel about strategy.

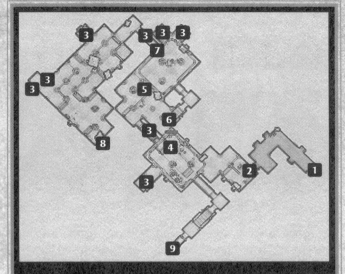

1. Natural Caverns

2. Scenic overlook: Your appearance here triggers the appearance of the emperor and his two surviving Blades below and a second ambush by two Mythic Dawn assassins. When you jump down two levels, you'll join the royal party at the emperor's behest. (Once you descend, you can't return to the Natural Caverns.)

3. Mythic Dawn assassins.

4. After the ambush, the emperor will wait here until you descend from #2. Once you do, you'll talk to Uriel Septim VII and select a birthsign. Baurus will supply you with a torch, Glenroy unlocks the door into the next section, and the party goes on its un-merry way.

5. Chest with 10 arrows and four lockpicks.

6. The royal party descends these stairs to the scene of the third ambush—this time involving three assassins…

7. …and then, via this hallway, to two smaller ones — which, depending on your movements, may or may not flow together into one.

8. The Sanctum

9. Imperial Prison: This is still locked when you're in the starter dungeon. However, when you return to the Imperial Subterrane in the Dark Brotherhood quest "Scheduled for Execution," you'll use this door to reach the prison.

The Blades fight off the second ambush.

Their exchange is followed by another assassination attempt. Since you're now set up with weapons and armor, you may be able to participate in the emperor's defense. However, since it's just two assassins this time, Baurus and Glenroy may already have dispatched them by the time you're ready. Use the bow and stay on one of the room's upper tiers. However many skinny Rats you offed back in the Imperial Substructure, you're not remotely ready to go toe-to-toe with the assassins.

Finally, Glenroy tries to coax Septim into moving onward, and the emperor protests that he wants to rest a little longer. That's your cue to show your face. Hop down to the party's level, and the ever-friendly Glenroy promptly orders Baurus to kill you as a potential ally of the assassins.

Don't worry. The emperor calls off the dogs. He knows better.

You join the royal party. Glenroy still doesn't trust you, but Baurus treats you almost like a normal person, and you can question him briefly about the Blades and Septim. And the emperor is almost…fatherly! Seeking to explain why he trusts you, Septim asks whether you're familiar with The Nines—the state religion whose deities include Tiber Septim, the first emperor of Tamriel. Evidently, Uriel feels your stars are linked and asks for your birthsign. See the "Birthsign" chapter for help on what to choose.

Alas, the emperor's own star flickers only dimly. He now states plainly what was only implied back in your cell: He has seen his own death. He seems even to have accepted it. But he'll make no predictions for your own destiny—save that it seems bright with possibility. ("In your face, I behold the son's companion.")

The party heads north, with Glenroy unlocking the door, then makes a U-turn, heading south for the stairs and the third ambush. If you're fast off the mark, you can make a useful contribution to the emperor's defense. Ready your bow, drop off the north side of the path, then jump onto one of the ledges that overlook the columned room below from north, west, and south. Let fly.

Again, it's not as though these Blades bruisers need your help, and you probably won't do much actual damage before they finish the job you start. But even simple hits on the two hard-to-see assassins in the raised areas above the columned room's northeast corner forces them to abandon their positions

and ruin the surprise. (By shooting at them, you can trigger them early—before the Blades arrive in the room where they're waiting. You can see into the room from a raised area, but they have to walk to it by a somewhat more roundabout path.) And your presence above distracts any on the lower level, giving Glenroy and Baurus the opportunity to take some free whacks.

A Mythic Dawn assassin

Try not to shoot your comrades. They forgive you this time, but future comrades may not be quite so tolerant. They make short work of the next three assassins, and the party moves south to the door to the Sanctum.

OBTAINING THE AMULET

Here it ends. And here it begins.

There's a strange mood in the air as the party enters the Sanctum. The emperor has just told you he's going to die, and this statement hangs between you like smoke. It's almost as though he's already dead and you're all just going through the motions.

Glenroy obviously smells trouble. He orders the party to hold up while he checks the path to the north. He signals it's clear and then leads east toward a gate. The gate is locked from the other side, and the Blade smells a trap.

He's right. The trap lies in a small, apparently enclosed chamber to the north. Perhaps this is "the Sanctum" itself and perhaps even the defensible position that Glenroy was arguing for back in the Subterrane.

The Blades read it as a "dead end." In fact, it's not a dead end—and that fact will be the emperor's undoing—but these two Blades don't know that. After all, it was Renault who opened the escape route in the first place and Renault who led the way down that dark track. And it may have been Renault, too, who knew this room's secret exit. And she's dead.

But there's no opportunity to deal with these subtleties. At this point Glenroy and Baurus suddenly run off to deal with assassins who've appeared to the rear, leaving you alone to defend the emperor.

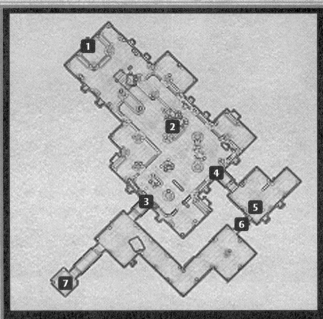

1. **Imperial Subterrane:** Glenroy will instruct the party to wait here while he checks the path ahead.

2. Glenroy signals to the party to follow him.

3. This gate is locked from the other side. Glenroy smells a trap.

4. The party tries this side passage instead. It leads to a dead end.

5. Baurus and Glenroy rush off to deal with an attack from the rear, leaving the emperor to your care. Septim gives you the Amulet of Kings and instructions to take it to Jauffre and find his remaining son.

6. A Mythic Dawn assassin steps out of a secret door here and kills the emperor. Baurus returns and kills the assassin before he can kill you (or so we hope) and provides you with the location of Jauffre (Weynon Priory) and the key to the sewers. He also fixes your character's class.

7. Sewers

You can follow the Blades. If you do, they kill the assassins in the big room to the south and Glenroy dies. But things won't progress until you return to the emperor. If you stay with the emperor, you have a moment before he speaks to you. If you've taken damage, this would be a good time to restore your health to full. If you follow the Blades out, Baurus will periodically shout at you to "stay back and protect the Emperor!" and the fight will continue indefinitely until you return to the room where the Emperor is waiting.

Sensing that his end is nigh, Septim places in your care an artifact called the Amulet of Kings and charges you to take it to someone named Jauffre. He does not further identify the amulet, or say who Jauffre is or where to find him, only that he knows where to find "my last son." The emperor also talks of "the jaws of Oblivion," and "the Lord of Destruction."

Baurus mourns his Emperor.

The conversation has no sooner ended than a stone panel rises in the room's northeast corner and a Mythic Dawn assassin appears and slashes at the emperor. Just like that, it's over. Septim is dead.

The assassin's still very much alive and kicking, and you're no more capable of killing this one on your own than you were back in the Imperial Prison. Stay out of range of his dagger until Baurus reappears on the scene and takes off the heat.

Baurus doesn't blame you, either; he blames himself. Nor does he accuse you of swiping the Amulet of Kings. He realizes that the emperor "saw something in you." And because the emperor trusted you, Baurus trusts you despite the fact that you're an escaped convict carrying a divine artifact, which you claim the emperor handed you himself seconds before a guy with a red hood and a magic dagger came through a secret door.

Baurus of the Blades

Baurus tells you that Jauffre is the Grandmaster of the Blades and lives as a simple monk in Weynon Priory. The priory is almost straight west from the sewers' exit—in the woods southeast of the city of Chorrol.

Getting Directions

You don't get a lot of directions in *Oblivion*. The compass has a directional marker, and assigned destinations are highlighted on the game map, so it's hard to get lost. The only time directions are required is when you're looking for a location to which the game hasn't expressly directed you. That won't happen often until the "Freeform Quests" chapter.

You probably still have lots of questions. But it's time to go. All you can do at this point is enter the secret passage opened by the assassin.

Baurus? He's staying to guard the emperor's body and fight off any pursuers. But you'll see him again before too long.

THE SEWERS

You're not out, but you're almost out. Descend the stairs and follow the depression in the floor west and north to a door for which Baurus gave you a key. Inside is a well entrance (a manhole cover) you activate to reach the final section. Beyond, a large chamber has a trench running down the middle. You find a couple of Goblins and a Rat in here. Dispose of them, and on the far side of the trench you find a wheel you can activate to open the second chamber entrance.

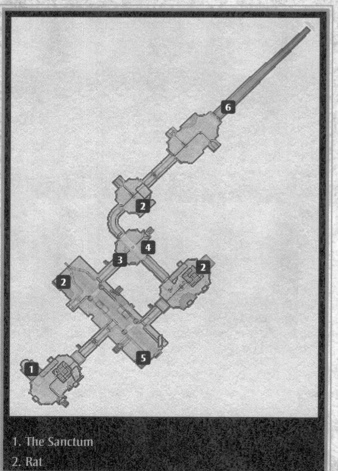

1. The Sanctum
2. Rat

3. Goblin

4. Goblin Berserker. Also, a chest containing 31 arrows and two lockpicks.

5. A chest containing 32 iron arrows and two lockpicks, a barrel containing six cheese wedges, and a crate containing three bags of flour.

6. City Isle: Specifically, just northeast of the Imperial Prison compound on an island in the northeast corner of Lake Rumare.

Enter the room and take the stairs leading up. Follow the path over the bridges and through the gate. You may find a few additional Rats to kill along the way, and eventually you come to the final gate.

Don't like your character? Maybe you made a mistake with your birthsign. Or your experience in the dungeon has taught you that you're want to play a little differently than you'd thought. When you activate this last gate leading outside, you're offered the opportunity to tweak your character's race, birthsign, and class. Essentially, you can change any of the decisions you've made to this point, even your name.

The sewer exit

Save your game here, as it allows you to quickly start a new game without playing through all of the previous dungeons.

Once you've made any changes you want to your character, head outside.

THE WORLD OF CYRODIIL

You exit the sewers just northeast of the Imperial City. You're on an island in the northeast corner of Lake Rumare, which serves as the capital's moat.

What comes next? It's up to you. You can try the Ayleid ruin just across the lake from where you left the sewers. At the moment, you have only one official quest: Deliver the Amulet of Kings to Jauffre at Weynon Priory.

But despite the sense of urgency that accompanied the emperor's and Baurus's last speeches, that mission will keep. The game will adjust its pace to yours. Cyrodiil is full of adventures large and small, and you can explore freely in any direction. Beginning now.

Your first view of the outside world.

DELIVERING THE AMULET

FAST TRAVEL VERSUS SLOW TRAVEL

The trip west should be uneventful. If you use "fast travel" to get to the city of Chorrol, it's virtually guaranteed to be. You appear just inside the gates. Exit and follow the road a short distance southeast to the priory.

However, it is recommended that you walk all the way to the priory—if only to get into the habit.

Fast travel is a great convenience. You simply select a destination and appear there, with none of the potential complications (like combat with wandering creatures) and potential distractions (like off-the-books adventures) of foot travel. You won't have to wait longer than it takes to load a new region.

While fast travel resembles teleportation, it is not instantaneous. Time does pass. How much time depends on a number of factors: how far you're traveling; active spell effects that influence speed; your current level of encumbrance; whether you're on horseback or, if not, on your own natural speed. (Running at the time you enter fast travel doesn't influence your subsequent speed.) Hence, the fast-traveler who leaves Anvil in the morning will find it is night upon arrival in distant Leyawiin.

You can speed things up a bit by un-equipping your armor and weapons before you use fast travel. However, fast travel does carry with it some limitations and conditions. You can't fast-travel out of combat. (Note that you're considered to be in combat once an enemy has decided to attack you—regardless of whether or not you're trading blows or you can even see the creature.) You can't initiate it while indoors. And you can't fast-travel when spell effects are damaging your health.

Most importantly, fast travel is limited to locations you know about or have discovered. At the start of the game that includes Anvil, Bravil, Bruma, Cheydinhal, Chorrol, the outskirts of Kvatch, Leyawiin, Skingrad, and the Imperial City's eight districts.

To discover a location, you must pass by it on foot. In this respect, fast travel is rather like flying with the shade down: You can't make out any details along the way.

Note, too, that quests don't require the use of fast travel. While you'll routinely work to mesh your schedule with those of wandering NPCs, only on occasion will the game require you to be in a particular location at a particular time—and you can't miss those appointments in any permanent sense. (Sooner or later, they roll around again.)

The more you walk now, the more locations appear on your map, and the more you will be able to use fast travel later. Even if you can't zap straight to a destination, increasingly you'll find you can fast-travel to a location nearby and then walk the remaining distance.

There are dozens upon dozens of locations out there—from small settlements to caves to fortresses to mines to tombs to shrines to isolated farmhouses. To experience *Oblivion* fully, walk every established route and blaze your own trails into the wilderness. Just because the game doesn't expressly dispatch you into a given region doesn't mean there's nothing there.

On this trip, for instance, you'd miss two locations on a straight route from the sewers' exit to Weynon Priory. One is Sinkhole Cave—a big bandit lair on the north side of Imperial City that, cleared out, makes a nice (if rather rough 'n' tumble) home for a beginning adventurer. The other, in the woods west of the northwest corner of Lake Rumare, is Yellow Tick Cave—a conjurer's hideaway that introduces the game's main enemy: the Daedra.

PRIORY PRIORITIES

Where's Jauffre? Depending on when you've arrived at the priory, he could be in one of three places.

NPCs follow schedules. Sometimes pretty elaborate schedules. They work during the day. Sometimes they go out to eat. They sleep at night.

Weynon Priory

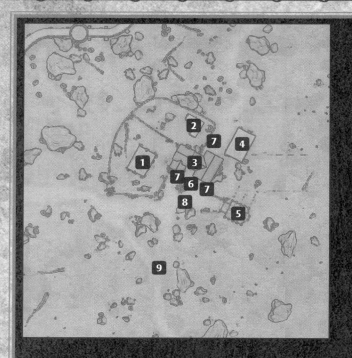

1. Weynon Lodge: The shepherd Eronor lives here.
2. Sheepfold
3. Weynon House: Your first stop on the Main Quest, this is home to the Blades' chief, Jauffre; Prior Maborel; and Brother Piner. You'll deliver the Amulet of Kings to Jauffre to complete the "Deliver the Amulet" segment. (Most of the time, he's upstairs—either sitting in the library or asleep.) Jauffre and his brother monks also supply you with equipment and transportation for the next Main Quest mission, "Find the Heir," and its attached "The Battle for Castle Kvatch" Miscellaneous quest. You'll return here in the Main Quest's "Weynon Priory" segment to find Maborel dead, Jauffre and Piner under attack, and the amulet missing. And then, with Martin and Jauffre, you'll set off for Cloud Ruler Temple—the base of operations for the rest of the Main Quest.

4. Stable: You'll find Prior Maborel's Paint Horse here. (Now your Paint Horse!)

5. Weynon Priory: When you turn over the Amulet of Kings in "Deliver the Amulet," you'll find Jauffre here between 6 a.m. and 10 a.m. When you return to the monastery in the "Weynon Priory" segment of the Main Quest, you'll find him under attack here by two Mythic Dawn agents. (A third is already dead.) Note that you can climb the ladder to the top of the chapel tower.

6. Prior Maborel: He's here in body, if not spirit, after the attack by Mythic Dawn agents in the "Weynon Priory" segment of the Main Quest.

7. Mythic Dawn agents appear at these locations in the Main Quest segment "Weynon Priory." Two more attack Jauffre in the chapel.

8. Eronor appears here when you arrive at the monastery in the Main Quest segment "Weynon Priory."

9. You'll meet the Odiil brothers here in the Miscellaneous quest "Goblin Trouble."

For most of the day, when you enter the priory, Prior Maborel gets up from the table and offers his help. You can tell him your business is private—which elicits an unsettling comment about "another mysterious visitor." (This may seem ominous, but it is simply a reference to other Blades calling on the Grandmaster of their order.) Or you can simply ask for Jauffre to be directed to his current location.

You can also ask Maborel about other topics—among them the priory itself, which elicits comments about Septim's death and references to a news account of the assassinations. (Maborel gives you his newspaper.)

Prior Maborel

A lengthy biography of the late emperor is lying on the table. Read it. It's a good idea to get into the habit of reading the game's books. Many contain background information that, even if not directly concerned with events in Cyrodiil, helps provide a context for them. Some have good stories. And some, called skill books, boost one of your skills by one point. (Skill is specified in the book—you don't get to choose, and it isn't random.)

Maborel may not tell you everything he knows. See the section "The Subtle Art of Persuasion" for details on how to get more information out of people.

In addition, across the table you find a letter from another monk, Brother Piner, to his mother in the Imperial City. No, it's not polite to read other people's mail, but it certainly sheds an interesting light on events. In it, Piner makes light of the assassinations' consequences.

"It's horrible and depressing," he writes, "but the Empire will survive."

Note that this is only the current version of the letter. You also find three crumpled papers next to it—earlier drafts that suggest something of the desperation of his mother's original message and the young monk's tense relationship with his old mom. They also give a taste of the mood abroad in Cyrodiil, and it is a shadow of things to come.

Jauffre, Grandmaster of the Blades

You're most likely to find Jauffre at his desk in the priory's library—the eastern room on the second floor. Turn over the Amulet of Kings and repeat the emperor's last words. The monk clears up some questions outstanding from your final exchange with Septim.

The "Prince of Destruction" the emperor mentioned is Mehrunes Dagon—one of the Daedra lords who rule the world of *Oblivion* and a recurring figure in the recent history of Tamriel. (He was an important figure in *Daggerfall* and had a cameo in *Morrowind* as well.)

Dagon shouldn't pose a threat to the mortal world. It is protected from Oblivion by magical barriers. So why did the emperor perceive a threat from Oblivion? Jauffre doesn't know, but he does seem to have an idea. The grandmaster seems to imply that those Dragonfires themselves are the wards that separate Oblivion from the mortal plane.

FIND THE HEIR

Jauffre also tells you about Septim's illegitimate son. His name is Martin, and he's a priest in the Chapel of Akatosh in the city of Kvatch. Jauffre charges you with the task of rescuing the heir—Jauffre correctly suspects he's in danger—and bring him back to the priory.

He offers some help of a practical nature by unlocking the nearby chest and offering free use of its contents. Take him up on it. If you're coming straight from the sewers, this is a major upgrade for your armor and weapons.

Talk to Brother Piner. He's one of the monks who wanders around Weynon Priory, who turns over a book, *The Warp in the West*, a compendium of intelligence reports about an apocalyptic event that achieved "the Miracle of Peace" in the empire's war-torn Iliac Bay region. This is a skill book; reading it will bump up your Block skill by one.

On the grounds, you're likely to run into Eronor, a Dark Elf who works here as a shepherd. Ask him about "assistance" and he contributes a repair hammer that you can use to repair your armor or weapons.

Finally, locate Maborel. He offers the use of his Paint Horse, which is housed in the stable on the north side of the building. This appears to be just a loan, but in fact it's a gift—even if you don't talk to Maborel about it, he effectively bequeaths it to you. (Alas, Maborel is not long for this world.)

The Horsie Set
There's a whole horse subculture in Oblivion.

You don't need a horse to get to Kvatch—or anywhere else, for that matter. But even the prior's horse—the slowest of the five types in the game—markedly speeds your progress. This represents a nice compromise between fast travel (instantaneous, but skips over the intervening countryside) and walking.

When on horseback, move along roads or across open terrain—not through dense forest such as along the direct route to Kvatch—to make the most of the speed advantage. (It's hard to maneuver your horse in tight places.) This also spares you the need to engage or avoid wandering creatures in the wilderness. You can simply race past them.

Horses can jump, too, clearing low walls and fences—and this is where this horse makes up for its comparative lack of speed. (In jumping, it's tied for second.) You won't have to steer around many of the smaller obstacles, as you might have to do on foot, and can chart a more direct route to your destination.

For more information, see the "Freeform Quests" chapter.

The Subtle Art of Persuasion
Finally, Weynon Priory offers the first opportunity to play the Speechcraft mini-game to elicit hidden information.

You won't pick up any deep secrets here, and what you learn doesn't relate to the Main Quest. (In fact, Speechcraft isn't required in the Main Quest at all—though it can come into play in the quests "The Path of Dawn" and "Spies.") But the earlier you master the game, the more options you have later on (see the "Skills" chapter for tips on mastering the game).

You've already talked to Prior Maborel. But perhaps you haven't heard everything he to say. He has "Brother Piner" and "Eronor" topics. It's possible he won't trust you enough to address them—despite your having turned over the Amulet of Kings to Jauffre, or Maborel himself extending to you the use of his horse.

And don't worry if you can't crack Maborel right now. You're not missing much here that you can't discover on your own. Maborel thinks Piner's on the impulsive side and reveals that Eronor has a relative in distant Leyawiin who crafts a pretty mean spell.

Right now, Leyawiin's in the wrong direction for an easy visit, but you'll bump into Dagail in the Mages Guild quests.

KVATCH

Are you ready for Kvatch?

Unfortunately, Kvatch is not ready for you. Most of the city is in ruins. Fast travel takes you not to the city proper but to a refugee camp to the south.

The mood is one of despair and barely muted panic. Hirtel, who speaks to you automatically upon your arrival, says that Kvatch has been destroyed by Daedra (a bit of an exaggeration) and that Martin must be dead. Then he takes off to the west. You find him later at the Flowing Bowl tavern in Anvil.

Hirtel, one of the survivors from the sack of Kvatch

Refugees from Kvatch

The five other NPCs have tales of grief and loss but say only that Martin didn't make it out of the city and suggest that Savlian Matius at the barricades to the north may know more.

The camp route has some advantages. It has beds. You can use these to level up if you haven't done so already. You'll probably need the extra stat points soon.

You may even do a little business here. Naturally, the Orc smithy Batul gra-Sharob and Nord alchemist Sigrid have nothing to sell, as they left it all behind when they escaped

from Kvatch. But the Batul gra-Sharob can repair your armor for a price and, in a very limited way, buy weapons and armor you don't need. Meanwhile, Sigrid can buy potions and ingredients.

How about getting there under your own power? If traveling by horse, detour southeast back to Lake Rumare and then southwest toward Skingrad and west to Kvatch—a long road (albeit one covered at high speed) that offers you your first real taste of Cyrodiil and its West Weald region.

Or you can walk directly to the city itself, passing through a trackless wilderness along the eastern edge of the Colovian Highlands. When your route bumps up against the foothills of the Imperial Reserve, you find in quick succession the Ayleid ruin Wendir, the abandoned Fort Carmala (which may be your first experience with Vampires), and what seems to be a ghost town called Hackdirt (which turns up in the Miscellaneous quest "A Shadow over Hackdirt").

Farther southwest is Fort Dirich (now under new management as an undead dungeon), the isolated farm of Weatherleah (the subject of another Miscellaneous quest, "Legacy Lost"), and the Sanguine shrine (where you get the Daedric quest "Sanguine"). Refer to the "Daedric Quests" chapter for more details.

Here, the woods end and the foothills begin. Pass Fallen Rock Cave (which figures in the Fighters Guild quests "Unfinished Business"), the Shardrock farm, and a second Ayleid ruin, Miscarcand. (You visit Miscarcand on official business much later in the Main Quest.) Now you've reached roughly the borderline of the Kvatch–Skingrad road. Kvatch is just to the west.

Are you too late? For Kvatch, absolutely. But look at it this way: You're here early for The Rapture! The walls are scorched, the trees are all burnt. A flaming, rippling, dimensional gate stands in front of the city gates. When you place your cursor over it, you see the word "Oblivion."

The Oblivion Gate at Kvatch

Uh-oh.

Did anyone get out of Kvatch? Many did not. Talk to Savlian Matius beyond the barricade south of the gate—he's running what's left of the town guard—to learn that some survivors took refuge in the chapel and that the count and his men are holed up in the castle. Matius plans to hold his ground to prevent the encampment of survivors to the south from being overrun.

Savlian Matius, captain of the Kvatch Guard

The good news: Matius has seen Martin. The bad news: He saw him leading a group toward the Chapel of Akatosh. He's still inside the city and you'll have to get him out.

BREAKING THE SIEGE OF KVATCH

Offer to help and Matius will give you what he supposes is a suicide mission.

He thinks it is possible to close this Oblivion Gate. After all, he reasons, the enemy opened and later closed the smaller ones that were used to launch its assault on the city. He sends you into Oblivion to help the men he's sent before you or, if they're beyond help, to "see what you can do on your own."

Pass through the gate to enter a hellish scene: an island in a vast sea of lava. Great dark towers loom to the north. In the distance, you see suggestions of movement. Non-human movement.

To the northwest, north, and northeast stretch three bridges. The northwestern and northern bridges lead to a larger landmass; However, the northwestern bridge is broken, and on the northern one, a great gate is slowly closing. You can't get through before it does, and you learn, on approaching the closed gate, that it can't be opened from here. Through a gap between the gates, you can see the bodies of four town guards.

In fact, two Kvatch guards survived the prior mission. Check the area between the northwestern and northern bridges to find a terrified fellow named Ilend Vonius. He discloses that another guard, Menien, has been taken to a large tower—presumably the central spire in the cluster to the north. He offers to come along on a rescue mission (or you can save his life for later battles by telling him to join Savlian Matius at the barricade).

But how to get across the lava to investigate? Forget the bridges—a path across the lava extends north from the area where you found Vonius. When you arrive on the far side, you're in enemy territory.

Leveled Enemies

Enemies encountered here vary. In an open-ended game like *Oblivion*, it's impossible to predict exactly when a player will take on any given quest. For instance, many players come straight out of the starter dungeon and start on the Main Quest right away. In that case, you'll find lots of Scamp Runts—the giant Rats of the Daedric world, here. Nevertheless, methodically clear them out—partly for the experience and partly just to avoid nasty situations where a bunch attack at once.

But many players go off and find their own adventures, coming to the Main Quest later with an improved character. To provide a suitable challenge for that advanced character, enemies in *Oblivion* have been "leveled." That is, the enemy you face in any given combat is adjusted to your character's current level. So, as you go up in level, the Scamp Runts turn into Clannfear Runts—little Daedric dinosaurs with spellcasting ability. At higher levels, you may run into the Scamp Runt's big brother, the Scamp, or a Flame Atronach, or the Clannfear's big brother. And so on.

This often makes referring to a specific enemy in a specific place inaccurate, so forgive the generic "enemies" and "Daedra" in some spots, and look at the maps for details.

At the top of the tower near the northwestern bridge, look for a gate switch against the west wall. Alas, it's not a switch for the Oblivion Gate—that would be too easy—but for the three bridge gates. But it does smooth your escape path if you decide you're overmatched—with the minor drawback that opening the gates on the northern bridge releases three Daedra. Kill these through the gaps between the gates before you start across. Watch where you stand on the lift platform on the way back down the tower—there are spikes!

Your next destination is the large central tower to the north. This is the sole entrance to a complex that also includes the eastern and western satellite towers. (The northern satellite can be entered only through a small cave in the island's northeast corner.)

This is the first of many such complexes in the Main Quest. They're all generally similar: a central Citadel, flanked by side halls in which you do much of the actual climbing, and topped by a Sigil Keep—wherein you find the Sigil Stone that must be displaced to close an Oblivion Gate.

KVATCH OBLIVION WORLD

1. Oblivion Gate: You'll arrive in Oblivion just north of this gate. Until you close the gate, you can use it to retreat to a point just south of Kvatch's main gate.

2. Leveled Daedra

3. Burned body and a steel claymore.

4. Two sets of gates (initially closed). Between them, you'll find the bodies of four Kvatch guards who died in an earlier attempt. The gates can be opened with a switch atop the tower at #12.

5. Ilend Vonius: A survivor of the ill-fated original mission, Vonius will try to fight off the Daedra near the entry zone, greet you on your approach, and disclose that one

of the party was taken to the main Citadel. Then he'll either flee back to Kvatch or, if you ask him to remain, follow you and fight at your side.

6. Avalanche trap trigger points. One near the bridge on the west side is especially nasty, as it triggers a slide onto the bridge itself and the boulders can sweep you and Vonius into the lava.

7. Stunted Scamp: Follows the Dremora (#8).

8. Dremora scout: Patrols the path south toward the central bridge to a point just north of the claw trap (#10).

9. Mines: Visible on the surface, this device begins to spin when the player comes within range. If one of the mines detonates, you'll get whacked with a Fire Damage spell tuned to your character's level.

10. Claw trap

11. Meat Harbor: Not essential. This tower, reached by a bridge from the Corridors of Dark Salvation level of the main Citadel, offers only loot and two leveled Daedra.

12. Blood Feast: Main Citadel. At the top is the Sigil Stone. Taking it closes the gate and spits you out back outside Kvatch. See separate map.

13. Reapers Sprawl: This tower can be reached only by a bridge from the Corridors of Dark Salvation level in the main Citadel. Atop the tower, you'll find prisoner Menien Goneld, who gives you instructions to complete the mission, and a Dremora Sigil Keeper, who talks (!) and has the key to the upper levels of the main Citadel. Two leveled Daedra can be found at the base of the tower.

14. Blood Well: A small tower with two leveled Daedra. At the top, a blood fountain (healing) and a switch that opens the two gates on the bridge back to the Oblivion Gate. This is useful only if you find yourself overmatched and need to beat a swift retreat.

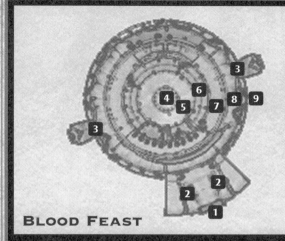

BLOOD FEAST

1. Exit to the exterior world.

2. Magicka Essences

3. Exits to the Rending Halls.

4. Vertical structures make for tricky mapping. So rather than clutter this map with enemies and fountains and "The Punished" sacks from five sublevels, we've opted to list the contents for entries 5–9 in text.

5. Entry level: Map points #1–3 all appear on the entry level.

6. Second level (reached after using the upper exit from the Rending Halls): Up the ramps, you'll find a single Dremora and two exits to the Corridors of Dark Salvation.

We've seen this Dremora wander down into the Rending Halls, so you may get a warmer welcome there than we've forecast.

7. Third level (reached after using the midlevel exits from the Corridors of Dark Salvation—#8 on that map): On this balcony (a dead end), you'll find a pair of "The Punished" loot sacks.

8. Fourth level (reached after using the upper-level exit from the Corridors of Dark Salvation): A Dremora mage—and no obvious exit. Ah, but there is: That round platform is a teleporter. Activate any one of the spikes along its northeast side, and you'll be zapped to the…

9. …Fifth level. Here you'll find another "The Punished" loot sack and the two entrances to the Sigillum Sanguis. Note that the teleporter goes both ways.

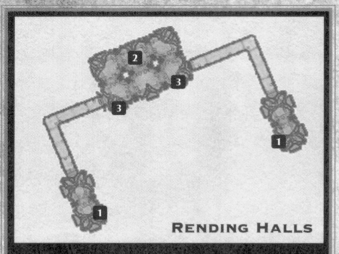

RENDING HALLS

1. Exits to Blood Feast's entry level.
2. Blood Fountain (healing)
3. Exits to the Citadel's second level.

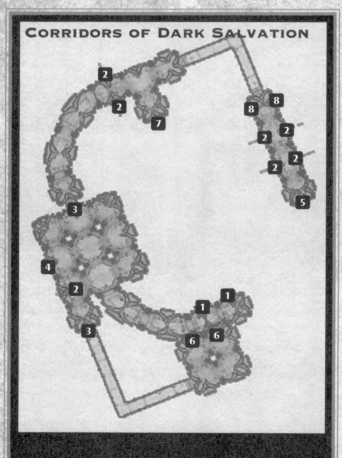

CORRIDORS OF DARK SALVATION

1. Exits to the Blood Feast's second level.
2. Spike traps. The first one you find is broken. (It has killed a Stunted Scamp.)
3. Locked doors; #4 leads to the key.

4. Exit to the bridge to the smaller, southeast tower, affectionately called Reapers Sprawl. Here you'll find a Sigil Keeper Dremora, who holds the key to the doors at #3, and prisoner Menien Goneld, who explains what you need to do higher in the tower.

5. Exit to the bridge to the smaller, southwest tower, Meat Harbor. You don't need to bother with this garden spot, but you'll find a pair of Daedra, some loot—and a broken elevator!

6. These exits lead onto a dead-end balcony in Blood Feast. (It's the Citadel's third level.)

7. Exit to the Blood Feast's fourth level.

8. The switches in these alcoves do not disable the traps down the hall at #2, but they'll show you how the trap works before they do an "Indy" on you.

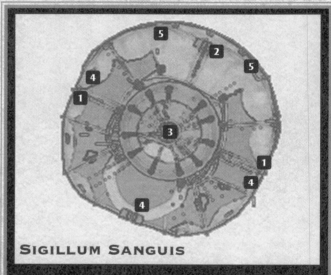

SIGILLUM SANGUIS

1. Exits to the fifth level of the Blood Feast. Note that these are on a lower level than they appear to be here.

2. Blood Fountain. Also deeper in the Sigil Keep than it appears on the printed page.

3. Sigil Stone: Activate it. Things get crazy and you'll find yourself outside Kvatch's regular old gate.

4. "The Punished" (loot sacks): The middle one's on the top level; the others are one level down.

5. Magicka Essences

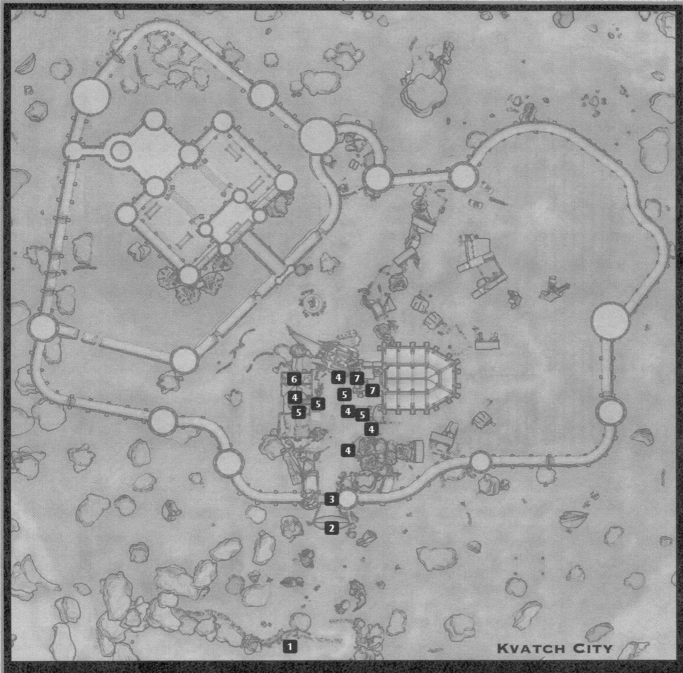

KVATCH CITY

1. Watch Captain Savlian Matius and a handful of troops. Matius sends you to destroy the Oblivion Gate in "Breaking the Siege of Kvatch." When it's gone, he orders up a new phase to the mission: Together with the remnants of the City Watch, you're to storm the plaza inside the Kvatch city gate. In the Main Quest mission "Find the Heir," this enables you to rescue the folks holed up in the Great Chapel of Akatosh and persuade Martin to follow you back to Weynon Priory.

2. The Oblivion Gate: Fiery and intact, or stumpy and ruined. You'll have to go inside the gate and close it to break the siege of Kvatch.

3. Kvatch's city gate

4. Leveled Daedra: As usual, these guys run the gamut from Stunted Scamps at low levels to Xivilai at Level 21. When they're dead, they stay dead.

5. Respawning leveled Daedra: These four bad boys, drawn from a very similar list, are designed to encourage the player to fight the battle with Matius and his gang. When you talk to Matius to kick the assault into gear, they are disabled. However, if you venture into Kvatch without talking to Matius, the Daedra in #4 do not appear and at least one of these respawning Daedra will. Moreover, they won't stay dead and Martin

and company won't feel sufficiently safe to leave the church. You'll have to get the City Watch involved in the operation first.

6. **The boss:** If you bring Matius's forces into Kvatch, you'll find this leveled Dremora mage on the upper floor of this ruined structure.

7. **The Great Chapel of Akatosh:** Within, you'll find Martin, two members of the City Watch, and survivors of the Daedric attack on Kvatch. After defeating the Daedra in the plaza outside with the help of Matius's troops, talk to Martin and he'll agree to return to Weynon Priory with you. Talk to Matius, and he'll ask you to help liberate the castle at the city's west end in the Miscellaneous quest "The Battle for Castle Kvatch." (You won't be able to explore the rest of the city until you agree.)

From the Daedric Citadel, enter the Rending Halls and then the Citadel again. Climb to the Corridors of Dark Salvation and cross the bridge to the eastern tower. At the top, await the unfortunate Menien and a Dremora Sigil Keeper who may make a rather bloodthirsty little speech before he surrenders his Sigil Key.

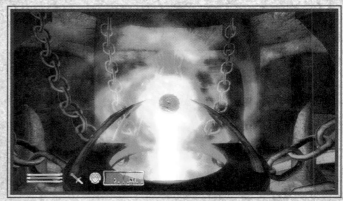

A Sigil Stone

Menian Goneld, captured by the Daedra.

Talk to the caged Menien. You can't rescue him, but he tells you what to do next: Find the Sigil Keep and take the Sigil Stone. He doesn't give the keep's location, but you doubtless noticed out in the main Citadel that you've only climbed part of the tower. Your newfound key will open the doors in your path.

Return to the Corridors of Dark Salvation and use the north door. Where the corridor levels out, watch for a spear trap. At the top, enter the Citadel yet again. You need to reach the lift on the high side of this tier. Here's where things get nasty: On the way, you're charged by two Dremora.

This must be the suicidal part Matius was talking about.

Fighting here isn't a serious option for a basic character. But sneaking (or simply running) can get you to the lift intact. At the top, climb to one of the two Sigil Keep entrances.

Activate the Sigil Stone at the top. This is the Oblivion Gate's anchor in the Daedra world. With the anchor gone, the gate is adrift. It collapses upon itself—but not, thank goodness, before depositing you back outside Kvatch's scorched walls. Your path into the city is clear.

Make your way back to the barricades and Matius. You have a couple of options. Matius proposes that you and his small command (which now includes Vonius) launch an assault to free Kvatch.

He seems in a hurry—everybody seems in a big hurry in *Oblivion*—but there's actually no rush. If you need a breather, ask your young commander to wait, fast-travel down to the refugee camp, and take a nap in one of the tents. (Most of the folks here now thank you for closing the Oblivion Gate.) When you're ready, climb back up the mountain, talk to Matius again, and give the go-ahead. The little force boldly charges into the city and helps you carve up the Daedra.

Kvatch in ruins

THE MAIN QUEST

Note that you have to kill all the Daedra in and around the plaza outside the chapel. That includes as many as three in the ruined building southwest of the chapel. Otherwise, Martin (sitting in a pew near the front of the church) won't agree to leave with you, and your reception from town guardsman Tierra will be notably hostile.

Note, too, that you can climb to the top of the ruined building and survey the destruction. The city to the west and north is largely gone. What isn't gone is burning. To the northwest, a castle is in flames.

If you talk to Matius after he enters the church, he asks for your help in reclaiming that fortress. To be sure, success in this mission will contribute to the army you raise in the later Main Quest segment "Allies for Bruma," but "The Battle for Castle Kvatch" isn't a required part of the Main Quest. It's a Miscellaneous quest, which is addressed in the "Miscellaneous Quests" chapter.

Martin, the lost Septim heir

If you've mopped up the Daedra, it's now short work to take Martin in tow and fast-travel to Weynon Priory.

Remember: Prepare for combat first.

KVATCH VARIANTS

It's possible some players will bypass Weynon Priory and simply show up at Kvatch. That'll work, too, but the quest unfolds a little differently.

You can still deal with Matius and rescue the survivors holed up in the chapel. But as you haven't yet learned about Martin, you can't ask refugees or guards about his whereabouts. When you find him, he's just "A Guy in a Church," and you get no special Septim-was-your-daddy dialogues. He'll be evacuated to the refugee camp. You must deliver the amulet to Jauffre to get Martin's name and then return to the camp to take him in tow.

Something similar can happen if you do put in at the priory first, fight your way into the church, but wait to talk to Martin until after you've explored. You may return to the church to find he's vanished.

After all, the chapel does offer some diversions. Oleta may be your first Main Quest encounter with a trainer—a character who can, for a steep price, bump up one of your skills (in this

case, Restoration). You can chat briefly with the two town guards: Berich Inian, who refuses to let you pass through the north door—this is reserved for the Miscellaneous quest "The Battle of Castle Kvatch"—, and Tierra, the ranking officer here. You can explore the lower regions of the church and, via a door at the east end of the undercroft, exit into the otherwise-inaccessible eastern section of Kvatch. Here, the destruction is virtually total.

What you may not realize initially is that Matius and the other town guards follow you into the church. In or out of your hearing, Tierra will report to Matius—there were more survivors, but they didn't stay—and then order the civilians to evacuate to the refugee camp. That's where you find Martin.

Finally, you don't have to go into Kvatch with Matius's troops. You can take down the Daedra around the church yourself, though we expect this will be a rather dicey business for a starting character.

Alas, you'll never be able to clear them out to Martin's satisfaction. As soon as you turn your back, they'll creep back. You need to call in Matius and company to keep them from respawning.

The Oblivion Crisis

This is not a quest, though it can provide the raw material for dozens of independent quests. At the moment, it's just an invisible event—the flicking of a switch in the game's dark heart.

When Martin agrees to follow you to Weynon Priory, you set off "The Oblivion Crisis." At this point, Oblivion Gates can open in certain locations in the wilderness all across Cyrodiil. You suddenly begin to find the gates during your travels on foot. Each is jumpstarted by the player's entry into one of the designated regions.

The gates pop up randomly, but typically the gate can appear in remote areas of Cyrodiil not otherwise occupied by a named location—though you'll find some close to cities. Listed below are some of the sites for potential gates closer to the major communities. Refer to the maps for a more complete list of all the possible Oblivion Gate appearances.

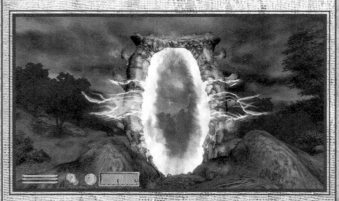
Oblivion Gates begin opening across Cyrodiil.

Near Bravil

- Northwest of Veyond's Cave, which is north of Bravil on the northwest coast of Niben Bay.

Near Bruma/Cloud Ruler Temple

- In the mountains straight east from Cloud Ruler Temple.
- South of Applewatch, in the mountains west of Bruma.

Near Cheydinhal

- Just southwest of the city proper.
- On a mountain northeast of Fort Farragut, which is just northeast of Cheydinhal.
- Northwest of Swampy Cave, which is southeast of Cheydinhal.

Near Chorrol

- East of the Odiil farm, which is east of Chorrol.
- Northeast of Nonwyll Cavern, which is in the mountains north of Chorrol.

Along the Gold Coast

- West of Malacath's shrine, which is just west of Fort Sutch.
- Southwest of the Gweden farm, which is southeast of Anvil.
- Southeast of Fort Urasek, which is southeast of Gweden farm.

Near Imperial City

- Just southeast of the Arcane University complex in the city's southeastern extremity.
- North of Fort Variela, in a Necromancer lair on the west side (middle portion) of the Upper Niben.
- Southwest of Fort Chalman, at the northwest corner of Lake Rumare.

Near Kvatch

- Southeast of the bandit encampment Dasek Moor, which is south of the Kvatch refugee camp.
- Northwest of the Shetcombe farm, which is northeast of Kvatch.
- West of Fyrelight Cave, along the road between Skingrad and Kvatch.

Near Leyawiin

- On an island in the Lower Niben Bay, just north of Leyawiin.

- Southeast of Darkfathom Cave, on the east bank of the Lower Niben.
- North of Rockmilk Cave, a little less than halfway up the west side of the Lower Niben.

Near Skingrad

- Southeast of Fallen Rock Cave, northwest of Skingrad.
- Northeast of Bleak Flats Cave, north-northwest of Skingrad.
- Just southwest of Goblin Jim's Cave, straight north from Skingrad.

These gates are not paper tigers. Daedra will appear nearby—sometimes just one and sometimes several. The gate will generate other Daedra. You can enter each gate, explore the red world on the other side (the gates link to the full range of random Oblivion environments), and then close the gate much as you did at Kvatch.

But you can't close it for good. There is always the chance that, if you re-enter that region, the gate will rematerialize—again linking to a random Oblivion world when you enter it.

In other words, you can't close down the random gates completely. This isn't a task to be completed but an undulating environmental hazard that follows the music of the Main Quest. As the story heats up, the chance of setting off new gates increases markedly. When you complete the Dagon Shrine quest, officially opening the war, the chance of gates opening rises to 100 percent.

At the same time, non-random Oblivion Gates will open outside six Cyrodiil cities: Anvil, Bravil, Cheydinhal, Chorrol, Leyawiin, and Skingrad. These don't count against the gate limits, and you can close these gates permanently at any point before the end of the Main Quest (which will slam them all shut for you). However, you can't collect a reward for most of the closings (Cheydinhal is an exception) until reach the "Allies for Bruma" segment of the Main Quest, when you parlay the gate closings into extra troops for that city's defense.

The figures for the random gates won't drop back to their post-Kvatch levels until the end of the "Paradise" quest. And the gates won't go away entirely until the end of "Light the Dragonfires!"

WEYNON PRIORY

You arrive back at the priory to find it under attack by Mythic Dawn assassins. The first person you see is the shepherd, Eronor. With an assassin close on his tail, he tells you how he mistook the attackers for travelers, and then suddenly weapons appeared in their hands and Prior Maborel was dead.

You're up against it here. Comparatively speaking, these cultists are not as tough as the assassins that took out the emperor, but there are five of them—three outside and two in the chapel with Jauffre—and time isn't on your side. It's important to fast-travel to the priory itself rather than to Chorrol this time. You have to kill the agent chasing Eronor to save your own life, and the two attacking Brother Piner near the Priory House to save his. That done, Piner will join you in the chapel in the fight to save Jauffre. (Eronor just runs for his life.)

In the chapel, time again is of the essence. If need be, make yourself the target, interposing yourself between Jauffre and his attackers, and use potions to keep up your health. Use that nice combat scroll you found in Jauffre's chest. And, rather than stowing Martin somewhere safe, let him help. He's a real asset in this fight.

Once rescued, Jauffre's thoughts go immediately to the Amulet of Kings. He hid the amulet in a secret room off the priory library. Either beat him there (it's supposed to be in the chest) or meet him there to learn the amulet has vanished. Jauffre seems on the verge of despair until he learns Martin is safe.

The Amulet of Kings was taken by the Mythic Dawn.

But where to keep him safe? The monk decides on Cloud Ruler Temple—an ancient Blade fortress high in the Jerall Mountains northwest of Bruma. Your next task is to escort Martin and Jauffre to this hideaway. (If Brother Piner survived the battles, he stays at the priory.)

You can either fast-travel directly to Cloud Ruler Temple (one of the few cases where you can fast-travel to a location you haven't previously visited) or take the road from Chorrol to Bruma, then head north to the fortress.

Cloud Ruler Temple

When you approach, the great doors open, a Blade named Cyrus appears, and Jauffre introduces Martin. The Blades at the top of the slope salute him as "Martin Septim," and Martin makes a brief, halting speech. When it's over, he thanks you for saving his life and confesses he doesn't know what to do.

The Blades hail Martin as the heir to the Septim Throne.

But Martin's instincts are good—for instance, he already knows that these Oblivion Gates are unnatural—and he has you and Jauffre to help him find his inner emperor. He'll rapidly embrace his new role.

Talk to Jauffre; he thanks you for your services in a more tangible way. You're one word away from joining the Blades.

Now, the organization of Blades is not a true faction in the fashion of the Fighters, Mages, and Thieves Guilds. (Those quests are detailed in the "Faction Quests" chapter.) It's more like a pseudo-faction. There's just the one rank and one set of equipment. You won't find unique Blade quests, or, from this point on, the sub-quests within the Main Quest function as Blade quests.

Membership confers the right to claim weapons and armor from the fortress armory, located below the library in the east wing. You find most of your kit in a chest—a near-complete suit of Blades armor and an Akaviri Long Sword—and the missing helmet and extra sets of gauntlets and greaves on the table in the middle of the room.

This armor is lighter and offers better protection than the armor you found in Jauffre's chest back at the priory. (However, keep what you can carry of your old armor, and sell it off the next time you're in town.) The sword's a touch heavier than the claymore and does slightly less damage, but it's a one-hander, so you can keep a shield or torch equipped at the same time.

Martin quickly settles in. You can often find him wandering the library, sitting before the fire in the Great Hall, or sleeping in the nice, big bedroom in the west wing. He's already being treated like a king. And he's starting to act the part—telling you to follow Jauffre's orders "while I'm getting oriented here."

THE PATH OF DAWN

Everyone seems to agree that the next objective should be the Amulet of Kings. Jauffre doesn't have a concrete plan for its recovery, but he puts you in touch with someone who may have leads to its location: Baurus.

You remember Baurus, right? You accompanied this Blade through much of the Imperial Prison and its underpinnings. He's now living in Luther Broad's boarding house in the Elven Gardens District of the Imperial City.

If you walk, in the Great Forest you find some places of interest along the sometimes-steep path down from Bruma to Lake Rumare: Bleaker's Way (an odd village of uncommunicative Nords and Dark Elves; it pops up in the Daedric quest "Mephala"), the massive Unmarked Cave, and the bandit cave Sercen.

The road west and south to the bridge into the capital is marked by a pair of abandoned but not quite empty forts. (These are rather like the strongholds from *Morrowind*.) Fort Caractacus and the nearby, curiously empty hamlet of Aleswell surface in the Miscellaneous quest "Zero Visibility." Fort Empire is a big critter dungeon.

If you fast-travel into Elven Gardens, you appear just inside the district's exterior wall. Pass the walkway and garden and make a left onto the first street. The boarding house is behind the first door to the northwest.

You may not recognize Baurus out of his armor. He's at the table right in front of you. Talk to him, or simply sit down, and Baurus tells you he's being watched. You're to follow the man who's following him. Note that you can't identify the man to whom he's referring (Astav Wirich) unless you look around *before* you sit down. In any case, Wirich gets up as Baurus passes and follows him into the basement. Once downstairs, Wirich shows his true colors—the red robe and bound mace of a Mythic Dawn assassin—and takes off after Baurus.

Baurus at Luther Broad's Boarding House

Help Baurus—unaided, he may not survive. You can start the fight off nicely (if in rather cowardly fashion) by throwing a combat spell into Wirich's back as he closes with the Blade.

Then search his body. You find a book—*Mankar Camoran's Commentaries on the Mysterium Xarxes, Book 1*—and Baurus now tells you what he's learned. The emperor's killers are members of a Daedric cult called Mythic Dawn that worships Mehrunes Dagon.

Thank you very much, Baurus, for your intuitive grasp of the obvious. The real tip: Baurus suspects a scholar named Tar-Meena at Arcane University can tell you more about the book you've found.

The university is in the southeast corner of the city. If you are a high-ranking member of the Mages Guild, you can find Tar-Meena in the Mystic Archives. Otherwise, she will conveniently be waiting for you in the lobby of the Arch-Mages Tower (the only part of the university open to the public).

Tar-Meena, head librarian of the Mystic Archives

It turns out that your book is one of four needed to locate the Mystic Dawn cult's secret shrine to Dagon. (This is an initiation test for cult novices.) Tar-Meena gives you the library's copy of Book 2 and directs you to a bookstore, First Edition, in the city's Market District to consult with the owner, Phintias, on where to find the remaining two.

The Market District is in the city's northeast corner. Fast-travel again; First Edition is the last door on the left.

Books 3 and 4 are "impossible to find," says Phintias. He's never seen Book 4. But it just so happens that he has a copy of Book 3—which he's promised to a customer, name of Gwinas, who's come all the way from the province of Valenwood to collect it. Phintias invites you to stick around and talk to him.

The bookseller has just handed you the solution. Buttonhole Gwinas inside the shop, as he's heading for the door, and reveal the Mythic Dawn's involvement in the emperor's murder. Gwinas now wants nothing to do with the group and gives you both Book 3 and a note revealing how to get Book 4—from the sponsor of Gwinas's Mythic Dawn membership.

Don't wander too far while you're waiting. Once Phintias makes that disclosure, Gwinas appears in the street outside and heads for the shop.

Gwinas can tell you how to get the final volume of _Camoran's Commentaries_.

When Gwinas leaves, he heads for his lodgings in Imperial City. You have to use bribery or Speechcraft to sweeten Phintias's mood—to a Disposition of 60—for the bookseller to reveal that Gwinas is staying at the Tiber Septim Hotel. (The Tiber Septim Hotel is in the Talos Plaza District on the west side of the city—in the southeast portion of the rotunda immediately east of the entry bridge.)

 You would only need to follow/find Gwinas at his hotel if you missed his arrival at Phintias's shop, which you could do if you weren't paying attention. Gwinas is enabled immediately after you first ask Phintias about the Mysterium Xarxes, so if you then leave or don't ask about Gwinas, you could miss his arrival or not realize his significance until later.

If you'd rather skip persuading Gwinas to hand over Book 3, you can alternately raise Phintias's Disposition to 70 when you first inquire about Book 3 and he sells you the book—earlier protestations of his word being his bond to the contrary. (You can even have some fun afterward bragging about this to Gwinas.) Or, if you're extremely good at lockpicking, you can steal the book from the store before talking to Phintias. It's in

the four-tumbler chest next to the cellar stairs. (In each case, you still have to get the note from Gwinas.)

As a final alternative, an accomplished pickpocket can steal the book and note from Gwinas—and an accomplished assassin can simply kill him and take them.

Head back to the Elven Gardens District, talk to Baurus about the "Mythic Dawn meeting" and "sewers," and then follow him. Apparently the meeting's right now. The Blade leads you down into the sewers. He takes the east tunnel, opens a gate leading south to a cistern, and then goes through another into a high-ceilinged chamber that recalls the ones you saw earlier in the sewers below the Imperial Prison.

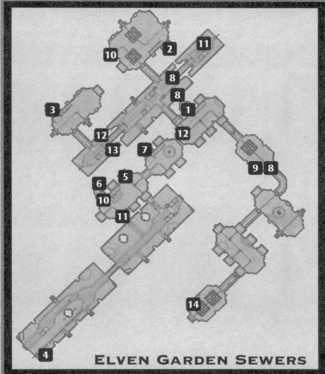

ELVEN GARDEN SEWERS

1. Exit to the Elven Gardens District: You'll appear here when you enter the sewers with Baurus in the Main Quest mission "The Path of Dawn."

2. Exit to Othrelos's cellar.

3. Exit to Irene Metrick's cellar.

4. Exit from the Sewer Waterworks: This is the entrance to the southern section of the Elven Gardens sewers.

5. Exit to the Sunken Sewers: Baurus stops here to debate who's going to take the point and the backup role in the meeting with the Mythic Dawn. This is the entrance used by the point man.

6. Exit to the Sunken Sewers: And this is the one used by the backup man.

7. Exit to Fathis Ules's cellar.

8. Slough gate: A remotely operated gate. And not that remote. The two turn wheels that operate the three gates—one operates two of them—are close to one of the gates.

9. Turn wheels: These open and close the not-so-remotely operated gates of #8.

10. Chest

11. A chest containing one and possibly two restoration potions.

12. Two sacks of food

13. A mostly submerged sack of food. Yummy.

14. A barrel containing two torches.

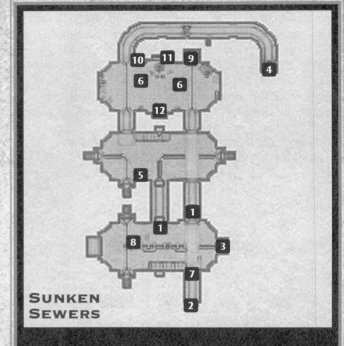

Sunken Sewers

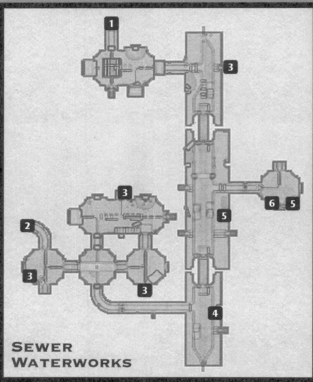

Sewer Waterworks

1. Exit to the Elven Gardens Sewers (northern section).

2. Exit to the Elven Gardens (southern section).

3. Chest

4. A sack containing a healing potion.

5. Crate

6. A barrel

1. These key-locked gates will be opened by Raven Camoran and one of his accompanying Mythic Dawn guards when they arrive for the rendezvous.

2. Exit to the Elven Gardens Sewers: This is the entry door used by the backup man in your meeting with Mythic Dawn operative Raven Camoran.

3. Exit to the Elven Gardens Sewers: This is the door used by the point man at that meeting.

4. Exit to the Talos Plaza Sewers: Opened with the same key that opens the gates at #1.

5. Raven Camoran

6. Mythic Dawn guards

7. If you insist on the role of point man, Baurus will take up position here.

8. Take a seat here. Camoran will be with you shortly. He'll unlock the nearby gate, walk around the table, and make a little speech. Until your cover is blown. After the fighting's done, claim Book 4 of Commentaries on the Mysterium Xarxes from his body.

9. A boss-level chest

10. Chest

11. Books 1 and 2 of Commentaries on the Mysterium Xarxes can be found on the bookshelf here…

12. …and Book 3, six gold, and two lockpicks on the desk here.

Here, you stop to sort out which of you will take "point"—that is, who will receive the book—and who will do backup duty. The point person proceeds through the west door into the Sunken Sewers, per Gwinas's note, and sits at the small table. The backup climbs the stairs to the south, enters the same room through the west passage, and keeps watch.

It doesn't make much difference which one you choose. Either way, Gwinas's sponsor, Raven Camoran, arrives out of the darkness and starts a little recruitment speech. Two more Mythic Dawn cultists appear in an adjoining room. Then, the speech ends prematurely with a fight. Either Baurus is recognized as the Blade that Wirich was stalking, or the Mythic Dawn's backup team discovers you've brought backup as well. (Gwinas was told to come alone.) Even failure to sit in the chair as ordered gets the cultists riled up. Obeying orders is apparently very big with the Mythic Dawn folks.

Raven Camoran

Kill the three of them, get the fourth volume of *Commentaries* from Camoran's inventory, and talk to Baurus again. He's headed for the fortress to serve under Martin.

You're on your own again with a brain-teaser to solve. How do you divine the location of the Mehrunes Dagon shrine from the books?

You can solve this yourself without help. At least give it the old Arcane University try. Looking at the books gains you a one-point boost in each of four magical disciplines: Conjuration, Destruction, Illusion, and Mysticism. (These are skill books.)

If you can't figure it out, Baurus offers that maybe Tar-Meena, the scholar who came up with Book 2, can provide more assistance. Leave the sewers the way you entered and pay her another visit at Arcane University.

You have to talk to her three times on three different days to get the solution. The first two conversations result in tips to help you solve it yourself.

The first such hint: She suspects the books contain a hidden message. But she wants another day to work on the project, which means you need to wait until after midnight to bug her again.

This time, Tar-Meena suggests that the first word in each paragraph may be the key to the books' meaning. But she wants one more day of study.

So try your own hand again. The scholar doesn't quite own the solution yet but has now given you a strong hint. Take the first *letter* of each paragraph of the four books to form a message: "Green Emperor Way Where Tower Touches Midday Sun."

If you still can't see it, when you return to the university the following day, Tar-Meena has sorted it out. She even interprets it for you. Green Emperor Way is an avenue on the palace grounds.

Specifically, it's in the palace cemetery. Fast-travel to the Palace District and you appear on a walkway leading northeast to a flight of stairs. Just before the stairs, turn right and walk over to the large, domed tomb. If you highlight the tomb, you learn it is the tomb of Prince Camarril.

Tomb of Prince Camarril in Green Emperor Way

Wait until noon. A glowing map appears on the tomb's door, with the Mythic Dawn shrine marked. Check your province map. The destination marker has appeared in the hills west of Lake Arrius in eastern Cyrodiil.

You don't have to visit Cloud Ruler Temple again to report your success or receive instruction for the next quest. (If you do, Jauffre offers his congratulations and his hope for the future. Baurus is back and guarding Martin. Martin offers a new comment on Mehrunes Dagon's reputed *Mysterium Xarxes*.)

Your next move should be obvious: Hit the shrine and get the Amulet of Kings back.

DAGON SHRINE

Your path into eastern Cyrodiil winds through rather desolate and, toward the end, difficult terrain.

Retrace your route along the north coast of Lake Rumare, and this time continue east at the bandit cave Sercen. After you pass the tumble-down Roxey Inn, the path begins to turn south. Head east-northeast cross-country and you hit Fort Chalman (now an undead dungeon), Exhausted Mine (now a Goblin lair), and, up in the hills, the farmhouse Harm's Folly (which plays into the Settlement quest "Revenge Served Cold") (see the "Miscellaneous Quests" chapter for details on Settlement quests). Then there's nothing for a long stretch until you reach the shrine on the far side of the mountains. (The slopes east of the farm can be prohibitively steep, and you may need to detour north or east to reach the cave.)

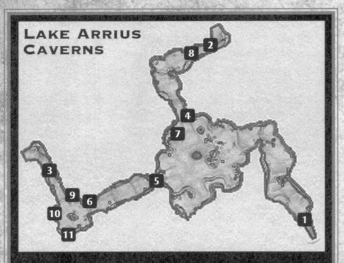

LAKE ARRIUS CAVERNS

1. Exit to Lake Arrius.
2. Exit to the shrine antechamber.
3. Exit to the shrine living quarters.
4. A key-locked door. In the Main Quest mission "Dagon Shrine," the doorkeeper (#7) will open it for you when you give the countersign, or you can kill him and take his key.
5. Secret door: This opens only from the other side. It's the escape route for the player. But it also allows a player who's dropped all belongings in this foyer (prior to Harrow collecting them) to recover his or her equipment and then return to loot the shrine and hit acolytes with pointy sticks.
6. The switch that opens the secret door at #5.
7. The doorkeeper: When you provide the countersign, he'll open the key-locked door at #4.
8. Harrow: The shrine warden waits for you here. He'll take your belongings and then lead you through the antechamber into the Dagon Shrine.
9. Miscellaneous loot: A Mythic Dawn robe, a copy of the book Hiding with the Shadow, and two crates.
10. A sack of grain and a barrel of valueless items.
11. A chest containing gold, with possibilities of other loot.

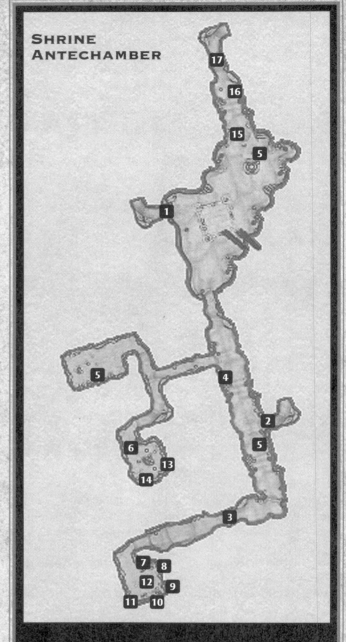

SHRINE ANTECHAMBER

1. Exit to Lake Arrius Caverns.
2. Exit to Dagon Shrine, with a leveled lock of two or more tumblers. (Harrow has a key.)
3. Door to storage room, with a leveled lock of three or more tumblers. If it gives you agita, the storeroom guard has the key, but he's not nearby. (See #7 in the "Living Quarters" map.)
4. Mythic Dawn guard: This guard stands watch here but also patrols to the portcullis at the north end of the antechamber.
5. Mythic Dawn guard
6. Mythic Dawn acolyte
7. A low platform containing a barrel (two torches) and a

boss-level chest. Under the platform, you'll find a Lesser Soul Gem.

8. Weapon rack containing an iron mace and iron short-sword.

9. A chest containing one or two restoration potions.

10. The crate with the iron shield on top could contain (in order of likelihood): Mythic Dawn garb, a potion, scroll, and magic jewelry. The rest is dreck.

11. The crate contains nothing of value, but the chest contains gold and might also contain other valuable loot.

12. The barrel and small crate hold only junk. But the chest's contents are identical to those of the one at #11, the large crate's to the one at #10. And the grain looks tasty.

13. The small crate could contain magic jewelry and a scroll. On the table is the book Gods and Worship.

14. On a stone shelf, you'll find the first three volumes of the Mythic Dawn Commentaries.

15. This portcullis can't be opened from this side...

16. ...but can from the other using this lever.

17. Exit to the living quarters.

Inside you can play it one of two ways: undercover or commando. You can give the countersign to the doorkeeper at the bottom of the first passage and wait for him to unlock the first door, or butcher him and take his key. In the next room, you can turn over your possessions to the shrine warden, Harrow, and allow him to lead you to the shrine for your initiation—or you can refuse and send him to join his buddy. If you killed the doorkeeper, you will have to fight Harrow—and everyone in the shrine will be hostile as soon as you start a fight with anyone.

Harrow, Warden of the Shrine of Dagon

Undercover is the way to go for a low-level character. It gets you all the way into the inner shrine with no one the wiser. Fighting instantly blows your cover. Word of the attack spreads like wildfire, and you have to kill pretty much everybody in the

antechamber to reach the shrine. You've seen what Mythic Dawn guys are like when they transform into warriors, and that can be too much for a lower-level character.

You don't have to hand over all your stuff to Harrow, though. Find some flat ground in the shrine's first room and dump everything you can before you talk to Harrow. (If you dump your stuff outside, you watch it tumble down the steep mountainside in a lovely demonstration of the game's physics engine.)

Alas, you can't drop your gold. Consequently, any gold carried to this encounter is forfeit (at least for the moment). Either invest it in equipment, potions, and spells before you leave, or return after you're done and take it back.

DAGON SHRINE

1. Exit to the antechamber. When you try to escape, you'll find this blocked by a portcullis.

2. However, this exit will be open. It's the way out. Fight your way out, or just run.

3. The portal back to Mankar Camoran's personal "Paradise" appears here.

4. Mankar Camoran: The #2 entry in Oblivion's Bad Guy Countdown makes his first appearance. He addresses his fanatical followers from here. On the podium before him sits the Mysterium Xarxes book (your objective) and a silver dagger, with which you can send intended sacrificial victim Jeelius (#5) to the next world.

5. Jeelius: A priest at the Temple of the One in the Imperial City, he's been kidnapped by the Mythic Dawn and is all set up as a sacrifice to Daedra lord Mehrunes Dagon. You just have to kill him. Or not.

6. Ruma Camoran: Camoran's daughter. We see Fairuza Balk playing her in the movie version. She'll direct you to sacrifice Jeelius.

7. Shrine guard: He appears here once the alarm is sounded.

8. Mythic Dawn acolytes

9. After delivering you to the shrine, Harrow watches the proceedings from here. If you want your belongings and cash back, you'll have to find him after all hell breaks loose.

10. Stairs down into the shrine (and up to the exit).

When you enter the shrine, you hear cult leader Mankar Camoran's speech. It serves both as confirmation of Baurus's earlier intelligence of Mythic Dawn's involvement in the assassinations and as a statement of intent for future campaigns.

"The time of Cleansing draws nigh," he declares. "I go now to Paradise. I will return with Lord Dagon at the coming of the Dawn!"

And so he does, taking the Amulet of Kings with him—but not the *Mysterium Xarxes*, which rests beside a sacrificial dagger on the podium at the west end of the dais.

The *Mysterium Xarxes*

Save him (simply refusing to kill him is not enough), grab the book, and run all out for the stairs to the north. He follows you outside the shrine and makes his way back to Imperial City. (You find him back at his duties—he's a priest in the Temple District—later in the game.)

Mankar Camoran preaches to his faithful followers in Dagon's Shrine.

Speak to Ruma Camoran, Mankar's daughter, and she orders you to kill the victim laid out on the altar.

Tough decision. With the death of Jeelius, your escape from the shrine will be somewhat easier. By killing him, you've proved yourself and Ruma Camoran and the acolytes at the base of the dais will disperse. But you've gone undercover to slam the door to Oblivion and save innocent lives—not take them. Truth be told, you're not going to be able to just stroll out of the shrine with *Mysterium Xarxes* under your arm in any case. Saving Jeelius won't make it that much harder. The alarm will go off, and releasing him just makes it go off with enemies in closer proximity.

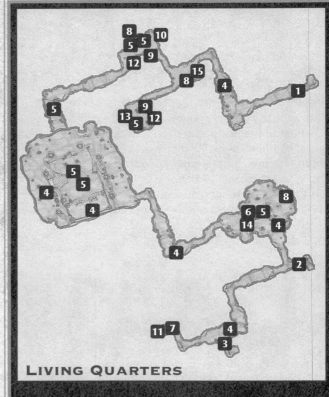

LIVING QUARTERS

1. Exit to Dagon Shrine.

2. Exit to the shrine antechamber.

3. Exit to the Lake Arrius Caverns and the secret door. This is the way out.

4. Mythic Dawn guard

5. Mythic Dawn acolyte

6. Mythic Dawn cook (!): By name just another acolyte, this Mythic Dawn cultist is actually the shrine cook—a

fact revealed only by the silver spoon in his inventory and (a 10 percent chance) by his possession of rare ingredients.

7. Storeroom guard: This guy's stuck down at the back end of the shrine, and he's taking advantage of his isolation by not doing his job. He's supposed to be guarding the storage room at the southern tip of the antechamber. Instead, he's sleeping 22 hours a day and using the remainder to grab a snack in the big room to the northeast. Pickpocket him or kill him for the storeroom key.

8. Crate: Chances at magic jewelry and a scroll.

9. Crate: Might contain a potion, a scroll, or a piece of magic jewelry.

10. A crate from #9 and a chest with one, possibly two bits of restoration-oriented loot.

11. Nice little cache. A Sneak skill book, Sacred Witness, a 75 percent chance of two restoration potions, and 50 percent chances of magic jewelry and Restore Magicka potions. (Our hunch: This is all stuff the lazy guard at #7 swiped from the storage room.) Locked, with two or more tumblers.

12. Chest containing gold and maybe more.

13. Boss-level chest. Locked, with two or more tumblers.

14. The stuff in the crates is useless. But not the bag of grain.

15. Shelves containing Nighteye and Fortify Personality potions, Bound Dagger and Restore Health scrolls, empty Lesser and Petty Soul Gems, a copy of The Book of Daedra, and a shopping list. "Beer, lots of beer," it begins. (On the adjacent desk, you'll find a recipe for a Cure Disease potion. It works, too—even if you're just a beginner alchemist.)

You can't leave as you entered; a locked gate now blocks this path back to the shrine's antechamber. Happily, a second exit on the north side of the room's upper tier is open, and the comparative safety of a separate antechamber is only a short way up the tunnel. Here, the enemy mood runs more to panic than outrage.

Your impulse is probably to obey your journal entry and cart the book back to Martin pronto. But now that you're suited up again, you can nip back into the shrine, using the secret exit, and do some looting—including reclaiming any gold or personal property that Harrow liberated from you earlier.

Harrow should still be in the shrine. You have to kill him to recover your gold. Another good source of loot is through the lower door of that pillared room where we shook off the pursuers.

However, reaching Harrow and getting out alive may not be a simple task—even with your reclaimed equipment. If you ran from the scene, there are still packs of Mythic Dawn guards and acolytes—not to mention Ruma Camoran—roaming the

intervening antechamber and the shrine itself. The longer you're here, the greater the chance they will catch up to you and try to kill you.

Back at Cloud Ruler Temple, talk to Martin to turn over the book for decryption. He expects it will reveal how to open a portal to Camoran's Paradise and, hence, to recovery of the amulet.

But that's going to take a while. In the meantime, Martin refers you to Jauffre to see a report of spies in Bruma.

SPIES

Cloud Ruler Temple may not be quite as safe or secret as the Blades' grandmaster once thought. The temple's gate guards have reported seeing strangers on the road for the past several nights. Jauffre can't mobilize the Blades for a general search of the mountainside without risking the fortress's security, but he can send you out to spy on the spies. He suggests you talk to Blade Captain Steffan and Captain Burd in Bruma at the base of the mountain.

Depending on the time of day, Steffan can be found patrolling the walls, guarding Martin, eating in the library or sleeping. He tells you the strangers usually appear at dusk near a runestone down the rocky slope. (Runestones are discussed in the "Freeform Quests" chapter.)

Burd can be found either in the Great Hall of Castle Bruma or the adjoining barracks. He hasn't noticed strangers in town. Indeed, with "the Oblivion Crisis," he says there hasn't been much travel lately—apart from Jearl's recent trip up from the south.

These two referrals set up alternate (and mostly separate) approaches to cracking the case. One involves surveillance, the other a concerted investigation in Bruma. And some stage, each will involve fighting. Jauffre wants the spies dead, and he wants to know what they know.

SURVEILLANCE

The surveillance part is fairly basic. Before 7 p.m., take up a position on the large snow-covered rock partway down the

The runestone outside Cloud Ruler Temple

slope south of the fortress road. (Those guards must have eyes like eagles. The fortress itself is a bit too far away to serve as a useful vantage point.)

Fix your gaze to the south and wait. Shortly after 7 p.m., two figures approach a runestone just east of the low hill to the south.

You won't see the two doing any actual spying, but their presence here is certainly suspicious. Maintain a careful distance; at 10 p.m., you can track them back to a cave entrance (Bruma Caverns) southwest of the city. This leads to a door to the basement of Jearl's house in the city's southwest corner. If you can pick the lock, you can put a beating on the Mythic Dawn spies Jearl and Saveri Faram.

If you can't pick the locks, let the spies spot you. They morph into Mythic Dawn warriors and attack—against their orders, as it happens. Kill them. Ultimately, you're going to have to kill them anyway. You find keys to the cave door and trapdoor on their bodies. (Jearl also has the key to her house.)

But where's the intelligence Jauffre asked you to collect? On a table in the cellar is a note from Ruma Camoran that lays out the enemy's operations and future plans in frightening detail. The Mythic Dawn order already knows Martin is at Cloud Ruler Temple, and the fortress's destruction is now a priority. The spies, Jearl and Saveri Faram (who are identified by name) are looking into what Martin's doing there and his potential escape routes. (The Mythic Dawn doesn't want a repeat of Kvatch.) The agents also have been active outside Chorrol—the first explicit hint is that a gate has already appeared there—and plans call for the opening of a Great Gate at Bruma.

The order is also interested in you—probably more now than when the note was written.

INTELLIGENCE

But let's assume you've missed the window for tracking the spies today and don't feel like wasting a day waiting. Then head for Bruma and Captain Burd.

Burd, Captain of the Bruma Guard

Jearl is a local, but her name is the only hard detail you have. However, when you talk to Burd, your journal suggests you have a chat with Jearl.

Jearl never leaves her house, which remains locked all day long, making your task difficult. Trying to pick her lock gets you fined by the town guard. You need more than the circumstantial evidence to break into a house with impunity. Can someone provide hard info on Jearl?

A survey of residents turns up a lot of interesting local problems—all outside the capacity of this chapter—but only one comment about Jearl, and it raises suspicions without providing probable cause. (Regner, who lives several houses to the east, says Jearl stays inside all the time.)

If you put the "strangers in town" question to Jorek the Outcast, a beggar who wanders Bruma, he says his memory "sometimes ain't what it used to be." With five pieces of gold, you can jog his memory. Jorek now recalls seeing someone he'd never seen before looking out Jearl's window when Jearl herself wasn't home.

In fact, two of Jearl's neighbors can offer similar tips. Ongar the World-Weary across the street and Arnora to the east have heard Jearl talking to someone, and, like Jorek, Ongar's seen someone at the window. But they talk only if you belong to the Thieves Guild or if you ratchet the speaker's Disposition up to 60. Raise their Dispositions by playing the persuasion mini-game, or by Charm-ing them.

Moreover, Ongar's door is also locked, and picking attempts produce the same swift response from the authorities. Ongar's only here from 6 a.m. to noon, and you can find him taking his meals at Olav's Tap and Tack or wandering the city for the rest of the day.

You now have your probable cause. Bring this information to Burd's attention and he authorizes a search of Jearl's home. You still have to pick the lock on the door and then another lock on the trapdoor to the cellar, where you find Ruma Camoran's note. (If you can't master both locks, your only recourse is to track down the spies themselves, as described in the "Surveillance" section above, and take their keys.)

Find Ruma's orders in Jearl's basement.

Report back to Jauffre, who says he'll contact Bruma's countess to report the threat to the city. Then he bumps you over to Martin for a progress report on his decryption of the *Mysterium Xarxes*.

BLOOD OF THE DAEDRA

Just as Camoran bound himself to the evil book *Mysterium Xarxes* to create his Paradise, so can Martin bind himself to it to create a portal into that realm. But he needs your help to secure the materials for this ritual. So far, he's identified only one: the blood of a Daedra lord infused in a Daedric artifact.

Ask Martin about "Daedric artifact" to learn these can be obtained through the cults devoted to the various Daedra lords—and that the book *Modern Heretics* offers a good account of the cults. The temple's library has a copy.

Note that his language is a little artful here; Martin means the temple has a copy—not that it's physically in the east-wing library. (It's on Martin's table in the Great Hall unless you've already taken it.)

Read *Modern Heretics: A Study of Daedra Worship in the Empire* to learn the location of the Shrine of Azura. Your journal suggests a visit to this shrine to learn how to acquire such a Daedric artifact, and a map marker shows the shrine's location. See "Azura" in the "Daedric Quests" chapter for details.

Azura's Shrine

On the surface, this all looks fairly straightforward, but this is one tricky quest.

The book, if you actually read it—and you *are* reading the books, right?—also mentions other Daedra lords and their artifacts: Hircine the Huntsman (the nemesis in *Morrowind*'s *Bloodmoon* expansion), and his artifact, Savior's Hide armor; Malacath and the hammer Volendrung; and Molag Bal and the Mace of Molag Bal. "Other Daedra Lords, their shrines, and worshippers, remain to be discovered in Cyrodiil by earnest and persistent researchers," The book's text reads.

In fact, any of the game's 15 Daedric artifacts will do for this quest. Which one should you collect for Martin's ritual?

PICKING AN ARTIFACT

Here is more information to help you chose your artifact:

If convenience and speed are paramount, you can fast-travel to Azura's shrine or possibly the Sanguine shrine. You passed the latter if you walked to Kvatch. Possibly others, too, if you've explored significantly on your own. Two more shrines— Namira's shrine east of Bruma, and Hermaeus Mora's shrine far west of the Blades temple in the mountains near the Skyrim line—are within easy walking distance.

But proximity is a deceptive virtue. You typically need an offering of ingredients to summon the Daedric lords, and many of the required ingredients are hard to come by for a low-level character. The monsters that yield them appear only when the player has reached higher levels.

So what do you do if you're still small potatoes? Some alchemists stock the ingredients, but figuring out which ones may be a long-term enterprise. The ingredients may turn up in general clutter, but again, they are rare and, naturally, they probably won't be there when you go looking for them.

Shops don't have fixed inventories. Like loot, shop inventories are drawn from large collections of items that reflect the player's current level.

If you want an easy quest, go to Nocturnal's and Hircine's shrines. It's a long trip to the Nocturnal shrine even if you first fast-travel to Imperial City—the shrine is east of the midsection of the Lower Niben—and it is open for business only at night. But you don't have to supply anything up front to get the quest, and the mission itself involves only a nominal amount of mayhem and quite a lot of sneaking about and eavesdropping.

Hircine's shrine is much closer—straight south from the Imperial City's southeastern extremity, on a hilltop in thick woods south of Sweetwater Camp. The offering (a wolf or bear pelt) isn't hard to find, and the mission (kill a unicorn) shouldn't be a stretch.

One last consideration: Each of these quests yields an artifact that you might put to good use yourself. If you give it to Martin, you throw it away—albeit to a good cause.

So are any artifacts clearly expendable? Martin seems to think so. He offers a unique comment on each when you turn it over. For example, he says that the Wabbajack staff you collect from the Sheogorath shrine's mission is the stuff of mischief. (You might think otherwise. This staff, which changes the target into a random creature, is an excellent way to bring a tough enemy down to size. Use it against a easier one, though, and it may have the opposite effect.)

In the big picture, they're all useful. But in the smaller one of an individual game, usefulness is relative to how you play. If you're a blunt-weapons guy, the sword Goldbrand may not impress you. A blademistress may look askance at the hammer Volendrung. And if you're not much of an enchanter, a reusable soul gem like the Azura's Star isn't likely to rise far above your horizon.

For more information on each quest, see the "Daedric Quests" chapter.

BLOOD OF THE DIVINES

By the time you turn over the Daedric artifact to Martin, he's figured out the second item required for the portal ritual: the blood of a god. Jauffre has suggested the blood of the emperor Tiber Septim, a mortal who became divine as Talos. Martin suggests you ask him where to find it.

Martin studying the *Mysterium Xarxes*

Security-minded Jauffre has another mission foremost in his mind. As forecast in Ruma Camoran's note from the "Spies" quest, an Oblivion Gate has appeared outside Bruma, and he asks you to show Captain Burd and his town guard how to close it.

However, if you then ask after "the armor of Tiber Septim," he steers you to a relic from the reign of Tamriel's first emperor.

 The "Bruma Gate" and "Blood of the Divines" quests run in parallel. It doesn't matter which one you do first. We tackle "Blood of the Divines" here and the "Miscarcand" quest that follows because, with "Blood of the Daedra," they make up a sequence of "ritual" quests. Look for the "Bruma Gate" section later in the chapter.

After his victory at Sancre Tor, Septim made a present of his bloody gear to the Blades. The Blades built a shrine around the cuirass deep in those catacombs. And in the years that followed, the location—where Septim received the blessings of the god Akatosh—became a mecca for Blade pilgrims.

Then an unspecified evil settled in Sancre Tor. It claimed the four mightiest Blades of Septim's time—note their names, Alain, Valdemar, Rielus, and Casnar—and Jauffre says it has been "centuries" since a visitor has returned from the shrine.

He leaves you with the key to Sancre Tor's outer door and he fears he is "sending you to your death."

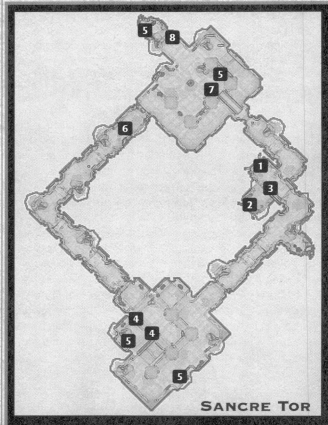

SANCRE TOR

1. Exit to the surface ruin. You'll get the key required for entry into Sancre Tor when you receive the "Blood of the Divines" quest from Jauffre.

2. Exit to the Entry Hall, which serves as a "hub" for access to the dungeon's other levels. Note that this is on a lower level than it appears on this map.

3. Dagger of Sparks: An enchanted weapon is required to fight off the ethereal creatures that inhabit the dungeon. This is a basic one.

4. Dart trap

5. Chest: Two are unlocked and two others have leveled locks with one or more tumblers.

6. This portcullis is raised using the nearby lever.

7. Undead Blade: Defeat this nasty skeletal warrior—the first of four—and the spirit of Rielus will appear. He'll tell you a tale. He's one of the four Blades sent to Sancre Tor by Emperor Tiber Septim to learn what manner of evil had crept into the Catacombs. He then walks to the Tomb of the Reman Emperors. You must beat all four undead Blades to claim Septim's armor.

Each of the undead Blades' Skeletons has a special item. In Rielus's case, it's the Amulet of the Ansei, with a leveled Fortify Block skill enchantment.

8. A chest containing one or possibly two items of restoration-oriented loot.

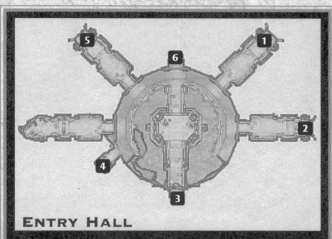

ENTRY HALL

1. Exit to Sancre Tor entry level.

2. Exit to Prison.

3. Exit to Tomb of the Reman Emperors.

4. Exit to Catacombs. This door is hidden from view. Head for the tomb and turn west just before you reach the door. You'll see a sewer tunnel leading to a grating. Hop over the wall and follow the tunnel. The hall to the Catacombs is off to the left.

5. Exit to the Hall of Judgment.

6. A chest containing one or two items of restoration-oriented loot.

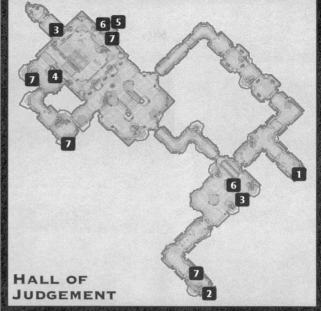

HALL OF JUDGEMENT

1. Exit to Entry Hall.

2. Exit to Catacombs.

3. Boss-level chest. The chest on the south side of the bridge is locked—a leveled lock with two or more tumblers. And the one on the "observation deck" at the north end of the level may seem impossible to reach…

4. …But if you can jump up here, then you should be able to jump to #6 and then to the deck. (It can be done by a character with maxed out Acrobatics and Speed stats.)

5. Undead Blade: Though not shown on the map, there's a small recess here. Beat down this Blade Skeleton and the spirit of Casnar will appear, make a brief speech, and then make for the Tomb of the Reman Emperors. (Mishaxhi is the undead Akaviri commander you'll encounter at Pale Pass in the Miscellaneous quest "Lifting the Vale." No, he won't recognize his Cleaver. But nice try.)

From the combat, you'll inherit Mishaxhi's Cleaver—an Akaviri claymore with a leveled Disintegrate Armor enchantment.

6. Chest containing one or two restoration-oriented items.

7. Chest. The one with the undead Blade has a leveled lock with one or more tumblers.

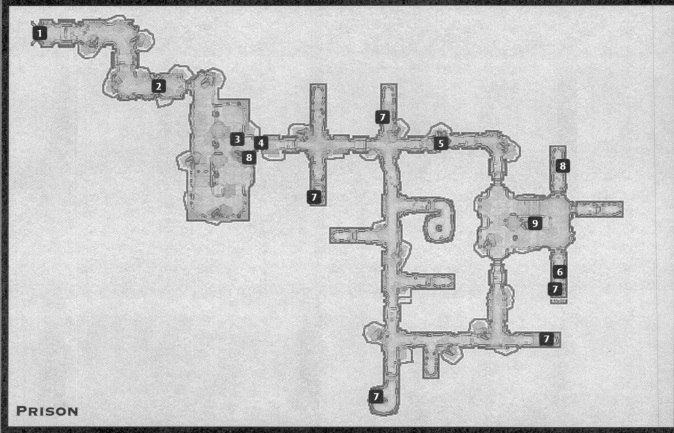

PRISON

1. Exit to the Entry Hall.

2. This portcullis is raised using the nearby lever.

3. Warden Kastav: Not an undead Blade, but the prison's chief. Take the warden's key. It unlocks the door at #4.

4. The door at #4. This can also be picked.

5. Cave-in. This passage is blocked.

6. Undead Blade: When this one's gone, the spirit of Valdemar appears. Again, you can have a little chat with it before it makes for the tomb. The Skeleton leaves behind Valdemar's Shield, which has a leveled Reflect Damage enchantment.

7. Chest. The one with the undead Blade has a leveled lock with one or more tumblers.

8. Chest containing one or two restoration-oriented items.

9. Boss-level chest. The leveled lock has two or more tumblers.

CATACOMBS

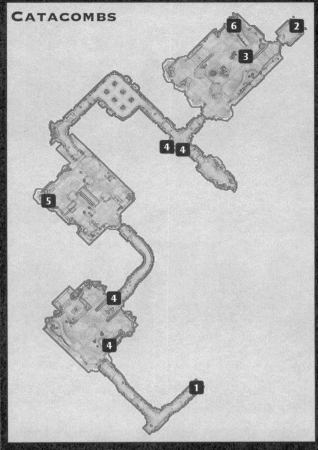

1. Exit to Entry Hall.

2. Exit to Hall of Judgment.

3. Undead Blade: When the Skeleton goes down, the spirit of Alain appears. He's the least grateful of the Blades—we suppose he's cranky after hundreds of years of being dead—and basically tells you to get out of his way as he heads off to the tomb. The Skeleton leaves behind Northwind—a one-handed Akaviri blade with a leveled Frost Damage enchantment.

4. Chest containing one or two restoration-oriented items.

5. Chest

6. Boss-level chest

TOMB OF THE REMAN EMPERORS

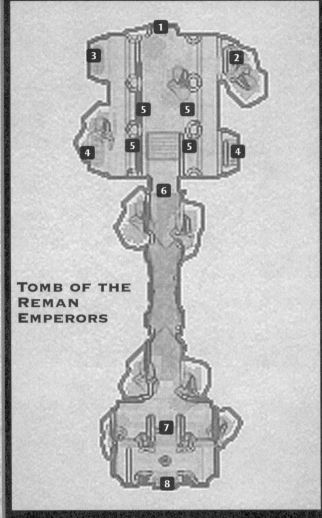

1. Exit to the Entry Hall.

2. The Tomb of Reman of Cyrodiil. You can read the inscription.

3. The Tomb of Reman II. Again, you can read the inscription.

4. The inscriptions on these tombs are illegible.

5. The spirits of the Blades take up positions on one knee at these locations. The last spirit to be freed will wait closer to the door and doesn't take his place until you enter the tomb. When you approach the Blades, the Underking's enchantment will be dispelled and the barriers to the inner portion of the tomb removed. After you take the armor (#7), the Blades stand. Speak to them individually, and they'll depart for Aetherius.

6. The barriers start here. You ain't goin' nowhere until you free the captive spirits of all four Blades.

7. The armor of Tiber Septim: So take it already. It's your objective in the Main Quest mission "Blood of the Divines."

8. The Tomb of Reman III. You can read the inscription.

Jauffre has never said anything quite like that before. Then again, in the Main Quest, you've never before visited a place quite like Sancre Tor.

Sancre Tor is a sprawling undead dungeon still bent to the evil will of a departed entity. Among other things, this means Ghosts and Wraiths. And that, in turn, calls for a magic weapon—something the Main Quest hasn't thrust into your hands up to this point. Any of the Dremora weapons from the Kvatch Oblivion Gate will do, if you happened to pick one up. If you don't have a magic or silver weapon yet, quest independently for one before you set out on this mission.

You've probably passed fairly close to Sancre Tor on your way northeast to Cloud Ruler Temple. On your way southwest, across foothills and forest, you pass the Ayleid ruin called Rielle, the small and waterlogged Boreal Stone Cave (whose lone inhabitant figures in the Miscellaneous quest "A Brotherhood Betrayed"), and the critter lair Sideways Cave.

Sancre Tor's entrance is in the southeast interior corner of a decaying keep—north of the tree line on a rough plateau at a break in the mountains. The exterior entrance to the keep itself is in its southwest corner.

The armor isn't that far into the dungeon—off the Entry Hall (which serves as a hub for Sancre Tor's six sections) in the Tomb of the Reman Emperors. But you can't reach it. A four-stage magical barrier blocks the way.

The Armor of Tiber Septim

By the time you reach the barrier, you may already have made a start at removing it. Spread around the dungeon are four undead Skeletons. *Blade* Skeletons. You must defeat them all. One's in a large chamber near the bottom of the initial section of Sancre Tor, the others are in the Hall of Judgment, the Prison, and the Catacombs—all of which can be reached from the Entry Hall. The Hall of Judgment and the Catacombs are also connected directly.

It doesn't matter which Blade you tackle first. After you defeat each Skeleton, the ghost of the respective Blade appears and fills in some of the specifics to the broad story.

The four were sent by Tiber Septim to learn what had invaded the Catacombs. They discovered, too late, that it was the Underking—Septim's former Imperial battlemage, Zurin Arctus. Arctus was determined to have his revenge on the emperor and claimed it here by blocking those who would visit

Sancre Tor to honor Septim and forcing the emperor's servants to an endless defense of the defiled shrine.

One of the guardians of Sancre Tor

The Underking himself is long gone, but the undead Blades are still in his grip. However, once you defeat their undead incarnations in combat, they join up to break the lingering spell that blocks your access to the tomb. Then you can claim the armor—wear it, too, if you like. It's a nice (if unenchanted) heavy chest plate.

Alas, you don't get to keep it. Give the armor to Martin, and he removes the needed blood, puts on the armor himself, and gives you another quest.

GREAT WELKYND STONE

The third item required for the portal ritual is a Great Welkynd Stone—a magical artifact found in the ruins of an Ayleid capital at Miscarcand.

This is the first explicit reference to the Ayleid people in the Main Quest.

Ayleid

Morrowind had the Dwarves. *Oblivion* has the Ayleids—a dead civilization, founded in time immemorial, whose artifacts are in demand by collectors, enchanters, researchers, and emperors-to-be. You'll be sent out several times in *Oblivion* to retrieve them—notably in the Miscellaneous quests "The Collector," "Nothing You Can Possess," and "The Secrets of the Ayleids."

Just as you could instantly identify the rusted Dwemer towers in *Morrowind*, you can recognize the gleaming Romanesque ruins of the Ayleids. To date, you've seen at least three—Wendir, in the deep woods southwest of Weynon Priory; Rielle; and Miscarcand itself.

If you walked from the priory to Kvatch, you probably found Miscarcand along the Skingrad–Kvatch road.

Glories and Laments Among the Ayleid Ruins, a travel guide on Martin's work table in the temple's Great Hall, deals with another site—Ceyatatar, in the forest between

Skingrad and Imperial City. In its images of decay, it hints at the elegance and sophistication of the Ayleid civilization—though not its brutality.

 None of this is required for the mission, but if you want to learn more about the Ayleids, check out *The Last King of Ayleids* at (among other places) Imperial City's First Edition bookstore; *On Wild Elves* in Arcane University's Mystic Archives; and *The Amulet of Kings* in the library at Cloud Ruler Temple.

You shouldn't have too much trouble in Miscarcand. The enemies (mainly Goblins, Zombies, and Skeletons) are manageable, the loot satisfying, and the path down to the Sel Vanau and Morimath sections and its Great Welkynd Stone uncomplicated. Just stay on the main path. Most of the time, it's on high ground.

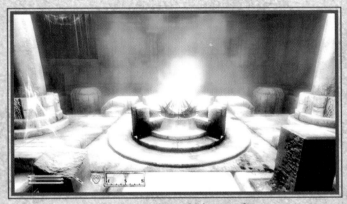

The Great Stone of Miscarcand

The king and a couple of his pals appear from a hidden enclosure on your way out, but the fight can be surprisingly quick (so long as you close quickly with this son of a Lich), and the hideaway even provides you with a speedier way up and out.

Back to Cloud Ruler Temple. That's the end of the ritual quests for now. The fourth component remains elusive. Martin doesn't know what it is and he won't know until you complete two missions that relate to the defense of Bruma. If you haven't completed "Bruma Gate," Martin directs you to do so now. If you have, see Jauffre, who sends you off on a massive expedition called "Allies for Bruma."

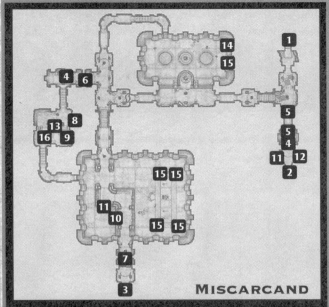

MISCARCAND

1. Exit to surface ruin.
2. Exit to Morimath level. Unavailable from the Miscarcand level until you recover the Great Welkynd Stone and return topside. Access is blocked by a removable wall that can't be lowered from the north side. (This is an escape hatch that allows to the player to avoid having to trek all the way through the ruin on the way out.)
3. Exit to Sel Vanua level.
4. Pressure plate: One lowers the wall at #5. The other opens the gate at #6.
5. Removable wall
6. This gate can be opened only by stepping on the pressure plate on the far side.
7. This remotely operated gate blocks the exit to the Sel Vanua level.
8. Push this button to open the gate at #7.
9. A boss-level chest with a leveled lock of two or more tumblers. You'll also find a Magicka-restoring Welkynd Stone (not to be confused with the Great Welkynd Stone you're seeking) between the broken crates nearby.
10. Chest
11. Big bad Goblin hit you? Aw. We're sorry. Want to make it all better? A restoration-related item (maybe two) can be found in these chests.
12. Another boss chest with a leveled lock of two or more tumblers.
13. You'll find gold in this chest, natch, but you'll also find three scales. They're fairly common among Goblins— currency?—but they're an ingredient useful to the Journeyman alchemist in Water Breathing potions and to an Expert one in Water Walking potions.

14. Two more scales in this crate, with small chances of a bit of gold and a Goblin weapon. But the real prize here is the Welkynd Stone next to the crate.

15. Welkynd Stones: In addition to the two we've already found close to other loot, there are five more here.

16. Two more scales and two bits of food in this sack.

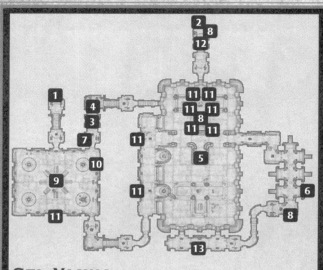

Sel Vanua

1. Exit to Miscarcand level.

2. Exit to Morimath level.

3. This gate can't be opened from the south side. (The button at #9 lifts the cover off the Varla Stone in the middle of the room.)

4. Pressure plate: This will open the gate at #3 on your way out.

5. An Ayleid boss chest with a leveled lock of two or more tumblers. A Welkynd Stone is nearby.

6. Another boss chest

7. Loot chest

8. A chest containing one or two restoration-related items.

9. Varla Stone: Recharges a magical item. To get it, you'll have to lift the cover off it by pushing the button…

10. …at #10

11. Welkynd Stone

12. This gate is pretty darn remotely operated. The button is all the way over…

13. …here!

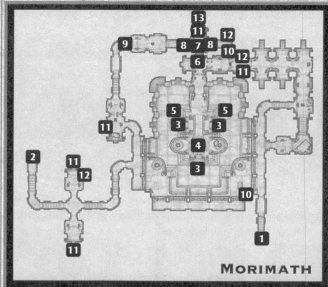

Morimath

1. Exit to Sel Vanua.

2. Exit to the Miscarcand level.

3. These staircases rise from the floor when you take the Great Welkynd Stone at #4. (This is not for your benefit. The staircases allow the two Zombies that materialize to the northwest and northeast (#5) when you take the stone to reach you quickly.)

4. Great Welkynd Stone

5. Zombies (summoned when the stone is taken)

6. Removable wall: The Zombies are the least of your troubles. Your removal of the Great Welkynd Stone also lowers this wall…

7. …and reveals the King of Miscarcand, who is located here along with a pressure plate for #8. This Lich operates at one level above your own, with a significant repertoire of nasty spells and powers and the Lich's standard resistances—including frost, magic, and poison—and 25 percent spell reflection. It has one notable weakness: fire.

8. Removable walls: Stepping on the pressure plate at #7 lowers them.

9. This gate is unlocked with the Miscarcand key from the Lich's body.

10. Boss-level chest: Leveled lock with two or more tumblers. You'll need a gift for jumping to reach the one on the platform to the southeast.

11. Chest

12. These chests each contain one or two restoration-related items.

13. Welkynd Stone

BRUMA GATE

You get to run a training mission. An Oblivion Gate has opened before Bruma. You're the one who closed one of these things at Kvatch. Now you're to instruct Captain Burd and his men on Oblivion Gate closing procedures. Meaning you're going to close it for them while they watch your back.

EXTERIOR WORLD

1. Oblivion Gate.

2. Citadel entrance.

3. Claw trap.

4. Turret: These babies turn themselves on if you get within about 60 feet and then blast you with fireballs.

5. Blood Fountain (healing)

6. Magicka Essences

7. Fleshy pod (loot)

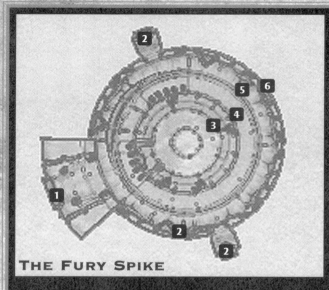

THE FURY SPIKE

1. Exit to exterior (ground level).
2. Exit to Rending Halls (ground level).

Mapping vertical structures is a ticklish affair. Everything's on top of everything else but it looks like it's all together. Rather than display each enemy and fleshy pod on a single level and risk confusing folks (one of the folks being me), we've handled this one a little differently—summarizing the contents of each of the Citadel's four discrete levels.

3. Ground level: No loot, blood fountains, or Magicka essences. Exits to the Rending Halls to the north and south.
4. Second level (reached from the middle exit of the Rending Halls): Up the ramps, on the north side, you'll find "The Punished" (i.e., loot sack) and a Magicka fountain. Dead end.
5. Third level (reached from the upper exits of the Rending Halls and the lower exit of the Corridors of Dark Salvation).
6. Fourth level (reached from the upper exit of the Corridors of Dark Salvation): Near each of the north and south entrances to the Sigillum Sanguis (each with a leveled lock of two or more tumblers), you may find a Daedra. Between them is the Dremora Sigil Keeper. Use his key to enter the Sigillum Sanguis. (Also look over his nice equipment.)

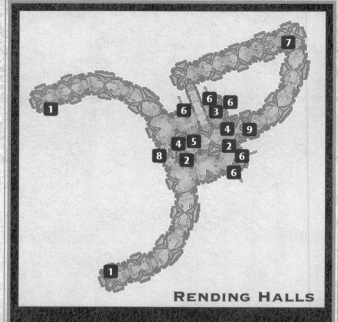

RENDING HALLS

1. Exit to The Fury Spike (ground level).
2. Exit to The Fury Spike (third level).
3. "The Punished": Also known as loot—identical in contents to what you'll find in hanging fleshy pods in the exterior world.
4. "The Punished": Same as #3.   However, these two appear on the hall's upper level—immediately opposite the exits to the second level of The Fury Spike.
5. Blood Fountain: This appears on a lower level.
6. Spike traps.
7. Look up. That's a blade trap. You don't want it hitting you. (Flip the lever on the left wall, which activates the trap before it can take you unawares.)
8. Exit to The Fury Spike (second level): This is a dead end with some loot and a Magicka fountain.
9. Doorway to halls' upper level.

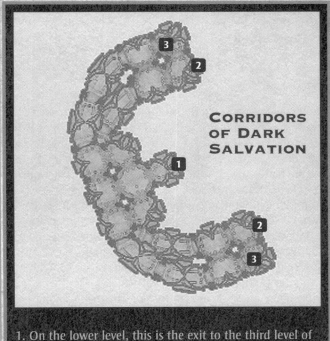

CORRIDORS OF DARK SALVATION

1. On the lower level, this is the exit to the third level of The Fury Spike. On the upper level, it's the exit to the fourth.
2. Magical essences
3. "The Punished" (loot). A Daedra loses his allowance, and you get it!

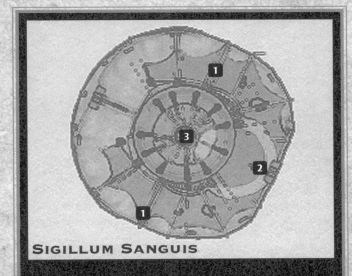

SIGILLUM SANGUIS

1. Exit to The Fury Spike. (It's on a lower level than it appears here.) Also, on the upper level, a Dremora archer occupies each of the exits.
2. "The Punished"
3. The Sigil Stone. Activate it and wait for the big finale! You and any survivors will appear outside Bruma beside the ruined gate.

Captain Burd and his men outside Bruma

The gate shimmers southeast of the city. You can enter and do a reconnaissance if you wish. However, this plan will probably be brief and bloody. The Daedra assembled on the other side—an array that is increasingly Dremora-oriented as you rise in level—may just eat you alive.

Better to wait, enlist the aid of Burd and two of his five town guardsmen (who can be found outside the town gate), and go in together. That way, the Daedra assembled on the far side can eat them alive.

That's a joke. You need to watch the guards' backs just as they (it is hoped) watch yours. If they die, you may die. Try not to hasten this process by hitting them instead of the Daedra.

As you move counterclockwise around a U-shaped island toward another of those great gray towers—home to the Sigil Stone that anchors the Bruma gate—your quartet faces a swarm of Daedra. The exact composition of this happy mob will vary a good deal, depending on your current level, but you're going to see a lot of Dremora.

If you're getting clobbered here, read it as a signal to come well-prepared with potions, ramp up your weapons and armor, and level up in side quests before you try it again.

The Sigil Tower

You find the tower similar to the one reached via the Kvatch gate, with one important difference. Chance plays a greater role in exactly how things play out. Many of the Daedra may or may not appear. You face numerous enemies in and out of the Citadel on your way up to the Dremora Sigil Keeper (this one at the top of the Citadel) and the Sigil Stone.

When it's over, you get Burd's gracious thanks and perhaps too-blasé assurance that he and his men can tackle things in the future.

Here the ritual and "Bruma" quest sequences draw together again, and we embark on the "Era of the Big Missions." The Main Quest is beginning to come to a head.

ALLIES FOR BRUMA

Your success with the Bruma gate opens up two overlapping quests—"Allies for Bruma" (from Jauffre) and "Defense of Bruma" (from Martin). Make good progress in the first before you try out the second.

Jauffre's still worried, and with good reason. The Daedra are numberless. The members of the Bruma guard are finite. If a Great Gate opens here like the one that opened (and then closed) outside Kvatch, then it's over. Something needs to be done to improve the odds. Jauffre asks you to serve as a sort of warrior/ambassador to Cyrodiil's other cities and to the empire's Elder Council (which rules Tamriel in the absence of an emperor) and collect more troops for Bruma's defense.

Even using fast travel directly to the castles, this is no small task. If you play the quest out now in its fullest form, it's by far the largest in *Oblivion*.

For one thing, you have to find the right person in places that may, in many cases, be unfamiliar to you. (Up to this point, the Main Quest has kept you out of most of Cyrodiil's cities.) Sometimes you need to see a count and sometimes a countess. In Skingrad, initially, you may go through a middleman. And at every stop, the ruler wants something big from you in return.

As we mentioned earlier, in "The Oblivion Crisis," lesser Oblivion Gates opened outside six of Cyrodiil's cities after you completed the "Dagon Shrine" quest. Understandably, none of their rulers feel comfortable sending their soldiers to another city's defense until their own is safe. At Anvil, Bravil, Cheydinhal, Chorrol, Leyawiin, and Skingrad, to secure a commitment of troops, you have to close a gate.

In Kvatch, where the Oblivion Gate has already been shut down, the situation is a bit different. Here, your old pal Savlian Matius wants your help in liberating Kvatch's castle.

Then again, if you've been aggressively closing those gates and have wrapped up "The Wayward Knight" and "The Battle of Castle Kvatch" Miscellaneous quests, "Allies for Bruma" will just be a victory tour to collect thanks and troops already earned.

 The troops are not sent automatically to the battlefield; you have to go back to each local ruler and make your request.)

 See the "Miscellaneous Quests" chapter for details on securing the Kvatch and Cheydinhal contingents.

You may not realize initially that the "Allies for Bruma" quest is entirely optional. You can do all of it, or part of it, or none of it. If you think you can kill anything the game throws at you or are impatient with the quest's vastness or just want to see a big battle now, talk to Martin to set things in motion and then follow his instructions.

Did we mention that you should probably prepare to be quashed like a bug? It's difficult to survive the conflagration that follows without some seriously tough fellows backing you up or aggressive and effective participation in the battle by a well-prepared player. Each of the mini-quests you complete boosts your chances.

How many quests is enough to win? There's no simple answer. Jauffre will measure your success if you check in with him occasionally (using the "aid for Bruma" topic) along the way. You need a majority of the possible allies to win his approval.

But that's all he's doing—counting allies—and your character's stats, skills, equipment, and your own aggressiveness also weigh in the battle's outcome. What kind of fighter or wizard are you? Is the only good Daedra a dead Daedra, or do you get anxious and heal up when a Scamp bites your big toe? If you have a full house of allies, you should be able to slip through with defensive fighting. If you're coming up short, you may have to spend more of your hit points to make up the difference.

Can you safely skip any of these trips? One, certainly: You don't need to go to Imperial City. Chancellor Ocato of the Elder Council is just going to turn you down. The Imperial legions are tied down in the provinces fighting the Daedric invasion and can't be spared.

And it's useful to note that some of those quests have greater practical yields than others. At Bravil, you win the services of a proper heroine, a Level 15 guard captain named Viera Lerus. At Cheydinhal, you can collect another hero—a Level 15 guard captain named Ulrich Leland—and one generic soldier. (If Leland has been killed in the Miscellaneous quest "Corruption and Conscience," you get only the soldier.)

Anvil and Chorrol each contribute two generic soldiers, and Kvatch, Leyawiin, and Skingrad provide one apiece.

We suggest you do the quests in that order and give the battle a trial run after Chorrol. Here's a rundown on your contacts in each city, their hours of easy availability, and where to find the Oblivion Gates.

Anvil: The castle is south of the city proper on an island. Countess Millona Umbranox can be found in the Great Hall from 8 a.m. to 4 p.m.—standard "audience" hours for most of Cyrodiil's nobles—and in the dining room from 8 p.m. to midnight. The Oblivion Gate is on a hillside northwest of the city gate.

Millona Umbranox, Countess of Anvil

Bravil: The castle is southeast of the city gates. From 8 a.m. to 4 p.m., Count Regulus Terentius is in the Great Hall. He's pretty much an ass in conversation, but he does send you a marvelous fighter. The Oblivion Gate is on a rise northwest of the city gate.

Chorrol: The castle is northeast of the city gate. Countess Arriana Valga keeps the standard office hours, but even when she's not hanging out in the Great Hall, she spends most of her time in public areas (notably the Chapel of

Arriana Valga, Countess of Chorrol

Stendarr and The Oak and Crosier tavern). The Oblivion Gate is on a low rise in the woods just south of the city gates.

Leyawiin: The castle's at the west end of the city. Count Marius Caro holds court in the County Hall from 8 a.m. to 4 p.m. and takes his dinner there from 8 p.m. to 11 p.m. The gate is northeast of the city.

Marius Caro, Count of Leyawiin

Skingrad: In other cities, you simply seek out the ruler and walk up and say your piece. With some extra art, you can do that here, too. Up two flights of stairs, pick the three-tumbler lock to the Lord's Manor and you can surprise Count Janus Hassildor—and get the same version of "no" you've received from the other local nobles.

It's tempting. Waiting for Hassildor to show up in a public area is a fruitless exercise. He doesn't, except under special circumstances. And if you can't unlock the door, you must go through an intermediary. The count has two stewards who serve as buffers between Hassildor and the public: an Argonian female named Hal-Liurz and an Imperial named Mercator Hosidus.

Both are prepared to blow you off until you throw the "aid for Bruma" topic at them. Tune changed; count summoned. You can wait as ordered or follow the steward upstairs; it doesn't matter.

In refusing your request, Hassildor makes a strange little speech—with references to "my kind" and "whatever you may think of me."

Hey, Count, we just met! But, come to think of it, he is a strange-looking guy. Those piercing eyes. Almost like…a Vampire.

In fact, exactly like a Vampire. It doesn't relate to the Main Quest, and, unlike other ravenous Vampires you encounter, Hassildor is not an imminent threat. But you deal with Count Dracula and his odd appetites again before you're finished with *Oblivion*.

The Skingrad gate appears east of the castle—down the hill to the right at the end of the bridge, near the large rock that marks the entrance to Bloodcrust Cavern.

THE GATES

Five of the six gates—the gates at Anvil, Bravil, Chorrol, Leyawiin, and Skingrad—are described here. The sixth, the gate outside Cheydinhal, is part of a Miscellaneous quest, and is described in that section.

CHORROL GATE

You arrive facing south in a small forest of Daedric towers—including an inaccessible one behind you that is sinking into the surrounding lava. Ahead of you may be as many as 10 Daedra.

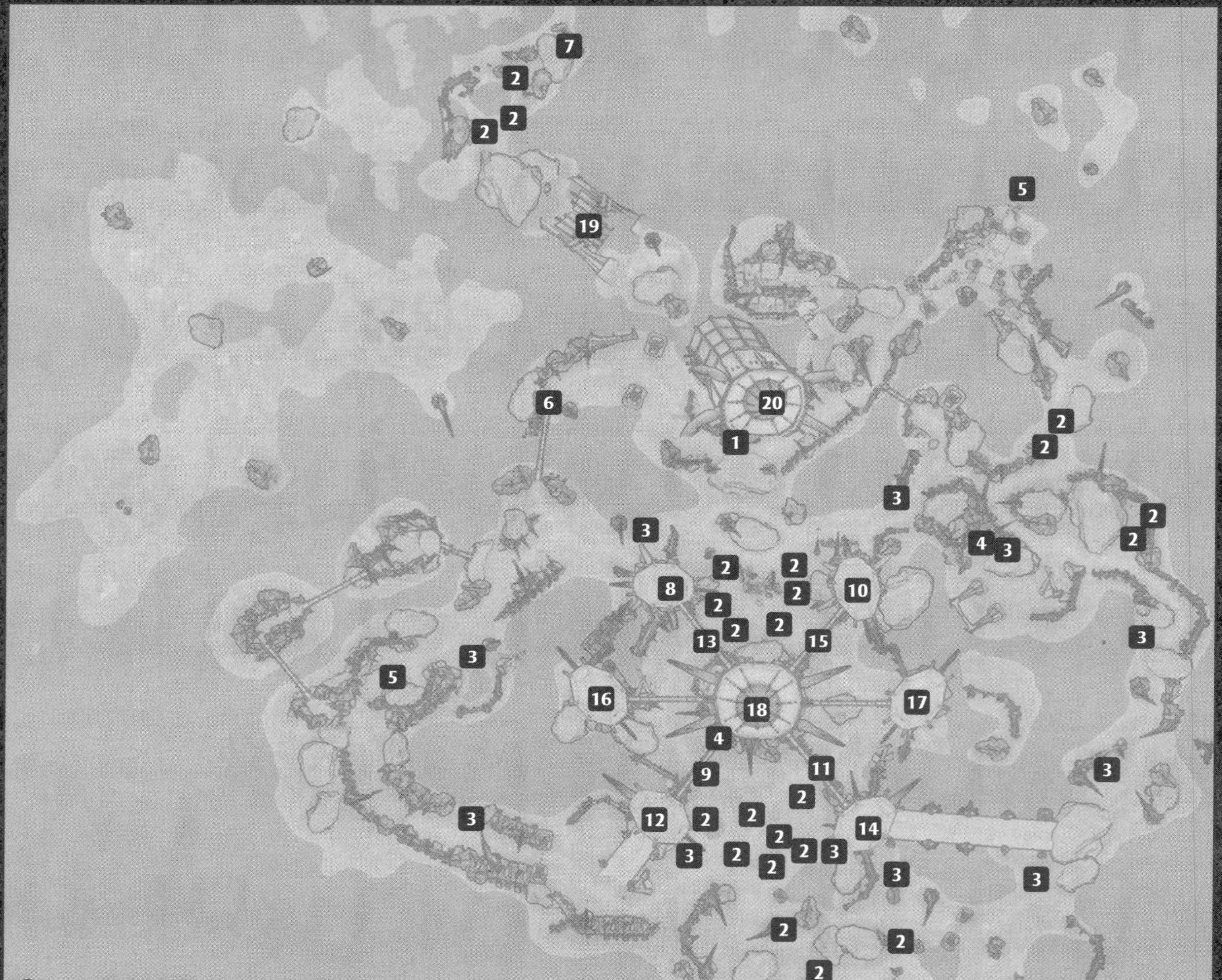

CHORROL OBLIVION WORLD

1. Exit back to Cyrodiil—specifically to a small ruin on a hillock south of Chorrol.

2. Mines

3. Turret

4. There's little loot in the exterior world, and what there is tends to be hidden away. At each of these locations you'll find a pair of fleshy pods. One contains one or two restorative items. The other has little you'll want beyond a bit of gold.

5. Blood Fountain (healing)

6. Two more fleshy pods. Again, you'll pretty much scrape the contents of one off your boot.

7. Fume Vaults: This modest-sized cave, guarded by three of the usual suspects (and likely a fourth that could be a Dremora) leads east and south under the lava to the out-of-kilter door to the lost Citadel at #20. Note that there's an Easter Egg on the cave's lower level that's reached by dropping down the hole west of the exit. Note also that you'll be dropping into lava, which equals instant death, and that a super-human Acrobatics stat is needed to get back out, so you'll need

to use a cheat or exploit to survive. In the far northeast corner of this warm enclosure is a boss-level fleshy pod.

8. **Tsunami:** Like Eruption (#10), this tower provides access to three of the other five satellite towers and limited access to the central Citadel. A switch at the top opens the Tornado Gate at #9.

9. **Tornado Gate:** It's opened by the switch atop the Tsunami tower at #8.

10. **Eruption:** A switch at the top of this tower opens the Landslide Gate at #11.

11. **Landslide Gate:** It's opened by a switch atop the Eruption tower at #10.

12. **Tornado:** Switches atop this tower open the Tsunami Gate at #13 and dump a (dead) prisoner out of his cage. The body falls all the way to the base of the tower.

13. **Tsunami Gate:** If the bridge wasn't in the way, you'd see it. It's opened by a switch atop the Tornado tower at #12.

14. **Landslide:** A switch at the top opens the Eruption Gate at #15.

15. **Eruption Gate:** It's opened by activating a switch at the top of the Landslide tower (#14).

16. **Hurricane:** Healing at the top, fighting and surface access at the base.

17. **Earthquake:** Ditto.

18. **Portals of Natural Disaster:** We're not mapping the place out, but we'll tell you how to get started on your way to the Sigil Keep. This can be a mite tricky: Though you get into the Citadel early on, you do so at a level that gives you access only to the smaller towers to the northwest, northeast, southwest, and southeast.

Open the gate at #13 or #15. This will give you access to the surface entrances of the towers at #16 and #17. Climb #16 or #17 to the top and take the bridge over to the Citadel. (A good jumper could also leap between bridges to reach these towers.) You're now at a slightly lower level than before and can enter the Rending Halls, which lead to the upper levels of the Citadel.

19. **Collapsed gate** (which can be used as a bridge over the lava).

20. **Embers of Hatred:** Major Easter Egg. This world's second Citadel is slowly becoming one with the lava around it. However, if you're willing to risk getting burned to a crisp—you'll have to jump over some lava en route—you can get in via the Fume Vaults at #7. This Citadel's unlike anything you've seen to date. The floor is tilted. There's no fiery beam down its axis and no Sigil Keep. And the entry level is guarded by two special Dremora called "hate keepers." They have great loot no matter what level you've reached. You'll have to kill both for their Keys of Dark Hate. The first key lets you through a key-required door into the Halls of Dark Hate—endearingly empty, save for the unique extra-potent Magicka and Health dispensers—and the second lets you out onto the Citadel's second level. Here you can teleport up to the third level (activate the spikes beside the pad) to reach two custom containers. One holds the Hatred's Soul bow (with leveled Fire Damage and Drain Speed enchantments), 13 soul-trapping arrows, and a Daedra heart. The other contains three bones and a mace called Hatred's Heart with a leveled Fire Damage enchantment.

Don't worry. Only three of those are guaranteed to appear and there is only either a 25 or a 50 percent chance that each of the other seven join them. Those include the four Daedra closest to you.

Flame Atronach

You can enter the small towers to the east, Eruption and Landslide, and west, Tsunami and Tornado. The one to the east is a better bet—the western one being guarded by additional Daedra. At the top of each, you find a switch to open one of the gates outside and an entrance to a bridge that leads south to the central Citadel, Portals of Natural Disaster. Once you have opened one of the exterior gates you have access to the third eastern tower, Earthquake, or western tower, Hurricane. Ascend either of these towers and at the top you will find yet another bridge to the Citadel. Here, as in the past, use the adjoining Rending Halls to climb most of the way up the Citadel to the Sigil Keep.

LEYAWIIN GATE

This is the hard one.

You appear, facing north, on an island in another sea of lava—conceivably with Daedra in every direction save the southwest. The path under the lava to the north lies through the cave entrance north and west of the gate on this same isle.

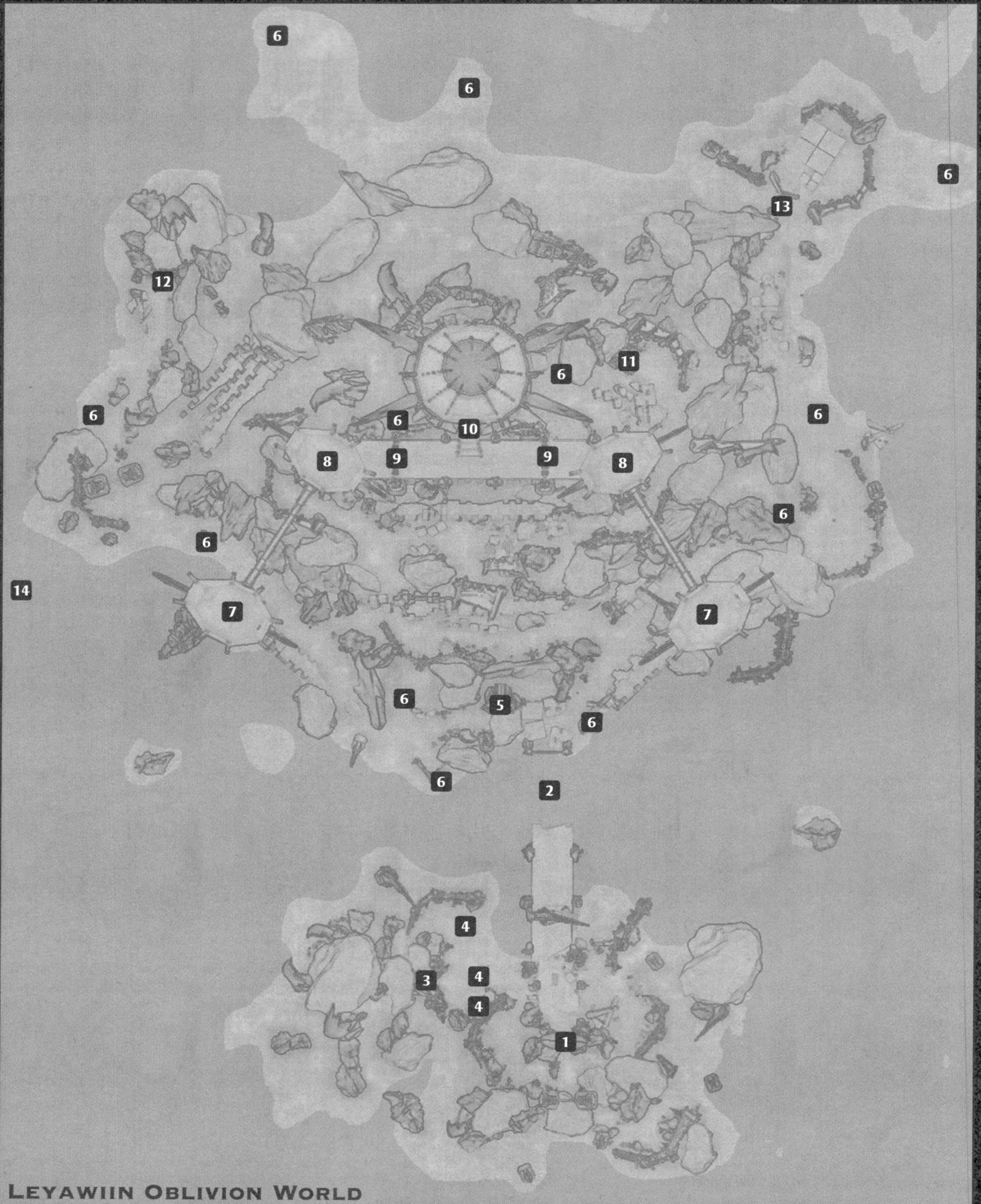

LEYAWIIN OBLIVION WORLD

1. Oblivion Gate: Exit back to the Yellow Road just east-northeast of Leyawiin.

2. The jump isn't quite as long as it appears here, but we humbly suggest that anyone without spectacular

Acrobatics skill and high Speed attribute stop trying and just use the cave at #3.

3. Nether Tunnels: A random cave consisting of two or three sections. "Nether Tunnels" isn't a place-name so much as a description of what happens to you when you activate the door. You're teleported to one of seven possible starting sections—all called either The Hate Tunnels or the Worm Gut Channels. When you activate the door at the other end, you're teleported again—this time to one of seven middle sections (called either Molten Halls or Fume Vaults) or seven end sections (called either Mire of Ash or The Scratch Paths). If you wind up in a middle section, when you activate the door at the other end you'll be teleported to an end section. If you wind up in an end section, the door teleports you out the exit at #5.

4. Mines

5. The exit from Nether Tunnels. (See #3.)

6. Turret

7. Spindle Shrine: At the top of each tower, you'll find a Magicka Essences fountain and entrances to bridges leading to towers to the northeast and northwest. The elevators are damaged, and you can reach the cellars only through the cave at #11.

8. Blood Well: At the top of each tower is a switch that opens the respective gate at #9. Atop the western tower, you'll also find a Blood Fountain (healing). Atop the eastern one is a dead Mythic Dawn guard—throw a switch to dump him out of his cage—and, at the base of the tower, a midlevel fleshy pod. The bottom of each tower is defended by two Daedra.

9. These gates are opened by throwing switches atop the Blood Well towers.

10. The Tower Portal: When you activate the door, you're teleported randomly to one of five Citadels. These vary a good deal. The Lust Keep and The Dreaded Refuge are roughly the same size as other Main Quest Citadels, with two side halls. The Gore Steeple is smaller, with just one. And The Flesh Spire and The Claw Monolith have three.

11. Molten Halls: This small cave connects with the cellars of both Spindle Shrine towers at #7.

12. Loot cluster—albeit of a rather tatty sort. Two of the three fleshy pods are of the cocooned-victim variety, but the third is standard midlevel Oblivion loot.

13. Another loot cluster—slightly better than the one at #12 by virtue of a fourth fleshy pod, which contains one or two restoration-related items.

14. Off the map to the west is a very long, sinuous island. We doubt many people will be able to get there except through cheats or exploits. (Though we won't rule out that an expert in Acrobatics with extremely high hit points and a wealth of healing magic might make it by skipping across the lava as can be done with water.) There's nothing here, honest. But in the north side of a wedge-shaped rock around the middle of the island, you'll find a door. It can't be activated, and it doesn't connect to anything. This is just scenery.

Oblivion Caves

A random teleport thing happens. In fact, it happens two or three times in this cave. The door into Nether Tunnels zaps you into one of seven starting sections of a giant, generic 21-segment dungeon. And the exit, innocently labeled "Oblivion Cave," zaps you again. Seven of its 12 possible destinations constitute the "middle" portion of the dungeon, and the remaining five are drawn from the end portion.

If you land in a middle section, its exit teleports you to one of five end sections. If you land in an end section, the exit zaps you to the south-central coast of the north island. Hence, you should be on the far side of the lava after traversing two or three sections of dungeon.

Make your way west to the southwestern or east to the southeastern tower. Climb it, cross the bridge to the northeast or northwest, and throw the switch atop the tower at the other side. These switches open the gates on the central bridge, which leads to the Citadel entrance.

That random thing happens *again*: entering the main tower's door teleports you into one of five Citadels.

One of these is much easier than the other two. Here you'll face just five Daedra in the Citadel itself, three more in the adjoining Dark Tower Corridors, and, if you haven't yet reached Level 14, none at all in the Sigil Keep. (If you have reached Level 14, things suddenly get very nasty indeed.)

However, in the tougher Citadels, you're guaranteed to face those same five Daedra and may face as many as 11 more (though for each of those 11, there's a 50 percent chance they won't appear). In the three adjoining sections, one tower has another 10 guaranteed Daedra and the possibility of a further 13 that may or may not appear, and the other has eight guaranteed and eight possible. In each of the Sigil Keeps, you'll face three Daedra.

Note that this little slice of heaven also has its own small dungeon (Molten Caves) that links the cellars of the small southwestern and southeastern towers.

Skingrad Gate

Initially, this is a bit similar in appearance to the Chorrol Gate with a couple of notable differences: no Leaning Tower of Oblivion behind you when you arrive…and not a Daedra in sight.

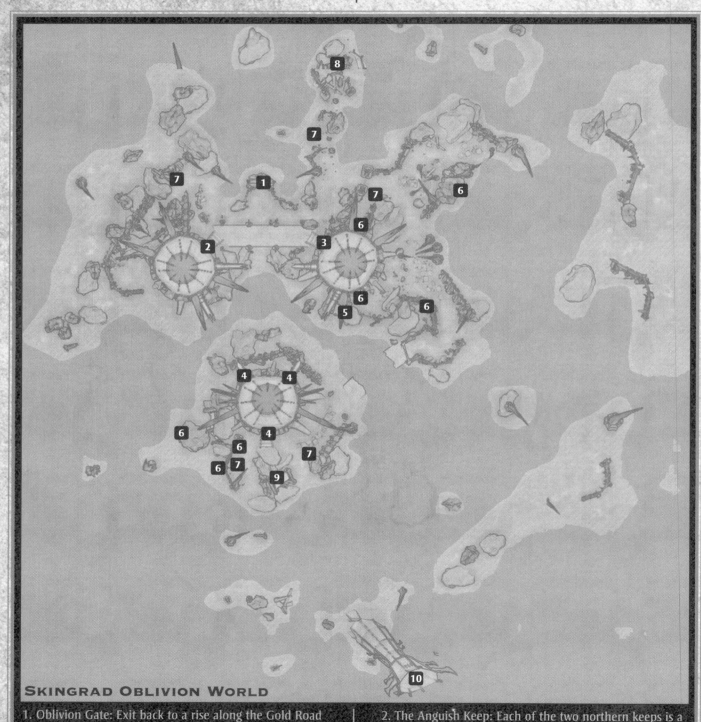

Skingrad Oblivion World

1. Oblivion Gate: Exit back to a rise along the Gold Road east of Skingrad.

2. The Anguish Keep: Each of the two northern keeps is a Citadel in its own right—with two side halls and a separate shrine at the top. (Only the main Citadel to the south has a Sigillum Sanguis and Sigil Stone.) In

this one, you'll face 3–7 Daedra in the Citadel proper; a further two in the Halls of Eternal Twilight (heavily mined, with a boss-level container behind a three- to five-tumbler lock); 1–6 in the Halls of Shame (two turrets, a Blood Fountain, and Magicka Essences); and 1–3 in The Anguish Shrine. In this last section, you must climb to the middle level and throw a lever to release one of two locks. When the first is released, a bridge extends and links the shrines atop the two northern keeps and you can cross over directly to the top of the second tower and release the second lock. When both locks are released, the shrine bridge retracts, but bridges from each keep will extend to the main Citadel to the south. The entrance to the main Citadel bridges is in the Citadel proper on the level between the Halls of Eternal Twilight and the Halls of Shame.

3. The Sorrow Keep: As above, but with these differences: In the Citadel proper, you face 6–7 Daedra; a further 3–5 in the Halls of Eternal Twilight (two swinging-blade traps and one midlevel fleshy pod); 2–4 Daedra in the Halls of Shame (two corner and two single spike traps, Health and Magicka dispensers, and another mid-level pod); and 1–3 in the Sorrow Shrine (two Magicka Essences and a third midlevel pod).

4. The Brooding Fortress: You'll have one of two experiences here. If you use the main entrance to the south, you'll have to fight your way up the whole Citadel. This means facing up to 15 Daedra in the Citadel itself, including at least three Dremora and two Dremora mages (with two midlevel fleshy pods as your reward); a Dremora mage and possibly two more Daedra in the

Rending Halls; 2–8 Daedra in Desolation's End (swinging-blade trap, two Magicka Essences, and a Blood Fountain); one or two more in the Corridors of Dark Salvation (four corner-based spike traps and a swinging-blade trap); and three more, including a boss, in the Sigil Keep (a boss-level fleshy pod and two Magicka Essences). However, if you use a bridge from a northern Citadel, you'll arrive in the Citadel proper on the level between Desolation's End and the Corridors of Dark Salvation, with the enemies below you none the wiser.

5. Blood Fountain (healing)

6. A midlevel fleshy pod

7. Turret

8. Magicka Essences

9. Molten Halls: Small cave with two or three Daedra that links the island with…

10. …Quake Ruin: This small tower is sinking into molten rock. That's why it's undefended; even Daedra don't want to live in a house with lava in the cellar. Within, around the elevator pad, you'll find two low-level fleshy pods and, a short a way up the ramp, a boss-level one. The tower ramp's steeper than usual, owing to the tilting of the tower, and you may have trouble reaching the prize. Try climbing on the reddish banister that runs along the wall. (And, no, there's nothing at the top of the tower.)

Dremora

That's just temporary. The Daedra are inside the Citadels to the east and west. Fight your way up both towers to their Sigil Keeps by the conventional Citadel route to release a pair of locks; this extends bridges to a third Citadel on an island to the south.

You arrive already high up in the main Citadel. Climb to the Corridors of Dark Salvation, then to the Sigil Keep.

On the south side of the main tower is the entrance to a small cave called Molten Halls (different from the Molten Caves in Random Daedra Hearts). This leads under the lava, against a fair amount of opposition, to a sunken tower to the south. Within lie, undefended, three sacks that contain a good deal of loot.

ANVIL GATE

You arrive in a northeastern extremity of a large circular landmass, with two small towers (useful for loot and combat only) on peninsulas to the southeast and south, and a Citadel on a mountain to the southwest.

The path up to the Citadel winds up the mountain past occasional Daedric defenders and passes through a nameless cave on its east side. Like the Leyawiin Gate, the Citadel door zaps you to one of five Citadels. See that section for the details.

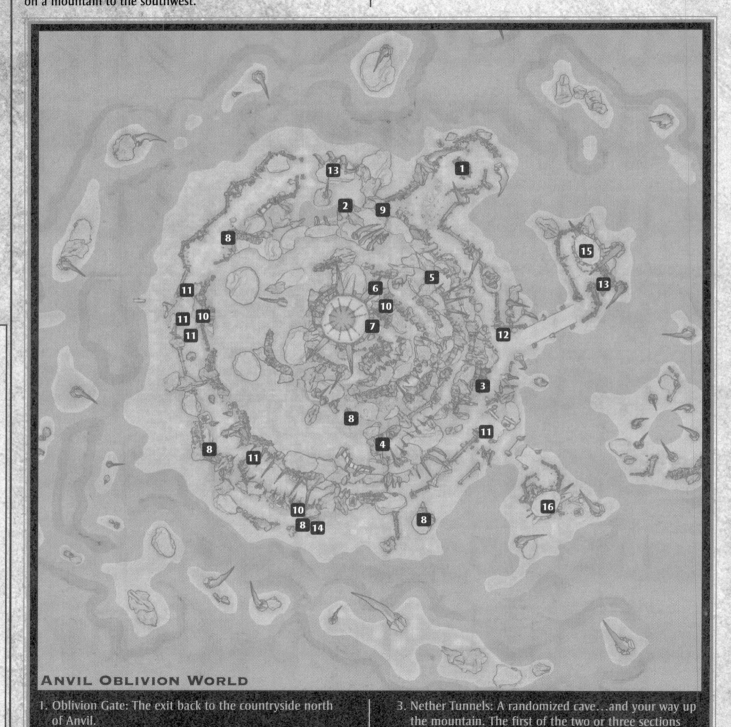

ANVIL OBLIVION WORLD

1. Oblivion Gate: The exit back to the countryside north of Anvil.

2. Lava pool. If you're standing beside the pool scratching your head, you probably missed the cave entrance at #3.

3. Nether Tunnels: A randomized cave…and your way up the mountain. The first of the two or three sections you'll pass through is called either The Hate Tunnels or Worm Gut Channels. "Nether Tunnels" isn't a place name so much as a description of what happens to you

when you activate the door. You're teleported to one of seven possible starting sections. When you activate the door at the other end, you're teleported again—this time to one of seven middle sections (called either Molten Halls or Fume Vaults) or seven end sections (called either Mire of Ash or The Scratch Paths). If you wound up in a middle section, when you activate the door at the other end you'll be teleported again to an end section. If you wound up in an end section, you'll be teleported out the exit...

4. ...which is here.

5. The Red Gnash Channels: Another cave, but without the randomization thing. It's defended by five Daedra, contains nominal loot, and has a slightly tricky exit northwest of the entrance. (You'll have to wind your way up to it.) It deposits you...

6. ...here. Now you just have to head counterclockwise and then double back on the upper path to the Citadel door at #7.

7. Tower Portal: Did you just hear the randomizer whirring? When you activate the door, you're teleported randomly to one of five Citadels. These vary a good deal. The Lust Keep and The Dreaded Refuge are roughly the same size as other Main Quest Citadels, with two side halls. The Gore Steeple is smaller, with just one. And The Flesh Spire and The Claw Monolith have three.

8. A potentially lucrative fleshy pod.

9. A disgusting fleshy pod—which seems more like the remains of cocooned mortal than an honest-to-Talos container.

10. An avalanche in waiting.

11. If the rocks don't kill you, maybe the mines will.

12. Or this turret.

13. Blood Fountain (healing)

14. Magicka Essences

15. Reapers Sprawl: Not essential; just loot and combat. You'll find a dead Mythic Dawn member (!) in a cage (which can be opened with a switch) at the top of the tower.

16. Meat Harbor: #15 without the cage.

BRAVIL GATE

The realm begins in the southern section of the map with a path to the south and to the west. Ahead of you is a locked gate barring you from entering the small isle the Citadel resides on. To the east and west of the Citadel are smaller towers that allow you access this isle.

The path to the south will have you fighting fewer Daedric enemies but will require you to do some lava jumping and navigation through a series of small islands. Once through these lava flats you will need to head on over to the eastern tower and within you will find a switch that opens the gates that allow you access to the Citadel. The path to the west will lead you through hills and caves loaded with Daedric encounters. Once inside the caves, navigate to the lowest portion and exit into the westernmost tower. If you head up one level you can exit this tower and onto a bridge that leads you to the Citadel. Also inside this tower is a switch that opens the gates to the Citadel. The Citadel is another randomly selected Citadel from the list of five that was explained earlier.

And that's that. You're at the end of a very long run. You should feel supremely satisfied. If you're wondering if you've done enough, you'll have one more opportunity to make things right.

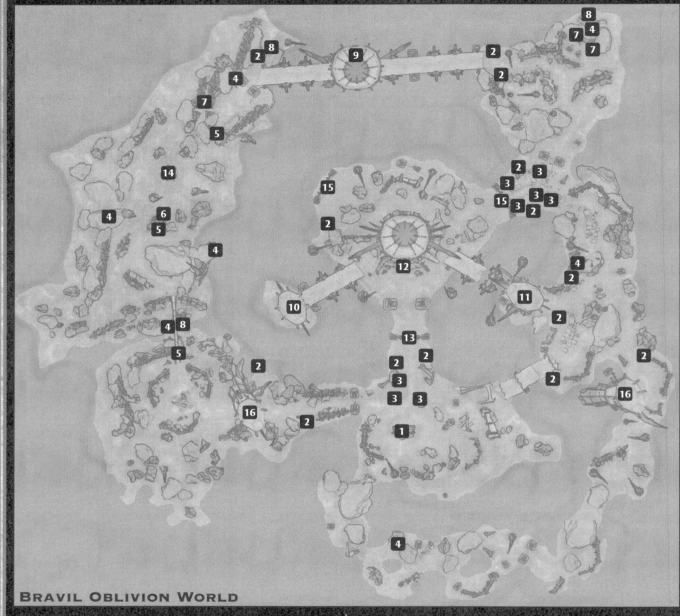

BRAVIL OBLIVION WORLD

1. Exit back to the countryside north of Bravil.

2. Turret

3. Mines

4. The good kind of fleshy pod—gold for sure, possibly other useful loot. A dead Zombie lies on the ground here.

5. Caverns of the Abused: Small, multi-entrance dungeon that goes under the volcano and, more significantly, allows you to get into the base of the Blood Well tower (#10) across the lava to the east.

6. Avalanche trap

7. Magicka Essences

8. Not-so-good fleshy pod, with a little gold and possibly some clothes, bones, and a poison potion. Afterward, we think you'll want to wash your hands.

9. A boss-level fleshy pod, a Blood Fountain (healing), and another of those turd-level fleshy pods. (By the way, despite appearances, there's no tower here; a Citadel top-piece has been used as part of the bridge architecture.)

10. Blood Well: See #5 for a sneaky entrance into this tower. A switch at the top opens the gate at #13.

11. Spindle Shrine: The switch at the top opens the main gate at #13.

12. Tower Portal: Activate it and foom. You're teleported randomly to one of five Citadels. These vary a good deal. The Lust Keep and The Dreaded Refuge are

roughly the same size as other Main Quest Citadels, with two side halls. The Gore Steeple is smaller, with just one. And The Flesh Spire and The Claw Monolith have three.

13. This gate opens once you throw the switch atop either of the towers at #10 or #11.

14. Volcano!

15. These gates should open in sequence (to no particular purpose) within seconds after the gate at #13 opens.

16. No, you can't get into these towers.

DEFENSE OF BRUMA

Talking to Martin at any time after completing both Bruma Gate and Miscarcand sets events in motion. However, the mission won't reach its climax until you give a final go-ahead.

From Martin, you learn that the true objective is to coax the enemy into opening a Great Gate before Bruma and then entering it to capture a Great Sigil Stone—the final component Martin needs for the portal ritual.

Granted, it's dangerous, but it's the only scheme available. And if it works, Martin will have the means to open a gateway into the "Paradise" of Mythic Dawn chief Mankar Camoran.

When your dialogue with Martin is complete, he sets off for Bruma, where he means to lead the defense. Follow him there, if you like. Baurus and Jauffre do the same. Along the way, Martin can talk to you in greater detail about "battle plans," and you'll better understand what's to occur on the plain before Bruma: You've learned from the letter acquired from the Bruma spies that three small gates must be opened before a Great Gate can introduce one of the great siege machines that laid waste to Kvatch.

However, your immediate task is to visit Countess Narina Carvain at Castle Bruma and ask her to meet Martin at the Great Chapel of Talos for a council of war.

Narina Carvain, Countess of Bruma

And now to have some fun. Bruma should look a little different than the last time you were here. It is now an armed camp. If you've been a diligent recruiter, you'll find the area immediately outside the castle walls crowded with troops and tents. You can identify the troops by city, chat with them (although the responses are pretty much "go team!"), or listen to them chat amongst themselves.

The allies rally to the defense of Bruma.

If it's daytime, Carvain is probably in the castle's Great Hall, where she keeps an audience schedule of 8 a.m.–12 p.m. and 3–8 p.m. She recognizes the desperation of the plan—her guard captain, Burd, calls it "madness"—but Carvain also seems to recognize things are not quite lost. She agrees to the meeting without qualifications and sets off for the chapel with Burd and her bodyguard.

Keep up with them and you'll be able to watch the church staff retreat from the nave and the exchange between Martin and Carvain in the ring of light at the east end of the chapel. When their conversation ends, talk to Carvain again. Her response depends on how many allies you recruited in "Allies for Bruma." If you completed all the mini-quests, she'll call you "a diplomat as well as a warrior" and you'll have two options: "I'm not ready yet" and "Let the battle begin."

If you didn't complete all the mini-quests, her response is adjusted to the number you've actually nailed and you'll have a third option: do more recruiting. This is what we meant about the two quests overlapping. You can continue "Allies for Bruma" here, come back later, and re-embark upon "Defense of Bruma" with more troops on hand. Or, if you're unhappy with your character's level or kit, you can use this break to go questing or shopping as well. Just as characters eternally made their rounds at Cloud Ruler Temple, they eternally stand in place in the Great Chapel of Talos.

When you're ready, give Carvain the high sign. The party slowly makes its way out the church's west door, and suddenly, there's a lot going on: Bruma's population is lined up from church to city gate to cheer and salute Martin; he exits onto the plain east of the city; and finally, on Martin's arrival, the whole allied force surges toward a dip northeast of Bruma where a lesser Oblivion Gate has opened. If you skipped Allies for Bruma entirely you'll find the Bruma Militia in the dip—a comparatively ragtag and panicky group of home guards.

Join the troops. Martin has barely finished his pep talk to the assembled allies when the Daedra start coming through the gate.

Tactics? Limited. Like all the big battles, this one's going to be a bit chaotic. Just keep an eye on Martin—he dashes off into combat with unnerving regularity—and help him if he gets in over his head. Try not to hit your own team. Don't bother trying to close the lesser gates—you can't even enter them here. Martin dies if you move too far away from him.

And don't try to fight the whole battle by yourself. This may be tempting if you have a high-level character. But your agenda here is just to keep Martin alive, and when you figure in Jauffre, Baurus, Burd, and a pair of Bruma soldiers on top of the allies, you may have as many as 16 defenders to tackle the enemy. That's plenty for the task at hand, and it leaves you free to assume a firefighter's role—rushing to where you're needed most. Let the Daedra come to you, rather than trying to stop them right outside the gates, as this will draw forward and engage more and more troops.

Step swiftly into the shimmering surface of the Great Gate soon after it appears. For at that moment, invisibly, a clock has started counting down. When you reappear under the red sky of Oblivion, you've begun the next mission: Great Gate.

The Battle of Bruma

However, before you set out, look around before you leave, and pick your moment of departure carefully.

Martin can't die while you're gone, but Jauffre and Baurus enjoy no such special protection. Neither is an essential character in the Main Quest at this point, but both are useful comrades in the final mission ("Light the Dragonfires!").

To ensure their availability at that time, confirm they're disengaged from combat with the Daedra before you move through the Great Gate.

GREAT GATE

You're at the southern opening of a horseshoe-shaped enclosure. Just to the north, a vast Siege Crawler moves inexorably south toward the Great Gate—its forward surface looks like a sun in eclipse.

The Daedric Siege Engine

It takes several minutes for this city-destroyer to cover the remaining short distance to the exit. It is indestructible and irresistible. If it moves through the gate and onto the plain outside Bruma, the city falls, your mission ends, and the battle is lost.

However, if you can claim the Great Sigil Stone from the Citadel to the north before the machine rolls on stage, you've won.

But how to get the Sigil Stone in such a short time? Move swiftly along the route we lay out for you. Do not linger over roads not taken or go searching for loot. Fight only when necessary. This buys you time for a few fights you can't easily avoid.

Beyond the open gate, Dremora archers on the bridges to the east and west snipe at you, so don't linger in the open. Step inside the first of two eastern towers (thus avoiding the Daedra lurking under the underpass beside the western one). Climb to the top and cross the bridge to the north.(Depending on which entry tower you chose you can also head east or west and then north, but the former route involves one less Daedra.) As you exit the towers, be mindful of your distance to the Siege Crawlers maw, since it is capable of showering you with fire blasts. In either of the northern entry-area towers, ride the elevator down to the cellar and use the northern exit.

You now see the Citadel and two flanking towers to the north. If you chose to pass through the eastern towers, you emerge from this exit facing a difficult jump over lava on a fallen bridge. If you survive the jump, you must scramble up the terrain through a gauntlet of defensive towers to the bridge in front of the Citadel. Once on the bridge, enter the eastern tower flanking the Citadel.

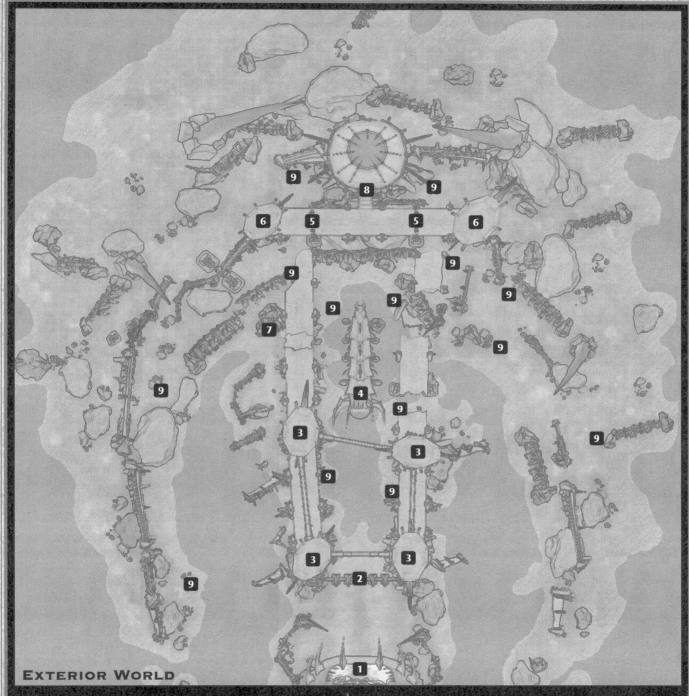

EXTERIOR WORLD

1. Great Gate

2. This gate opens when you arrive on the scene.

3. World Breaker Guard: Guard towers—all similar, but not identical. All four have exits to bridges leading to the two adjacent towers. Three of the four have a resident Dremora—all but the northwestern one. (It has a Magicka fountain and a torture cage.) And the two northern ones have exits onto broken northbound bridges.

4. Daedric siege crawler: If it gets out the Great Gate before you can destroy the gate, kiss Bruma goodbye. If you destroy the gate, this city-killer blows up on the battlefield outside Bruma and you'll find a conventional Sigil Stone (which you can keep) on the ground near its front end.

5. You must open one of these gates to reach the Citadel door. To do that, you have to throw a switch…

6. ...at the top of one of these two towers. Each is inhabited by a Dremora and a leveled Daedra and has a Blood Fountain. (The western one also has Magicka Essences.)

7. The Smoke and Scorch: Getting safely to a tower out in the open is difficult—owing mainly to the turrets (#9).

However, this small cave can funnel you directly into the cellar of either tower. It's defended by three leveled Daedra.

8. Entrance to World Breaker.

9. Turret

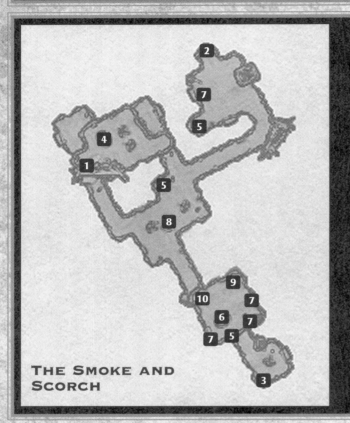

THE SMOKE AND SCORCH

1. Exit to exterior world.

2. Exit to World Breaker Guard—the western of the two towers marked #6 on the "Exterior World" map.

3. Exit to World Breaker Guard—the eastern of the two towers marked #6 on the "Exterior World" map.

4. You begin the cave on the upper level. This is a hole down to the lower level.

5. Daedra. Note that the southernmost of the three is on the lower level—not the upper as it appears here.

6. Hole up to treasure room. But how do you get up here? You can't—not conventionally, anyway.

7. Fleshy pod. Note: Of the three southern pods, the western and northern are on the lower level and the eastern is up in the treasure room (#6).

8. Fleshy pod: This contains one or two restoration-related items. It's surrounded by a nasty version of the claw trap you've seen on the surface in Oblivion.

9. Fleshy pod: The low end of Oblivion loot pods, this victim-turned-into-container probably contains a bit of gold, low-end clothing, bones, and possibly a poison potion.

10. A boss pod!

If you chose to pass through the western towers, a much smaller jump exists here, but multiple Daedra await you on the other side. After you pass the Daedra, scramble up to the bridge in front of the Citadel and enter the western tower flanking the citadel. Unlike the leap of faith on the eastern side, if you miss this jump you fall to a broken portion of bridge that leads you down to a cave called The Smoke and Scorch. Inside the cave you find only a few Daedric encounters and some Fleshy Pods. Progress through the caves to exit to the base level of either the eastern or western towers flanking the Citadel.

Activate the gate control at the top of either of these towers. This opens the gates on the bridge leading to the main Citadel known as World Breaker. Then drop halfway back down the tower and make a run past three Dremora for the Citadel entrance.

No random Citadels here, just the one, and a comparatively simple and depopulated one at that. Inside and on the first level you will find the first of two Sigil Keepers. Each carries a key to the Sigil Keep. Use the door on the north side of the entry level to reach the Vaults of End Times.

Inside the Vaults of End Times you will find a hall that contains three blades suspended from the ceiling. You can release these blades using the switches found on the walls just before them, then jump over the blades or wait for them to raise to run under them. After the hall you will enter a room with a single Daedra and 3 doors. The door to the right contains another Daedra, the door in the middle leads you to a Blood Fountain and a Magicka Fountain, and the door to the left will lead you up to the next level of the Citadel.

You will exit the Vaults back out to the center of Citadel to find a long, spiraling hike up to the Sigil Keep and few Daedric encounters. At the top you will find another Sigil Keeper. If you defeated the Sigil Keeper from the bottom of the Citadel you already have the key you need to enter the Sigil Keep but if you chose to pass the first Sigil Keeper this is your final chance to obtain the key needed to enter the Sigil Keeper. Inside, with two Daedra in a smaller area you need to fight again. Then just do what you've done so many times already.

And then you're back in the dip northeast of Bruma. The battle is won. The gates crumble. The remaining Daedra die. You can collect a range of congratulatory comments from Jauffre, Martin, and Burd, not to mention some admiring comments from the troops. The allied forces begin to disperse.

And Martin begins to plot out the portal ritual.

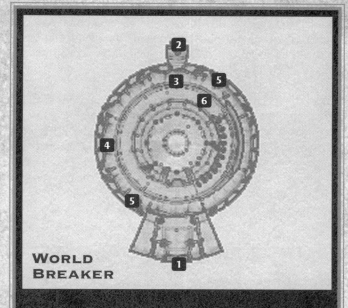

WORLD BREAKER

1. Exit to exterior world.

2. Exit to Vaults of End Times (lower).

3. Dremora Sigil Keeper (ground level). Has the Sigil Key that unlocks the upper-level doors at #5.

4. Exit to Vaults of End Times (upper level).

5. Exits to Sigillum Sanguis (upper level). Three-tumbler locks. Unlocked with Sigil Key from the body of either of the two Sigil Keepers.

6. Dremora Sigil Keeper (upper level).

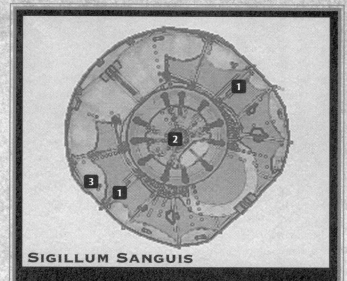

SIGILLUM SANGUIS

1. Exits to the upper level of World Breaker. These doors are on a level lower than appears here.

2. Great Sigil Stone: Activate it to destroy the Great Gate and strand the emerging siege crawler. You'll reappear among surviving allies in the gully outside Bruma. You have to give this stone to Martin—it's a component in the portal he'll open to Camoran's Paradise—but you'll be compensated with the conventional stone that powered the destroyed Daedric siege crawler.

3. "The Punished" (a loot sack)

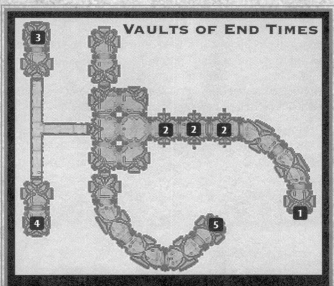

VAULTS OF END TIMES

1. Exit to World Breaker (lower level).

2. Blade traps

3. Blood Fountain (healing)

4. Magicka Essences

5. Exit to World Breaker (upper level).

PARADISE

Now to launch an invasion of your own.

Back at Cloud Ruler Temple, talk to Martin again. With the Great Sigil Stone, he's all set to spin his magic and asks if you're ready for the portal ritual. Once you enter Camoran's Paradise, you won't be able to return through the portal and will have to find another way back. (In fact, you're sent back automatically to the fortress when Camoran dies.) So make sure you're well-equipped and well-supplied enough to live off your own resources for a while before you say "yes."

This large quest—a series of three smaller, linked quests—isn't quite on a scale with "Allies for Bruma," but in that mission, you knew at least part of the ground you were covering. Paradise is a wholly unknown area—all strange and unmapped terrain.

When you're ready, just tell Martin. He backs off a bit and casts his spell. A fiery portal appears. Enter it. You reappear within a little white stone enclosure in the middle of an Eden-like region.

Martin opens the portal to Camoran's Paradise.

Mankar Camoran himself gives you your first lesson in Paradise's geography. Big-mouthed supervillain that he is, the unseen Camoran can't help letting the Scamp out of the bag,

and he'll tell you about his "Gaia Alata" in a series of monologues. Among other things, you'll hear about a "Savage Garden, where my disciples are tempered for a higher destiny." And that he'll await you at Carac Agaialor—"my seat at the pinnacle of Paradise."

His little lesson sets you up with conversation topics that you can use to draw out the "Ascended Immortals" in your immediate neighborhood—peaceful Mythic Dawn cultists who have died in Camoran's service and await return to Tamriel after Dagon's expected victory.

The Immortals respond to you in one of three ways: You're seen as an ensnared enemy, as another annoyance in a land of annoyances, or as a potential savior.

Camoran's Paradise

Either way, they clarify that you're already in the Savage Garden. For them, this is a true Hell; they are continually killed by the Daedra, reborn, and then killed again. The only way out is the Forbidden Grotto, and the grotto door can be unlocked only with the Bands of the Chosen. These are given by Camoran to a few favored servants.

But these favored ones never return, and no one seems to know what becomes of them.

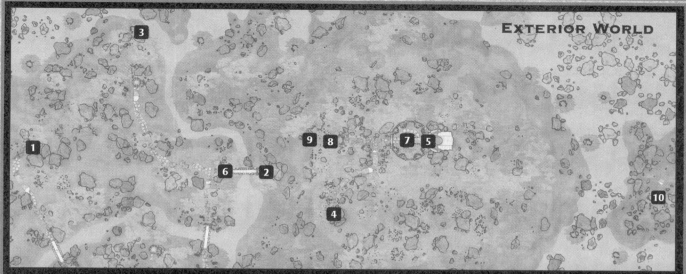

1. You arrive here.

2. Entrance to the Flooded Grotto. You'll find Kathutet (#6) in here after you've dealt with Anaxes in #3.

3. Entrance to Anaxes's lair. You can free the Xivilai (who has by been trapped here by Ascended Immortals) to win the Bands of the Chosen, which allow you to pass from the Flooded Grotto into the Forbidden Grotto.

4. Exit from the Forbidden Grotto: Once you exit from this second section of this grotto onto the hilltop, you can come and go freely from one to the other.

5. Entrance to Carac Agaialor: Inside, you'll fight Mankar Camoran and his two children. Camoran's death destroys his Paradise and sends you back to Cloud Ruler Temple with the Amulet of Kings.

6. Kathutet: A Dremora. He'll set you a task. Either free the Xivilai, Anaxes, from his lair (#3) or defeat Kathutet himself in combat. Either one will get you the Bands of the Chosen, which allow you to pass from the Flooded Grotto to the Forbidden Grotto. If you free Anaxes,

you'll find this gent inside the Flooded Grotto upon your return.

7. Raven and Ruma Camoran: Yes, you killed him and maybe her, too. You can kill 'em again right now. But like the proverbial bad penny, Mankar Camoran's two bad kids keep coming back, so don't waste your strength. Talk to them. They'll lecture you on the wonders of the forthcoming apocalypse and send you in to see Papa.

8. Statue of Mehrunes Dagon: He's about as big as a house and he's swinging a big old axe. This is known as "foreshadowing."

9. You can't get here from the hilltop region. And you wouldn't find anything if you could. If you wander far off the beaten path on the hilltop, you're zapped back to the exit from the Forbidden Grotto (#4).

10. Altar with a boss-level Ayleid chest: Well, they had to hide some loot here, didn't they?

FREEING ANAXES

Water encloses this pleasant starting zone on three sides. The side that isn't enclosed is to the east.

In fact, this whole section of Paradise is essentially a funnel pointed east at the door of the Flooded Grotto (which leads to the Forbidden Grotto). When you approach the white stone bridge leading to the door, you run into a Dremora named Kathutet.

Kathutet

He makes you a proposition: To enter the Forbidden Grotto, you have serve him or beat him in a fight.

Serving him means freeing a Xivilai named Anaxes from where the Ascended Immortals have imprisoned him. Anaxes's location is to the northwest, in what turns out to be his home (the Lair of Anaxes)—a cave on the western bank of the stream that flows past the grotto entrance. He's lodged behind a boulder at the back of the cave.

Beating him in a fight is the more direct and quicker route to Kathutet's Bands of the Chosen, but comes with the caveat that Kathutet is five levels above you, and thus a formidable adversary.

If you choose to free Anaxes, do so by activating both logs bracing the boulder, then the boulder itself. Stand to the side while doing so, or you may get killed by the rolling boulder.

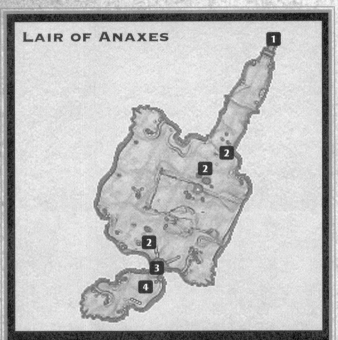

LAIR OF ANAXES

1. Exit to the exterior world.
2. Ascended Immortals: They'll tell you the story behind their imprisonment of the predatory Xivilai Anaxes and beg you not to free him.
3. A boulder, propped up by two logs, that keeps Anaxes trapped in an enclosure at the south end of the lair.
4. Anaxes himself. Kathutet (at the entrance to the Flooded Grotto) enlists you to free him. You can do so, in which case he'll kill the Ascended Immortals here and Kathutet will give you the Bands of the Chosen on your return. Or you can kill Anaxes, in which case you'll have to kill Kathutet and take the Bands.

Note that you can also release and then kill the Xivilai—a task made easier by the fact that, once released, this Level 20 monster is focused on killing the three guards and pays no attention to you. However, doing so requires you to battle and kill your annoyed quest-giver in order to get the Bands.

Afterward, find Kathutet inside the Flooded Grotto, near the door to the Forbidden Grotto. If you've done the job, he keeps his promise and turns over the Bands—but also advises that you're still going to die at the hands of his brother, Orthe—and that no one escapes these caves. Put on the Bands and open the door.

FORBIDDEN GROTTO

The Forbidden Grotto turns out to be a prison. The favored few are caged or dead…or both.

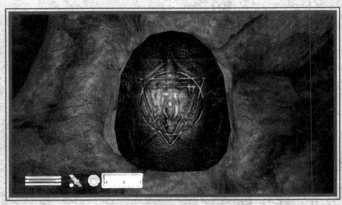

The Forbidden Grotto

You can't help them—but you can torture them by pushing levers that lower them into the lava below. Indeed, unless you find help here, you won't even be able to help yourself.

This three-section cave is a real challenge. It offers baddies of various stripes, many of them Daedra ranging from Scamps at low levels to Atronachs, Clannfear, Daedroth, and Spider Daedra at higher ones. However, most of them are spread out through the tunnels and, with a little art, can be ambushed and killed off separately.

But there is one place where you may run into trouble—and another that will stop you cold.

The first is a large room in the first section of the grotto, occupied by three Dremora—Ranyu, Amkaos, and Kathutet's brother Orthe. Unlike Kathutet, these Dremora have not read your press clippings. If you go waltzing into this room, there's every chance you'll end up dead.

You can avoid them by enlisting Eldamil as a confederate. In fact, you'll have to work with him. Eldamil is your only way out of the Forbidden Grotto

If you choose to kill Eladmil anyway, he'll reappear later on in the caves.

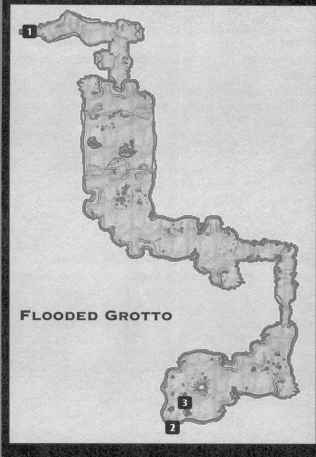

FLOODED GROTTO

1. Exit to exterior world.

2. Exit to the Forbidden Grotto: You must be wearing the Bands of the Chosen (acquired from Kathutet at #3) to open the door.

3. Kathutet: When you return from freeing (or killing) Anaxes, you'll find your Dremora pal here. He'll either be pleased and supply the Bands of the Chosen, or he'll be really, really annoyed and suddenly decide your body has room for several new orifices.

Eldamil

FORBIDDEN GROTTO

1. Entrance from the Flooded Grotto. Why not the usual "exit"? Because once you're in, you can't get out this way.

2. Prisoner (in torture cage): As you'll quickly divine, the grotto isn't the promised land but a torture chamber.

3. At these locations, you can participate in the torture by pushing this lever to raise one nearby cage and lower the other into the lava below. In a bit, you can be the guy in the cage.

4. "The Punished": A loot container, on loan from Oblivion, that looks rather like a beating heart. This contains one or two restoration-oriented items.

5. Eldamil: A former lieutenant of Mankar Camoran who now regrets his role in the Daedric invasion of Tamriel, Eldamil is instrumental in getting you out of the grotto alive. (You can turn him down initially, but you have to hook up with him sooner or later.)

6. Orthe: Eldamil's Dremora boss. Agree to let Eldamil help you, and Orthe will come and check up on his underling. (See #8.)

7. Ranyu and Amkaos: Orthe's Dremora buddies.

8. Assume the role of a prisoner and enter this torture cage when Eldamil directs you to do so. You'll be pinned there. Eldamil lowers the cage toward the lava and raises it again at the last second, opening the door on the far side of the trench. Eldamil then distracts the three Dremora to the north as you make your way out the east exit. (They'll kill him, but he'll be resurrected in the next part of the grotto. Such is the way of Paradise.)

9. Then again, suppose you don't accept Eldamil's help? In that case, the east exit is blocked by an immovable rock

and you'll have to find another route. You'll find this portcullis closed and locked...

10. ...and will need Orthe's key to unlock it. You'll find it here, along with a restoration-related item, in a loot sack christened "The Forbidden." (This involves either killing or running desperately from the three Dremora.)

11. The exit to the next section of the Forbidden Grotto. (The Bands of the Chosen will get you through this one.) Again, once through the door you can't get back again.

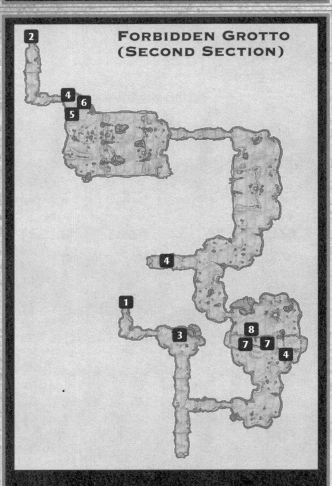

FORBIDDEN GROTTO (SECOND SECTION)

1. Entrance from the first section of the Forbidden Grotto.
2. Exit to the top of the hill and the rather spartan Camoran family home at Carac Agaialor.
3. The resurrected Eldamil is waiting for you here. Even if you turned him down earlier, he'll remove the Bands and, if you wish, follow you and fight at your side.
4. "The Punished": A loot container that contains one or two restoration-oriented items.
5. Medrike: This Xivilai holds the key to the exit.
6. Loot container
7. Prisoner in a torture cage.
8. Lever: Lowers one cage into the lava and raises the other. Share the pain.

This former advisor to Mankar Camoran is near the entrance to the first section's second large room, garbed in Mythic Dawn attire. When you find him, he tells you that he helped plan Uriel Septim's murder and opened the Great Gate before Kvatch—but now he's had a change of heart and wants to help you.

Eldamil's appearance may be a little too timely, his confession a little too earnest, his involvement in the Mythic Dawn's plots a little too broad...but he's legit. He proves it to you by getting you past Orthe—in a way that you would not survive if he were a Camoran loyalist.

Once Orthe is gone, Eldamil opens the gate leading to the east side of the chasm. Don't vault the trench, even if you're a gifted jumper. You'll only have to vault right back again when you hit a dead end at the end of the grotto's second section.

Eldamil can't follow you across the trench, but he meets up with you at a stone circle early in the grotto's next section and removes your Bands of the Chosen. (To get across the trench, Eldamil puts you in a cage that drops a ramp across the trench and also opens a stone door on the far side. If you try to jump across the trench without using Eldamil's help, the way will be blocked.) A good thing, too: the same Bands that got you into the Forbidden Grotto prevent you from getting out. Attempts to move from the grotto's second section to the third with Bands in place are greeted by an explosion of light...and no teleporting-to-the-next-section action whatsoever.

After Eladmil removes the Bands, he asks if he can help. Say "yes" now, or get killed several times and come back and say it later. If you agree, he follows you into the third section of the grotto, where he helps you kill a Xivilai by the name of Medrike—a cousin to Anaxes—and then out the final door to the Terrace of Dawn.

CARAC AGAIALOR

You're on top of the mountain. It's very similar to the section of Paradise where you first arrived. You can explore, but there's really not much to see apart from Camoran's villa and grounds.

Just follow the violet mana blooms up the slope to the north to find a statue of an axe-wielding Mehrunes Dagon. You also discover a path leading east through three arches, to a temple-like structure.

When you enter the grounds, you'll find Camoran's children, Raven and Ruma. They're supposed to be dead—Raven was Gwinas's sponsor in the Mythic Dawn in "The Path of Dawn," and Ruma attended your initiation ritual at the Dagon Shrine. You had to kill Raven and, between saving the sacrificial victim and grabbing the *Mysterium Xarxes*, you may have killed Ruma, too. But in Paradise, everyone who has died in the service of Mankar Camoran lives again. Anyone who dies in Paradise eventually respawns—except Camoran himself.

Ruma and Raven await you at Carac Agaialor.

Mankar Camoran in his throne room.

You can talk to Raven and Ruma, but their responses run to taunts rather than conversation. Your business is with their father.

He's seated on his throne inside his palace, waiting your arrival. When you approach, Camoran begins another speech: a forecast of a future under Mehrunes Dagon. You can let him say his piece, or you can attack him.

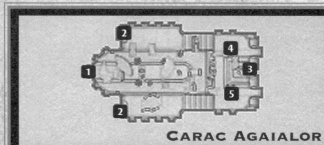

CARAC AGAIALOR

1. Entrance from the exterior world: It's sealed behind you when you enter.

2. Exits onto the balcony: Also sealed. Damn.

3. Mankar Camoran: Your job here is killing him. You can lay into him directly or wait until after he makes his bwa-ha-ha speech. He puts up a good fight—summoning leveled heavy-duty Daedra and healing himself on a regular basis. When he's dead, the place begins to crumble, like all good bad-guy Citadels, and you're transported back to Cloud Ruler Temple with the Amulet of Kings.

4. Ruma Camoran: You may already have killed her at the Dagon Shrine. And you may have to kill her more than once here. She'll resurrect again and again until you've killed her dad.

5. Raven Camoran: You or Baurus definitely killed him in the Elven Gardens Sewers. Now he's back; as with Ruma, you can't get rid of him until Mankar Camoran is dead.

We recommend attacking him immediately. And don't waste your time fighting Ruma and Raven; like everyone else in this Paradise, they are effectively unkillable. Killing them can buy you a temporary breathing space, but they will soon "respawn" out of a glowing cloud on one of the resurrection pads inside the palace (this is also where they will respawn if you kill them outside the palace). Concentrate your fire on Mankar. This might be the time to put away that magic sword for a change and just use your unenchanted weapons—he has a permanent spell absorption, spell reflection, and damage reflection that make him particularly dangerous to attack with magic or with enchanted weapons. Ruma and Raven will of course do their best to distract you from killing their father, but Eldamil can be some help, at least in the initial phase of the battle.

When it's over, you end up with the Amulet of Kings in your inventory (whether you actually take it yourself or not) and back at Cloud Ruler Temple. Give the Amulet to Martin. Once he has it on, it doesn't slip off. He is Septim's son, if you ever doubted it, and he's almost the emperor. All that remains is to restore the Dragonfires in the Temple of the One and, with them, the waning barriers between Oblivion and Tamriel. Martin's already been in touch with Imperial Chancellor Ocato about a meeting—he's behaving like a good politician already—and urges that the two of you set off right away before the enemy can recover from this setback.

LIGHT THE DRAGONFIRES!

One last trip. With Martin in tow, fast-travel from Cloud Ruler Temple to Imperial City's central Palace District. If Jauffre's still among the living after the battle for Bruma, he comes along as well.

Outside the palace, you meet up with Baurus. (If Baurus fell in battle in the sewers or outside Bruma, he'll be replaced by Captain Steffan. If Steffan somehow wound up dead, too…well, you get jack squat.)

Chancellor Ocato meets Martin in the Elder Council chambers.

THE MAIN QUEST

While Baurus stands watch outside, enter the Elder Council Chambers and speak to Chancellor Ocato.

He announces that the council's already had a sit-down on this matter, has recognized Martin's claim to the throne, and…

…and Ocato is interrupted. A messenger brings word of an attack. Oblivion Gates have opened across Imperial City. Daedra are inside the walls.

At that moment, all hell breaks loose. Two Dremora have killed the guards outside the council entrance and entered the corridor outside the chamber.

The mission has suddenly changed from a coronation procession to a scramble for survival. You and a small army must fight your way to the Temple of the One and its Dragonfires.

Almost immediately, the fight in the corridor flows outside. The Dremora were just an advance unit. Up from the south and east comes the main body, including more Dremora and a group of Daedra drawn at random from a list that includes everything from Scamps to Xivilai.

This battle is the usual close-quarters chaos, but you should prevail. Even if you lost Jauffre and Baurus at Bruma, you have a lot more guys on your side now: Ocato (who is the Imperial battlemage), the two guards who were stationed at the interior door to the Council Chambers (and who stick with the party as long as Martin lives), and five Imperial legionnaires who appear out of the north and join the fray. Their fates are not predetermined—they live or die according to the tides of combat—and the more that survive the easier the rest of your trip will be. If their captain is among the survivors, he'll have a brief exchange with Martin. The Legion compound has been cut off, and this small unit was the last to escape, meaning "this is all the reinforcements you'll get."

Happily, this is also all the Daedra you face in the Palace District. You've jumped the quest's first major hurdle, and your reward is a sense of the Imperial City's dire predicament. From your position outside the Council Chambers, note the flames above the walls in adjoining districts. The capital is burning.

Your path leads only to the Dragonfires. The only operable doors in the Palace District are the ones leading to the Temple District (in the southwest corner) and the one back into the Council Chambers. The only operable door in the Temple District is into the Temple of the One. (After you pass through the door from the Palace District, it is barred behind you by the guards.) You can't make a detour through other parts of the city in the hope of saving it piece by piece or finding a safer passage. You

can't spirit Martin to safety as the Blades did his father, though it is an elegant thought. And, needless to say, you can't use fast travel across this hostile environment.

You're now operating within special versions of the Palace and Temple Districts. They exist only during this quest. When it's over, you can no longer reach them. Loot the corpses that you want to loot now, and don't drop anything of consequence either outdoors or in the temple. Otherwise, they're gone for good. If you're overburdened afterward, dump the extra in the Council Chambers. This room doesn't change its state once the Main Quest is complete, so you'll be able to recover your goods later.

Head southwest into the Temple District, or just follow your companions, who may already be headed that way en masse. Here, the Daedra have opened a pair of gates—one east and the other west-northwest of the Temple of the One. When you approach them, they start pumping out lots of Daedra.

Don't bother with the gates. As with the standard Oblivion gates at the Bruma battlefield, you can't even enter them. Only deal with the Daedra when necessary to your survival. The more you kill, the more Daedra the gates pump out. They're set up to maintain a more or less constant number of enemies in the district.

Advance swiftly to an enemy you *can* beat—but, oddly enough, can't kill. He's not far away. Closing in on the gates gives you your first look at the Main Quest's final "boss" monster. The vast, red, axe-wielding form of Mehrunes Dagon blocks the entrance to the Temple of the One.

Mehrunes Dagon attacking the Imperial City.

The journal entry reporting this discovery is rather panic-stricken, and with good reason. Dagon's appearance here changes the whole equation. It makes lighting the Dragonfires irrelevant. Forget containing Oblivion. Oblivion has already arrived.

Talk to Martin. This may be a little tricky with all the chaos going on around you, but it's the most important conversation you have with him. He tells you that mortal weapons may hurt Dagon, but that he can't be killed. You then raise the possibility of casting him back into Oblivion and using the Amulet of Kings.

And this gives Martin an idea. He doesn't say what the idea is, only that "I now know what I was born to do." Perhaps Martin, like his father, has had a prophetic dream. For this recalls another moment, not so long ago, when Uriel Septim looked into your face in the dim light of an Imperial Prison cell and realized his dream was real and that he would die that day. Martin just asks you to trust him—and get him to the temple's Dragonfires.

How? Martin has already given you a hint. You can't kill Dagon, but you can hurt him. If he can be staggered by heavy damage from a single blow of a weapon or spell, you and Martin can race past the reeling giant into the temple.

Once in the temple, Martin's finally safe—and it's no longer your fight. All that's required is to talk to him one last time to set him in motion and begin the end sequence. He says he's sorry he won't be around to help rebuild Tamriel. He thanks you for your friendship. And he says goodbye.

"But now I must go," he says, "The Dragon waits."

Martin moves within the circle of the dead Dragonfires. Just as he reaches them, Dagon breaks through the temple's roof. You won't actually see Martin smash the Amulet of Kings—this reference appears only in your journal—but the Dragonfires are re-lit in a great gout of flame. Martin disappears from view behind the fires and emerges transformed into a vast dragon.

Mehrunes Dagon battles the avatar of Akatosh.

The dragon and the Daedra lord struggle. And then Dagon is gone—cast back into Oblivion.

The city has been saved. The Oblivion Crisis has ended.

But at the cost of another emperor. For Martin, too, is gone.

EPILOGUE

Is he with his great ancestor Tiber Septim, as a journal entry speculates? Or simply dead? Did he pass into Oblivion with Dagon? Is he a dragon still?

You can hear a bit more about Martin in dialogue after this event, and from his own lips in a video sequence.

For all the fires, it turns out the Imperial City fared pretty well in the battle. When you leave the temple, the two gates have been closed. The Daedra are gone. The fires are out. You can move freely again to the Palace District and other parts of the city.

And you'll discover, over time, that the Daedric invasion hasn't cut you off from anything that was present in the Imperial City beforehand. Quests, shops, and characters are as they were before.

Indeed, the only lingering damage is to the Temple of the One. Its dome is gone. Its walls are in bad shape. And at the center of the temple, where the Dragonfires burned for centuries, now stands a great stone statue of a dragon.

Is it purely representational—a symbol of Martin's heroic sacrifice? A sentinel vigilant against future Daedric invasions? Or is the point not so much the statue as what it has replaced—a tacit indication that Tamriel no longer needs Dragonfires, divine amulets, or even emperors to protect it against Oblivion?

Statue of the Avatar of Akatosh in the Temple of the One.

You won't get a clear answer within the game. No one seems to know the meaning or source of the statue. But when a big statue suddenly shows up without the obvious benefit of an earthly agency, it stands to reason that the gods were somehow involved.

The victory over the Daedra seems total. When you venture back out into Cyrodiil, you find that all the random Oblivion Gates in the wilderness and any Oblivion Gates left open after "Allies for Bruma" have been closed.

In fact, the only existing Daedra are the ones occupying Castle Kvatch. If you haven't completed the Miscellaneous quest "The Battle for Castle Kvatch," you can still do so now.

If they survived, the other named characters from the final expedition (Jauffre, Baurus, or Captain Steffan, and Chancellor Ocato) return to their respective hangouts—the Blades at Cloud Ruler Temple and Ocato in the Elder Council Chambers.

What will become of them? Much of this lies outside the scope of *Oblivion*. But the Elder Council will run the empire, at least in the short term, and presumably that means Ocato, as the council's chief, will become an even more significant political force. Ocato seems like a straight arrow, but, given the empire's unhappy history with ambitious Imperial battlemages, this possibility may give you pause.

Presumably, the Blades, their official functions rendered superfluous by the absence of an emperor, will now revert to their origins as a monastic order.

However, none of these men have roles in the rest of *Oblivion*—though Ocato's name does pop up (as a victim) in a Thieves Guild quest.

Of course, other quests will bring you back to the area around Cloud Ruler Temple. You'll always be welcome. You can still chat with old friends, sleep in the barracks or in Martin's old bedroom, read the books in the library, and generally use the place as a base of operations.

But the Main Quest having run its course, the old friends won't have much to say. You may detect in the fortress that same sense of inevitability we picked up back in the Sanctum at the beginning of our story.

The place seems rather cold and dark. Things have changed. They will never be the same again.

OVERVIEW

The Fighters Guild functions as a middleman: It matches "contracts" for tasks that require rough handling to the talents of its members. If you have a gift for beating up bad people, you'll fit in well.

The requirements for membership are almost nonexistent. You can even have a bad reputation. In fact, we get the impression the guild rather likes its members to have a bad reputation—short of out-of-control bad guy. Your Infamy score (which is calculated based on any bounty you've ever had on your head) must be under 100 to join. (You can't reduce Infamy, but you can counterbalance it with Fame gained by performing other quests.)

Once you're in the guild, you can be as bad as you want to be, as long as your offenses don't involve guild members. Stealing from a guild member will get you canned—if the theft is detected. Attack a guild member and, oddly enough, there's a window of forgiveness. (We expect this sort of thing happens a lot when you bring a bunch of aggressive types together.) You'll be warned after each of the first two hits. After the third, the member attacked will respond in kind and you'll get booted.

You can apply to Guild Master Vilena Donton for readmission. She'll enroll you in a penitential 20-step program: collect 20 pelts from the black and slightly tougher brown bears in the wilderness and in caves. If you offend again, she'll give you a last chance: collect 20 Minotaur horns. And if you offend *again*, you're gone for good.

Vilena Donton, Master of the Fighters Guild

Fighters Guild branches can be found in every Cyrodiil city except Imperial City. However, you can join and receive quests at only three of them. You must speak to Guild Master Vilena Donton (on the top floor of the Chorrol branch), Azzan (on the ground floor of the Anvil guild), or Burz gro-Khash (on the second floor of the Cheydinhal guild).

Assuming you've met the requirements, simply ask about joining the Fighters Guild, confirm that you want to sign on, and you're in at Associate rank.

A few immediate benefits: You now have a free place to sleep in most towns. You get a +10 Disposition bump in your dealings with other guild members. You can grab with impunity free weapons lying around the guilds.

And, of course, you can earn gold and glory by performing Fighters Guild quests. If you're talking to Donton, you'll be referred to Azzan or gro-Khash for work. If you're already talking to one of them, just ask for a contract.

Minor variations are permitted in the order of the quests, but the broad structure remains the same throughout your tenure: After each tier of two or three contract quests, you'll be sent to Modryn Oreyn, the Champion, who offers one or more "duties" quests. These typically cast you in the role of guild cop or "fixer." (Toward the end, this changes to the role of guild maverick.) Increasingly, these will revolve around the activities of the Blackwood Company, an unscrupulous competitor that has been stealing business from a troubled guild.

Completion of quests is periodically rewarded with promotion (via the Advancement topic) to higher ranks. When you reach Guild Master, you get to run the joint!

We look at the quests in the order you receive them. When it comes to the contract quests, you can generally go to either Azzan in Anvil or Burz gro-Khash in Cheydinhal for an assignment. As you begin new chunks of the contract quests, both will have something for you to do. In each section, Azzan's quests are followed by gro-Khash's; you may do them in the order you choose.

EARLY CONTRACT QUESTS

A RAT PROBLEM

Not the kind you think. Someone or something is killing the Rats in Arvena Thelas's cellar. And Thelas, who lives just down the street from the Anvil guild, doesn't want them killed. She loves them; they're her pets.

This is Azzan's first contract quest for you, so speak to him about contracts to receive it. Then, head to Arvena Thelas's house. After you speak to her, go down to the cellar, where you find, improbably, a Mountain Lion attacking the Rats! Now, how'd a creature like that get into an enclosed basement in an enclosed city?

Azzan, Anvil Fighters Guild

Kill the Lion and report back to Thelas. She worries that more lions will follow and sends you off to find a hunter, Penarus Inventius, and to remove the threat. Your compass will lead you to Inventius. Often, he's in his house, right down the street, although he may be off hunting in the wilderness.

Pinarus Inventius, Lion hunter extraordinaire

Inventius is surprised by your news of a Mountain Lion in Anvil. However, he's seen a few in the wilderness and agrees to lead you to their last known address. Inventius takes you outside the city (if you didn't find him out there to start) and up the hill to the northwest. At a rock formation on the path's south side, he tells you this is where the lions will appear and ventures that there shouldn't be more than four.

He's right on both counts. By now, you may already have had a run-in with two of the lions. The other two should be on the far side of the rocks.

When the battle ends, return to Thelas to find her worries undiminished. Evidently there's *another* Mountain Lion down in her cellar.

By the time you return from killing it, she has worked up a theory. Thelas thinks someone's out to get her and has fastened on a neighbor, Quill-Weave, as a likely suspect. (She's seen Quill-Weave sneaking around the rear of the house at night.) She sends you off to spy on her.

This may seem like another wild goose chase. Thelas started out sounding sweetly flaky. Now she sounds a bit paranoid.

But she's right. Shortly before 8 p.m., position yourself to watch Thelas's backyard. (The bush outside the wall on the yard's west side is a good spot.) Soon an Argonian woman creeps in through the east entrance and leaves a piece of meat in the middle of the yard. If she can see you, she won't leave the evidence, so make sure to stay out of her field of view.

Quill-Weave, very bad neighbor

You get a journal entry about confronting Quill-Weave. Do so, and she cops to her plan: She expected the Rats would leave the basement and the town guard would chase them away. Tell her about the Mountain Lions and she pleads that she didn't mean for this to happen and offers you free training in Acrobatics if you keep her secret.

Instead, be honest with Thelas, who will then supplement the standard Fighters Guild cash reward (keyed to your current level) with free Speechcraft training. If you claim that Quill-Weave wasn't involved, she seems discomfited, suspecting perhaps that you're holding something back, and you'll get only the gold.

It's a slightly better choice, unless you're a fiend for Acrobatics. Quill-Weave won't provide your reward until you've made an appropriate report to Thelas, and she doesn't wait around. If you're delayed in getting back to her, you may find she's vanished into her home (two houses west of Thelas's) and will have to wait on her appearance (she eats out) or pick the lock. (If you're truly unlucky in your timing, you may have to wait awhile, as Quill-Weave also visits her friend Casta Scribonia in Chorrol on the seventh of each month.)

In any case, get back to Azzan at the guild. Ask about advancement for a bump in rank (to Apprentice if you've done just the one quest) or contract for another job. And start listening to the rumor mill for word of your exploits.

THE UNFORTUNATE SHOPKEEPER

This is a basic but rather difficult guard-the-store mission. Norbert Lelles, who runs Lelles's Quality Merchandise in Anvil, has been experiencing a run of break-ins. You're to stay in the store overnight to intercept the thieves.

For this mission, it helps to have a little advance knowledge of Anvil's layout. Otherwise, the compass directions may seem baffling. The guild is in the residential district. Lelles's shop is in the separate commercial one along the docks in the northwest part of Anvil (See the Anvil map in the "City Maps" chapter).

Head to the back door of Lelles's shop. He must know you're coming, because he's left it open for you. Doesn't seem like the greatest idea for someone who's having problems being robbed. Lelles is puzzled about how the thieves keep getting into his store. He gives you the lowdown on the robberies, and then he heads to the Flowing Bowl while you take care of business.

The three thieves come piling through the front door in a bunch sometime between 11 p.m. and 4 a.m. Handling them is tricky. Individually, each might not be so bad, but they all tend to arrive at the same time. Spells to incapacitate some or all members of this party would be ideal, but you can get through this with fighting. We suggest falling back slowly to the stairs, which enables you to take on the baddies one at a time.

Disgruntled employees

When they're dead, head to the Flowing Bowl and talk to Lelles, who reveals that the three are former trusted employees. We guess that's the secret to their success: They had keys. If you hang out in the shop until morning, when Lelles opens up, you can quickly convert the thieves' belongings into cash.

Azzan won't have anything further for you. If you started the Fighters Guild quests with him, he'll bump you over to Burz gro-Khash in the Cheydinhal branch. If you started the quests with gro-Khash, you'll be sent to Vilena Donton and then Modryn Oreyn for the first of the duties quests.

THE DESOLATE MINE

This is your initial Fighters Guild quest if you start out working for gro-Khash in Cheydinhal, or the third if you start by working for Azzan in Anvil.

The rather grumpy gro-Khash wants you to deliver a bow, a hammer, and a sword to a trio of unarmed Fighters Guild members in the Desolate Mine northwest of the city. A little inventory management, a little walking, a little conversation, and, if it works out correctly, much butchering of the Goblins.

The trip itself is short, though you might run up against one or two Goblins or critters right outside the mine entrance. Inside, speak first to Rienna. She takes the bow and directs you to distribute the other weapons to comrades Elidor and Brag gro-Bharg.

Burz gro-Khash, Cheydinhal Fighters Guild

Each has a weapon preference. Give the sword to the High Elf and the hammer to the Orc. The three set off to mess up the mine's population of Goblins.

You're expected to follow along and help them. The Goblins are spread out around the mine, and it shouldn't be too difficult. Here's an incentive: If any of the other Fighters Guild members die, you'll be docked 20 percent of the reward when you return to gro-Khash. And you'll have the unsettling experience of hearing about their deaths in the rumor mill. (On the other hand, if everyone survives, your success will be celebrated in rumors as well.)

You're done here. If you haven't performed Azzan's initial two quests, gro-Khash sends you off to Anvil. If you have done them, you're sent to Vilena Donton in Chorrol for the first of the duties quests.

You can request promotion to Apprentice if you've completed just the one quest or to Journeyman if you've also performed Azzan's.

DOING YOUR DUTIES

UNFINISHED BUSINESS

You must complete the first round of Fighters Guild quests from Azzan and Burz gro-Khash to get this one. The initial contact is Vilena Donton in the Chorrol branch—who explains the guild's standards of decorum and diligence—but the actual quest comes from Modryn Oreyn, who can typically be found on the Chorrol guild's entry level.

Modryn Oreyn, Fighters Guild Champion

Oreyn sends you off to contact a new guild member named Maglir. Maglir was assigned a contract in Skingrad, but he has "defaulted"—failed to complete the task—and you're to find out what's gone wrong.

Find Maglir at the West Weald Inn in Skingrad near the West Gate. The young man is matter-of-fact about having defaulted—saying simply that, given the dangers involved, he wasn't paid enough for the mission (recovery of Brenus Astis's journal from Fallen Rock Cave). And with that, he hands you the ball and offers you the chance to run with it.

Maglir, guild weasel

Strictly speaking, you've done what you were asked to do. You can return to Oreyn and make your report. But he's only going to send you back to get the journal, so don't waste your time.

If you don't have a magic, silver, or Daedric weapon, get fixed up with one before you head for the cave—a quick jaunt northwest of Skingrad. It's populated by a mixture of 15 undead and critters.

Three cave-in zones give Fallen Rock Cave its name. The first is in the entry hallway. These are designed as obstacles for the player rather than snares for the residents, but they can be avoided without difficulty. (Just don't run into the rockfall zones. Use your weapon to bat the rocks out of the way.) Make your way carefully to the cave's innermost room, which holds the journal and its late author.

Read the journal if you like. *Various Studies on the Fauna of Cyrodiil* offers intriguing (though incomplete) tidbits on Rats, Minotaurs, Trolls, and what the diary calls a "land dreugh."

You can either return to Maglir or go directly to Oreyn. Maglir doesn't really care how things end up. Either be honest with Oreyn and claim the credit (and have it come back to bite you later) or help out your fellow Fighters Guild newbie by telling Oreyn that Maglir did complete the quest—sacrificing the the Fame bump (you do get the reward).

Will Oreyn buy it? Your journal doesn't seem to think so, and the rumor mill begins to percolate with reports that you've covered up for Maglir's mistake. But the lie won't injure you. In any case, Oreyn does give you another quest.

DRUNK AND DISORDERLY

Three Fighters Guild members have been making trouble in Leyawiin. You're to find out what's behind it.

The trio—Dubok gro-Shagk, Rellian, and Vantus Prelius—can be found at the Five Claws Lodge. You walk in with their argument already in progress, a table overturned, and a cask knocked from its base. Spend a minute listening to the three (along with the proprietor of the bar, Witseidutsei) yell at one another. Pretty funny stuff. When you appear, Witseidutsei identifies you as a Fighters Guild member and begs you to remove your comrades.

Drunk guys with swords

Talk to them to learn they're not simply drunk. They're angry over being displaced by the Blackwood Company. This discussion—and it is just a discussion; these fellows are very decent to you, if a bit surly—ultimately leads to Prelius's suggestion that you find jobs for them.

It's not that hard. With a Disposition of 40, any Leyawiin resident—even the Five Claws proprietor—will steer you to Margarte. Or you can approach Margarte directly. The trick is finding her, as she's a roamer and spends her afternoons collecting ingredients in the countryside west of the city.

She's a "trade consultant" by profession, but her hobby is alchemy. She needs Ogre's Teeth and Minotaur horns for experiments, and she doesn't trust the Blackwood folks enough to hire them. However, she's not quite ready to trust the Fighters Guild, either.

As a test, she sends you out as her own personal errand boy. She wants five portions of ectoplasm, and she doesn't care how you get it. You can buy some at All Things Alchemical in Skingrad or head out to nearby ruins and find some undead types that like to haunt the places. Ghosts and Wraiths seem to be made of the stuff.

Ectoplasm can be found in the Undercrofts of Chapels, even at low levels.

After you bring the ectoplasm to Margarte, she allows the Fighters Guild to work for her. Report back to Prelius. Everybody's happy—not least Witseidutsei. You may even run into the trio again in the countryside as they go about their ingredient-collection errands. And if you visit the Five Claws the next day, you'll find everything's back to normal. Oh, and feel free to bring Minotaur horns and Ogre's Teeth to Margarte from now on. She'll give you 500 gold for either, in groups of five.

Oreyn is disturbed at the news of the Blackwood foothold in Leyawiin but pays you off and promotes you to Swordsman. You'll be hearing about this Blackwood outfit again soon.

Newheim the Portly, mugged for his mug

Oreyn has no further assignments for the time being and kicks you over to Azzan and gro-Khash for further contracts.

MORE CONTRACTS

DEN OF THIEVES AND NEWHEIM'S FLAGON

You may notice a familiar face in the Anvil Fighters Guild: Maglir from the Unfinished Business quest is back. Evidently Oreyn hasn't gotten around to dealing with him yet, or your lie about his default carried some weight, because he's still in the guild. And for this mission, he's your partner.

For a contract, it's all rather vague. Azzan reports recent thefts in Anvil and indicates the thieves are believed to be hiding nearby. Basically, he says, "Ask around."

In fact, ask around about thieves right inside the guild and you'll leave with a lead: Newheim the Portly was among the victims.

Newheim gets around a good deal—even out to the harbor from 8 a.m. to 10 a.m. —but when you catch up to him, he fills in the blanks in the contract nicely. The thieves, all Bosmers, stole an heirloom held by three generations of the Portlies: a flagon that keeps ale "cold and sweet." (This is a separate, optional quest—Newheim's Flagon—nestled within the larger Den of Thieves quest.) And the bandits can be found in the Hrota Cave north of Anvil. It's close. Head out the gate and up the steep slope toward a large grass-topped rock. The cave entrance is in the southeast face of the great dark rock just to the north.

Within, you must clear out the Wood Elves while keeping your own pet Wood Elf, Maglir, alive. Highlights include three falling-rock traps (including one in the first side corridor as you enter), a log trap (like the one from the Natural Caverns in character gen), a swinging-mace trap, a secret door, and assorted containers.

Oh, the flagon? It sits on top of a barrel in the northeast corner of the central pit in the last large room.

The wrap-up is simple: a cash reward from Azzan, a bump up to Protector (if you've already finished Amelion's Debt for gro-Khash), and a referral either to gro-Khash in Cheydinhal or to Modryn Oreyn in Chorrol. If you return the flagon, Newheim provides three bottles of his special brew.

AMELION'S DEBT

This is advertised as an heirloom-retrieval mission, which sounds similar to one you may have just performed for Newheim the Portly outside of Anvil. If you're flush and feeling charitable, it may be a good deal simpler. Pay close attention to the characters you meet here.

Biene Amelion, distressed damsel

Burz gro-Khash sends you to speak with Biene Amelion in the small settlement of Water's Edge—far down on The Lower Niben's west side. That's a long way from Cheydinhal, so fast-travel to Leyawiin's West Gate and march north on the coast road, past Undertow Cavern and White Stallion Lodge. Biene Amelion is in the northernmost of the three houses.

Amelion's father, Marcel, was a gambler, and not a very good one. He fell deep in debt. And that now he's gone—kidnapped to force payment (or maybe he just skipped town, the rat)—the burden has fallen to his daughter. She wants to sell her grandfather's enchanted sword and cuirass to pay it off. You can either retrieve them from the family's ancestral tomb or pay the debt (1,000 gold) from your own pocket.

If you have the money and inclination to pay the debt, great; that makes things simple. Just return to gro-Khash for reward, promotion, and a referral either to Azzan in Anvil or back to Modryn Oreyn in Chorrol.

If not, you have a dungeon crawl on your hands. Amelion marks the tomb on your map. It's to the southeast—on the eastern shore of The Lower Niben—and consists of two sections. The first is a large cave with 4–7 undead enemies (enchanted, silver, or Daedric weapon required) and a good deal of loot. The second section, the Sarcophagus Chamber, has 1–8 baddies—the one being anything from a Ghost up to a Lich, depending on your level—and the cuirass and long sword of Brusef Amelion neatly laid out atop a grave. If you're handling the affair as a run 'n' grab, look for an emergency exit nearby, which allows you to keep running all the way to the exit.

Of course, if you just run through, you'll miss all of the other pieces of Brusef's armor scattered about the tomb. It looks like someone or something just didn't want to leave his poor old bones alone. The boots, gauntlets, helm, and shield are all in the first part of the tomb, while the greaves are in the Sarcophagus Chamber. These pieces are all yours to keep. After all, you didn't agree to return those, and what's a little grave-robbing among friends?

You can get everything from the tomb and keep the equipment, as long as you give Biene enough coin to pay off the debt. She's cool with that. The sword's not bad, as it has a nice frost damage enchantment on it. Either way, you've done a nice thing, and perhaps making the money back should not be the first thing on your mind.

If you've also completed Den of Thieves for Azzan, put in for a promotion to Protector when you return to gro-Khash.

THE PLOT THICKENS

THE MASTER'S SON

You must complete Den of Thieves for Azzan and Amelion's Debt for gro-Khash before this "slightly off-the-record" quest comes up on your radar. It's back to Modryn Oreyn for some guild duties, and you start to learn what's really going on in your beloved Fighters Guild.

You're looking for Galtus Previa, who vanished in Nonwyll Cavern while searching for gems. More significantly, you're searching in the company of Guild Master Vilena Donton's younger son, Viranus.

Viranus Donton, the Master's son

You're to make sure that Viranus succeeds—succeeds meaning "doesn't die." (If he does die, your career with the Fighters Guild is at an end.) The young man needs field experience. Evidently his mother "coddles" him too much, though Oreyn says this is understandable given the death of his brother, Vitellus, in a botched guild mission.

As you make your way through the quest's early steps—picking up Viranus at his home in Chorrol and talking to him about the mission—you realize that Viranus's mother doesn't know word one about this quest. Privately, Oreyn is trying to groom Viranus for a future role to which he's not yet suited.

However, you'd think Oreyn would have picked a more modest challenge. Nonwyll Cavern, in the mountains north of Chorrol, may give even you some bad moments. The cave is inhabited by Trolls. The inner cave? *More* Trolls, plus Ogres and a Minotaur.

Needless to say, Galtus Previa is no longer among the living—though not for the reasons you think. His body lies in the innermost room of the inner cave, with a broken shield nearby. Just noting the body gets you a journal entry and enables you to observe, "There were creatures inside" when you get back to Oreyn. (Your reward is a magic blade adjusted to your character's level.) But Oreyn notes in turn that Previa hadn't been eaten and seems dissatisfied with that theory.

The late Galtus Previa

The broken shield? Ah, that's another story. Later on, you'll recognize it. We think Oreyn does already. "I'll be looking into this," he says.

MORE UNFINISHED BUSINESS

Maglir has screwed up again. Once again the little Wood Elf has defaulted on a contract—this one with a mage in Bravil. Once again, Oreyn dispatches you to find out what went wrong and set things to rights. And, once again, you find the "eight-pint hero" in an inn rather than out in the field—this time at Bravil's Lonely Suitor Lodge.

The explanation: Maglir has quit the guild and gone to work for the Blackwood Company. However, he hasn't forgotten your treatment (or perceived mistreatment) of him in the original Unfinished Business quest, and your handling of its disposition with Modryn Oreyn dictates his response to you now. If you gave him credit for that contract, he'll bump you along to the guild client in this one—Aryarie at the Bravil Mages Guild.

Maglir, Blackwood Company weasel

However, if you properly claimed the credit yourself, Maglir is confrontational and threatening. (Or tries to be, anyway.) In that case, either drop back to Chorrol and get the name from a sputtering Oreyn or do a house-to-house search to find Aryarie.

The task is to collect 10 portions of Imp gall from Imps in Robber's Glen Cave. This modest hideaway is a short jaunt northwest up the main road to Imperial City and is slightly

richer in loot (14 chests) than it is in Imps (13). Each Imp yields one portion of gall.

Despite the delay, Aryarie is pleased and offers up a noncontractual Ring of Shielding. Oreyn advances you to the rank of Defender and offers you another job—this one arranged on the sly. He asks you to meet him at his home at night. If it's daytime when you arrange to rendezvous, he'll meet you at the house—a humble shack in the city's southwest corner—shortly after 8 p.m. If it's already night, he'll head out directly and you can meet him there now.

AZANI BLACKHEART

Your contact with the Blackwood Company to date has been minor—a burst of anger from members of the guild's Leyawiin branch and, more recently, the news of Maglir's defection (good riddance).

Naturally, there's more to it. Oreyn finally tells the tale of a failed guild expedition (arranged at the behest of a wizard named Argoth) to retrieve an artifact from Azani Blackheart. Oreyn lost 15 of the 20 men so assigned—including Vilena Donton's elder son Vitellus, who died fighting a gallant rearguard action. Then the Blackwood Company apparently went in and performed the same mission successfully.

It may all have been a setup, for Argoth has turned up dead, and the artifact is missing.

The mission had a devastating effect on the guild. Since then, Oreyn says, Donton has been gun-shy—reluctant to commit to war with the Blackwood Company for fear of sacrificing the whole guild—with the result that the organization is dying only slowly, but dying nevertheless.

Oreyn decides to take the matter into his own hands and expose the Blackwood Company as imposters. It's strictly off the books—Donton doesn't know—and Oreyn can't order you to join him. But if you refuse, he cautions that guild contracts are going to dry up.

In fact, they dry up *immediately*. Burz gro-Khash and Azzan still have more quests to offer, to say nothing of four more duties quests from Oreyn, but you'll cut yourself off from the lot unless, sooner or later, you tell Oreyn, "I'm in."

Oreyn proposes to meet you at the Leyawiin guild and then explore Blackheart's putative stronghold at Arpenia, a fortress in the forest above the east side of The Lower Niben. You can walk it with him, but it's certainly quicker just to fast-travel; this destination is enabled as soon as you need it.

Your approach to this Ayleid ruin is notable only for its lack of notability. No guards outside. Inside, you won't face any real challenges either. (This is not to say it's safe; the place is alive with traps.) Arpenia is deserted, with none of the detritus of battle or occupation.

This seals it for Oreyn. In the middle of the first big room, he speaks to you: He's convinced the Blackwood Company's assault was a sham. The two sides must have struck a deal. The mercs built a second story on their reputation at the expense of the Fighters Guild. Blackheart removed an enemy and kept his artifact.

Here the mission shifts from investigation to a renewed assault—an ostensible effort to complete the guild's original contract with the late Argoth. Oreyn says Blackheart is crazy for Ayleid ruins, and Oreyn knows of another, Atatar, to the northeast. This time, he'll lead.

His hunch is correct. Blackheart is here. Atatar is big—well stocked in traps and enemies (more than 20 bandits and critters, all told), especially on the first three levels, with Blackheart himself, a Redguard warrior several levels above your own, waiting at the bottom with a Daedric claymore and Elven armor.

Azani Blackheart, Ayleid Ruin aficionado

And the artifact? Oddly, it's never identified and you won't find it. (We get the feeling this might show up again someday.) In any case, Oreyn's more interested in Blackheart's ring, as this is the evidence that will establish your victory. Give it to your comrade, and you're done. Oreyn bumps you up to Warder and sends you to Azzan or gro-Khash for more contracts.

DO SOME CONTRACTS, EARN SOME CASH

THE WANDERING SCHOLAR

When you return to Azzan, you learn that a scholar, Elante of Alinor, is researching Daedra worship. You're to accompany her into Brittlerock Cave, near the fort at Sutch, and protect her while she goes about her work.

Elante, a bit overdressed for spelunking, waits for you just inside the entrance. She indicates that a Daedric shrine can be found in the caves—naturally, it's in the inner cave—and asks you to handle any "difficulties" on the way down.

These "difficulties" are not insignificant; numerous Daedra of various shapes and sizes await you.

Elante of Alinor, Daedric scholar and likely victim

At the bottom of the caves, Elante decides to stay. You can either head back the way you came or go through the door near the shrine. If you choose the latter, prepare to fight your way through more Daedra (and pick up more of that sweet loot). Either way, make your own way back to Azzan for your reward and the usual bumps in Fame and your reputation within the guild. (If Elante dies, the reward and Fame bump evaporate, but the quest is considered complete.)

Azzan can promote you to Guardian (if you've already finished "The Fugitives" for gro-Khash), but he has nothing more for you at the moment.

THE FUGITIVES

Burz gro-Khash has one quest for you on this go-round. There's been a prison break in Bravil, and the fugitives, rather than sensibly making themselves scarce, are hanging around and tormenting the city that jailed them. You're to kill them, says your journal. "Maybe you'll get lucky and they'll surrender," says gro-Khash. (He's joking.)

Finding them is your first problem. No one in Bravil is willing to talk without extra inducement. Use persuasion or bribery to coax an NPC's Disposition up to 60, and you learn that the four are in Bloodmayne Cave.

If you're in the Thieves Guild, you have an alternative—find another member to give you the scoop with no Disposition requirements, plus extra info: the prisoners' names and the little fact that the four are murderers. (Try Luciana Galena or S'krivva; both have homes in Bravil.)

Fortunately, their prisoners aren't together. Ashanta and Hlofgar are in the initial section of the cave (which is near the river northwest of Bravil), and Dreet-Lai and Enrion are in the inner one. The first three are pitched one level above yours. Enrion is three above—and he's supplied with a magic weapon.

Get back to gro-Khash for the standard reward. For the first time, he seems impressed. Maybe this grumpy old Orc has a soft spot for slaughtering murderers.

Ask him about advancement, and he promotes you to Guardian (assuming you've already done The Wandering Scholar for Azzan) and sends you to Azzan or to Modryn Oreyn for another duties quest.

Oreyn dispatched a team of guild fighters—including Viranus Donton, whom you shepherded through an earlier quest—to clear this mine of Trolls. He hasn't heard from them since. You're sent to investigate.

The mine's far to the southeast on the Elsweyr border. Fast-travel to Leyawiin and make your way southwest up into the hills.

There are two entrances, one at either end of the mine. Use the western one, to which the game directs you. You'll figure out the story more quickly and the battles should prove much more manageable.

You find three dead bodies by the time you reach the bottom of the entry passage. In fact, apart from a single Troll and a range of critters, everyone in this section of the mine is dead: five guild members—and two from the Blackwood Company.

Who exactly was the guild fighting here? Did the Trolls kill everyone? Or did the guild members and Blackwood folks kill each other?

It's the latter, though you won't know this for certain until you find Viranus Donton's body and journal in a large southern chamber. (Evidently, the Troll-removal operation was going well when the Blackwood Company stormed in and started killing Trolls and men indiscriminately. For fun, there are other passages in the journal that give some great insight into Viranus and his personal life.)

Viranus Donton: not cut out for guild work

To find said journal, you must fulfill the guild team's original mandate: kill the nine remaining Trolls. Try to catch them in the tunnels between the rooms, where they have no room to maneuver, and you can face them one at a time.

With the journal in hand, make your way back to Chorrol. Oreyn instructs you to lie low and perform contracts (contact either Azzan or gro-Khash for your next assignment). "You still have a career ahead of you," he says. Oreyn, on the other hand, may not. He faces the unenviable task of telling Vilena Donton about the death of her remaining son.

Bad news travels fast. If this is your first contact with a quest-giver since completing Trolls of Forsaken Mine, you'll learn that Oreyn's little chat with Vilena Donton did not go well. He's been kicked out of the guild. And you, as his instrument, have been demoted two ranks to Defender.

This quest—your last for Azzan—is the recovery of a sacred stone that has been stolen from the church in Bruma. You'll get the story from Cirroc at that city's Great Chapel of Talos.

The healer is in and around the church for most of the day. He reports that the Stone of St. Alessia—a ward against evil—is presumed to have been taken by a group of four or five men who were seen leaving the chapel on the night it vanished. They headed east. (Your journal clarifies that this means "out of town.")

Follow the road east from the gate and drop down a rocky slope to a lone Khajiit named K'Sharr. He freely confesses participating in the theft but says the stone is gone—his party was jumped by Ogres and he's the only survivor—and points you east-southeast to the Ogres' digs in an Ayleid ruin called Sedor.

K'Sharr, robber robbed of stone

Once inside the ruin, it's not far to the stone: up the stairs, around a curving hallway, down another flight, across a large chamber and short hall, and there it is. Granted, you'll probably have to mess up some Ogres along the way, though we like a speedy character's chance at a dash 'n' grab. If you're the more stealthy type, try sneaking by.

Then retrace your steps to the exit, to Cirroc (who gives you three Restore Health potions), and to Azzan for your reward.

And promotion? Even after all that's happened? Possibly. Here's how it works for the remainder of the contract quests: After you complete two of these three remaining contracts, either Azzan or gro-Khash will restore your previous rank of Guardian. Upon completing all three, you'll be promoted to Champion—Oreyn's old position in the guild.

The Noble's Daughter

Lord Rugdump: nobleman, gentleman, scholar

This quest is rather strange and sweet. Lady Rogbut, the daughter of Orcish nobleman Lord Rugdumph, has gone missing. You're to find her. Start by talking to the lord at his estate northwest of Lake Arrius. His pleasant hilltop mansion is within easy walking distance from Cheydinhal.

The lord thinks Ogres made off with his daughter and suggests you search for her east of his estate. His directions are spot-on; the trio of monsters and their captive can be found almost directly east of the front door. Approach them from the hillside to the south. The slope will make it hard for the Ogres to get at you, and you can swing away at them without taking damage in return. Watch your flank; while you're banging on one Ogre, another may be approaching from your blind side.

The young lady, more embarrassed than frightened, follows you back to the manor. The lord is overjoyed, misuses new words, and presents you with Rugdumph's Sword. It's an odd sword: It has a Silence spell (very useful against those mages), along with a spell that absorbs Speechcraft.

Back in Cheydinhal, gro-Khash is pleased, pays you off, promotes you back to your old rank (provided you've completed The Stone of St. Alessia for Azzan), and says he may look up the daughter sometime—a strange and sweet ending. Except for the Ogres.

Mystery at Harlun's Watch

Burz gro-Khash's final quest involves the disappearance of residents in the small community of Harlun's Watch, just south of Cheydinhal.

Your contact, Drarana Thelis, is in the southernmost of the hamlet's three houses. She tells you how odd, flickering lights appeared several nights earlier by the Swampy Cave, how a party was dispatched to check them out, and that its members haven't been seen since.

Check out the swamps to the southeast, just west of the cave, and you'll account for the night lights: Will-o-the-Wisps! (Note that you'll need the wisps' glow dust in the Daedric quest "Azura.")

Swampy Cave: bad place to visit

However, that doesn't explain the disappearances. Wisps aren't likely candidates as killers. What say we visit Swampy Cave? It's packed with Trolls—more than 20 of them, between Swampy Cave and the attached Swampy Cavern. But nothing clearly indicates the fate of the missing residents—until you penetrate to the southern tip of Swampy Cave, where you find the intact body of one Eduard Denile. Evidently, the wisps weakened the searchers and the Trolls finished them off.

Your journal instructs you to clear out the Trolls. That means both sections of the cave. In some spots, they're arranged in clusters, so look for chokepoints where you can face one Troll at a time.

Return to gro-Khash for your reward and promotion to Champion (if this is the last of the contracts you do), and to learn the Orc has no more work for you. If you've performed The Stone of St. Alessia quest for Azzan, you've exhausted all the available guild contracts.

However, Modryn Oreyn wants a word with you.

The Blackwood Company

Information Gathering

Meet Oreyn at his house again. Any hour will do—we hear he has a lot of time on his hands. Expelled or not, the former Champion is determined to take down the Blackwood Company and wants your help: You're to kidnap Ajum Kajin, a Blackwood leader, from the company's new base in Glademist Cave, east of Chorrol, and bring him to Oreyn for…well, let's just call it "interrogation."

You must put all seven Blackwood guards to the sword at some point to get Kajin to accompany you, so go in swinging. Kajin is in the cave's innermost room. Order him to follow you back to Oreyn's house; provided the guards are all dead, it's as good as done. (If not, he'll summon the remainder to attack you.)

Back at the house, speak to Oreyn. He wants three pieces of information: the Blackwood Company's size, the identity of its leader, and the secret of the group's strength. You can browbeat Kajin to get the info, or you can sweat him. However, you're not to kill him.

Ajum-Kajin will talk with encouragement.

Either of the suggested methods will work. You can get the first two bits of info (100 members and Ri'Zakar) either by raising Kajin's Disposition first to 70 and then to 90 in the Speechcraft mini-game or by pounding on him repeatedly with your bare hands. (A weapon speeds up this process, but you risk killing him.) Of course torture is a despicable practice, in this world or any other, but in this situation it does happen to be the quickest way to make this fellow spill his guts.

These approaches will take you only so far. You'll never get the third piece of information from Kajin. He'll say "I choose death!" and a short time later his body bursts into flames and he slumps to the floor. He has killed himself rather than give up the Blackwood Company's secret recipe.

Oreyn is not dissatisfied. You've gotten some good info. But to get the final piece, you'll have to become the thing you hate.

INFILTRATION

Oreyn now dispatches you to Leyawiin to join the Blackwood Company and get that last bit of data. This is easier than you might think. Find your way to the Blackwood Company's building (just south of the Fighters Guild in the western part of the city), climb the stairs within, and speak to the company's No. 2 man, Jeetum-Zee.

Jeetum-Ze, Blackwood Company recruiter, pharmacist

He questions you a bit, but seems more curious than suspicious, and asks you to follow him to the Training Hall. Apparently, he's been getting a lot of Fighters Guild members joining his ranks, so your defection isn't that odd. Once you're downstairs, he briefs you and three others on a mission to remove Goblins from the hamlet of Water's Edge.

Here, you come quickly to the source of the Blackwood Company's power: the sap of the Hist tree. In the dialogues that follow, you realize this powerful narcotic is illegal and that the Blackwood Company isn't smuggling it in from the Argonian homeland of Black Marsh. Rather, through magic, they have found a way to keep one of the Hist alive in Cyrodiil.

You may think this a good time to make your excuses and bring the sap back to Modryn Oreyn, but you'll be treated as a pariah if you do. (He's staying in character, and guild members just think you've gone over to the other side.) You have to let this scenario play out. Drink the sap down—otherwise you're going nowhere—and you'll automatically fast-travel to Water's Edge.

Follow your Blackwood comrades west, behind the houses, where seven uncharacteristically passive and unarmed Goblins await. There's something amiss here, and you can hold back. (You've been to Water's Edge, after all, and maybe have already guessed where this is leading.)

But you're going to have to join in eventually. Once the Goblins are dead, talk to your fellow Blackwoods. They tell you that they still smell Goblins and order you to check the houses.

Sure enough, indoors you find four more Goblins—also passive and unarmed—standing around innocently, almost as though they live here. Kill them all and you get a message that Water's Edge has been cleared of Goblins. Then you fast-travel automatically again—and what do you see next but the smiling face of Modryn Oreyn. You're back at his house in Chorrol. He explains that your guild brothers found you unconscious on the streets of Leyawiin.

Tell Oreyn about the Hist sap. He says he'll look into it and, in the meantime, sends you back to Water's Edge to check on its people.

When you look behind the houses where the initial Blackwood assault on the seven Goblins took place, you find not a single Goblin corpse. Instead, you find the bodies of seven sheep.

And clustered near the shed, near the newly returned Marcel Amelion, are the bodies of Biene Amelion, Jolie and Eduard Retiene, and Marie Alouette. Four Goblins in the houses. Four human faces now looking blankly up at the sky.

Water's edge victims

What can you say to Amelion? Nothing meaningful. What can Oreyn say when you return to him? Nothing that can assuage your sense of guilt. You *know* what happened here. You have participated, albeit unwittingly, in an atrocity against your own people. The only way to atone for this crime is to take out the Hist tree. And that's the final mission.

THE HIST

You're to return to the Blackwood Company's headquarters in Leyawiin and destroy the Hist tree. Oreyn advises that Blackwood leader Ri'Zakar is an experienced mercenary who knows to keep it under lock and key.

If a tree burns in Leyawiin…

In fact, Ri'Zakar and his lieutenant are themselves under lock and key in their respective third- and second-floor chambers. You'll have to kill Ja'Fazir, who attacks you when you enter the Blackwood Company hall, for the key to Jeetum-Zee's room, take down Jeetum-Zee for the key to Ri'Zakar's room, and vanquish Ri'Zakar for the cellar key. These three are each a tough fight. Rest up between them, as each gets progressively more difficult.

In the cellar, you find the Hist tree itself, tended by two very tough Argonian mages and sustained by strange machinery. Kill the mages—they both have some nasty spells, but you can use the tight quarters to your advantage—and get the two pipes. (One is on the table on the south side of the room, the other on the floor nearby.) These enable you to activate the pumps and destroy the tree.

On the way out, you find our favorite Wood Elf, Maglir. He greets you, whining about his ruined life, and you have to kill him.

Maglir, about damn time

Oreyn awards you with the Helm of Oreyn Bearclaw. We're not sure how he came by it. (It was awarded to the hero of Morrowind by the Daedric lord Malacath.) But perhaps it's not a good idea to look a gift helm in the nametag.

He also bumps you over to Guild Master Vilena Donton to explain everything that's happened. By design, she's been entirely out of the loop, and this contributes a little to her annoyance should you confess to working with the dismissed Oreyn (and even if you don't).

But that fleeting anger is overwhelmed by gratitude for your gallant deeds, and with this in mind Donton promotes you to Guild Master—with a recommendation that you appoint Oreyn as your second-in-command. "The guild has passed me by," she says. "You are its future."

Oreyn hems and haws a bit—but finally accepts. "Someone has to keep you in line," he says.

IF YOU ARE THE FUTURE, WHERE DID WE LEAVE OUR KEYS?

Now, it would be a sad state of affairs were you to ascend to the Guild Master rank just as the guild runs out of things to do.

So it doesn't. Your single-handed reduction of the

Blackwood Company to (in Oreyn's words) "just another band of mercenaries" opens up the markets for contracts and fighters. The Fighters Guild is back in business.

As boss, you receive a cash stipend and a share in the guild's loot. When you're promoted to Guild Master, you're given the key to a chest in your top-floor quarters in the Chorrol guild. Once a month, you'll find your gold and items within.

Both are random. For the gold, the game generates a number from 1 to 100 and multiplies it by 10, so, conceivably, you could receive 10–1,000 gold pieces in a given month. The items are all drawn from a big list that includes magic weapons, armor, jewelry, and potions.

Finally, in broad strokes, you can now determine how the guild operates—instructing Oreyn either to pursue more contracts (which will boost your stipend) or to increase recruitment (which means more items). It's good to be boss, isn't it?

FACTION QUESTS: THE MAGES GUILD

OVERVIEW

The folks in the Mages Guild are more self-involved than others—in some part because the use of magic in Tamriel is regarded with suspicion. Hence, you won't be performing contracts for other people, but assisting in the guild's research and administration.

Like the Fighters Guild, the Mages Guild has powerful enemies and your focus will be to beat them back.

Joining is simple. All you have to do is ask. Speak to one of the seven branch leaders: Carahil in the Anvil guild, Kud-Ei in Bravil, Jeanne Frasoric in Bruma, Falcar in Cheydinhal, Teekeeus in Chorrol, Dagail in Leyawiin, or Adrienne Berene in Skingrad. (Unlike the Fighters Guild, the Mages Guild has an outpost in the Imperial City at the Arcane University. However, this is closed to you until you complete a series of "recommendation quests.")

Polus, who is in the lobby of the Arch-Mage's Tower at Arcane University in Imperial City.

The Arcane University, located in the Imperial City, is the seat of power for the Mages Guild. At later stages of the quest line, you'll come to call it home.

What you retrieve as your penance depends on your offense. If it's theft, Polus charges you to replenish the guild's alchemical stocks by collecting 20 Dragon's Tongue Flowers and 20 Redwort Flowers.

Dragon's Tongue is hardly easy to come by. Fort Redwater, along the Black Marsh border, has a large number of the flowers growing outside. If you can't find all you need there, look for clusters of the bright yellow flowers just northeast of Leyawiin. As a last resort, there are a few flowers scattered in many places throughout the West Weald between Skingrad and Bravil.

Redwort Flowers are also in short supply in Cyrodiil. The highest single concentration can be found a short distance southeast of Fieldhouse Cave in County Leyawiin, near the Black Marsh border. If luck is with you, you'll be able to get all the Redwort you need in one place. If not, try the Ayleid ruins of Wendelbek and Morahame (both on the eastern side of Niben Bay, along the Panther River). If all else fails, scour the West Weald between Skingrad and Bravil, as the flowers grow in small numbers throughout the area.

Guild halls are located in every city in Cyrodiil, and the guild can be joined from any of these locations.

There's one requirement: The guild doesn't want criminals in its ranks, so you must clear any bounties on your head first.

That done, you're in. If you'd like to stay in, observe the same basic rules that hold true in other guilds. Don't steal from guild members. Don't kill them. If you do, you'll be kicked out and have to apply for readmission to Raminus

FACTION QUESTS: THE MAGES GUILD

If you kill a guild member, you have to find 20 portions of Vampire dust and 20 Daedra hearts. The Daedra hearts may not be a huge issue if you're into the Main Quest (which is all Daedra, all the time). You'll find them on the bodies of Dremora and Xivilia. And if you're not that far in the Main Quest, you can buy from some alchemists (some of the time) what you can't pocket in the wild.

The Vampire dust is trickier, for a couple of reasons. It is found in the remains of Vampires, and the game throws you into their path on only a few occasions—notably at Bloodcrust Cavern in the Mages Guild "Information at a Price" quest and Gutted Mine in the Daedric "Azura" quest. In addition, visits to Lipsand Tarn and Fort Carmala are possibilities in the "Fingers of the Mountain" recommendation quest and the Main Quest, respectively. (Carmala's on your route from Weynon Priory to Kvatch.)

The other problem: The more you deal with Vampires, the greater the risk of catching the Vampire disease (porphyric hemophilia). See the "Vampires" section of the "Freeform Quests" chapter for more details.

If you're a repeat offender, you'll be a repeat ingredient-picker. Just don't screw up a third time, or you're out for good.

RECOMMENDATION QUESTS

You can embark immediately on a series of seven recommendation quests—one from each of the branch leaders named above. With each quest you complete, the respective branch leader will send a recommendation to the Council of Mages on your behalf. Completing all seven nets you a promotion, enables you to perform more difficult assignments, and allows you to climb to higher ranks in the guild. We've arranged them from easiest to most difficult, but you can do them in any order.

BRUMA RECOMMENDATION

The mage J'skar seems to have vanished into thin air. No one's seen him for days. Bubbly branch leader Jeanne Frasoric says this won't do—what if someone from the Council of Mages should drop by?—and asks you to bring him back to the material world.

Jeanne Frasoric, the ArchMagister of the Bruma Hall

You have one lead: Guild member Volanaro suspects that a spell misfired. Seek him out in the guild's cellar to discover this is just the cover story he's fed Frasoric.

The truth is rather more mean-spirited. Frasoric is not much of a mage, and the Bruma guild members don't respect her. Volanaro asserts that "she's managed to butter up the right people just enough to keep her position." And they deal with the situation by making her life miserable with pranks—like J'skar's "disappearance."

If you raise Volanaro's Disposition to 70, he'll strike a deal with you. He'll help if you'll substitute one prank for another: steal Frasoric's *Manual of Spellcraft* from the desk in her top-floor office. He'll even teach you a low-level Unlock spell for this purpose.

Jeanne's Desk

Both the door and desk locks are easy (should you feel disposed to pick them instead), and you should be in and out of the office in no time. Give the book to Volanaro, and he'll meet you in the cellar at 10 p.m. to dispel the Invisibility spell on J'skar.

J'skar, visible again

You can also find J'skar on your own. He's still hanging around the guild. Just explore; you may hear him chuckle. You might even see a door open and close on its own. Or, most likely, the cursor will see what you can't and his name will pop up in the corner of the screen.

If the search is unsuccessful, cast a Detect Life spell and J'skar will show up as clearly as Frasoric or Volanaro. (It's an indicator of Frasoric's modest magical competence that she didn't do this herself.) Zap him with a Dispel spell to remove the Invisibility, and J'skar (with a crabby remark tailored to the current stage of the quest) will march off to present himself to Frasoric. She bubbles a bit more, and her recommendation is yours.

BRAVIL RECOMMENDATION

Bravil resident Varon Vamori has been riding on guild member Ardaline hard for some days—even stealing her Mage's Staff. Branch leader Kud-Ei isn't clear on the reason—it sounds like the way that passionate eight-year-old boys treat unresponsive eight-year-old girls—but says it must stop. You're to have a chat with Mr. Vamori's inner child and use "whatever means necessary" to recover the staff.

Kud-Ei, ArchMagister of the Bravil Hall

Despite her ruthless-sounding words, Kud-Ei intends a Beguile scroll to be your main instrument in your exchange with Vamori.

Varon Vamori: scoundrel or scorned?

And, sure enough, that does the trick. While he feigns various levels of ignorance of his beloved at lower Dispositions, at a scroll-assisted one of 65, Vamori confesses that he likes Ardaline and that her lack of interest in him feeds a rage inside him. Hence the theft of Ardaline's staff. And hence, with measures of shame and awkwardness thrown in, his subsequent sale of that staff to a friend, Soris Arenim, who lives in Imperial City's Talos Plaza District.

If persuasion will get you to the necessary dispositions in this quest, hold on to your Beguile scrolls for some other time. Or, you can sell them for a bit of extra cash.

You can dash off in pursuit of the staff straight away, but a stop at the Mages Guild to consult Kud-Ei first will net you two more Beguile scrolls. And they'll come in handy—for Arenim is even less willing to discuss the matter than his friend. Indeed, if you mention "Mage's Staff," he'll end the conversation. (He thinks you've come on behalf of Vamori, who is feeling guilty and has made several attempts to recover the staff.)

Soris Arenim, current owner of Ardaline's staff

Again, the scroll works wonders. With a Disposition of 70, Arenim offers to sell you the staff for only a portion of what he paid: 200 gold.

That may seem a lot of money for an item that, to judge from Kud-Ei's comment about the staff being "more symbolic than practical," has nothing special to recommend it. Can you get him to knock down the price?

How about knocking it down to 0? Wives are well-known in popular myth for failing to understand their husbands' obsessions and for being eager to give away purported treasures cluttering up the basement. So it is, we think, with Erissare Arenim. Use the other Beguile scroll to raise her Disposition to 65, and she'll tell you that it's in a locked chest in the cellar, and the key is upstairs in her husband's desk. Or you can save the scroll for some other close-mouthed character and take the key and staff.

Kud-Ei doesn't want to know how you got the staff, but is delighted, and teaches you the Captivate spell (which is weaker than Beguile), and promises to supply your recommendation.

CHEYDINHAL RECOMMENDATION

A low-level mage has dropped a Ring of Burden down the well behind the guild. Falcar (who hangs out on the top floor) was experimenting with the ring, and he asks you to retrieve it.

Falcar, ArchMagister of the Cheydinhal Hall

The well's locked, and Falcar sends you to Deetsan for the key. She'll provide it and, if Falcar's not nearby, will also supply some useful background. (If she won't talk, either wait until afternoon, when Deetsan is downstairs and Falcar up, or until he goes to sleep in his cellar quarters.)

You're not the first to be assigned this task. An eager Associate named Vidkun was sent down the well and hasn't been seen since. With this in mind, Deetsan teaches you Buoyancy—a combined Feather/Water Breathing spell. At least you won't drown.

But you may become over-encumbered. Down in the well, you find the unfortunate Vidkun suspended near the ceiling. When you take the ring from his body, you gain 200 points against your maximum Encumbrance. Before you descend, lose enough equipment so this puts you at least five points below the maximum. (This allows for the Buoyancy spell wearing off before you can lose the cement ring; it reduces your Encumbrance by 5 points.) Otherwise, like Vidkun, you'll be stuck in a bad place.

Back in the guild, Falcar has vanished. Other guild members direct you to Deetsan. She tells you to just drop the ring anywhere (evidently, this was just Falcar's perverse joke), expresses sadness at Vidkun's death, and explains the blowup that occurred in your absence.

Deetsan confronted Falcar over the well affair. Enraged first to learn Deetsan had helped you in your mission, then by her threat to report him to the Council of Mages, the guild chief launched into an incoherent rant ("your days are numbered") and stormed out.

Deetsan actually cares about the people she works with, unlike Falcar.

So where's your recommendation? Deetsan asks you to search Falcar's cellar quarters for the letter or anything unusual. You won't find the letter, but the dresser near the bed contains two Black Soul Gems. Deetsan takes these from you without explanation of their presence or function—but comments ominously, "This is worse than I'd expected"—and says she'll write your recommendation.

Black Soul Gems are the tools of Necromancers, and become important later on in your questing

What's going on here? You won't find out within the confines of this quest. For now, let's just say that Falcar and his Black Soul Gems will be making a comeback.

ANVIL RECOMMENDATION

Merchants traveling along the Gold Road between Imperial City and the Gold Coast region have been found dead. Others are missing. The Council of Mages has asked Anvil branch leader Carahil to bring the murders to an end, and you are the cheese in her trap.

Carahil, ArchMagister of the Anvil Hall

Carahil sends you to the Brina Cross Inn—the common thread among the victims. You'll receive further instructions there from Arielle Jurard—one of the battlemages dispatched by the guild.

She makes the assignment sound dangerous, but it isn't. You're not required to kill the killer yourself. And should you choose to do so, you'll find it easy.

The inn is north of Anvil near Brina Cross—the point where the roads to Anvil, Kvatch, and Fort Sutch meet. You find Jurard in the common room. She tells you to take a room, posing as a traveling merchant, and says she'll meet you there later.

 See Chapter 21 World Map/ Gold Coast Map marker #12.

The Brina Cross Inn. Any one of these people could be a killer.

Seek out the proprietor, Christophe Marane, and ask for a bed. He asks your business. You can respond either that you're a traveling merchant or that you'd rather not say. (It doesn't matter; Marane isn't the killer or a tipster, and he is concerned about the murders.) He directs you to a room at the rear of the inn, and Jurard shows up there shortly after you do.

She lays out the sting. In the morning, you're to head east along the road. You'll be followed at a discreet distance by Jurard and another battlemage. When the robber makes a move, you're to protect yourself. For now, rest up for tomorrow's exertions.

In the morning, make sure you're armed and armored and have an offensive or healing spell at the ready. Leave the inn, make your way past the waiting battlemages, let yourself out the gate, and follow the road east-southeast.

The road rises into the pines and there is a dark figure in the distance. It's Caminalda, whom you may have spoken to at the inn. She's the one who seemed over-lavish in her greeting. Her tone is now hostile. Now you can run.

Caminalda reveals herself as the culprit.

But you don't have to be scared. By forcing conversation with you, Caminalda has made a tactical error: You're too close and she now has to face what all mages dread—melee combat without a melee weapon. She's also unarmored and just a level above your own, so you should be able to quickly cut her down to size.

Not much loot for a robber— just her fancy duds and some gold. But you'll also find Caminalda's room key from the inn. The room holds a chest and the chest holds more gold. Return to Carahil for her recommendation, and you can move on.

SKINGRAD RECOMMENDATION

Branch leader Adrienne Berene says she wants to consult the mage Erthor about some notes he borrowed. We suspect from her cranky manner that she wants the notes back.

Adrienne Berene, ArchMagister of the Skingrad Hall

Erthor isn't around. From Sulinus Vassinus, you learn he was forbidden to practice in the guild after that "awful scamp incident" last year. He has set up shop in Bleak Flats Cave and checks in with the guild now and then.

However, Vassinus hasn't seen Erthor lately. No one has. Druja can fill in the blanks: She adds the cave to your map (it's northwest of Skingrad) and suggests reminding Berene that the whole Bleak Flats Cave thing was her idea. Berene then teaches you (gratis) the Weak Fireball spell. The implication is that Erthor must have dug himself a hole, and that you're going to have to dig him out.

See Chapter 21 World Map/ West Weald Map marker #14.

To find the cave, head west out of Skingrad along the road, then north cross-country when the fences end. It's a big hole. Inside the cave await deranged Zombies. You must kill them before Erthor will agree to follow you out. He doesn't say where they came from, but we suspect we've just witnessed this year's "somewhat-less-awful Zombie incident."

FACTION QUESTS: THE MAGES GUILD

Erthor, safe and sound again

Something is clearly bothering Kalthar. What might it be?

Either take Erthor in tow or send him to the guild under his own power, to win Berene's assurance that she'll get around to writing your recommendation in her own sweet time.

Don't feel compelled to escort Erthor all the way back yourself. He can make it under his own power, giving you time to return to town at your own pace.

LEYAWIIN RECOMMENDATION

Dagail's a strange lady. When you approach the Leyawiin guild leader for a recommendation, she makes a bewildering if poetic little speech. The only useful nugget you'll extract is that you need to talk to Agata.

Dagail, ArchMagister of the Leyawiin Guild

Agata explains the weirdness: Dagail has "visions." (Actually, to judge from Dagail's own words, she hears voices.) Once useful, the visions have grown less coherent, and now, without the protection of her Seer's Stone amulet, they are "crippling." You're to ask around the guild to find out if anyone's seen the missing amulet. Comments from Sdrassa and Alves Uvenim point to Kalthar. Kalthar is full of resentment over Dagail's (in his view) undeserved position in the guild and mentions similar problems experienced by her father. You get a journal entry suggesting you bring Kalthar's familiarity with the amulet to Agata's attention.

She supposes Kalthar overheard a conversation between herself and Dagail—but says they never mentioned Dagail's father. In other words, Kalthar seems to know too much. Agata says she'll keep an eye on him while you question Dagail about a connection between her father and the Seer's Stone amulet.

You won't have to ask the question. Dagail has already seen it in a vision and answers thus: "Blood ran blue and dragons flew high. Under broken towers and broken bodies it now lies, waiting to be found."

Your journal interprets this riddle for you: You need to find the fort at which Dagail's father was stationed. And your compass and map now point you to Fort Blueblood, southeast of Leyawiin.

See Chapter 21 World Map/ Blackwood Map marker #30.

It's a large two-section dungeon full of enemies—all outlaw Marauders save for the two mythic beasts (ranging from Imps to Ogres, depending on your level) that guard the amulet. Along the way, you find good loot—half of the 26 containers hold something useful or saleable—and a drawbridge.

The remains of Dagail's father, Manduin, are in the innermost room. The amulet's inside a coffin resting on the ground near the far wall.

The Marauder boss holds the key to Manduin's resting place.

In the second large room on your way back out, you're confronted by Kalthar. He reveals that he took the first amulet and planned to return it after Dagail stepped down and he'd advanced within the guild. And now he demands the other one.

You have to fight him. Kalthar's a battlemage, but he won't be much trouble. Use the stairs on the near side of the bridge to reach the portcullis you saw after you entered the fort. (It can be opened only from this side.) Backtrack to Leyawiin and return the amulet. Dagail's voices grow quiet, and the recommendation is yours.

CHORROL RECOMMENDATION

Teekeeus asks you to clear up "a small matter." It proves to be anything but small. The branch leader acknowledges an "unpleasant history" between himself and former guild member Earana. He discusses their quarrel only in the broadest terms: Teekeeus sees Earana as a renegade who disobeys regulations. Earana thinks Teekeeus abuses his powers. (For more details, ask around the guild. Between Atragar and Alberic Litte, you learn the two got each other bounced from Arcane University in Imperial City.)

Teekeeus, ArchMagister of the Skingrad Hall

At any rate, now Earana's in town and Teekeeus supposes she wants something from him. You're to find out what it is so she'll go on her way. "I do not want her here, spreading her lies," Teekeeus says.

Earana has a bone to pick with Teekeeus, and expects you to do the picking.

Earana can be found on the street outside the guild or at The Grey Mare inn. Interesting; she barely refers to Teekeeus—save a warning not to mention your conversation to him or anyone else in the guild. She gives you another quest: She wants a book, *Fingers of the Mountain*, which is in a ruin called Cloud Top in the mountains north of Chorrol. She promises to make the search worth your while.

When you report to Teekeeus on your conversation, it develops that the branch leader wants the book, too. Do you get the feeling you've been misused?

This small surface ruin is a fair march northwest of the city, and a good climb, as well. If you've been to Nonwyll Cavern in the Master's Son Fighters Guild quest, fast-travel there, then walk west. You find the book on a charred corpse among the broken columns.

See Chapter 21 World Map/ Colovian Highlands Map marker #22.

Who gets it? It's up to you. Earana has the prior claim. And Teekeeus has been disingenuous in his dealings with you. Earana doesn't want anything from Teekeeus. Rather, Teekeeus has used you as an unwitting instrument in his dispute with Earana.

But Earana's promised reward is as yet ill-defined, and you do need Teekeeus's recommendation to climb within the guild. (If you give the book to Teekeeus, it's a done deal.) On that basis, your decision may seem a foregone conclusion.

Not to worry. You can collect the recommendation and still keep your promise to Earana, and vice versa.

If you give the book to Earana, she'll ask for a day to translate the work before you visit her at the inn. When you do, she turns over some notes. They're drawn from smeared marginalia, but your task is clear: Find a Welkynd Stone (a lesser version of the Great Welkynd Stone you'll collect in the Main Quest) in an Ayleid ruin, return to Cloud Top, and cast a Shock spell at a magical pillar at the site to obtain a major-league Shock power—at significant personal risk.

If you don't already have one, purchase a Shock spell from Athagar, who is in the guild's foyer. In Ayleid ruins, Welkynd Stones are all over the place. The two ruins closest to Chorrol are Wendir (which the undead have taken over) in the south-western forest and, more convenient to your destination, Lipsand Tarn, in the northern mountains. (It's north of Nonwyll Cavern and northeast of Cloud Top.)

More convenient equals more dangerous. For, along with the 25 Welkynd Stones in Lipsand Tarn, there are more than a few Vampires and a Vampire "patriarch." This carries some unique risks—a 1–2 percent chance that you'll catch porphyric hemophilia—the Vampire disease.

Welkynd stones are useful to any character relying on magic, but have a particular use in this quest.

Take a few Welkynd Stones. (They can also be used to restore lost Magicka.) If you take just the one you need, don't equip it or you'll use it and lose it.

Nor is vampirism the only danger. Casting your Shock spell on the pillar has a nasty side effect: You get zapped by lightning. As the notes from Earana advise, you should counter this effect. Possible approaches include increasing your resistance to shock, reflecting the lightning, or fortifying your health and taking the damage. But if you survive the ordeal, you have a nice lightning spell called Fingers of the Mountain.

Don't be fooled by its mundane appearance. This stone packs quite a punch.

The quest has a second act. It pops up if you return to the other party and explain that you've given the book to the other person. Each person deals with this fact with equanimity: He or she tells you to steal it back.

If you're talking to Teekeeus, the steal-it-back directive is an order. If to Earana, it's a request. Refuse her request, and the second act ends early. She'll have nothing further to do with you.

Neither of the thefts is difficult. If you gave the book to Earana, she hustled off to stow it in her chest in her room at The Grey Mare. Wait her out. (She eats between 1 and 4 p.m. and sleeps from midnight to 8 a.m.) Bring the book to Teekeeus, and the recommendation is a done deal.

If you gave the book to Teekeeus, he headed for his room in the guild's top-floor living quarters, where he placed it in a locked chest behind a locked door—each with locks that can be opened with a key he keeps on his person. There's traffic through this area only late at night and early in the morning. Turn the book over to Earana, and she'll proceed to translate it as described above.

If you inquire after the book, Teekeeus notes that it's gone missing. Perhaps your involvement in its disappearance is implied. Or perhaps it isn't, and that's your conscience talking. But it doesn't effect your recommendation, which is in the bag.

RAMINUS POLUS'S QUESTS

A MAGE'S STAFF

With the seven recommendation quests complete, talk to any branch leader about recommendation to be referred to Raminus Polus at Arcane University in Imperial City. He's in the Arch-Mage's Lobby—through the door ahead of you when you fast-travel to the University District.

Necromancers have overrun Wellspring Grove, and will attack you on sight.

Polus is appalled by the mages' deaths and mystified by the assault. Necromancers don't like the limelight. He takes up the matter with the Council of Mages while you see Delmar at the Enchanting Center south of the Arch-Mage's Tower to arrange your staff's creation.

Raminus Polus will be your contact for the next several Mages Guild quests.

Polus promotes you to Apprentice, gives you the Robe of the Apprentice—a symbol of your rank—and sends you to acquire material for another symbol: the wood for a Mage's Staff. It comes from a grove near Wellspring Cave, east of Imperial City near the shore of Lake Rumare.

See Chapter 21 World Map/ Heartlands Map marker #43.

This sounds like a mundane retrieval mission. It is not. The cave has been invaded by Necromancers. There are nine of them—six in the cave and three in the cemetery at the rear—and they have killed the grove's two guild attendants, Zahrasha and Eletta.

Locate and activate both bodies. Zahrasha's is near the front of the cave, and Eletta's is in Wellspring Grove near the cave's rear exit (on an island in the lake). You must kill the Necromancers to claim the chest in the middle of the grove.

Why the attack? It's a mystery. The closest thing you get to an explanation is the greeting from Noveni Othran, the only named Necromancer present. Othran, who is in the Grove, regards you as a "plaything." "I'll make your corpse dance," she says, "and then tear itself apart!"

Creating Your Staff

The staff is a symbol, but not just a symbol. It is enchanted with one of nine spells attached to three magical disciplines. You choose the discipline and the spell. If you select Destruction, you'll have access to the Fire, Frost, or Shock spells. If you choose Illusion, then you get Charm, Paralyze, or Silence (which prevents enemies from casting spells). If your discipline is Mysticism, then your spell choices are Soul Trap, Telekinesis, and Dispel (which knocks down protective spells enemy casters have active).

Possible Staff Effects:

Fire	Silence
Frost	Soul Trap
Shock	Telekinesis
Charm	Dispel
Paralyze	

Delmar runs the Chironasium, and will produce a staff of your choosing.

Your choice should be dictated by what you have and your style of play. Don't duplicate a spell effect that's in your repertoire unless you'll make it stronger. For instance, if you already have the Fingers of the Mountain spell from the Chorrol segment of the recommendation quests, do you need Shock? If you're a fighter at heart and a mage on the side, you want a spell with more direct effects than those offered by the only intermittently useful Charm and Telekinesis. (A nice compromise between finesse and force is Paralyze, which guarantees you a quick leg up in combat.)

Twenty-four hours after you place the order, talk to Delmar. The staff is ready; it is in the cupboard at the back of the room. (You'll also find a bunch of scrolls. Take them. You're guild, so it's not theft.) Dash to Polus for promotion to Journeyman and a new mission.

ULTERIOR MOTIVES

The guild is following up your discoveries at Wellspring Cave with a heavy-duty investigation. Related to that investigation is a book which was loaned by the guild to Skingrad count Janus Hassildor, and now must be recovered. This errand is yours.

Polus cautions that the count is reclusive and will be difficult to meet with (as you've learned if you visited the castle in the "Allies for Bruma" segment of the Main Quest). Steward Mercator Hosidus in the castle lobby says the count won't see you, and the steward won't broach the subject with the count again until the next day.

Mercator Hosidus is the steward of Castle Skingrad, and is annoyed by your arrival in town.

Nor is that the only delay. The next day, Hosidus says the count will meet with you—but not now and not at the castle. He wants to meet near the Cursed Mine to the west of town. after 2 a.m. That's odd, but it's nonnegotiable, and even an accomplished lock picker who breaks into the count's living quarters and questions the nobleman with the strange eyes won't learn anything to contradict this assertion.

The meeting spot is east-southeast of the mine in the farm country along the Skingrad–Kvatch road. Fortunately, the royal party is early. Unfortunately, it doesn't include the count. It consists of Hosidus and his Necromancer pals, Mondrar Henim and Arterion. In pursuit of unspecified plans, they mean to kill you.

While Hosidus is a couple of levels above you, his friends are both one below. But it's a moot point, because the fight has scarcely begun when Hassildor turns up and kills his steward and his companions.

The count scolds you for thinking the meeting legitimate. Even so, it served a purpose: Hassildor knew Hosidus was involved with Necromancers, but hadn't identified his colleagues. He insists that he is not one of them—and says that this is what the guild wanted to know. You were not sent for the borrowed book—there is no book—but to spy on Hassildor. Once again, a Mages Guild quest-giver has lied to you.

Count Hassildor chastises you for meeting with Mercator.

It's your turn to scold. Return to Polus, and he apologizes—both for putting you in harm's way and for not telling you the truth about the count's nature. (He's a Vampire.) But the real point here is that the guild is nursing a fragile compact with Hassildor; it keeps his secret and Hassildor shares intelligence with the mages. You were sent to Skingrad because Arch-Mage Traven worried that sending a high-level guild member would provoke an adverse response from the count and send Necromancers diving for cover.

As if to make up for the fibs, you're promoted to Evoker and given a Spelldrinker amulet with a constant Spell Absorption effect that's adjusted to your character's level.

VAHTACEN'S SECRET

"I have a new task for you," says Raminus Polus, "and I assure you there are no Necromancers involved."

You're to lend a hand with research at the Ayleid ruin Vahtacen. Irlav Jarol (one floor up in the Arch-Mage's Tower) is nominally in charge of the project, but other work for the Council of Mages has distracted him, and he asks you to look into a report by Skaleel of a blocked passage.

Irlav Jarol is one of the few remaining members of the Council of Mages, and oversees research projects at Ayleid ruins.

Your second stop is at a spell seller. Make sure you have Fire, Frost, Damage Magicka, and Fortify Magicka available as spells or scrolls. Any variety will do.

Fast-travel to Cheydinhal and go south-southeast to Vahtacen. (If you've done the Mystery at Harlun's Watch quest for the Fighters Guild, you'll have a shorter trip if you first travel to Swampy Cave east of the ruin or Harlun'sWatch to the northwest.) The northbound passage leads through caves to the underground ruin. Skaleel waits at her camp in the first large room.

 See Chapter 21 World Map/ Nibenay Basin Map marker #37.

The ruin has been a problem. The researchers have found a giant pillar in a room at the bottom of the explored ruins. It responds to magic. Several mages who've cast spells at it were zapped back. They think it's a lock of some kind, but they haven't found the key.

Denel, who's down in the room with the pillar, repeats some of this story—but also fills in some important blanks. He points you to inscriptions on tablets in the corners of the room: "av molag anyammis" in the southwest; "av mafre nagaia" in the northwest; "magicka loria" in the northeast; "magicka sila" in the southeast.

This pillar is unlike anything else in Ayleid ruins, and is the key to this site.

The researchers would have a shot at deciphering these phrases with an Ayleid reference work, and Denel says Skaleel may have such a book. She's in a snit over Jarol's inattention to the project; this has made her slow to volunteer her help, and made other researchers shy about asking for it. In the role of tactless newcomer, you can do what they can't. Go up the passage and ask Skaleel for "Ayleid reference" and she'll turn over *Ayleid Inscriptions and Their Translations*.

You can read just enough of this book on your own to see it might help. On page 1, you see that "av molag anyammis" means "from fire, life."

This is a double clue: One of the spells you must cast on the pillar is a Fire spell, and it comes first in the sequence. In fact, shoot a Fire spell at the pillar now. The strength of the spell and where you hit the pillar don't matter. Segments of the pillar rise and fall to reveal stairs leading down to a glimmering doorway.

You can't reach the door until you've cast four spells in the correct order—and, alas, this is the only part of the book you can figure out on your own. You need Delen's help with the rest. Talk to him about "Ayleid reference" and he'll take the book and ask you to read him the inscriptions for translation. You can do them individually or all together. Translate "magicka sila" either together with or after "magicka loria." On its own, it will be slightly mistranslated until you find its context.

In "av mafre nagaia," "mafre" means "frost." "Magicka loria" means "magic darkens" or "wanes." And "magicka sila," translated in isolation as "magic shines," emerges in context with "magic wanes" as "magic waxes." Hence, spells that do Frost damage and that damage and fortify Magicka will fill out the sequence.

Execution is tricky. First off, do you have these spells? (Scrolls work, too.) We hope so, since neither Skaleel nor Denel sells them. If not, trek to Cheydinhal, or perhaps farther, to find them. Any Fire, Frost, and Damage Magicka will work. (Note that the "damage" in "Damage Magicka" should be taken literally; Drain Magicka and Absorb Magicka spells won't work on the pillar.)

Moreover, most Fortify Magicka spells are cast on your character, and this one needs to be a targeted spell in order to hit the pillar.

Diligent explorers will be rewarded in Vahtacen. Denel stands near a chest containing a good many scrolls. Some useful, some not. Included amongst them are one of each get you through this challenge.

Finally, you must cast the spells in the correct order, following the inscriptions clockwise around the compass from the room's southwest corner: Fire, Frost, Damage Magicka, and Fortify Magicka. But you're not told this anywhere, and you may have to experiment.

What happens if you choose poorly? Like the mages before you, you'll get zapped by some or all of the four Dark Welkynd Stones in the corners of the room—with the severity of the shock tuned to the number of stones that have a direct line of sight to your location. (To avoid getting blasted at all, cast your spells at the pillar from a position down the southern corridor.)

When you've cast all four, the pillar disappears into the floor and ceiling. Descend the stairs into Vahtacen Tarn. (If you ask Denel and Skaleel first, you'll be unanimously selected for this task.)

This is larger than the small cleared portion of the ruin above the pillar. Watch for traps in the center of the first two large rooms and the corners of the third, and more than one dozen Ghosts or Wraiths all the way through.

The last room has a raised area in the center and no evident way to reach the top. East and west of this raised area, configurations of stones in the floor suggest that staircases can be raised at these points.

The switch is on the right at the top of the northern stairs. Now you can grab the Ancient Elven Helm and go back upstairs to Skaleel by one of three routes. She knows the helm is a real find and directs you to take it to Jarol. He's happy, and Polus is happy that Jarol is happy.

The cage protecting the Helm can be raised by hitting the button on one of the columns nearby.

NECROMANCER'S MOON

You should also be happy. The helm has been removed from your inventory for study, but you get a promotion to Conjurer and a snazzy new robe.

The Council of Mages is gathering information on the Necromancers. Among other places, they've sought data in Arcane University's Mystic Archives, but without luck. Polus thinks this course may yet prove fruitful, and he asks you to take a specific tack with archivist Tar-Meena: Ask about the Black Soul Gems you found in Falcar's quarters in the Cheydinhal recommendation quest.

Drop by the archives for a chat. The harried Tar-Meena is grateful to be asked about something specific and tells you to find a book called *Necromancer's Moon*. It's on a small table to the right of the door as you enter.

Tar-Meena runs the Mystic Archives, and is under pressure from the Council of Mages to offer information about what's going on.

Read it and consult with the archivist, who calls attention to a reference to "the Shade of the Revenant" and says it's OK to borrow the book. Bring it to Polus. He refers you to Bothiel (who's in the lobby) on this same reference.

And this rings a bell in Bothiel's head. She recalls that Falcar asked about the same thing some time back. He had a file of notes on the topic and dropped one. Bothiel smartly did not drop it in the recycling bin, and now passes this "Hastily Scrawled Note" to you. It mentions five primary sites—the Dark Fissure, Forts Istirus and Linchal, Pothole Caverns, and Wendelbek—and asserts that "altars have been raised; Anchorites have been called."

Polus recognizes the Dark Fissure as a cave in the mountains near Cheydinhal. He asks you to go there with the nebulous instructions to find "any connection to what we've learned"—and to not get yourself killed.

See Chapter 21 World Map/ Nibenay Basin Map marker #52.

It's easy to reach, though mountainous terrain requires a roundabout route. You've been to Vahtacen, and the Dark Fissure is across the river to the east-southeast and closer to Swampy Cave (which you may have visited in the Mystery at Harlun's Watch mission for the Fighters Guild). You'll recognize it from a distance from the altar out front and the column of spectral light beaming from the heavens.

The Necromancers have created altars to worship the King of Worms.

There's no need to explore the cave. (Polus cautioned you to watch your step.) Watch as a Worm Anchorite emerges from the fissure and uses the altar to exchange Soul Gems for Black Soul Gems. You'll get a journal entry about what you've seen. Report to Polus for promotion to Magician and a referral to Arch-Mage Traven—the source of your remaining guild quests.

If you get trigger-happy, and take down the Worm Anchorite before he has a chance to perform his ritual, don't worry. He carries a note that details what the Necromancers are up to, and Polus will accept this in lieu of witnessing the actual event.

Black Soul Gems

Evil-doers rejoice! You too can make use of the Necromancers' altars to create black soul gems of your very own. Simply visit any altar on a night when the spectral lights shine down on them, and bring along some grand soul gems. Place them in the altar, and cast any Dispel magic at the altar, and the gems will be converted to black soul gems, suitable for trapping the souls of any human (something normal soul gems can't do).

HANNIBAL TRAVEN'S QUESTS

LIBERATION OR APPREHENSION?

Traven is either in his third-room quarters or the second-floor Council Chamber. The guild has long had a man working undercover within the Necromancers' organization, but Arch-Mage Traven has not heard from informant Mucianus Allias for

some time. This has inspired fears for his safety and concerns about the reliability of his information. Has his cover been broken, or has he gone over to the other side?

Hannibal Traven, Arch-Mage of a guild under siege. He'll be your contact for the remaining Mages Guild quests.

The guild has dispatched battlemages to Allias's last known location—the Ayleid ruin Nenyond Twyll, south-southeast of Imperial City—to bring him in for questioning. But Traven fears for Allias's safety at the hands of the mages—first that he'll be seen as just another Necromancer in a Necromancer stronghold and second as a perceived defector. You're to make sure Allias returns safely to Arcane University.

See Chapter 21 World Map/ Great Forest Map marker #36.

It turns out that the battlemages beat you to Nenyond Twyll, then the Necromancers beat the battlemages. The mages are dead, save for Fithragaer, whom you may meet a short distance into the ruins (if the undead don't kill him first). He says the Necromancers were waiting for the battlemages, and that Allias ("this traitor") must have told them they were coming.

With that, he orders you to follow him, but don't! He runs into the trap at the foot of the stairs, and dies.

This leaves you to batter a path through the undead, a half-dozen Necromancers, and two Necromancer bosses (not to mention a range of nasty traps) down to Mariette Rielle, who tells you before she attacks that it's all for nothing. Allias has been reduced to a Worm Thrall—essentially, a Zombie slave.

You must find the undead edition of Allias to confirm this assertion. This is tricky, as he's not standing around with the other baddies, but is concealed behind a secret door at the east end of the huge bottom chamber in Nenyond Twyll. The switch to open the door is in an alcove north of the door.

Return first to Traven, then to Polus (to whom you'll continue to go for promotion), who promotes you to Warlock. This carries with it free access to the Council Chamber—meaning folks there will no longer act indignant at your presence there.

Mucianus has met an unfortunate fate, and is beyond your help when you arrive.

The vampire hunters gather in the Two Sisters Lodge twice a day.

INFORMATION AT A PRICE

Janus Hassildor, the guild's Vampire ally in Skingrad, has important information, but he won't hand it off to just anyone. He has requested that you pay him a visit. Why you? Traven doesn't know, and Polus ventures it's "rather unlike him."

The reason is plain to you after your last encounter on a dark country road: Hassildor thinks you can be trusted—and has some doubts about the trustworthiness of the rest of the guild. And he's right.

Go through Hal-Liurz in the Skingrad castle lobby, and the count will see you. He isn't going to cough up the info at "hello." He wants you to "take care" of "a small nuisance" first.

Vampires have taken up residence in nearby Bloodcrust Cavern. Moreover, their presence has drawn to Skingrad a group of at least three Vampire hunters. Both of these groups present problems, but the count can't act against either without the risk of calling attention to himself and his special status. However, you operate under no such constraints and can kill the Vampires and either kill, help, or preempt the Vampire hunters.

You have several options. The best solution, and the least labor-intensive, is to help the Vampire hunters succeed in their mission by telling them where the Vampires are.

You can do that right now, without a visit to the cave; you'll have to locate the Vampire hunters first. Hassildor didn't know their whereabouts. (In matters vampiric, he maintains a low profile.) But they must be staying at an inn. There are two in Skingrad: the West Weald Inn (at the west end of the northern part of the town) and the Two Sisters Lodge (in the south part at the center of the cluster of buildings west of the church).

If you go to the first, proprietor Erina Jeranus will point you toward the Two Sisters. And at the Two Sisters, Mog gra-Mogakh confirms the hunters come in to eat in the afternoon and go to bed around midnight. (You can get a similar tip from Mog's sister, Ugak, at the Grateful Pass Stable west of the city.)

Stake out the inn until they show. They'll be in the dining room between 1 p.m. and 4 p.m. and in their rooms on the top floor from 11 p.m. to 7 a.m.

Tell the leader, Eridor, you have information for him, and that the Vampires are in Bloodcrust Cavern. He'll thank you for the tip. The four hunters take off for the cavern. Potentially, you have killed two birds with one stone—or, at worst, killed one bird and nicked another.

See, the Vampire hunters may or may not complete the job. This is not a scripted event, and there is no way to predict its outcome. All you can do is wait for journal entries that the Vampires have been cleared out of Bloodcrust and that the Vampire hunters either are dead or have left town. If you don't get both in a day's time, poke your head into the dungeon to see what's gone wrong—and mop up.

It's easy enough to directly follow Eridor and his men on their trek to the cave. Once inside, stay far enough behind that the vampires attack them first; you can be waiting in the wings to finish off whoever survives.

Alternatively, you can take care of the Vampires yourself. Present yourself at Bloodcrust Cavern east of the castle and kill them. It's not that tough. They're spread out, none is more than a level above your own, and seven are at your level. Take a portion of Vampire dust from one of the bodies—even if you already have Vampire dust from a Vampire encounter elsewhere in the game.

The vampires in Bloodcrust Cavern can be formidable enemies…unless you let someone else do the fighting for you.

This has its risks. In each encounter with a Vampire, there is a small chance you'll be infected with porphyric hemophilia—the disease that causes vampirism.

Now seek out Eridor and tell him the Vampires are dead. He asks for proof. If you have even a single portion of Vampire dust from Bloodcrust Cavern—the other nine Vampires can still be alive—you can provide it. Eridor and his pals give up and leave town. That's persistence for you.

A third possibility for players who enjoy difficult approaches is whacking everybody on your own. Be especially careful about killing the Vampire hunters. Not because they're particularly hard guys (Carsten is two levels above your own, Eridor and Vontus Idolus are each one level above, and Shamar is your equal), but because you may bring the law crashing down on your head. Hassildor has already cautioned twice that he can't rein in the Skinguard guard on your behalf.

However, Eridor's useful in this cause. Ask him where he's looking for the Vampires and he'll tell you: "Shamar's up by the statue, Vontus is out in the high pasture, and Carsten has the town exit near the castle covered."

It's possible (though difficult) to rub out the men at each of these locations without the Skingrad guards being any the wiser. Your best bet is a single killing blow—delivered from behind with a poisoned weapon. Kill Eridor in his bed at the Two Sisters—when he'll be initially unable to respond and without armor.

In any case, when both sides of the quest are complete, return to Hassildor for the promised information payoff: A powerful Necromancer named Mannimarco has arrived in Cyrodiil. Other Necromancers are flocking to him—some guild members have even defected—and the count suspects he has bad things planned for the mages.

If you've played earlier Elder Scrolls games, the name Mannimarco may ring a bell. He's a powerful Necromancer who's been around a very long time, and was directly involved in the events that occurred in Daggerfall.

You won't get a promotion after this quest. You won't even get another quest immediately. Traven says his attention is occupied by the Council of Mages. Try him on the third day after you wrap up "Information at a Price."

A PLOT REVEALED

Traven reports that the Council of Mages has been thrown into "disarray" by the presence in the province of Mannimarco—a.k.a. "King of Worms." As Hassildor intuited, the Necromancer has targeted the Mages Guild—Traven does not say in what way—but Mannimarco's reasons are unclear and the guild has received no demands.

Of course, the whole concept of "demands" implies a plan for continued coexistence of the guild and the Necromancers. And you're about to find out that this isn't the case.

Traven sends you to Bruma. He has not heard from Jeanne Frasoric, the bubbly leader of the guild branch there, for several days and worries that "something may be amiss, given recent developments."

You could say that. The Necromancers have invaded the Bruma guild, killed Frasoric, Volanaro, and Selena Orania, and set the place on fire. You must kill the undead creatures (ranging from Zombies to Wraiths) on the ground floor and in the cellar to reach a single Necromancer (Camilla Lollia, who's pitched one level above your own) in Frasoric's upstairs quarters.

The Bruma Mages Guild has been almost completely destroyed by Mannimarco and his minions.

Once Lollia goes down, J'skar, whose invisibility provided the source material for your Bruma recommendation quest, decloaks nearby. He witnessed everything that happened—and since then has been playing hide and seek with Lollia, whom you may have heard taunting him. He saw the King of Worms standing over Volanaro, sucking his soul out of his body, and saying "something about Echo Cave and destroying the Mages Guild."

J'skar reveals what he saw while hidden during the fighting.

And with that, the frightened mage takes off for the protection of Imperial City. You'll find him later, no longer invisible, in the lobby of the Arch-Mage's Tower. You needn't share his fears—Mannimarco won't return to the Bruma guild—but should follow in his wake and get the intelligence back to Traven.

Again, the Arch-Mage needs three days to sort out a response. In the meantime, Polus promotes you to Wizard and provides the spell Wizard's Fury—a blast of Fire, Shock, and Frost damage that's tuned to your current level.

THE BLOODWORM HELM AND THE NECROMANCER'S AMULET

"At the worst possible time," begins Traven, "the council is in ruins." The mages have split over the council's response to the Necromancers' challenge—not on whether but how to fight back. Some higher-ups in the guild want to "fight fire with fire"—that is, use the dark weapons of necromancy against the Necromancers.

But the "fight fire with fire" folks—both regulars from your visits to the second-floor Council Chamber—have handled the disagreement in impolitic fashion. Two groups have swiped artifacts from Arcane University—the Necromancer's Amulet and the Bloodworm Helm—and carted them off to distant locations in the Cyrodiil hinterlands. In each case, Traven fears that the takers may fall victim to the Necromancers. And in the next two quests—straightforward retrieval missions running in parallel—you're charged with recovering the artifacts.

Both artifacts must be turned in to Traven to complete the quests, but no one ever said you couldn't use them before turning them in. Acquire one, and feel free to equip it in order to help you get the other. They both have significant bonuses for spellcasters.

The Bloodworm Helm crew, led by Irlav Jarol (who figured in Vahtacen's Secret), has taken that artifact to Fort Teleman to research its potential uses again Mannimarco.

See Chapter 21 World Map/ Blackwood Map marker #35.

Teleman is to the southeast near the Black Marsh border. If you've visited the Ayleid ruin Atatar in the Fighters Guild quest "Azani Blackheart," fast-travel to that location and make your way southeast down the river. If not, fast-travel to Leyawiin and head northeast through the Blackwood forest.

Jarol's the only guild member in evidence here, and he's dead—whether as a result of inappropriate experimentation or hostile action, we can't be sure. There's no shortage of enemies, drawn from an unholy alliance of Daedra and Necromancers. Hack your way through the two sections here to a big room at the bottom, take the helm from Jarol's corpse, and bring it back to Traven, who promises to keep it in a secure place in the Arch-Mage's Tower.

Irlav Jarol has fallen to the Necromancers.

The other godforsaken spot is Fort Ontus in the Colovian Highlands near the Hammerfell border. If you walked from Weynon Priory to Kvatch in an early stage of the Main Quest, you've passed close to this dungeon and should be able to fast-travel to Weatherleah, Rock Bottom Caverns, or Fort Diritch, then go west into the hills.

See Chapter 21 World Map/ Colovian Highlands marker #11.

The dungeon residents—all guild turncoats dressed like Necromancers—are not hostile. (Not yet, at any rate.) They all tell you to talk to Caranya. She's down in the second section. Getting to her may seem difficult owing to the heavy-duty locks on the first door into that section and the first gates you find into Caranya's sanctum after you enter Fort Ontus Halls.

This just means you haven't gone far enough into this section or looked hard enough. You can open the portcullis southwest of Caranya using the lever on your side.

Caranya has no intention of giving up the amulet. She means to pass it along to Mannimarco. With a colorful remark about the King of Worms sucking out your bone marrow, she attacks you.

Caranya's a tough character, with spells drawn from the Necromancer boxed set, and it's a tough fight. But she's made the same error as Caminalda in the recommendation quests: She let you get close to her, and that may be her undoing.

Take the amulet from her body and go out of the fort the way you came. Those once-peaceful guild turncoats attack you. You can also use the exit at the north end of Caranya's room, but you'll face heavier opposition that way.

The mages in Fort Ontus turn hostile as soon as you defeat their leader. You'll need to fight your way back out.

First stop: a bewildered Traven, who says Caranya was among his "most trusted advisors." Then to Polus for promotion to Master-Wizard. That makes you his equal in rank. Where can you go from here?

AMBUSH

You've checked the guild insurrection and now can turn your attention to taking on the Necromancers. You're to rendezvous with a group of battlemages dispatched to intercept a unique Black Soul Gem and prevent its delivery to Mannimarco. You don't know what the gem does, but Traven thinks it may be a means of saving the beleaguered guild. (In short, he's joined the "fight fire with fire" crowd.) And that's all he'll say until you complete the quest.

See Chapter 21 World Map/ West Weald marker #23.

The battlemages—Thalfin (the leader), Merete, and Iver—are waiting for you outside the Ayleid ruin of Silorn near Skingrad. Your nearest fast-travel destination is Bloodcrust Cavern. From the cave, make your way southeast across the headwaters of the Strid River into the ruins. Speak to Thalfin, and she'll lead you to a point closer to the site and brief you.

Thalfin has been leading the now-botched mission at Silorn, but lets you take over when you arrive.

The original plan called for a direct assault on the site. But that's impossible due to an enchantment on Silorn's door, and, after an abortive attempt that cost the party one member, the mission has been recast as an ambush. From activity at the site—two guards are patrolling outside—Thalfin judges the Necromancers should emerge soon.

She also tells you that, on Traven's instructions, you're in charge and asks for orders. You can either prepare for the ambush—assigning the three battlemages to two spots in the ruins to the west—or wade in and take care of business yourself.

To get the ambush rolling, talk to each of the battlemages about "Abilities." You'll learn that Thalfin is more comfortable with an axe than a spell; Merete has a talent for "large-scale spells"; and that Iver is a proficient healer. Hence, the non-fighter Merete belongs in the northern spot, at a safe distance from the action, and the healer Iver in the southern, so he can apply his spells at close range. (Thalfin doesn't express a preference, but she's better off to the south.) If you pick the wrong spot, each suggests that they could be better used and you can reassign them after they're at their stations.

When everyone's in position, speak to Thalfin again. Keep an eye on the base of the stairs leading up to Silorn's entrance. Two Necromancers emerge from the ruin, join the two out front, and head east in single file.

Be careful when approaching the ruins. Getting too close will alert the Necromancers to your presence, blowing your cover. In the event that you find yourself exposed before getting your allies set up, run back to them and let the Necromancers come to you. Your guild-mates will jump in to help out.

The ambush draws gem-bearer Falcar out of the ruin. (Yes, Falcar, the Cheydinhal guild leader-turned-Necromancer.) Fix him in place with a Paralyze or Burden spell, kill him, and claim the gem without the need to fight your way into the depths of Silorn.

Be quick and accurate. When combat starts, Falcar tries to retreat into Silorn. If you're in the right position, this works to your advantage, as it separates him from the mob and gives you a clear target. Disregard Thalfin's cautions, circle around the statue, and come up on the Necromancers from the rear, blocking his retreat.

If this doesn't work, you'll have to do it the hard way. Silorn consists of three levels inhabited by lots of Necromancers and undead. Falcar is at the bottom. Take the gem from his body and return to the guild.

With Falcar defeated, only one last challenge remains

You've saved Traven. With the gem in hand, Mannimarco would have launched an assault on Arcane University. The special Black Soul Gem was designed to hold Traven's soul.

CONFRONT THE KING

But you've saved Traven only so that he may sacrifice himself for the greater good. After you accept a final assignment to confront the King of Worms in Echo Cave, Traven reduces himself to a Colossal Black Soul Gem.

Take the gem from the folds of his robe and fast-travel—to Cloud Ruler Temple if you've completed the Weynon Priory mission in the Main Quest, or to Bruma if you haven't—then go west to Echo Cave.

See Chapter 21 World Map/Jerall marker #4.

The cave door is locked; you can't pick it. Guard Bolor Savel holds the key. He says he will die defending it. Oblige him, which isn't hard, take the key, and enter.

Bolor Savel is only the first obstacle in your path to finally meeting Mannimarco.

Echo Cave is a big nasty Necromancer dungeon with Necromancers and undead spread over three levels. It's also home to Mannimarco—in the large room on the depopulated third level (Echo Necromancer's Chamber). The King of Worms is several levels above you. He has high-level Paralyze, Shock, and Summon Lich spells, and will give you a good run for your money. He's standing next to a switch that sets off "claw" traps all over the room.

Mannimarco himself awaits you in Echo Cave.

Ordinarily, he'd be able to turn you into a Worm Thrall (like poor Mucianus Allias) with his Enthrall spell. But the presence of the Colossal Black Soul Gem in your inventory is sufficient to prevent this. Thus robbed of his critical weapon, he's beatable. Close in and finish him off.

Loot the chests afterward—lots of good stuff—and play with Mannimarco's Staff of Worms, which has a nice reanimation effect on dead bodies. Return to the Arch-Mage's Tower, now your tower.

ROOM AT THE TOP

The Worm has turned. The Necromancers have lost their center of gravity, and the Mages Guild is intact—though its membership is reduced in number.

You're in charge. You were already de facto Arch-Mage before you set out on that final mission, so, on your return, Polus doesn't so much promote you as recognize your new status.

With the title comes a range of privileges. You now have access to the full range of guild facilities, including the Arch-Mage's quarters on the top floor of the tower. That's now your quarters.

 The Arch-Mage has access to his very own Spellmaking and Enchanting Altars. If you want, you never have to visit any of the other facilities in the Arcane University.

Once a week, you can have the guild supply you with additional portions of any ingredient, however rare or common it might be. You just have to put one portion of the ingredient you want in the chest in your quarters. Twenty-four hours later, there will be additional portions of that ingredient in there. But don't wait too long to grab them. After a week, they'll be cleaned out.

Magic with a practical use: this chest will provide you with ingredients of any one type once a week

Finally, you can enlist a single apprentice from Arcane University to follow you and fight alongside you. Ten of these generic characters wander the campus at any given time. If the apprentice dies in your service, or is dismissed by you, you can come back for replacements ad infinitum.

These are not the toughest folks in Cyrodiil, and they may serve mainly as buffers in combat. Each has one random Destruction spell and a full load of Warlock spells—meaning at least one spell from each of the following disciplines: Destruction, Alteration, Illusion, and Restoration. But they're also several levels below you.

The Apprentices may not be your strongest allies, but will eagerly follow you into battle if you so choose.

What can you do with your new pal? Well, Mannimarco is gone and the formal Mages Guild quests are at an end. But the Necromancers are around, and you can make mopping them up a personal project. The "Hastily Scrawled Note" from the Necromancer's Moon quest identifies five "primary sites," and we count numerous additional Necromancer sites.

FACTION QUESTS: THE THIEVES GUILD

OVERVIEW

Icon	Guild Rank	Fenced Items Requirement	Quest Requirement	Available Fence
	PickPocket	None	May the Best Thief Win	Ongar the World Weary
	FootPad	50 gold	Untaxing the Poor	—
	Bandit	100 gold	The Elven Maiden	Dar Jee
	Prowler	200 gold	Ahdarji's Heirloom	—
	Cat Burglar	300 gold	Misdirection	Luciana Galena
	Shadowfoot	500 gold	Taking Care of Lex	Orrin
	Master Thief	700 gold	Arrow of Extrication	Fathis Ules
	Guildmaster	1,000 gold	The Ultimate Heist	—

Initially, you may wonder if there is a Thieves Guild in Cyrodiil. Unlike the Fighters and Mages Guilds, it has no branch offices—not even the unofficial ones that exist within the seedier pubs in Morrowind. It has no obvious local representatives. And word of mouth suggests it doesn't exist.

The Thieves Guild does exist, but it isn't a conventional guild with an imperial stamp of approval. Secrecy is the organization's watchword; membership is exclusive and the initiation exercise rigorous.

Thieves Guild membership carries with it two unique advantages. By appealing to either of two doyens (guild lieutenants)—Armand Christophe in Imperial City and S'krivva in Bravil—you can reduce your current bounty by half. In other words, you'll spend half as much money to pay off fines to redeem your bad behavior.

S'krivva, the next Doyen

The guild also gives you access to five fences, who are parceled out over the quest line's course. They're the only merchants in the game who will buy your stolen loot. (They'll buy standard loot as well, but because fences strike hard bargains, you're better off selling your standard dungeon sweepings to regular merchants.) Moreover, you can buy back from a fence items you've sold to him or her. You'll lose some money on the deal, but it's fair payment to have the rights of ownership stripped away.

Even thieves have rules. The handling of bad treatment of fellow guild members will be familiar from the Fighters and Mages Guilds. Don't beat up on your fellow thieves and don't steal from them.

Punishment works differently here. You won't perform missions to redeem yourself, but pay fines.

Armand Christophe, your first Doyen

Fines
200 gold for theft
500 for assault
1,000 for murder
Plus additional 1,000 bloodprice for any unnecessary murders.

Moreover, no "three strikes and you're out" rule accompanies these penalties. You can offend to your heart's content and stay in the guild as long as you have the cash to back it up. And, finally, unlike the fines imposed by guards, the theft and assault fines do not accrue over multiple offenses. You can smack one guild member with your sword, or 10, or 100, and, if you're still alive after said whacking, you'll still have to pay only 500 gold. (Once you've assaulted one Thieves Guild member, they kick you out of the guild. At that point, they can't fine you again for assaulting a member because you are no longer a member.)

If this all seems permissive, the guild also has a no-killing-on-the-job rule that has no parallel in the other guilds. The Thieves Guild is about stealing stuff, not killing people. "We're not the Dark Brotherhood," says Christophe.

It works this way: If you're instructed to steal item X from the house of Y, then the person of Y, and any other persons occupying Y's house, must remain inviolate for the term of the quest. If they don't, the guild will hear about it instantly, you're out, and you'll have to pay a "blood price" of 1,000 gold per death for readmission.

However, note that the job doesn't start until you pass the door of the target structure. If you kill someone on the street outside the house of Y, the guild doesn't care.

This could get expensive. If you take on a Thieves Guild mission and leave it unfinished while performing other work that directs you into the same area, and you happen to kill some people, you'll owe the blood price, even though you were "on the clock" for Thieves Guild quests.

FINDING THE THIEVES GUILD

There are two routes into the Thieves Guild. One way is to read a wanted poster for the "Gray Fox." They are all over Imperial City. A few of the 20-plus locations: next to the Arena entrance, next to the exit from The King and Queen Tavern in Elven Gardens, on the left wall inside the Divine Elegance shop in the Market District, next to the exit from Talos Plaza District to the Temple District, and beside the lighthouse entrance in the Waterfront District.

The Gray Fox wanted poster

Reading this document gives you the topics "Gray Fox" and "Hieronymus Lex." You have to talk to a beggar whose Disposition is at least 70 before the beggar will ask, "Are you looking for him?" Choose the option that you want to work with the Gray Fox to get a tip to visit the Garden of Dareloth in the city's Waterfront District at midnight.

The second approach comes in the form of an invitation from the guild that you get only after you commit a crime and spend time in jail.

Any crime will do. It doesn't have to be a theft. (If it's a murder, you'll also win the interest of the Dark Brotherhood faction.) The offense doesn't have to be big or dramatic. Take something small that doesn't belong to you, which also ensures that the fine or jail sentence will be small. Do so under the eyes of the item's owner, so the offense will be detected. You'll know from the owner's reaction that it was.

The ultimate destination for all thieves, and one way into the Thieves Guild.

Wait for a guard to show up or go find one and talk to him. Select "Jail." Go to sleep to run out your sentence. When you wake, you find yourself outside the prison. And then…

…depending on where you are in Cyrodiil, it may take a while before the next step kicks in. If you're already in Imperial City, Myvryna Arano may reach you within minutes. If you're not, and you want to forge ahead with the Thieves Guild quests, wait where you are. She'll hand you a note that contains information on a secret meeting in the Garden of Dareloth at midnight.

 The messenger seeks you out only in the eight cities—not in the wilderness, dungeons, or rural-route locations like Weynon Priory, Cloud Ruler Temple, and the small settlements. If you're at the province's southern or western extremes— in Leyawiin or Anvil—it could be up to eight hours before Myvryna drops off her message. If you fast-travel between cities, it could take her even longer to find you. So if you want the note, stay in one city until she finds you.

To get to the Garden of Dareloth, fast-travel to the Waterfront District. The marker on your compass points you to the front door of a closed-up house. Though not identified as such here, this is Dareloth's house. Use one of the nearby arches to cut through the bank of houses and circle around to the back to find the real target. Wait there for the appointed hour. Congratulations. You've found the Thieves Guild.

ARMAND CHRISTOPHE'S QUESTS

MAY THE BEST THIEF WIN

Finding is not joining. You are not yet a member. Unlike the Fighters and Mages Guilds, the Thieves Guild requires a demonstration of your practical skills—rather than just a general indication of a level head. After two other would-be members, Methredhel and Amusei, show up around midnight, you can speak to Christophe about "Thieves Guild" and he'll give the three of you a challenge: Steal the diary of Amantius Allectus.

Christophe tells you virtually nothing about where to find the journal—just that it's in the Imperial City—but offers that beggars will help you for a price. Just one rule: You're not to kill Allectus or each other. (In fact, you can't kill either of your rivals—they are essential characters—but you can fight with them, to no good effect.)

Amusei, Armand Christophe, and Methredhel in the Garden of Dareloth

You have nothing to fear from Amusei. At this stage of the quest line, the Argonian is useless. He wanders fruitlessly in Talos Plaza.

Methredhel is another matter. During Christophe's speech, she exclaims that she'll have the diary before dawn. And when the speech ends, she runs for the causeway that leads northeast to the Temple District. She knows where she is going.

Do not follow her: For any but the fastest characters, this will cement her lead over you.

Make sure you have lockpicks. (If you don't, Christophe will sell them to you for 5 gold each.) Wake the beggar Puny Ancus, who's sleeping near the wall north of the meeting place, and bribe him to tell you what he knows about Allectus. He

reveals that Allectus lives at the Temple District's east end.

Fast-travel there, run to the east gate, turn south down the last lane before the gate, and pick the two-tumbler lock of the first door on the right. The diary is in the desk on the ground floor. (Read it; it's a short and gruesome account of the writer's attempt to develop a Vampire plant.)

Let's suppose you're not so quick off the mark. You arrive at Allectus's house to find the diary missing. Methredhel has beaten you to the punch. Indeed, if it's the same day, she's still here and will taunt you with her triumph. Then she'll vanish through a cellar trapdoor into the Temple Sewers, and you won't be able to follow her.

Vanish to where? Back to Christophe to claim her prize? No. Methredhel is subject to the same meeting constraints as you and won't reappear in the garden until late that night. Rather, she has retreated to her home and stowed the diary someplace safe. Or so she thinks.

Your journal prompts you to steal the diary back. You've only to bribe a beggar to learn that Methredhel lives at the north end of the Waterfront District.

This will be a fairly easy burglary. The door and chest locks are adjusted to your character's level, and Methredhel and her roommate, Adanrel, go out for dinner after 6 p.m. every day.

Let's suppose, again, that you missed the chance to steal back the journal. Methredhel is no fool. She returns the diary the next night and joins the guild. What then?

You get one more shot. This time, Christophe sends you to get Rohssan's sword. Bribe a beggar to learn that Rohssan runs an armory (A Fighting Chance) on the east side of the Market District. The sword's in a chest in Rohssan's upstairs quarters. You'll need to deal with the leveled locks on the door and chest and a guard dog within, but that's that.

Rohssan's watchdog

One way or another, with diary or sword, you've satisfied the guild's requirements. Meet Christophe behind Dareloth's house at the appointed time, and you're in at the rank of Pickpocket. You'll get most of the guild's commandments, as outlined previously. At some point during the quest, question him about the Gray Fox for your next bit of data: He's the thieves' guildmaster, though apparently he's uncomfortable with the title.

However, Christophe won't give you an assignment. Just as you had to prove yourself an able thief before you were admitted to the guild, you'll now have to demonstrate your commitment by fencing stolen items before you'll receive a mission.

INDEPENDENT THIEVERY

Christophe's advice on this score is broad. He charges you to find "a likely looking house," then to "break in and steal some stuff."

Where? Anywhere you like. You're operating under few restrictions. All of Cyrodiil is your beat. The no-killing restriction isn't even in effect, because this is not a quest. If you like, you can do all your freelance burglaries now. After you fence items worth a total of 1,000 gold, you'll be able to do the next 10 quests without interruption.

For now you have to sell to a fence at least 50 gold in stolen property before you can undertake the Untaxing the Poor mission. In the interests of efficiency and easy distance, move your operations to Bruma—the location of the only identified fence. That's Ongar the World-Weary, who lives on the south side of town.

Castles contain the most loot. But they also have lots of guards, and your chances of getting pinched go up. Shops are decent targets, too, but they're heavily locked and the best stuff is locked in keyless chests that are inaccessible. Middle-class houses offer few temptations—though they sometimes contain smidgens of loot—and lower-class houses have none.

Upper-class houses are guaranteed to contain something salable. If you do the Dark Brotherhood quests first, you'll make a number of these burglaries easy, as you'll see later in this chapter.

In targeting upper-class houses, you will bump up against the Dark Brotherhood quests; burglarizing quest locations may or may not cause problems for you later. In many cases, quest items appear only when the quest is running, so you can't take anything critical. Here are a few suggestions of houses you can try that contain upper-class loot:

Anvil: Heinrich Oaken-Hull's house is north of the Chapel of Dibella's east end.

Bravil: Ungolim's house is on Bravil Plaza's north side.

Bruma: Lyra Rosentia's house is in the town's northeast corner.

Honmund's house is north of the Great Chapel of Talos.

Baenlin's house is south of Lyra Rosentia's.

Cheydinhal: The Orum house is across the river from the Chapel of Arkay.

Chorrol: Rimalus Bruiant's house is in the town's north-central part.

Imperial City: Dorian's house is in Talos Plaza's south-eastern quadrant.

Jakben, Earl of Imbel's house is in the southeast corner of Talos Plaza's traffic circle.

Umbacano Manor is on the northeast corner of Talos Plaza's traffic circle.

Leyawiin: Alval Uvani's house is in the town's south-central part.

Rosentia Gallenus's house is in the town's west-central part.

Skingrad: Nerastarel's house is at the east end of the south part of town.

Summitmist Manor is also at the east end of the south part of town.

See the "City Maps" chapter for exact location of each house.

FENCING

Don't rush off to Ongar. Fences drive hard bargains. Ongar has a Mercantile skill of 60. That's probably better than yours. You're not going to get as much as you expect for your loot. Can you tweak this payoff?

Absolutely. It will pay off in your encounters with merchants in legitimate and illicit goods. The techniques covered here will work equally well when you need to enhance some other skill in a hurry.

Your first step is to boost your Mercantile skill—your ability to bargain. There are several ways to do this: permanently, by training with a character for a price or reading a Mercantile skill book; semipermanently, by finding and equipping an item with a Fortify Mercantile enhancement; or temporarily, by acquiring and casting the appropriate Absorb Skill spell or scroll.

Master Trainer

Those who can train you up to 40:

Foroch, who holds court at the Gottshaw Inn (southwest of Kvatch)

Mach-Na, who runs Mach-Na's Books in Cheydinhal

Those who can train you up to 70:

Margarte, the alchemy hobbyist in Leyawiin

Seed-Neeus at Northern Goods and Trade in Chorrol

Those who can train you up to 100:

Consult the "Master Trainer Quests" in the Miscellaneous Quests" chapter.

The other step is to chat Ongar up in the Persuasion mini-game. Make him like you. If he likes you, you'll get better prices. Take advantage of the ground you gain with him by coming back for more.

The first fence, Ongar the World-Weary

Granted, you will earn connections to new fences who have more gold than Ongar's rather sad 300. But they also have a progressively higher Mercantile skill—peaking at 100—and hence they're more and more stingy about parting with that extra gold. Start with Ongar and exhaust his gold before you move on to his comrades. Indeed, given your investment in his good nature, there's no need to move to the other fences at all. His barter gold will replenish in 1–3 days.

Fence	City	Barter Gold	Mercantile Skill
Ongar the World-Weary	Bruma	600	60
Dar Jee	Leyawiin	800	70
Luciana Galena	Bravil	1,000	80
Orrin	Castle Anvil	1,200	90
Fathis Ules	Imperial City Elven Gardens	1,500	100

UNTAXING THE POOR

The Imperial City doesn't usually collect taxes in the Waterfront District. The people here are poor, and Christophe says the receipts would barely cover the cost of their collection.

Hieronymus Lex, a "law and order" type in Imperial Watch, has broken the tradition. The Gray Fox, who has placed the Waterfront's people under his protection, wants to restore it. You're to play Robin Hood and steal the tax money and records.

The Gray Fox's nemesis, Hieronymus Lex

Your pal Puny Ancus can help you. Wake the poor fellow. He discloses that Lex has an office in the South Watchtower. Your compass and map now point you to a spot near Amantius Allectus's house in the Temple District.

Above the ground floor, you're trespassing, so be quick about it. Two ladders—the second to a locked trap door—take you up to Lex's quarters. Don't worry about the captain. He's out virtually all day on rounds, and if he's here, the erstwhile painter, the captain, is likely sleeping. Unlock the desk's leveled lock and get the gold and the records. Read the records, too, for a hint on the next quest.

Cart the stuff to Christophe without getting pinched—which could be tricky, depending on your timing—and he tells you to keep the gold, promotes you to Footpad, and, if you've fenced a total of 100 gold in stolen items, offers another mission.

THE ELVEN MAIDEN

On its surface, this is a very ordinary mission. Christophe dispatches you to collect a bust of the late Countess of Cheydinhal.

Fast-travel to Cheydinhal's West Gate. Seek out one of the city's beggars—Luckless Lucina or Bruccius the Orphan. It will cost you a small bribe to learn the bust is near the countess's guarded and haunted tomb in the undercroft of the Chapel of Arkay.

The bust of Llathasa Indarys

Inside the undercroft door, wait and watch the patrolling guard's movements. When she's in the eastern extremity, swoop in and grab the bust from the shelf in the western extremity. Then swoop back out again, before the guard can do anything, and leave the church. Fast-travel to the Waterfront. (The Ghost—or Wraith, depending on your level—appears only if you open the sarcophagus in the niche behind the bust.)

The Waterfront's full of guards! Usually, there are two at any given time. Now, with reinforcements pulled in from the nearby Temple District, there are four. And they are looking for Christophe and the bust.

This makes your midnight rendezvous an unlikely event. Christophe is hiding in the cellar of one of the Imperial Trading Company buildings. Your journal suggests asking fellow thieves about his whereabouts. You won't learn anything but the obvious on that score, but you'll hear that Methredhel is looking for you. Hang around for a while and she'll find you.

It turns out no one commissioned the theft of the bust. The mission was designed to nail a mole inside the guild. Unsurprisingly, this turns out to be Myvrynra Arano. (You can also pick up this morsel from Hieronymus Lex if you're nearby when he lets it slip in conversation with a guard.) Methredhel instructs you to pin the theft on the spy. Plant the bust in her Waterfront District home, then tell Hieronymus Lex she's the thief.

Arano lives in a shack west of Lex. This proximity and the guardsmen running back and forth past the house creates some trouble in getting past the leveled lock undetected, so be patient and wait for your moment. When you activate the cupboard near the bed (not the one to the left of the fireplace), the sculpture is automatically inserted.

As Methredhel suspected, you'll also have trouble persuading Lex of Arano's guilt. Boost his Disposition to 70, and he'll blow what's left of Arano's cover. Follow him into Arano's place. He searches the cupboard, confronts the informer, and charges her with the theft. Arano's revealing protests are to no avail. She goes to jail forever.

Will Christophe come out of hiding for your late-night meeting? He will. Along with your 100 gold reward, you'll get a promotion to Bandit and the identity of the second fence. Dar Jee, who lives in Leyawiin, has 400 in gold and a Mercantile skill of 70.

You also receive a referral to S'krivva in Bravil for future work. This quest's nugget of conventional wisdom on the Gray Fox is brought to you by any Wood Elf or Khajiit member of the guild: The Fox's identity is a secret.

S'KRIVVA'S QUESTS

AHDARJI'S HEIRLOOM

S'krivva's home is near Bravil's North Gate, but Christophe's advice was on the mark: Don't bug her there unless the door's unlocked. (She's a drug dealer on the side—she makes a regular skooma delivery every Saturday—and she values her privacy.) You're better off catching her at the Lonely Suitor Lodge (9 a.m. to 9 p.m. on Tuesdays and Thursdays and 8 p.m. to 10 p.m. daily for dinner).

 The door is unlocked a lot: 6 a.m. to 8 p.m. on Sundays, Mondays, Wednesdays, and Fridays; 6 a.m. to 9 a.m. on Tuesdays and Thursdays; and, on Saturdays, 6 a.m. to 10 a.m. and again from 2 p.m. to 8 p.m.

If you've fenced 200 gold in stolen loot, the Khajiit will have an assignment for you. Ahdarji, the widow of a former guild fence, has lost a beloved ring to a "street scavenger" (that is, a freelance thief) and is offering a reward for its return.

Find Ahdarji through beggars in her hometown of Leyawiin.

For a small bribe, either Rancid Ra'dirsha or Deel the Scalawag reveals that she lives on the west side of town, lunches at the Five Claws Lodge (specifically, from noon to 2 p.m.), and takes her dinner at the Three Sisters Lodge. (Indeed, she lingers there until midnight.)

You'll never guess who took the ring: Amusei, your ineffectual rival in "May the Best Thief Win." Ahdarji wants him dead but, after you explain about the guild's no-killing rule, settles for making him suffer.

On that score, the city guards have beaten you to the punch. Ask a guard with a Disposition of 45 or pay off a beggar to learn Amusei has been jailed for trying to blackmail Leyawiin's countess. The beggars throw in the wisdom that the guards can be bribed to allow a visitor to see a prisoner.

Armed with this knowledge, make your way to the castle dungeon, where you will be refused admittance to see Amusei before you can even ask. Bribery (20 gold) will work here. So will picking the pocket of the guard for the key to the cells. So will not asking for permission and making your way stealthily down the hall, picking the lock on the door to the cells and chatting with Amusei.

Offer him a lockpick, and he'll tell you how a fence told him the ring was too hot to handle. It had already been stolen before Amusei touched it. Inscribed "To Alessia," the ring belonged to Leyawiin's countess. Amusei planned to sell it back to her, and that's how he got pinched. She has the ring now.

"The countess rarely leaves the castle," says the thief. "Good luck getting it back." (Amusei will escape his cell when the quest ends.) A direct assault on the royal quarters isn't impossible, but you'll need to be an accomplished sneaker to pick the lock on the second door while avoiding detection by the two flanking guards.

Consult your journal. It suggests you check with Ahdarji or the beggars again. These options are mentioned in an almost incidental way, but in fact this is an either/or proposition and an important one.

If you talk to Ahdarji, she reveals that her attachment to the ring is more than sentimental. It is professional. The ring allows the wearer to read the count's private messages. Now she'll pay double (200 gold) for its return.

An extra 100 gold is not that much money; talk to a beggar instead. If you do, you'll get the name of a contact within the castle (countess handmaiden Hlidara Mothril). You'll pay 10 gold and also get a suggested place and time for your approach. (Ms. Mothril eats dinner in the castle at 8 p.m.) Not to mention a reference to a hidden torture chamber used for interrogation of Argonian immigrants from Black Marsh. There's an element in Leyawiin that loathes Argonians.

You'll find the lady in the dining room in the castle's County Hall a little after 8 p.m. Mothril is not a willing participant in the burglary, and she needs encouragement to spill the beans—a Disposition of 60 to speak about Alessia Caro's schedule (she goes to bed after 11 p.m. and is away in Chorrol from the 15th to the 17th); 70 to discuss the ring (the countess wears it all the time but puts it in her jewelry box at night); and 80 to note that the secret passage links the cellar to the royal quarters. (You can also learn about the countess taking off her ring at night from a stray remark to her lady in waiting—but you'll have to be close by at the time.)

Use the door in the castle lobby's southwest corner to reach the cellar. In the storage room at the hall's end, throw the switch in the barrel against the west wall to open a secret door nearby and follow the hall beyond first to the torture chamber, then to the royal quarters.

Entrance to the secret passage in Castle Leyawiin

If you observe basic caution, you shouldn't have to deal with anything worse than locks along the way. The only serious obstacle is the jewelry box (atop the dresser near the bed), which will have a tough lock, depending on your level.

Grab that document, *Divining the Elder Scrolls*, from the jewelry box as well. Its point is that the Elder Scrolls are prophecies. (This is our bit of Gray Fox arcana for this mission, though the connection won't be apparent for some time yet.)

Leave as you entered and make your way to Ahdarji and S'krivva for their separate rewards and promotion to Prowler.

MISDIRECTION

Hieronymus Lex, the Imperial Watch captain with the no-tolerance position on the Thieves Guild, has sent guards from all over the city into the Waterfront District with a view to capturing the Gray Fox. The Fox is safe, but the guild's work isn't getting done, and S'krivva wonders how long this can go on.

If you've fenced goods worth 300 gold, S'krivva sends you to the city to locate Methredhel, who is handling the guild's response to this crisis.

Sure enough, if you visit the Waterfront, there is a crush of guards asking after the Gray Fox; a curfew in effect; Christophe under effective house arrest; Lex, in his old spot near Myvrynra Arano's house, declaring the district "closed for business"; and no one saying anything much about anything.

You can draw a bead on Methredhel's location—Dynari Amnis's house in Talos Plaza—by bribing a beggar with 15 gold in any other Imperial City district. (Traditional Waterfront informer Puny Ancus has been consigned to the Abandoned

Shack for the period of the lockdown, and he's got the same "curfew" line as everyone else.)

Methredhel has a plan to force Lex to redeploy his resources and thus loosen his grip on the Waterfront: Five guild operatives will simultaneously stage burglaries at prominent locations across the city. You're to steal Hrormir's Staff from the Arch-Mage's room at Arcane University and, just in case the mages are slow-witted today, leave a note from the Gray Fox in his nightstand suggesting that other precious items may also disappear unless university security is beefed up.

The theft is easy. Visit the topmost room in the central Arch-Mage's Tower either as instructed—when Hannibal Traven is sleeping (1 a.m. to 7 a.m.)—or when he's downstairs in the Council of Mages chamber (9 a.m. to 11 p.m.) Take the staff from the table and activate the nightstand to insert the note. (The requirements are the same if you're an Arch-Mage.)

While you're at it, collect the document *Fragment: Song of Hrormir*, from the top of the little bookshelf to the right of the Altar of Enchanting. This is more Gray Fox trivia—an extract from an epic tale that alludes to the theft of the Gray Cowl from Daedra lord Nocturnal. ("Mortal man hast taken it from me unaware.")

The Archmage's room and Hrormir's Staff

Did you wonder why this seems easy? Those guards running around in the Waterfront slums aren't new characters added to the game for this purpose. They're drawn off from other Imperial City districts—specifically Arcane University (two from the day shift and two from the night) and Temple District (one from each shift).

This has useful implications for a player struggling to meet the requirements for fencing, and you may want to stretch out this quest and take advantage of the reduced police protection to build up some credit with fences Ongar and Dee Jar. Admittedly, the Temple District doesn't have any pure upper-class homes, but a number are on the cusp between middle- and upper-class loot. And the university is thronging with stealable items.

In any case, return the staff to Methredhel, and she'll dispatch you to the Waterfront to spy on Lex—sticking to him closely enough to overhear any conversation. The assumption here is that he'll eventually receive an order to restore the borrowed guards to their original duties.

Lex is still between Arano's old place and Christophe's shack in the slums. You'll scarcely have approached him when a Dremora appears to the north, walks up to the captain, and delivers a note.

Lex gets new orders.

Keep an eye on that note. Lex drops it and it skitters away from him. Retrieve it to discover that it's from Raminus Polus of the Mages Guild—and isn't so much an order as a threat. But the threat works. Lex calls off the dogs. You can watch as the city watch clears out and the people return.

Return to Methredhel (still at Amnis's place) and she gives you one last job: Return Hrormir's Icestaff to the Mages Guild. Not directly—that would be too dangerous—but to a "safe chest" in the home of former university researcher Ontus Vanin.

The house is in the north wall in the district's southwest corner, and the chest is upstairs against the southeast wall. Hit it in the p.m. on a weekday, and Ontus won't be home. He takes lunch and dinner out and in between, shops until he drops—in stores with a magical bent. The staff is automatically inserted when the chest is activated.

You're done. If you stop in to see Methredhel on your way to Bravil, you'll find she's already returned home to the Waterfront District. Your reunion with S'krivva will be accompanied by a reward of 300 gold, promotion to Cat Burglar, and the identity of a third fence. (That's Luciana Galena in Bravil—with 600 gold and a Mercantile skill of 80. She's at the Lonely Suitor Lodge from noon to 2 a.m.)

LOST HISTORIES

A thief named Theranis was sent to Skingrad to retrieve a book called *The Lost Histories of Tamriel* for the Gray Fox. He has not returned. If you've fenced goods worth 400 gold, S'krivva will send you in his footsteps.

Fast-travel to Skingrad and find the beggar Foul Fagus or Nigidius the Needy. Bribe one or the other with 20 gold, and he'll tell you that Theranis was bragging at the Two Sisters Lodge about having stolen something from Castle Skingrad. Theranis didn't figure on Watch Captain Dion being present for this confession. Result: Theranis was imprisoned.

The beggar doesn't rate your chances of seeing Theranis on visitor's day that highly. He suggests two options: Get arrested or break into the jail.

But there is also a third: get a job in the castle. This is both the easiest solution and the most involved. Ask at the castle—or ask a Breton, High Elf, Imperial, Nord, or Orc in town—about "Work in Castle Skingrad" for a referral to Shum gro-Yarug, the count's butler. Follow up with a question about the butler himself to learn he leaves the castle for the West Weald Inn at 10 a.m. and moves to the Colovian Trader at noon.

You're hired as the "slop drudge" who brings food to the prisoners. Shum gives you a description of tasks and prohibitions, then you can go to work. Look for the dungeon door up the stairs to your left in the castle courtyard. Identify yourself to the jailer, and he admits you to the cell block.

Getting tossed in the clink is quicker. If you don't have Open spells, make sure ahead of time that you have lockpicks, so one will accompany you into your cell. Lift a bit of fruit from the table in the castle lobby and select "Jail" when the guard runs up and does his law-enforcement spiel.

Finally, sneaking and lockpicking will work. It's the hardest of the three approaches—the jailers have a high Sneak skill and the leveled locks start at three tumblers—one well within the abilities of an accomplished thief.

One way or another, you're in jail. And Theranis isn't here. But tell the lone inmate, Larthjar the Laggard, that you're here to rescue him. This bumps his Disposition up 20 points and he'll tell you what became of your quarry. (This is not the right moment to critique Larthjar. If you do, his Disposition falls 40 points.)

Larthjar relates that the "Pale Lady" has taken Theranis from the jail three times, and this time he has not returned. A bad sign. No explanation of who this "lady" might be, but Theranis's Argonian cellmate was taken a short time ago and put up a hell of a fight. There's a good deal of blood about.

If you got yourself arrested, open the cell door with a pick or spells. Follow the blood trail that leads from the cell next door to the blank wall at the hall's end. Activate the "strange candle" on the right to open a secret door and enter the wine cellar at its end. When the hall ends in a wall, use the handle to the left to open a second secret door. You're in the butler's quarters—and now take in the full meaning of his line about staying out of the wine cellar.

The bloodstains continue into the cask room. Activate the rightmost of the three sconces to open the front of the central cask. Down the passage beyond, you're attacked by the Pale

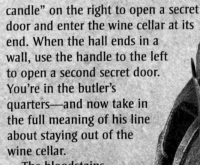
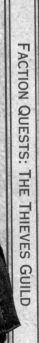

Lady—a flimsy Vampire—and find Theranis (dead; activate his body for a journal entry) and the Argonian prisoner (Amusei, in trouble again—this time for stealing a fish). Amusei's grateful for your rescue and says he'll join the guild. He has a message for the guild from Theranis, which he'll pass along if you get him out.

The Pale Lady in her secret chamber.

Two escape routes present themselves—through the jail or through the wine cellar and the castle proper. Both can work if you have a decent Sneak skill and hit the patrols right—the patrolling guards have a high Sneak—but the wine cellar route is the better one, with fewer chances of detection. Avoid bringing Amusei down the main castle staircase, and instead make for the courtyard through the northeast door on the lobby balcony.

Outside the castle, cross the bridge and head down the path toward Skingrad. Halfway down the hill, you get an journal entry. Talk to Amusei about the book and get Theranis's message: "Look under the bush near the well, behind Nerastarel's house."

Nerastarel's house is in the southern part of Skingrad—north of the South Gate. The message is correct. The book is near the well behind the house, between a bush and a rock. Read it if you like; it's a brief account of how, "once a prophecy contained in an Elder Scroll is enacted in Tamriel, the text of the parchment becomes fixed…. It becomes a historical document declaring the unequivocal truth of a past event." (This doubles as the Gray Fox tidbit for this mission.)

Why is the Gray Fox looking for this info so urgently? Return the book to S'krivva for a payment of 400 gold.

TAKING CARE OF LEX

Though twice thwarted, Hieronymus Lex is still a problem for the guild. If you've fenced 500 gold worth of stolen items, the Gray Fox (via S'krivva) asks you to "eliminate" him. To be sure, the guild's rules on killing are still in force. "Eliminate" is an unfortunate choice of words. S'krivva means eliminate Lex as a threat—by getting him a new job.

As it happens, Anvil's countess is looking for a guard captain. The commander of the Imperial Watch has sent her a list of candidates. This list does not carry a strong recommendation for Mr. Lex, who, through his own heavy hand and the guild's own concerted efforts, appears as something of a screw-up.

This letter has arrived in Anvil and currently resides in the desk of Dairihill, Countess Umbranox's steward. (She wants her cousin to get the position and has lied to her ladyship about the letter's arrival.) The Gray Fox wants you to steal that list and arrange manufacture of a new one that makes this perennial thorn in his side sound like the best thing since sliced bread.

Now, why give Lex this particular job? S'krivva doesn't know, but says the Fox "has extended his protection to the Umbranox family and Lady Umbranox in particular." (This is the quest's one new disclosure on the Gray Fox, and you'll get a wrap-up of earlier ones when you visit the Anvil court.)

You need an accomplished forger, and you'll have to find one on your own. S'krivva says only that she doesn't know of one in Bravil. And then, the crowning touch: You're to sneak into the Imperial Prison and use the legion commander's seal to make it all nice and official before you deliver the list personally to the countess.

Orrin opens the secret passage in Castle Anvil.

First off, you need that letter. How this unfolds depends on whom you approach. Most people in Castle Anvil will tell you the steward's office is in the private quarters and that Dairihill is not there much—she spends her mornings in the audience chamber and takes dinner at 8 p.m. with the countess. That enables you to set up a burglary timed to her absence. You'll have get through two locked doors, slip by a guard, and open a locked desk.

But there's an easier way. Start in Anvil proper. Speak to one of the beggars—Penniless Olvus or Imus the Dull—to learn nothing about "Dairihill's Office," but that the castle has "secret ways and secret people." "Find the blacksmith," says the beggar.

Your journal doesn't know what to make of this. But, indeed, there is a blacksmith north of the castle lobby. Orrin's a Thieves Guild member—and, soon, one of your fences—and will show you a secret door that bypasses the guard and one of the locks. It's in the little wine cellar north of the main smithy room, and is opened by activating the right-hand column of two that bracket a niche in the north wall. (You can find and use it on your own.) At the top of the stairs within, press the left-hand column to open a second secret door. The steward's office is around the corner to the west. You'll have to master leveled locks on the door and desk before you can grab the list of candidates.

There are two exits from the secret passage. One leads to the castle staff's private chambers. The other leads to a secret cave under the castle. It has an outside entrance to the harbor. Nobody lives here, so you can make it your own if you want.

"Hieronymus Lex, overly fanatical—not recommended," reads the entry.

Now to find a forger. Again, the Anvil beggars are helpful. For a bribe of 15 gold, either will point you to an individual, known only as "A Stranger," who lives near the Anvil Mages Guild. (In fact, right next door to the Mages Guild—in the falling down Abandoned House.) A Stranger, whoever he is, will need 24 hours for the forgery and a fee of 500 gold to turn over the document giving Lex his highest phony recommendation.

The Stranger, who is a master forger and much, much more.

Now for the seal. The Imperial legion commander's office is in the northwest part of the outer ring of the same Imperial Legion District that houses the prison. This won't be easy. The area is patrolled, the building is often inhabited (it's the Mess Hall), and it is locked up tight as a drum. The three locks on the path to the seal, in quick sequence, will test any player's lockpicking skills: the left-hand outside door, the door inside and to the right, and the lock on the trunk to the left of the legion commander's desk.

You won't take the seal, but use it automatically on the forged letter when you select it. It's off to Anvil for a morning audience with the countess. (You can talk to her at 8 p.m. when she comes down for dinner, but she doesn't like mixing business and pleasure.) Looks like you got there just in time; she was prepared to give the job to the steward's cousin. She approves the assignment and asks you to deliver the

reassignment order to Lex personally. "The look on his face should be priceless," reads your journal.

Can this play out differently? Sure. We like to tell Dairihill about the letter, watch her sputter, trapped by her own deceit, then withhold the letter, give it to the countess, and finally come back to Dairihill for our 20-gold tip for the delivery. Life is sweet.

So where's Lex? He's on his rounds. You can catch up to him on the road or wait for him to catch up to you at the South Watchtower in the Temple District (where he stops for lunch for two hours at noon) or The Bloated Float on the Waterfront (where he stops for dinner for two more hours at 6 p.m.).

He sees the Gray Fox's dirty hand in his transfer. And he's right—but doesn't he sound paranoid now? You can't help but feel a bit sorry for him.

Lex takes off for Anvil. If you're curious, check in at the castle to find he's in town guard armor and has joined the patrols.

After traveling to Anvil twice and the Imperial City twice, you are done with this marathon. Go to Bravil and S'krivva for promotion to Shadowfoot, a reward of 500 gold (plus 500 gold reimbursement for the forgery), and access to a fourth fence— your pal Orrin from Castle Anvil. With 800 gold and a Mercantile skill of 90, Orrin's easiest to find in the castle smithy.

That's your last mission from S'krivva. But patience. Before long, provided you've fenced stolen goods worth 600 gold, you're going to see a familiar face.

THE GRAY FOX'S QUESTS

TURN A BLIND EYE

If you stay put in Bravil, Methredhel will appear a couple of hours after you complete Taking Care of Lex, and she tells you the Gray Fox has a job for you. No details, just that you're to meet him at Helvius Cecia's house in Bruma (see Bruma city map in the "World Maps" chapters). This formula will be used for each of the remaining quests.

Methredhel's behavior during this search recalls that of Myvrynra Arano if she sought you out after your release from prison in Finding the Thieves Guild. That is, she's sent out from the Waterfront District. She'll look for you only in seven of the eight cities—not in smaller settlements, the wilderness, dungeons, or in Bruma. (In each case, you'll get no message and no further prompting in the city where the meeting is to take place.) And if you leave a location when she's en route to it, she won't target your new location until she's reached the old one.

If you want the mission now, wait for her to catch up. If you don't, this will take a while.

The house is in Bruma's southeast corner. Cecia is waiting for you outside. The Fox, with the Gray Cowl hiding his face like a veil, is sitting by the fire downstairs. Greet him politely—smart-mouth him and you'll knock his Disposition down 5 points—and the guild leader will get down to business.

The first meeting with the Gray Fox.

It's a retrieval mission. The Gray Fox wants a great crystal called Savilla's Stone from the Temple of the Ancestor Moths—an "extensive and well guarded" monastery in the mountains of northeast Cyrodiil. (Essentially, it's a retirement home for blind Moth priests.) He is not specific about the stone's powers—saying simply it confers "...advantage." After you recover the stone, you're to meet the Gray Fox in Bruma again.

You're forbidden to shed "innocent blood" in this quest, but no blood price attaches to the deaths of the stone's guardians. This doesn't sound so strange at a distance, but it may when you reach the monastery and the "guardians" prove to be the blind priests. This sounds like the Gray Fox shaving the rules to suit his purposes. He must want the stone something bad. (Indeed, by the end of the quest line, the concept of "blood price" will have vanished.)

Your first step is to feel out the beggars. For 20 gold, any beggar will give you more background information than you'll get out of the monks at the site. The Moth priests serve in some Elder Scrolls–related capacity at the Imperial Palace. When their age advances or sight declines to the point at which they can't work, they go to the temple. Here, they live in a secret labyrinth and are said to be masters of fighting in darkness.

This is the second time in a row the Gray Fox has sent you on an Elder Scrolls errand. What is going on here? You can't find out yet—not until the end of the Thieves Guild quests—but a small slice of knowledge is a secondary reward for successful completion of this mission.

It's a long trip—especially by Thieves Guild standards. After all, you've been hanging out in cities and have probably been using fast-travel between them. If you've already performed the Daedric quest "Azura," you can do that here, too. From Azura's shrine, make your way east-northeast to the temple.

First, visit the three monks in the Monk's Quarters. Hjar, Holger, and Hridi are peaceful and blood price applies here. Play friendly. They'll play dumb to most of your questions, and you'll need to boost their Dispositions to 70 to get answers—Hjar fills in a few more details about the "blind monks," and Holger confirms that Savilla's Stone is in the catacombs.

Temple of the Ancestor Moths

They talk, but they don't say a heck of a lot. To understand what the monks are about, get the book *Pension of the Ancestor Moth*. You'll find one copy here and another in the temple proper at the far end of the nave.

The monks interpret the Elder Scrolls. So profound is the scrolls' wisdom that their readers are driven deeper and deeper into blindness. When the blindness becomes total, the monks come to the temple to nurture the Ancestor Moths, spin their silk into cloth, and embroider the cloth with the Moths' history. (The monks on the surface serve as facilitators.) The blind monks are also good with swords.

This takes place in that secret labyrinth. And if you can get Holger's Disposition up to 80, he'll lead you up the hill to the chapel and the adjacent crypt and unlock the crypt door, or you can pick it.

Through the locked door at the other end of the crypt, there are four levels of catacombs—three lightly populated with enemies and one (the third) heavily laden with traps.

It's OK to kill these folks. They'll try to kill you the moment they detect your presence, and, blind or not, they are good with those Akaviri Dai-Katanas. You'll face a "boss" equal to your level (on the bottom level), two sub-bosses (on the first and second levels), four Priests at your own level (all on the first), and four Rats.

Suppose you're not of a mind to kill a bunch of sightless, silk-weaving, retired priests—even if the Gray Fox says it's OK. You can avoid them. There aren't that many. And though the deep darkness here is a great equalizer, remember that you still have an advantage: If you carry a light source, you can see your enemies. (If you don't have one, you'll find three torches in a barrel in the crypt opposite the entry stairs.) They can't see you. All they can do is hear you, and you can control how much they hear. Sit a spell as the priests file by. (They'll observe their usual schedules for work, meals, and sleep.) Take an alternate route. The place is big enough that you can do that on the upper two levels. Take your shoes off, walk rather than run, and sneak rather than walk.

You shouldn't have much trouble with the traps in the Caverns of the Moth. Keep an eye out for tripwires and jump over them.

Savilla's Stone is on the central dais in the Shrine of the Moth. Unfortunately, it's not the only stone up there. The Dark Welkynd Stone on the pedestal nearby will zap with a Frost spell an exposed character within a certain range. If you have to fight the boss here, lure him away first and do battle on the earthen shelf that surrounds the room. Approach the stone from under the cover of a nearby pillar and the walls of the dais.

You can't hide from the stone using magic or your Sneak skill. However, you can cast a Frost-Shield spell to reduce damage. And you can time your dash for Savilla's Stone. The Dark Welkynd Stone can fire once every six seconds. That gives you a five-second window between shots to come out of cover, grab the stone, and get back under cover. Or dodge the bolts. Or use a Telekinesis spell to grab the stone from a distance.

You don't need to sneak back through the catacombs. The ramp in the east wall of the shelf leads up to an emergency exit that places you beside a well behind the Monk's Quarters. And on the way to the exit, in a chest on a little rise, there is a unique document—*Instructions: The Gray Cowl*—that sheds new light on your boss and the predicament of life at the top of the Thieves Guild.

The blind monks of the Ancestor Moths

You've come across speculation that the Gray Fox's Gray Cowl was stolen from the Daedra lord Nocturnal. This document suggests that she allowed it to be stolen and states that Nocturnal has revealed that the cowl carries a curse of utter anonymity. "His true nature shall be unknown to all who meet him," it reads. "His identity shall be struck from all records and histories…. He shall be known by the cowl and only by the cowl."

Get to Bruma. With the Gray Cowl document in your inventory, you can ask whether the cowl belonged to Nocturnal. Give him your source, and the Gray Fox confirms the document's accuracy.

A wonderful tool for a guildmaster who must live in shadow. But a terrible fate to be consumed by that shadow.

Arrow of Extrication

You must play the waiting game. Stay put. The same rules apply as before—except that this time, the messenger will seek you out in Bruma but not in Chorrol.

The messenger is Amusei, who has managed not only to join the Thieves Guild, but also to ingratiate himself with the Gray Fox.

You're to meet Mr. Fox at Malintus Ancrus's house in Chorrol (see the Chorral map in the "World Maps" chapter). It's at the southwest corner of town and, as before, the owner is waiting outside with an admonition not to keep Mr. Fox waiting.

The Gray Fox has been experimenting with Savilla's Stone and discovered he needs "something special" for his plans. You're to steal the Arrow of Extrication from Bravil court wizard Fathis Aren. You can kill Aren if need be—the Fox doesn't care anymore—but not in Castle Bravil.

Accept the mission, and it's off to that rustic city once again. (Blow off the Gray Fox, and everyone hears about it, and you'll take a guild-wide 5-point Disposition hit, plus an additional 5-point hit in dealings with the Gray Fox himself.)

Guards in Bravil (and castle folk generally) offer that Aren is a gloomy Gus said to hang around with Daedra, and that he has a room in the castle's north wing. A beggar with a Disposition of 70 or better, or one newly bribed with 20 gold, will mention that Aren also has a ruined tower outside town where he stores his choicest treasures. (If you pay for this intelligence, you'll also learn that the tower is southeast of Bravil.) Fathis alone can open the tower door, but beggars Wretched Aia and Cosmus the Cheat suggest a secret passage that links castle and tower.

So it sounds as though the castle is the place to start. It's easy to find the north wing. Pick the leveled lock on the middle door on the balcony above the castle lobby, and you're there. (The two guards flanking the door have a good Sneak skill and may take exception.) Inside, hang a left, pick another leveled lock, enter, and you get a journal entry that you've found Aren's chambers.

You can search the chests or cut to the chase; it doesn't matter (the treasure is random and will be different each time). If you open both chests, a pop-up message tells you that the arrow isn't in this room and you should look for a secret chamber. To find the secret passage, activate the right-hand column of those flanking the niche opposite the door. Beyond, another locked door leads to the Wizard's Grotto. Here begins the dungeon crawl.

The secret passage in Fathis Aren's room.

The grotto's the first of two sequential dungeons—the other is the Wizard's Lair—that link the castle to Fathis Aren's tower southeast of Bravil. It's a large waterlogged region with lots of distractions, and at one particular spot it's easy to miss the correct path.

At the first junction, kill or sneak past the creature there and unlock the gate that's straight ahead of you. Take the left of two ramps curving down to a broad watery channel to the south, and continue south until you see the floor fall away ahead of you.

This deep pit can deposit you in the calm waters of Niben Bay. Beware of the giant Slaughterfish in the underwater cave. The fish has some nice treasure in its belly, but the exit you want is near the top of the east wall—initially hidden by overhanging rocks.

Once past this point, everything is obvious. You unlock more gates and face Conjurers and Daedra. In the Wizard's Lair is a large room with stairs in the back right corner that lead up to the tower entrance.

Aren is waiting near the top of this tall and tattered surface ruin. (Also waiting, along the way, are other Daedra—all keyed to your level, with Stunted Scamps at Level 1 and Xivilia at Level 22.) You can't get to the big boss directly. Parts of the ring pathway on his level are missing, and it's too far to jump. So climb to the top of the stairs against the north wall, then drop a level on the gap's far side.

You can kill Aren, but a proper thief won't bother. His Sneak skill is a pathetic 5, and you can creep past him into his little alchemy lab, open the chest in the right rear corner, and swipe the tower key and the Arrow of Extrication.

But that's not the Arrow of Extrication. Aren doesn't have it. The "key-shaped arrowhead" is as good as it gets. The Gray Fox is disappointed, but talks about having the arrow repaired, as though it were a broken toaster. You'll still get your 500-gold reward, promotion to Master-Thief, and access to the last of the five fences—Fathis Ules. He's based in the Elven Gardens section of the Imperial City.

 He travels to Chorrol, where he'll hang at The Oak and Crosier, for the Miscellaneous quest "Sins of the Father."

Ules has 1,000 gold and a daunting Mercantile skill of 100. After the quest line ends, he'll become a fixture at guild headquarters.

The Fox doesn't drop any hints about his plans for these artifacts—alone among the Thieves Guild quests this one contains no hints about the guildmaster—but he alludes to making use of your talents in the near future and vanishes when you leave Ancrus's house. The "near future," in this case, means when you've fenced 800 gold in stolen goods.

BOOTS OF SPRINGHEEL JAK

If you hang out in Chorrol after completing Arrow of Extrication, Amusei may take as long as 36 hours to show up with a request from the Gray Fox for a meeting at Ganredhel's house in Cheydinhal (see the Cheydinhal map in the "World Maps" chapter). (The same rules apply to this search as applied in the prior two ones—except that Amusei now will find you in Chorrol and won't find you in Cheydinhal.) The house is near the front of the Chapel of Arkay.

Springheel Jak is a famous thief who died 300 years ago— and is said to have been buried with his boots on. You're to locate the grave and recover the magical boots. You have one lead: Jakben, the Earl of Imbel, is Jak's only known descendant. He lives somewhere in the Imperial City, and his house might contain a clue to the grave's location.

The first step is to bounce Jakben's name off a beggar and see if it sticks. An investment of 10 gold will be rewarded with information that the Earl of Imbel lives along the central rotunda of Talos Plaza and that he's a rather odd bird. He only goes out at night. (Refuse to bribe and you'll be misdirected to Bruma.)

It's easy enough to break in. The earl's out, and his servant, Gemmlus Axius, is asleep on Monday, Wednesday, and Friday nights from 10 p.m. to 2 a.m.

Alas, you're not going find much information. You can liberate an Imbel family genealogy from a locked desk in the earl's top-floor study, but it doesn't mention Jak by name or even hint at his gravesite. A journal entry suggests that you need to persuade the earl personally.

Another option is to question Axius. He'll give different replies depending on whether his master or Axius himself is home or not. (The servant goes shopping in the Market District on Tuesday, Thursday, and Saturday mornings and visits the Temple of the One from 8 p.m. to midnight on Sunday nights.)

Some of the replies are lies. But taken together, they present a picture of a dangerous man.

Moreover, look at what's not present in the house: a second bed. There's just the one for Axius. Unless the earl sleeps standing up, there's something you're not seeing here.

A mysterious entrance in Earl Imbel's basement.

That would be the catacombs, reached through a manhole in the cellar. It requires a key, and, as you'll learn from Axius if you wake him, Jakben has the only one.

And what would Jakben be doing sleeping in the catacombs? Well, Axius is pretty clear about that, too, though he doesn't use the key word: The catacombs are the family crypt and Jakben is a Vampire. That's why he's out prowling for his "supper" in the middle of the night and that's why you're supposed to be in danger when he returns.

Oddly enough, when you do meet the earl (which may take a while; he's rather elusive), he's as timid as his servant. He acts like a terrified robbery victim, and when you ask about "Springheel Jak's boots," he turns over the key to the crypt.

Skip the crypt. It's not essential. The earl is wearing the boots. You can kill him up in the house, take the boots (which boost your Acrobatics skill 50 points), and return them to the Gray Fox. Quest over. But if you attack him, his timidity will vanish and all of a sudden you're fighting a well-equipped Vampire Spellsword.

The real Jakben, Earl of Imbel

A visit to the crypt nets you another document that you can use to put a unique question to the Gray Fox at quest's end. Is it worth the trouble? Two Vampires are here. A third is likely, and five more are possible on top of that.

Kill 'em all, sneak around, and loot the coffins and chests, or just go after Springheel Jak's coffin, which is south of the entrance behind two locked doors and a Vampire patriarch.

Here is Springheel Jak's diary. It discloses that Jakben is Springheel Jak and that he once partnered with a famous thief—whose name he can't seem to recall. Is this the Gray Fox? That would fit: Jak died 300 years ago and you've heard that the Fox has been around for 300 years.

 If you haven't already killed Jakben, opening the coffin will be that undead gentleman's cue to charge on stage.

Get back to Cheydinhal and collect another 500 gold and, if you've read the diary, a bit of obscure Thieves Guild lore. The Gray Fox denies knowing Jak. He is not immortal. The cowl is handed down from master thief to guildmaster. There have been dozens since the first stole Nocturnal's cowl. "I am hoping to be the last," he says.

THE ULTIMATE HEIST

You'll need to have fenced 1,000 gold in stolen goods for this last mission. If you got the last 200 gold through the fence Fathis Ules, don't wait in the Elven Gardens for the messenger. It's one of the spots Amusei won't look for you. For the quickest turnaround, travel to the city's Waterfront District.

Amusei invites you to meet with the Gray Fox one last time—at Othrelo's house in the northeast corner of the Imperial City's Elven Gardens (see the Imperial City map in the "World Maps" chapter).

You're to steal an Elder Scroll from the Imperial Palace, something nobody has ever attempted, much less accomplished. The Gray Fox talks about the greater glory of the participants in this operation, but admits that he needs the scroll himself. He doesn't say why.

If you succeed, your reward will be "worth far more than mere money"—meaning, doubtless, the leadership of the guild and stewardship of the Gray Cowl. The Gray Fox has confessed himself weary of the burdens of the latter. You can't be promoted any further without displacing him.

It's a long and elaborate quest, and you'll have to perform a string of difficult tasks in a particular order. This is confusing, and at the end of the briefing, the Gray Fox gives you a book, *Plan for the Big Heist*, that lays it all out point by point.

The Elder Scrolls are kept behind a door that cannot be opened. Savilla's Stone, which you liberated from the Temple of the Ancestor Moths in Turn a Blind Eye, has revealed a hidden path around that door—a forgotten escape route called the Old Way.

However, the entrance to the Old Way is sealed. To unseal it, you must enter the palace cellars and activate the Glass of Time. "Whatever that is," the great thief adds.

He can't tell you much about the Old Way. The visions in Savilla's Stone are cloudy. The Fox has learned what items you'll need in your passage, but not the obstacles you'll face. Hence, you'll take with you the boots of Springheel Jak, which allow you to jump to an otherwise-unreachable position and protect you against damage when falling from a great height, and the Arrow of Extrication, which unlocks the last door. If you forgot to bring a bow, one of the skeletons in that room has one.

The Gray Fox has engineered events so that, when you reach a reading room in the palace, you'll receive the scroll from the blind priests. They'll think they're turning it over to a "notable" named Celia Camoran. But she'll be "unavoidably detained" and you'll step into her place. Thus, you're not to speak to the priests.

Some final caveats: Blood price vanishes during this mission. No guild penalties accompany any murders you may perform en route. However, killing is still not a good idea, as you may acquire a bounty—though the guild doyen can still halve it afterward—and a load of guards will be in the immediate area.

However, none of the plan is written in stone. "Of course, the chances of something going wrong with this plan are very high," says the Fox. "When that happens, you'll just have to get creative."

THE PALACE BASEMENT

Your first step is to find the "Glass of Time" in the palace basement. Fast-travel to the Palace District, enter the Elder Council Chambers, and hang a left. Follow the ring corridor to the locked door that leads to the crypt. Be stealthy here, as one guard is stationed close by and a second patrols the area.

The Glass of Time.

There's no sarcophagi here—just palace junk of various descriptions, albeit entertaining junk like the giant chair, giant club, giant crystal ball, and giant hourglass at the end of the ring corridor. Oh, and a guard that is likely to be patrolling down there.

The giant hourglass is the Glass of Time. Activate it for a journal entry directing you to search for the door to the Old Way.

ARBORETUM, ARENA, AND PALACE SEWERS

That was easy. Now it gets tougher. The Old Way is three sewers away, and one of those sewers is home to Vampires and their pals.

Start in the city's Arboretum. Near the exit that leads east into the Arena District, a grate leads down to the South East Tunnel just north of the path. Use it. In the sewer, follow the passage north and east to a gate with a leveled lock. In the room beyond, use the wheel in the west wall to open the door in the east. Beyond the door, drop into the trench and head either north or south.

Passages from both the north and south rooms lead east to a region called Beneath the Bloodworks—that is, the Arena Sewers. (The Bloodworks is the Arena's lower-level practice area.) Both take you to the exit to the Palace Sewers, but the northern route is longer and more dangerous, so take the southern route.

The Arena and the Palace Sewers beyond are Vampire and undead lairs. Open the door to the east and descend the stairs into a room with gates to the east and south. The east path is blocked by a remotely operated gate at the moment, so open the gate to the south, kill the Wolf, climb the stairs in the room beyond, and follow the corridor to another gate.

Turn the wheel in the room beyond (which opens the closed gate blocking the east path), open the gate to the north, drop off the bridge, and head east through the newly opened mechanical gate. Cross a trench room with a closed northern exit to a gated room with another wheel in the north wall. Turn the wheel to open the north exit from the trench room.

The door to the Old Way.

Use that exit and take the western passage to a locked gate—opened with the key you received from the Gray Fox. In the middle of the room beyond, a manhole leads to the Palace Sewers. Activate the cover, and your journal offers advice to look for the entrance to the Old Way.

You won't have to look far. In the Palace Sewers, open the gate and descend the stairs. Head north through a second gate to a pair of cisterns and across a trench. On the far side of the trench, just right of the bridge, an area where the sewer wall has collapsed reveals the "strange door" to the Old Way.

THE OLD WAY

The Old Way is a tomb. Numerous undead—from Skeletons to Wraiths, according to your level—roam its halls, which are further complicated by swinging-mace traps and some heavily locked doors.

Make your way south to the entrance to the Lost Catacombs. But how do you get out? It's a little tricky. Explore thoroughly, don't make assumptions, and keep an eye peeled for holes that have been knocked in the dungeon walls.

The entrance to the Lost Catacombs is artfully concealed. In the southwest corner of the level is a well. Look south from the well. There is a section of sandy sub-structure, with niches in the walls where loose soil has been collecting, similar to the starter dungeon. The last niche on the left is not a niche at all, but a makeshift ramp leading down to the final door.

THE LOST CATACOMBS

Part palace crawlspace, part cave, part Ayleid ruin, this level is a standard run' n' gun with undead baddies and Rats. You can see the exit from a good ways off; you just can't open it. The iron gate down to the Hall of Epochs is operated remotely, and there aren't any remote controls in sight.

Use your Springheel-enhanced jumping ability to reach the switches on the balcony. (Either the east or west switch will do.) Use the ruined staircase against the east wall as a launching pad if this proves difficult. Push the buttons, and the door opens.

You need Springheel Jak's Boots to jump onto this balcony.

Unfortunately, those same switches also activate the two Dark Welkynd Stones that flank the exit. They fire chain-lightning at you in strength commensurate to your level. There's not much cover here, aside from the corners near the switches, so it's easiest to dodge these bolts or draw their fire and run for the door while they regenerate.

HALL OF EPOCHS

At the top of the first flight of stairs in this large Ayleid ruin, you get a journal entry speculating that there must be a secret way to open this door, that it must involve the Arrow of Extrication, and that you'll have to stand in a special spot with a clear view of a pillar for the keyhole to open.

Unlock that side gate in the east wall of the upper level. This puts you on a balcony. Push the block at the balcony's south end to open a secret door in the room below that leads to a large chamber. In the southwest corner are descending stairs and another set to the east in the room at the bottom. Go all the way to the bottom. At the east end of this room, behind the altar, is a second block. Push it.

Nothing happens in the immediate neighborhood. But as you retrace your steps, beginning at the bottom of the second flight of stairs you start seeing new Zombies. When you return to the big room with the statue, the stone walls at the north end of the room have been removed.

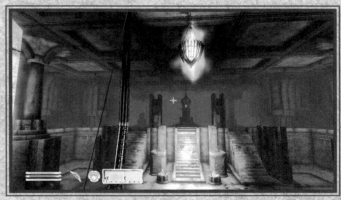
Use the Arrow of Extrication to open the secret door.

Formerly, these walls blocked access to a bridge that you passed under on your way into this room. Now you can walk onto the bridge itself. Sure enough, in the center is a pressure plate. Stand on the pressure plate and your journal says, "This must be the spot." The statue at the far end of the room does a 180-degree turn, and a hatch opens in its belly to expose what must be the keyhole. If you can fire the Arrow of Extrication into it, you'll reveal the door.

Your Marksman skill does have an impact on the accuracy of this shot, but not a big one, and you should be able to hit the target reliably with a low skill if you know where to aim—the spot where the figure's hands hold its sword. Save the game before trying this.

If the arrow hits its mark, you hear a distinctive sound and the statue rises to reveal a flight of stairs leading down into the fireplace of the Palace Guard barracks. If you miss, pick up the arrow and try again, or reload the saved game. Go into sneak mode and activate the revealed door.

THE ELDER SCROLLS LIBRARY

Most of the guards here are sleeping. That's a good thing. Who knows what they'd do if they saw you walk out of the fireplace?

However, you may also find guards coming and going on their rounds. If they detect you, they won't bother trying to arrest you; they'll just attack. So stay hidden and wait until any shift change is completed, then move out on the tail of the newly awakened guard.

Bear left down the hall. The little ramp at the end leads to the Palace Library. Make sure a guard isn't watching when you pick this lock and another leading to the inner library's corridor. A third door leading into the library proper is down the hall to your left, but you have to pull the lever at the end of the hall to the right to open it, and a blind priest is sitting practically on top of it.

Inside the library, take a seat at the round table at the foot of the stairs. When you hear footsteps, a blind priest appears on the stairs and brings you the scroll. Pick it up from the table. (You can try to read it, but it's all gibberish.)

Now make your escape. The remotely operated door by which you entered has closed behind you and can't be operated from this side. But a second door—up to this point impassable—can be found on the library's upper level. Now that you have the scroll, you can pick the lock on the second door. If you can reach the door without the priests detecting your presence, you should be fine. Sneak up the spiral stairs and keep your mouth shut. Talking to the priests still means instant exposure, drawn swords, pursuit, and possibly death.

But, once out of the library, how are you to get out of the palace tower? The passage down from the guard barracks is impassable. Go *up* and look for an unconventional route. Remember, the Gray Fox mentioned that the boots of Springheel Jak not only allow you to reach otherwise-inaccessible areas—they've already done so in the Hall of Epochs—but they also prevent you from taking damage in a long fall. You just have to find a place to fall.

Your options are limited, as you're running out of tower. Only the modest quarters of the blind Moth priests and the lavish ones of Chancellor Ocato are above you now.

Ocato's chamber holds the exit. Dive into the flue beneath the loose grate in the chancellor's fireplace. If you've avoided detection and Evangeline, the chancellor's apprentice, is asleep (midnight to 6 a.m.), so much the better. The activation point in the near right corner of the fireplace is hard to target on the fly, and you're likely to be running hard if the priests are pursuing you and Evangeline is shooting fireballs at you.

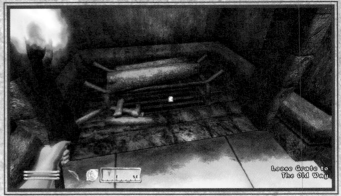

Jump down the fireplace to escape from the Imperial Palace.

The result? If you're wearing the boots, you land safely in a spot a short distance from where you entered the Old Way. The boots will be destroyed in the process. If you're not wearing the boots, a lesser character may very well die—it's a long way down—and a greater one certainly will take damage. In that case, though, you keep the boots.

Either way, you won't be further pursued and have only to return through the sewers to Othrelo's place in the Elven Gardens and turn over the Elder Scroll to the Gray Fox. He is beyond delighted.

In fact, the quest isn't quite over. The Gray Fox has one last task for you. He asks you to bring a ring to Countess Umbranox in Anvil, tell her only that it is a gift from a stranger, and to report back on her reaction.

The Gray Fox reveals himself.

You won't have to report back. When you check in with the countess during her morning audience, you notice that A Stranger is in his traditional place on the bench in the Great Hall.

Approach the countess once she is seated on her throne and offer her the ring. In the end, Corvus responds by renouncing his life of crime and passes both title and cowl to the new guildmaster.

That would be you. Congratulations, Mr. Fox.

Corvus Umbranox is the man who took up the Gray Cowl a decade ago. He is/was the husband to Millona and is/was the Count in Anvil. You discover all of this during the conversation between the two of them in this scene.

EPILOGUE

How do things work out for the Umbranoxes? The countess does not respond to her husband's renunciation in words, but when you leave the Great Hall, Corvus's throne vanishes from castle storage and appears on the dais beside his wife's and a chair for Corvus now appears in the castle dining room.

You can have a good deal of fun with your new equipment. The cowl carries three enchantments. It boosts your Sneak skill by 25 points. It has an automatic Detect Life spell that identifies all nearby non-player characters as luminous forms—respective of intervening walls. And the Feather spell increases your maximum Encumbrance by 200 points, so you can carry a lot more loot (or anything else).

> The cowl is also a second identity. Look at the stats page—the one that shows your Bounty, Fame, and Infamy. Now look at it again with the cowl in place. The cowl gives you an instant Infamy of 100 and an instant Bounty of 500 gold. (You can pay this off, and halve it by going to Christophe or S'krivva, but you reacquire the bounty when you put on the cowl again.)
>
> Any bounty you accrue as the Gray Fox vanishes when you remove the cowl. You become yourself again and, owing to the cowl's magic, no one who witnessed the cowl's placement or removal is any the wiser as to your being the Gray Fox. (However, any quest activity performed as the Gray Fox will be attached to your "normal" character.)
>
> Thus, you can confine your crimes to your Gray Fox identity and insulate your original character from the adverse effects of committing crimes, all the while accruing all the advantages.

In the Imperial City's Waterfront District, Dareloth's house has effectively become your house. The front door remains barred, but you can now enter the basement through a door in the "garden" at the rear. You can find some loot upstairs in a four-tumbler chest.

There's also a point of interest here. The Arrow of Extrication is back in the Hall of Epochs (unless you retrieved it), and the boots of Springheel Jak may have been destroyed during "The Big Heist." But Savilla's Stone is here. (No, you can't do anything special with it.) So are the three documents you turned over to the guild in quests. The tax records from "Untaxing the Poor" and Hieronymus Lex's orders reassigning him to Anvil from "Taking Care of Lex" are both on the desk upstairs, and *The Lost Histories of Tamriel* book from the quest

"Lost Histories" is on the bottom shelf of a bookshelf nearby. (The Gray Fox wanted poster is on the wall.)

And something else: You've got visitors! After all, this is the guild headquarters. Fathis Ules now shows at Dareloth's house at 7 p.m. and hangs out until 5 a.m. He doesn't bring a casserole or a bottle of wine, but he is Johnny-on-the-spot for fencing. No longer will you have to travel all over Akatosh's green earth looking for these guys.

Armand Christophe drops by at noon and stays till midnight. Isleif the Open Handed will visit on weeknights; Methredhel on Monday, Wednesday, and Friday nights; Amusei on Tuesdays and Thursdays; and one of Methredhel's roommates, Carwen, and a pickpocket named Jair on weekends.

The new Thieves Guild headquarters.

You get a variety of reactions from different types of non-player characters if you appear or speak to them while wearing the cowl. Martin and Millona Umbranox respond angrily, while Corvus Umbranox seems happy. "The cowl suits you," he says. "Me? I am much happier without it." Others will be honored or fearful.

Without a bounty on your head, guards recognize you as the Gray Fox but say they'll look the other way this time. With a bounty, they confront you fiercely but won't follow through unless you resist arrest. (You can also bribe the guard for the full amount of your bounty. Paying it off legitimately or going to jail is not an option.)

You may also wonder what the new Anvil guard captain, Hieronymus Lex, would think about having the former Gray Fox as his boss. After all, his wish at your last parting that providence would throw the Gray Fox into his path in Anvil has come true.

Well, he doesn't think about it, because he doesn't know. Only the countess does. And, of course, Lex will never know, because the title is now yours and Corvus Umbranox and the Gray Fox are thus two different people. Confronted by the Gray Fox, Lex will behave like any other guard.

Poor fellow. He just can't win.

You won't have been playing *Oblivion* for very long before you overhear a street rumor about how the Dark Brotherhood comes to killers in their sleep. The rumor is true. To get an invitation to join this assassin's guild, you'll have to kill someone. How should you choose a victim?

Though you're never expressly told this, it'll have to be someone who doesn't really deserve to die. This means the victim must belong to at least one non-evil faction.

Now, you could walk into the street and kill just about any non-essential character and fulfill this requirement. However, in doing so, you could make your game somewhat more difficult in the short or long term. For example, you wouldn't want to kill a shopkeeper. You never know when you'll need to visit one. The beggars are important in the Thieves Guild quests. Avoid killing members of factions you are a member of—if only to avoid the potential guild and criminal penalties. The city guards—especially in packs—are more than most players can handle.

Ideally, kill someone you're probably going to have to kill anyway. We suggest one of those local Mythic Dawn agents listed under "Dagon Shrine" in the "Main Quest" chapter. The two in Imperial City appear only at the end of that segment, but the others are all around beforehand. (Yes, they're Mythic Dawn, but each also belongs to a non-evil community faction, and so the game regards them as non-evil.)

The two weakest victims are Tanasa Arano and Tolisi Girith (both Level 5)—servants at the Riverview mansion in Cheydinhal. Your best shot at a clean kill is when they're asleep in the cellar (2 a.m. to 6 a.m.) or on Sundays, when both leave the house and spend virtually the whole day (9 a.m. to 11 p.m.) at Newlands Lodge.

Once the killing has been performed, simply go to sleep in a bed or on a bedroll. You'll wake at the prescribed hour to find an ominous black-robed figure standing beside you. This is Lucien Lachance—a Speaker for the Dark Brotherhood.

You sleep rather soundly for a murderer. That's good. You'll need a clear conscience for what I'm about to propose.

Lucien Lachance

Enter Lucien Lachance, Speaker for the Black Hand...and your new best friend.

Note that Lachance won't appear in The Bloated Float (the floating inn in Imperial City's Waterfront District), Cloud Ruler Temple, Camoran's Paradise, or the Dagon Shrine, though he will show up in the rest of the Lake Arrius Caverns complex. Nor will he make his initial appearance at the Inn of Ill Omen between Bravil and the Imperial City. (That's the destination for the first Dark Brotherhood quest. If you sleep there after that quest is complete, Lachance shows up.)

He also won't appear if you activate the bed in your prison cell. In doing so, technically, you're not sleeping but signifying your desire to serve out your sentence rather than escape.

A Knife in the Dark

Lachance speaks before you can move. The three conversation threads all work out the same way—with slightly different wording, but no variations in Lachance's Disposition or the equipment you'll receive at the end.

It becomes apparent that the Brotherhood is more than just a guild. It's also a cult of death that worships the "Dread Father, Sithis." To join the Brotherhood, you must kill a man named Rufio at the Inn of Ill Omen. The Speaker provides a bit of intel if you ask about Rufio. The target is "old and weak and sleeps his days away," says Lachance. "You could kill him before he even has a chance to wake."

If the proposal gives you the creeps, just leave it alone. If you don't kill Rufio, you'll never hear from Lachance again. And if it *really* offends you, you can kill Lachance. (Well, you can try. He's an accomplished assassin with fairly nasty stats.) If you succeed, you'll cut yourself off from the Brotherhood for good.

If you want to join, fast-travel to Bravil. You'll find the inn roughly halfway up the road to Imperial City.

 If you've performed the Daedric quest "Hircine," you can speed this up a bit by fast-traveling to Hircine's Shrine instead and making your way cross-country to the southwest. Or, if you've performed the Mages Guild quest "Ambush" fast-travel to the Ayleid ruin, Nenyond Twyll, and make your way east-southeast.

Speak to proprietor Manheim Maulhand to learn that Rufio's the lone guest, and that you'll find him downstairs in the Private Quarters. The trap door is in the niche in back of the stairs. Rufio's room is at the end of the hall. The door is unlocked, and you're likely to find him in bed. (Rufio sleeps 20 hours a day; from 2 a.m. to 6 a.m. he wanders the inn.) He's exceptionally weak, and one light blow will surely do him in.

Your first Dark Brotherhood assignment couldn't be any easier.

If you like, wake him first and respond to his assertion of "I ain't done nothing!" with "Oh, but you have, Rufio" to get an unpleasant taste of why he's in hiding. (Return to the inn later, after the quest is complete, and his murder will have registered with inn hands Maulhand and Minerva.)

How do you recontact Lachance once the deed is done? As before, Lachance will find you. Simply sleep in a bed again—even at the Inn of Ill Omen—and he'll appear when you wake.

Lachance now sends you to an abandoned house in the east part of Cheydinhal. Enter the basement, try to open a black door (which looks more like a spooky painting), use the password "Sanguine, my brother" to enter the Sanctuary, and then speak to Ocheeva.

Before you go, ask a few more questions. You learn that the Black Hand that runs the Brotherhood consists of a Listener and four Speakers. You're not to dishonor the Night Mother, betray the Brotherhood, disobey orders, or kill or steal from another member.

Lachance also alludes to the penalties for infractions. You will be visited by the Wrath of Sithis—literally. When you sleep after committing one of these infractions, an undead spirit with precisely that name will drop by for a chat and you'll have to defeat it for readmission to the Brotherhood. A tougher version will appear after second and third infractions, although after the third time you're fighting only for your life. Winning the battle won't get you back in the Brotherhood.

Beyond the Black Door lies the warmth and safety of the Dark Brotherhood Sanctuary.

The abandoned house is east of Cheydinhal's Chapel of Arkay; it's the third house in from the East Gate. Pick the front-door lock to gain admittance.

> The option to present the correct phrase at the Sanctuary door is only available after you've met with Lucien Lachance and killed Rufio.

Ocheeva waits for you just inside the Sanctuary. Talking to her completes the quest. She refers you to Vicente Valtieri for assignment and gives you two pieces of enchanted armor that fortify your Sneak, Illusion, Marksman, Blade, and Acrobatics skills by a total of 10 points.

Talk to everybody here: Gogron gro-Bolmog, Telaendril, Antoinetta Marie, and Teinaava. (M'raaj-Dar dislikes you on sight—his insults are slightly different if you're a Khajiit—until about halfway through the quest line.) It's fun and it's good to get into the habit of talking to everyone. Via "contract," each of your colleagues, at a Disposition of 30 or better, offers hints of how best to perform a given quest.

> M'raaj-Dar may not like you, but he'll still sell you some very useful assassin-friendly weapons and items. Particularly nasty are the Poisoned Apples. If you can slip one into an NPC's inventory, or remove any nearby food and leave a Poisoned Apple in its place, the next time that NPC eats will be their last. The foul fruit will kill any non-essential NPC who eats it, so practice using it effectively, and it will prove to be an assassin's best friend. Just be patient! A Poisoned Apple does damage over time, so you'll have to observe your victim eating for a while before they drop.

VICENTE VALTIERI'S QUESTS

A WATERY GRAVE

First thing to know about Vicente Valtieri: he's a Vampire. However, he's sacrificed his Vampire agenda for a Dark Brotherhood one, and you have nothing to fear from him. Valtieri explains how the contract system works—most notably, that some missions come with a bonus for meeting "certain parameters." However, your first quest has no such bonus. You must kill pirate captain Gaston Tussaud aboard his ship, the *Marie Elena*, which is docked in the Imperial City's Waterfront District.

If you've spent time wandering the Waterfront District, you already know about this ship. It's at the east end of the docks. If you approach the stairs that lead down to the top deck, the first mate, Malvulis, warns you about snooping and, with other pirates, will attack if you get too close.

The *Marie Elena*, lying at anchor on the Imperial City Waterfront.

Baenlin enjoys a quiet moment before his body is shattered by a Minotaur head.

A direct approach is out of the question. However, Valtieri observes that the pirates have been loading a lot of cargo lately and that you might be able to smuggle yourself aboard in a crate. At the east end of the docks, you'll find an open crate. You can't activate it, but just stand nearby for a short while and you'll get a message inviting you to climb inside. Do so and you find yourself on the ship's empty lower deck.

Make your way up to the middle deck and then aft. A pair of pirates are quarrelling spiritedly over the wisdom of having a woman (Malvulis) on board. When they're done talking, one pirate heads your way—the other will bed down in the aft chamber—so backtrack to the trap door and wait until the coast is clear. Then advance and climb to the captain's quarters.

Stay hidden and put a big hurt on him quickly with a spell or sneak attack. However swiftly you put down Tussaud, two pirates on the ship's top deck hear the ruckus and enter the cabin. These fellows are weaker than the captain, but you don't want to get into a two-on-one. Quickly take the key from Tussaud's body and unlock the chest atop the dresser in his bedroom. Now you can exit via the rear door onto a balcony at the rear and swim back to shore.

An alternate approach is to jump to that same balcony from the east end of the dock, pick the lock on the door, and enter the captain's cabin directly.

Fast-travel back to Cheydinhal and check in with Valtieri.

ACCIDENTS HAPPEN

Make sure this particular accident happens to a Bruma resident named Baenlin. It's a specific type of mishap, and if you meet the specs, you'll get a significant bonus.

On the second floor of Baenlin's home is a secret door. Beyond the door, there's a space between the wall and roof where ties connect a mounted head to the wall above Baenlin's favorite chair. Loosen those ties between 8 p.m. and 11 p.m. and Baenlin will wind up wearing the head. Kill him any other way, or kill Baenlin's Nord manservant Gromm, and you'll sacrifice the bonus.

Baelin's place is the second house on the street to the right just inside Bruma's east gate. Use the basement door around the back. Be careful making your move to the second floor. Neither Baenlin nor Gromm goes out at all. Wait until Gromm is busy in the kitchen—to the right, across the living room, as you come out of the cellar—or upstairs with the old man.

At the top of the stairs to the second floor, make a U-turn to the right and enter the bedroom. Activate the section of wall to the right of the desk (the one with the peephole), enter the crawlspace, wait for the appointed hour, and activate the fastening.

In fact, you can kill Baenlin a little ahead of schedule or a little later; he typically sits in the chair under the Minotaur's head from a little after 7 p.m. to midnight.

Then exit back through the cellar and return to the Sanctuary. If you dropped the head on Baenlin, you get the dagger Sufferthorn, with leveled Damage Health and Damage Strength enchantments plus the gold. If you took a more conventional route, you get just the gold. Either way, you advance in rank to Slayer.

Pay another visit to Baenlin's house the next time you're in Bruma. The body has vanished. There's a new tenant—Caenlin. He doesn't have much to say beyond a dismissive reference to his uncle's death. (This is the one rare case where you're pretty clearly meeting the Brotherhood's client.)

And what of Gromm? If you didn't kill him, you're likely to find him crying in his beer at Olav's Tap and Tack down the street. He loved the old man and mourns that he couldn't protect him.

SCHEDULED FOR EXECUTION

You've already met your next target. His name is Valen Dreth. He occupied the cell across from you in the Imperial Prison at the beginning of the game. At that time, he was unfailingly unpleasant. Now you have a chance to pay him back.

That's not the only familiar reference. Valtieri mentions that a prisoner recently escaped the jail using secret tunnels connected to the sewer system. The grate you passed through effortlessly on your way out has since been locked, but your quest-giver provides the key. Avoid killing the guards to get a bonus.

Retrace your steps to the sewer exit—near the dock just down the hill from the Imperial City Prison in the northeast corner of Lake Rumare. Once inside, there's only one path. A trench room in the second section has a remotely operated gate to the southeast end and a locked gate to the northeast. The door beyond the locked gate leads to the third and final section of the sewers. Few surprises here, except for a body at the edge of a cistern (which will be explained soon enough) and a new lock on the manhole that leads up to the sanctum.

The dungeon is effectively identical in layout to the starter dungeon, but this one has guards looking into the emperor's assassination. There are eight—four in the Sanctum, two in the Imperial Subterrane, and two in the Imperial Prison. They all have a low Sneak skill, but most are positioned directly in your path.

The gate that blocked the royal party's access to the sewers at the beginning of the game is now open, but detour through the room where the emperor died in order to read Captain Gepard Montrose's report on the "inconclusive, to say the least" investigation. (It's on the table. The guards have dumped the assassins' bodies into the sewers.) And if you're really good, you can also pick Montrose's pocket for the keys to Dreth's cell and the Imperial Prison.

Stay in sneak mode and make your way slowly and surely up to your old cell, where you can listen to Dreth trade taunts with a guard. When the guard heads for the stairs, approach Dreth's cell.

So long as you kill Dreth quickly, it doesn't matter what you do here. Talk to him or don't talk to him. Shoot him through the door with bow and arrow (as Telaendril suggests) or open the lock with either your pick or Montrose's key and kill him with a melee weapon. As Valtieri said, Dreth has wasted away in prison and he goes down immediately.

You dare torment me? Valen Dreth? Let me out of this cell, you fetid piece of Guar dung!

Valen Dreth

You're going to die in here!

Make your way back the way you came or, if you have the prison key, just head up the stairs and out. You'll get the usual leveled gold for the mission and the Scales of Pitiless Justice as your bonus.

Valtieri now has a special assignment for you ("The Assassinated Man"). And Teinaava wants a favor that is actually a side quest: "The Renegade Shadowscale."

The Renegade Shadowscale

Technically, this is a Miscellaneous quest, but it's effectively a Dark Brotherhood side quest—available only to members who've completed the quest "Scheduled for Execution" and only until quest-giver Teinaava dies in "The Purification."

He sends you to kill an Argonian named Scar-Tail who's hiding in the Bogwater swamp and asks you to return with your victim's heart as proof. This Shadowscale fled Black Marsh and refuses to perform his duties as a royal assassin.

 You can get some background about Shadowscales from Ocheeva.

Bogwater is southeast of Leyawiin. It'll be a shorter walk if you've completed the Daedric quest "Nocturnal" (fast-travel to Tidewater Cave and walk east), the Mages Guild quest "Leyawiin Recommendation" (fast-travel to Fort Blueblood and head south), or the Miscellaneous quest "Whom Gods Annoy" (fast-travel to Darkfathom Cave and proceed southeast).

You'll find Scar-Tail around his campfire on a slope above Topal Bay. It's an easy kill. Your intended victim has already fought off one attempt on his life by an agent of the Argonian Royal Court and has only a few hit points left.

The Shadowscale Scar-Tail will provide little challenge in combat, but perhaps you can work out a deal?

Talk to him and he'll offer an alternate approach: Let him live, take his treasure (the usual leveled gold you'll get for finishing a quest) from a hollow in the smaller of the rocks near his fire, and present the heart of the dead agent to Teinaava.

Either way will work. The dead agent's body is just west and slightly south of the campfire, beside a big tree. Teinaava recognizes either heart as Argonian and turns over the Boots of Bloody Bounding, which fortify your Acrobatics and Blade skills.

THE ASSASSINATED MAN

You're to fake the murder of Francois Motierre in Chorrol. Evidently Motierre owes money to "the wrong kind of people," and those people have dispatched an "enforcer" to do him in. If the enforcer believes Motierre is already dead by your hand, he won't do the job. So the plan is for you to "kill" Motierre in the enforcer's presence with a knife laced with the rare poison Languorwine, which simulates death. (Valtieri will supply the knife as well as an antidote with which to wake Motierre later.)

With each contract fulfilled, the Dread Father Sithis is provided a precious soul to do his bidding in the Void. But in this particular contract, with no one actually being killed, Francois Motierre had to make a special arrangement with Lucien Lachance—so he offered up the life of his own mother. He's certainly done his family proud.

The Motierre place is just up Chorrol's central street, on the left near side of the traffic circle. Pick the lock on the front door. Motierre waits for you just inside. He says time is short. The enforcer, an Argonian named Hides-his-Heart, is already on his way to kill him.

He goes over the plan sketched by Valtieri—adding that you'll need to leave Chorrol without hurting the enforcer and return the next day to revive Motierre while his body is on display in the undercroft of Chorrol's Chapel of Stendarr.

 Because this quest requires you to keep someone alive, rather than killing him, it's the only Dark Brotherhood contract that can be failed. Keep Motierre alive at all costs.

When he's done speaking, position yourself beside Motierre with your poisoned blade at the ready. A few seconds later, you'll hear Hides-his-Heart muttering his threats through the keyhole.

The best way to handle this is to poison Motierre shortly after Hides appears through the door and then make a swift exit. If you linger, things may get complicated. The enforcer and the debtor have a little conversation. It's revealed that you're a competing assassin. Hides tells Motierre he's been

naughty and tells you to back off. Motierre gives you cues to act. And Hides at last tells you to defend yourself.

Up to this point, you can take down Motierre and get out of the house without starting a fight. If you stay longer, the result is very likely combat, probably pursuit, and either your death at Hides's hands or Hides's death at the hands of the vigilant City Watch —which is just as bad in the game's eyes as if you'd killed him yourself.

We'll assume that everything's gone okay and that you're now standing just outside Chorrol's South Gate. Now wait until after midnight for Motierre's body to be discovered and removed to the chapel crypt.

You find him lying peacefully in the southern extremity of the undercroft. Activate his body and he automatically revives.

Motierre looks dead enough, but you can rectify that by administering the Languorwine antidote.

Here Motierre finally thinks to mention that his dead ancestors will regard his rising from the dead as a desecration of their resting place and will rise to defend it. You'll have to kill or evade three Zombies before escorting him to The Gray Mare, where Motierre can book passage out of Chorrol. One Zombie is right behind you, one's in the undercroft's north wing, and the third is to the northwest in the main undercroft. Finally, have the dead man follow you out of the crypt and south to the inn.

Back in the Cheydinhal Sanctuary, Valtieri gives you the amulet Cruelty's Heart. He hands you to Ocheeva for future quests. Along with a promotion to Eliminator, he supplies the key to the well beside the Abandoned House. It'll drop you right into the northwest corner of the Sanctuary's main room.

 If Motierre or Hides dies during the quest, you won't get the promotion or the key, but you can still move on to the next quest. You'll get both perks after you complete "The Lonely Wanderer quest."

If you wish, Valtieri will also turn you into a creature of the night. You just have to talk to him about "Vampire" and then confirm. Think about it before you take the leap.

THE LONELY WANDERER

You must kill a High Elf named Faelian. He lives in Imperial City. He likes to go for long walks, and that's all Ocheeva knows. She suggests you consult your colleagues.

She also urges discretion in your pursuit. Imperial Legion captain Adamus Phillida is to the Dark Brotherhood what Captain Hieronymus Lex is (or was) to the Thieves Guild. If you want a bonus, avoid doing anything that would get the captain hot and bothered—like killing Faelian in front of witnesses.

The best advice from your colleagues comes from Valtieri: He says the Imperial City's Elvish community is tight-knit. Somebody within it must know of Faelian. Ask any Elf in the Imperial City with a Disposition of 50 or better about Faelian to learn he lives at the Tiber Septim Hotel in Talos Plaza and is a "rather distasteful fellow."

From here, you have several options. Based on this intelligence, you can stake out the Tiber Septim, wait for Faelian to return to the hotel (at 8 p.m.) or leave again (at 1 a.m.) and buttonhole him outside. (He won't talk in the hotel proper.)

You'll quickly see that Faelian can't form an intelligible sentence, but he's fairly focused about acquiring his drug of choice (skooma), and leaves you with the impression that he'd be friendly if you could supply it. He'll even give you a connection: Nordinor in Bravil sells the stuff during the wee hours.

Faelian is under the influence of skooma all day, every day.

Of course, skooma is skooma, and you don't have to go all the way to Bravil to find it. If you're holding, that skooma will do as well as any. And if you're up for a burglary, you can find three vials of the stuff in an unlocked chest in the big room upstairs at skooma addict Trenus Duronius's house in the western Temple District.

Duronius goes out on weekday mornings—leaving as early at 8 a.m. and staying out as late as 3 p.m. The front-door lock has three tumblers.

Rendezvous with Faelian anywhere outside the hotel and tell him that you have skooma, and he'll invite you to meet him at his "special place"—Lorkmir's house in the Elven Gardens District—between 11 a.m. and 5 p.m. He'll even supply a key. A journal entry reports that this is the spot for your hit.

Alternate approach: You can figure this out intuitively by following Faelian on his rounds. From around 2 a.m. to 8 a.m. he's at the Abandoned Shack in the Waterfront District, where he always seems to have company, and then wanders the Elven Gardens District until he pops into Lorkmir's place at 11 a.m. It's on the north side of the central street in the western portion of the district. Break in and explore a bit while you're waiting for Faelian—if only to satisfy yourself that you won't be interrupted. The place has been plundered and Lorkmir has been knifed in the cellar. No clear evidence pointing to the killer is present—the knife beside Lorkmir is unowned—but Faelian's the natural suspect. He has a key. Lorkmir doesn't.

But these are long and rather tedious approaches. With a Disposition of 50, the hotel's hostess, Augusta Calidia, will confirm Faelian lives there with his wealthy girlfriend, Atraena. Calidia says he's around only at night, and she speculates he spends every waking hour either using the drug or looking for more. (Your journal makes it clear that the hotel itself isn't a sufficiently secure location for a hit.)

To further narrow the search, talk to Atraena. This sad, pretty woman spends all her time in the hotel. With a Disposition of 50, she'll tell you everything—most notably, how Faelian visits Lorkmir's house to use skooma. This gives you the house as a destination.

Ocheeva gives you the standard leveled-gold reward for killing Faelian and an enchanted steel bow as the bonus.

BAD MEDICINE

The warlord Roderick lies deathly ill in the mercenary stronghold of Fort Sutch—kept alive only by a potent medicine. Infiltrate the fort and replace the medicine with a poison supplied by Ocheeva. The Brotherhood's client wants it to appear that Roderick died of his illness, so it is essential that you remain undetected. If you're spotted, the defenders' guard will be up, the poisoning attempt will fail, and you'll have to kill Roderick the "old-fashioned way." Poison = bonus. Old-fashioned way = no bonus.

Worst case, you'll have to fast-travel to Anvil, walk north along the Anvil–Kvatch road and, when the road curves east, cut north cross-country. You'll pass the abandoned Atrene Camp and Lord Drad's Estate, and just down the slope to the north you'll see the fallen-down abbey tower.

But depending on where you are in the game, a shorter route may be available. If you've completed the Mages Guild quest "Anvil Recommendation," fast-travel directly to Brina Cross Inn and make your way north. If you've performed the Daedric quest "Malacath," fast-travel to the shrine and head east.

Near Fort Sutch is a ruined tower connected to the fort by flooded tunnels that Ocheeva suspects are unguarded. The tunnel entrance is a trap door in the foundation southwest of the tower. You'll have to pick the lock, but that's the extent of the security until you get into the fort proper, where two guards, Neesha and Ulmog gro-Cromgog, block the corridor. They are discussing Roderick's perilous health.

You may think you have to get past these two, but in fact, you need them to open a locked gate *behind you* that leads to Roderick. Sneak up just close enough to overhear what they have to say. When they're done talking, backpedal up the hall and hide in the second niche down the side hall. The guards will open a key-required gate and leave it open behind them. When Neesha bears left to Roderick's sickbed, you'll see the medicine cabinet straight ahead of you.

Neesha positions herself near Roderick's bed, and gro-Cromgog patrols the area near the medicine cabinet. With a decent Sneak skill, and possibly a little concealing magic, you should have little trouble getting around them.

Roderick's poison lies within the medicine cabinet. Replace it with the bottle of poison, and he's as good as dead.

This time, simple activation isn't enough; you must take the medicine out of the cabinet and put in the poison. Then scoot. Retrace your steps to the gate and then to the trap door.

If you don't have the stats for sneaking, you'll need some speed. Wait until the guards open the gate, then make a run for Roderick's sickbed, thump him once, and drop into the big room below and make your exit.

Return to Ocheeva for the usual gold reward. If you avoided detection, you'll also get the bonus: an enchanted shirt, The Deceiver's Finery.

WHODUNIT?

Youdunit. In a quest straight from old mysteries, you're the homicidal party-pooper in a gathering at Summitmist Manor in Skingrad.

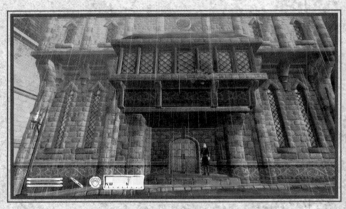

Inside, the ill-fated houseguests await.

The five other guests think it's all in fun. They have agreed to be locked in the house until one of them finds a hidden chest that contains gold and (they believe) the exit key.

In fact, the chest doesn't exist and nobody's getting out alive. Each guest has somehow wounded the anonymous host, and they have been gathered here for your killing pleasure. And if you kill each of the five without witnesses, you'll get a bonus.

The house is two doors in from the north of the city's two eastern gates. The doorman, Fafnir, supplies the key and you're in. In the lobby, elderly Matilde Petit briefs you on each of the other guests: a young Dunmer lady, Dovesi Dran; a Nord, Nels the Naughty; retired soldier Neville; and young nobleman Primo Antonius. She asks about you. Tell Petit you're an assassin sent to kill her, and her Disposition shoots up to maximum. She loves a good joke.

You can play this mission all kinds of ways, but there are three general styles:

1. A Disposition workshop, with lots of meeting and greeting, finding out what everyone really thinks of everyone else, and, when the murders start, watching the guests' suspicions percolate. Most of the pre-departure tips are geared to this approach. This mission is an elaborate construct with a little romance and lots of hatred stirred into the mix, and it would be a shame to let it go to waste by just killing everybody right away.

The characters have a huge number of unique responses adjusted to various circumstances and Disposition ranges. Don't regard this is a rush job. Take your time and play it out to fully enjoy it.

Use your silver tongue to turn the houseguests against each other...

...and they just might do the dirty work for you.

2. A killing field in four walls. Conceivably, you could tear through it in a few minutes. The killings are easy, and none, with the possible exception of Neville (who should be hit with a sneak attack), should take more than one blow. Just prowl around and wait until each guest is alone—which will be increasingly the case as you thin their numbers. Try to lure the players to the other sections of the house, and kill them where their murders won't be witnessed by other guests. (It's a three-story house, with lots of doors in the living quarters on the top floor to establish privacy.)

3. Set the stage and then get the rest of the guests to kill each other! This requires some art. The elderly Matilde won't attack anyone, but with Dispositions of over 70 and the right circumstances, each of the other four can be persuaded to attack her or each other. One for instance: Antonius's burgeoning passion for Dran can be channeled into a preemptive attack on her if three guests are dead, Dran lives, and Antonius's Disposition is at least 70.

Back in Cheydinhal, you get the usual gold for the killings and, if you earned the bonus, the Night Mother's Blessing, which provides boosts in multiple skills.

PERMANENT RETIREMENT

In a mission handed down by the Brotherhood's ruling council, you're to assassinate the Imperial Legion "pest" Adamus Phillida. To send a don't-mess-with-us message, and win your bonus, cut off Phillida's ring finger and place it in the desk of his successor.

An enchanted arrow called the Rose of Sithis—one shot, one kill—is provided for this purpose. But Ocheeva mentions a caveat: It can't pierce Phillida's armor. You'll have to use it when he is unarmored. Surveillance may be useful.

The Rose of Sithis is specially commissioned and crafted to kill one person—in this case, Adamus Phillida. When fired on anyone else, it only wounds.

Gro-Bolmog suggests you have greater freedom of action than Ocheeva implied. You don't have to use the deadly arrow, but we think the Orc is steering you wrong here. If you attack Phillida with a melee weapon, he'll immediately put on his armor and you're suddenly fighting a guard captain 15 levels above your own.

After a career of thwarting the Brotherhood's plans, Phillida has retired to Leyawiin, where he lives in the City Watch barracks. You can follow him through his day or simply talk to his lone bodyguard, who says the old man keeps a regular, safe routine—including a daily swim. The swim, in a pool at the east end of the city, doesn't take place until 3 p.m.

After a lifetime of service to the Legion, Phillida finally lets his guard down. Show him the error of his ways.

Don't forget to take the severed finger and the raft of useful keys on Phillida's body. You must physically place the finger in the locked desk in the locked ground-floor office at Imperial Legion headquarters in the outer ring of the Imperial Prison District.

In Cheydinhal, Ocheeva turns over the standard reward—plus a 500-gold bonus for giving the finger to the Imperial Legion commander.

And that's not the end of it. The killing makes the papers; check out the new *Black Horse Courier*. The next time you're in Leyawiin, drop by the City Watch barracks. Phillida's poor bodyguard has committed suicide over his failure. Check his body for a note.

OF SECRET AND SHADOW

Ocheeva has received sealed orders for you from Lucien Lachance. The letter directs you to meet him at Fort Farragut. Leave Cheydinhal by the east gate and climb the hill to the ruined tower.

Fort Farragut is populated with six Dark Guardians (like the one that tirelessly patrols the Cheydinhal Sanctuary) and a range of nasty traps. You don't have to deal with them at all. Instead of the big door inside the tower, use the trap door inside the giant dead tree just northeast of the ruin, and you'll wind up at the base of a rope ladder in Lachance's Sanctum.

The hollowed-out tree hides a ladder down to Lachance's private quarters. Find it before you enter Fort Farragut, and you can avoid confrontation with the Skeletal Guardians.

LUCIEN LACHANCE'S QUESTS

THE PURIFICATION

What Lachance tells you changes everything. There is a traitor in the organization, and that traitor is somehow linked to the Cheydinhal Sanctuary.

You're in the clear, and the traitor's activity predates your arrival. But your colleagues are all suspect, because Lachance now charges you to undertake an ancient rite known as

Purification: the systematic killing of everyone back at the base. "And, hopefully, we kill the traitor in the process," he says.

Alas, there's no alternative path here—save not doing the quest and thus giving up the whole quest line. You can still consult with your colleagues about the quest via "contract," but you can't reveal your orders—your comrades only marvel at their secrecy—and the only relevant advice you'll receive is disheartening. Ocheeva tells you Lachance's word is law.

M'raaj-Dar has finally come to reason and wants to be your new best friend. Sadly, it's too little, too late.

Lachance provides two tools to help in the extermination. The Poisoned Apple is helpful if you clear out the food first and then wait until someone eats.

 Search Lachance's quarters thoroughly, and you'll find a barrel filled with the deadly Poisoned Apples!

 Valtieri doesn't eat; Telaendril eats in the Sanctuary only on Mondays, Wednesdays, and Fridays; and M'raaj-Dar eats at 4 a.m.!

We suggest you summon Rufio's angry ghost in the training room so it can do the maximum possible damage—there may be as many as three people here. Once the ghost is engaged, backstab or perform power attacks on its opponents. Valtieri and Ocheeva can be attacked in their sleep or in the privacy of their rooms. Then you'll just have to mop up.

 The Poisoned Apple affects *any* NPC who eats it, so the player could save it and use it on some other unsuspecting NPC elsewhere in the game!

Postpone an attack on M'raaj-Dar until he's done practicing his spells in the training room. He'll be low on Magicka and will have to fight you conventionally.

Depending on the day of the week, you may have problems finding Telaendril, who spends parts of Tuesdays and Thursdays outside the Sanctuary in Cheydinhal proper and weekends in Leyawiin (where she wanders near the east city gate). If that's the case, either wait for her return or seek her out. You'll find her schedule on Ocheeva's body.

Return to Fort Farragut. Lachance explains that your orders will now be deposited at "dead drop" locations around the province—the first in a hollow rock on Hero Hill. He rewards you with the black, glowing-eyed horse Shadowmere. And he promotes you to Silencer—his private assassin.

May Shadowmere serve you as he served Lucien Lachance.

THE "DEAD DROP" QUESTS

AFFAIRS OF A WIZARD

The first drop is some distance to the southeast over steep slopes. Inside a great rock, you find instructions to kill a powerful Necromancer named Celedaen, who is in the process of turning himself into a Lich. (Necromancers in the *Elder Scrolls* universe sometimes do this in the hope of achieving immortality.) The orders suggest Celedaen is too powerful to confront directly, but that the cave must contain records that give some hint of a weak point.

Leafrot Cave is a long way to the south, and the direct route goes through pathless and quite possibly unexplored terrain. Assume you'll have to get there under your own power. You'll find it much easier to follow the road west to Lake Rumare, then head south and southeast, and finally cut east, cross-country, just north of the Ayleid ruin Morahame.

You won't have to descend far into this small cave, at the edge of one of the Panther River headwaters, to find the Necromancer's notes. His journal, *The Path of Transcendence*, is on the table against the east wall in the first room. Celedaen is using a magical hourglass to extend his life. Your journal suggests that its removal would kill him. It does. Just sneak up on him in the inner cave and pickpocket him. You can kill him conventionally, too, but he's 20 levels above yours and he has

the Necromancer's power to summon undead allies, so that could get nasty.

You'll find your reward (500 gold) and instructions in a sack on the southwest side of the tree in the middle of the traffic circle south of Chorrol's north gate.

NEXT OF KIN

There won't be any when you're done. Kill off the whole Draconis family: the mother, Perennia, and her children, Matthias, Andreas, Sibylla, and Caelia. Lachance knows the location only of Perennia and suggests you elicit from her the whereabouts of her kids before you send her soul to Sithis.

She's at Applewatch—a farm just west of Bruma. You can get there most easily by going east-northeast from Chorrol along Orange Road and heading north cross-country when the road's course shifts from northeast to east. Or just go cross-country the whole way. It's hilly terrain, so leave the horse behind.

It couldn't be easier. Perennia's a little dotty, thinks you're with a shopping service she's hired, and gives you a list of the children's addresses and suggested gifts and 100 gold for this purpose. Kill her and, if he gives you trouble, her dog Jake. Or kill her first and take the list from her body; it doesn't matter.

The old Draconis matron Perennia is definitely the easiest family member to dispose of.

You can handle her family in any order. Andreas is probably the easiest to defeat. He doesn't wear armor and is armed only with a dagger. Just wait until he goes to sleep (around 2 a.m.) or until the Imperial Legion trooper who seems to be permanently stationed at Andreas's Drunken Dragon Inn isn't nearby. It's southeast of the Ayleid ruin Atatar from the Fighters Guild quest "Azani Blackheart."

Matthias is best killed between midnight and 5 a.m., while he's sleeping upstairs at his home in the southwestern part of the Imperial City's Talos Plaza District. Pick the lock on his front door.

You can kill Caelia while this City Watch guard is on night patrol in Leyawiin—unlike other watch troopers, she's only one level above yours—but it's easier to wait until she appears a little after 7 a.m. at the Three Sisters Inn, where you can dispatch her in privacy. She'll be in a private room on the second floor; pick the lock.

Go through the modest dungeon of Muck Valley Cavern to reach Sibylla. Within easy walking distance of Cheydinhal, it contains six to eight critters. (Sibylla went to the cave to live with the animals and has gone savage.) You shouldn't have much trouble with them, but Sibylla may prove a fair opponent. She's a level above you and wields a mace with authority.

Once everyone's dead, click on the grate in the well in Castle Skingrad's courtyard for your usual 500 gold and new orders. Sometime after you find the traitor's diary in "Following A Lead," return to Applewatch. You'll find the graves of the five family members arrayed in an arc just southeast of the farm house. You can claim Caelia's un-enchanted steel longsword from her grave and read the inscriptions on each. Only the one on the mother's grave alludes to her being a murder victim: "May her spirit forever curse the murderer who stole her precious life."

This isn't just an idle reference. When you read the inscription on Perennia's stone, her ghost appears, approaches you from behind, and attacks. It won't be higher than Level Four and, with an enchanted weapon, you'll have no trouble putting the mother down a second time.

BROKEN VOWS

Actually, it never got to the vows stage. The Khajiit nobleman J'Ghasta has declined an offer of marriage over the young lady's dowry. The girl's family is disappointed and wants satisfaction.

Your compass points you to J'Ghasta's home a bit south of the city's east gate. When you get past the lock, however, it may appear he isn't home.

Recall that your orders mentioned him spending much of his time practicing unarmored combat. A trap door leads down to the Secret Training Room on the lower floor just behind the stairs.

J'Ghasta is a master of Hand-to-Hand combat, and has honed his body into a lethal weapon.

This is perhaps your most straightforward mission. Just because J'Ghasta's a good hand-to-hand fighter doesn't mean you must be one as well. Kill him with your weapon of choice. Then find your way to Old Bridge—it's along the Red Ring Road south of Imperial City—for your usual reward and orders. Your fastest route is to swim south from the Imperial City's Waterfront District.

FINAL JUSTICE

Your next target is an Argonian hunter named Shaleez. You'll find him in the Flooded Mine just north of Bravil.

Shaleez wanders through the mine a good deal during the day. You may have an easier time finding her if you visit between 10 p.m. and 5 a.m., when she's asleep. Between those hours, hang a right at the first junction; climb a ramp into a large, semi-flooded room; ascend another around the corner to the southeast; and drop the hammer on her. You'll find a couple of nice magical weapons on her body.

Again, travel to collect your reward and new orders. Fort Redman's on the east bank of the Lower Niben. It's closer to Leyawiin than to Bravil, and you make better time if you've been to Water's Edge (which is across the water to the southwest) for the Fighters Guild quest, "Amelion's Debt," or performed either the "Sheogorath" or "Nocturnal" Daedric quest. The one shrine is to the northwest and the other is to the east-southeast.

A coffin (containing the 500 gold, a schedule for an Alval Uvani, and your orders) is just right of the door into the fort. Fort Redman proper is a Vampire lair, and you find a single bandit in the tower itself.

A MATTER OF HONOR

Uvani is your next target. He's a traveling merchant, hence the schedule. Thus, you can figure out where to make the hit. There are two issues in this difficult mission: avoiding the glare of publicity and avoiding getting killed.

Uvani can kill you *easily*. He's not just a merchant but a battlemage who is a master of Destruction magic. You'll need something special to cancel out this advantage: mead. Uvani is allergic to the honey it contains. If he drinks it, about five seconds later he'll be paralyzed forever and at your mercy.

You'll find mead all over the game—including eight portions in the cellar of Summitmist Manor in Skingrad (which you cleared out in "Whodunit?") and five in the living quarters section of your former Sanctuary in Cheydinhal.

But how do you get Uvani to drink the stuff? It's tricky. Watch him. You'll see that, at meal times, he'll often sneak around. He likes to *steal* his food. Your challenge is to make sure the only food available for him to steal is the mead.

If you didn't use the Poisoned Apple in "The Purification" quest, that will work here as well.

In other words, you'll have to clear out all the edibles in the immediate area. At the inns along Uvani's route, that means you risk getting caught stealing yourself—or committing murder when you attack the paralyzed Uvani.

Looks like Alval Uvani has had his first, and last, drink of mead.

There's another option. The only private spot mentioned in the schedule is the merchant's home in the southwest corner of Leyawiin. You can pick the lock, clear out the cupboards, and wait for Uvani there.

However, Uvani doesn't make it home very often. Leyawiin is at the end of the last and longest leg of Uvani's itinerary, and the merchant may reach the city so behind schedule that he immediately turns around and heads back to Bravil. You may have to wait here quite a while for the perfect situation.

An impatient player may give up and opt for the dangerous compromise of killing Uvani in the wilderness between cities. However, your victim won't steal mead found en route, you can't ambush him (his Sneak skill is 100), and it'll have to be a straight, stand-up fight. You can win this battle—especially if it's fought in rough terrain where Uvani will have more trouble hitting you, but he'll probably only have to hit you once to end it.

Pick up your money and orders from the hollow stump in the garden reached through the passage between Rindir's Staffs and Edgar's Discount Spells in the western part of the Imperial City's Market District.

THE COLDEST SLEEP

Next stop: Gnoll Mountain, east of Bruma. Kill Havilstein Hoar-Blood, who has himself killed the chief of a Solstheim mead hall.

This is a comparatively straightforward hit—a tough one, though, as Mr. Hoar-Blood is five levels above your own and has a magic battle axe supplied with a variety of nasty enchantments. Note, too, that the mountain is fairly high and quite steep over some sections of slope and that you face an unexpected and simultaneous second opponent in Redmaw, Hoar-Blood's pet wolf.

Havilstein Hoar-Blood enjoys a quiet moment before he's murdered in cold blood.

Kill 'em in the right spot and you'll have some macabre fun watching the bodies zoom down the mountainside.

Your orders for the next mission are in the Ayleid ruin of Nornal, southeast of Cheydinhal. The easiest way to get there is to fast-travel to Muck Valley Cavern, where you removed Sibylla Draconis in "Next of Kin," and then head south. Yes, you have to go inside this time, but not far. Just descend the stairs, following the curving corridor at the bottom, and turn right at the first junction. Dive into the water, pick the lock on the gate, and the chest is right in front of you.

Nornal is a huge, four-level marauder base. You may explore it in the Miscellaneous quest "Vampire Cure."

A KISS BEFORE DYING

In Bravil, a Wood Elf named Ungolim spends his days inside his secure house and his evenings outdoors praying to an ancient statue that his fondest wish might be granted. Evidently he's in love with a married woman. The woman's husband has learned of Ungolim's passion and has summoned the Brotherhood to settle the affair…or so your orders state.

You're warned that, as in the case of J'Ghasta in Bruma, Ungolim suspects his life is in danger, may attack you on detection, and has bribed the guards to look the other way. Your journal suggests stealth.

Ungolim seeks the blessing of the Lucky Lady, unaware that his luck has just run out.

That'll work. If you're very good at sneaking—Ungolim's own Sneak skill is 55—you can creep up on your mark and whack him as he wanders near the statue in the northern part of town.

Activate the statue of the Lucky Lady to receive a blessing that boosts your Luck by 10 points for 1,000 seconds.

Before you can loot Ungolim's body or set out to collect your next orders, you're approached by Lucien Lachance, who says, in essence, "What the hell are you doing?"

By Sithis, what have you done? What madness has claimed you? You have betrayed me, you have betrayed the Dark Brotherhood! Why?

Lucien Lachance

Lucien Lachance arrives unexpectedly to show you the error of your ways.

You may have already suspected that something was amiss. After all, you started working for Lachance to eliminate a traitor, but recently, you've been performing missions that are, to judge from the official descriptions, comparatively mundane. And then there was your discovery at Unvani's house in Leyawiin.

In fact, they were not mundane at all. It turns out that everything you know is wrong. Since wiping out the Draconis family, you've been consistently directed to the wrong "dead drop" locations and, rather than performing Lachance's missions, have been decimating the ranks of the Black Hand. J'Ghasta, Shaleez, Uvani, and Hoar-Blood all were either Brotherhood Speakers or their Silencers, and Ungolim was the Listener.

Lachance now tells you to lie in wait near your next fake "dead drop" location and confront whoever delivers the orders.

FOLLOWING A LEAD

To date, your orders have always been at the dead drop when you arrived. Not on this occasion. You arrive in Anvil to find the barrel near the statue in the pond empty. Just wait. Before long, you see a Wood Elf named Enilroth heading in your direction. Sure enough, he deposits the orders in the barrel. If you speak to him, he'll tell you what he knows.

The Wood Elf boy Enilroth, doing the traitor's dirty work.

Any of the three conversational approaches will do. (The only differences are in the wording of the responses.) Enilroth says he was given his marching orders by a robed, faceless man the previous day as he passed by the Anvil lighthouse. Enilroth believes the man lived in the lighthouse cellar and speaks of an awful smell coming from those rooms. He refers you to Ulfgar Fog-Eye, the lighthouse keeper, for a key.

The orders direct you to assassinate Arquen—a "High Elf whore" whose whereabouts are uncertain. However, don't go looking for info on Arquen at the locations mentioned; you'll find her a little later in this quest. Nor should you detour to Fort Farragut. Lachance said the place is being watched, and apart from looting it, there's nothing special you can do there.

Enilroth keeps the 500 gold. You can liberate it only by picking his pocket after your exchange—not before; the gold doesn't appear in his inventory until you talk to him—or taking his life.

At the lighthouse, you can bully Fog-Eye into giving you the basement key either by following up a request (the first reply) with a threat or a demand, or by simply demanding it (the second reply). However, if you ask for the key and then say nothing, he'll get ticked off and attack.

The evidence you're seeking is on the little table next to the central pillar in the cellar's back room. To judge from this diary, the traitor is a lunatic obsessed with obtaining revenge against Lachance and the Night Mother for his own mother's murder. The diary also supplies the location for the Miscellaneous quest "The Ghost Ship of Anvil."

Someone clearly has issues....

Take the mother's head from the little shrine in the same room. It doesn't do anything, but it gives you a little Easter Egg in the next big scene.

You're too late to save Lachance from paying for the traitor's mischief. At Applewatch, you find him dead at the hands of the Black Hand. Its remaining members are still here—Arquen (who turns out to be not a prostitute, but a Speaker), Banus Alor, Belisarius, and Mathieu Bellamont.

Not to worry. As Lachance told you, you are not suspected of complicity in the plot. Indeed, with Lachance's death, you're promoted to Speaker.

But the Black Hand acts as though, with Lachance's death, the crisis has largely passed. You've read the diary and know better. One of these "fingers" of the Black Hand is the traitor and is waiting for the planned consultation with the Night Mother to strike.

Which one? This is where the head from the lighthouse basement comes in handy. Simply drop it anywhere inside Applewatch. Three of the four Brotherhood members take no notice of it when you speak to them. But one, Bellamont, seems to recognize it and is momentarily thrown off guard.

However, you can't expose him. (In time, he'll expose himself.) Just talk to Arquen about the Night Mother between midnight and 3 a.m., and she'll ask if you're ready for the trip to the Night Mother's resting place. If you agree, you'll be teleported, and the five of you reappear beside the statue of the Lucky Lady in Bravil.

HONOR THY MOTHER

When you arrive, you can't move. Arquen recites an invocation, and for a moment the statue seems to come to horrifying life. Its contortions reveal a trap door down to the Crypt of the Night Mother—the entrance to this last and shortest of the Dark Brotherhood quests.

The members of the Black Hand gather to invoke the Night Mother's Blessing.

After your companions descend, you can move again. Follow them. First activate the statue to receive its blessing. You need a little extra luck, and this is the last time you can extract the blessing.

After you descend, listen as Arquen appeals to the awakened Night Mother for guidance—and this dark legend straightens her out. Lachance was an obedient servant of Sithis. A traitor remains within the Black Hand.

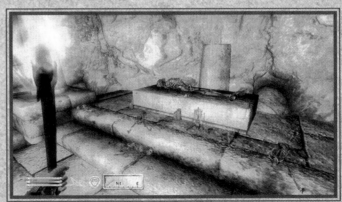

The Night Mother and her damned children, first offerings to the Dread Father Sithis.

Bellamont chooses this moment to strike. He kills Alor and Belisarius on the spot. He tries to attack the Night Mother, who can't be killed, and then you. With Arquen's help, beat him down. He's 20 levels above your own, with a Longsword of Burning, so this could prove difficult.

When he's dead, the Night Mother speaks to you. She explains everything, invites you to loot the place (the three sarcophagi contain nice random magical equipment), boosts your Blade of Woe dagger (with Damage Health, Damage Willpower, and Demoralize enchantments), and then zaps you back to the Cheydinhal Sanctuary.

Once you arrive, speak to Arquen and she'll lay things out. She's going to get the Sanctuary up and running again. You'll serve as the Brotherhood's Listener—the conduit between the Speakers and the Night Mother. You've reached the top of the Brotherhood's ladder. From here on out, it's all gravy.

EPILOGUE

WHISPERS OF DEATH

This isn't a quest so much as an extended reward. Check in with the Night Mother's statue in Bravil on a weekly basis, return each time to Arquen with the "whispers" (the identity and location of a single client), and you'll collect from her your cut of the week's receipts. These are the same sums that you received as rewards in your early Brotherhood missions—25 to 300 gold, depending on your level. Note that none of the 19 possible clients is real; their identities and locations are selected at random from lists. None of them are located within Cyrodiil.

When the Night Mother speaks, death follows.

Initially, the Sanctuary is empty save for you and your lieutenant. It won't remain that way for long. Once you start to collect assignments, the hideout is repopulated with up to three generic low-level members: a Khajiit swordsman and an Imperial archer—both two levels below you—and a Breton mage at your own level with a repertoire of 10 spells. If you took out the old Sanctuary's Dark Guardian, you find another one of those patrolling the halls as well.

These kids are very much in awe of you, and you can freak them out a bit with pop quizzes on the nature of Sithis and the Night Mother. If you ask about rumors, they'll often repeat your deeds in the Brotherhood back to you.

As Listener of the Dark Brotherhood, you are feared and respected above all others.

You can order one of these acolytes to follow you in your travels. (In theory, if you're also Arch-Mage of the Mages Guild, you could have both an apprentice and a murderer tailing you around.) The murderers have a somewhat more elaborate command set than the Guild counterparts. In addition to the usual "follow," "stay," and "go away," Brotherhood underlings also follow in stealth mode and follow "with utmost haste."

ARENA

A faction of a slightly different color: bright red.

These are grim times for Cyrodiil. The emperor and his sons are dead. Daedra are coming out of the woodwork. Kvatch is largely gone. The guilds are under siege. Only in the Imperial City's great Arena can the people give up their cares for a few hours to the intense sport of gladiatorial combat.

There are two ways to participate in the Arena. You can win money as a gambler, or fame and money as a combatant.

It has no entry requirements—anybody can play—and just one great, over-arching quest: If you can defeat 27 opponents over the course of 22 matches, you'll become the Arena's new grand champion.

Either way, present yourself at the entrance to the Arena—on the east side of the Imperial City—between 9 a.m. and 9 p.m.

The Imperial City Arena, as it has stood since the days of Gaiden Shinji.

THE GAMBLER

This appears pretty straightforward. Speak to Hundolin, the gatekeeper. This agreeable fellow will accept your wager on either the Yellow or the Blue team for 25, 50, or 100 gold as many times as you wish while the Arena is open for business. If you win, see Hundolin again and you'll get double your money back.

The gatekeeper, Hundolin, is only too happy to take your wager.

Once you place your bet, enter the right-hand Arena door onto a balcony overlooking the killing floor with a cheering crowd around you.

You can't reach these folks and couldn't interact with them even if you could. However, you can chat with eight NPCs who visit the balcony at various points during the week: Gwinas, Pista Marillin, and Winson (every day); Roderic Pierrane on weekdays; Wumeek on Monday, Wednesday, and Friday; and Elisa Pierrane (wife to Roderic) and Ulen and Dralora Athram on weekends. (Note that Gwinas has a bit part in the Main Quest and won't show up at the Arena while its "The Path of Dawn" segment is running.)

Make it a point to visit the Arena at various times and speak to all of them. Mostly, it's for fun. One is flaky, at least one is addicted, one's going to catch hell from his wife (though she never catches up to him), and, as you'll see, one has useful information. (Some gamblers have to travel significant distances and so may take a while to appear.)

When you step into the room, an announcer starts talking, two portcullises in the Arena open, gladiators clad in yellow and blue emerge, and the fight begins.

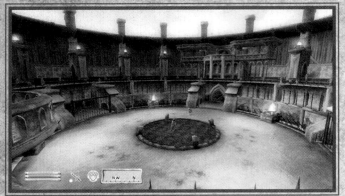
You could win a fortune in the Arena—or lose your shirt trying.

Hundolin said the chances of winning are 50/50. That is true. However, that's where the parity ends. The fighters are equipped at random and it's in these load-outs that much of the battle is won and lost. Each combatant is guaranteed to receive light or heavy raiment (armor) and will probably (a 90 percent chance for each item) receive each of the following: a melee weapon that could range from a dagger up to a two-handed Elven weapon; a shield; and a helmet. Hence, the actual odds could be distinctly uneven in any given battle.

LUCK

Can you can influence the result? Not directly. An invisible barrier separates the balcony seats and the Arena floor. And, of course, you don't know who has what equipment until you watch the fight.

However, if you speak to fellow gambler Dralora Athram, you learn that Luck seems to have an impact on the outcome. Mrs. Athram says her enchanted amulet helps her win her bets.

If only you had an amulet like the one Dralora Athram possesses...

It's not just talk. The game does check your Luck attribute when you step into the spectators' area; when it reaches 50, the fighter on whom you bet begins to accrue additional hit points. The more Luck, the more points and, in general, the better the odds—though naturally hit points alone won't make up for critical shortfalls in your fighter's ordnance. (For

instance, if the gladiator doesn't have a weapon, he or she may well get creamed—though that's not a sure thing either.)

So how to improve your Luck at the spur of the moment? Spells, potions, scrolls, and magic items all work. The trick is finding them just when you need them.

Two Fortify Luck spells are available from Trevaia at the Chapel of Dibella in Anvil. One raises Luck by 10 points for 60 seconds, the other by 15 points for 90 seconds.

Three types of Fortify Luck potions carry respective boosts of 10, 15, and 20 points for 30 seconds, and two Fortify Luck scrolls offer boosts of 50 and 100! All turn up in loot and their respective vendors, but not predictably—they appear on lists of items that are adjusted to the player's level—and it's impossible to say precisely where they'll appear.

Weak Fortify Luck potions are available at Renoit's Books in Chorrol and at the Cheydinhal Mages Guild.

Or, if you're a Journeyman-level alchemist, you can make one. You'll need two of the three ingredients that have a Fortify Luck effect. It's the tertiary effect of the common bonemeal and primrose leaves and the secondary effect of the rare green stain shelf cap.

Now, if you're a Journeyman alchemist, you probably have at least reached the rank of Apprentice in the Mages Guild and so have access to the Arcane University. If so, you're all set. You'll find bonemeal in the Arcane University's Chironasium, upstairs at the Mystic Archives, and upstairs at the Praxographical Center, and the other two ingredients grow wild on the grounds.

If you're not an Apprentice, you're shut out of the relevant areas of the university campus, and you'll have to collect the ingredients the hard way.

The cellar of Agarmir's house (near the southern tip of the city's Talos Plaza District) holds 13 portions of bonemeal. You must pick a three-tumbler lock to get into the house and a leveled one (minimum two tumblers) to reach the cellar. Agarmir spends much of his time out and about, so it's an easy burglary. (Agarmir is himself a thief who is involved in the Miscellaneous quest "Unfriendly Competition," so don't whack him before his time if you want to complete that mission.)

Primrose leaves grow in fair quantity in the wilderness, with an 80 percent chance of harvesting the ingredient from each plant. It grows in greatest quantity (nine plants) in eastern Cyrodiil at the eastern headwaters of the Panther River. The closest location is Pell's Gate. Just swim south from the waterfront to Old Bridge and then south along the river to find three plants.

Green stain shelf cap is an iffier affair. They can be hard to spot. (They grow out of the sides of trees and rocks.) You have just a 50 percent chance of harvesting the ingredient from any given plant. And it can be found conveniently only in the north-central part of Leyawiin (two plants). So you may wind up searching in the distant wilderness. The greatest concentrations can be found south of the Onyx Caverns (six plants)—it's east-northeast of Leyawiin near the Black Marsh border—and in a small surface ruin south of the Ayleid ruin Piukanda (three plants). The latter is just up the slope northwest of Lake Rumare.

Finally, the game has three different amulets with Fortify Luck enchantments. The strongest, which carries a 10-point boost, turns up unpredictably in loot and shops, but the other two can be found in the wilderness—and one of them is right under your nose.

The weakest, with a 6-point boost, can be found beside a statue inside the ruined tower above Fort Linchal, which is northeast of Kvatch. A middle-rank amulet, with an 8-point boost, is atop a pillar in the ruin of Fort Teleman—near the Black Marsh border south of the southern headwaters of the Panther River. A character with a good Acrobatics skill can reach it by jumping atop the wall, following it to a spot near the pillar, and jumping the gap.

(Naturally, this raises the issue of how you can boost your Acrobatics skill. The same general rules apply, but you can also use trainers and skill books—and it's a good deal easier to find an item enchanted with Fortify Acrobatics.)

Finally, you can just kill Mrs. Athram and take her amulet. We guess it wasn't that lucky after all! She gets around, and the easiest approach is to kill her—and probably also her husband and fellow Arena gambler, Ulen—in their bed at home. Pick a three-tumbler lock to enter their house on the north side of the plaza's central rotunda.

Kill Dralora Athram while she's sleeping, and the lucky amulet will be yours.

THE COMBATANT

The heart of the beast. Use the left-hand door and descend into the Arena Bloodworks—so named for the blood that sometimes drips down from the killing floor above.

The Arena Bloodworks, training hall of some of the best warriors Cyrodiil has ever known.

This is the training area for Arena fighters. Talk to Owyn at the east end of the north room. He'll talk some intimidating talk and, if you nevertheless sign on as a fighter, assign you the unflattering rank of "pit dog" and give you a choice of light or heavy raiment. You'll have to wear this in every Arena battle save the last.

How to choose? It's best to be guided here by your armor skills and whether you want to travel light. The raiments are identically enchanted—adding 2 points to your Personality attribute and 5 to your Athletics skill—but the heavy raiment weighs 27 pounds more than the light. (Ignore Owyn's comment about figuring you for a "heavy raiment type." It's just a tease, not an assessment of your stats.)

And the rest of your ordnance? Don't worry; you're not going to be thrown to the wolves of randomness like those Blue and Yellow team guys in "The Gambler" section—although you have in fact been assigned to the Blue team. (Owyn mentions this under the "Rules of Competition" topic.)

Instead, you're thrown to the wolves of standardization. The raiment is full-body armor, and its use prevents the use of any cuirass, greaves, boots, gauntlets, or bracers you've acquired in your travels. (If you remove the raiment during the match, you're disqualified and will have to refight the match. If you do it again, you're stripped of your rank and barred from future matches.)

However, you can use whatever weapons, shield, helmet, and enchanted jewelry you please.

If you do not have a weapon, you'll find several here: four iron claymores on wooden racks in each of the two principal rooms; three iron warhammers on another rack in the entry room; and an iron longsword beside a bedroll on the east side of the entry room. (You'll want something better—that is, enchanted—if you plan to make the Arena a career.) You can also find an Athletics skill book, *The Ransom of Zarek*, in a cupboard against the Bloodworks' north wall.

THE MATCHES

If you're suited up, the Arena is in operation (for now, the same 9-to-9 schedule as for gamblers), and you don't have a bet riding with Hundolin, tell Owyn you're ready for a match. He offers a short briefing. A gate opens nearby; pass through it into the adjacent "Red Room" and the passage that leads up to the Arena floor. At the top of the stairs to the portcullis, the announcer begins his spiel. You're on.

When the gates are lowered, the battle begins, and it rages until someone lies dead.

To fight in the Arena, you must go through Owyn, the curmudgeonly blademaster.

TATICS

It's always a fight to the death—no yielding—and anything goes. Spells are fine. Bows and arrows are fine. Running away screaming is fine.

There are many ways to win. A lot of them involve standard combat tactics, and we cover those in the "Combat" chapter. Here, we discuss tactics specific to the Arena.

The Arena floor is an enclosed, circular area from which you can't retreat—the door back to the Red Room locks behind you—and that contains no extra supplies. Be prepared in advance with potions, spells, weapons, and those few pieces of armor you're allowed. The longer you can postpone your sojourn in the Arena, the better stuff you'll acquire in your adventures and the better you'll do here.

It's wide open. You can jump up on the abutments beside the gates, but they're not sufficiently elevated to put you out of range of a melee weapon. And the spikes along certain sections of wall don't do any damage.

However, four blocks, arranged in a square around the central grating, do provide potential stumbling blocks for pursuers, and four pillars closer to the walls can be used to slow pursuers and also offer cover from ranged weapons and spells.

The Blue and Yellow team gates are directly opposite each other. You can't shoot through them with arrows or spells, but you can open up at a distance the moment the gate comes down. This is the farthest your opponent will ever be from you. Don't waste the opportunity.

Finally, note that these gates remain down during the fighting. Don't back into this passage; it's a potential death trap, but it's also a place to ensnare the more elusive of your opponents.

Those opponents are a varied lot, but they're all unfailingly aggressive and very fast. It's vital that you have either excellent native speed yourself or spells or enchantments to enhance it or to slow down your opponents. If you can outpace the Yellow team, you can win many matches—even against otherwise superior opponents—simply by keeping a safe distance, slowly wearing down your adversary with spells, and then stepping up to deliver the coup de grâce.

Afterward, you'll learn something of Arena protocol: You can't loot the bodies of your opponents or claim weapons and shields they may have dropped when they died. You also can't enter the Yellow team's reported Red Room. (It doesn't actually exist.) All you can do is descend again to your own Red Room, activate the Basin of Renewal to magically replenish your Health and Fatigue, and report back to Owyn for a reward and, at the end of each of the seven tiers, a promotion.

Along the way, you can chat with a supportive Blue team gladiator and the unpleasant Yellow team hero, who work out in the Bloodworks. The latter has different taunts at each level—all of which contribute to making killing her in the last hero-level match the more enjoyable.

THE OPPONENTS

The Pit Dog Matches

Mostly easy. You face a female Wood Elf supplied with a longsword and a light shield and helmet; a male Imperial with a heavier shield and helm; and an Argonian archer. All are a level above your own, but only the rugged Imperial stands a real chance of beating you. You receive 50 gold after each of the first two victories and 100 gold and promotion to "brawler" after the third.

The Brawler Matches

Your first and third opponents are an axe-wielding Nord and an axe-wielding Khajiit each two levels above your own. In between, you face (simultaneously) Wood Elf twin sisters—each a level up on you—who are armed with a bow and a claymore. Watch out for the bowwoman. She has a Chameleon potion; all of a sudden, she vanishes and you start getting hit by arrows that come out of nowhere. Stay behind the pillars and switch over to healing spells until the potion runs its course. You'll receive 100 gold after each of the first two victories and 150 gold and promotion to "bloodletter" after the third.

The Wood Elf twin sisters must both be defeated before you'll be declared victor.

The Bloodletter Matches
Here, it starts to get tough. Your opponents aren't quite so hardy as those in the brawler bouts, but they're generally better equipped: The opening Redguard may use a mace. The Breton lady that follows has a shortsword, heavy armor, and Endurance and Speed potions. You'll receive 150 gold after each of the first two victories and 200 gold and promotion to "myrmidon" after the third.

The Myrmidon Matches
The Shimmerstrike dagger used by your first opponent carries a weak Frost Damage enchantment. The High Elf (light armor and a longsword) and Orc (heavy armor and a silver battleaxe) that follow are comparatively nondescript. You receive 200 gold after each of the first two victories and 250 gold and promotion to "warrior" after the third.

The Warrior Matches
The Nord swordswoman who opens this round is a good challenge—three levels above your own and as fast with her longsword as Owyn asserts. The second round puts you up against the first of two magic users. Owyn's advice is spot on: Close with her quickly. (It's better to face her longsword than her daunting array of spells.) Finally, you face an Orc with a big old warhammer with which she probably won't have to hit you more than twice. Maintain a safe distance, but stay close enough that you can dart in for a telling blow. The hammer is heavy (75 pounds) and slow to swing, and you'll have a window for a quick hit after each miss. You receive 250 gold after each of the first two victories, 300 gold and promotion to "gladiator" after the third.

The Gladiator Matches
The three Argonian prisoners are unarmed and present little threat—unless they can box you in and gang up on you. (They're all of a higher level than you, and each has a respectable Hand-to-Hand skill.) So stay away from them and the walls. Follow a path between the pillars. In the course of pursuit, the pillars eventually will separate one from the others. When this happens strike swiftly and then withdraw and take them down one by one. They're followed by a Khajiit with healing potions and a Breton (somewhat easier) with a longsword. You receive 300 gold after each of the first two victories and 350 and promotion to "hero" after the third.

The Hero Matches
This final round opens with what will probably be a long and bloody fight against a former member of the Blades (several levels above your own) who seems to have all his old equipment, including his Akaviri longsword. Make sure you have some extra healing potions set aside for this match.

He once served the emperor, and now this ex-Blade is putting his training to good use—against you.

The second battle can be short. You face a magic user five levels above your own and supplied with a pack of Fire Damage spells and a Grey Aegis shield with a potent Resist Magic enchantment. You don't want to get involved in a spell-trading contest. As with the earlier mage, close with her quickly. You receive 350 gold after each of the first two victories.

The third match is nasty indeed. You finally face the Yellow team champion—that bad-tempered woman from the Bloodworks—and a pair of allies. She's seven levels above you, and the allies, a magic user and an archer, are, respectively, two levels above and even with your own. However, they're well-equipped allies—the archer has a high-quality bow and arrows, and the spellcaster has a nice array of Destruction and Restoration spells.

In short, trouble.

You're not alone. A Boar, Porkchop (previously seen only in his Bloodworks pen), fights on your side. Make the most of him. That may be tough, since you have no direct control over his movements. And if he goes up against the champion, he may live up to his name in the opening seconds of the match. But, ideally, he'll either occupy one of the three while you're taking on the others or gnaw at someone's backside as you slice into the front (or vice versa).

Go after the allies first. Otherwise, they're bound to pelt you with spells and arrows and wear you down. Yes, you may take a whack or two from the bad-mannered girl while you perform these tasks, but the magic user has few defenses in melee and the archer none. And you did bring healing potions, yes?

Success is rewarded with 500 gold and promotion to "champion."

GRAND CHAMPION MATCH

One more bout: You can challenge the Arena's grand champion—the half-Orc Agronak gro-Malog—known to (and loved by) Cyrodiil's people as "The Gray Prince."

The Gray Prince has never been defeated. Could you be the one to end his reign as grand champion?

For this task, Owyn hands you off to battle matron Ysabel Andronicus, who holds court at the other end of the room. To date, she has been at best curt to you. She's still a bit curt, but now she'll at least answer your questions.

The rules that held in standard Arena matches are more or less abandoned here. In this match, you can wear whatever armor you please. Andronicus says gro-Malog probably has his own Raiment of Valor (an emblem of his grand-champion status) heavily enchanted and suggests you do the same.

Gro-Malog's raiment is indeed enchanted: It boosts his Health, Fatigue, Athletics, and Personality by 10 points each. On top of that, he has a longsword and shield and he knows how to use his equipment. (His Blade and Heavy Armor skills are both very high, as are his hit points and Fatigue. In short, he's a very tough opponent.)

Prepare for the battle by beefing up on…well, everything: armor, weapons, potions, spells, and so on. The same tactics you've used in earlier bouts will serve you well. Indeed, maintaining a healthy distance or a respectable Block skill (the higher than better) is more important than ever, as gro-Malog has some killer power attacks.

But suppose he's beyond your ability to beat. There is a second route. Talk to gro-Malog about "the Gray Prince" and perform the Miscellaneous quest "Origin of the Gray Prince." (See the "Miscellaneous Quests" chapter for details.)

The upshot: You're sent to find proof of gro-Malog's "noble birthright" but wind up discovering that he's half Vampire! If you're already champion when you complete the quest—you can do it at any time and with or without an Arena affiliation—he'll beg you to challenge him. When you do, his response will be listless.

Then check in with Andronicus and select a nickname. Female characters have two choices: Lady Luck or The Iron Maiden. Pick carefully—the nickname has no effects for good or ill, but it will stick—and make your way up to the Arena as before.

The Tamriel Terror, huh? I like it! Yeah, that'll do nicely. All right, it's time to see if you're crazy good or just plain crazy.
Ysabel Andronicus

Choose a name that best defines your character.

Now, past experience in Morrowind may suggest you're still in for a fight. Characters who used you to end their lives in that game had a nasty habit of fighting back. And in the Arena, initially, it seems as though nothing's changed. Right out of the gate, gro-Malog charges at you…

…and then stops. He sheathes his sword, stands there, and begs you to end his life.

Hit him once and he'll go down, not to get up again. Strip the raiment from the late champion—you can also claim the rest of his possessions if you like—and present the armor to Andronicus to receive 1,000 gold and your own light or heavy raiment. (These have the same enchantments as gro-Malog's raiment and the same weights as the two you chose between when you first signed on.)

You've done it. We bow down before you.

EPILOGUE

Is there more? You bet. After she names you grand champion, Andronicus invites you to return to discuss your future.

This turns out to mean weekly matches in which you go up against monsters and wild animals. These combats—which continue indefinitely—can take place at any hour of the day. (Betting continues on its 9-to-9 schedule.) You'll always have three options, varying in difficulty, and success is rewarded with gold commensurate with both the number of creatures killed and your current level.

At Level 5 or lower, you can choose among a battle with a single Boar, a Boar and a Wolf, or two Wolves and a Goblin

Skirmisher. At Levels 6–8, you can face a Goblin Berserker, two Trolls, or two Goblin Berserkers and a Troll. At Levels 9–11, you'll go up against one Mountain Lion, two of 'em, or two of 'em plus a Spriggan. At Levels 12–14, it's a Bear, two Minotaurs, or a Bear and two Minotaurs. (Note that the Bear looks like the Brown Bear from the wilderness but has slightly different stats—most notably, 75 more hit points.) At Levels 15–17, you're going against an Ogre, two Ogres, or two Ogres and a Land Dreugh. And at Level 18 and higher, your opponents range from one to three Minotaur Lords.

That's the big perk. The small one: You now have a groupie. You'll meet the Adoring Fan just outside the Arena entrance after you ascend to the championship. This Wood Elf, with hair like a yellow chocolate kiss, watched you kill the Gray Prince and now worships you devoutly. In dialogue, he offers to carry your weapon, shine your shoes, and give you a backrub. All he'll actually do is follow you, stay put, or make himself scarce on your instructions.

Yes, oh great and mighty Grand Champion? Is there something you need? Can I carry your weapon? Shine your boots? Backrub, perhaps?

Adoring Fan

As grand champion, you'll earn the adoration of your own personal fan!

Even so, he's not entirely useless. At night, or if you enter a dark area, he'll bring out a torch. And he serves effectively as an early-warning radar for combat. The moment someone gets an idea to eat your brain, Adoring Fan is off, returning once the danger has passed. Unless, of course, you get sick of his devotion and attack him yourself, in which case this character will defend himself vigorously—and, we may say, fruitlessly, since he's six levels below your own. (However, you can't kill him in any permanent sense; he eventually respawns outside the Arena.)

One other minor effect: Your great deed enters the realm of gossip and rumor. You'll hear about it again and again from other people. Most of them will be in happy states of shock and awe.

But one, the Blue team gladiator, who made so many admiring and encouraging comments as you climbed the Arena ladder, is clearly incensed that you've killed his friend and mentor.

"Congratulations, grand champion," he says bitterly. "I hope it was worth it."

DADDY!

One final note. South-southwest of the Arena, under a small Romanesque colonnade, a Redguard named Branwen and an Argonian named Saliith practice hand-to-hand combat. They're training to be combatants in the Arena, and they do so every day from 6 a.m. to 1 a.m.

Every day, Branwen and Saliith work toward their one goal—becoming Arena combatants.

There's a little more to it. It doesn't rise to the level of a quest, but it does supply a touch more information about the otherwise anonymous blademaster, Owyn.

Enter the Bloodworks and look on the floor just to the right of the raiment cabinet near Owyn to spot a crumpled piece of paper. It's a letter from Branwen to Owyn in which she claims to be his daughter.

"One night with a scullery maid is all it takes," she writes. "Or maybe your father deserted you, too, and never taught you the basic lessons of life?"

Owyn,

I know you don't believe me. I know you think I'm just some stupid kid who doesn't know what she's talking about. But the truth is the truth — you ARE my father.

One night with a scullery maid is all it takes. Or maybe your father deserted you, too, and never taught you the basic lessons of life?

Take   Exit

The crumpled note on the floor near Owyn speaks volumes about Branwen's predicament—and Owyn's opinion on the matter.

Neither Owyn nor Branwen will comment on this message. (We suspect Owyn's comment is in the crumple.) But you can find some nice loot in the Arena hopefuls' camp. Wait till they turn in and then pick the lock on the five-tumbler chest in their little camp. (You can also pickpocket or—ugh—murder Branwen for the key.) The chest contains 100 gold, the Blade skill book *Song of Hrormir*, and an enchanted bracer (Bands of Kwang Lao) that boosts your Hand-to-Hand skill by 20 points.

Other illicit activities: The five-tumbler lockbox in the Arena foyer contains 500 gold—a lucrative target for a late-night burglary. Just mind the guards.

THE DAEDRIC QUESTS

There are 15 Daedric quests, but that's a deceptive number. Many of the quests are effectively two or three missions—and one comprises five.

Before you get the specific task from a Daedra lord, you must find the shrine and then make the appropriate offering.

And you won't always get help finding the shrine—in six quests, you get none at all—and the help you do get will be available from no more than two people and then only if you have the correct topic. (Of course, it's possible to stumble across the shrines on your own while exploring, but if someone gives you the location, it will be written to your map and save you a lot of time.)

How to get the necessary "Daedra cults" and "Daedra shrines" topics? If you're just starting out, you can't. You have to read the book *Modern Heretics: A Study of Daedra Worship in the Empire*, and it's available only to characters who've made some progress in the game. To get it, you must either complete the "Weynon Priory" segment of the Main Quest or finish the recommendation quests for the Mages Guild.

Completing the "Weynon Priory" segment gives you access to Cloud Ruler Temple—a Blades fortress high in the Jerall Mountains northwest of Bruma. The book lies on a table in the Great Hall and on a shelf in the library in the east wing. Finishing the recommendation quests gives you access to the initially locked-off areas of the Imperial City's Arcane University, where the book is on a shelf on the ground floor of the Mystic Archives.

The offerings are often a challenge, too. In 10 quests, you must provide an item—some of them ultra-obscure. In another you have to provide three that are ultra-mundane. And in another you must adjust your stats to the liking of the Daedra lord.

Finally, the Daedric quests are restricted by level. For example, to do Sanguine's quest, you must be at least Level 8. The reason? The rewards for these quests are the most powerful weapons, armor, and items in the game. It wouldn't do to have some little Level 1 character running around with the Mace of Molag Bal, now would it?

DAEDRIC QUESTS, LEVEL RESTRICTIONS, AND REWARDS

Quest	Artifact	Level Requirement
Azura	Azura's Star	2
Boethia	Goldbrand	20
Clavicus Vile	Masque of Clavicus Vile	20
Hermaeus Mora	Oghma Infinium	20+*
Hircine	Savior's Hide	17
Malacath	Volendrung	10
Mephala	Ebony Blade	15
Meridia	Ring of Khajiiti	10
Molag Bal	Mace of Molag Bal	17
Namira	Ring of Namira	5
Nocturnal	Skeleton Key	10
Peryite	Spell Breaker	10
Sanguine	Sanguine Rose	8
Sheogorath	Wabbajack	2
Vaermina	Skull of Corruption	5

* Has the level requirement as well as the requirement to have finished all of the other Daedric quests.

AZURA

Reading *Modern Heretics* also gives you the location of Azura's shrine. For a lot of players, this is the first Daedric quest.

After all, the "Azura" quest is semi-incorporated into the Main Quest under the heading "Blood of the Daedra," which actively puts forward the quest as the way to obtain a Daedric artifact that Martin needs to create a gateway into Camoran's Paradise.

However, you don't have to go along with the program. You can perform "Azura" separately from the Main Quest. The artifact can come from any of the 15 Daedric quests, and you can do Azura's quest at any point among them—except for last, which is reserved for the "Hermaeus Mora" quest.

The shrine is in the Jerall Mountains north of Lake Arrius, which is itself north-northeast of Cheydinhal. If you've performed the Fighters Guild quest "The Noble's Daughter," fast-travel to Lord Rugdumph's Estate and make your way northwest. If you've done the Thieves Guild quest "Turn a Blind Eye," fast-travel to the Temple of the Ancestor Moths and make your way southwest and then south down the valley. The shrine is on a mountain shelf just above and west of the valley floor.

At the shrine, the goddess's followers are much more peaceful than the savage Daedric creatures you've encountered. But they are suspicious of your intentions and either won't talk to you or won't tell you anything.

The communion of the faithful at the shrine of Azura.

Just ring for service.

However, speak to the Dark Elf Mels Maryon, raise his Disposition to 50, and you'll learn how to summon the goddess: offer glow dust at the shrine at dawn or dusk.

Glow dust can be found in the remains of the Will-o-the-Wisp. However, these ethereal creatures show up only in mythic creature dungeons at Level 10 and in swampy areas at Level 9. (The closest location would be Kingcrest east-southeast of the shrine.)

You can sometimes buy this rare ingredient from alchemists. Another option is to wait for the "Blood of the Daedra" segment of the Main Quest, when three Wisps turn up on and around the downslope north of Azura's shrine, or the Fighters Guild quest "Mystery at Harlun's Watch," when three more turn up near the entrance to Swampy Cave.

And if none of these possibilities work out, happily, there is one loose portion of glow dust knocking around in the game. It's in the Bruma Mages Guild—on a table on the left side of the room in the cellar's northwest corner. (Join the guild first by talking to Jeanne Frasoric, and it won't even be considered stealing.)

Maryon didn't give any hours for your offering—just "dawn" and "dusk." That's 5 a.m. to 7 a.m. and 5 p.m. to 7 p.m. This is one of the rare occasions when the game requires your presence at a specific time.

Activate the shrine with the glow dust in your inventory (assuming you're at least Level 2), and Azura will ask you to do her a service: Relieve the suffering of (that is, kill) five of her followers who long ago killed the Vampire Dratik and were themselves infected with vampirism in the process.

The Gutted Mine they inhabit is just over the mountain to the southwest. It's small, but it is filled with five "Afflicted Brethren" just looking for your blood. Each is marked on your map and compass.

The only possible hitch is that two of them are in a lower section behind a secret door in the mine's northwest corner—operated by a nearby pull cord. And they can infect you with the Vampire disease (porphyric hemophilia), so bring a Cure Disease potion or two.

Note that the Orc Vampire has on his body a worn note. It's interesting in and of itself, but there's no special bonus for returning it. Simply return to the shrine at any time, and Azura will award you Azura's Star—a reusable Grand Soul Gem.

And you may miss this, but that stuff she says about lighting candles in memory of her lost servants? It's true. Five orangish candles are placed high on the great rock behind the shrine when you kill the fifth Vampire.

BOETHIA

With the "Daedric shrines" topic, you can get the location of Boethia's shrine southeast of the city from Bora gra-Uzgash, who runs Borba's Goods and Stores just east of Cheydinhal's West Gate. (Ms. gra-Uzgash is a homebody and only goes out for dinner, which she takes at Newlands Lodge from about 8 p.m. to 10 p.m.)

In fact, the shrine's waaay southeast. You'll cut your journey in half if you've visited Drakelowe on the upper Corbolo River for Miscellaneous quest "Vampire Cure." Otherwise, you face a long trek over increasingly difficult terrain along the mountains' western fringe.

At the shrine, speak to Haekwon, a Redguard. He tells you to make an offering of a Daedra heart. You'll find these in the bodies of the most human-like Daedra—the Dremora and Xivilai. Your journal informs you that you must be at Level 20 to begin this quest.

The Xivilai makes a couple of nasty appearances in Camoran's Paradise in the Main Quest but is otherwise a leveled enemy that appears only after you've reached Level 20 or 21. However, the Dremora is standard equipment in and around the Daedric citadels in Oblivion.

Or, if you have the right spell, you can summon one of these Daedra and then plunder it for its heart. Athragar in the Chorrol Mages Guild sells a Summon Dremora spell, Volanaro in the Bruma Mages Guild offers a pricey Summon Dremora Lord spell, and Borissean at the Arcane University's Praxographical Center has a Summon Xivilai spell.

Finally, two Daedra hearts are rattling around inside the game world—one in a four-tumbler display case in the company offices on the top floor of the Anvil Fighters Guild, the other on a table in the big room at the bottom of the entry stairs on the top level of Ceyatatar (a large Ayleid ruin north of the Gold Road about two-thirds of the way from Skingrad to Lake Rumare).

Got everything? Potions? Spare weapons and armor? Repair hammers? Filled Soul Gems?

Activate the Boethia shrine with the heart in your inventory and the god tells you scornfully that you are not of his flock—but gives you a chance to prove yourself. He then opens a portal to Oblivion and challenges you to take part in his "Tournament of Ten Bloods": a series of one-on-one duels with members of the nine other Tamriel races. (Yours is the tenth "blood"; you won't fight a character of your own race.)

You'll complete a circuit of nine small, square arenas, linked by gates and arranged in a great circle about a statue of Boethia, with the invisible god himself cast as the announcer and commentator (and rather enjoying himself, we think).

Arrive at the tournament loaded with potions, repair hammers, spare weapons and armor, and filled Soul Gems or Varla Stones to recharge your magical gear. These are tough opponents. And there are nine of them. And you must fight them, one after the other. And you cannot rest or return home for sandwiches and Band-Aids. Your only advantage is your kit. They are all obviously overconfident swaggering bullies who have come with only a few Poison or Paralyze potions apiece. So make every point of Encumbrance count when you come to the Tournament of Ten Bloods.

Welcome to Boethia Stadium.

But you are fighting each one-on-one, after all, so how hard could it be? And there is plenty of lava, and Boethia forgot to put guard rails on his bridge spans. And there are lots of nice tight places to sneak around and bushwhack your opponents from, and narrow paths near the lava where someone could have an accident.

When the ninth opponent goes down, another portal appears. Once you've finished looting the losers, enter the portal, return to the shrine, activate it, and you'll receive a splendid enchanted sword called Goldbrand, which has a Fire Damage enchantment that does a fixed 22 points of damage per strike. (No, you can't convert it into Eltonbrand as you could in *Morrowind*.)

CLAVICUS VILE

No one tells you where to find this shrine, but as it's just southwest of the Imperial City—enclosed by a northern loop of the combined Gold and Red Ring Roads—you're less likely to need that kind of help.

At the shrine, talk to the Khajiit, Ma'Raska. He explains that you need 500 gold to transact business with the god. Your journal tells you that you have to be at Level 20. If you've got the gold on hand, activate the shrine directly.

Clavicus Vile and his cute puppy, Barbas

Vile wants a sword containing the soul of the warrior Umbra. (You may have encountered and dispatched this somber individual in the mountains behind Suran in *Morrowind*.) You're to begin the quest in Pell's Gate—a village near the Red Ring Road south of the Imperial City and east of the shrine.

You won't have gone far before you hear a voice. Don't turn around; there's no one there. The voice is Barbas, the Hound of Clavicus Vile, and it's coming from a figurine of a dog that appeared in your gigantic backpack at the end of Vile's speech.

Barbas insists you've made a bad bargain. Umbra's trouble. Your journal elaborates, saying that the sword in Vile's hands might cause "great ruin" to the lord's realm. "So, just leave things be," Barbas says. "Walk away. It's your best bet, really."

You can walk away at any time—just as you can with any quest. But you haven't yet done anything to walk away from.

At Pell's Gate, look up Irroke the Wide. (He lives on the east side of the settlement but spends his day wandering in the area.) At a Disposition of 60, he'll open up and explain that his apprentice Lenwin found the Umbra sword, seemed to be taken over by it, adopted the name "Umbra," and finally signed on with mercenaries and vanished. However, he's had a report that she's been seen recently at nearby Vindasel—an Ayleid ruin just to the west-northwest along Red Ring Road.

It's not hard to get down to Lenwin/Umbra—nothing but critters and the usual Ayleid traps block the way—and she's pretty much as Irroke led you to expect. She gives you a choice: leave or fight.

In fact, you have three options.

Leaving is celebrated by Barbas as a wise decision, and perhaps it is wise. It probably saves your life. Umbra is one of the toughest characters you'll meet in the game. She's extremely difficult to kill one-on-one. And if Umbra the person hits you solidly with Umbra the sword, she may not need to hit you again. (Don't worry about consequences. While Vile is ostensibly ticked off at you for backing out of your deal and says some threatening things if you activate the shrine, there are no actual bad results.)

She seems quite nice, but she has some rage issues.

Then again, this soul-trapping blade is one of the best in the game, and Umbra is clad from head to foot in ebony armor. Those are two excellent reasons for killing her. (Also, Barbas is right: It's a bad bargain.)

We vote for not telling her that you're going to fight. Just do it: Hit her with a nasty scroll from your dungeon-delving—you should always have one of these on hand—to knock down her Health, and when she's trying to catch her breath, beat on her with, say, Goldbrand (from the "Boethia" quest), and you'll wonder what all the fuss was about. (Also look for some nice loot in the chest beside the northwest pillar.) Make sure to hit her hard and fast, though: she regenerates Health like a Troll.

At this point, Barbas restates his case of not giving the sword to Vile. You can refuse to give it to him formally (returning the shrine and denying his request) or simply go off and do other business and leave the quest unfinished. It doesn't matter.

Or, if you keep even your bad bargains, simply return and turn over the sword. The "masque" you receive in exchange—

in fact, a full helmet with a glum face molded on the front—raises your Personality by 20 points.

Nice. But think of what you just gave away.

HIRCINE

You hear about Hircine's shrine (and the ones dedicated to Mephala and Vaermina) from Ontus Vanin, a minor player in the Thieves Guild quest "Misdirection" who lives in the southwest corner of the Imperial City's Talos Plaza. Just swim across Lake Rumare from the Waterfront District, make your way east on the Red Ring Road to the Ayleid ruin Sardavar Leed (or fast-travel there if you visited it in the Miscellaneous Quest "The Collector"), and head up the hill south-southeast to the shrine.

Speak to Vajhira, a Khajiit, and tell her you're a hunter. She says to offer a Bear or Wolf pelt at the shrine. Your journal tells you that you need to be Level 17.

Scenic views from the shrine of Hircine

Providing the pelt could be a simple task. You may already have one. Or a Wolf or Bear may be nearby. The most common location for Wolves, their tougher cousins Timber Wolves, and both the Black and tougher Brown Bear is Cyrodiil's forests. The area around the shrine is considered forestland, and a creature can be found directly north, south, east, and west of the shrine.

However, the appearance of a Wolf or Bear at these locations is not a given, and perhaps this would be a good spot to look at how the game generates creatures.

In this case, they're drawn from a list of 14—each of which can appear once the player reaches a particular level (a Wolf beginning at Level 1 and a bear at Level 7).

But none of the creatures is ever alone in the spotlight. At Levels 1–3, the odds are 25 percent that a Wolf will appear. (The creature could also be a Deer, a Rat, or an Imp.) At Level 4, the Timber Wolf and a second Deer join the crowd, but the creatures from Levels 1–3 can still appear. Hence the chance that a Wolf will appear is now 2 in 6. At Levels 5 and 6, four more creatures—including a third Deer and a second Imp—can appear, so the chance of a Wolf showing up drops to 2 in 10.

Even so, with four creature opportunities around the shrine, you'll probably get a Wolf or Bear at one of them. But suppose you don't. Where do you go?

If you're committed to the hunting route, your best solution is seek out the creatures in different terrain, where they appear at different player levels and perhaps at better odds. For instance, Wolves can also be found at creature locations in mountain forests, snowy mountains, and farmlands beginning at Level 1 and in mountain regions, highlands, hills, and Vampire lairs beginning at Level 4.

Or you could set about stealing the one of the four existing Wolf and Bear pelts. There's one Bear pelt on a barrel on the right at the top of the stairs in the Cheydinhal Fighters Guild and another on a table downstairs at Dro'shanji's house in Bravil.

The search for Wolf pelts leads to some interesting places. One is in the possession of Sakeepa, a shepherd who works out of the Aleswell settlement along the northern central portion of the Red Ring Road. Unless you've completed the Miscellaneous quest "Zero Visibility," he'll be extremely hard to find: Sakeepa is invisible. So is everyone else in Aleswell. And if you do spot him, he may not be easy to pickpocket, as he has a respectable Sneak skill of 21.

The other is at one of the most remote locations in the game: Dive Rock, way, waaay up in the northern Jerall Mountains near the Morrowind line—an undocumented quest location we'll visit more thoroughly in the "Freeform Quests" chapter. For now, suffice to say it's well east of the Temple of the Ancestor Moths, and that the pelt's in a sack beside the fire just east of a very scenic overlook.

With the pelt in your inventory, activate the shrine; the Daedric god of the hunt then sends you on one. You're to kill a Unicorn in Harcane Grove to the south-southeast and return with its horn.

Naturally, the Unicorn isn't alone. It is watched over by three Minotaurs of the grove that, by a strange coincidence, are each just a bit tougher and meaner than you. Rather than wading in, wait until there's some distance between the big critters and their charge, then either take them down separately or go straight for the gusto now kill the Unicorn and take her horn.

Or, if you have managed to kill the Minotaurs without incurring the wrath of the Unicorn, or if you can Charm or Calm her enough to prevent her from attacking you, you can hop on and ride her. Take her for a spin around Cyrodiil. Note the admiring glances of the guards and townsfolk. Then kill the unicorn and take her horn.

Now deliver the Unicorn horn to Hircine's shrine. Hircine makes a bloodthirsty little speech and gives you the Savior's Hide—light armor with a strong Resist Magic enchantment.

MALACATH

In Anvil, you can pick up the location of Malacath's shrine from the hunter Pinarus Inventius, who lives at the west end of the city (but can frequently be found wandering outside it), and the mage Thaurron, who hangs out at the Mages Guild.

It's easy to find even without directions. Take the road north out of the city, then the turnoff for Lord Drad's Estate; at the estate, just hook north and west around the hill behind the manor house. You'll run right into the shrine.

At a Disposition of 50, Shobob gro-Rugdush explains that Malacath likes Troll fat. You get it by killing a Troll with a character of Level 4 or higher. (Trolls are always leveled, and the ones with Troll fat start appearing at Level 4.)

Shobob gro-Rugdush, one of Malacath's beauties

Where? These ape-like creatures turn up regularly in the wild and in dungeons. However, you're guaranteed to find them in and around Veyond, a big Ayleid ruin northeast of Leyawiin; on both levels of Nonwyll Cavern and Forsaken Mine (from the Fighters Guild quests "The Master's Son" and "Trolls of Forsaken Mine," respectively); on the second level of Newt Cave, south of the Yellow Road near the mouth of the Corbolo River; and both outside and inside Tidewater Cave, southeast of Leyawiin on Topal Bay. (This last is part of the "Nocturnal" quest, so you could do that one first and pick up the Troll fat en route.)

If you visit the undead or possibly Necromancer lair Howling Cave, east of Bloodcrust Cavern (which is itself just east of Castle Skingrad), you'll find Troll fat on a table in the southeast corner of the big room at the beginning of the second level. Or check out the dead Trolls on the second and third levels of Veyond or in the water under the bridge just east of the mouth of the Panther River. Or start checking alchemists' inventories.

With the fat in inventory (and at Level 10 or higher), activate the shrine. You'll get different responses depending whether you're an Orc or a non-Orc, but the upshot is the same: Malacath says Drad has claimed the Daedra's Ogres as his own. You're to free them from their enslavement.

Go have a chat with Drad. If you tell him, "I admire your efforts," he'll explain his philosophy—the Ogres are beasts so no legal issues attach—and disclose that they're working in Bleak Mine to the east. If you declare yourself against slavery from the get-go, he'll stop talking to you and you'll have to talk to Lady Drad to locate the mine.

The mine's your next stop; the door is halfway up the slope east of the manor house. Pick the three-tumbler lock or borrow the key from a small table around the corner to your left as you enter the manor house. If you're not sneaking, be prepared to go almost directly into a difficult combat. The place is guarded by a small army of Dark Elves—quite a few of them grim veterans five levels above your own. And they keep watch vigilantly just inside the mine entrance.

You have a few options here. Killing all the guards first, then picking the keys to the poor Ogre slaves' cells from the guards' lifeless bodies, is the best way to preserve the delicate, peace-loving Ogre slaves from harm.

Another approach is to enter with a crate of lockpicks, or considerable skill in lockpicking, or an Open Hard Lock spell, then sneak past all the guards, open the cell doors, and spring the Ogres from their pens. The guards then amble about in puzzlement, surprised by the unaccustomed Ogre traffic in the passageways, and pretty soon they find you and try to beat you to death. The Ogres, grateful for your aid, join the fracas on your side. If the Ogres die in their struggle for freedom Malacath doesn't seem to mind. (But if *you* kill one of the Ogres, Malacath is not well pleased.)

Once all of the Ogre slaves have been released from their cells, they ponderously and wordlessly leave the mine and make their way west to the estate, and you get a journal note to return to the shrine.

Under new management

But pause for a moment at Lord Drad's Estate to admire the fruits of your labors. The Drads are now working the farm under the gentle stewardship of the freed Ogres!

At the shrine, Malacath is satisfied; the great hammer Volendrung (with Paralyze and Drain Health enchantments) is yours.

MEPHALA

In Imperial City, you'll hear two reports about a Mephala shrine—one from our pal Ontus Vanin in Talos Plaza (using the usual "Daedra shrines" topic) and the other from Luther Broad, who runs a boarding house in the Elven Gardens District (using the "Imperial City" topic).

If you've been to the Roxey Inn near the northeast corner of Lake Rumare, fast-travel there and make a quick jaunt up the steep hillside to the northeast; the shrine is at the top.

Speak to the Dunmer attendant, Dredena Hlavel; request an audience and she instructs you to make an offering of nightshade between midnight and dawn. You must be at least Level 15 to begin this quest.

Mephala, Webspinner and Plot-Weaver

You may already have had some experience collecting nightshade in the Miscellaneous quest "Vampire Cure." If so, you may have some left over and that'll do handsomely.

If not, we'll repeat in short form our advice from that quest: In the wild, the nightshade plant can be found in greatest supply in Camoran's Paradise from the "Paradise" segment of the Main Quest; in the wilderness halfway between Bravil and Skingrad; and in the region south of Bravil and west and northwest of Fathis Aren's tower (a.k.a. Temple of the Emperor Zero). You can also find it loose at The Main Ingredient in the Imperial City's Market District; in the library at the Chorrol Mages Guild; in a niche in the Sanctum portion of the Imperial dungeons when you revisit it for the Dark Brotherhood quest "Scheduled for Execution"; and in the Crypt of the Night Mother under the Lucky Lady statue in Bravil (only available in the Dark Brotherhood endgame).

Activate the shrine with the nightshade in inventory and you'll learn that Mephala does indeed spin a strange web. She wants you to go into Bleaker's Way, where the oil-and-water Dark Elves and Nords live side by side in peace, and sow discord between its two families by killing their respective leaders and in each case planting evidence that implicates the other family.

Nothing happened when you activated the shrine? Then you were probably too late—the offering period ends at 6 a.m.—or you've already been spinning your own nasty web in that community. Any crime committed against a member of either the Ulfgar or Dalvilu factions before you get the "Mephala" assignment kills the quest. In that case, Hlavel won't tell you about the nightshade, the nightshade won't work on the shrine, and you and Mephala won't bring strife to Bleaker's Way.

The quiet village of Bleaker's Way

Or did you get a strange journal entry that something you'd done in Bleaker's Way had spoiled Mephala's plan? This means that, after getting the quest but before making the offering, you ran off and made mischief in the village. That also kills the quest, but you get an explanation.

The village lies on a mountain shelf just west-northwest across the Silver Road. It's big for an off-the-map settlement—seven houses and the Goodwill Inn—though rather a quiet one at times. If you hit town at one of these odd hours, just talk to Kirsten at the inn in the northeast corner of town to learn that the local leaders are Hrol Ulfgar and Nivan Dalvilu.

Happily, most of these folks don't lock their doors during the day. Take advantage of this simplicity to drum up the "evidence" you'll plant on the bodies. Dalvilu's place is just west of the inn. A Dalvilu ceremonial dagger lies on a low table against the wall to the right as you enter. Ulfgar's house is at the west end of the village. Grab the Ulfgar family ring beside a *Guide to Leyawiin* on the table near the base of the attic stairs.

Then slip into (or remain in) the respective houses before dark and await the owners' returns. The two men run around town 2 p.m. to 6 p.m., return home, meet with each other from 8 p.m. to 10 p.m., and then call it a night.

Killing Dalvilu should be easy enough; he's only a level above yours. But Ulfgar is six up on you, with a decent set of combat skills, and he'll put up a heck of a fight.

Note you can't do the usual "activation" thing to place the ring and dagger at the scenes; you have to transfer them into the victims' inventories.

When both items have been placed, a journal entry advises you to report to someone (and anyone will do) that you've seen Dalvilu and Ulfgar attack each other.

Then step back and watch the chaos unfold. By the time you've completed this report, the battle may already have been joined, with Nords Ulrika Ulfgar, Beirir, and Kirsten fighting Dark Elves Arvin, Malyani, Redas, and Satha Dalvilu in the streets (and conceivably any ancestor guardians, should the Dark Elves invoke this power). The Dark Elves have a distinct advantage in numbers, and we've yet to see the Nords win without the player first, uh, leveling the playing field.

However, don't kill everybody or you'll sacrifice your reward—a very nice Ebony Blade, which, while not quite on a par with Goldbrand in combat damage, has Silence and Absorb Health enchantments.

MERIDIA

We'd count this as an easy mission, except that no one tells you about this shrine west of Skingrad.

However, it's sufficiently close to the city that it may pop up on your radar in other quests in the area—such as the Mages Guild mission "Ulterior Motives" or the Settlement quest "Bear Season." Chart a course west-northwest from Skingrad's West Gate to find the Meridia shrine between Cursed Mine and Shardrock farm.

At the shrine, speak to Basil Ernarde, a Breton, to learn Meridia hates the undead and that a suitable offering will be drawn from their remains. That's deliberately vague, because the god will accept more than one item—either bonemeal from the remains of a Skeleton or ectoplasm from a Ghost. Check your journal to learn that you must be at least Level 10 to begin this quest.

What's a nice Daedric Princess like you doing in a place like this?

You won't have to go far to find an offering. Under a bush just southwest of the northern of the two benches west of the shrine is a portion of ectoplasm!

With the offering in inventory, activate the shrine and Meridia will send you off to wipe out a band of Necromancers in Howling Cave east of Castle Skingrad.

You might have already been here. (We've mentioned Howling Cave in "Malacath" as a source of Troll fat. If you haven't done that quest yet, get the fat while it's hot.) The northern passage leads to a secret door and the secret door to five Necromancers—all three levels above your own and abetted by seven or eight undead creatures. When the fifth goes down, you'll be directed back to the shrine, where Meridia gives you a Ring of Khajiiti, with Chameleon and Fortify Speed enchantments.

MOLAG BAL

No one tells you about the Molag Bal shrine west of the Imperial City. If you were to head straight west out the bridge from the Talos Plaza District, you'd first hit Breakneck Cave and then the Ayleid ruin Narfinsel. Head south-southeast at Narfinsel to find the shrine in a clearing in the woods.

Speak to the Redguard, Amir, to learn you must find a Lion pelt to use as an offering.

Molag Bal, Harvester of Souls—The Corruptor

That's actually a Mountain Lion's pelt. In Hircine's quest, with a similar requirement, you may have found suitable creatures nearby. In Molag Bal's, you won't. Mountain Lions do not live in the woods. You can find them in the plains (Level 10 or higher); mountains (guaranteed at Levels 10–13, with a 50 percent chance at Level 16 or 17), highlands (Levels 10–15); and even rainforest regions (Levels 10–14). Of course, you can't begin this quest until you're at least Level 17, so finding the pelts shouldn't be a problem. Plus, there are others to be found…

"A Rat Problem," one of the first Fighters Guild quests, can supply as many as six pelts. Or you can seek out the game's two dead Mountain Lions. One has been killed by a leveled Troll in a corner of the second large room on the second level of Newt Cave—south of the Yellow Road near the mouth of the Corbolo River. The other should appear just southwest of Fort Ash. (It may be inaccessible below the scenery if a random Oblivion Gate appears at this location.)

With the pelt in inventory, activate the shrine and get another distasteful mission. Bal tells you about Melus Petilius, who has forsworn violence. You're to induce him to break his oath and attack you with the Cursed Mace (which Bal obligingly provides).

Petilius lives near the settlement of Brindle Home—a hamlet in the deep woods to the southwest. At a Disposition of 60, any of the residents will praise him to the skies. (Petilius sounds like a proper hero.) But he apparently was undone by the death of his wife, Vena. While Petilius was off defending the village, the poor woman died. He moved to an outlying cabin (which you can see off to the southwest) and visits his wife's nearby grave daily.

Petilius is solid as a rock on that oath if you talk to him at home. Zero out his Disposition. Punch him in the face. Cut him with your weapon of choice. Nothing.

You need to get Petilius's goat in a more stressful setting—say, at his wife's grave. He heads there a little after 10 a.m. Simply follow him southeast across a meadow to the stone, deposit the mace nearby, give him a spanking, and then talk to him.

So much for his oath. He'll pick up the mace and beat you to death with it. You'll reappear back at the shrine, and Bal, sounding rather bored, will award you the Mace of Molag Bal. It's a powerful mace on its own, and it digs into your enemy's Strength and Magicka by 5 points with each strike.

Now you can torment Petilius on your own. Return to his wife's grave to find him praying. You can speak to him to freak him out—or simply execute him and reclaim the Cursed Mace.

NAMIRA

Again, no one tells you about the Namira shrine east-southeast of Bruma.

Unless you've been playing the game in reverse, when you talk to Hrolfrodi the Harrier at the site you learn that you are too attractive to worship here. You must make yourself more "loathsome" to summon the Daedra. (You'll also learn that you must be at least Level 5 to begin the quest.)

Ms. Harrier doesn't explain further. Basically, she's telling you you've got too much Personality. So, after a game spent raising your stats as high as possible, in this quest you suddenly find yourself lowering one of them to a value of 20 or lower.

Excuse me. You're just not ugly enough yet.

This is a little tricky. Two potions that lower your Personality are knocking around loose in the game, and others turn up in loot and alchemist shops and, indeed, can be cooked up by you.

But you'll discover here that a pure Damage Personality potion can't be consumed by you but used only to poison your weapon. However, you can drink such a potion as long as it has at least one positive effect—that is, the game doesn't read it as a poison—but you'll have to make that one yourself.

To do that, you'll have to be able to recognize third-level effects of ingredients, and to do that, you'll have to be at least a Journeyman in the Alchemy skill. Damage Personality is the second effect for flour; the third effect for bog beacon asco cap, both types of cinnabar polypore cap, emetic russula cap, leek, pumpkin, summer bolete cap, and sweetroll; and the fourth effect for lettuce and wheat grain.

However, your best bet is to go to town on cheap wine. It's all over the game. We count 48 bottles in Bruma alone, including 20 in the chapel hall of the Great Chapel of Talos, seven in Baenlin's house and cellar, and six in the Jerall View Inn and its basement. Each bottle consumed will knock 10 points off your Personality for two minutes—while also dragging down your Agility and Intelligence for the same period and giving a boost to your Fatigue.

Play it safe and don't drink the wine (or potion) until you're back at the shrine, and then talk to Hrolfrodi and activate the shrine swiftly. You'll have to appear like a boozehound to the shrine as well as to the quest-giver.

Namira sounds like you're still a little too popular but nevertheless sets you a trial. A group of devout Namira worshippers lives in the absolute darkness of the Ayleid ruin Anga to the south. Some do-gooder priests of Arkay are planning to shed some light on their plight. You're to use a spell called Namira's Shroud to help these "Forgotten" kill the priests.

This is really pretty simple. Namira's Shroud is a darkness spell. When cast on one of the four priests, the priest's torch goes out, and he's suddenly fair game for light-hating NPCs. The Forgotten zero in directly on the highlighted priests—usually three-on-one—and kill them with little trouble. When the fourth priest goes down, you'll get a journal entry to return to the shrine. (Your Personality should long since have returned to normal, but you don't have to get drunk again.)

Don't kill any priests yourself, or you'll sacrifice the reward from Namira—a Ring of Namira with very nice Reflect Damage and Reflect Spell enchantments. Indeed, the only blows struck in Anga arrive if you penetrate to the secret room in the southeast corner—which holds two boss-level chests—and go toe-to-toe with two leveled undead.

NOCTURNAL

We think Nocturnal must be sort of a soft touch. People keep stealing things from her. Ages ago, the original Gray Fox stole Nocturnal's Gray Cowl. And now, two Argonians in Leyawiin have made off with the Eye of Nocturnal. You're to track them down and get it back.

This is one of the easier Daedric quests. You're given the location of the shrine by Alves Uvenim in the Leyawiin Mages Guild. And like the "Peryite" quest, this one, just up the road that runs east of the Upper Niben from Leyawiin, requires no offering for you to speak to the goddess. It does, however, require that you be at least Level 10 to begin.

You'll lose the compass pointer when you re-enter Leyawiin and get blank looks when you get the "Eye of Nocturnal" topic at all. However, speak to any male Imperial in Leyawiin on the "Leyawiin" topic to learn that Weebam-Na and Bejeen have been bragging about scoring a "valuable jewel."

Nocturnal, the Night Mistress

You may recall Weebam from the Miscellaneous quest "Mazoga the Orc," in which he has a funny cameo. (If Weebam-Na somehow died in that quest, you won't get this one at all.) His house backs onto a pond in the downtrodden district between the Great Chapel of Zenithar and the castle.

Here, he's kind of weird and sensitive. "Never heard of the thing," he says. "Neither has Bejeen. You ask too many questions."

Bejeen seems as nervous as her roommate, and in each case your journal suggests you eavesdrop on their conversation. Leave and return sneaking, and you'll overhear a brief debate about whether the Eye is safe from the Trolls in Tidewater Cave.

At this point, you'll get a journal entry about investigating the cave, and it appears on your map on the Topal Bay coast southeast of the city.

You can confront the two Argonians about "Tidewater Cave" and get a journal entry that you've alerted them to the fact that you overheard their conversation. However, that's just dialogue, and the Argonians don't try to move their treasure.

Tidewater Cave is a critter cave—3–10 encounters with beasts ranging up to Bears—but the featured attractions are the two leveled Trolls outside and three within. (They're tough but are weak against fire damage.) Inside, make your first left and then a left at the T intersection to find the Eye at the end of the underwater passage. Back at the shrine, exchange it for a Skeleton Key—an unbreakable lockpick that boosts your Security skill by 40 points.

PERYITE

This shrine you're likely to discover only in your travels. No one mentions the site on the southeast bank of the Silverfish River east of the Imperial Bridge Inn—indeed, no one talks about the god Peryite at all—and it's not close to any of Cyrodiil's cities.

Strange place. The five worshippers, arranged in a circle west of the shrine, are all frozen in place. Try to activate one to learn he or she is unconscious.

"Hel-LO! I'm here for my quest! Yoo-hoo! Anybody listening?"

No offering is needed here. (Probably because there's no one to tell you what it should be!) Just activate the shrine (when you've reached at least Level 10) and Peryite speaks. The followers tried to summon the god with a spell. It evidently backfired or a resentful god fired back (his words are a little ambiguous), and now the bodies of the five rest in the mortal plane while their souls reside in Oblivion. Peryite now wants you to reunite body and soul, and will send you to a special Oblivion realm for this purpose—one of two occasions in which you'll visit Oblivion during the Daedric quests. (The other is in the "Boethia" quest.)

You may worry that you need soul-trapping magic and Soul Gems for this purpose. You don't; these aren't souls in the same sense as you've come to understand them in Cyrodiil. You merely must run a gauntlet of leveled Daedra and find and activate each of the five souls. Each has its own marker on your compass and map.

You arrive facing north on the remains of a ruined bridge, with a sinewy landmass extending away to the southwest, southeast, and northeast.

You can collect the souls in any order. All five lie along a great circuit around this realm. You'll find the soul of Ilvel Romayn to the southwest near the door to a small tower; that of Er-Teeus to the north of Romayn's, near the entrance to a small dungeon called the Sightless Grotto; and that of Kewan well to the northeast—through the dungeon and then a fair trek northeast and east. (He's near the right-hand wall shortly before the path begins to turn south.

You can take a couple of routes from here. Around the rocks just southeast of Kewan is the entrance to another dungeon. It's hard going—17 leveled Daedra over two levels with some good loot—but deposits you onto an island to the southeast near a leaning tower. When you exit, you'll see the soul of Maren the Seal straight ahead of you near a great fire. (However, it's easier to reach Maren by an overground route and use stepping stones out to the island.)

Either way, once you're back on the mainland, head south through the archway with the two suspended corpses. Lots of

Daedra here, and near the fire at the west end you'll find Mirie. Backtrack toward your starting location. In the open area north of where you arrived awaits a luminous blue portal.

Enter it to return to the shrine. The worshippers are back in their bodies, doing worshipper-type things, but seem none too grateful for this event. Peryite's more appreciative and turns over Spell Breaker—a shield with a strong Reflect Spell enchantment.

SANGUINE

You can get two reports in Skingrad of a Sanguine shrine in the Imperial Reserve—from Fadus Calidius of the Skingrad Fighters Guild (using the "Daedra Shrines" topic) and Falanu Hlaalu at All Things Alchemical (using the "Daedra cult" topic).

If you traveled cross-country from Weynon Priory to Kvatch in the Main Quest, you probably found the shrine on your own. (It's southwest of the Weatherleah estate you visited in two of the Chorrol Miscellaneous quests and southeast of Fort Dirich from the Settlement quest "A Venerable Vintage.")

At the shrine, Engorm, a Bosmer, tells you that Sanguine would look favorably on a gift of Cyrodiilic brandy. You also learn that you must be at least Level 8 to begin the quest.

Sanguine, Lord of Hard-Partying

Four flasks can be found—and a fifth bought—in Imperial City. You'll find two flasks on the small table just inside the door to The Gilded Carafe in the Market District, a third upstairs on a table at the nearby Mystic Emporium, and a fourth on a desk on the second floor of Sevarius Atius's house in Talos Plaza. And you can buy Cyrodiilic brandy at The Main Ingredient in the Imperial City's Market District.

Three brandies can be found in Anvil—two in the castle (one on a table in the private quarters and the other on a desk in the royal quarters) and the other atop a shelf on the second floor of Heinrich Oaken-Hull's house. Three more turn up in Bruma—two in the castle (one in a display case in the Great Hall, the other on a table in the Lord's Manor) and the other in Baenlin's house on top of a desk in the south second-floor bedroom. And three more are in Chorrol—two in the castle (on shelves in the Great Hall and private quarters) and a third on a table beside the fireplace in Francois Motierre's house.

Two brandies can be found in Bravil—one on a shelf in the north wing of Castle Bravil's private quarters and a second on a shelf on the second floor of Ungolim's house. Two more are in Cheydinhal—on desks in the lord's quarters at Castle Cheydinhal and Rythe's house. Two are in Leyawiin—one on a shelf in the private quarters at Castle Leyawiin and the other on a desk in the west wing of the second floor of Ahdarji's house. And two more can be found in and around Skingrad—one on a desk in the Lord's Manor in Castle Skingrad and the other on a table in Milvan's house.

Finally, if you've already brought the "priest who would be emperor" to Cloud Ruler Temple in the Main Quest, you'll find a flask on the shelf in the west-wing bedroom next to Martin's.

With the brandy in inventory, activate the shrine and get an unusual quest. Countess Alessia Caro of distant Leyawiin is about to hold a dinner party. Sanguine thinks it will be as "stuffy" as the countess herself. You're to liven things up with the "Stark Reality" spell he provides. Think "stark naked" and you'll be getting close.

You can fast-travel directly to Castle Leyawiin, but you can't just march into the dining room. A guard is glued to the dining-room door (in the south wall of the throne room) all day and he isn't disposed to discuss the matter.

However, at 6 p.m., he eases up a bit. Ask him about "Dinner party." If you're got up in nice duds, he'll let you in.

What's "nice"? It's determined by a formula that adds up the "clothing value" of each article you're wearing. This is a hidden stat, but a suit of upper-class clothes or a couple of nice pieces of armor would fulfill the requirement nicely.

And at a Disposition of 70, the guard simply lets you in even without suitable attire—with the parting comment that he hopes he won't regret it.

He will regret it. Once you cast the spell, the stuffy little countess and her four guests lose their clothes and start running around in their undies. We'd love to stick around for whatever follows, but it's not practical. You see, the spell has also hit you. Look at your inventory. You don't have an inventory. It's all been blown away (but not forever).

For now, your cover is blown, the guards burst in, and you'll either have to make a very quick and efficient exit—don't use the south-wall door to the servants' wing; it's a dead end—or simply submit to arrest to avoid getting killed.

Back at the shrine, Sanguine rewards you with a Daedra-summoning staff called the Sanguine Rose…and unlocks the chest containing your belongings. Who knew running around in your skivvies could be fun and rewarding?

SHEOGORATH

No one gives you the location of Sheogorath's shrine, and it's one of the more difficult ones to find. However, it's one of the easiest to get. You only have to be Level 2.

It's near the Elsweyr border a little less than halfway between Bravil and Leyawiin. Follow the road south and southeast out of Bravil. When it passes the Ayleid ruin Bawn, it turns south-southwest, crosses a nameless river, and forms a C

as it climbs and then drops down a hill north of Fort Nomore. Head southwest after you pass the fort. You'll soon see the statue on a rise below a great rock.

Sheogorath's the mad Daedra prince, and his followers are probably crazier than he is. Make sure to talk to them all. They're…interesting. But they nevertheless manage to point you to the Dark Elf Ferul Ravel, who, slightly less mad, tells you to supply a triple offering of a head of lettuce, a Lesser Soul Gem, and yarn.

The strange crew at the shrine of Sheogorath

The lettuce and Soul Gem are easy to find in nearby Bravil, and in Border Watch lettuce and yarn are likewise easy to obtain.

In Bravil, look for four heads of lettuce on the second floor of the Fighters Guild, three in the castle's dining hall, and two in the homes of Andragil, City-Swimmer, Luciana Galena, and Ranaline. One of the gems can be found in A Warlock's Luck, on the table just south of the entrance, and another's on a shelf in the rear ground-floor room in the Mages Guild.

In Border Watch, a small settlement south of the shrine and west of Water's Edge, you'll find two heads of lettuce on the top shelf in the right near corner of the dining room in J'riska's house and two samples of yarn near the rug in M'dirr's house—one out in the open and one in the upright barrel. (You may want to learn the lay of the land in Border Watch, as you'll be back here momentarily.)

With the three items in inventory, activate the shrine for a quest rather in the messing-with-mortals spirit of the Sanguine one. Apparently not much happens in Border Watch beyond shoddy housekeeping, but its Khajiit residents are alive to apocalyptic implications in ordinary events. You're to heat things up by making one of their most dire prophecies come true.

Once in town, ask anyone about "K'Sharra Prophecy" for a referral to the village shaman, Ri'Bassa. (If he's not home, try the inn up the hill; he's the fellow in the hooded robe.) Tell Ri'Bassa you're a "traveling scholar"; his Disposition rises 10 points and he'll expand on the legend a bit—though he won't disclose the three portents unless it reaches 60. (If you ridicule the prophecy, it drops 10, he'll clam up on you, and you'll have to work that much harder to reach 60.)

The portents are plagues of vermin (Rats), famine (the death of livestock), and fear. Ri'Bassa won't talk about this third one (which you don't need to worry about; Sheogorath handles it himself) but does invite you to ask about the community itself and suggests you stay at the Border Watch Inn, celebrated for its cheese collection. In fact, it has a cheese museum. Yes, a cheese museum.

Ri'Bassa has quietly given you the methods of simulating the first two portents. Rats and cheese go together, and there's a lot of cheese on display at the inn. But not just any cheese will do. Speak to S'thasa, who runs the inn, to learn she has a rare Olroy cheese that, if used in her cooking, would serve as a magnet for rats. It's the orangey wedge in the display case with the blue backing at the front of the inn.

Prize cheeses on display at the Border Watch Inn Cheese Museum

Either pickpocket S'thasa for the display-case key (not always an easy task) or pick the five-tumbler lock while she's asleep (10 p.m. to 4 a.m.). Then, take the cheese, place the wedge in the cooking pot outside the inn, and wait a bit. A horde of Rats appears east of town and climbs the stairs toward the pot.

This gets kind of complicated. You don't have to kill the Rats—Ri'Bassa will ultimately take care of them if you don't—but you can do so using your weapons, if you feel so inclined.

Now you just have to attend to the Sheep. Poor Sheep. The pen's just south of the inn. Again, you can butcher them with your weapons or activate the feed trough with the Rat poison Ri'Bassa left on the stairway up to the inn in your inventory. Note that only five of the Sheep appear initially; the sixth doesn't show until you've lured in the Rats.

When the last one keels over, Sheogorath speaks to you and raises the curtain on the final act. Return to the stairs and descend to the first cross path. You're pinned in place, the wind picks up, the sky reddens as if an Oblivion Gate has opened nearby—and the center of the village is bombarded by a host of flaming German Shepherds! It's raining dogs in the village of cats! The kitties are convinced that Border Watch is doomed. (Despite all their grim talk, they stay put after the quest ends. Perhaps they have another prophecy that covers this eventuality.)

When the bombardment ends, you get a journal entry to return to the shrine. Do so, and Sheogorath turns over a "fun little toy" called Wabbajack.

For 20 seconds, this staff will transmute almost any creature into another creature. There's no telling what that other creature will be. It could be something big and horrific, like a Daedroth, that wants to eat your face. Or it could be a Rat that you can kill with one blow. Hence, when used against tougher enemies, it's an effective way to dial back nasty encounters. Would you rather face a Xivilai or a Mudcrab?

The staff won't work against a non-player character or an already-Wabbajack-ed creature, but its attempted use either against an NPC or any owned creature, like a Horse, Sheep, or Dog, is regarded as assault. And in the eyes of the law, killing a Wabbajack-ed creature is the same as killing the original. (However, if you, say, turn a legionnaire's horse into an Ogre and the legionnaire kills the Ogre (and thus the horse), you're liable only for the original assault.)

It is a fun toy, though, and it can lead to some rather interesting encounters.

VAERMINA

Ontus Vanin in Talos Plaza can clue you to the location of Vaermina's shrine. It's southwest of Cheydinhal on the east shore of Lake Poppad.

At the shrine, speak to the Dunmer, Aymar Douar, to learn you need to come up with an offering of a Grand Black Soul Gem. You must be at least Level 5 to begin the quest.

Vaermina, Mistress of Nightmares and Dark Portents

This is a quest in itself—one that will be that much tougher if you haven't had much to do with the Mages Guild to date.

So let's bring you up to speed: Black Soul Gems are produced by Necromancers to capture the souls of non-player characters—standard Soul Gems can hold only the souls of creatures—and are a persistent theme in the Mages Guild's quests. You'll discover them in the Cheydinhal Guild's recommendation quest, watch their manufacture in "Necromancer's Moon," and carry a giant one for protection in the finale, "Confront the King."

There are two ways to get a gem. If you're lucky, Grand Black Soul Gems will turn up in Necromancer loot. The closest Necromancer lair to the shrine is Dark Fissure—almost straight east across the Reed River headwaters. A boss and boss coffin can be found on the cave's third level.

Or you can make one. Ideally, you'll have completed the Mages Guild quest "Necromancer's Moon" first. That way, you'll have access to the book of the same name and a pair of notes that lay out the procedures. (If you're an apprentice in the Mages Guild, you can find the book in the Mystic Archives outside the confines of the quest.)

First, you'll need an unpopulated ordinary Grand Soul Gem and any Soul Trap spell. The locations of the former are outlined under the "Grand Soul Gem" section under the Miscellaneous quest "Vampire Cure." The latter can be purchased from any low-level Mages Guild spell vendor.

Now, visit an altar outside one of four Necromancer lairs: Dark Fissure; Fort Istirus (east of Kvatch); Fort Linchal (north-northeast of Kvatch); or Wendelbek (between the two northern headwaters of the Panther River).

And now, probably, you'll have to wait—up to six days. The altars can transform gems only on one day of each week. You'll know the day has arrived when a beam of spectral light descends from the sky. When it does, place the Soul Gem in the altar and cast your Soul Trap spell on the altar. Foom. The Soul Gem is now a Black Soul Gem. Take it and get back to the shrine.

When you activate the shrine with the gem in your inventory, the goddess asks you to retrieve her stolen Orb of Vaermina from the tower of the wizard Arkved, which is on a hilltop south-southeast of the shrine. "In my Orb, Arkved has found more than he bargained for," she says.

Arkved's Tower is actually the seven-level dungeon below the tower. At least, we think it is. Defended by Daedra and rather poor in loot, it is a very strange place—like something out of a dream. The first level displays some furniture on the ceiling. On the second, you traverse a vast dark void. (You'll need a torch.) The third holds giant furniture and exits into an Oblivion-like wilderness. The fourth level, Hall of Changes, is a crazy house of halls that lead to closets and doors that open on blank walls.

This leads to both the fifth level (a dead-end platform in a great dark hall of hanging corpses) and the sixth (a comparatively conventional stretch of dungeon—the last stretch of which is littered with Zombie bodies). The sixth brings you to "Death Quarters," where, rather than facing a great battle with the thieving wizard, you discover the wizard "unconscious."

Arkved is locked in a nightmare. The wonders and horrors of this state are transparent in the writings he's left behind; read the note and crumpled sheet of paper on the table beside the Orb and the second crumpled sheet on the floor beneath.

(Read also the Illusion skill book *Palla, Volume 1*. Great story, and this is the only copy. The second volume, also rare, can be found in the royal quarters in Castle Anvil Castle, in Heinrich Oaken-Hull's house in Anvil, and in the library of the Leyawiin Mages Guild.)

You can kill Arkved or leave him be; all you have to do here is take the Orb of Vaermina. The door in the northeast wall leads to a previously nonexistent trap door that deposits you under some bushes in the surface tower.

Back at the shrine, Vaermina awards you the Skull of Corruption. This staff creates a short-lived (30 seconds) "corrupted clone" of its target, with the same appearance, gender, race, stats, and inventory as the original.

As with Wabbajack, the Skull can be used casually as a toy to foment interesting strife around Cyrodiil. (The twins do not play friendly; the newcomer is always attacked as an enemy.) But, again like Wabbajack, the staff does have a practical use when brought to bear against the stronger enemies, who become their own worst enemy.

Note that using the staff against an innocent is a crime. However, killing the clone is not. Indeed, that's the only way to interact with it. You can't talk to it, pickpocket it, or loot its body for duplicate keys.

HERMAEUS MORA

To get this quest, you must fulfill four conditions:

1. Complete the other 14 Daedric quests.
2. Have reached the "Blood of the Daedra" segment of the Main Quest, in which you're assigned to collect a Daedric artifact. (This is designed to ensure that a player who's performed the other 14 quests and has been careless with his Daedric loot can still find an artifact available for use in the Main Quest. However, we'll tell you right now that you won't want to give this artifact away.)
3. You've reached Level 21 or higher.
4. Go to sleep. It doesn't matter where.

When you wake, an emissary named Casta Flavus is beside your bed. He tells you that the Daedra lord Hermaeus Mora has summoned you, writes the shrine's location to your map, and directs you to travel there. (Flavus vanishes from the game when you activate Mora's shrine.)

The shrine's deep in the western Jerall Mountains. Even when you know its location, it's difficult to reach. The slopes along the most direct approaches from the south and east may prove prohibitively steep, though it's possible to get there by approaching from the Vampire lair Lipsand Tarn to the southwest.

But there are two discrete paths up the shrine. The one that's easier to find starts just up the slope northwest of the Main Quest dungeon Sancre Tor. You're soon on a broad, winding track that leads upward through a series of battlements—and past a series of hostile critters.

Who can chart the tides of fate? Hermaeus Mora.

The other path is guarded by Bandits as well as critters, marked by bridges rather than battlements, and is much harder to find and follow. (It begins on a stony valley floor well east of the Ayleid ruin Ninendava on the south side of the mountain that's south of Echo Cave.) Note that there's a western fork off this path that leads to Ninendava, so it's possible to lose your way.

There's no offering requirement here. Simply activate the shrine and Mora commissions you to collect 10 souls—one from each race—and supplies a special Soul Trap spell (Mora's Soul Trap) for this purpose. (If you visit the shrine on your own, without the invitation, you'll get a vague message that you "haven't followed the path" to speak to the Daedra lord.)

This is a nice way of saying that you're to go on a killing spree.

You can collect the souls anywhere and wreak as much in the way of chaos and consequences as you wish. But we suggest that you simply make the rounds of certain Daedric shrines using fast travel and kill the worshippers.

Why? Well, the shrines are in remote locations, so you're unlikely to get caught. Most of the worshippers are easy kills, with no armor and poor weapons, and are likely to be no more than one level above your own. And, as you've completed the other Daedric quests, these characters no longer serve any useful purpose and hence you won't kill anyone likely to come in handy in the rest of your game.

The actual soul collection is simple. No Soul Gems required. Just cast Mora's Soul Trap—make sure it's Mora's and not one of the standard spells—and then kill your target. When the target dies, a journal entry indicates that you've collected a soul of the target's race. (If you don't get one, you either already have that race or you're using the wrong spell.)

The fastest route starts right here. At Mora's shrine, pick up a Dunmer soul from Norasa Adus, an Imperial soul from Bruscius Longus, and a Khajiit soul from Ri'Jirr.

Where to next? Ideally, you want a location with as many souls as possible. Two of the shrines, Peryite's and Sheogorath's, each have five worshippers, and, in each case, you still need souls from four of the five.

At Peryite's shrine, you can collect an Altmer soul from Mirie, an Argonian soul from Er-Teeus, a Nord soul from Maren the Seal, and a Redguard soul from Kewan. Alternatively, at Sheogorath's shrine, you can pick up an Altmer soul from Angalsama, an Argonian soul from Beewos, a Breton soul from Gregory Arne, and a Nord soul from Ortis.

Okay. Dark Elf, Khajiit, and Imperial. Three down, and seven to go.

Now you have seven souls and are missing a Bosmer, an Orc, and either a Breton or a Redguard. The most efficient way to handle this is to hit Clavicus Vile's shrine, where you can get the Bosmer's soul from Anedhel and the Orc's from Gul gro-Burbog, and then Meridia's shrine, where you can pick up either a Breton's from Basil Ernarde or a Redguard's from Demetrius.

And you're done. Scoot back to Hermaeus Mora's shrine. The Daedra prince doesn't care that the souls come from Daedra worshippers (including his own) and turns over the Oghma Infinium.

This is the ultimate skill book. Read it, and you'll be offered a chance to follow the path of steel, shadow, or spirit. These correspond to the combat, stealth, and mage stat sets. The steel path bumps up your Strength and Speed attributes and Blade, Blunt, and Heavy Armor skills by 10 points each. The shadow path does the same for your Speed attribute and Acrobatics, Light Armor, Security, and Sneak skills. And the spirit adds the points to your Intelligence attribute and Alteration, Conjuration, Destruction, and Restoration skills.

Once you've read one, the book vanishes. With that, the quest line is done. There's no aftermath—but you've got some amazing equipment with which to face the rest of the game.

MASTER TRAINER QUESTS

You'll have to climb into the game's higher reaches before you come upon these missions. Complete them, and make use of the additional training they permit, and your character will enter the realm of the superhuman.

You can improve your character's 21 skills by gaining experience in the world, reading "skill books," and by paying a non-player character to train you in a given discipline.

Each skill has five trainers. Two are low-level trainers who can bring a given skill up to 40. (Athletics is the exception; it has just one low-level trainer.) Two are medium or "advanced" trainers who can bring the skill up to 70. And one is a master trainer who can kick the skill up to its maximum of 100.

The low-level trainers don't refer you up the chain to the medium ones. You'll hear about most of the low- and mid-level trainers from folks you meet in your travels, though you won't always hear about them as trainers. Sometimes you'll hear something that suggests they're adept at some skill-related activity.

Many of these trainers are affiliated with guilds, and you must be a guild member for full access to their services. Fighters Guild members always require guild membership for training. Mages and Thieves Guild members never do, but sometimes the mages are sequestered in areas of the guilds that a nonmember can't reach without trespassing.

The master trainer's identity is known only to the medium trainers in a discipline, and they'll reveal it and that trainer's location in response to a query about "Training" only when your skill in the discipline reaches 70. (You can find the master trainers on your own, but then you won't have the necessary topic.) Then go find the master—sometimes at the ends of the earth and sometimes right under your nose.

In 20 of the 21 quests, the master may set you a task or test before he or she trains you. The one exception is Acrobatics, which is a freebie. (Alteration is also a freebie for Argonians.)

A number of these tests play off your stats and experiences in the game world—the number of people you've killed, for instance—and you already may have fulfilled their conditions. Should you fail a test, you can retake it immediately—save in the "Speechcraft" quest, in which failure is not an option.

ACROBATICS TRAINING

The low-level trainers for Acrobatics are Quill-Weave, who lives on the main drag in Anvil, and Ida Vlinorman, who lives in the northeastern quadrant of the Imperial City's Elven Gardens District. (Quill-Weave has a part in the Fighters Guild quest "A Rat Problem.") Vlinorman doesn't have any quest tie-ins, but there's a story abroad about her being involved in an illicit sport called "chapel climbing," which she'll confirm if you question her about "Imperial City."

The medium trainers are the dog-hater Tsrava, who lives at J'Bari's house in the south-central part of Leyawiin, and the dog trainer Ganredhel, who has a place of her own in the southeast corner of Cheydinhal.

Each points you to a master trainer named Aerin who's supposed to have taken up residence at a camp in northeastern Cyrodiil. It's in the northern foothills of the Valus range—north of Cheydinhal, east of Azura's shrine, and northeast of Lord Rugdumph's Estate.

Surprise. Aerin isn't here. In fact, there's no one named Aerin in the game. But an amiable fellow named Torbern is here, and it just so happens that he's an unparalleled Acrobatics trainer. Speak to him about "Training" and you're done. However, you may never get master-level training that easily again.

Torbern awaits you at Aerin's Camp, when you're ready for Acrobatics training.

ALCHEMY TRAINING

The low-level Alchemy trainers are Felen Relas at the Anvil Mages Guild and S'drassa in the Leyawiin Mages Guild. (S'drassa is the quest-giver for the Miscellaneous quest "Tears of the Savior.")

The mediums are Ardaline at the Bravil Mages Guild—you'll recover her staff in the Bravil guild's recommendation quest—and Brotch Calus, who has a house just east of Bruma's Great Chapel of Talos.

The latter two will bump you to Sinderion, who works out of the cellar of Skingrad's West Weald Inn and is the quest-giver for the marathon Miscellaneous quest "Seeking Your Roots."

Sinderion doesn't seem too high on training. But he'll entertain the idea in exchange for bottles of Cyrodiil's best two wines: both the Tamika and Surilie Brothers wines from the year 399.

There are around 30 bottles of each wine in the game. The closest in each case are in the wine cellar of Castle Skingrad—reached through a door (two-tumbler lock) off the dining room. Sinderion's tickled to have them, and you've got your training.

Two bottles of wine are all that Sinderion requires for training.

ALTERATION TRAINING

The quest for master-level Alteration training is a challenging one—unless you're Argonian.

The low-level trainers are Dovyn Aren, who has a home next door to Acrobatics trainer Ida Vlinorman in the Imperial City's Elven Gardens District (but also spends a lot of time in Fathis Ules's house in the southwest part of the district), and Deetsan at the Cheydinhal Mages Guild. (Deetsan figures in the Cheydinhal guild's recommendation quest—and takes over the branch after the departure of the Necromancer, Falcar.)

The medium-level trainers are Athragar at the Chorrol Mages Guild and Abhuki, who runs the Faregyl Inn just off the Green Road south of Imperial City. When they can't train you any more, they'll point you to master trainer Tooth-in-the-Sea on the Niben Bay coast north of Bravil.

At night, Tooth sleeps on a bedroll on the east side of the great rock that contains the entrance to Flooded Mine. During the day, from a little after 6 a.m. to 6 p.m., he's at the bottom of Niben Bay at a spot northeast of the mine and southeast of Veyond's Cave.

Approach Tooth about "Training" before 1 p.m. He'll test your water-breathing magic before he consents—unless you're a fellow Argonian. Argonians have a natural water-breathing ability and are exempted from the test.

You'll become well acquainted with the hazards of underwater travel in your quest for Alteration training.

You must hang out with him underwater for three hours in game time. During this period, remain close by the trainer; if you stray sufficiently far to surface for air, whether you actually surface or not, you'll fail. After the period elapses, he offers his congratulations and the training button will be available. (If you approach him after 1 p.m., he'll kick the test to the following day.)

How do you stay alive underwater? The ideal solution is to use a helmet with a constant Water Breathing enchantment. There are six of them, but can you find one? It's hard. These don't exist within the game world but occasionally pop up in leveled loot: the Black Marsh Helmet at Level 3, Helmet of the Deep at Level 5, Cave Diver's Helmet at Level 8, Helmet of the Drowned at Level 12, Seastrider's Helmet at Level 17, and Helmet of the Flood at Level 22.

You may find one on the bandit chief Black Brugo (from the Miscellaneous quest "Knights of the White Stallion"), Rigmor (from the Miscellaneous quest "Nothing You Can Possess"), Blackwood Company guards (from the Fighters Guild quest "Information Gathering"), or any Marauder boss.

If you can't find one, you can use spells or potions. (The three hours compresses to about six minutes in real time—the duration of 12 castings of a 30-second Water Breathing spell.) This spell can be purchased from Ungarion at A Warlock's Luck in Bravil, Trayvond the Redguard at the Cheydinhal Mages Guild, or Edgar Vautrine at Edgar's Discount Spells in the Imperial City's Market District.

The weak Water Breathing potions have the same duration as the spell, but you can reduce the busy work somewhat by buying or finding eight standard or four strong Potions of the Sea. The former can be found in chests in the captain's cabin on the pirate ship *The Sea Tub Clarabella* at the Anvil docks; on an outdoor balcony reached from the royal quarters in Castle Anvil; in a recess off the second level of the tower above Fort Vlastarus, located near the Gold Road east of Skingrad; on the third and fourth levels of Veyond's Cave, a Troll lair on the coast north of Bravil; and in leveled loot beginning at Level 5.

The strong potion is found in Chancellor Ocato's Imperial Palace quarters during the Thieves Guild quest "The Ultimate Heist"; can be received as a reward in the Settlement quest "No Stone Unturned"; can be purchased in the Bruma, Chorrol, and Leyawiin Mages Guilds, The Gilded Carafe in the Imperial City's Market District, The Sleeping Mare in Pell's Gate, and All Things Alchemical in Skingrad; and begin to appear in leveled loot at Level 10.

And you can make potions yourself. You'll need be at least an Apprentice-level alchemist and have at least two of the five relevant ingredients. Water Breathing is the second effect of both the standard and the Rumare Slaughterfish scales (the latter from the Settlement quest "Go Fish"), white seed pods, and onions, and the third effect of Dreugh wax.

However, be careful which ingredients you choose. All but the white seed pods are accompanied by a significant Health hit. The seed pods are found in goldenrod plants—most plentiful in the area around Fort Wariel northwest of Kvatch.

ARMORER TRAINING

The low-level Armorer trainers are Eitar, who lives with his wife Margarte (herself a medium-level Mercantile trainer) at their house just east of Leyawiin's Great Chapel of Zenithar, and Tadrose Helas, the busy smith at the Bravil Fighters Guild.

The midlevel trainers are Rohssan, who runs the A Fighting Chance shop in the Imperial City's Market District, and Rasheda, the proprietor of Fire and Steel in Chorrol.

At a Armorer skill of 70, both will mention that you can get further training from Gin-Wulm. He's allegedly a smith at The Best Defense in the Imperial City's Market District, but he seems to devote most of his time to wandering in the Market and Elven Garden Districts.

Gin-Wulm has a vested interest in armor; it runs in the family.

Gin-Wulm is rather indignant at the presumption of your request, and gives you a quiz: "What does the name Hazadir mean to you?"

Unless you've read the book *The Armorer's Challenge* (or have it in your inventory), you'll only be able to answer "Nothing"—which gets you exactly that.

However, the master trainer hints that the book is available at nearby First Edition bookstore. (It's also on top of a bookshelf on the second floor of the Cheydinhal Fighters Guild.) Now you can answer, "He won the Armorer's Challenge" to secure training.

ATHLETICS TRAINING

The low-level Athletics trainers are cheese-loving shepherd Uuras, who has a house in the southwest corner of Skingrad, and the henpecked Mahei in Leyawiin.

The medium ones are Hauls-Ropes-Faster, a drunken pirate who sleeps by day at The Fo'c'sle in Anvil and wanders the Waterfront at night, and Honditar, who has a little place just southwest of Chorrol and has a minor part in the Miscellaneous quest "Shadow Over Hackdirt." At an Athletics skill of 70, ask about "Training" and both will kick you to master trainer Rusia Bradus, who lives with her husband, Silgor, on Anvil's main drag next to the Abandoned House.

See the world, one location at a time. Rusia won't train you unless you've gotten around.

Bradus is a world traveler who measures your achievements by the number of locations you've discovered. If you've discovered 30, she'll train you. If fewer, she'll send you out to see more of the world first.

BLADE TRAINING

The low-level trainers in the use of bladed weapons are Naspia Cosma, the steward at Castle Cheydinhal, and Right-Wind at the Bruma Fighters Guild.

The midlevel ones are Sherina and Rhano at the Leyawiin and Anvil Fighters Guilds, respectively. At a Blade skill of 70, they'll bump you to Alix Lencolia—a blademaster who, passing through Cyrodiil on his way south, has stopped at the Faregyl Inn south of Imperial City.

Alix Lencolia: Do-gooder or fame-seeker? You make the call.

Just as Bradus watches your "discoveries" stat, Lencolia monitors your fame and infamy. He doesn't care whether you're more one or the other—just so long as your name has gotten around Cyrodiil. He won't train you until your Fame or Infamy hits 20. If you don't have it, go out and complete "good" quests for Fame or "evil" ones for Infamy. (You can also boost your Infamy by acquiring a bounty. When you pay it off, the Infamy you've acquired remains in place.)

BLOCK TRAINING

The basic trainers for Block are Fadus Calidius at the Skingrad Fighters Guild and Huurwen at the Anvil Fighters Guild. At the next level are cheerful Lum gro-Baroth at the Chorrol Fighters Guild—not to be confused with his sad-sack brother Kurz—and grape-grower Ambroise Canne, who has a house in the southwest corner of Skingrad.

The Block master, Andragil, who lives above Dro'Shanji in the north-central part of Bravil, wants to test your prowess first. Basically, you need take a beating from Andragil's warhammer without responding in kind. Un-equip any weapons and don't equip any for the term of the test—45 seconds—and don't get yourself killed. (It's okay to punch her, though this rather violates the spirit of the exercise.) We also recommend a nice shield. It's not required, but you'll have a better chance at staying alive.

Survive a beating from Andragil to prove you've got what it takes for Block training.

If you're quick on your feet, this may also prove a test of speed. Just keep Andragil's dinner table between you until the clock runs out. When the lady shoulders the hammer, it's done and you've got your training.

BLUNT TRAINING

The low-level blunt-weapon trainers are angry merchant Bugak gro-Bol at Southern Books in Leyawiin and Vigdis at the Anvil Fighters Guild.

The midlevel guys are Christophe Marane, proprietor of the Brina Cross Inn northeast of Anvil—like other inn operators, Christophe gets no word-of-mouth at all on his training—and Azzan at the Anvil Fighters Guild (and quest-giver for many of the early guild missions). Once your Blunt skill hits 70, each will point you to Irene Metrick, who has a house in the southwest quadrant of the Imperial City's Elven Gardens District.

Now, Ms. Metrick is a woman of mystery. (We discuss her a bit in the "Freeform Quests" chapter.) The medium trainers make references to some horrific acts in her past. "How many people have you killed in your lifetime, eh?" she asks. "Not as many as I, my little friend."

Follow in Irene Metrick's bloody footsteps to earn her trust and receive training.

Evidently, she's killed well over 50—and that's the minimum number you'll have to whack before she'll train you. Note that she does mean people—non-player characters, as distinct from creatures. (The game tracks both on your stats page.)

 If you raise Metrick's Disposition to 60 and ask about "Imperial City," she'll identify four other trainers—including medium Sneak trainer Othrelos and medium Security trainer Mandil.

CONJURATION TRAINING

The low-level Conjuration trainers are Fathis Aren, the court mage at Castle Bravil, and Sulinus Vassinus at the Skingrad Mages Guild. Vassinus has a minor role in the Skingrad guild's recommendation quest. Aren figures in the Thieves Guild quest "Arrow of Extrication"—and can be killed therein, so either don't kill him or put off that quest until he can't help you any more as a trainer.

The medium trainers are Alberic Litte of the Chorrol Mages Guild and, oddly enough, Arentus Falvius—the high priest at Bruma's Great Chapel of Talos. When your skill outstrips their ability to further train you, Falvius and Litte will send you to Olyn Seran, who can be found at Molag Bal's shrine—located in the Great Forest west of the Imperial City.

Seran wants you to put on a little magic show: You're to summon a Faded Wraith before him.

Olyn Seran wants a demonstration of your abilities as a Conjurer before he'll agree to training.

Now, this is nasty. While you can buy this pricey spell from Athragar at the Chorrol Mages Guild and Caranya and Gaspar Stegine at the Arcane University, you can't cast it until you have a Conjuration skill of 75.

Sounds like a Catch-22 situation: You need the training to help you get the spell and the spell to get you the training.

Fortunately, this spell is also embedded in a scroll. Unfortunately, that scroll is not for sale anywhere and doesn't exist at any fixed locations in the game. It appears only in loot—notably, loot from magic users like Necromancers and Conjurers. (The closest such hideaway is the small Necromancer lair Elenglynn to the west-southwest.)

DESTRUCTION TRAINING

The low-level trainers in Destruction are Chanel, the castle mage in Castle Chorrol, and J'skar, who works out of the Bruma Mages Guild. Note that, in the Miscellaneous quest "Canvas the Castle," you can get Chanel booted out of the game, so either avoid this event—it's not required—or postpone it until the mage can't train you any more. By contrast, you'll need to complete the Bruma guild's recommendation quest before you can train with the invisible and uncommunicative J'skar.

The medium trainers are Marc Gulitte at the Anvil Mages Guild and Delphine Jend at the Bravil guild. They're a bit different from the run of medium trainers; they won't give up the location of master trainer Bralsa Andaren unless you can coax their Disposition above 80.

We suspect they're hesitant because Andaren is off her freaking nut. She's made camp near a shrine to Kynareth west of the Weatherleah estate in the Imperial Reserve and is evidently killing off the wildlife.

Bralsa Andaren needs 20 Bear pelts before she'll agree to train you in the art of Destruction magic.

Why? Andaren apparently has a bone to pick with Kynareth, and she asks you to help her in exchange for training. You'll have to bring her 20 Bear pelts.

This is not a small task. As discussed under "Hircine" in the "Daedric Quests" chapter, Bears appear only at certain levels and in certain regions. They're most common in forests but begin to appear there only at Level 7—with a second chance at a Bear kicking in at Level 15. However, if you're Level 18 or higher, you

stand your best chances of finding them in mountain forests, where Bears can appear at Levels 7, 12, and 18.

So it's hard to give directions here. But if you're at Level 7, you'll have a slightly better chance of finding bears near Elenglynn (an Ayleid ruin west-southwest of the Imperial City); Fingerbowl Cave (north of the Imperial City and just northeast of Aleswell); Fort Carmala (south of Chorrol); Fort Sejanus (north of the Yellow Road southeast of the Imperial City); Piukanda (northwest of Aleswell); Pothole Caverns (south of the Faregyl Inn, which is itself just off the Green Road south of the Imperial City); and in the Nibenay Basin wilderness west of Fort Facian (just east of a stubby southeastern inlet that divides the Corbolo and Reed Rivers).

If you're Level 14 or higher, you can also check near the Ayleid ruins Kemen (in the mountains just east of Cheydinhal) and Rielle (in the mountains northwest of Bruma).

If you're more interested in completing this quest than holding on to your hard-earned cash, there's a simpler way to fulfill Andaren's request. Traders sell Bear pelts, and you can buy five at a time. Visit a few towns, gather what you need (keeping in mind that pelts can be heavy), and report back to her when you have all of them.

HAND-TO-HAND TRAINING

The low-level trainers in the Hand-to-Hand skill are Nahsi at the Bravil Fighters Guild and Rufrius Vinicius at the Anvil guild.

The medium folks are Davela Hlaren, who runs the Imperial Bridge Inn—on the north bank of the Silverfish River east of the Yellow Road—and Thieves Guild member Ra'qanar at Castle Cheydinhal.

The latter two direct you to master trainer Helvius Cecia, who has a house in the southeast corner of Bruma. He's in the Thieves Guild as well, and you've already met him if you've performed that guild's "Turn a Blind Eye" quest. (His house is used for your meeting with the Gray Fox.)

You'll have to put up your dukes and show Helvius Cecia what you know before he'll train you.

Cecia's got a test for you, too: Barehanded, smack him around for 30 seconds and reduce his Health by about 40 percent to prevent him from getting "bored." Don't worry; Cecia's guild affiliation is ignored for the term of the test, so you won't get booted if you're in the guild. Once you've hurt him enough, he'll speak to you and you're in.

But stop fighting when he tells you to stop. Once he talks to you, he becomes a guild member again. Keep fighting, and it's assault, with the usual potential consequences flowing from assault.

HEAVY ARMOR TRAINING

The Heavy Armor basic trainers are Brodras at the Leyawiin Fighters Guild and Bumph gra-Gash at the Bruma guild.

The medium trainers are Valus Odiil in Chorrol—quest-giver for the Miscellaneous quest "The Killing Field"—and Varnado, a coworker of Armorer master trainer Gin-Wulm at The Best Defense in the Imperial City's Market District. They'll put you in touch with master trainer Pranal—a retired gladiator who's settled at the Roxey Inn, on the Red Ring Road at the northeast corner of Lake Rumare.

Pranal has only one interest in life these days: Malene, the proprietor of the Roxey Inn.

Pranal has taken a shine to the Roxey proprietor, Malene, and will train you if you put together a little gift for her: a silver pitcher and a set of four glasses. He'll provide 50 gold to cover the cost, but no details as to the items' appearance or where to find them.

Along with the offerings for the Daedric mission "Sheogorath," this is the closest thing to a "clutter" quest in *Oblivion*. It's not that difficult. Just remember that Pranal said "glasses"—not cups, mugs, goblets, or tankards. There's just one type of glass in the game (silver), and it can be found all over the place.

If you're not particular about how you acquire the glasses, you can rip them off from a variety of castles, chapels, guilds, nice houses and inns, and Arkved's Tower—the big, strange dungeon from the Daedric quest "Vaermina." If you are particular, you can buy them at Lelles' Quality Merchandise in Anvil, Bravil's The Fair Deal, Bruma's Novaroma, Borba's Goods and Stores in Cheydinhal, Chorrol's Northern Goods and Trade, the Imperial City's Three Brothers Trade Goods and The Copious Coinpurse (both in the Market District), Leyawiin's Best Goods and Guarantees, and Skingrad's Colovian Traders.

There are two types of silver pitchers in the game. Either will do to complete the set. However, neither is for sale, and you'll either have to steal the pitcher or find it in leveled loot.

You can steal the pitchers from many of the same places that you found the glasses. By contrast, the loot can appear in a certain type of chest spread over all three classes of houses (most common in the middle-class ones); in the legion commander's chest you'll open in the Thieves Guild quest "Taking Care of Lex";

in two chests in Fathis Aren's Castle Bravil quarters and one in his tower outside the city, which you'll visit in the Thieves Guild quest "Arrow of Extrication"; in two chests in the section of the Imperial Sewers that you used for the final Thieves Guild quest, "The Ultimate Heist"; the chest that contains Lithnilian's notes in the Settlement quest "No Stone Unturned"; in chests and sacks that appear at the small wilderness encampments; and in certain of the lone chests that appear out in the wilderness. (See the "Freeform Quests" chapter for details.)

With the glasses and pitcher in inventory, speak to Pranal about "Gift." He'll ask you to give 'em to Malene. Via "Gift," she'll accept them gladly—while disclosing that she doesn't like Pranal that way—and you've merely to use the topic again with Pranal to start on the road to 100.

ILLUSION TRAINING

In Illusion, the low-level folks are Hil the Tall, a priest at Cheydinhal's Chapel of Arkay, and Jantus Brolus, who lives at Istrius Brolus's house in Bruma.

The medium-level trainers are Carahil at the Anvil Mages Guild and Kud-Ei in the Bravil guild. At an Illusion skill of 70, they'll bump you to Martina Floria at the Arcane University's Chironasium.

Martina Floria is one of the high-ranking members of the Mages Guild; she spends all her time in the Arcane University.

Now, with that skill level, we're betting you're well into the Mages Guild quests. If not, now's the time, as access to most of the university (including the Chironasium—"Enchanting Center" in the common tongue) is limited to guild members of Apprentice rank or higher. You'll have to complete the guild's recommendation quests to get the full run of the campus.

Floria wants 10 Welkynd Stones to train you. These aquamarine lava lamps, which restore Magicka, can be found almost exclusively in Ayleid ruins—but not always in sufficient numbers to fulfill Floria's demand in one trip.

The stones are most plentiful in the Necromancer lair Wendelbek, between the northern headwaters of the Panther River, where 58 are spread over four levels. But that's quite a trek to the southeast and much more stone than you need for the task at hand. Better to visit Vilverin, on an island just east of the northeast exit from the Imperial Sewers (21 stones over three levels); Sardavar Leed, on the Red Ring Road south of the city (16 stones on one level); Fanacasecul, on the Red Ring Road just south of the bridge to the Imperial City's Talos Plaza District (10 stones on one level); or Sercen, on the Red Ring Road just east of the junction with the Silver Road (10 stones on one level).

LIGHT ARMOR

The low-level Light Armor trainers are Dul gro-Shug, who has a house in the northeast quadrant of Imperial City's Elven Gardens District, and Olfand, who works out of Nord Winds in Bruma.

The medium trainers are Luciana Galena, a Thieves Guild fence who has a house in the southern section of Bravil (right above the house for sale), and the Argonian-hating Ahdarji, who has a house in Leyawiin (just west of the castle's southern gate) and figures in the Thieves Guild quest "Ahdarji's Heirloom." At a skill of 70, they'll bump you over to the master, J'Bari, who shares a house in south-central Leyawiin with midlevel Acrobatics trainer Tsrava.

J'Bari wants a new Elven cuirass. You'll definitely find one on Azani Blackheart, from the Fighters Guild quest of the same name.

J'Bari wants a new Elven cuirass in exchange for his services.

And if you're Level 15 or better, you might find it in loot from a wide range of characters. We can't give a full list of possibilities—you know how the whole leveled loot thing works by now, yes?—but it includes:

- Bandits in general, notably the ones on the top level of the Ayleid ruin Vilverin (opposite the northeast exit from the Imperial Sewers)
- Vampires in general, notably, three in Bloodcrust Cavern (near Castle Skingrad) from the Mages Guild quest "Information at a Price" and the Imperial and Nord Vampires in Gutted Mine from the Daedric quest "Azura"
- The Black Rock pirates (see the "Freeform Quests" chapter)
- Dead treasure hunters;
- three of your opponents in the Tournament of Ten Bloodsfrom the Daedric quest "Boethia"
- At least three of your opponents from The Hunter's Run, which you'll visit in the Miscellaneous quest "Caught in the Hunt"
- The two Camonna Tong thugs at Walker Camp north of Cheydinhal
- The Bandits Ayisha, J'Baasha, and Mensa Selas at Fisherman's Rock, from the Miscellaneous quest "Mazoga the Orc"

- The burglar Dranas Lerano from the Fighters Guild quest "The Unfortunate Shopkeeper"
- The Daedra worshipper Rona from Mephala's shrine
- The hunter Schlerus Sestius of Pell's Gate
- Shaleez from the Dark Brotherhood quest "Final Justice"
- Thrangirfin from the Fighters Guild quest "Den of Thieves"

MARKSMAN

The low-level archery trainers are Edla Dark-Heart, who lives at Regner's house on the south side of Bruma, and the vintner Shameer, who has a place of his own just west of Skingrad's Great Chapel of Julianos. (Conventional wisdom has Dark-Heart as an assassin on the run from a Skyrim murder charge.)

The midlevel ones are vineyard worker Reman Broder, who has a house in the southwest corner of Skingrad, and hunter Pinarus Inventius in Anvil. (The latter figures in the early Fighters Guild quest "A Rat Problem.")

At a player skill of 70, and a Disposition of 80, either man will point you to Alawen at Troll Candle Camp east of Anvil.

Alawen knows that an archer is only as good as his or her equipment.

It's hard to find Alawen and hard to talk to her when you do. If you don't find her in the camp by day, she's probably off hunting. She hunts with remarkable persistence and stamina. Even if you can keep up with her, you won't get her to talk to you, so intent is she upon her task. So we suggest you visit the camp between 10 p.m. and 4 a.m. when she should be sleeping. If she's not there, wait. It's a good bet she's returning from a hunt that has taken her far afield.

When you do talk to her, make sure you've got an Elven bow. If you don't, she's only going to send you off to get one.

Alas, no Elven bows are lying around waiting for you. It's another leveled item that may turn up at weapon shops if you reached Level 13 or in leveled loot beginning at Level 9. Focus on Bandit and Marauder dungeons, as they frequently have archers. The closest of these locations are Fort Strand east of Anvil and Belletor's Folly south of Kvatch.

Your best bet for buying one is probably The Archer Paradox in Bravil. Your best bet for finding one is Githriian—one of the baddies from the Fighters Guild quest "Den of Thieves" who has two chances of possessing the bow. Or, if you've reached Level

16 and are playing the Dark Brotherhood quests, try the Dark Guardian bowmen in Lucien Lachance's hideaway in Fort Farragut.

MERCANTILE TRAINING

For basic Mercantile training go to Foroch, at the Gottshaw Inn southwest of Kvatch, or Mach-Na, who runs Mach-Na's Books in the business district in the western part of Cheydinhal. (Foroch's skills are unadvertised and Mach-Na is known mainly for his grumpiness.)

The medium-level trainers are Margarte, who shares a house just east of Leyawiin's Great Chapel of Zenithar with her husband, Eitar (himself a low-level Armorer trainer), and Seed-Neeus, who runs Northern Goods and Trade near Chorrol's south gate. (Margarte figures in the Fighters Guild quest "Drunk and Disorderly," and Seed-Neeus has a part in the Miscellaneous quest "Shadow Over Hackdirt.")

They'll refer you to master trainer Palonirya, who runs Divine Elegance in the Imperial City's Market District. Palonirya looks in your pocketbook. If she finds at least 10,000 gold there, she'll train you.

Palonirya loves gold. And hey, who doesn't?

Yes, it's a lot of dough, but you can get it in one long quest by collecting Ayleid statues for Umbacano in the Imperial City's Talos Plaza District. See "The Collector" in the "Miscellaneous Quests" chapter for the details.

Note that this soon has a nice after-effect. Once your Mercantile skill reaches 75, you'll get a new topic when in dialogue with shopkeepers: "Invest 500 gold in this shop." Select this option and the money will be subtracted from your cash and the shop's "barter gold"—the amount of cash it has on hand to buy your goods—will jump by 500. That's the limit per shop, but you can do it with as many shops as you like.

MYSTICISM TRAINING

Try Angalmo in the Chorrol Mages Guild or Druja in the Skingrad guild for basic Mysticism training. (The former's skills are unadvertised. The latter figures in the guild's recommendation quest.)

At the next level, trainers are Ita Rienus in the Bravil Mages Guild and Boderi Farano in the Arcane University's Mystic Archives.

(You'll need to be at least an apprentice in the Mages Guild to contact Farano.)

They'll refer you to Dagail in the Leyawiin Mages Guild. Dagail's a bit off-center until you restore her stolen amulet in the Mages Guild Leyawiin recommendation quest, but she's got enough on the ball to know how many Oblivion gates you've closed. If you've zapped three—the minimum requirement to get through the Main Quest—she'll train you. If you've closed fewer than three, she'll send you out to close more.

Dagail is attuned to the mystic nature of the world and needs you to help restore the balance.

Once you've completed the "Dagon Shrine" segment of the Main Quest, you'll find quest-related gates outside each of Cyrodiil's second-tier cities and as many as 50 random gates in the wilderness.

RESTORATION TRAINING

The low-level trainers in Restoration are the healers Cirroc at Bruma's Great Chapel of Talos—he figures in the Fighters Guild quest "The Stone of St. Alessia"—and Marie Palielle at Skingrad's Great Chapel of Julianos.

The medium-level instructors are the healers Marz in Bravil's Great Chapel of Mara and Ohtesse in Cheydinhal's Great Chapel of Arkay. They'll refer you to master trainer Oleta at the Chapel of Akatosh in Kvatch.

Free Oleta from the ruined chapel in Kvatch to receive Restoration training.

Much of Kvatch has been virtually destroyed by the Daedra. As a result, this quest could play out a few ways.

If you haven't gotten into the Main Quest yet, Oleta is trapped in the chapel. You'll have to remove the Oblivion gate outside the walls and kill off the Daedra that occupy the plaza outside the chapel to reach her. See "Breaking the Siege of Kvatch" in the Main Quest chapter for details. She'll consent to train you when the city is safe.

That requires completing the Miscellaneous quest "The Battle for Castle Kvatch," in which you clear Daedra from the castle at the west end of the city. Talk to Savlian Matius after he enters the church to get that operation going, and see the "Miscellaneous Quests" chapter for details.

Don't take alarm if you can't find Oleta in the chapel on your return. Once you complete "Breaking the Siege of Kvatch," Matius instructs officer-in-charge Tierra to lead the survivors down the hill to the refugee camp to the south. That's where you'll contact Oleta for training.

SECURITY TRAINING

Obtain training in Security from low-level instructor Malintus Ancrus or Samuel Bantien. Ancrus is a current thief in Chorrol—his home in the city's southwest corner is used for your meeting with the Gray Fox for the Thieves Guild quest "Arrow of Extrication." Former thief Bantien has a house in the southwest quadrant of Imperial City's Talos Plaza District.

The midlevel trainers are thieves Dro'Shanji, who has a place below Andragil's in north-central Bravil, and Mandil, who lives in Othrelos's house in the northeast quadrant of the Imperial City's Elven Gardens District.

They'll direct you to J'baana. He's in the Imperial Prison District. We're guessing the master of Security needed a little more Sneak skill.

J'baana is a master thief who's taken a liking to life on the inside.

Don't bother talking to the jailor about access to the cells. J'baana's imprisoned after a fashion, but he's not really in prison. You'll find the Khajiit wandering around out of doors behind key-locked gates in the enclosed northeast portion of the Imperial Prison District. You can either talk to him through one of the gates—J'baana can appear at either of them—or enter the rear yard by either stealing the Imperial City Prison key from a jailor or picking the five-tumbler lock on the rear door inside the central bastion. (And good luck with that, huh?)

J'baana sends you on a FedEx errand: You're to retrieve a message from Thieves Guild doyen S'krivva in Bravil. She lives just southwest of the city's north gate. S'krivva seems rather caught out by your appearance but gives you a note to take back to the trainer. (Read it if you like; these two evidently are up to no good.) Just deliver it to J'baana (who isn't pleased) and the training is yours.

Now, here's the funny thing. J'baana is even less nominally imprisoned than he appears. He has all the keys—prison, Imperial Watch, and Imperial Watch office—and 30 lockpicks besides. He could escape at will but apparently stays because he enjoys his abode.

The low-level sneakers are City-Swimmer, who has a little place

SNEAK TRAINING

above S'krivva's just southwest of the Bravil city gate (and apparently a second home in the city's canals), and Glistel, who lives with low-level Security trainer Malintus Ancrus in the southwest corner of Chorrol—much to the outrage of her neighbors.

The midlevel trainers are Othrelos, who has a house in the northeast part of Imperial City's Elven Gardens District, and Mirabelle Monet, who runs the boarding house on the Anvil Waterfront (The Fo'c's'le). They'll point you to master trainer Marana Rian. She has a home in the northwest part of the Temple District but spends her evenings wandering in the Arboretum and Waterfront District.

Marana Rian is about the only person in Cyrodiil who will *ask* you to steal from her.

Her test is simple: Steal the coin she has in her pocket. This shouldn't be hard, since your Sneak skill is 70. Then talk to her again about "Training," and you're in.

SPEECHCRAFT TRAINING

We've saved the biggest of the training quests for last.

The low-level orators are the bard Alga, who lives with partner Honmund at his house in Bruma, and Uravasa Othelas, a priest at Bravil's Great Chapel of Mara.

The medium trainers are bard Varon Vamori, who has a house in Bravil (and a part in the Bravil Mages Guild recommendation quest), and the big-talking Gruiand Garrana, at Cheydinhal's Great Chapel of Arkay.

When you hit 70, they'll point you to Speechcraft master Tandilwe at the Temple of the One in the Imperial City's Temple District.

Tandilwe has the well being of Cyrodiil's most impoverished residents on her mind. She'd like you to take an interest as well.

Before she'll train you, Tandilwe wants you to undertake a pilgrimage: You're to talk to each of the beggars in Cyrodiil. There are 19—five in the Imperial City and two in each of Cyrodiil's seven second-tier cities. All you have to do is enter dialogue with each.

If you're a Thieves Guild member, you may already have dealt extensively with these wretched folks, who often serve the role of informants in those quests. If so, you'll get credit for those conversations, and, if you can remember to whom you have and haven't spoken, you don't need to repeat them now. Moreover, any beggars you may have killed before the quest begins are not held against you. (However, kill a beggar during the quest and you'll be unable to complete it.)

The beggars follow regular schedules. They all sleep from 10 p.m. to 6 a.m. on bedrolls in remote sections of town, spend their days wandering near two or three fixed locations, and return to their bedrolls shortly after 6 p.m. to eat. (The only thing that changes their schedules is bad weather—and that only in Anvil, Bruma, Cheydinhal, and Leyawiin.) Hence, if you can't find a person, find his or her bedroll and wait.

In Anvil, the beggars are Imus the Dull and Penniless Olvus. Imus sleeps behind the Flowing Bowl on the Waterfront. During the day, he can be found near the Waterfront District entryway, outside the Chapel of Dibella and on the docks. And in the event of rain, he'll take cover under the overhanging roof of Heinrich Oaken-Hull's house. Olvus sleeps just east of the main gate. He hangs out near that gate and the chapel, and, in rainy weather, under the overhanging roof of Morvayn's Peacemakers just west of his camp.

In Bravil, the beggars are Cosmus the Cheat and Wretched Aia. Cosmus sleeps behind the Lonely Suitor Lodge in the southwest corner of town and spends his day near the Great Chapel of Mara, A Warlock's Luck shop, and the city gate. Aia sleeps behind The Fair Deal in the northeast corner of town and spends her day near the city gate, the Lonely Suitor, and the chapel.

In Bruma, the beggars are Fetid Jofnhild and Jorck the Outcast. Jofnhild sleeps behind the rocks beside the North Gate and hangs out near that gate, on the stairs to the southeast, and at the Great Chapel of Talos. When it rains, he takes shelter under the overhanging roof of Honmund's house just north of the chapel. Jorck sleeps behind Anora's house on the south side of town and spends his day near the chapel, the East Gate and Nord Winds. When it rains, he heads for the front porch of Bradon Lirrian's house in the southwest part of the town.

In Cheydinhal, the beggars are Bruccius the Orphan and Luckless Lucina. (While Aldos Othran sleeps on a bedroll against the south wall, he's not a beggar. See the Miscellaneous quest "Corruption and Conscience.") Bruccius sleeps within a ring of buildings just southeast of the West Gate and spends his day near the Northeast Gate, the Great Chapel of Arkay, and outside Borba's Goods and Stores. Lucina sleeps in the southwest corner of town and spends her day near the West Gate, the town statue, and the chapel. In rainy weather, both Bruccius and Lucina make for the porch of Riverview in the southeast corner of town.

In Chorrol, the beggars are Lazy Kaslowyn and Nermus the Mooch. Kaslowyn sleeps among boulders against the south wall in the southwest part of town and spends his day near the fountain, the Chapel of Stendarr, and just down the street to the southeast. Nemus sleeps beside the rocks just north of the chapel and spends his day near the South Gate, the North Gate, and the chapel.

In Imperial City, the beggars are Fralav the Faker, Simplicia the Slow, No Coins Draninus, Ragbag Buntara, and Puny Ancus. Fralav sleeps near a well in an enclosure in the southwest corner of the Elven Gardens District; he spends his days near the gates to the exterior and the Palace District. Simplicia sleeps near a well in an enclosure in the southeast corner of the Market District and spends her day near the district's center and the exterior gate. Draninus sleeps at the south end of an alley in the northwest quadrant of Talos Plaza and spends his day on the north or south side of the district's central rotunda. Buntara sleeps in an enclosure near the northernmost portion of the Temple District and spends her day near the Palace and Waterfront gates. Finally, Ancus sleeps behind the boarded-up house in the Waterfront District and spends his day near the lighthouse and at the north and south ends of the docks. (Amusei sleeps on a bedroll near Ancus's, but he's not a beggar. He's involved in a handful of Thieves Guild quests.)

In Leyawiin, the beggars are Deeh the Scalawag and Rancid Ra'dirsha. Deeh sleeps near the well just northeast of the West Gate and spends his day near the North Gate, the Great Chapel of Zenithar, and the West Gate. In rainy weather, he hangs out in the small garden in the plaza in the southwest part of town. Ra'dirsha sleeps in the southwest corner of town and spends her day near the East Gate, the garden Deeh likes, and the chapel. In bad weather, she takes refuge on the little porch at the Five Claws Lodge, just north of the chapel.

Finally, in Skingrad, the beggars are Foul Fagus and Nigidius the Needy. Fagus sleeps behind a stable, which is itself behind the West Weald Inn—on the south side of the northern half of the city. He spends his days near the Great Chapel of Julianos, the Northeast Gate, and outside the West Weald Inn. Nigidius sleeps just across the street—next to the Skingrad Fighters Guild—and spends his day near the Northeast Gate, the intersection south of the town statue, and the chapel.

You shouldn't have any trouble talking to the beggars. The only potential problem is disease. The beggars are a regular cauldron of bacteria. All of them are carrying something, and three of them have two diseases. You can keep yourself safe with Cure Disease potions, spells, or scrolls.

MISCELLANEOUS QUESTS

ANVIL

WHERE SPIRITS HAVE LEASE

At The Count's Arms, from noon to midnight, you'll find a young man named Velwyn Benirus who's looking to unload his grandfather's dilapidated mansion in the northeast corner of town. (You can also learn about the house and Benirus through the rumor mill.)

The price: 5,000 gold. If you've looked into Cyrodiil's real-estate market —see "Houses" in the "Freeform Quests" chapter—this somewhat rundown mansion may seem like a bargain.

Well, yes and no. Info on the mansion is thin to nonexistent. You can assemble a little history on your own: Via "Rumors," you'll hear from a passerby a report that he or she heard someone scream inside the manor the previous night, and speculation that the house will never be sold.

In any case, if you give him the money, Velwyn gives you the key and deed. And he'll take off directly for parts unknown. (You'll have to track him down later.)

A cursory inspection of your purchase suggests you've just bought a fixer-upper at a nice price. One odd thing: In the farthest, deepest room of the capacious cellar is a "sealed portal" in the south wall that doesn't respond to your poking and prodding.

Benirus Manor beckons

The first time you try sleeping in the house, three Ghosts materialize and attack you. Kill them with an enchanted weapon; a journal entry announces the house is haunted and mentions a crash downstairs. A vase has fallen from atop a cabinet in the parlor. Under the vase rests a skeletal hand, along with a page from a creepy diary that refers to a secret room that only a Benirus can open. Read the diary—you learn Velwyn's granddad was a Necromancer and a grave robber—then take it and the skeletal hand.

You need Velwyn to open the door. Unfortunately, he took the money and ran. Passersby point you to The Count's Arms again, and folks there indicate he's bound for the Imperial City. As is often the case, your map knows more than you do. It directs you to the city's Elven Gardens District, where you learn from passersby that Benirus is staying at The King and Queen Tavern.

Buttonhole Velwyn there; he acknowledges that he should have mentioned that the house was cursed. Via the topics "Lorgren Benirus" and "Lift the curse," he agrees to meet you at The Count's Arms and straighten things out. Return to Anvil and speak to Velwyn at the inn. He directs you to follow him back to the house. Once inside, you assume the lead.

Seven Ghosts mark your route—two on the ground floor and five in the cellar. You may be able to dash past them and then stand guard against pursuers as Benirus waves his hands over the symbol on the cellar wall. When he opens the secret door, the Ghosts vanish—Velwyn, too; he heads back to the inn—and you're free to explore the crypt/laboratory beyond the door.

The resting place of Lorgren Benirus

With the skeletal hand from the parlor in inventory, activate the altar. When Lorgren's spirit completes its speech—it's a tissue of lies, but you'll have to comply to kick things along—activate the Skeleton itself. Kill it quickly before the Lich starts conjuring undead nasties.

When activating the remains of Lorgren, position yourself on the far side of the altar (with a nice enchanted weapon) to better intercept the great dark form when it materializes.

Then loot the place. You'll net Lorgren's Staff, *The Tome of Unlife* (worth around 350 gold), 40–1,490 gold (depending on your level), and an assortment of gems and jewelry.

When you emerge from the basement you discover that your

haunted mansion is transformed. The errant shutters and fallen painting have been rehung. The exterior walls are intact. There's food on the table and a fire in the hearth. It's not just a house; it's a home.

All you have to do is visit The Count's Arms for a fourth time and check in with Velwyn, and you're done. He'll eventually make his way back to The King and Queen Tavern in the Imperial City.

The siren's lair

THE SIREN'S DECEPTION

Again, you can pick this one up either from the rumor mill or directly from Maelona, whom you'll find strolling through town…and whose husband Gogan is said to be "intimately involved."

A gang of women has been luring Anvil's men to remote places, seducing them, and robbing them. When they robbed Gogan, they stole a ring that has been in Maelona's family for generations. She'll give you 100 gold to get it back. (Gogan can offer a bit of help as well; he'll identify the women who approached him as a fetching Nord and an Imperial.)

Visit the Flowing Bowl, where the robbers have been fingering their marks, at any time during its operating hours; it's the westernmost structure on the city's Waterfront. You'll barely have sat yourself down when the lovely Faustina Cartia or Signy Home-Wrecker enters and makes a beeline for you.

Signy Home-Wrecker and Faustina Cartia work their magic in the Flowing Bowl.

If you're male, Signy observes that you're alone and offers to remedy the situation with a wink and a nudge. If you're female, Faustina invites you to join the gang. Either way, you're set up for an 11 p.m. rendezvous at the Gweden farmhouse southeast of Anvil, which the respective lady will add to your map.

Make your way southeast of Anvil to the hilltop farmhouse. It will be locked until 11 p.m., at which time you can enter and have a chat with little Faustina.

There are minor variations at this point, depending on your character's gender and decision, but everything results sooner or later in the summoning of Signy and a Khajiit, Tsarinna, and a fight.

The fight can be a bit tricky, as the gang attacks inside the small farmhouse and there isn't a great deal of room for casters or marksmen to back off and do what they do best.

 Faustina is armed with a nasty dagger named Witsplinter, which saps your Magicka and intelligence—a nice prize when she finally goes down for the count.

When the three robbers are dead, who should walk in but Maelona and Gogan in Anvil city guard garb! Maelona explains that they've been working undercover to bring this gang of "sirens" down and turns over your reward of 100–600 gold (depending on your level).

This completes the quest, but you're not quite done. Take the Gweden bedroom key from Cartia's or Tsarinna's body. This lets you out of the house and into the cellar. A side room in the cellar holds a nice little Easter Egg: The proceeds of past robberies enable you to identify as past victims Heinrich Oaken-Hull, Pinarus Inventius, and Ernest. Alas, you can't return the items to their owners and embarrass them with their wives, but some are worth a fair amount of dosh—notably a two-tumbler jewelry box containing the "Oaken-Hull Family Jewels"; Inventius's iron cuirass and prize Minotaur horn; and Astia Inventius's amulet.

You'll come away with a leveled 40–1,490 gold, an emerald, and a gold nugget. Not too shabby!

THE GHOST SHIP OF ANVIL

Ready for a short item-retrieval mission? On the deck of the *Serpent's Wake*, the northern of the two ships docked in Anvil harbor, awaits a fretful sorceress named Varulae. The ship has just returned from a trip to Summerset Isle to retrieve a crystal ball that belonged to Varulae's mother…and the crew's been murdered. They are now "Spectral Sailors"—armed with sharpened cutlasses and adjusted to your level—and they haunt the ship. You're to get the crystal from a chest on the bottom deck and return it to Varulae.

The *Serpent's Wake* looks peaceful enough from the outside, but Varulae knows better.

Using the key provided, let yourself into the cabin, take the captain's key from his body, loot the chest (100 gold, a piece of leveled magic jewelry, and a jade necklace), beat on the thing here, and drop down the hatch to the mid-deck. Nothing much to see here—two baddies and two dead crew members behind closed doors—so trot to the hatch to the lower deck at the far end of the hall and descend to the hold.

Beware the Spectral Sailor's vicious sharpened cutlass.

Clean the clocks of two more baddies, take the crystal ball from the chest near the ladder—and, if you like, some loot at the far end of the hold—and get topside again. The sorceress offers up the enchanted cutlass Redwave (which has a leveled Drain Health enchantment) and then makes her way to The Count's Arms in Anvil, where she'll hang out for the rest of the game.

The murders of the sailors? You're not given any direct clues on the ship as to how they occurred, but you are in the Dark Brotherhood quest "Following a Lead." In that mission, you'll retrieve a traitor's diary from a macabre apartment beneath the Anvil lighthouse. In the middle of that book, there's a story about sailors visiting the lighthouse and ridiculing the writer as a "human rat."

"So I snuck on board, later that night, and I slit their throats. Every last one of them…The ghost ship of Anvil they'll call it now!"

BRAVIL

THROUGH A NIGHTMARE, DARKLY

You learn through the Bravil rumor mill that a friend of Kud-Ei has gone missing. Speak to the Argonian herself at the Mages Guild for the details: Her friend Henantier's reckless experiments have finally gotten him in trouble. Confirm your readiness to help recover him, and she'll lead you to a house just across the way where her friend lies in a restless sleep.

Using his Dreamworld Amulet, this obstinate spell-researcher traveled into his own dreams. He created the amulet to see if he could use these dreams as a training ground to help better himself and face his weaknesses head on. Three days later, he's still in there. You're to follow him and find out what's happened.

Getting to Henantier's Dreamworld is simple: As Kud-Ei instructs, equip the amulet (which she'll provide) and go to sleep in the adjacent bed. You appear near Henantier in a twisted version of his house—a strange hybrid environment with portals leading to four tests (Courage, Patience, Perception, and Resolve). Your only possessions: the amulet and your spells. But the amulet casts a constant-effect Silence spell on you, so you can't cast the spells. You can use only those things that you find in this strange place.

Henantier has been frightened into inaction but manages to disclose that he's lost things here and needs your help to find an exit. The "things" he's looking for are elements of his own sanity that have been ripped from him, represented by four Dreamworld elements. Only by returning these lost parts of his own mind to Henantier can you restore his sanity and open up a way home. At the end of each test, an element can be found: a gleaming sphere of energy the size of a crystal ball.

Killing Henantier in the Dreamworld will bring about your own demise as well.

THE TEST OF COURAGE

The entrance to this easiest of the tests is downstairs at the front of the dream house. All you have to do is swim down a long underwater passage without either 1) drowning (which is prevented by the timely use of two weak Water Breathing potions found en route) or 2) getting turned around while making the two somewhat awkward turns and going in the wrong direction. You surface in a pool at the bottom of a ruined tower; the Element of Courage is right in front of you for the taking. Do so, and you'll be teleported back to Henantier's dream house.

THE TEST OF PATIENCE

The cave-style door near Henantier's bed leads to the Test of Patience—an Ayleid-like ruin that's one big nasty trap.

You get the solution right at the beginning. You have to restore four elements of Henantier's vanished sanity to open a path back to the real world. These elements are represented by the gleaming spheres found at the end of each test.

Farther ahead lie three grids of pressure plates and arrow traps. You can't get around them. (Try to bypass the traps by dropping down onto the lower level and you'll die.) Granted, a character with a great Speed attribute and Acrobatics skill could blow across them and take low to modest damage. But the player who recognizes the scroll as a map can find a way across with no damage at all by following the path of a particular runic character from the bottom edge on each map all the way across each of the grids. Use the accompanying maps to make your way across.

Take your time; rushing through this test can be fatal.

THE TEST OF PERCEPTION

The Ayleid ruin-like door upstairs leads to the Test of Perception. This consists of a heavily trapped pathway that is notable for its supreme darkness—illuminated only by Dark Welkynd Stones that give off a dim red light when the player is in range. You can get through the test in this darkness, but the torch in the "Perceive" container at the start of this track makes the task much easier. Move slowly and watch the ground carefully, and you'll be fine.

Northeast of your starting area, on the fourth block, a pressure plate triggers a falling-rock trap. You can't prevent the three great blades in the circular area beyond from being set in motion, but you can avoid them easily. In the broad area beyond the circle four gas-emitter traps await, and another fallen-rock trap lies two blocks farther along.

Just beyond this trap, a slope formed of jumbled blocks leads up to a broad avenue with five great blades overhead. Just hurry past the lot, or move in baby steps into the gaps between the descended blades. And watch for another falling-rock trap in the round structure right after them.

One more leg to cover to reach the Element of Perception: a hillock of ill-fitting stones dotted with four pressure plates that set off a Frost Damage spell commensurate with your level from nearby Dark Welkynd Stones. As before, grab the element and you're whisked back to Henantier's dream house.

THE TEST OF RESOLVE

Veterans of the Imperial City's Arena will instantly recognize the scene. You're on the nasty side of the Red Room door, looking up the ramp toward the portcullis. Only, this is no more the Arena than the dream house is Henantier's house. The pillars are tilted, the sky red, the stands empty, and the whole place looks scorched. It's the Arena transported to Oblivion.

Take everything from the "Prepare" container just ahead of you: full leveled suits of light and heavy armor, a leveled shield, leveled sword, leveled staff, and a leveled blunt weapon. Get suited up and make your way up the ramp to meet the two Minotaurs.

The Minotaurs are each a level below your own, and the Staff of Lightning may be all you need. Just keep a respectable distance from the monsters and don't waste any of the weapon's charges. (If need be, mop up using whichever of the other weapons is best suited to your skills.) Once they're dead, stairs rise from the ground just outside the portcullis. At the top sits the Element of Resolve.

The Test of Resolve

Once you've assembled all four elements, talk to Henantier about "Dreamworld" and you'll quickly find yourself back in the bed at his real-world house. You lose the amulet and everything you collected in the Dreamworld and get back all your old belongings—plus a reward of six leveled scrolls from your grateful host.

THE FORLORN WATCHMAN

You learn from either the Bravil rumor mill or personal experience that the ghost of an old man walks the near shore of Niben Bay at night.

If you start with the rumor, you'll learn that Gilgondorin at Silverhome-on-the-Waterwill know more. The proprietor of that inn, just inside the city's North Gate, knows the watchman's schedule: He appears nightly at 8 at Bawnwatch Camp. Gilgondorin obligingly marks this on your map. The camp is on a small island a bit southeast of Bravil.

The watchman won't speak to you at first, but if you follow him southeast to a point just up the hill behind Fort Irony, he identifies himself as "the man once known as Grantham Blakeley," asks you to look for him "in the mouth of the panther," and looks southeast across the bay.

The forlorn watchman's somber vigil

Your journal suggests returning to Gilgondorin for his read on "the mouth of the panther." He tells you it's the mouth of the Panther River—the point where it flows west into Niben Bay is choked with sharp tooth-like rocks—and it's just east across the bay from where Grantham ended his spectral walk. Swim across to find a cargo ship, the *Emma May*, which ran up on these rocks years ago.

Don't bother with the top deck; it offers no access to the ship. You can enter the upper deck through a gaping hole in the ship's starboard side. Inside, you'll find spirits (ranging from Ghosts up to Wraiths), hatchways down to the middle deck and up to the captain's cabin, and, in a side cabin, a logbook that suggests the combination of a storm and a mutiny was the ship's undoing.

The captain's cabin contains another spirit, gold (40–1,490, depending on your level), and three potions; the middle deck has two more spirits and as many as three more potions; and the lower deck the holds the Wraith of the mutinous Gable. The small key on his body unlocks the door behind him and the shackles of the skeleton (the unfortunate Blakeley) in the room beyond.

Grantham Blakeley's remains

Once the skeleton is unshackled, Blakeley's ghost puts in another appearance and mentions that the room contains "a map to my gratitude" before marching into the next room and vanishing, his spirit set free by your action. (Meanwhile, you can collect a nominal reward from two chests—one underwater near the entry hatch and hard to see without first moving into deeper water.)

The map's right behind the pillar to which the skeleton was shackled. "X" turns out to mark a spot a short ways east across two bends of the river. The chest is underwater—sandwiched between four rocks just south of a small dock—and contains a hodgepodge of nice loot.

There is no compass target to the treasure, but if you simply follow the river along, you will come across the chest.

CAUGHT IN THE HUNT

You pick up from the rumor mill or from Ursanne Loche that her husband, Aleron, is missing. Ms. Loche, who lives above Henantier's place, reports that Aleron's a gambler heavily in debt to an Orc usurer named Kurdan gro-Dragol. Aleron was to have met gro-Dragol the previous day at the Lonely Suitor Lodge, but he hasn't returned and Ursanne, knowing what she does of the Orc's character, fears for her husband's life.

The Lonely Suitor is on the other side of the river. No sign of Aleron but Kurdan's upstairs and quite as unfriendly as Ursanne suggested. Coax his Disposition up to 60 and learn that he wants a favor to disclose Aleron's whereabouts: Retrieve his father's axe from Fort Grief Island out in Niben Bay or (he implies not so subtly) Aleron won't make it home ever again. He gives you a chance to prepare yourself and bids you to return to him when you're ready to go.

When you're prepared, Kurdan provides the transportation out to Fort Grief Island. Just activate the little boat beside the dock behind A Warlock's Luck shop (back across the bridge, a hard right and down the stairs), and you're there.

The ruins at Fort Grief Island

Surprise, surprise! Inside the surface ruin is Aleron Loche. Kurdan has created an event called "The Hunter's Run" (evidently inspired by Richard Edward Connell's "The Most Dangerous Game") in which humans are prey. You'll have to venture into the dungeon alone (Aleron's no fighter), brave the many traps, kill the three hunters, and return with the key to the now-locked outer gate.

The first, an Imperial at your own level, is right at the start of the dungeon, so that'll have to be a stand-up fight. The others—a Nord two levels above yours and an Orc three higher—may require some art; use the dungeon architecture to good effect. Lure the Nord forward into nearby arrow and pit traps. Make the Orc chase you around the pool at the bottom of the stairs while you wear him down with spells. If he falls in, so much the better.

Search The Hunter's Run well; there is a fair amount of loot scattered about, presumably from previous victims of Kurdan's game.

You need the keys on the Imperial and Nord to open the door to The Hunter's Abyss (the second level) and supposedly the key on the Orc to open the gate out of the tower. That last one's fake but, happily, you'll probably find the real one before you have a chance to try the phony.

When you leave the dungeon you're forced to watch in horror as Kurdan murders the defenseless Aleron. You're going to have to kill the Orc and a Khajiit archer henchman who appears on the ledge above you. It's probably best to lure Kurdan somewhere the archer can't get a bead on you, take him down, and then finish off the henchman.

After you dispatch Kurdan and his crony, take the real key from his corpse and make your way to the gatehouse just inside The Hunter's Run. Turn the lever and the gate outside will open, allowing you access to the boat once more.

Take the boat back to Bravil and call on Ursanne Loche to report her husband's death. She rewards you with a Speechcraft skill book, *Biography of the Wolf Queen*.

TWO SIDES OF THE COIN

The rumor mill suggests that Arnora Auria needs help recovering some money stolen from her by her boyfriend, Jorundr. The truth is a good deal more complicated.

Should you approach Arnora herself (she lives at the south end of the city), boost her Disposition to 60, and then speak to her about "Jorundr" and "Stolen gold," you'll get the impression (confirmed by a journal) that her proposal is not quite on the up-and-up.

Arnora Auria

Agree to help, and she lays it out for you: Arnora asserts that, against her will, she has served as Jorundr's accomplice in a series of small crimes. Last year, Jorundr started taking on bigger targets and killed a guard in one of these capers. He was caught, and when Arnora returned to their hideaway, he'd been arrested and the gold they'd stolen had been moved. You're to visit the prisoner in the dungeons under Castle Bruma and find out where he put it.

It's easy to see Jorundr. Just ask the guard about "Visit a prisoner" and he'll unlock the door to the cells.

Until you're on the other side of the bars, Jorundr won't trust you.

But Jorundr won't talk. He thinks it's all a trap arranged by a corrupt guard named Tyrellius Logellus. Persuasion and bribery aren't possible here, and your journal suggests that you'll have to get yourself arrested to earn his trust. The easiest way is to try to pickpocket the watching jailor; select jail when you're arrested and, poof, you're in Jorundr's cell.

Now that you're a fellow cellmate, he lays out a very different story—one in which Arnora was the one pushing for bigger scores; she killed the guard and turned in Jorundr. The one common element between the two tales: Jorundr moved the gold. Now he wants Arnora dead and makes you this proposal: Kill her and bring him her amulet, then he'll tell you where the gold is hidden.

At the end of the chat, a third element enters the picture: Logellus himself. He wants Jorundr to reveal the location of his stash. (He's not interested in you, and you can't deal with him just yet.)

You can handle the Jorundr/Arnora situation in one of two ways: Kill Arnora as ordered or tell her of Jorundr's plan.

Our money is on Arnora as the greater of two evils, but the first course is also slightly easier and no less lucrative than the second. Confront her, and come clean about Jorundr's scheme. Tell her you're doing things Jorundr's way, and she will pounce. She's a spellsword three levels above your own, likes to use a Chameleon spell, and may remain alive long enough to summon the city guards.

The amulet on her body is a fake and Jorundr will identify it as such. Instead, take her chest key and unlock the one beside her bed downstairs and take the "true" amulet. Jorundr then discloses that the gold is buried outside the city near the North Gate. The chest, in a cluster of rocks on the slope to the right of the road, contains a leveled mixture of gold, gems, jewelry, and skill books. All done!

If you decide to tell Arnora about Jorundr's plot and choose her scheme, things work out a bit differently. She gives you the real amulet willingly and tells you to get the loot location from Jorundr. What she didn't count on was the dirty guard, Logellus, overhearing your exchange in jail. When you go to claim the treasure, he's on the scene as well. You can talk to him—he'll claim he's killed Arnora —or go straight into combat, in which case you'll learn he's probably killed Arnora from a journal note after his death. He's tough, but not as tough as other city guards, being just five levels above your own.

Get the treasure and check in at Arnora's house to confirm her death and complete the quest. (You can also visit Jorundr again to let him in on the plot and Logellus's death.)

 Jorundr's loot includes two skill books. This offsets the skill loss from having to be arrested to get him to talk.

A BROTHERHOOD BETRAYED

The rumor mill is churning in Bruma: a Vampire hunter named Raynil Dralas has slain a Vampire within the city walls! Should you walk into Bradon Lirrian's house west of the Great Chapel of Talos, you'll be confronted by a guard, Carius Runellius. He explains that this is a crime scene and orders you to leave.

However, if you boost his Disposition to 70, he explains that the late Bradon was a Vampire. The guard has recently found the bodies of two Bruma beggars with puncture wounds in shallow graves outside the city. Vampire hunter Raynil Dralas arrived in Bruma right around this time and the city enlisted him to track down the culprit. Which he did. The city guard's own follow-up investigation has established a strong circumstantial case for Bradon's vampirism—including the discovery of another beggar's body in the cellar.

Bradon Lirrian

The crime scene

Case closed…almost. Bradon's wife, Erline, insists her hubby was no Vampire and offers some compelling arguments. However, none of this makes an impression on Runellius, who says the authorities have confirmed with a neighboring city that Raynil Dralas is indeed a noble and worthy Vampire hunter. If you're to put a dent in this case, you'll have to find Raynil himself.

And that's easier said than done. Most folks on the streets know nothing of his whereabouts. You'll have to speak to either Hafid Hollowleg at the Jerall View, Fjotreid at the Bruma Hammer and Axe, or Petrine at the Bruma Wildeye Stables to learn he's staying at Olav's Tap and Tack. (With a Disposition of 70, Olav himself will confirm this and even provide a key to Raynil's room.)

Raynil is gone, but you'll find the journal of someone named Gelebourne behind the dresser on the right side of the room. Take it. The document recounts the exploration by Gelebourne, Bradon, and Raynil of an Ayleid ruin, their successful extraction of a potent artifact, and the extraordinary steps they took to secure it. Apparently, all three of them were a part of some sort of adventuring brotherhood in the past.

Suddenly, things become crystal clear, and more so when you check back with Olav and learn that Gelebourne was the previous "Vampire" hunted by Raynil. Raynil had been killing

MISCELLANEOUS QUESTS

his comrades for their chest keys and has used the "Vampire hunter" reputation from the killing of the first to secure his vindication in the killing of the second. Bring the journal back to Runellius at Bradon's house and you'll put the case on a new heading: He'll muster the guards for a city-wide search for the suspect. You're to meet him at Olav's inn in an hour.

When you do, Runellius reports that Raynil was spotted by a scout, who unfortunately lost him in the mountains west of the city. He sends you off to Boreal Stone Cave to intercept him, and the haste he urges on you isn't just a dramatic device, so listen to what he says.

This is one of the game's rare time-sensitive events; you must carry it off within a day, or Raynil will escape with the artifact.

The small cave is a short distance west, and Raynil is waiting in its first room. He won't surrender, and he is a challenge to kill. Claim the three keys from his body and open the nearby chest to find the artifact is an "unremarkable" amulet.

The elusive Raynil Dralas

It's only unremarkable until you get it back to Bradon's widow. Evidently the dead man did not trust his comrades and masked the amulet's true nature behind a word of command. The widow speaks that word and restores the amulet to you as the Phylactery of Lithness, which has a leveled Speed enchantment. The quest is done—but you can still check in with Runellius at Olav's inn and exchange information.

LIFTING THE VALE

You'll need a Fame of 10 to get this quest. Countess Narina Carvain collects Akaviri artifacts. You'll learn this from the local rumor mill or from the countess's herald, Tolgan, who seeks you out when you're outdoors in Bruma and provides an enticement of 25 gold to meet the lady.

Tolgan, herald of Countess Narina Carvain

You're supposed to see her during audience hours, but you can in fact talk to Carvain whenever she's in one of the castle's public areas. It turns out the countess is missing one important Akaviri piece from her collection. The Draconian Madstone, which immunizes the wearer from poisons, was last reported to be in the ruins at Pale Pass. If you wish, Carvain will relate a good deal of that location's significance in the First Era war with the Akaviri invaders—the upshot being that the enemy command post at the pass was never discovered and remains lost to this day.

Carvain gives you the first milestone on your trip—Dragonclaw Rock, at the end of the road that leads north and east from Bruma. You'll have to get the rest using the diary of an Akaviri courier and a map. It's easy: Go west up the hill to the Sentinel statue and then north along the slope to the Serpent's Trail.

The area around the Sentinel is fairly alive with creatures, so be on your guard.

This small dungeon is inhabited by four nasty Ogres and six or seven creatures. In a long, straight section of corridor, you'll find a skeleton with the orders mentioned in the courier's journal. Take the orders with you. You can't read them, but they'll come in handy at Pale Pass.

The door at the other end of the passage takes you into that hidden valley. You'll have to kill or elude a dozen more Ogres on the path down to the ruin. Just stick to the old, overgrown road and eventually it will wind its way to the ruins.

MISCELLANEOUS QUESTS

The former headquarters of the Akaviri invasion force in the First Era is your destination.

The dungeon itself is infested with Skeletons—five levels of undead Akaviri defenders. You need to reach their commander, Mishaxhi, in the Venom of the Serpent level. There's some variety to the routes, but they all converge in a large room with a central drawbridge with arrow traps at its entrance and four Skeletons at its exit.

The commander of the Akaviri headquarters, Mishaxhi

Mishaxhi thinks you're the messenger from the Akaviri homeland; as long as you have the orders from the skeleton in the Serpent's Trail, you're fine. Just talk to him and select the second option and the commander will walk into the wall behind him and vanish. As he does, a secret door rumbles to life, revealing a treasure vault. The Madstone's on the pedestal, and there's some nice loot in the big chest on the left. The side door is a shortcut to Scales of the Serpent.

If you select the other options, or the second one without having the orders in your inventory, Mishaxhi attacks you. You'll have to kill him. (He's just one level above you, but he has the full Blades kit.) After he "dies," his body vanishes and the secret door opens.

Carvain rewards you with a Ring of the Vipereye, which has leveled Fortify Agility and Resist Magic enchantments. Note that after the quest is over, the Madstone appears in the hall next to her throne in a locked display case.

The vale also contains an undocumented quest. (See "A Ring of Keys" under "Undocumented Quests" in the "Freeform Quests" chapter.)

CHEYDINHAL

CORRUPTION AND CONSCIENCE

You may want to save this quest until after you've completed "Defense of Bruma" in the Main Quest. Ulrich Leland is one of your toughest soldiers in that battle—but he won't be if he gets jailed or killed in this quest beforehand.

Corrupt captain of the Cheydinhal guard, Ulrich Leland

Since the ascension of Leland to guard captain, the city guard has developed a heavy hand—dealing out big fines for even the smallest of infractions. You'll be referred by the rumor mill to one of the more vocal complainers—Llevana Nedaren, who lives just south of the Great Chapel of Stendarr. And she, in turn, will mention an especially egregious abuse of authority—how a fellow Dunmer, Aldos Othran, lost his home—and cite a potential ally in combating these abuses.

That's Garrus Darelliun, the No. 2 man in the guard. He can be found in County Hall at the castle on the north side of town. Boost his Disposition to 60 and Darelliun confirms Nedaren's story about the fines and discloses that he thinks Leland is putting the money in his own pocket.

Darelliun would like to bring his boss up on charges, but needs a witness. Aldos Othran is the most likely candidate, but he can't approach him directly. You can. Othran follows one of three routes around the city during the day, but you'll always find him at his bedroll beside a campfire in the southeast corner of town from a little after midnight to 10 a.m.

He'll be drunk, but a question about "Ulrich Leland" will make an impression. Regrettably, it makes the wrong impression. Othran asks you to follow him back to his former home, where he has words with the guard and eventually pulls a knife on him. The guard kills Othran.

MISCELLANEOUS QUESTS

This is the last mistake Aldos Othran ever makes.

Things can develop in two directions from here.

Your journal suggests you bring Othran's death to Nedaren's attention. She's enraged and from her rage comes another bad plan. You're to lure Leland to Nedaren's home with a report that she holds evidence incriminating him. "I'll do the rest," she says.

Your journal won't like the sound of this, and will suggest that you talk to Darelliun instead. But your journal isn't the boss of you, and, heck, it can be fun to make bad things happen to bad people.

Leland also follows different patrol routes through the city, but you can find him in the castle barracks for dinner a little after 7 p.m. and he'll go to bed there about 10. Raise his Disposition to 55 or better, and he'll agree to follow you to Nedaren's place.

Nedaren lays a trap for the captain—first paralyzing him and then siccing two Rats on him. The rats kill Leland. Problem solved, and you didn't even get your hands dirty.

There's another way. Darelliun agrees with that doubting journal entry, and proposes an investigatory approach. He supplies the key to Leland's quarters on the lower level of the barracks. You're to search it for evidence, and you won't have to search far; an incriminating letter ("Who knew that Indarys would be so easy to dupe?") is lying atop a book on the table to the right as you come in the door.

Whichever approach you used, once you have the letter or a corpse, Darelliun is your next stop. Either way, he'll ask you to meet him at the Bridge Inn in two hours for the finale.

If you used Darelliun's plan, Leland is arrested and jailed. He'll spend the rest of the game in Cheydinhal's dungeons. (Visit him there if you like. Man, is he ticked.) Darelliun is promoted to replace him. You get a leveled reward of 150–650 gold.

If you took the Rat-chow route, Nedaren's the one who winds up in prison, and she's in the slam for the life of your game. Darelliun seems to have considered jailing you as a co-conspirator, but settles for trimming your reward to a leveled 75–575 gold.

Beware if you elect to take out Ulrich Leland on your own, as he's 15 levels higher than you, and a bounty is put on your head if you're seen!

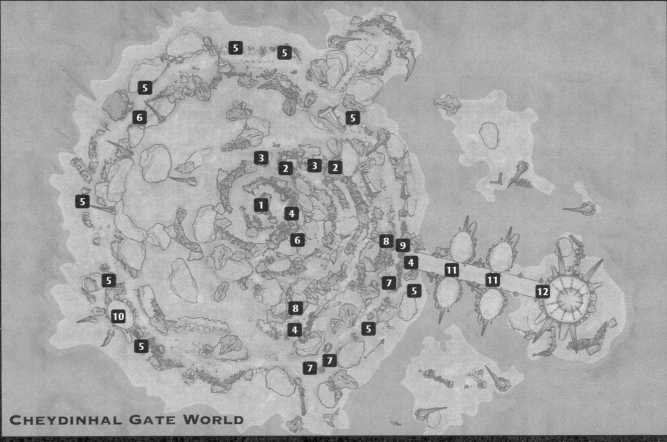

CHEYDINHAL GATE WORLD

1. **Oblivion Gate:** Gate back to Cheydinhal, which places you west of the city near the Cheydinhal Stables and the Knights of the Thorn Lodge.

2. **The Bowels:** Unusual cave with three "pancake" sublevels, each atop the next. A nice amount of loot (five containers), just two defenders (of a piece with the outdoors Daedra), and another dead member of the Knights of the Thorn (#4). Given that the sublevels are connected by holes in the floor, you'll be able to explore it effectively only from the upper of the two entrances.

3. Avalanche trap

4. **Fallen Knights of the Thorn:** This order of amateur crusaders, led by the son of Cheydinhal's count, piled into Oblivion in search of glory. Instead, they found death. The bodies of three knights lie scattered around the landscape, and the fourth is in one of the two caves. You'll find a steel shield, bow, claymore, and dagger beside the body at the west end of the bridge to the Citadel

5. Turret

6. Middle-rank fleshy pod, with gold guaranteed, and the possibility of other useful loot.

7. Mines

8. **The Bowels:** Same name and general configuration as the cave in #2, but a separate dungeon. Little loot, five enemies, a nasty trap on the top level, and a couple of holes that will drop you into lava on the bottom one.

9. **Farwil Andarys and Bremman Senyan:** The two survivors of the Knights of the Thorn's ill-fated mission. Speak to Farwil, and they follow you and fight at your side the rest of the way. Close the Oblivion Gate and bring the count's son home safely to Cheydinhal, and you'll get a nicer reward.

10. **Blood Well:** Atop this small tower, you'll find a boss-level fleshy pod, a Blood Fountain (healing), Magicka Essences, and a Daedra. The two below may be tougher, as they may include Dremora. (You can't enter the towers that flank the bridge to the Citadel.)

11. These two sets of gates open when you speak to that blowhard Farwil Andarys at #9.

12. **The Chaos Stronghold:** Lots of fighting in here. You'll find 7–10 Daedra in the Citadel itself (at least six of them Dremora), another three Dremora in the Rending Halls, 4–6 Daedra (at least two of them Dremora) in the Corridors of Dark Salvation, and 1–3 (including a Dremora boss) in the Sigillum Sanguis.

MISCELLANEOUS QUESTS

You won't be able to perform this quest until you've completed the "Dagon Shrine" segment of the Main Quest and Oblivion Gates open outside Cyrodiil's cities. You can either handle it on your own or wait until Jauffre asks you to as part of the Main Quest's "Allies for Bruma" segment. In that quest, you're dispatched to recruit troops from each of Cyrodiil's cities. In each case, you're asked by the local authorities to perform a mission; most of the time, that mission involves closing an Oblivion Gate. And so it does here.

This time, someone's beaten you to the punch. Talk to Amminus Gregori, who patrols the area near the gate—northwest of the Black Waterside Stables just west of the city. He reports that Count Andel Indarys's son, Farwil, and his six men—the all-talk-and-no-action "Knights of the Thorn"—went through the gate two days ago. The count's offering a reward for either his son's recovery or confirmation of his death.

Farwil isn't dead yet, but four of his comrades on this ill-considered venture can't make the same claim. After stepping through the Oblivion Gate and arriving on a mountaintop, you'll find their bodies as you make your way to the bottom and around to the east where the two survivors (the annoying Farwil and sensible Bremman Senyan) are waiting. Farwil refuses to be rescued and orders you to finish what he started.

The wayward knight, Farwil Indarys, and his companion

In substance, this isn't much different from any of the other gate-closing missions in the Main Quest, except that you need to keep the young man alive to get the best ending. Follow the nearby causeway east across the lava to the main Citadel. Kill the leveled Daedra in your path. Activate the Sigil Stone at the top, and you'll find yourself back outside Cheydinhal with the gate in ruins.

The Sigil Stone at the top of the main Citadel is your only way out.

Make sure you are well equipped before you enter this gate. Once you get about halfway down the mountain in Oblivion, you can't go back.

If he survives, Farwil names you an honorary Knight of the Thorn—a dubious honor that carries with it a legitimate medallion with a leveled Speechcraft enchantment. His father gives you a choice of two weapons: Thornblade (with a Disintegrate Armor enchantment) or the Staff of Indarys (with Damage Strength and Shock Damage enchants).

If Farwil doesn't make it, the count nevertheless rewards you 75–450 gold for your efforts. If you recovered his son's signet ring, he'll give you an additional 200 gold and allow you to keep the ring.

Suppose you haven't wrapped up "The Wayward Knight" by the time you complete the Main Quest? That event closes all the remaining Oblivion Gates in Cyrodiil—including the one outside Cheydinhal. However, it does not strand Farwil & Company in Oblivion. (Unfortunately.) Along with Senyan and a third knight, Jhared Strongblade, the young nobleman will be deposited outside the gate. Characteristically, Farwil gives himself credit for the gate's destruction. The count's as happy as if you'd rescued his son yourself, but as you haven't actually completed the quest, you don't get the reward. Lazy-bones.

A BRUSH WITH DEATH

You learn either from the rumor mill or from Tivela Lythandas (who lives in the southwest corner of town) that her husband, Rythe, a celebrated painter, has gone missing. Funny thing, though: He vanished while working on his latest painting inside a locked studio. Tivela provides a key to this ground-floor chamber, and you're off on a rather wild adventure.

You'll find Rythe quickly. The painting on the easel in his studio has unusual properties: Activate it and it teleports you to a wilderness region that recalls Cyrodiil's Great Forest...but something's different.

Rythe Lythandas's painted landscape

In the near distance appears a man. It's Rythe. It seems you're both stuck in his painting. He explains that a Bosmer attacked him in his studio, stole his enchanted Brush of Truepaint, and entered the painting with Rythe in hot pursuit.

He goes on to explain about the Brush of Truepaint's ability to allow the painter to create a masterpiece from within the canvas itself; the only limit is the painter's imagination. The brush has allowed Rythe to paint his "strikingly realistic" paintings for years (cheater). Apparently, the thief knew this too, and broke into the Lythandas homestead with every intention of making off with the unusual artifact. Unfortunately, the careless rogue added his own signature: a half-dozen Troll-like guardians.

These Painted Trolls are quite real, and want you dead.

Those guardians have killed the thief and are still roaming the forest. You must defeat them and reclaim the brush from Senannala's body. The painted Trolls are quite tough, but fortunately, Rythe provides you with a bit of an edge: several bottles of turpentine. Apply one to your weapon of choice for additional damage. Follow your quest compass to the unpainted area and the thief.

Search the Trolls' corpses after they fall to score a rare and valuable ingredient, Painted Troll fat.

Take the brush back to Rythe. He takes it gladly and begins walking south. Follow him. He paints a door back to his studio, appears there soon after you do, and, after a short conversation with his relieved wife, rewards you with the Apron of Adroitness, which boosts your Intelligence and Agility.

CHORROL

SEPARATED AT BIRTH

Reynald Jemane has been turning up sober in Cheydinhal. This wouldn't be unusual were it not for the fact that, in Chorrol, he's typically drunk...and that the Cheydinhal Jemane doesn't recognize the acquaintances of the Chorrol Jemane.

The Chorrol Jemane spends most of his day drinking at The Grey Mare. Chat with him at the inn or his home in southwest Chorrol and you'll see this is an odd story. Drunkenly, he'll deny having been in Cheydinhal and, with 50 gold, commissions you to look into his doppelganger.

The estranged Jemane brothers meet.

Folks in Cheydinhal don't recognize Reynald's name. But they do know a Guilbert Jemane who's staying at the Newlands Lodge. Turns out Guilbert looks like Reynald without a drink in his hand. The two men are twins, and in simply talking to Guilbert about Reynald, you've been instrumental in reuniting them. Guilbert sets off directly for Chorrol.

Fast travel to Chorrol and report to Reynald. He denies having a brother until you throw up Guilbert's name to him.

This short quest (part of a small series—see "Legacy Lost" and "Sins of the Father" below) isn't done until Guilbert shows up in Chorrol. Be warned that, without your intercession, this can take a very long time—days and days sometimes—so if you're the impatient type and anxious to watch the reunion, follow Guilbert on his trip. It should take less than a day.

LEGACY LOST

Provided you've performed the quest "Separated at Birth," you can help the Jemane brothers recover their birthright in this one.

The brothers and their parents were separated as children when Ogres attacked Weatherleah, the family's estate in the wilderness south of Chorrol. Now they want to return to their ancestral home, but first they ask you to find out if it's still inhabited by monsters.

Guilbert acknowledges his directions are vague. In fact, they're just wrong, and if you go looking for Weatherleah now, you'll have to do so without the aid of compass and map markers.

Your journal suggests you ask around town. Do so, and you'll learn that Sabine Laul at the Chorrol Fighters Guild has explored the Chorrol backcountry and might know Weatherleah's location. Look for her in the guild's cellar. Ask about Weatherleah and she'll mark the location on your map.

Weatherleah, the ancestral home of the Jemane family

This small broken-down farm sits in the trackless wilderness south of Chorrol. On your arrival, a journal entry says the place is still overrun with Ogres. That's all Guilbert asked about, and you can return to Chorrol and make your report. However, he's only going to send you back to clear the place out, so kill off the three leveled Ogres and it's all good.

Return to The Grey Mare for Guilbert's thanks and a further request for you to escort the brothers to their new home. The trip should be uneventful—though there's a chance of encounters with wilderness creatures en route—and when the brothers reach the estate, you get a journal entry. Speak to Guilbert for a leveled reward of gold (75–450) and an invitation to visit again.

That's not just an idle bit of dialogue, by the way. When you reach Redguard Valley Cave in the "Sins of the Father" quest, Weatherleah undergoes a transformation. The brothers fix the farm up big time, mending fences, planting crops—and presumably clearing the Skeletons out of the attic. But not out of the closet, as you'll see in the next quest.

SINS OF THE FATHER

About two and a half days after the "Legacy Lost" quest is complete, Fathis Ules will approach you outdoors with some gossip about the Jemane legacy. Ules asserts that the brothers' father, Albert Jemane, was a professional thief who once performed a mission on behalf of the Thieves Guild, kept the stolen article for himself, and hid it at Weatherleah. He expects that, when the Ogres sacked the farm, they took the item back to Redguard Valley Cave—almost straight south from Chorrol's South Gate.

Fathis Ules, a Thieves Guild fence, sheds some light on the Jemane family history.

If you wish, you can revisit Weatherleah en route to the cave and visit the supposed sins of the father upon his sons. They resent the imputations and why not? You don't have any evidence apart from Ules's claim.

You may find the cave entrance guarded by one or two leveled Goblins, but inside, Redguard Valley Cave is all Ogres: seven like the ones that occupied Weatherleah and one chieftain three levels above your own. From his body, retrieve the Honorblade of Chorrol—a very nice unenchanted ebony longsword.

Note that Redguard Valley Cave isn't linear; you can drop into the second pit in your path, hang a right, and take on the boss.

What do you do with it? You can keep it yourself (though this prevents you from completing the quest). Ules will give you 750–3,000 gold for it, depending on your level.

Your journal suggests you take it to Castle Chorrol. Royal steward Laythe Wavrick confirms the sword was indeed stolen by a daring thief and gives you the Escutcheon of Chorrol—a shield with leveled Fortify Endurance and Reflect Damage enchantments.

Finally, if you returned the sword to the castle, visit Weatherleah again. By this time, Guilbert has put a few facts together and understands that his father was not on the up-and-up. He gives you four leveled Soul Gems as compensation.

THE KILLING FIELD

Valus Odiil stands in The Grey Mare inn and asks piteously if you have seen his sons, Rallus and Antus. The boys apparently have gone off to fight "creatures" (Goblins) that have appeared on his farm outside Chorrol and expect their father to join them at Weynon Priory. But age sits heavy upon Odiil, and he asks you to go in his place.

Valus Odiil wants you to help his sons.

The priory is just down the road to the east. The brothers are waiting on the road nearby. Listen to their exchange, and then speak to the even-tempered Rallus. He leads the way southeast and then east down the hill toward the farm. In the middle of the field, he stops and you get a journal entry.

Last stand on the Odiil farm

And here come the Goblins, 10 of them arranged in three leveled waves consisting of plain Goblins at Level 1, Skirmishers at Level 4, and Berserkers at Level 8, with a boss (a Skirmisher, Berserker, or Ambusher) to top it off. When they're all dead, talk to Rallus again and the brothers will set out for Chorrol to meet their old dad. Then Valus returns home and the boys return to the farm.

During the skirmish, stay in the field with the brothers. That way, you'll be able to help each other out in battle.

If Odiil's sons both survive the battle, their father will award you a nice enchanted sword called Chillrend with leveled Frost Damage and Weakness to Frost enchantments. If one dies, you'll receive 150 gold. And if both died, you'll get nothing. "What little money I have must now be spent on burials," Odiil says.

SHADOW OVER HACKDIRT

The easiest way to set things in motion is simply to be polite when you meet Dar-Ma. This outgoing young Argonian woman hangs out around Chorrol's northern traffic circle for a couple of hours every morning. If you come near her, she approaches and introduces herself. If you're pleasant in the brief conversation that follows, you'll get 20-point Disposition bumps with both Dar-Ma and her mother, Seed-Neeus, who runs Northern Goods and Trade just inside the city's South Gate. If not, you'll knock 10 points off Dar-Ma's and 20 off her mother's.

Dar-Ma

Hackdirt, a not-so-friendly little town

Let three days pass and then leave Chorrol (fast-travel to another city, for instance). When you return, Dar-Ma is gone. She's on a delivery errand to a solitary village called Hackdirt in the woods south of Chorrol. However, she's not yet overdue for her return, so wait two more days in or out of town and then talk to her mom.

If you were nice to Dar-Ma earlier, Seed-Neeus will have a Disposition of over 50 and you'll immediately learn from her that Dar-Ma has gone missing. (If not, you'll either have to boost her Disposition above 50, quit the conversation, and then speak to her again, or pick up word of the disappearance on the streets and then speak to the mother on the topic "Missing daughter.") Specifically, Dar-Ma made the trip on her horse, Blossom, and the delivery was to one Etira Moslin.

A little research about Hackdirt gives you your first taste of the "shadow" of the title. Emfrid at The Grey Mare says it was once a bustling mine town that has turned Ghost town. And Honditar, who has a little place outside Chorrol just southwest of the city, speaks of unspecified trouble at Hackdirt 30 years earlier when "Legion had to be called in, people killed" and the town reportedly was burned to the ground.

Hackdirt is virtually straight south from Chorrol's South Gate. It's the most hostile little place this side of Hla Oad. Everyone here is suspicious of "outsiders." No one will tell you anything unless you have evidence, and then they'll just lie.

Moslin runs Moslin's Dry Goods on the village's west side. She is indignant—says Dar-Ma never showed up at all. If you ask further about "Hackdirt" or "The Brethren," she's rude and even makes some vague threats. Your journal suggests she's hiding something and urges you to explore further.

You don't have to explore that far. In a burned ruin behind the shop, you'll find Blossom the horse. However, Moslin claims the horse is her own, and after this second interview another journal entry concludes you'll get nothing out of her and suggests you move on.

Other avenues? Presumably Dar-Ma had to stay somewhere. But Vlanhonder Moslin, who runs the Moslin Inn at the north end of the settlement, don't know nuthin' about nuthin'. You can shake his story a bit if you head upstairs and retrieve the lady's diary from the dresser in the badly disarranged guest room on the right. (Dar-Ma keeps thinking she hears footsteps outside her door.) Then he allows she was there, but claims she left without her belongings.

You can also explore the Chapel of the Brethren at the south end and read a bit of the mostly runic *Bible of the Deep Ones*. You can't decipher it—nor can anyone else—but it establishes that these folks are onto some weird stuff.

Now, you can kill either of these people, take their keys, unlock any of the seven trapdoors into the caverns beneath the village (five in the buildings and two outdoors), slug your way through the half dozen Brethren in the cave, and rescue Dar-Ma from her cell. But then you won't know which trapdoor to use or what time to make your move, and you won't get the whole story.

In fact, there's just one person in town who's prepared to help you: Jiv Hiriel, who lives in a shack in the southeast corner. Speak to him about Dar-Ma and then meet with him at his house between 6 p.m. and midnight. (If your initial contact with him is between those hours, give him about a half hour to get his act together before you try him again.) He'll signal he's prepared to talk by leaving the door unlocked and then positioning himself before the fire.

Jiv Hiriel, your one friend in Hackdirt

Some of what Hiriel says is sketchy. For instance, you never do find out exactly what "The Deep Ones" are—though you'll hear their horrific sounds if you stay down in the caverns long enough. But this much is clear: The townspeople intend to sacrifice Dar-Ma in an effort to bring them back. Hiriel provides the same universal trapdoor key and suggests you use the hatch in Moslin's Inn in the middle of night when the townspeople are gathered in the caverns.

It's excellent advice. The Brethren will attend that meeting as well, and, provided you use the inn trapdoor, that keeps them out of your way. These shirtless guys—armed with clubs and Night-Eye and frost-resistance abilities—may all be one to three levels below your own, but they often operate in a pack. (If you do wind up fighting them, note that they are weak against fire attacks.)

"The Gathering" takes place from 1 a.m. to 5 a.m. Stay out of sight until 1:15 a.m. or so—Hiriel's place should be a safe haven—and drop down the hatch in back of the inn's bar. In the cavern, just hook around the corner to the left, let Dar-Ma out of her cell (the trapdoor key works here as well), and make your way topside and over to Blossom. You shouldn't see a soul in Hackdirt. Dar-Ma mounts up automatically. Tell her to follow you and she methodically makes her way home to Chorrol, where you'll get a 5-point boost in your Mercantile skill from her mom.

Countess Valga is busy with an investigation. With a Disposition of 50 or better, she'll tell you about it—a painting of the count has been stolen from her bedroom—and send you off with a key to the castle's private areas and instructions to speak to castle residents and gather physical clues.

Suspects in the disappearance of the countess's painting: Chanel and Orgnolf Hairy-Legs

From Valga, you learn that the only residents who had access to the locked bedroom and haven't accounted for their whereabouts at the time are court mage Chanel and porter Orgnolf Hairy-Legs. In other words, they're your prime suspects.

She also points you to guard captain Bittneld, steward Orok gro-Ghoth, and herald Laythe Wavrick as witnesses. You can go off and search for the principals or simply wait in the Great Hall. Sooner or later, most of the folks involved in the case flow through the audience chamber.

Gather your evidence from these Castle Chorrol residents: Bittneld, Orok gro-Ghoth, and Laythe Wavrick.

Speaking to everyone makes it easy to get on the wrong path. Wavrick points to Hairy-Legs's drinking problem, and notes that lately he has been asking people for money to support his habit. With a Disposition of 60 or better, gro-Ghoth offers that he didn't see either Chanel or Hairy-Legs on the night of the theft and reports a minor run-in with the latter over his drinking.

However, Bittneld observes that Chanel has been spending a lot of time in the West Tower, and when he spoke to her about it, she indicated it had to do with her spell research. "I suppose at the time it sounded good enough for me," he says.

Hairy-Legs isn't likely to do himself any favors in your initial interview. This red-nosed man belligerently refuses to answer any questions. However, with a Disposition of 60 or better, he says that on the night of the theft he was quarreling with a delivery boy over a wine shipment and spent the rest of the evening in his room reading. (Reading wine bottle labels, we suspect.) He's not your boy, and an accusation against him will only damage your reward.

And Chanel, with a Disposition of 60 or better, indicates she was in the courtyard taking star readings and then studied her charts over wine in the dining room before bed.

But she also says something a little unusual. Ask her about "Stolen painting" and she offers a brief critique: "Whoever painted it could not do the man justice. He was kind and noble, which is difficult to convey on canvas."

The fact that two witnesses mention it was a stormy night contradicts Chanel's "star readings" story. This should help you swing the investigation's focus to her.

After you've spoken to all these folks, a journal entry tells you to focus on physical clues. And this more or less clears Hairy-Legs. Searches of the chest in his modest second-floor chamber and the North Tower where gro-Ghoth found him drinking reveal nothing but the suspect's over-fondness for wine.

However, the West Tower—down the hall to the south and then right from Hairy-Legs's room—is another matter. Behind the boxes in the tower's lower room stands a painting of a chapel. Someone in the castle is a painter. From Bittneld's encounters and Chanel's own remarks, you know the painter is Chanel, but you don't have enough evidence yet to make an accusation stick.

Chanel said she spent time in the dining room on the night of the theft. It's northeast of the Great Hall. Check the north corner of the rug and you'll find paint stains. And check the lectern on the table opposite the door in Chanel's room—just up the southern stairs from the Great Hall—to find paint supplies. The journal takes the position that these were concealed and reports that you now have enough clues to make your accusation.

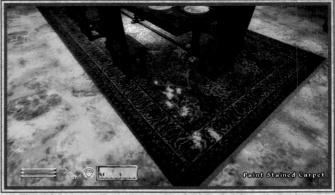

This is one of the hardest clues to find. It's in the dining room under the table off of the Great Hall.

Chanel concedes its truth, but won't confess outright (which is required to get the countess to buy the accusation) unless you raise her Disposition to 70—at which point she admits her love for the count, her authorship of the portrait, and her jealousy over the time the countess spent with it. (You also get the rolled-up painting here.)

So, now you have a dilemma. Should you tell the truth to the countess, or should you conceal the truth and let Chanel keep her only keepsake of the count?

Talk to Valga. If you rat out Chanel, you'll restore the painting to the countess (it reappears in her bedroom) and receive a leveled reward of 200–700 gold and some gems that range downward from a flawless diamond at Level 17 or higher to a plain or flawed pearl or flawed topaz. If you accused poor Hairy-Legs en route, you'll receive only a significantly reduced allotment of gold (50–300). (Accusing Chanel prematurely just knocks down her Disposition by 20 points, which makes it that much harder to elicit her confession.)

Chanel is gone. She vanishes from the castle immediately and for good.

But it doesn't have to be that way. If you take pity on her—after all, her crime was essentially an act of love—you can claim to Valga that you've accused neither suspect. You'll still get 25–150 gold for your trouble. You'll keep the painting, which you'll give back to a grateful Chanel, who asks you to return in three weeks for a painting of your own. (Your journal will remind you.)

It's a very nice nighttime scene from Chorrol. And if you drop it (the only way to inspect it), you'll find it comes with its own attached easel, so you can display it in your home!

THE IMPERIAL CITY

THE COLLECTOR

This is the most lucrative quest in *Oblivion*, with a total payout of 10,000 gold, and it's one of the hardest missions to find. To get the quest, you have to perform the first chunk of it before you even know it's part of a quest. Specifically, you have to recover a statue from one of 11 Ayleid ruins. Not every Ayleid ruin has a statue—for instance, none of the ones in western Cyrodiil have them—and no one tells you where to look for them until you're already into the quest.

An Ayleid statue

The best candidate for easy collection of a statue is Culotte, about halfway down the east bank of the Upper Niben. You'll face no more than four Zombies and one half-hearted trap, and it's convenient to the Imperial City. When you find yourself traveling southwest along a raised path across a huge chamber with many biers on both sides, you're on the right path. This leads to a small chamber with three pillars. The statue—sort of a spiky hourglass without the glass—is on the floor between them.

Now you just have to sell it. For the sake of argument, let's suppose you do so in the Imperial City's Market District. Leave the shop and wait around outdoors. Within a couple of hours, you'll be approached by a man named Jollring who reports that he's acting on behalf of his master, Umbacano. (This is a process similar to the invitation you may receive to join the Thieves Guild. Jollring will travel to any city to find you—this can take a long time if you're in Anvil or Leyawiin—but will wait to approach you until you exit any interior locations.)

Expect a visit from Jollring after you sell an Ayleid statue.

From the servant and the note he bears, you learn Mr. U is a collector of Ayleid antiquities who wants more statues like the one you sold and is willing to pay handsomely for them. You're invited to his home in Talos Plaza to discuss the matter.

Either follow Jollring back to Umbacano's house or meet him there. (The door is unlocked during daylight hours.) Speak to him in the entryway and tell him you want to see Umbacano. This unlocks the door to the private quarters upstairs and you can have a little chat. It seems the 10 remaining statues were once kept in the Ayleids' Temple of the Ancestors but were scattered to Ayleid cities before that empire fell. Which cities, Umbacano doesn't know.

We've already located the one statue in Culotte. Here are the remaining sites:

- **Fanacas** is in the mountains north of Cheydinhal. It's a smallish Vampire lair, with a Vampire patriarch or matriarch (which you may face on your way out), four Vampires, and one wild animal. You spend a lot of time winding your way around water, but you only have to go into it (and then make a hard left) at the very end to reach the statue room.

- **Mackamentain** is at the south end of the Nibenay Basin—which means in the middle of nowhere. Follow the Yellow Road southeast from the Red Ring Road. After the road turns straight south toward the Silverfish River, head east cross-country to find the ruin just northwest of a small lake. It's a three-level, underpopulated Necromancer lair; you face a collection of undead creatures and a Necromancer Adept at your own level. The statue is near the Necromancer in the final room on a bier—along with a nice treasure chest. An exit back to the first level can be found at the northwest end of the room; then open a secret door to reach the dungeon exit.

- **Moranda** is roughly halfway between Chorrol and Bruma, on a hill enclosed by the large southeastern bulge of the Orange Road. The first two levels offer enemies ranging from Imps to Trolls (depending on your level). The four-tumbler gate down the stairs to the right as you enter is an express elevator to the heavily gas-trapped third level. Two passages lead north from the room at the base of the stairs. The right-hand one leads to a caged Varla Stone. (The button to raise the cage is in the niche to the southwest.) The left-hand one leads to the statue, which is in the corresponding niche off that room.

- **Ninendava** is east-northeast of Main Quest dungeon Sancre Tor and northwest of Moranda. You'll face 7–14 undead creatures (which may include Vampires). The statue is on a shelf in a niche behind a four-tumbler door in the ruin's northeastern extremity. If the lock gives you trouble, the key is atop a book on a table in its western extremity.

- **Sardavar Leed** is just south of the Red Ring Road south of the Imperial City between forts Homestead and Alessia. Some combination of Daedra or Conjurers guards the entrance—it's a Conjurer's lair—and six conjurers, 8–12 Daedra, and a Conjurer Adept await inside. The statue's in a niche in the Adept's gated enclosure in the interior of a somewhat confusing second level.

- **Vilverin** is on a small island in the northeast corner of Lake Rumare—just across the water from the exit from the starter dungeons. This large four-level dungeon is an adventure in itself, with a couple of little side stories—in a dirty scroll on the top level and an undelivered letter on the bottom—and quite a bit of good loot. This includes 21 Magicka-restoring Welkynd Stones on the first three levels and two enchantment-restoring Varla Stones on the last two. (You'll have to raise the covers off the Varla Stones to claim them.)

  The entrance is guarded by two Bandits, but it's a mixed-use hideaway: weak Bandits (10 levels below the player, save for the one-level-below ringleader) mainly on the top level; undead on the second and third; and a Necromancer, his creations, and the statue at the bottom.

  You'll run into a few obstacles on the way down. On the second level, it may seem as though there's no obvious entrance to the third. (This is how the poor Khajiit bandit mentioned in the scroll got stranded down here.) Use your map to locate the secret door and activate it, or simply make a U-turn from the entry door and then step on the pressure plate that's hidden behind the altar at the end of the hall.

  On the third level, there's a room with a locked door at one end and six buttons on two pillars at the other. You can pick the lock—it will be four or five tumblers—but you can also find a key. Five of the buttons open corresponding compartments in the walls that each contain a leveled Skeleton. The sixth button—the one in the upper right—opens a niche in the right wall with the small container that holds the key.

  Naturally, the statue's surrounded by swinging-blade traps. However, the blades swing in sync, and so are easy to pass without harm. The Necromancer, Jalbert, is set at your level and shouldn't give you much trouble. (He often has nice equipment; replay this last level if you don't like the load-out.) You can leave by the passage in the south wall—either by picking the three- to five-tumbler lock on the gate or taking the key from beside the chest—or climb the tumble-down section of the east wall...which leads right into an arrow trap.

 Check the "World Maps" chapter to find the exact locations of all 10 of these sites.

- **Welke's** off in the eastern wilderness—just east of the point where the southernmost headwaters of the Panther River join the main body of the river. It's a rambling three-level tomb with plenty of nasties (some of which may turn out to be just Rats) on the top two levels and a "boss," which could be anything from a

Ghost to a Lich, depending on your level, on the bottom one. The statue's on a bier in the middle of this room.

- **Wendelbek** is northeast and across the Panther River from Welke—just east of the second westernmost of the river's four northern headwaters. As you may know from the Mages Guild quest "Necromancer's Moon," it's a Necromancer's lair. The four winding levels are inhabited by Necromancers, Zombies, and a Necromancer Adept. However, you can skip the Adept and the last two Necromancers, as you only have to reach the third level to find the statue—on a bier on a balcony overlooking the stairs down to the fourth level.

- **Wendir** is in the woods south of Chorrol. If you walked to Kvatch from Weynon Priory, you probably passed right by it, and it's already on your map. It's a tomb; at least 15 undead creatures walk its dark halls. You can avoid many of them on the upper level if you stay on high ground, and the same advice on the lower level will take you more quickly to the statue—on a bier on a south-facing balcony in the northern part of the level. It's guarded by a boss-level undead creature ranging from a plain Ghost to a Lich. One other thing: Bring lots of lockpicks. A lot of stuff is locked in Wendir.

- **Wenyandawik** is northwest of Bravil—south and a little east of the Inn of Ill Omen from the first Dark Brotherhood quest. Initially, it seems oddly empty. Only temporary: This tomb contains plenty of undead, Rats, and an undead boss (up to a Lich). The gate on the right side of the giant first-level room leads to two more of those valuable Varla Stones and, through the secret tunnel at the end of the hall, to the boss and the statue (on a pedestal).

When you bring back each statue, follow the procedures you used on your first visit to Umbacano. You'll receive 500 gold per statue. Umbacano will then place each statue in a cabinet in his private quarters. You can burglarize this house later in an undocumented quest. Umbacano employs a raft of guards, and one of them can be bought off. Get Umog gra-Marad's Disposition up to 75. Then you'll be able to bribe her with 100 gold and she'll step out for a drink at the Tiber Septim Hotel while you do your thing.

Umbacano, collector of Ayleid antiquities

You'll get some help from your employer. When you turn over the next statue, Umbacano provides names and map locations of five of the sites. When you return the third, he'll give you an early start on the "Nothing You Can Possess" quest. When you hit nine, he offers a bonus of 5,000 gold for the tenth statue—and he's as good as his word.

NOTHING YOU CAN POSSESS

You won't get this quest until you've recovered two Ayleid statues for Umbacano (three overall) in the marathon quest "The Collector."

Once that second statue is in his hands, the collector invites you to perform "Another Task." Agree and he'll provide a sketch of the entrance to an Ayleid city, called the "High Fane" in old books, and ask if you recognize it. Umbacano wants you to recover a carved panel from the High Fane's central chamber, to which he will provide a key.

Things can go in a couple of directions from this point. If you've already visited the Ayleid ruin Malada or have read the book *The Cleansing of the Fane*, you will recognize the sketch. This will make your job somewhat easier, as you'll know immediately where you're headed.

If you haven't, you won't recognize the sketch and will have to locate the site. You'll have immediate help: When you leave the house, you'll be approached by a man named Claude Maric, who identifies himself as another treasure hunter in Umbacano's employ. You can avoid him if you already know about Malada, but if you don't, he'll provide a tip and some positive info.

Claude Maric, a rival treasure hunter

Ask about "The High Fane" and then *The Cleansing of the Fane*, and he'll direct you to look for the book at a Market District bookseller. In fact, *Cleansing*—a.k.a. *The Chronicles of the Holy Brothers of Marukh, Volume IV*—can be found at First Edition in the Market District, Mach-Na's Books in Cheydinhal, in the Arcane University's Mystic Archives and Enchanting Center or upstairs at Herminia Cinna's house in the city's Elven Gardens District.

And with a Disposition or 60 or better, Maric will identify the High Fane as Malada and write its location to your map.

But he advises you to stay away and read the book first. (Actually, the book is rather encouraging; it reports that the "concourse of devils" from the temple was destroyed in the First Era.)

Maric's other info is all accurate, but you may distrust him. You'll have to read your journal or talk to Umbacano again to learn that he's not simply a fellow treasure hunter but your direct competitor in a race to retrieve the carving. Sure, he's helpful…but is he trying to get you to do the job for him? (Yup.)

Malada is in the Valus Mountains in far eastern Cyrodiil—roughly halfway between the Black Marsh border and the north-south stretch of the Silverfish River. That's a long haul from the city. If you've already visited Mackamentain for "The Collector" quest, just fast-travel there and head east-southeast. Or if you've visited Peryite's shrine in the Daedric quests, zap there and then head northeast.

Malada, or "The High Fane"

You're not alone. Follow the dirt path through the defile west of the site and you may hear a distant conversation. Turn right at the end of the defile and climb a little slope, and you'll find Brucetus Festinius and Rigmor. They are uncommunicative. The man tells you he's here for the "scenery and fresh air" and the woman that they're doing "a bit of hunting and sightseeing…not that it's any of your business."

Note that there are three bedrolls in the camp. The couple's compatriot is nearby. Follow the road below the camp to the southeast to find a Khajiit archer named S'razirr on the ridge overlooking the ruin.

S'razirr, one of Maric's thugs

Do you smell an ambush-in-the-making? If so, you're on the mark. It'll happen when you emerge from the dungeon. But some options require that you prepare now:

1. Strike a deal with S'razirr. Boost his Disposition to 65 and ask after Claude Maric to learn S'razirr is indeed working for the treasure hunter and thinks Maric is cheating him. He'll propose a deal: Pay him half of your fee—a quarter, if your Speechcraft is over 50—and he'll fight on your side in the battle, evening the odds at two-to-two. (Maric himself won't fight under these circumstances.)

2. Strike the deal with S'razirr and whack Rigmor and Festinius. Under these conditions, you'll have to fight Maric.

3. Preemptively remove all three of Maric's colleagues. This eliminates the ambush entirely. Maric is a coward and won't fight you on his own. And lest you worry that you're murdering innocents, you'll find confirmation of Rigmor and Festinius's involvement in a note on Rigmor's body.

Malada's part free-roaming zoo and part tomb. On the top level await plenty of standard dungeon critters, two undead creatures and their boss, and on the bottom, eight more undead. It's not particularly tough. Grab the carving out of the wall directly ahead of you, back away so the wall doesn't collapse on top of you, and make your way back as you came.

When you emerge, Maric and his group are arrayed around the entrance. Maric approaches and, rather in the manner of Rene Belloq from *Raiders of the Lost Ark,* asks for the carving. What do you do?

That depends what steps you've already taken to prepare for the battle. But even if you haven't taken any steps, you still have some options:

1. Face the music of a three-on-one assault. If you twice refuse to turn over the carving, Maric instructs his colleagues to kill you. (Maric himself won't fight unless he's either attacked or you selected the second option above.) This isn't that tough a battle. Festinius and

S'razirr are both at your level. The only challenge is Rigmor, who's decked out in heavy armor and has big old hammer.

2. Run like hell. Or let a horse run for you. Maric's Bay Horse is concealed behind the section of ruin just south of the dungeon entrance. If you beat him to it, you can steal it and get out of range quickly; the ambushers will give up pursuit. But try this only during daylight hours. Riding a horse down an unfamiliar mountain road at night is extremely dangerous—not least to the horse.

3. Wimp out and give the carving to Maric. This saves your life but blows the reward if Maric makes it back to the Imperial City with the artifact still in his possession—which is likely to happen, as he'll be on horseback. You should bring a horse of your own or Speed-enhancing magic.

4. Give the carving to Maric and immediately carve him a new one. A few good blows, knocking his health down to less than 25 percent, and he'll surrender and give you back the carving. (A couple more good blows and he'll be Soul Gem material, which is okay, too, but you won't be able to count on his help in the "Secret of the Ayleids" quest that follows.)

Then it's back to Talos Plaza. You'll be paid according to your level—a minimum of 500 gold if you're at Level 5 or less and up to 2,500 gold if you're at Level 21 or higher.

And did you ally with S'razirr? Then you have a debt to pay. Meet him at the nearby Tiber Septim Hotel. You can either pay him, claim that you don't have the dosh—S'razirr knows you've been paid off by Umbacano and doesn't believe you—or simply refuse to pay him. If you fail to deliver, S'razirr is incensed, follows you everywhere, and, when you leave the Imperial City, tries to kill you. You can settle up with him in either cash…or blood.

SECRETS OF THE AYLEIDS

Wait on this one until you've finished "The Collector" and collected your 5,000 gold bonus. "Secrets" ultimately takes Umbacano out of the picture, and if you complete it before "The Collector" is complete, you'll sacrifice the money.

Umbacano also covets the crown of the last Ayleid king. Owner Herminia Cinna has spurned his offers for this relic. You're to obtain it for him, by hook or by crook, and what you don't spend of the 1,000 gold Umbacano provides will be your reward.

Decline the mission, and it won't be offered again. Umbacano instantly hires someone else to retrieve the crown, but nevertheless offers you the second leg of the mission: escorting him through the Ayleid ruin Nenalata to its throne room. We'll deal with that a bit later.

Acquiring the crown involves a fairly simple burglary. (You can't buy it.) Cinna's house is at the southern corner of the Elven Gardens District's east end. You'll have lots of opportunities to break in, as she takes extended walks in the Palace District on a regular basis and also in the city's Arboretum on Sunday morning. You must get by a three-tumbler lock on the front door, a leveled lock (one to five tumblers) at the top of the stairs, and a four-tumbler lock on the Ayleid cask in the southeast corner of the room beyond. (The key to the cask is in the four-tumbler desk in the far corner.)

Herminia Cinna keeps the Crown of Nenalata locked in this Ayleid cask.

Track down Cinna herself for a second option. She says Umbacano is a dangerous man—not merely a collector but a seeker after the Ayleids' vast magical power. Cinna doesn't know exactly what the Nenalata crown does, but she knows enough to understand that the powers it taps should not be exploited.

Herminia Cinna, a scholar of the ancient Ayleids

She offers another approach: Bring Umbacano another crown. Cinna has learned of one that went to the grave with the ruler of the Ayleid city of Lindai. As Umbacano hasn't seen Cinna's crown, she doesn't think he'll know the difference. She'll even add Lindai to your map—it's in the forests east of Chorrol—and provide the key to the royal burial chamber at its bottom.

It's a comparatively simple affair—a two-level tomb with 11 to 15 undead, lots of gas traps on the first level, and the crown in an unlocked Ayleid cask on a pillar in the second-level crypt. (It has leveled Fortify Alteration, Fortify Illusion, and Resist Magic enchantments.)

Give it to Umbacano. There's one perilous moment when he seems on the verge of questioning its provenance, but he doesn't and, for the moment, everything seems okay.

Of course, you don't know when you retrieve this doppelganger that Umbacano has special plans for the crown—and that by providing a fake one you've signed his death warrant. Then again, if you give him the real one, you just may be signing your own.

Either way, as mentioned earlier, Umbacano now asks you to meet him in three days' time at Nenalata—across Niben Bay from Bravil at the mouth of the Silverfish River—for the final phase of his research. (If you didn't kill Maric in "Nothing You Can Possess," he'll join you there as well.)

This is a fairly straightforward tomb-raiding operation until you reach the third level. Stairs in a large room descend into a well with an empty panel in its east wall. Umbacano places the carving from Malada into the panel, intones some words, and advances into the throne room beyond, with a speech about restoring the lost glory of the Ayleid civilization. He'll sit on the throne, place the crown on his head…and either transform into an evil Ayleid king (if you brought him the Nenalata crown or skipped the first part of the mission) or die in a nasty fashion (if you returned the Lindai crown).

Umbacano transformed into the King of Nenalata

In the former case, you'll have to put down the king and, in each case, a half dozen ticked-off Skeletons (Liches, if you've reached Level 18) from adjoining rooms. (The stairs behind you have vanished into the floor, and an exit won't open in the north wall of the north chamber until the monsters are gone.) Take the crown (the Nenalata one carries leveled Fortify Alteration, Fortify Conjuration, and Reflect Spell enchantments), the king's staff (which has leveled Dispel and Drain Willpower enchantments), and Umbacano's two house keys (which will make it a lot easier to steal back the statues you sold him in "The Collector").

If he survives, Maric will head back to his regular hangout at the Roxey Inn with a couple of interesting lines about the late

Umbacano. Back in the house in Talos Plaza, Jollring and the security guards note that their master hasn't returned, but they remain on duty.

Alas, Umbacano and Maric may not be the only casualties. If you skipped the first part of the mission, you'll find Herminia Cinna dead in her house—evidently done in by whoever stole the Nenalata crown in your stead. (The killer is never revealed.)

ORDER OF THE VIRTUOUS BLOOD

In the outdoor portion of the Temple District, Ralsa Norvalo will approach a player with a Fame of 5 or greater with a request that you meet her husband, Gilen, at Seridur's house (in the district's southeast corner) on an urgent but unspecified matter.

Inside, speak to Seridur. He leads you to the cellar and identifies the men gathered here as Vampire hunters belonging to an organization they call the Order of the Virtuous Blood.

The Order of the Virtuous Blood's hideaway in the basement of Seridur's house

They claim they've just found a Vampire living in their midst: district resident Roland Jenseric. The evidence: Seridur says he found Jenseric struggling in his garden with a woman he's been seeing. Overpowered by Jenseric, he returned later to find the woman dead with puncture marks on her neck.

Problem is, the order's members say they are but scholars and not equipped to handle a big, bad Vampire. That's where you come in. You're to locate Jenseric (who has vanished) and kill him. Seridur suggests you start with a search of his home.

In Jenseric's house, on a book on the table on the ground floor, you'll find a letter from Jenseric's girlfriend, Relfina, that mentions meeting at a cabin in the Great Forest east of the city. A journal entry says this is his likely hideout, and a map marker shows its location just north of the Blue Road out to Cheydinhal. Fast-travel to the nearest location—Cheydinhal in a pinch but possibly Vilverin if you've visited it for "The Collector" quest.

You can play this two ways: Take what you're told at face value and whack Jenseric straight away, or look more closely at the evidence.

On arrival at the cabin, your journal spits out an entry about being cautious. Ignore it. Jenseric is unarmored, no match for you. Then go back to Seridur's house and confirm you've done the deed for a reward of 250 gold.

Roland Jenseric's hideout

But did you notice that Jenseric didn't attack you on sight? He wants to talk. If you let him, he'll claim it's the other way around. He claims that Seridur is the Vampire. He has no direct evidence beyond the disputed attack on Relfina but suggests you make inquiries with the other members of Seridur's "order" and Phintias at the First Edition bookstore in the Market District. And he suggests you'll never see Seridur out of doors during the day.

You may already have some information on that last score. Try to see Seridur during daylight hours before you set out to find Jenseric; bodyguard Cylben Dovolas says Seridur's asleep after a long night of "study"—with the slightest bit of hesitation before "study"—and will rise at 5 p.m.

However, when you get back to the Imperial City, you won't find Seridur, period. Phintias says he sometimes visits a burial site called Memorial Cave, on the southeast shore of Lake Rumare.

When you enter, a journal entry confirms it's a Vampire lair. Your 13–18 encounters will run the gamut from wild animals to undead creatures to Vampires. However, the only Vampire you're guaranteed to face is Seridur, in the innermost portion of the cavern. He'll make a speech like a big bad villain—he's planning to kill Jenseric and the other members of the order next—and then you'll kill him.

 Seridur is a tough opponent. Not only is he armed and armored, but he also has the spell capability of a Nightblade and standard Vampire enhancements such as resistances to disease and paralysis, minor resistance to normal weapons, weakness to fire, and the chance to infect with porphyric hemophilia.

Then get back to the cabin. Naturally, Jenseric is relieved not to be dead. Surprisingly, he plans to carry on with the order. He asks for time to make arrangements, but he'll be ready by

MISCELLANEOUS QUESTS

the time you get back to the Imperial City. Meet him in Seridur's cellar. Here you'll collect a leveled Ring of Sunfire (which has Reflect Spell and Resist Disease enchantments), honorary membership in the order, and the promise of future rewards if you return Vampire dust from the remains of any Vampires you kill. Start now with the dust of any Vampires you axed in Memorial Cave. You'll net 250 gold a pop.

IMPERIAL CORRUPTION

In the Temple District, you can pick up two reports of a corrupt Imperial Legion guard. Luronk gro-Glurzog and Ruslan, who both live in the district's northeast section, say they were accused of stealing at Jensine's "Good as New" Merchandise in the Market District and then shaken down for cash to avoid being sent to jail. They'd recognize the guard's face but don't know his name.

Jensine does. With a Disposition of 70, she'll name Audens Avidius. Apparently this watch captain has been pulling a similar stunt with shopkeepers, who are too frightened to complain.

You must bring the matter to the attention of the authorities. Try a guard. They'll tell you to talk to either watch captain Hieronymus Lex or, if Lex has been transferred to Anvil (part of the Thieves Guild quest line), to Servatius Quintilius.

 However, don't complain to Avidius himself, or at least save your game first. Should you do so, Avidius decides that you have assaulted him, puts your bounty at 1,000 gold, and attempts to place you under arrest.

Audens Avidius attacks

Unless parts of the Thieves Guild quests are running (in which case the captain is in the Waterfront slums), Lex is probably on patrol and so, depending on the time of day, could be just about anywhere. Follow your compass until you find him. He's too obsessed with his fruitless pursuit of the Gray Fox (the Thieves Guild's chief) to help you, and kicks you along to watch captain Itius Hayn, whom you'll find the same way you found Lex. You can find Hayn on your own to skip this step, but there isn't a quest target to help you.

Hayn won't trust you enough to discuss the matter. You'll have to coax his Disposition up to 70 for him to address the prerequisite for bringing charges: two witnesses who are willing to testify.

You can't get Jensine's Disposition high enough for her to even think about it. But at Dispositions of 70, Ruslan and gro-Glurzog accept your proposal and speak to Hayn first thing in the morning (8 a.m.). Follow them and watch if you like. Whether you do or not, all three witnesses now like you a lot.

Once both witnesses have contacted Hayn, Hayn will acknowledge this fact (via the "Corrupt Imperial Watchman" topic). And if it's early enough in the day—8 a.m. to 6 p.m.—the captain will set off immediately to arrest Avidius on his rounds. Follow him and you can watch this event as well. You'll hear Avidius issue a threat against you. (It's a threat he'll expand upon should you visit him in prison.) The corrupt guard then exchanges his watch armor and weapon for street clothes and is led off to the Imperial Prison.

You'll get a Fame bump and Disposition boosts with all the good-guy principals in the quest. Carmalo Truiand replaces Avidius as watch captain.

But the quest isn't over. Avidius remains imprisoned for at least 10 days. After 10 days, and if you're at Level 5 or higher, he'll escape—vanishing from his cell and reappearing just outside the door into the prison district —and come after you as the architect of his downfall. (If you haven't reached Level 5, he'll wait until you do and then escape.) This event gets picked up by the rumor mill.

Avidius really hates you and will seek you out anywhere—even in Oblivion. Mind that he's no longer many levels above your character (he's at your level) and no longer has his watch armor or weapon (just an iron dagger).

When the angry man is dead, the quest is over. A note on his body sets forth his plans for a crime spree—killing everyone he holds responsible for his imprisonment.

UNFRIENDLY COMPETITION

Several merchants in the Market District are complaining about unfair competition by Thoronir at The Copious Coinpurse. Tertullian Verus at Three Brothers Trade Goods, Claudette Perrick at The Gilded Carafe, and Ogier Georick at The Main Ingredient all complain of prices far too low to be legitimate, and Georick suggests Thoronir's inventory must be stolen.

If you inquire further, you'll be referred to Jensine at Jensine's "Good as New" Merchandise, who's heading up a committee (the Society of Concerned Merchants) looking into Thoronir's business practices. She'll enlist your aid as an investigator.

You can take three approaches in conversation with Thoronir, and get a 10-point Disposition bump for the tactful one and a 20-point drop for the blatant one, but these gambits do not reveal any useful information about the secret source of his goods. Your journal suggests watching him after his shop closes.

The Copious Coinpurse: "The shop where your purse is just as full after you buy!"

Thoronir closes shop at 9 p.m. The Wood Elf goes around the corner to The Merchants Inn for dinner. At 11 p.m., he leaves and makes his way northwest, then southwest toward the gate to the Imperial Palace, then west again along the moat. He ducks into a small garden, where he meets a Nord named Agarmir. Their conversation makes clear that something untoward is going on here—but not precisely what.

Your journal now suggests following Agarmir. The two men split up when they get back to the street. Follow Agarmir south into the Palace District and then west into Talos Plaza. He has a house in the district's southwest corner.

Your ever-helpful journal suggests you wait until he's out and about and then explore the place. (You can't get in when he's home; the door is barred from the inside.) If it's the weekend, he'll be out from 8 a.m. to 2 p.m. for a walk and lunch. On weekdays, you'll have to wait until late in the afternoon.

Pick the three-tumbler front-door lock and the two- to five-tumbler cellar lock. Descend into the cellar; another journal note surmises from the bonemeal and muddy shovel that Agarmir's a grave robber. You'll confirm this when you read the "Macabre Manifest" on the table—a list of the recently deceased and the property that was buried with them.

Take the book with you as proof—Thoronir won't believe you without it in your inventory—and return to The Copious Coinpurse. The proprietor is eager to make amends and agrees to help you catch Agarmir, who is off on some unspecified mission. Your journal's solution: The last entry in the manifest is presumably the most current, so check out the graveyard in the Palace District.

Fast-travel there and then follow your compass pointer until you get a journal note that the entrance to the Trentius Family Mausoleum has been unsealed. Enter: Agarmir and his fellow Nord, Rolgarel, have prepared a grave...for you. It's a trap; the door has locked behind you and the only way out is to kill Agarmir for his key.

This shouldn't be that hard if you're cautious. While the room's modest dimensions give the aggressors a natural advantage, the columns provide cover. Move quickly and don't let yourself get boxed in.

Agarmir and his friend spring a deadly trap on the player.

 Agarmir is armed with a blade named Debaser, which saps Willpower and Endurance. Make sure you pick it up after the fight has ended.

Take Agarmir's shovel from beside your intended resting place; that's the evidence you'll require. Everything else is gravy. Agarmir's sword, Debaser, has leveled Willpower and Endurance enchantments. Rolgarel may have some nice equipment. And if you're of a grave-robbing persuasion yourself, you can take Calliben's Grim Retort from the middle niche on the left-hand wall. (This mace carries Absorb Strength and Absorb Blunt skill enchantments.)

By the time you get back to The Copious Coinpurse, Thoronir's decided to give his ill-gotten gains and inventory to the temple and to join the merchants' society. And he has a reward for you as well: the Weatherward Circlet—a ring with leveled Resist Frost and Resist Fire enchantments. (We won't ask with whom it was buried.) And don't forget to return to Jensine for a leveled reward of 100–600 gold.

AN UNEXPECTED VOYAGE

Surprise, surprise...

The first time you sleep at the Waterfront inn The Bloated Float, the shipshape hotel promptly puts out to sea. What's going on? Lynch, who's waiting outside your door, will give you a hint or two before you use him as a sheath for your sword…if you first claim to be a passenger and then claim to be a member of his gang. (If you tell him to butt out or claim to be a member of the city guard, he'll draw on you.)

The Bloated Float: Cyrodiil's first and only inn on the water

He lets on that four members of the Blackwater Brigands have hijacked the Float, that the ship's owner, Ormil, is with his boss, and that he's locked bouncer Graman gro-Marad in the storage room across the way. The brigands' intentions are not clear, but there seems to be an expectation of riches.

You can simply kill the baddies on sight and beat the quest. But if you're patient and draw them into conversation first, you'll be equipped to persuade their leader to surrender both herself and her enchanted sword.

However, you have run out of options with Lynch and will have to kill him or be killed by him. It shouldn't be that hard. Like all the lower-level thieves, Lynch is two levels above yours, but poorly armed and armored. After he dies, take his instructions and the storage-room key from his body.

Gro-Marad indicates he can get the ship back to port if you can get him to the top deck. And the instructions provide the name of a second thief (Minx) and sketch out more of their plan: scuttling the ship and a meeting in Bravil three days hence.

On the tavern deck, find Minx. Tell her Lynch sent you to assist the brigand boss, Selene. Before you run out of lies, you'll learn Selene is holding Ormil in his locked cabin behind the bar.

Kill her for the key to the top deck, climb the stairs, unlock the door, and speak to Wrath, who mans the rear deck. In his greeting, he reveals the purpose for the brigand raid: They're trying to find the "Golden Galleon." To squeeze a bit more info out of him, tell him you're waiting for orders and that you were added to the gang three days ago. And once he's dead, take the key to Ormil's cabin from his body.

Return to the tavern deck and tell gro-Marad the top deck is secure. He'll make his way up to the wheel, but won't steer the ship home until Ormil is free. Then, using the key from Wrath's body, unlock the door behind the bar and enter Ormil's cabin. That lady is Selene. Kill her or speak to her.

The only way to rescue Ormil is through Selene, and that isn't going to be easy…unless you've been paying attention.

Killing her is tougher than with the other brigands. She's four levels above your own, equipped with the Blackwater Blade—a sword with a leveled Absorb Fatigue enchantment.

This is where some of the tidbits you picked up from her cohorts come in handy. Put your weapon away. Say to Selene: "I took the key from Wrath"; "I'm here to join the gang"; "…three months ago?"; "to find the Golden Galleon"; "You mean in Bravil?"; and "I've killed all of them." (You'll still get these options even if you haven't talked to her underlings, but it'll be guesswork and even one bad choice starts a fight.) With the right choices, she promptly surrenders and turns over her sword. Speak to Ormil and he'll ask you to escort Selene to the room beside your own on the bottom deck.

Return to the cabin and he'll tell you the whole story: The Golden Galleon doesn't exist. With business at the Float flagging, Ormil made up a tale about a golden statue the ship's previous owner had hidden in the inn to excite interest.

Ormil suggests you rest. It's the only way to get back to port. When you wake, you'll be back at the Waterfront, Selene will have vanished, and folks are eating and drinking up on the tavern deck. Check in with Ormil again before you disembark. The authorities apparently wanted the brigand; whether she's dead or alive, Ormil will supply a leveled reward of 75–450 gold.

ORIGIN OF THE GRAY PRINCE

You can perform this quest at any point up until you challenge the "Gray Prince" for the Arena grand championship.

In the Bloodworks, down the ramp to the left from the Arena entrance, you'll find a sturdy Orc named Agronak gro-Malog. He's the Arena's current champion, worshipped by the crowd as the Gray Prince, but gro-Malog is still dissatisfied with the hand he's been dealt. He asserts that he is a lord's son who has been denied the trappings that ought to attend his high birth. You're to supply the evidence that proves it.

Agree to help, and the half-Orc reveals that he's the illegitimate child of one Lord Lovidicus. He and his mother—an Orc servant in the lord's Crowhaven fortress in the western reaches of Cyrodiil—fled to the Imperial City when the lord's wife threatened to kill them. Before the mother's recent death, she gave gro-Malog a key that would, she said, "unlock the truth" of his birthright at Crowhaven.

The Crowhaven ruins are on a seaside hilltop northwest of Anvil. Just fast-travel to that city, follow the road northwest out of town, and then head cross-country when the road begins to turn east. You'll find 2–5 undead Skeletons on the surface—Liches, beginning at Level 18—and the door into the dungeon in the tower's northwest corner.

The early stages of the top level hold just Wolves and Rats. Then you start finding coffins. This isn't a fortress; it's a tomb. And if gro-Malog was born here…what is he?

At length, you come to a gate. To the right, the entrance to the Crowhaven Burial Halls. To the left, a smaller door leading into a catacombs and, beyond, stairs leading up to a door that can be unlocked only with Agronak's key.

What secrets lie beyond this ancient locked door?

This is Lord Lovidicus's quarters. Inside, you won't have gone far before you're attacked by the lord himself. He's five levels above you, but unarmored and armed only with a dagger, so you should prevail if you're well equipped.

The thirst of Lord Lovidicus can only be quenched with your blood.

In the second section of the quarters, the lord's journal lies on a table. Read it and then take it. It reveals everything. Gro-Malog's father, while indeed noble, was also a Vampire. His pregnant mother, learning this, locked the undead father-to-be in his quarters and ran. He has been there ever since. You have to wonder what his mother was thinking when she gave her son the key 30 years later.

No need to explore the bottom level—a regular Vampire lair—unless you're so disposed. Just get out and fast-travel back to the Bloodworks. Gro-Malog is as good as his word on the promised combat techniques, and you'll get permanent 3-point increases in your Athletics, Blade, and Block skills.

But the poor Gray Prince is wholly undone by his father's journal. No more talk about being an unacknowledged nobleman. He now calls himself a "wretched, vile spawn of evil." He'll never be himself again, and when it comes time for you to fight him for the Arena championship, he'll basically lie down and allow you to kill him.

KVATCH

THE BATTLE FOR CASTLE KVATCH

This quest is a spin-off from the Main Quest.

You can perform this combat quest any time after you've completed "Breaking the Siege of Kvatch" segment of the Main Quest. However, do it no later than the "Allies for Bruma" segment to get the maximum benefit.

This mission kicks off when you speak to Kvatch guard captain Savlian Matius after you've battled your way into the burning city's Chapel of Akatosh. Matius then asks for your help for the second phase of the assault—reaching the castle at the west end of the city. Give the go-ahead and he'll take off out the church's north door toward the castle gate with swordsman Ilend Vonius and bowmen Merandil and Jesan Rilian in close formation behind him.

If any soldiers were lost in the previous Kvatch quest "Breaking the Siege of Kvatch," sections of this battle will be more difficult. It's in your best interest to help them all survive as long as possible.

The party will cut through four leveled Daedra and then stop before the bridge into the castle proper. Talk to Matius again to learn the gate is locked. That's where you come in. You're to open it from the inside—following the passage within the wall from the North Guard House to the gatehouse. The entrance from the Guard House is locked as well, but Berich Inian, who is still standing guard at the chapel's north door, has the key.

Berich Inian holds the key you'll need to complete this quest.

Throw this lever to raise the gates and gain access to the castle.

So zip back to the chapel and speak to Inian about "Guard House Key." He wants to know why you want it. Both of your responses will work—and Inian accompanies you either way—but the brusqueness of the first costs you 5 Disposition points and gets a similarly brusque answer. (If you're polite, Inian will describe your route through the city.)

Talk also to the three generic Imperial Legion troopers who have just appeared in the chapel. One of the two swordsmen will tell you that they saw the smoke of the burning city while patrolling the Gold Road and offers their help. Tell him to follow you and suddenly you've got a squad.

Just in time. In the chapel crypt, the area outside the crypt exit at the east end of the church and the crooked path north to the Guard House, you'll find 20 more leveled Daedra. They just keep coming and coming. Take it slow here, try to keep your small group together, and methodically clear out each area before you move on to the next. If you lose Inian en route, take the key from his body.

 Weaker players, or those not skilled in melee combat, shouldn't be afraid to use Inian and the Legion guards as shields. Let them soak up damage while you help them out from behind. It's not necessary that any of them survive, but the longer they're with you, the easier these fights will be.

Once you reach the Guard House, the mission suddenly gets easy. There's nothing but fire and darkness in your passage west within the north wall, up the ladder to the castle gatehouse, and up the stairs to the great wheel that opens the gates.

To be sure, there are eight leveled Daedra in the courtyard and five more in the entryway—these last will be either Scamps, Flame Atronachs, or Daedroth—but with your help, the combined Legion and city guard forces should master any challenge in the outer regions of the castle.

When the entry area has been cleared, Matius will stop and hold position. If they've survived, so will Inian, Tierra (who joins the party when the gates open), and Vonius.

Speak to Matius. He assigns you to handle things the rest of the way. However, you may not be alone. If they've survived, the three legionnaires and the city guard bowmen, Merandil and Rilian, will continue to follow you into the Great Hall (four Daedra) and, down the hall at the Great Hall's far end, the count's quarters. (You can skip the sleeping quarters.)

The fate of Count Goldwine

The count's quarters hold a mini-boss—a Scamp at Levels 1–3, a Fire Atronach at Levels 4–9, and a Daedroth at Level 10 or higher—and the body of Count Omellius Goldwine. (No, you can't save him.) Take the signet ring from the body, return to Matius, report the count's death (respectfully, to avoid a 20-point Disposition hit), and surrender the ring to complete the quest.

Savlian then tells you he's tired of fighting and gives you a Kvatch cuirass off his own back. (It carries leveled Fortify Strength and Endurance enchantments.) And when you reach the "Allies for Bruma" segment of the Main Quest, come see Matius again. He'll supply a soldier for the big battle with the Daedra that follows in "Defense of Bruma."

LEYAWIIN

TEARS OF THE SAVIOR

S'drassa, the hooded Khajiit in the Mages Guild, collects crystals. He's looking for a specific type called Garridan's Tears—the frozen blue tears of knight Garridan Stalrous—and he offers "a fair bounty" in gold. For background on the tears, he refers you to Julienne Fanis at the Arcane University in the Imperial City.

The collector of all things crystal, S'drassa

Ordinarily, you'd find Fanis at the university's Lustratorium (the Alchemy Center). However, for the term of this quest, she's based in the lobby of the Arch-Mage's Tower. She'll give you either the long-form legend of the knight or quickly direct you to the First Edition bookstore in the Market District for a book called *Knightfall*.

The store does indeed have the book. It's an account of Garridan's search for the Everflow Ewer—a bottomless pitcher of water—at Frostfire Glade in the mountains southeast of Bruma. References in your book will place it on your map. But there's more to it: The book mentions that refined frost salts are needed to enter this region, and your journal refers you back to Fanis. She sells 'em. Buy one portion, and you're equipped to enter the glade…but not exactly ready.

Did you read the book? Frostfire Glade is so named because the cold at the center of the glade is so intense that it damages the player. You need protection, and S'drassa can help: Check in with him before you set out and he'll give you five powerful Philter of Frostward potions.

The glade is reached though the small Frostfire Cave, populated by five or six leveled creatures ranging from Rats to Bears. The use of the frost salts at the exit into the glade is transparent; simply activate the door with the salts in your inventory.

You emerge into a misty closed-off valley. Use the Philter of Frostward potions to keep warm or you will be sustaining frost damage for every second you spend in the mist. At the center of the glade, just north of the entrance, Garridan and a giant Frost Atronach are locked forever in a frozen embrace. Nearby is the glade's only living defender (a leveled Frost Atronach). Arrayed around the great ice sculpture are the five Garridan's Tears.

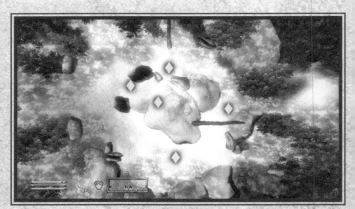

This aerial view of Frostfire Glade shows the locations of all five Garridan's Tears.

Bring all five tears back to S'drassa. (You won't get any credit if you recover fewer.) He'll pay you a leveled 500–2,500 in gold. Note that after the quest ends, the tears appear in a display case near S'drassa in the Mages Guild.

WHOM GODS ANNOY

You'll hear stories around town about animal noises and foul odors coming from Rosentia Gallenus's house. Pick the four-tumbler lock and pop into the big orange house in the south-central part of town to see Gallenus herself. (She's too embarrassed to leave the house.)

The source of the problem is her new Daedric staff. It summoned Scamps that follow her around endlessly, regenerate instantly if killed, and are methodically ruining her house. She'd love to dump the thing, but that's another element of the curse: She can't seem to let go of it.

MISCELLANEOUS QUESTS

Rosentia Gallenus proves you shouldn't play with artifacts made by the Daedric prince Sheogorath.

You're to consult Gallenus's friend, Alves Uvenim, at the Mages Guild to the west. This Dark Elf lady reveals that it's the Staff of Everscamp—a prank by the Daedric lord Sheogorath. It can be handed off only to a willing recipient and can be disposed of entirely only if returned to a Sheogorath shrine in Darkfathom Cave just southeast of the city.

It's an easy errand—albeit a rather slow one, as you'll take a 20-point Speed hit as long as you possess the staff. (Note that you can't use the staff yourself.) The cave is home to 7–12 leveled Daedra—up to Xivilai at Level 20—and the quick path to the shrine is always down and to the right.

 Head for Darkfathom Cave as soon as you can. The Everscamp isn't useful at all, and you move slower while stuck with the staff.

At the shrine, you get a message that your urge to possess the staff has vanished. Drop it anywhere on the dais—it doesn't have to be on one of the altars—and the Scamps will remain here.

Drop the staff near this altar to get rid of the annoying Everscamps.

Scoot back to Leyawiin and Gallenus for your reward—the Ring of Eidolon's Edge, with leveled Block and Blade skill enhancements. (Note that Gallenus, now staff-less and Scamp-less, may now be out and about town again.)

MAZOGA THE ORC

Weird quest. Mazoga the Orc stands around just inside the entrance to the County Hall in Castle Leyawiin. If you speak to her, she asks if you're the count. If you say yes, you're a liar. If you say no, you're useless to her. What's going on?

She's a knight. Really. Just ask her.

Castle guards know a little more. They'll tell you Mazoga claims to be a knight, say the count wants the matter looked into, and suggest you speak to him. That'll give you the quest.

You can talk to Count Marius Caro in the hall during audience hours (roughly 8 a.m. to 4 p.m.), and he'll invite you to perform "Service to Leyawiin." Evidently Mazoga won't say what she's doing here. You're to find out and get back to him. Simple as that.

Having spoken to the count, you now have a "The Count sent me" topic, and Mazoga talks to you after her fussy fashion. When you get through the amusing preliminaries, she'll ask you to fetch her an Argonian named Weebam-Na. All she'll say is that he's a hunter and is supposed to know about the woods nearby. (If consulted, various locals, including the count, will note that Mr. Na has a house in town.)

The quest gets stranger. Weebam-Na lives in a modest shack east and slightly south of the chapel tower. He talks like Jackie Mason. "Did I forget how much I like you that I should do this favor for you?" (If you ask about Leyawiin, he embarks on a funny rant about Rats and ways to serve them.)

Bump Weebam-Na's Disposition up to 50 and he'll remember how much he likes you and head for the castle. Here, he'll have a conversation with Mazoga that is approximately as odd as the conversation you had with her. She wants to be guided up the Lower Niben to Fisherman's Rock. Weebam-Na wants to know why. Mazoga won't say. Weebam-Na won't guide her.

If you talk to her, she asks you to escort her. Why? This time, she offers up the fact that Mogens Wind-Shifter camps there, with the suggestion that ultra-violence to the person of Mr. Wind-Shifter may follow.

It's an easy trip up the east bank and then downhill toward a bonfire and four intimidating-looking folks at water's edge. Things get straight to the ultra-violence when Mazoga accuses Wind-Shifter of killing her friend and Wind-Shifter denies it. (Don't start with the ultra-violence until Mazoga has said her piece, or Mazoga will be "disappointed" in you.)

Hardy outdoorsmen sharing anecdotes around the fire.

Fortunately, they look tougher than they fight—Wind-Shifter is three levels above yours, but his comrades are all one below—and Mazoga is, after all, an Orc.

When all four are dead, she'll clear up the mystery: Her best friend Ra'vindra reported Wind-Shifter's gang of highwaymen to the authorities and was killed by Wind-Shifter in retaliation. That day, Mazoga became a self-appointed knight determined to make wrongs into rights. (For some alternate post-combat dialogue, beat Mazoga to the scene and kill Wind-Shifter yourself.)

Mazoga offers no reward beyond her invitation to loot the bodies, and they don't have much. The real reward comes when you report back to Caro in Leyawiin and he offers you both positions as...

KNIGHTS OF THE WHITE STALLION

But first you have to pass a trial: Find and kill Black Brugo—the leader of the Black Bow Bandits. (Note that Mazoga must be alive for you to get this quest. Otherwise, Caro judges that you're unworthy.)

The count suggests that Mazoga may have Bandit contacts who can put you on to the highwayman. But it turns out that Mazoga (back in her usual spot in the castle foyer) knows Black Brugo and his routine. He works out of a small Ayleid ruin called Telepe, northwest of the city, and shows up there daily between midnight and 6 a.m. to collect his take.

Ask Mazoga to follow you (or not) and make your way out the West Gate and over the hill north of the Five Riders Stables.

Leave early, as you have a little business to transact at Telepe before the ambush. You may find one or two lookouts on the surface. Eliminate them and also the two Bandits in the right-hand room just down the stairs inside. (If you're lucky, they're sleeping.) Take their black bows. In fact, take every black bow you find during this mission. Caro will pay a bounty for each.

Be sure to greet the welcoming committee with lethal courtesy.

In the left-hand room, push the button in the east corner to open the gate out in the corridor. Beyond the gate, an Ayleid coffer with a three-tumbler lock contains 300 gold and a brief note. This is Brugo's take. (You can also wait until he's opened the coffer and simply take the money from Brugo, or kill him first and use his key.)

Now wait for Brugo and cohorts Alonzo and Roxy Aric to appear. They'll make for the button and then try to claim the gold from the coffer. Hammer 'em. Alonzo and Aric are easy prey, being two and three levels below your own, but Brugo is four levels above yours and a real challenge if you're on your own.

When you get back, tell Caro about Black Brugo's death, and Caro inducts Mazoga and you into the Order of the White Stallion, and gives you a key to White Stallion Lodge, a County Leyawiin shield, and a promise of 100 gold for each black bow you bring him. You should have at least five by now.

Sunrise across the Niben from White Stallion Lodge

Return to Mazoga in the lobby to announce your joint promotions. She'll march off directly in the wilderness to continue her knightly deeds. See "Fun with the Black Bow Bandits" in the "Freeform Quests" chapter for details.

If you didn't take Mazoga along for the ride, and just used the pretty lady's information for your own ends, you've made an enemy. Mazoga's Disposition drops 50 points. You're now "a manky sroat." And she'll hang out in the castle forever.

SKINGRAD

PARANOIA

Walking through Skingrad, you'll eventually pick up the topic "Glarthir." Talk to folks to learn that he's a local nut who hasn't strayed over the line into criminal activity—yet. You'll get a good variety of comments, with more, and more detailed ones, at Dispositions of 50 and 60.

But note that two of the 60s—Bernadette Peneles and Erina Jeranus—seem to warn you off Glarthir. They suggest Glarthir's eccentricity is getting worse.

Glarthir, Skingrad's resident eccentric

Glarthir himself is activated when you walk by his place on the corner west of the Great Chapel of Julianos. He approaches you and asks you meet him behind the chapel at midnight. Do so, and he offers you a mission. He claims he's being followed. He's not sure who's doing the following, but, whoever it is, he asserts that he is a threat to their plans. (Read your journal afterward; it expands upon what you've actually heard.)

Beginning at this point, the quest can unfold in radically different ways.

HELPING GLARTHIR

Glarthir assigns you to watch three people he thinks are watching him. The first is Bernadette Peneles, who lives across the street from his house. Then you're to report back to Glarthir at the same time and place with your findings. (If you don't show up, Glarthir keeps showing up at midnight indefinitely.)

Bernadette Peneles is spying on Glarthir, isn't she?

If you've already used the Glarthir topic around town, shortly after this first rendezvous you'll be approached by Dion, the captain of the Skingrad city guard. He wants to know what you think you're up to with this troubled man. You can respond with three levels of cooperativeness, but it all works out the same way. Dion says Glarthir is crazy and that getting involved in his schemes isn't good policy. If Glarthir asks you to do anything "strange," you're to bring it to the attention of a city guard.

You can let Dion know right now that Glarthir thinks there's a plot against him. Dion then concurs with earlier assessments that Glarthir is getting worse and revises his "strange" prerequisite to "dangerous." But paranoia isn't a crime, and Dion can't move against Glarthir yet.

And it is paranoia. No one on Glarthir's enemies' list is actually spying on him. They glance at him when they pass on the street, and perhaps that's all it takes for Glarthir to work up a case against them.

However, if you haven't made independent inquiries about Glarthir, you may not know this for a metaphysical certainty. You don't have to follow Peneles or, indeed, any of the three "spies"; it's not a condition for making your reports to Glarthir. But if you want to satisfy your suspicions, be in position outside Peneles's house at the appointed hour the following morning.

On a typical day, Peneles heads to the chapel for a quick morning prayer (coincidentally walking past Glarthir out on his morning constitutional in the plaza in front of the chapel), then heads out the city's West Gate. She turns south at Tamika Vineyards, finds her way through a gap in the fence, and starts tilling the soil. This goes on until 11 a.m., when she breaks for lunch and heads for the rival Surilie Brothers Vineyards' shed on the north side of the road. At about 1 p.m., she returns to the city and does yard work behind Tamika's house until 7, when she eats her dinner on the spot. At 9, she heads home and stays home.

This woman clearly has no interest in Glarthir. You can either tell Glarthir so, or lie and tell him that Peneles is spying on him, or claim your work isn't done. In the first two cases, Glarthir pays you the promised 150 gold and sends you off to spy on Toutius Sextius, who lives on the corner across the bridge north of the chapel. In the last, he'll angrily defer the pleasure until your next midnight meeting.

Toutius Sextius, another suspicious character

Sextius spends most of his day exploring Castle Skingrad and the area around the city. Follow him, or don't follow him; again, it doesn't matter. If you report that he's a spy and previously reported Peneles as a spy, you'll collect 200 gold. (Glarthir likes to have his delusions confirmed.) If you say he isn't one, and previously reported that Peneles isn't either, you'll get 150 and Glarthir will mutter about "what price betrayal." He seems to be having doubts about you.

But he'll nevertheless ask you to tail Davide Surilie, who Glarthir suspects of being the ringleader in this "plot." Glarthir's next-door neighbor, Surilie spends his days working at his vineyard as methodically as Peneles does at hers.

Davide Surilie, the ringleader of the conspiracy?

If you've tried to cure Glarthir with common sense, and acquitted all three of the "spies," when you meet with him next, he'll say they're all in on it—and you as well—and attack you. You'll have to put him down hard. Being that he's an unarmored, unarmed Wood Elf, this should be about as tough as killing a midlevel Wolf. Take his gold—he has just under 350—and his key so you can loot his house at your leisure.

However, if you mark even just Surilie as a spy, you'll get 200 gold. And if you've identified any spies at all, you'll get a note ("List of Death") in which Glarthir orders the deaths of any conspirators for a reward of 1,000 gold.

You can handle this list several ways: You can make the hit(s) as ordered, take Glarthir's note to the authorities, or warn the individuals who are threatened—or some combination of these.

The killing will be easy. You only have to take out one of the three to get the full fee, so just designate one of them as the "spy." If you followed the marks, you'll know where how they spend their days, and none of the three is a fighter or carries weapons or armor.

If you take the "warning" route, Peneles and Sextius will both ask you to alert the guards. But Surilie says he and his brother will settle the issue with Glarthir themselves. And they will, too—though they may require your help to get past the front-door lock on Glarthir's house.

If you select the "authorities" route, any city guard will do. He'll take off after Glarthir, and let's just say the little Elf doesn't get the "go to jail" and "pay gold" niceties to which you've become accustomed. He'll die. He can scarcely do anything else.

NOT HELPING GLARTHIR

If you decline to help Glarthir, he goes over the edge. He makes for his house, retrieves a battleaxe from a table on the third floor, and immediately embarks on a killing spree. He goes after Peneles, Sextius, and Surilie in that order.

You can handle this several ways.

You can wait until Glarthir assaults his victim and then take him out. (You take him out before he attacks, but it's murder.)

Glarthir takes matters into his own hands.

Or pickpocket him for his key and lockpicks or pick the five-tumbler lock on Glarthir's front door and then steal the battleaxe before he can grab it. True, he may find another weapon, but that'll be tougher without the lockpicks. He may wind up fighting with his bare hands, his victim may survive his initial attack to flee into the street, and that may bring the guards into the fray—in which case the battle's over before it's begun.

Or if you have a really great character, or are just feeling stupid and suicidal, you can run interference for him and see how far Glarthir can go. Our testing suggests that, unassisted, Glarthir can kill Peneles but is likely to get stopped by guards on or around the bridge north of the chapel as he heads for Sextius's place. So you'll basically have to kill off the whole Skingrad guard nightshift for him to get to Surilie.

EPILOGUE

You may have noticed that, at various points on the helping-Glarthir side of the quest, you're told of him scribbling on a piece of paper. Those notes wind up on a table against the east wall in his cellar; late in the quest, when you get Glarthir's key, you can read them.

Depending how things unfold, there will be as few as three (if you didn't help him) and as many as seven (if you reported on Toutius Sextius). One of the documents that will always appear is an account of Glarthir's own surveillance on Surilie at his vineyard west of the city. It refers to the wine-maker going off by himself—possibly to bury secret evidence—and to a later finding that ground had been disturbed. It's easy to read this as just another bit of paranoia and equally easy to read it as the one small slice of reality.

We think it's all in Glarthir's head. But there does happen to be one bit of minor loot nearby. North of the vineyard are two ponds. Sunk beside the central rock of the eastern one is a chest containing bit of gold, probably some clutter, and a small chance of a lockpick. And on the south side of the pond is a nirnroot plant. Activating it just happens to give you another quest.

SEEKING YOUR ROOTS

As you wander Cyrodiil, you may notice a strange plant that emits a noise and slightly glows with an inner light. The stuff grows all over Cyrodiil. We count 305 of the two varieties of the nirnroot plant from Anvil to Leyawiin, and any one of them will do.

The elusive and rare nirnroot

Wherever you find your first sprig, you'll get a journal entry proposing that you take it to an alchemist. Any alchemist will do, too. They are: Felen Relas at the Anvil Mages Guild; Ardaline at the Bravil Mages Guild; Selena Orania at the Bruma Mages Guild (assuming the Necromancers haven't wiped it out in the Mages Guild quest "A Plot Revealed"); Eilonwy at the Cheydinhal Mages Guild; Angalmo at the Chorrol Mages Guild; Julienne Fanis at the Lustratorium in the Imperial City's Arcane University (or the lobby of the Arch-Mage's Tower if the "Tears of the Savior" quest is also running); Ogier Georick at The Main Ingredient and Claudette Perrick at The Gilded Carafe,

both in the Imperial City's Market District; S'drassa at the Leyawiin Mages Guild; and Falanu Hlaalu at All Things Alchemical in Skingrad.

You should now have compass and map markers for all these folks when you enter their appropriate town. Each will express interest in your sample and refer you to Sinderion in Skingrad—pointing to him but not telling you his exact whereabouts. (Only Hlaalu at All Things Alchemical in Skingrad's northwest corner tells you he's at the West Weald Inn near the city's West Gate.)

Sinderion works out of the inn's cellar. (You can also get the quest by talking to him directly.) His proposal: Bring him 10 samples of nirnroot and he'll give you an Elixir of Exploration and make others available at a discount. He'll even suggest the best location for finding the rare plant: Shadeleaf Copse in the Great Forest just to the northeast. Three plants are arrayed around the central pond: near the rocks on the north, south, and west shores.

And the other six nirnroots? That's a problem.

You've just stumbled onto the biggest quest in *Oblivion* and quite possibly the most difficult as well. Over the course of four mini-quests, you'll have to collect 100 samples of nirnroot to enable Sinderion to create four versions of the Elixir of Exploration that are stronger and more diverse in their effects. The first, weak potion has Fortify Health and Night-Eye effects that last for five minutes. The second version, which requires 20 nirnroots, adds a Fortify Fatigue effect. The third, which requires 30, also boosts your Blade, Blunt, Destruction, Restoration, Security, and Sneak skills by 5 points each for a minute. And the final, "grand" version, which requires 40 roots, doubles the duration of those same skill boosts.

Why's it so hard? Well, it's not like picking mushrooms. Nirnroot rarely grows in profusion in any one area. Moreover, while other flora periodically respawn, nirnroot plants never do. You can't go back to Shadeleaf Copse over and over again.

Unfortunately, while Sinderion gives you some broad advice, he doesn't give you any other nirnroot locations. No one does. "Seeking Your Roots" is a scavenger hunt that runs almost entirely off your own initiative.

The designers have compensated a bit for nirnroot's scarcity by making it easier to detect. Nirnroot plants give off a dim glow and make a soft sound rather like wind chimes.

Nirnroots can reliably be found near water and rocks. But there's a lot of water and rock on display in Cyrodiil. Where should you look?

NIRNROOT IN THE WILD

Most nirnroot is in the distant wilderness. Alas, it's very spread out. There are only two regions with three plants, and Sinderion sent us to one of those. Nine more regions have two plants each, and the other areas, if they have nirnroot at all (highly unlikely), have but one.

Happily, there are a handful of wilderness areas into which nirnroot-bearing regions have been concentrated. The northern reaches of the Blackwood swamps, near Cyrodiil's border with Black Marsh, are the nirnroot mother lode.

Three dungeons serve as the western anchors for searches in this region: Fort Doublecross, Fort Teleman, and Fieldhouse Cave. The easiest to reach is Doublecross. Fast-travel to Leyawiin, follow the road east and north out of the city, and head northeast cross-country when you see the Ayleid ruin Veyond.

Only two plants grow in close proximity to the ruined tower. But fanning out across the dark pools in every direction but west are two dozen additional plants. They'll run out to the north and south when the water runs out, but to the east you'll keep finding them until you reach the hills at the map's edge.

Fieldhouse Cave is northeast. There may be a good deal of overlap with the nirnroot stocks east of Doublecross, but we count four more samples near the entrance: one east-northeast of the cave entrance, beside a cluster of rocks, and the three others along a rough line that begins with the plant at the west edge of a circle of rocks west of the cave and then extends southeast.

Teleman is east-northeast of Fieldhouse Cave. We've found nine additional nirnroots in the same general area. Three are immediately southwest—one on the water's edge just south-southwest of the tower, another at the tip of the peninsula that extends farther southwest, and the third beyond the large boulders across the narrow channel to the west of the second plant. Three others lie west and northwest of the fort—the first at water's edge west of the tower, the second near some rocks across the water still farther west, and the third beside the fifth large rock (counting from the one beside the second plant) to the north. The last three of the nine are more distant—one well south of the tower at the southern end of an inlet, the second southwest of the tower at the west end of a larger inlet, and the third at water's edge southeast of the second.

There's not much nirnroot in western Cyrodiil. However, explore the Abecean coast west of Anvil to find at least seven samples: two at the south end of an island just off the coast, a third on the pointy mainland peninsula north of the island, a fourth farther north along the shore, a fifth still farther north on a small peninsula that extends southwest, a sixth at the north end of the island just off the coast here, and a seventh on yet another island (this one marked with a noninteractive shipwreck) a good deal farther north.

Find three more by following the western stretch of the Strid River along the Elsweyr border. And a similar march along Topal Bay southeast of the Lower Niben nets six—four on two islands just off the coast and two on the mainland—and a trip southwest another three.

There are more of them here than you'd think. Lots of folks keep nirnroot as a houseplant. If you were to collect all these, you'd have 62 nirnroots and could complete the first three mini-quests.

Merely a curiosity to some, the nirnroot can actually be found inside as a houseplant.

The nirnroot houseplants are still the property of the building's owner, so be aware that if you are seen taking one, it will be counted as a crime.

In and around Anvil (11 nirnroots), plants sit atop a dresser on the second floor of Heinrich Oaken-Hull's house; beside the statue near the Main Gate; just behind the rocks on your left as you leave the city on the way to the castle; atop a dresser in Dairihill's bedroom in the castle's private quarters; growing at the north end of the pool in the Smuggler's Cave under the castle; on a beach on the south side of the little island just south of the outside entrance to that same cave; beside the stairs leading up to the docks from the west; next to three rocks at the north end of an inlet west of those same stairs; on the west side of that same inlet; on a windowsill in Ulfgar Fog-Eye's quarters below the lighthouse; and in the northwest corner of an island just south of the lighthouse.

In and around Bravil (12 nirnroots), look for nirnroot on a dresser in Andragil's house; on a stool at the foot of a bed in City-Swimmer's house; on a dresser on the third floor at Silverhome-on-the-Water; atop a dresser in the Great Hall of the Chapel of Mara; atop a wardrobe on the second floor of the Fighters Guild; in the Wizard's Grotto (which, with the Wizard's Lair, connects the castle with the Temple of the Emperor Zero); along the city's west wall behind the Mages Guild; along the city's south wall behind the House for Sale; along the wall in the southwest corner of the castle grounds; at the southern end of the bridge over the Larsius River just west of the city; near the center of the arrowhead-shaped island just southeast of the city; and on the coast northeast of the ruined fort (itself northeast of Bravil), where you'll find the city's

Oblivion Gate after the "Dagon Shrine" segment of the Main Quest.

In Bruma (three nirnroots), you'll find nirnroot on a dresser in an upstairs bedroom at Baenlin's house, atop a stack of boxes at Regner's house, and atop a bookshelf in the Lord's Manor in the castle.

In Cheydinhal (four nirnroots), it sits on a dresser in an upstairs bedroom at Mach-Na's Books, on a hall table at the head of the stairs at Riverview; beside the western abutment of the eastern bridge on the island in the middle of town; and at the south end of the chamber below the Mages Guild well (which you'll visit in the guild's recommendation quest).

In Chorrol (two nirnroots), look for nirnroot on a bedside table in Vilena Donton's quarters at her home and on a dresser upstairs at Casta Scribonia's house.

In the Imperial City (12 nirnroots), there's nirnroot growing on the wall at the north end of the southern of the two sections of moat on the north side of the Arboretum; on a stool in the captain's quarters in the South Watch Tower, which can be reached from both the Arboretum and the Temple Districts; on a plant stand in the Arch-Mage's quarters and on a bookshelf in the Mages Quarters at the Arcane University; on a table at The Gilded Carafe and atop a cupboard in a bedroom above the Mystic Emporium in the Market District; on a barrel upstairs at Sam Bantien's house in Talos Plaza; on a dresser upstairs at Salomon Geonette's house in the Temple District; on the table in the captain's cabin aboard the pirate ship *Maria Elena*, docked at the Waterfront District; near the water on the east side of the southernmost island of the Waterfront District; and just east of the north exit from the City Sewers, with another nirnroot farther northeast along the coast.

In Leyawiin (16 nirnroots), grab nirnroot from a window seat on the second floor of Ahdarji's house; a dresser in Jeetum Zee's room and a plant stand on a balcony in the Blackwood Company Hall; a dresser on the ground floor of Margarte's house; just east of Best Goods and Guarantees in the northeast corner of town; and find two more flanking the entrance to the castle grounds.

Moreover, just outside the city are no fewer than nine nirnroots. One is on the east side of a little inlet that's to the north immediately after you leave the city by the East Gate. Two others are east and south-southeast, respectively, of the Coast Guard Station on the peninsula north of the city. Two more flank the channel east of the castle, and three of remaining four can be found along the narrow strips of land that separate the city's south wall from the Lower Niben. (The fourth is on the mainland farther southwest.)

In Skingrad (two nirnroots), you'll find it on a windowsill on the top floor of Toutius Sextius's house and on a dresser on the top floor of the Surilie brothers' house.

There is some nirnroot in smaller communities: on a shelf behind the bar at the Border Watch Inn (Border Watch is a Khajiit village north-northwest of Leyawiin near the Elsweyr border); atop a dresser at Torbal the Sufficient's House at Brindle Home, a hamlet in the Great Forest west of the Imperial City; atop a dresser on the second floor of Natch Pinder's house in Hackdirt (a spooky village in the woods southwest of Chorrol); on a dresser at Shafaye's house and at the southwest exterior corner of The Sleeping Mare inn in Pell's Gate, a village on the Red Ring Road south of the Imperial City; and on a little nub of a peninsula just northeast of the hamlet of Water's Edge—a short walk north from Leyawiin on the west side of the Lower Niben.

NIRNROOT AND DUNGEONS

Often, it's located outside near a dungeon entrance. And, very occasionally, it's inside. You'll find it:

- Beside the rocks atop the waterfall just west of the entrance to Charcoal Cave, just off the Green Road from the Imperial City to Bravil a short distance south of the Red Ring Road.

- Along the coast just southwest of the Ayleid ruin Culotte, an undead dungeon on the east side of the Upper Niben channel about halfway down its length.

- Behind the rocks just northeast of the wreck of the Emma May at the mouth of the Panther River—a location you may have visited for "The Forlorn Watchman" quest.

- Just north of the southern east-west wall in the surface ruin of the Ayleid site Fanacasecul, an undead dungeon along the Red Ring Road just west-southwest of the Imperial City.

- Among the rocks on the mainland coast south of the entrance to Fatback Cave—a Goblin lair located at the southern tip of the large Lake Rumare island that holds the Imperial City.

- In a field of green stain cup mushrooms at the foot of a tree northwest of the entrance to Fieldhouse Cave—a Conjurers' lair located, er, right on top of the "t" in "County Leyawiin"! (See "Nirnroot in the Wild" for more details on this area.)

- Inside the small tower north of the entrance to Fort Cedrian—a Marauder stronghold just after the Corbolo River crossing on the Yellow Road southeast of the Imperial City—with another inside the dungeon itself, in a corner of the big room at the end of the first level.

- Up against the outside of the northeast wall of Fort Cuptor—a Necromancer lair near the southwest shore of Lake Canulus in eastern Cyrodiil.

- Both against the north exterior wall and southwest of the entrance to Fort Doublecross, a Necromancer lair northeast of Leyawiin. (See also "Nirnroot in the Wild" for more details on this area.)

- Just north of the entrance to Fort Entius—a Conjurers' lair on the west bank of the northernmost section of the Silverfish River.

- Among the rocks just southwest of Fort Gold-Throat—a Goblin lair beside the northwestern headwaters of the Panther River.

- Beside a large rock just north of Fort Irony—a Goblin lair in the northeast corner of the peninsula that extends into Niben Bay southeast of Bravil.

- Under the stairs in the tower above Fort Redman—a Vampire lair on the east bank of the Lower Niben, northeast of the west-shore hamlet of Water's Edge.

- Up against the west exterior wall of Fort Redwater—a Vampire lair at the junction of the two easternmost branches of the Panther River.

- On the water to the west and north of Fort Roebeck—a Conjurers' lair on the southwestern branch of the White River south of the Imperial City, with a third nirnroot in the dungeon's upper level.

- Against the southeast interior wall of the tower above Fort Teleman—a Necromancer lair south of the southern extremity of the Panther. (See also "Nirnroot in the Wild.")

- On the top level of The Hunter's Run—a dungeon under Fort Grief in Niben Bay that appears in the "Caught in the Hunt" Miscellaneous quest.

- Behind a flight of stairs in a trench in the North Tunnel of the Imperial City Sewers—a section that leads to the sewers' north exit.

- On the north side of a small pond northwest of Leafrot Cave—a undead dungeon northeast of the northern branch of the easternmost headwaters of the Panther. (A second plant can be found near two big boulders in a gully west-southwest of the cave.)

- Beside a rock southwest of the entrance to Memorial Cave—a Vampire lair on the southern shore of Lake Rumare, which you may recall from the "Order of the Virtuous Blood" Miscellaneous quest.

- On the stairs leading up to the entrance to the Ayleid ruin Morahame—a mythic critter dungeon across Niben Bay from Bravil.

- Right beside the entrance to Redwater Slough—a Vampire lair just downriver and on the opposite bank from Leafrot Cave and just northwest of Fort Redwater.

- Just east of the entrance to Reedstand Cave—a critter den well southeast of Bravil. (Heading south from that city, you'll find it east of the road shortly after you pass Fort Nomore to the south.)

- Down by the water south-southeast of Tidewater Cave—a critter den (and Troll hangout, if you've done the "Nocturnal" Daedric quest) on Topal Bay southeast of Leyawiin.

- At the edge of an "island" in the middle level of Veyond's Cave—a Troll lair on the coast north of Bravil.

- Just west of the entrance to the Ayleid ruin Welke—on the north bank of the Panther River's southernmost feeder stream. (Others can be found to the southwest and northwest, across the Panther.)

- Southwest of the entrance to Wellspring Cave on the east shore of Lake Rumare. (You'll visit this location in the Mages Guild quest "A Mage's Staff.")

- In the west-northwestern outbuilding of the Ayleid ruin Wendelbek—a Necromancer lair near the headwaters of the second westernmost of the Panther River's feeder streams.

ADDITIONAL SITES

- On the coast northeast of Bawnwatch Camp—located on an island southeast of Bravil which you'll visit for the Miscellaneous quest "The Forlorn Watchman."

- Against an exterior wall just north of the entrance to Cadlew Chapel—a small priory north of the mouth of the Silverfish River.

- Among the rocks at the north end of the Silverfish River bridge to the Imperial Bridge Inn, with a second near the docks on the south side of the river.

- On a dresser in an upstairs bedroom at Lord Rugdumph's Estate north of Cheydinhal.

- On the northwest shore of Lake Canulus, southeast of the Nayon Camp (a Bandit cookout).

- On the north side of a small pond north of the Nocturnal shrine—just off the Yellow Road on the east side of the Lower Niben, about halfway between Leyawiin and Lake Rumare.

- Atop a dresser at the Odiil farm, southwest of Weynon Priory.

- At the east end of the Old Bridge, northwest of Pell's Gate.

EPILOGUE

With the grand elixir in hand, you're done. Sinderion has run through his avenues for research. You can return to him for more potions—but at a price, and not in perpetuity. They'll run out eventually. However, he'll now buy nirnroot from you at 250 gold for each 10 you can supply.

THE SETTLEMENT QUESTS

THE POTATO SNATCHER

You can get this little quest by finding either the quest-giver (S'jirra) or the quest object (six jumbo potatoes).

S'jirra is in Faregyl—an inn off the Green Road south of the Imperial City, near the southeastern headwaters of the White River. This cook apparently left the potatoes outside to dry. The next thing she knew, they were gone and someone was running west into the woods.

The someone was a hungry Ogre. You'll find it in the woods west-northwest of the inn, near the Ayleid ruin Nenyond Twyll. Simply kill it, take all six potatoes from its body, make your way back to the inn, and S'jirra will reward you with one to five loaves of her famous potato bread. You can buy additional loaves at 25 gold each.

Potato thief!

RAID ON GREYLAND

Just outside Leyawiin's West Gate, you'll meet an Imperial Legion trooper named Lerexus Callidus, who's on the trail of skooma dealers.

But he's got a problem: Callidus is either known to the dealers or he's conspicuous in his Legion armor. In any case, the lookout at the nearby Greyland settlement always spots him, and the leader—a Dark Elf named Kylius Lonavo—always gets away.

You wouldn't have these problems. Callidus effectively deputizes you. You're to go in and deal with (that is, kill) Lonavo.

Greyland's a small house just west of the city and south-southwest of your current position. Don't worry about the lookout. Lonavo's not alone—there'll always be a Marauder melee fighter with him—and he's got a leveled magic claymore. Paralyzing or burdening magic would be handy here so that both enemies can't attack you at the same time.

Kylius Lonavo's skooma den

Take Lonavo's ring as proof for Callidus and his sword for yourself. From the legionnaire, you'll collect a bounty based on your level.

REVENGE SERVED COLD

As in "The Potato Snatcher," you get this quest from either the quest-giver or the objective, whichever you find first.

The quest-giver is a fellow named Corrick Northwode who lives at Harm's Folly—a small Heartlands farm that's roughly equidistant from the Imperial City to the southwest and Cheydinhal to the southeast. (If you walked to Lake Arrius Caverns from the Imperial City for the "Dagon Shrine" segment of the Main Quest, you should have hit Harm's Folly in the foothills.)

Northwode's wife was killed in a Goblin raid while he was away buying supplies. He wants revenge on the Goblins—and the return of his wife's amulet as a keepsake. He won't tell you that the Gobs are in Exhausted Mine until you end the chat.

Northwode makes the dungeon sound complex. It's not. The mine is fairly thronging with cackling Goblins and Rats, but most of them are sufficiently spread out that you'll be able to tackle them one at a time. The leveled "Netherboss" in the final room isn't much advanced over what you've already been facing. Just take the necklace from the boss's body and get back to Northwode for your reward.

This Goblin boss slew Corrick's wife and has her necklace. It's payback time.

NO STONE UNTURNED

On the north bank of the Silverfish River, a short distance east of the main north-south road down the east side of Niben Bay, is the Imperial Bridge Inn. Within, you'll find a High Elf sorcerer named Lithnilian who lost his notes on those Magicka-restoring Welkynd Stones normally common only to Ayleid ruins when he was attacked in Bramblepoint Cave. Can you recover them for him?

If you already have the notes, great. They mention the owner's presence at the inn, and the quest is over. If not, Bramblepoint's a three-level mythic enemy cave to the west-northwest near the Niben shore with a variety of creature types. Fair loot, too. Get into the habit of checking for it, as the notes aren't in the open but in a chest in the southwest corner of the southernmost room of the bottom ("Deep") level.

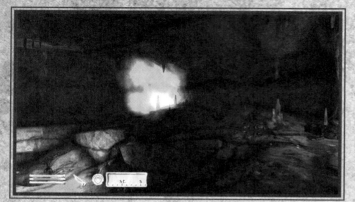

The Welkynd Stone patch deep inside Bramblepoint Cave

Read the notes if you like. You can't do anything with the raw Welkynd Stones in the cave, but a contented Lithnilian will provide at least three leveled potions when you return them. Then he'll move upstairs to the balcony and sit down to read them.

THE GRAVEFINDER'S REPOSE

"Raelynn the Gravefinder must die," says Malene.

The proprietor of the Roxey Inn, on the Red Ring Road at the northeast corner of Lake Rumare, reports that since the Necromancer took up residence in Moss Rock Cavern and undead began appearing near the cave entrance, it's no longer safe to walk in the woods at night. Kill Raelynn, and Malene suspects you'll put an end to the problem.

The cavern's up the hill just north of the inn. The absence of actual undead creatures outside the entrance isn't a signal of an easy task. Inside, you face undead and Necromancers, and you'll find some decent loot. One boss creature keeps Raelynn company in the cave's innermost chamber.

It's your job to dispatch this nasty Necromancer who's performing her evil experiments in Moss Rock Cavern.

Raelynn is much tougher than the average Necromancer, so proceed with caution when taking her on.

Once Raelynn's dead, return to the inn for a leveled reward.

BEAR SEASON

If you were to draw a line between Skingrad and Kvatch, just north of the middle of that line would be the sheep farm Shardrock. Speak to shepherd Thorley Aethelred and he'll complain of Bear attacks on his flock. You're to "thin the population a bit"—kill six of them—to scare the rest away.

Finding the Bears may take a while. They're not scrunched together in a cave, but spread out in a rough circle around the farm: four to the north, three beyond the pond to the east, three to the south, and one among the rocks to the southwest. And they can sometimes be hard to see, owing to the plants and rocks and even overcast weather. So listen for their bawl and the thump of their passage.

Help Thorley Aethelred get rid of the West Weald Bears plaguing his Sheep.

Take fangs from each of the six so Aethelred will know you've done the job. He'll reward you with one of a selection of seven books. Four are skill books (Athletic, Block, Hand-to-Hand, and Heavy Armor), and the remaining three—two volumes from the Feyfolken series and the spooky *Palla, Book II*—are simply rare.

THE SUNKEN ONE

Southwest of Shardrock, just northeast of the ruined city of Kvatch, is Shetcombe farm. When you step inside the house, you'll get a journal entry that the place seems to be have been recently abandoned and a suggestion that you search for a clue to where the owner has gone.

That may prove a little tricky until you let the cursor do the walking and realize that the object in the clay bowl on the central table isn't food. It's the crumpled first page of Slythe Seringi's journal.

Written as he watched Kvatch burn, the diary outlines Seringi's plan to bring an offering to "The Sunken One" in nearby Sandstone Cavern. Seringi takes the view that this entity has brought about the destruction of Kvatch and might next turn its attention to the Imperial City.

In fact, this fellow's nuts, but in a well-meaning way. He wants to save the world and is willing to put himself at risk to do so.

The cave's just northeast of the farm; the entrance on the north side of a large rock may be guarded by several mythic enemies ranging from Imps to Spriggans to Ogres. More enemies await on the first level, along with (atop a chest in the trench leading to the entrance to the second level) the second page of Seringi's journal. Things don't seem to be going well.

No, definitely not. On the second level, a large room has a pit in the center. East of the pit is a descending passage. Seringi's body is here, as is the crumpled third page of his journal (he was attacked by a creature and blames himself for the destruction of mankind that must follow) and his offering to the Sunken One (gold, gems, and nuggets). That will serve as your reward—along with the loot in here, which is respectable.

Slythe meets his end in the depths of Sandstone Cavern.

And the "Sunken One"? A Storm Atronach who pops in at the last minute after you read Slythe's last note. Be careful, as it appears at the only exit from the fissure where the unfortunate pilgrim lies.

A VENERABLE VINTAGE

Again, you can pick up this mission either from the quest-giver or by independently finding the quest objective.

Nerussa runs the Wawnet Inn just west of the bridge into the Imperial City. If you ask her about "Wine" you'll learn she's a wine collector, too, and has been unable to lay hands on Shadowbanish Wine. This brew, which doubles as a Night-Eye potion, was made especially for the Imperial Legion and can be found in the province's many ruined forts. Bring Nerussa six bottles and she promises to pay you well.

Nerussa at the Wawnet Inn, lover of fine and rare wines

There are 40-plus forts in Cyrodiil. You can find Shadowbanish in or around only eight of them. (However, there are two bottles in every wine chest, so you must visit only three.) Those eight are:

- **Fort Aurus**, a Conjurers' lair on the northeastern shore of Niben Bay just south of the mouth of the Corbolo River. The wine chest is in a western corner of the dungeon's easternmost room. It's guarded by a Conjurer.

- **Fort Carmala**, a Vampire lair in the woods south of Chorrol. The chest is against the north wall in the dungeon's northeastern extremity. It's guarded by a Vampire patriarch!

- **Fort Dirich**, an undead hangout southwest of the Weatherleah estate (see "Legacy Lost" under Chorrol). The chest is against the southwestern wall of the crypt's southernmost room. It's guarded by an undead boss.

- **Fort Grief**, a surface ruin on an island in Niben Bay— just south of Fort Aurus. (The dungeon under the fort is used in the Miscellaneous quest "Caught in the Hunt.") This unguarded chest is against the west wall on the top level of the ruined tower.

- **Fort Irony**, a Goblin lair on the southwest shore of Niben Bay—on a peninsula southeast of Bravil. The chest is beside the central pillar in the dungeon's southernmost room. It could be guarded by a Goblin...or maybe just by a "nuisance beast."

- **Fort Magia**, another undead conclave just south of Wellspring Cave (from the Mages Guild quest "A Mage's Staff") on the east shore of Lake Rumare. Guarded by an undead boss, the chest is beside a sarcophagus in the northwest corner of the dungeon's bottom level (Garrison Blocks), half in and half out of the water.

- **Fort Scinia**, a mixed-use dungeon in the mountains southeast of Cheydinhal, near the Morrowind border. The chest waits unguarded on the floor at the east end of the entry hall for the second level (Hall of Legends).
- **Fort Vlastarus**, a Vampire lair just off the Gold Road east of Skingrad. The chest is beside the central pillar in the western of the dungeon's two northernmost rooms. It's guarded by a Vampire, undead creature, and a Wolf or a rat.

 See the "World Maps" chapter for the location of each fort.

When you return to the Wawnet Inn, exchange the six bottles for 1,000 gold. And if you dig up any of the remaining 10 bottles in the future, come back to Nerussa. She'll pay 100 gold for each. Or drink one and gain the benefit of a long-lasting Night-Eye potion.

GO FISH

Just across the road from the Wawnet Inn is a house called Weye. The tenant, Aelwin Merowald, is a fisherman who was recently disabled by a Slaughterfish bite and asks you to collect the 12 remaining Rumare Slaughterfish scales needed to fulfill a lucrative contract with an alchemist.

If you inquire further, you'll be pointed to a spot just to the north in the northwest part of Lake Rumare. (If you laugh at him instead, his Disposition will plummet 60 points and you'll have trouble learning the location of Merowald's savings in conversation. We'll discuss that in a bit.)

You should be able to find all the fish you need here. However, this is not your ordinary Slaughterfish. It's a Tamriel Barracuda, and the ones you'll encounter at higher levels can take and deal out a lot of punishment.

Happily, it has a weakness against shock attacks, so make sure you bring appropriate weapons (along with healing and Water Breathing potions).

When you collect the 12th scale, you get a journal entry to check in with Merowald. He'll take the scales and you'll get the Jewel of the Rumare—a ring with Fortify Athletics and Water Breathing enchantments.

And you'll recall Merowald saying he's made a bundle off his deal with the alchemist? Raise his Disposition to 70 and he'll reveal that the money's in the house under a special lock, and that the key is on his person.

Yes, you can be a creep and steal his retirement money. There's gold in the chest in the southwest corner. You can't get it without the key and you'll have to pickpocket or kill Merowald to get it.

Aelwin Merowald looks over Lake Rumare.

WHEN THE VOW BREAKS

You can get this quest either by speaking to Maeva the Buxom or by finding a special mace on her husband's body in Fort Strand.

Maeva lives at the Whitmond farm just north of Anvil. She'll immediately start in about her "good-for-nothing husband." Apparently Bjalfi the Contemptible has lived up to his name, made off with a Buxom family heirloom—the mace Rockshatter—and headed off to join a gang of Marauders to "find his fortune." She doesn't sound like she misses the man much, but she does want the mace back.

The Marauders operate out of the ruined fort on the hill east of the city. Bjalfi's down on the second level (Great Dome). There are two paths—left and right at the first junction—and we think the left-hand one's a bit shorter and safer. Either way, at the bottom, you'll have to face Bjalfi and a Marauder Warlord (who are at your own level) and possibly one or two additional Marauders. But this path has a swinging-mace trap into which you can lure your opponents.

The traitor and layabout Bjalfi the Contemptible

You can keep Rockshatter if you like—it has a nice shock-damage enchantment—but you won't be able to finish the quest. If you surrender it to Maeva, she'll turn over her dowry.

MISCELLANEOUS QUESTS

VAMPIRE CURE

To get this quest, you'll have to be a full-blown Vampire, not merely infected with porphyric hemophilia. (See the "Vampires" chapter for details.)

Even then, the quest does not come to you. You must find it by speaking about "Cure for vampirism" to a chapel priest or healer—or, if you're a member of the Dark Brotherhood, to Vampire Vicente Valtieri. The chapel folks can themselves only offer that death is a certain cure, but suggest you speak to Raminus Polus at the Arcane University.

If you're an Apprentice in the Mages Guild, you already know to find Polus in the lobby of the Arch-Mage's Tower. Polus doesn't have the cure himself, but he kicks you over to Count Janus Hassildor of Skingrad, whom he says has been doing research on the subject. (And Hassildor's a Vampire himself.)

Janus Hassildor, Count of Skingrad

You may already know from contacts in the Main Quest and Mages Guild quests that the count is reclusive. You'll have to go through his steward, Hal-Liurz. (The other steward, Mercator Hosidus, may be dead by now if you've been following the Mages Guild quest line.) She'll go see the count, and the count will come down to meet you.

The cure is for his wife. While the count willingly accepted the changes that came with his vampirism, Rona Hassildor struggled with them and slipped into a coma when she refused to drink blood. Hassildor's own search has pointed to the witches of Glenmoril, and he's received a report of a woman near the Corbolo River who may be one. You're to find her.

You're pointed to a solitary home called Drakelowe on the Corbolo's upper reaches. The only nearby quest location is Arkved's Tower from the Daedric quest "Vaermina." If you haven't done that one and haven't explored other locations, just fast-travel to Cheydinhal and head south.

See the "Nibenay" map in the "World Maps" chapter, map marker #38.

The house sits high on the river's east bank. The lone resident, Melisande, asserts that she is no longer a witch but says she can help with the cure. However, she wants a favor before she'll even discuss the details: You're to bring her five empty Grand Soul Gems.

Melisande, Glenmoril Coven retiree

GRAND SOUL GEMS

There's an easy way and a hard way to do this. The easy solution is to just buy the gems. Most Mages Guild branches have a vendor who is guaranteed to have a Grand Soul Gem for sale. In Anvil, it's Felen Relas; in Bravil, Ardaline; in Bruma, Selena Orania; in Cheydinhal, Eilonwy; in Chorrol, Angalmo; and in Leyawiin, Alves Uvenim. If you've reached a high enough level, there's a chance the gem will respawn in a vendor's inventory, so you could simply wait around.

The hard way is to find them in the wild. (They'll turn up in leveled loot, but those appearances are unpredictable.)

However, there are eight empty Grand Soul Gems lying around loose in the game. One's right under your feet. Descend to the basement through the trapdoor in the south fireplace. Plentiful evidence indicates that Melisande is still very much a witch—including, in the room at the end of the hall, a dish of Soul Gems. Right next to it lies a Grand Soul Gem.

You'll find two more in five-tumbler display cases on the ground floor of the Chorrol Mages Guild, plus two others at the Arcane University—one in the lobby of the Arch-Mage's Tower and the other in the Mages Quarters.

The last three are in dungeons convenient to Drakelowe. Squandered Mine is just up the mountainside to the northeast. Crayfish Cave is just downriver to the south-southeast. And the Ayleid ruin Nornal, which you may have visited to collect the instructions of the Dark Brotherhood quest "A Kiss Before Dying," is a short distance west.

See "Nibenay" in the "World Maps" chapter, map markers 39, 40, and 17.

Two of the three are relatively easy. Squandered Mine's three levels are occupied by Level 1 Bandits and critters—save for the leveled undead creature that guards the Soul Gem. (It's behind a secret door on the south side of the bottom level.)

Crayfish Cave, a big critter den, is also easy once you understand the dungeon's somewhat unconventional structure. (The first level is a hub that gives access to each of the additional four levels.) The Soul Gem is on the fourth level, Crayfish Steep, which is reached by heading right from the cave entrance. When you leave the water on this level, head southeast and northeast up two ramps. At the top of the second ramp, continue straight on, past a side room containing a dead adventurer. A secret door opens ahead of you, and beyond it the Soul Gem sits on a low pedestal.

However, Nornal is rather tricky. The gem's down on the bottom level. On the second level, you'll find yourself in a water-logged room while an archer takes potshots at you from a balcony to the southeast. To get out, hop on the fallen column at the northeast end of the room—a task that won't be easy until you hit Journeyman level at Acrobatics—and then jump to small ledges to the east and south, edge around the corner, and vault the balcony railing. (Note that you can remove the cages from atop the pillars in the lower room by pressing buttons in the northwest part of the lower room and on the balcony floor. Under them lie three Varla Stones.)

And on the third level, there isn't a conventional way out of the water that fills the lower portion of the level. You'll need water-walking magic or a master-level Acrobatics skill (which allows you to skip across the surface of the water). However, from there it's pretty much smooth sailing through Bandits, their camp, and a secret door. The gem's on a pedestal.

When you return the five gems, you'll learn Melisande can indeed cook up a vampirism cure—eventually. But the Soul Gem hunt was only the first errand in a series. Now she needs six garlic cloves, two bloodgrass shoots, five nightshade leaves, Argonian blood, and the ashes of a powerful Vampire.

GARLIC, BLOODGRASS, AND NIGHTSHADE

You can find garlic just about anywhere—in shops, in loot, and lying around in people's homes. Loose garlic is most plentiful in Weynon Priory, where three cloves lie in a bowl on Jauffre's desk in the library and three more are in a bowl on the shelves at the other end of the room; the Imperial Legion mess hall, with six cloves on a shelf against the west wall; M'dirr's house in Border Watch, with four cloves in a bowl on the table; The Dividing Line in Leyawiin, with three cloves on a storage-room shelf; Lord Drad's Estate, with two cloves in a bowl on the dinner table and a third on the table beside it; and three cloves on the dinner table in Satha Dalvilu's house in Bleaker's Way (a fair-sized village just west of the Silver Road between Bruma and Lake Rumare).

Garlic

In addition, there's an 80 percent chance of harvesting a clove from a garlic cluster, which can be found in greatest quantity in Skingrad in the cellars of Glarthir's and Lazare Milvan's houses, Summitmist Manor, and the House for Sale, and also the cellar of Rimalus Bruiant's house in Chorrol.

Apart from a few locations in the Cyrodiil wilderness where it spills out through random Oblivion Gates, the bloodgrass plant grows only in Oblivion. It's most plentiful in three regions reached through the Cheydinhal gate in the Miscellaneous quest "The Wayward Knight." (Note that there's only a 50 percent chance of harvesting it from a given plant.) However, if you haven't yet completed the "Dagon Shrine" segment of the Main Quest—which opens the Cheydinhal gate—you can find a lot of it in the section of Oblivion reached through the Kvatch gate and also in the Daedric quests "Boethia" and "Peryite."

Bloodgrass

You can find loose bloodgrass in Cyrodiil at just two locations, but you'll have to be well along in the Dark Brotherhood and Thieves Guild quest lines to find them. One is on a table high up in the Temple of the Emperor Zero (a.k.a. Fathis Aren's Tower) south of Bravil, and you'll have only one shot at the Brotherhood one; it's on the altar in the Crypt of the Night Mother under the Lucky Lady statue in Bravil, which is accessible only during the Brotherhood endgame.

The nightshade plant, which yields nightshade 80 percent of the time, is most plentiful in another one-shot region:

Camoran's Paradise from the "Paradise" segment of the Main Quest. In Cyrodiil, you'll have your best luck searching in the trackless wilderness halfway between Bravil and Skingrad and the areas south of Bravil and west and northwest of the Temple of the Emperor Zero.

Nightshade

Loose, the ingredient is most easily found on a display table at The Main Ingredient in the Imperial City's Market District (four portions); as a dinner-table decoration in the second-floor library at the Chorrol Mages Guild (three portions); in a niche in the sanctum when you revisit it for the Dark Brotherhood quest "Scheduled for Execution" (two portions); and, again, the Crypt of the Night Mother from the Brotherhood endgame (two portions).

Argonian Blood

Any Argonian will do—enemy or friendly, named or generic—and any circumstances. You just have to use the enchanted dagger provided by Melisande for this purpose. (The enchantment forces the target to bleed when struck.)

The quickest way to go about this is to head north to Mach-Na's Books in Cheydinhal and slash the proprietor once. The surly old lizard is rated "essential" by the game—meaning you can't kill her—but she bleeds as well as any other Argonian. Yes, you'll probably get in trouble with the law, but you can always make things right by just paying the bounty.

If you don't like attacking an innocent, there are many ways to go about this, depending on where you are in the game. While you don't have to kill your mark, you can sync this assault with other events in the game where you do have to kill an unimportant Argonian. (You can face Argonians in the Arena, in the Main Quest, in a variety of Dark Brotherhood and Fighters Guild quests, and in any number of dungeons.)

Vampire Ashes

Melisande has a particular Vampire in mind: Hindaril in Redwater Slough on the eastern reaches of the Panther River.

The Vampire/undead lair is small as dungeons go. If you're a good lockpicker, make a left at the first T intersection to reach Hindaril, who is imprisoned behind a five-tumbler lock. If not, first make a right at the T, swim through the underwater passage, and retrieve the key from a chest on the rise at the northeast corner of a large pool at the far end.

Hindaril is a tough opponent—five levels above your own—but he has a peculiar weakness: He is not expecting company and so is not armed when you appear on the scene. When he spots you, he'll run to his coffin and retrieve a weapon. However, if you're fast and beat him to the punch, he'll have to fight you with his bare hands.

Hindaril, the ancient Vampire

Take Hindaril's ashes, and take a peek in his coffin. If you get the right roll, you'll find tons of stuff inside.

Also check out the coffin suspended high on the north wall in the dungeon's first large room; a good jumper should be able to leap atop it from the east side of the pit. It holds a Shortsword of Jinxing with a Damage Magicka enchantment.

If you happened upon Redwater Slough before taking on this quest and have already killed Hindaril, never fear. His ashes should still be in your inventory and can immediately be turned over to Melisande.

Simply return the ashes to Melisande, talk to her about them and then "Cure for vampirism," wait around for 24 hours, and you'll have two potions—one for yourself and one for Rona Hassildor. Make for Castle Skingrad again, tell steward Hal-Liurz that you have the cure, and she leads you to a hidden door in the castle courtyard.

Beyond, in the Chamber of the Lost, you'll find Rona Hassildor in bed, dead to the world, the count sitting by her side, and, surprisingly, Melisande. Evidently the witch has agreed to revive the countess long enough for her to drink the potion. She does. The countess has a touching exchange with her husband—and then keels over and dies. You can't talk to her during her brief return to the living, but you can disgrace yourself afterward by looting the body of its small supply of gold. (You're really just here as a witness.)

Rona Hassildor, the long-suffering countess of Skingrad

Do as the count instructs: Give him a day to put his wife's affairs in order and then see Hal-Liurz. (Sleep in the countess's deathbed, if you like!) When you see the count again, he'll give you a rather meager reward of leveled gold. But then, the real reward from your hard work is the ability to forever rid yourself of the effects of vampirism, should you so choose.

Traveling southeast along the Yellow Road from the Imperial City, just before the bridge over the Corbolo River, you'll find a small camp at Crestbridge. Speak to Barthel Gernand to learn that his party was chased from the intended site of a new settlement at Cropsford by a Goblin war party.

Crestbridge Camp

Gernand's wilderness guide, Mirisa, reports that the location up the road to the northwest is positioned right between two warring tribes based out of Timberscar Hollow (the Rock Biter Goblins) and Cracked Wood Cave (the Bloody Hand Goblins) and that the solution to Gernand's problem lies in settling the Goblins' dispute. You can either sneak into Timberscar and steal back a totem (a staff topped with a tribal head) that was stolen from the Cracked Wood Goblins or kill the Cracked Wood Goblins' shaman leader.

Killing the leader is likely to require killing not a few additional Goblins en route. These may include a Rat farmer three levels below yours (but no higher than Level 8); six standard Goblins one level below your own; a Skirmisher at your own level; a Berserker; a War Chief two levels above yours; and the Goblin Shaman herself. Your best tactic is not to let them gang up on you by fighting in the big rooms.

You can make your assault on Cracked Wood Cave much easier by waiting until nightfall, when a raiding party, including the tough war leader, heads out to attack the Timberscar Goblins. Likewise, if you follow the war party at a discreet distance and enter Timberscar behind them, reaching the totem staff may be easier once the two Goblin tribes are embroiled in combat. However, don't let them detect you, or you may find yourself fighting both tribes at once—they hate you more than they hate each other.

MISCELLANEOUS QUESTS

The totem-retrieval mission is decidedly the easier route. The Rock Biter population is slightly tougher—two standard Goblins are replaced by an extra Skirmisher and an extra Berserker—but the path to the totem requires fewer and easier contacts. (Use the central and northernmost of the three exits from the large central room to find it.)

The stolen Totem Head in Timberscar Hollow

Return to Crestbridge and use the "Goblin war" topic with Gernand. Alas, there's no real reward beyond the settlers' gratitude. Once you're out of sight, the party will pack up, head northwest to Cropsford, and set up its tents. The houses will go up, the tents will vanish, and about two weeks after their arrival the work will be complete. Visit at different stages in the settlement's development to collect different comments from Gernand, his daughter, and her husband. (Mirisa heads south for the Imperial Bridge Inn on the north bank of the Silverfish River, where she takes up life as a Deer hunter and venison provider.)

Technically, the quest is complete, too. But if you decided to retrieve the staff, you still have some options.

To return it to the Goblins, simply drop it outdoors near the Cracked Wood Cave entrance or inside the cave. The Goblins will find it and restore it to its proper place. (Note that, except for the shaman, the Goblins respawn, so even if you wiped out most of the mob in Cracked Wood Cave and then had second thoughts, they'll still recover the staff—as long as the shaman remains alive.)

You can keep the staff. It's not simply a tribal symbol, but a weapon; it does shock damage.

And if you speak to Mirisa, she'll suggest that you can use the staff to incite war between Goblin tribes.

Mirisa's a fun sort of girl.

Much of this is beyond the provenance of this quest. (See "Fun with Goblins" in the "Freeform Quests" chapter for details.) But once the settlers are on station at Cropsford, you could perversely re-ignite the war between the two tribes from the quest. Gernand and company won't comment formally on this event, but if you're present to watch, they may get slaughtered as the Goblin war parties once again pass through Cropsford.

ZERO VISIBILITY

On the Red Ring Road north of the Imperial City, a short distance west of the junction with the Silver Road up to Bruma, you'll stumble upon a little village called Aleswell. At a glance, it seems abandoned. But if you look around a bit—notably, inside the Aleswell Inn—you'll see translucent forms moving about and realize the folks are simply invisible. (You can also pick up this quest from Roxey Inn proprietor Malene as a rumor.)

Most of the residents—there are five—don't want to talk about the problem. They all refer you to Diram Serethi. Diram, who's also in the inn, blames the invisibility on Ancotar—a wizard who works out of nearby Fort Caractacus. But he's vanished, too. Diram suspects he's hiding—and he's right.

Caractacus is down the slope to the southeast. Like Aleswell, it also appears empty. Like Aleswell, it isn't. Climb the stairs and check out the little room on the north side of the first level. On the desk, you'll find Ancotar's journal and the heart of the problem: Annoyed by interruptions by Aleswell residents complaining about his experiments, Ancotar turned himself invisible. In so doing, he carelessly turned everyone in Aleswell invisible as well.

 Diram Serethi warns you to watch out for the invisible creatures that infest the fort ruins. Take him seriously. An invisible Wolf or Bear can be a nasty surprise for the unwary.

Now you just have to find Ancotar and see if the damage can be undone. That's a bit of a problem. Unlike Diram, the invisible wizard wanders around a lot, and it can be difficult to be looking in the right direction when the slight refraction effect of the invisibility spell flickers into view or to follow it when it moves past you.

Ancotar's laboratory in Fort Caractacus

Ancotar is ticked off by this interruption, too, and you can use his shrill voice as an additional guide. We found it easiest to spot him at the top of the stairs opposite the room with the journal. (And if that doesn't work, just use a Detect Life spell.)

He'll provide a scroll containing a powerful area-effect counter-spell and admonish you to stand in the center of town when casting so as to affect everyone. And he'll start to say something else…and stop himself. Bump his Disposition up to 70 and he'll provide a ring (Ancotar's Ring of Protection) that provides some kind of insurance. "Not that I think anything will go wrong," Ancotar says. "Serious side effects are highly unlikely."

Bastard. If you don't wear the ring, a serious side effect is guaranteed. Your Luck attribute will take a 50-point pounding. This won't wear off even in a year or two, and you'll have to cast a Restore Luck spell on yourself or visit a chapel to have it repaired.

However, as long as you're in the village when you cast the spell, all's well in Aleswell. You don't have to figure out the geographic center of the community. Diram hails you as "the savior of Aleswell" and says you'll always have a free bed at the Aleswell Inn. (His sisters are even grouchier than they were when they were invisible.)

But suppose you are overanxious and cast the spell before you return to Aleswell or vengefully decide to spoil Ancotar's own invisibility by casting it while he's nearby? He'll be pissed, and in the latter case he'll be pissed twice over, but Ancotar will nevertheless provide a replacement scroll. Do it again, however, and you and the folks of Aleswell are out of luck and you'll be as unwelcome a visitor in the village as you were welcome before.

(One other little wrinkle: If you're a member of the Mages Guild or have an Illusion skill of better than 50, Ancotar will talk a little shop with you. You don't get anything extra materially, but it's an amusing little mage rant against the idiocy of the "normal" world.)

ATTACK ON FORT SUTCH

After "The Oblivion Crisis" accelerates at the end of the Main Quest segment "Dagon Shrine," but before the Main Quest ends, you'll be able to perform this unusual combat quest out in Cyrodiil's northwestern wilderness.

It's unusual not so much for what you do—going into Oblivion and fighting Daedra—as for how the game charts your progress. Though events are ticked off invisibly, you won't get any journal entries at all. The game won't even tell you you're on a quest.

The trigger event for this mission is delivery of the Mysterium Xarxes to Martin and Martin's subsequent request that you speak to Jauffre about Mythic Dawn agents who are spying on Cloud Ruler Temple. Among other things, this opens Oblivion Gates outside six of Cyrodiil's cities, and also near Fort Sutch—a ruined fort in the wilderness well north of Anvil.

You may already have been to the Fort Sutch dungeon in the Dark Brotherhood quest "Bad Medicine." This one takes place on the surface above it. If not, take the road north from Anvil. When it starts to turns east, follow the side road north to Lord Drad's Estate and then head north across the pastures to a broken tower.

At the base of the ramp into the tower is an Imperial Legion captain. As you approach, a soldier runs up to him and yells that there are too many Daedra and the company needs to fall back. If you can, speak to the captain before he rushes off, and he'll ask you to help his troops defeat the creatures emerging from the fiery gate to the northeast. (The soldiers will just tell you the captain's the only one who knows what's going on.)

The Imperial Legion takes on the Daedra near Fort Sutch.

The seven legionnaires—the captain, three swordsmen, and three bowmen—face a surge of leveled Daedra. You can help or you can watch. (Heck, you can even become part of the problem.) Three Daedra are already advancing on the tower when you appear on the scene. They'll keep coming through the gate at regular intervals, with the last and nastiest being a Dremora, which emerges as you close in on the gate.

When all the Daedra all dead, speak to the captain again and he'll invite you to try to close the gate. However, he's been ordered to hold position, and there's a general unwillingness to proceed further among the troopers under him, so don't expect support à la "Bruma Gate" in the Main Quest.

You can enter the gate at any point. It will take you to one of four Oblivion worlds—each well supplied with enemies and each very different from the others. Once the gate connects with a given world, the game remembers the connection and the gate links to that location until it is destroyed.

Save your game before you enter the gate. That way, if you don't like where you've landed or want to take on a particular challenge, you can restore and re-roll.

FREEFORM QUESTS

ADVENTURERS

Track down one of the adventurers in Dzonot or Talwinque (best odds).

What, you thought you were the only person in Cyrodiil with an interest in dungeon delving? In 16 dungeons, you have a small chance of encountering a random adventurer.

Generated when you enter his dungeon or dungeon level, this anonymous fellow—always called "Adventurer"—is an Orc two levels below your own. He's probably a warrior, but possibly a battlemage or spellsword. He'll have leveled armor, loot, and an enchanted blade. The warriors also have a shield and the spellcasters a decent repertoire of magic.

You don't have to kill them. They're not hostile and, indeed, have a bit of amiable dialogue. They're seeking treasure in the name of the Orcish realm Orsinium and Orc lord Gortwog. If you watch them, that's really all they do. They don't sleep or eat, and they never leave their parent dungeon. Every four hours, they embark on a two-hour search for loot. They're trying to collect 1,000 gold in valuable "miscellaneous" items—typically gold, gems, or cups.

You have a 25 percent chance of finding the adventurer in Dzonot Cave and the Ayleid ruin Talwinque.

There's a 10 percent chance of an encounter in Arrowshaft Cavern, Doomed Mine, Fort Black Boot, Fort Chaman, Fort Doublecross, Fort Nomore, Fort Urasek, Gray Rock Cave, the Ayleid ruin Hrotanda Vale, Kingscrest Cavern, the Ayleid ruin Niryastare, Nornal, and the Ayleid ruin Rielle (northwest of Bruma).

Refer to the "World Maps" chapter for additional help finding these locations.

AYLEID WELLS

At 35 wilderness locations around Cyrodiil, you'll find Ayleid wells. When activated, each restores 400 points of lost Magicka and also fortifies it by an additional 50 points for five minutes. (This works even with your Magicka at the maximum, so you can still get the fortify boost.)

Need it again? Wait until midnight when the well recharges.

The wells are relatively rare in western and southern parts of the province and most plentiful in the central and eastern regions. Their locations are:

Near Bravil
- Southeast of Anutwyll, which is on the Green Road just north of Bravil.
- East of the Ayleid ruin Wenyandawik, which is northwest of Bravil.

Near Bruma
- On the Orange Road southwest of the city.

Near Cheydinhal

- Northeast of Cheydinhal and southeast of the Ayleid ruin Fanacas.

- East-southeast of Cheydinhal and northwest of Hero Hill.

- West of the Ayleid ruin Belda, which is north of the Blue Road about midway between the Imperial City and Cheydinhal.

Near the Imperial City

- Southwest of Fort Empire, near the northwest corner of Lake Rumare.

- South of Fort Virtue, on the Red Ring Road at the southwest corner of Lake Rumare.

- Northeast of Cracked Wood Cave, which is on the Yellow Road southeast of the Imperial City.

- At the junction of the Red Ring and Yellow Roads.

- Just northeast of Wellspring Cave on the east shore of Lake Rumare.

- Just southeast of the Ayleid ruin Culotte on the east shore of the Upper Niben.

- On the Red Ring Road at the northeast corner of Lake Rumare, between the Ayleid ruin Sercen and the Roxey Inn.

- Directly above the Ayleid ruin Vilverin, on an island in the northeast corner of Lake Rumare.

- Northeast of the Ayleid ruin Sardavar Leed, near the south shore of Lake Rumare.

- Southwest of the Imperial City, near the western headwaters of the White River.

Near Kvatch

- North of Sandstone Cavern, which is northeast of Kvatch.

- West of Kvatch, just north of the northward bump of the Gold Road between the Brina Cross and Gottshaw Inns.

- North of Kvatch and west of Fort Linchal.

Near Leyawiin

- West-southwest of Onyx Caverns, which are east-northeast of Leyawiin near the Black Marsh border.

- Northeast of Tidewater, which is south-southeast of Leyawiin.

Near Skingrad

- Northeast of Goblin Jim's Cave, which is north of Skingrad.
- East of Derelict Mine, which is east of Skingrad on the Gold Road.
- Near Fat Rat Camp, on the Gold Road west of Skingrad.
- Northwest of Fallen Rock Cave, which is itself northwest of Skingrad.

In the Wilderness

- Well northwest of Kvatch and east of the Ayleid ruin Niryastare.
- Just west of the Ayleid ruin Ondo, which is on the east bank of the north-south stretch of the Silverfish River.
- North-northwest of the westernmost headwaters of the Panther River.
- Between Fort Naso and Sercen Camp and east of Squandered Mine, in the region east of the southern stretch of the Reed River.
- Just southwest of the Ayleid ruin Mackamentain, east-southeast of the Yellow Road bridge over the Corbolo River.
- South of the Yellow Road bridge over the Corbolo River.
- Southeast of the Mouth of the Panther, near the south bank of the Panther River.
- In the West Weald region west of Wenyandawik and south of Pothole Caverns.
- North of Lake Arrius and east of Gutted Mine.

- Southeast of the Ayleid ruin Nornalhorst, which is east-southeast of Skingrad.

FUN WITH THE BLACK BOW BANDITS

When you kill Black Brugo to complete the Miscellaneous quest "Knights of the White Stallion," you're not done with the Black Bow Bandits.

Black Bow Bandit

If you catch up with your partner, Mazoga the Orc, again afterward, she'll say, "I'm going to get me some black bows. Tag along if you like."

It's not just fancy talk. Most of the time, post-quest, Mazoga is in or around White Stallion Lodge—a rustic cabin northeast of Telepe on the Lower Niben's west coast to which you obtained access by your good works in "Knights." But three days a week, the Orc lady does indeed go hunting for five black bows.

Black Bow Bandit

At 2 p.m. on Monday, she heads for the small Ayleid ruin Telepe, where the Bandits you killed in the Miscellaneous quest have respawned. (You can never run out of Black Bow Bandits.)

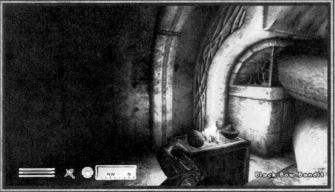

At the same time on Wednesday, she makes for Rockmilk Cave—a four-level lair across the Niben from Fisherman's Rock. There's already a war going on here, involving 17 Black Bows

(including a boss) and eight conventional Bandits on one side and 14 or 15 Marauders on the other. Check out the debris in the cave-in trap on the top level; there's a dead Bandit in there. And the big tent on the bottom level is home to a Black Bow dog, with the sweet name of "Pumpkin."

On Thursday, Mazoga's off to Undertow Cavern—a two-level cave just off the road between Leyawiin and the lodge. It's really just a Bandit hideaway, but a token Black Bow Bandit can be found on the upper level and nice loot (and lotsa water) down below.

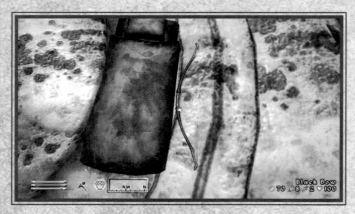

Don't forget to turn any black bows you capture in to Leyawiin's count for the 100 gold bounty.

Across Cyrodiil, within rings of rough stones, stand 21 ancient monuments known as Doomstones.

You'll hear different things about these pillars from various folks. Upper-class characters will assert (via "rumors") simply that they are a mystery.

In one issue of the *Black Horse Courier*, Anvil author Quill-Weave (the troublemaker in the Fighters Guild quest "A Rat Problem") is quoted as saying that she finds "no evidence at all to support the popular notion that these Runestones were once artifacts of great magical power." (You can find this issue at the *Courier*'s office in the Imperial City's Market District; at The Count's Arms inn, Heinrich Oaken-Hull's house, and Lelles' Quality Merchandise in Anvil; at The Oak and Crosier in Chorrol; and at Rosentia Gallenus's house in Leyawiin.)

And if you've achieved Apprentice rank in the Mages Guild, you can even attend a lecture series on Doomstones on the Arcane University campus. Yes, the university has lectures! The students start to gather on the benches outside the Praxographical Center a little after 9 a.m. and 3 p.m., and the talks are offered at 10 a.m. and 4 p.m.—whether you're present or not. There are five talks in the series, with one chosen at random each day. Hence, a lecture can repeat, and it may take a while to hear all five.

Regrettably, the lectures don't all contain solid info. One of them is fairly on the mark, the others various distances from it, and it's conceivable that if you set out after one lecture, and it's the wrong one, you'll go off half-cocked.

In fact, there are two types of Doomstones: "Birthsign" and "Heaven" stones. When activated between 6 p.m. and 6 a.m., each of the 13 Birthsign stones strips you of any Doomstone powers you've acquired from another Birthsign stone and gives you new ones. (Note that you keep the powers and abilities that came with the birthsign assigned during character generation.)

The "Heaven" stones, marked with red runes, are slightly trickier, as you have to have a certain level of combined Fame and Infamy (with both considered as positive values) to activate them. (If you don't have it, you'll get a message that "The Hero's fate is known when the Hero's fame has grown.") The payoff here is that the new powers don't cancel the old and that, if you visit all seven stones, you'll accumulate a formidable array of special powers.

THE BIRTHSIGN STONES

Apprentice Stone: Located just south of Skingrad. Gives the greater power Void Seed, which fortifies your Illusion and Alchemy skills by 20 points for two minutes.

Atronach Stone: Located west-northwest of Skingrad and north of the Shardrock farm. Gives the greater power Arcane Well, which has a two-minute Spell Absorption effect and fortifies Intelligence by 20 points for two minutes.

Lady Stone: Located west of Anvil. Gives the greater power Lady's Warding, which fortifies both Willpower and Endurance by 20 points each for two minutes.

Lord Stone: Located high above the Brena River, north of the Ayleid ruin Niryastare, near the Hammerfell border. Gives the greater power Ysmir's Scales, which provides two minutes of 50-point frost resistance and also fortifies the Light and Heavy Armor skills by 20 points for the same period.

Lover Stone: Located east of the Yellow Road on the south bank of the Silverfish River, east-southeast of the Imperial Bridge Inn and west-southwest of Peryite's shrine. Gives the greater power Lover's Bower, which fortifies Personality and Luck by 20 points for two minutes.

Mage Stone: Located north of the headwaters of the Silverfish River. Gives the Magicka Manifold greater power, which fortifies Magicka by 50 points for two minutes.

Ritual Stone: Located along the east side of the Lower Niben, northeast of Fisherman's Rock and east of Fort Redman. Gives the greater powers Mara's Mercy and Mara's Milk. The first allows you to restore 150 lost hit points to another character, the other 100 hit points to yourself.

Serpent Stone: Located southeast of Leyawiin, halfway between Tidewater Cave and the Bogwater campsite. Gives the greater power Cobra's Dance, which paralyzes the target for 5 seconds while damaging its Health by 4 points for 20 seconds.

Shadow Stone: Located east-southeast of the Yellow Road bridge over the Corbolo River. Gives the greater power Fingernail Moon, which gives you a two-minute 15 percent Chameleon spell.

Steed Stone: Located just south of the Blue Road, southeast of Roland Jenseric's cabin, about halfway between the Imperial City and Cheydinhal. Gives the greater power Hellride, which fortifies your Speed attribute and Acrobatics skill by 20 points for two minutes.

Thief Stone: Located on the Silver Road just north of its junction with the Ring Road. Gives the greater power Cheater's Nip, which fortifies the Agility and Luck attributes by 20 points for two minutes.

Tower Stone: Located just north of the Red Ring Road on the southwest shore of Lake Rumare, west-northwest of the Old Bridge. Gives the greater power Warden Key, which casts an Open Hard Lock spell and fortifies your Armorer skill by 20 points for two minutes.

Warrior Stone: Located just northwest of the Ayleid ruin Silorn, which is southeast of Skingrad near the headwaters of the Strid. Gives the greater power War Cry, which fortifies your Strength attribute and Blade, Blunt, and Hand-to-Hand skills by 20 points for two minutes.

THE HEAVEN STONES

Jone Stone: Requires a combined Fame/Infamy of 10. Located well north of Skingrad and east of Sanguine's shrine. Gives the greater power Jone's Shadow, which casts an Invisibility spell and fortifies your Sneak skill by 30 points—both for two minutes.

Aetherius Stone: Requires a combined Fame/Infamy of 20. Located just northwest of Skingrad, south of Bleak Flats Cave. Gives the greater power Gates of Aetherius, which fortifies Magicka by 50 points and gives the player a 20 percent resistance to magic—both for two minutes.

Jode Stone: Requires a combined Fame/Infamy of 30. Located east-southeast of Anvil, just southeast of Troll Candle Camp. Gives the greater power Jode's Blood, which fortifies your Health by 40 hit points and your Blade, Blunt, and Hand-to-Hand skills by 20 points—all for two minutes.

Sithian Stone: Requires a combined Fame/Infamy of 40. Located north of Kvatch—roughly at the center point between Shattered Mine to the west, Mongrel's Tooth Cave to the north-northeast, and Fort Linchal to the southwest. Gives the greater power Sithian Web, which fortifies your Illusion, Marksman, Mercantile, Security, and Speechcraft skills for by 20 points for two minutes.

Magnus Stone: Requires a combined Fame/Infamy of 50. Located east of the Haunted Mine in the Nibenay Valley, south of the center point of the southern tributary of the Panther River. Gives the greater power Children of Magnus, which fortifies all six magical skills—Alteration, Conjuration, Destruction, Illusion, Mysticism, and Restoration—by 15 points for two minutes.

Shezarr Stone: Requires a combined Fame/Infamy of 60. Located northwest of Leyawiin and just north of the Ayleid ruin Telepe. Gives greater power Shield of Shezarr, which casts a 10 percent Reflect Spell and fortifies the Armorer, Block, and Light and Heavy Armor skills by 20 points for two minutes.

Dragon Stone: Requires a combined Fame/Infamy of 70. Located just east-northeast of Lake Arrius Caverns, which are north-northwest of Cheydinhal. Gives greater power Dragon Dream, which fortifies Health by 40 points, Magicka by 50, and Fatigue by 100 for two minutes.

DRUGS

Skooma doesn't have quite the presence in Cyrodiil as it did in Morrowind, but it is here. You'll find drug activity in or around three cities: Imperial City, Bravil, and Cheydinhal.

Skooma's like a jolt of adrenaline—boosting your Strength and Speed attributes by 60 points for 20 seconds. Naturally, there's a big downside: Your Agility is drained by 60 points for the same period, and your Intelligence takes two points of semi-permanent damage. (The damage doesn't go away after 20 seconds. You must go to a chapel to have it repaired.)

The game offers chests of the drug and loose skooma potions. Five of the chests are in the Temple District home of Trenus Duronius, who's got it *real* bad, and eight of the potions can be found at Riverview in Cheydinhal. (It's probably the reason owner Voranil is so unpleasant to his hired help.)

In Bravil, Thieves Guild quest-giver S'krivva sets out to make a skooma delivery at 10 a.m. every Saturday to a spot southwest of the Lucky Lady statue near the middle of town. Nordinor from The Fair Deal sells the junk from midnight to 4 a.m. from a spot between The Fair Deal and Silverhome-on-the-Water. (You may even buy five potions from him in the Dark Brotherhood quest "The Lonely Wanderer.")

Reistr the Rotted

A skooma den operates above Carandial's house just south of the statue. Grim place. The four folks here are addicts. Their brains are frazzled. Only Roxanne Brigette is semi-normal.

She's also one of two folks—the other is Antoine Branck, who works at the city's stables—who'll tell you via the "Bravil" topic that Count Regulus Terentius's son Gellius is a skooma addict as well.

How does she know? Because she's seen him here. Every Saturday at noon the young lord makes his way to S'krivva's house, northeast of the statue, to buy the drug and then hangs out in the skooma den until midnight. (If you want hard evidence, check the chest behind the bed in his room in the north wing of the private quarters in Castle Bravil.)

Skooma is also sold outside the Imperial City by Shady Sam. He's hard to find. Make your way north from the stables outside the Talos Plaza District; he's behind some rocks outside the walls of the Elven Gardens District. He sells potions—with poisons a specialty—and lockpicks.

The third city where skooma is available is Cheydinhal. Bazur gro-Gharz, who has a house on the east side, mentions in his greeting that he has protection from the Orum Gang. And if you ask after "Cheydinhal," he asserts that "Boss uglies in Cheydinhal are the Orums." (There's another reference to the gang in the "Gray Fox, Man or Myth?" issue of the *Black Horse Courier* newspaper.)

Gellius Terentius

Perhaps you passed it off as just colorful talk, but there is in fact an Orum Gang of Orcs operating a skooma-smuggling ring out of the city.

At a little after 6 a.m. on Tuesday mornings, Oghash gra-Magul, who has a house next to gro-Gharz's, sets out for the

Imperial City's Waterfront District. She picks 10 portions of skooma from a barrel (with a leveled to two- to five-tumbler lock) beside the porch of Myvryna Arano's house in the western slums, leaves 250 gold in the barrel, and returns to Cheydinhal.

R'vanni

You'll never see anyone drop off the drugs or collect the money at this end; it's placed and removed automatically. However, you can hear about a gang of Khajiit insurgents called the Renrijra Krin whose members are working as Bandits and skooma smugglers, and can put two and two together. (You'll pick up references to the Krin from Drels Theran at Castle Bravil, Betto Plotius in Leyawiin, and Redguards generally.)

Then, at 6 a.m. on Fridays, gra-Magul heads out to Walker Camp (beyond the Ayleid ruin Fanacas north-northeast of Cheydinhal) to meet a pair of Camonna Tong thugs—a courier and his escort. The courier gets all the skooma and gra-Magul gets all the courier's gold.

Black Bow Bandit

At about 10 p.m. that night, gra-Magul returns all but 100 gold—her cut, we expect—to the gang's boss, Dulfish gro-Orum, at his home across the street from the Fighters Guild.

The courier isn't the end of the line. After the exchange, he heads north to Kingscrest Cavern and deposits the skooma in a hollowed-out rock just north of the cave entrance. As at the Waterfront, no one collects the drugs from this location; they're removed by the game automatically. (Note this trip also brings you close to Aerin's Camp and master Acrobatics trainer Torbern.)

Where do you come in? Wherever you like. You can just take it all in. Or you can rub out gro-Gharz (who is a gang member), gra-Magul, the Tong courier and his buddy, and Dulfish and his wife, Magub (who works at Borba's Goods and Stores). (S'krivva and Nordinor can't be killed.) If you're feeling extra-frisky, take on the whole gang together. It gathers for lunch at Cheydinhal's Newlands Lodge a little after noon and again for dinner a little after 8.

Of course, they're all five levels above you, so you'd better bring something extra to the party.

MORROWIND

Wonder what happened in Morrowind after you left? You'll hear a good deal about it in Cyrodiil.

Apart from a report (by Elves) that slavery has been abolished and the Khajiit and Argonian slaves freed, it's mostly bad news.

I signed on for the Raven Rock colony. Went there as a builder. Hung around afterwards, but the money ran out.

Dranas Llethro

Dranas Llethro and Hillod the Outlaw, who live in the Abandoned Shack in the Imperial City's Waterfront District, both worked on the Raven Rock colony on Solstheim (from the *Bloodmoon* expansion). Evidently it came to a bad end. "The money ran out," says Llethro.

Talk to Nords or Orcs and you'll learn the former are on the warpath—fighting with House Redoran with the help of Orc mercenaries. It rumored they're trying to run Imperial forces off Solstheim entirely.

Vivec has vanished—perhaps taken by Daedra. And it's rumored that the Nerevarine—the hero of Morrowind—has left the province altogether on a trip to Akavir.

NON-QUEST DUNGEONS

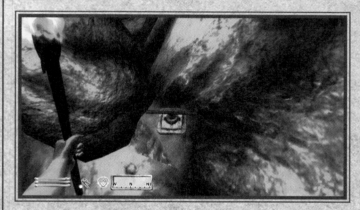

A great many dungeons in Cyrodiil are unassociated with any quest. They include ruined Imperial forts, Ayleid ruins, caves, and mines. You'll find these annotated in the "World Maps" chapter.

Most of these dungeons have no backstory. You just go in, kill whatever looks at you funny before it kills you, sidestep the traps, grab whatever good things wait at the bottom, and get out.

But just because a dungeon doesn't have obvious quest hooks doesn't mean there's nothing out of the ordinary at work there. Consider for instance the Goblin tribal dungeons (see "Fun with Goblins") or the unplundered hideaways of the Black Bow Bandits (see "Fun with the Black Bow Bandits"). Others of interest include Black Rock Caverns, Lost Boy Cavern, and Sideways Cave.

BLACK ROCK CAVERNS

You'll know this is something special from the moment you find the entrance behind a waterfall above a rockbound pond northwest of Chorrol. But once inside, it may be a challenge to find something else that makes it unusual. It appears to be just a two-level Bandit cave with standard enemies and loot.

Black Rock Pirate

However, search carefully; in the big room on second level, turn the handle hidden behind rocks against the southeast wall near the south corner.

Hmmm. All it appears to do is close a door in the southwest wall that leads back to one of the two entrance to the first level. What's that about?

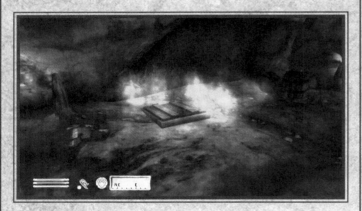

It's designed to force you to exit via the other door. When you return to the top level, two Black Rock pirates—a bowman and a melee fighter, each a level above yours—materialize on a rise to the right and attack.

Kill the bad men, and check out the area where they appeared. There used to be a big rock here. Now the rock's gone and another handle has appeared in its place. Turn it.

Nothing obvious happens, but return to the big room on the second level; a big rock on its northeast side has been replaced by a trap door leading down to "Lost Black Rock Chasm."

Follow the trail of Skeletons and dead Bandits down to a dead end. Use the handle on the right-hand wall to remove the blocking rock. And here you'll find a ruined pirate ship.

Kill off the four pirates—three are a level above you and one is four higher—and loot the place to your heart's content. Beyond what's on the baddies, you'll find loose gems on a brazier, cutlasses, and containers. (One of the chests is on the ship and another is hidden behind it.) And one of the chests near the brazier contains both a leveled piece of enchanted light armor and an enchanted weapon!

LOST BOY CAVERN

You aren't the first visitor to this Necromancer lair, hidden in a leafy trench east of northward bend in the Silverfish River and northwest of Lake Canulus. A certain Vangaril has been here before you and has left a "Weathered Journal" on the rocks beside the door for any who would follow.

Vangaril came to the four-level cavern in hope of freeing the soul of his friend Erandur, who has become a Lich. Their tale unfolds in additional documents uncovered as you make your way through the Necros and their undead minions. To learn it all, collect the crumpled papers on a table on the south side of "Canyon" level and in a coffin niche in the southeast corner of the "Yawning Halls" level; the folded page that appears both in a chest at the far west end of the fort-like "Hidden Bastion" level and atop the chest behind the throne in the final room; and the three letters to the Mages Guild in a little laboratory on the south side of that level.

The final confrontation is behind the locked double doors (two to five tumblers) at the east end of the level. If you're Level 23 or higher, you'll face the Lich. Vangaril seems to have completed his task…and then to have been fused together

Erandur-Vangaril

with his friend in the jointly operated Lich "Erandur-Vangaril." Kill it (them?) and take both its leveled staff and the enchanted blunt weapon on the body.

However, if you're Level 22 or below, you'll find only an unkillable Ghost here. (It takes a while for the men's souls to merge.)

SIDEWAYS CAVE

There's quite a story behind this dungeon, located just across the water southeast of the Imperial City's northeast sewer exit, though it's only hinted at in the dungeon itself.

The first level is a standard mythic enemy lair—until you reach the secret door in its northeast corner and it drops to reveal an Ayleid door leading into the "Hidden Lake" level. This is a flooded Ayleid ruin with all sorts of flotsam strewn about.

As you round the last turn to the entrance to the third level, the buried Ayleid ruin "Lost Abargarlas," stick to the right side of the channel. Atop a slab, a tablet bears a rough translation:

"Meridia-child, Earth root power, sea wave like (earth like a flood?). People-out (escape? present tense? imperative?)."

This is the first of three such translations. The second tablet is just inside the door to the third level: "Fourth Star Hour (time?) Terror-of-the-Most Meridia come (came?)."

At the top of the stairs, bear north. You eventually come to a stony hallway with three gates that open automatically at your approach. At the east end of the chamber beyond them, you find the translator (dead), a passage back to Hidden Lake,

and a third translation: "Stone-Settlers (builders?) not rest (wake?) Meridia. Terror of the Most Terror. Haste to safehome."

Conjurer

Can you put it all together? The big picture is that, long ago, Ayleid settlers stumbled onto this grotto. They made it their own—in the end, too much their own. In doing so, they uncovered a forgotten shrine to the Daedra lord Meridia. Meridia's vengeance for this violation was swift: She crushed Abargarlas with her stone roots and, incensed that some survivors escaped, buried the grotto almost entirely.

OTHER DUNGEONS OF SPECIAL INTEREST

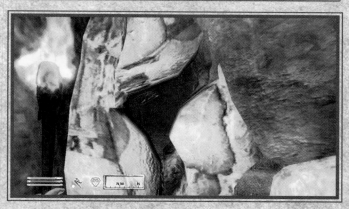

See the "World Maps" chapter for additional help finding these locations.

CEYATATAR

Ceyatatar is populated by Conjurers and located off the Gold Road midway between Skingrad and the Imperial City. An underground waterfall can be seen on the first level of this Ayleid ruin and reached from the second level. In the "boss" room on the third, you can exterminate Scamps with poison gas and find a hidden trap door to the Great Forest.

CRUMBLING MINE

Make some progress into this Bandit den under the walls of Chorrol and you'll see from the foundations that you're underneath the city proper. The Bandits realize this as well. In fact, they're counting on it. If you penetrate to the mine's innermost recess, you'll see through a crack in the wall that they're working to break into Chorrol's putative sewer system!

CURSED MINE

On the third level of this Bandit hideaway west of Skingrad is a good-sized silver-mining camp.

FORT ASH

You must complete an unusual (albeit very easy) switch puzzle at the beginning of the second level to get through three iron gates. Turn the handles on both sides of the first gate to open the first and third gates and the handle on the wall west of the left handle to open the middle one.

FORT CUPTOR

Avoid the floor grates on the second level ("Battlemains") of this Necromancer lair on the southwest shore of Lake Canulus. They drop you into a sewer maze and you'll have the find the switch (on a ledge up a short set of stairs on the west side of the maze) to open the exit gate (to the northeast). Other notable features include a Skeleton that ambushes you from behind a drapery and the partially dissected skeleton of a child.

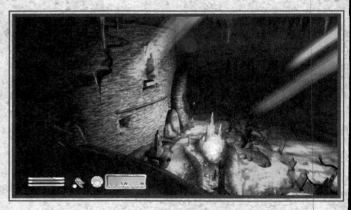

FORT RAYLES

Getting into this Conjurers' lair northwest of Chorrol is a bit tricky. The entryway is in an unusual spot—up on the second level of the surface tower. And you can only explore a bit of a top level before a puzzle blocks your path. You must have a bow to solve this. To open the portcullises to the east and west, fire arrows—any arrows will do—into the gems embedded in the foreheads of the two statues to the north.

The east gate leads to the portion of the "Hall of Winter"

level with the boss—once you solve another puzzle. Blocking the way is another remotely operated portcullis and four sets of dart traps to cover the approach. Use the rightmost of the three switches down the hall to the west to open the closed gate. Watch the central grate on the floor in the boss room; it's a breakaway and a long way down.

FORT URASEK

You can watch (or help) a pair of Marauders escape from the key-required jail on the bottom level of this Goblin lair on the east-central shore of Lake Rumare. The key's in the guard's sack near the entrance. (But they're Marauders, so don't expect 'em to be appreciative if you help.) The throne at the south end of that level is booby-trapped. Sit on it, and you'll get a face full of mace.

UNDERPALL CAVE

This undead dungeon along the Orange Road northeast of Chorrol starts out as a cave, only to turn into large fort (Underpall Keep) with north and south wings. The Necromancer behind it all can be found on the shores of a giant underground lake.

EASTER EGGS

M'AIQ

An inexhaustible source of bad info in Morrowind, M'aiq the Liar has emigrated from Vvardenfell to Cyrodiil—and seems to have acquired a somewhat firmer grasp on the truth.

M'aid knows much, tells some. M'aid knows many things others do not.

M'aid the Liar

Finding him is beyond difficult. In Morrowind, M'aiq at least had the good grace to stand still. In Cyrodiil, he moves around.

Beginning in a position in the Nibenay Basin—east of the Yellow Road bridge over the Corbolo River and just north of Trossan Camp—the Khajiit moves between Leyawiin and Anvil and every so often, for a five-hour stint, searches for calipers—a device used to measure thickness and distance. They appear in a lot of dungeon loot, so there's no telling where he might end up. He also runs about as fast as anyone else in Cyrodiil, so he's rather tough to catch up with.

If and when you find M'aiq, speak to him, as you probably won't find him again soon. As in Morrowind, he holds forth on a number of interesting topics: children, Colovian fur helms, companions, crossbows, dragons, fighting with one's feet, fishy sticks, nudity, werewolves, and more.

But he doesn't lie about most of them. He merely offers his take on each topic. Basically, M'aiq provides a little commentary on all the hot-button issues that *he* feels are unimportant. He's just a run-of-the-mill, opinionated Khajiit with a burning need for…calipers. To each his own.

M'aiq prefers to adventure alone. Others just get in the way. And they talk, talk, talk.

M'aiq the Liar

Now, you'll recall that, in Morrowind, M'aiq told the truth about one thing: He was the only person to supply the location of the lost shrine of the Daedric prince Boethia. Many players will doubtless wonder whether M'aiq alone holds some secret information this time around.

No. He's just chock-full of opinions. We promise.

FORT SURPRISE

A handful of ruined Imperial forts have unusual loot in hard-to-reach spots. We've mentioned a few of these in the context of quests where a particular magic item would come in handy. And a few, we haven't.

At Fort Coldcorn, in the Great Forest northwest of the Imperial City and east of Chorrol, note that there's an upper level to the surface tower but no stairs to reach it. Instead, you must jump from pillar to pillar and then up to the upper level—a task for which you'll need to be a Journeyman-level acrobat. (An Acrobatics skill of about 60 should be sufficient.)

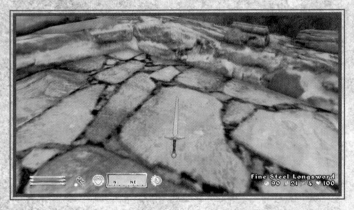

Fine Steel Longsword

Jump over the low portion of the east wall to a porch where you'll find a chest. (A good acrobat could also jump from the hillside above directly onto this porch.) It contains some gold, along with a range of other possible items, a "Key of Hidden Wealth," and a note: "The sword leads the way. Half a mile. It's just past the big rock on the right."

The sword is a longsword lying on the "porch" floor and pointing resolutely northeast. (We just hope you didn't bump the longsword on your way onto the "porch.") Just follow it up the green hill. Sure enough, near the edge of a gully, you'll see

a distinctive turtle-like rock to the right and, behind it, a chest that responds only to your new key. Inside lies a dagger and a "Note of Bounty."

The hidden wealth may not be much. The dagger will be just a regular dagger if you're at Level 1 or 2. But at Level 3 or higher, it will be enchanted. And the note? "Blessed are those who explore the unbeaten path…"

Similar challenges (minus the sword) can be found high on the walls and pillars of Fort Strand and Fort Variela.

The latter is on the west coast of the Upper Niben between the Imperial City and Bravil. You need an Acrobatics skill of 70 to make it to the top of the lowest pillar, and it's all downhill from there. The jewelry box above the eastern arch contains that "bounty" note, a leveled piece of jewelry, probably a potion (75 percent chance), and possibly a scroll (50 percent chance).

Fort Strand is on the hill just east of Anvil. You need an Acrobatics skill of about 60 for this one. Atop the northwest wall sit potions of Agility and Detect Life and a "Note of Exception": "Nothing in life is free…except for this."

No jumping is required on the hillside southwest of Fort Facian, east of the southern headwaters of the Panther. Here, you'll see three Runestones. At the base of the middle one lie seven gold coins and a jewelry box. The box contains a piece of leveled jewelry and a potion, and there's a 25 percent chance it will also contain a scroll.

North of Fort Gold-Throat, on the westernmost of the northern headwaters of the Panther, is a pillar and section of wall. Against the east side of the pillar is a chest. It contains ingredients typically used by Conjurers, a filled Soul Gem (75 percent chance), and the same note as from Fort Coldcorn.

Finally, just off the west shore of Niben Bay, southeast of Bravil and east of Fort Irony, there's a chest beside the ruins on the bottom that contains a leveled gem and, if you're Level 2 or better, a leveled potion.

FLORA AND INGREDIENTS

In a sense, the rarest plants in Cyrodiil are among the easier ones to find, as they're all food-related and hence can be found reliably on certain small farms in the wilderness.

For instance, the rarest is the watermelon vine, with just nine instances in the game—three in the central field at the small agricultural settlement of Aleswell on the Red Ring Road north of Lake Rumare, two in the field at the Odiil farm outside Chorrol, one at Water's Edge on the west side of the Lower Niben, one in a small fenced patch behind the Harborside Warehouse on the Anvil docks, and the last at Gottlesfont Priory in the Great Forest west of the Imperial City.

Watermelon Vine

The others are the wheat stalk (16 instances), pumpkin vine (25 instances), and tobacco plant (43 instances). The rarest non-food plant is dryad's saddle polypore (19 instances), which can be found in greatest concentration outside the Ayleid ruin Wendir, south-southwest of Chorrol; just east of the junction of the Orange and Silver Roads; and just southwest of Lake Arrius. It's followed closely by the green stain shelf cap with 20 instances. (We've already covered this plant under "The Gambler" in the "Arena" chapter.)

Human Heart

Most of the ingredients these plants yield are anything but rare. For instance, there are 120 watermelons across Cyrodiil. And while there are just six instances of loose wheat grain—including two on a table at Southern Books in Leyawiin and two more on one in Baenlin's house in Bruma—it's available from food vendors and in loot and so can't really be reckoned uncommon.

Nirnroot Plant

However, two ingredients cannot be harvested or purchased. You'll find two human hearts on a table in Cadlew Chapel (a Necromancer lab at the mouth of the Silverfish River), two more in Lucien Lachance's sanctum in Fort Farragut, and the fifth, along with some human skin, at a grim little altar in the cellar of Claudius Arcadia's former Talos Plaza home. (Arcadia's in prison for praying to the Dark Brotherhood's Night Mother.) Another bit of human skin can be found on a shelf in the Leyawiin Mages Guild's laboratory. (Remember that there's a party in the Mages Guild that favors using necromantic magic against the Necromancers.)

FLORA IN OBLIVION

Oblivion is an incredibly savage environment. Even the plants are against you.

There are four varieties of harrada root plants. Two look rather like the innocent roots you've seen hanging in Cyrodiil's dungeons. And those two are indeed harmless.

Harrada Root

However, the other two—one that lies flat on the surface and one that grows upright—will attack for 5 points of damage every two seconds when the player is within about 12 feet of its roots. You can't kill the plant and you can't resist the damage, so your best move is to move!

The upright variety is found in the greatest concentrations within random caves, but you'll also find it in the Oblivion world entered through the Kvatch gate—notably around the big rock west of the small southwestern tower and in the cave that leads into the small tower north of the central Citadel. The horizontal one is most prevalent in the Main Quest segment "Bruma Gate" north of the main Citadel. (Note that four harrada plants—one attacking plant and three peaceful—can leak into Cyrodiil with the opening of certain Oblivion gates. The random gate that can open off the Green Road south of the Imperial City, between the Faregyl Inn and the Inn of Ill Omen, comes with one attacking and one peaceful plant.)

You can harvest harrada from an attacking plant. And, needless to say, its four effects (in order) are all nasty: Damage Health, Damage Magicka, Silence, and Paralyze.

Moving may be easier said than done when dealing when the spiddal stick. It fires off an area-effect Drain Speed spell every 30 seconds when the player is within six feet. You'll take a 4-point hit on your Speed for 10 seconds. Note that these spells are cumulative, and that the spiddal is generally found in clusters, so don't let them hammer you.

It's found in greatest concentrations in the randomly selected Oblivion worlds but also turns up in large amounts in worlds reached through the Cheydinhal, Bruma, and Kvatch gates—the largest cluster being in the Cheydinhal world, about halfway down the southwest face of the mountain atop which

you arrive. Moreover, just to complicate things, about 20 percent of the 290-plus spiddals are dead. The dead ones are found largely in the randomly selected worlds but also appear in the Daedric realms from the "Boethia" and "Peryite" quests. In the Boethia realm, all four spiddals are dead. In the Peryite realm, seven of the 10 are dead.

Again, a couple of plants can leak into Cyrodiil through random Oblivion gates northwest of Skingrad and south of Kvatch near Dasek Moor. And again, both the live and dead spiddals yield an ingredient with generally nasty effects: Damage Health, Damage Magicka, Fire Damage, and Restore Fatigue.

The third Oblivion plant, and by far the most common, is bloodgrass. It doesn't attack, and the effects of its ingredient form are largely positive: Burden, Chameleon, Fortify Health, and Resist Paralysis.

FUN WITH GOBLINS

The Bloody Hand and Rock Biter Goblins from the Miscellaneous quest "Goblin Trouble" are just two of the seven Goblin tribes. Each tribe has its own home cave and totem staff, and you can amuse yourself by stealing any or all of their totems, shuffling them around, and making the Goblins go nuts on each other to recover them. (The one hitch is that you can't tell the staffs apart in your inventory. The only way to distinguish them is by placing one and seeing which tribe goes after it.)

Dust Eater Goblin

One fun idea: Put six of the heads in one location and then sit back and watch the chaos. There's no limit to the distance Goblins will travel to recover a totem, but they have no special gift for selecting a safe route. Hence, if they run into bruisers en route—for example, Imperial Legion troopers—they may get slaughtered. And since Goblins hate other Goblins, if they run into another tribe, they're likely to fight then and there.

White Skin Goblin

The other five tribes are based at:

Barren Mine: Located east of the Lower Niben south of the Mouth of the Panther River and just south of a westward squiggle in the main north-south road. The Dust Easters are a small tribe of six Goblins of strength comparable to those in the "Goblin Trouble" Wilderness quest: two guards, a Skirmisher, a Berserker, a War Chief, and a Shaman. The tribal head is located in the innermost room of this modest-sized, one-level cave.

Skull Breaker Goblin War Chief

Derelict Mine: Located on the Gold Road just east-northeast of Skingrad. A chat about "Goblin hunting" with Ah-Malz at the Skingrad Fighters Guild will write it to your map. Unlike the single-level lairs in which Goblins typically take up residence, this is a large, three-level dungeon with 20 Sharp Tooth Goblins of strength comparable to those in the "Goblin Trouble" Wilderness quest: eight guards, seven Skirmishers, three Berserkers, a War Chief, and a Shaman. And it's involved in a *second* Goblin war—this one with the White Skin Goblins of Goblin Jim's Cave. The totem stolen from that cave is on the second level. The Sharp Tooths' own totem is on a table in a big room near the end of the third.

Goblin Jim's Cave: Located north of Skingrad. A chat about "Goblin hunting" with Fadus Calidius at the Skingrad Fighters Guild will write it to your map. Similar in structure and strength to Derelict Mine, this base for the White Skin Goblins is home to 11 guards, seven Berserkers, a Skirmisher, a War Chief—and Goblin Jim himself. (He's not a Goblin but a Breton witch!) No totem, however; it's been stolen by the Sharp Tooth Goblins of the Derelict Mine.

Skull Breaker Goblin War Chief

Plundered Mine: Located just east of the Silver Road where it begins to turn west toward Bruma. Home to the Three Feather Goblins, this two-level cave has eight guards, three berserkers, four Skirmishers, a War Chief, and a Shaman. The totem's on a crate outside a tent in the pit in the last room on the second level.

Wenderbek Cave: Located northeast of Cropsford along the upper stretch of the Corbolo River. The Skull Breaker tribe consists of five guards, a Berserker, a Skirmisher, a War Chief, and a Shaman. The totem's in the doorway to this one-level cave's big room.

GOLD MINES

You'll find silver in no fewer than 16 mines in Cyrodiil. But what about gold?

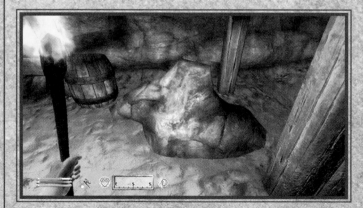

Gold nuggets are much harder to find. There are just eight gold veins in the game, and they're confined to two mines—Desolate Mine and Abandoned Mine. When you activate one of these veins, you have a 75 percent chance of extracting a nugget—the same as with silver.

Desolate Mine, with five of the veins, is a Goblin lair straight northwest of Cheydinhal. (You'll visit it in the Fighters Guild quest "The Desolate Mine.") Most of the veins are deep inside the mine. Descend to a T intersection and make a left. This puts you in a big room with two exits on its far side. Take the left-hand passage. The first two veins are in the near right corner of the first small room; down a longer, trapped stretch corridor, a single vein is in the upper left corner of the last room.

Gold Vein

Return to the first room. The right-hand passage leads to another large room. The exit in the far right corner leads down a passage (again, long and trapped) to the boss chamber, where you'll find the last two gold veins beside the niche on the right side of the room.

Abandoned Mine is a Bandit lair northeast of the northeast spur on Lake Canulus. The veins are close together on the top level. After you enter, go as far north as you can and descend a ramp to the east. Open the wooden door at the bottom. Look for the first vein in the rock wall opposite the door and the two others at the south end of the room to the southeast.

HIGHWAYMEN

You already know that traveling through the wilderness can be dangerous. Here and there, you're assaulted by wild animals, Bandits, and even undead creatures. Most of the time, they simply attack you with no preamble.

Your money or your life.
A Highwayman

But there's also a different class of baddie out there that's rarer than the others. They're formal highwaymen—all Khajiits two levels higher than your own—who surprise you along the roads and greet you with one of three differently worded demands for money.

ScreenShot: File 'Freeform21.bmp' created.
Skull Breaker Goblin War Chief

There are three possible responses, depending on your circumstances. If you have 100 gold, you can simply pay the robber. However much dosh you have, you can challenge the robber to take the money from you. Or, if you have less than 100 gold, you can plead poverty.

However, the highwayman won't believe this last claim unless you're dressed in a manner that supports your story. Your equipped armor and clothing must have a "clothing value" of less than 10. This a hidden stat, but sorting out what works here is a good deal less complicated than in the Daedric quest "Sanguine," where you have to dress for success. Suffice it to say that extremely simple clothes, or no clothes at all, will work brilliantly. The robber will leave empty-handed and you'll leave intact.

Highwayman

Four of the robbers are guaranteed to appear. One ambushes you on the Chorrol side of Fort Ash on the Black Road. Another waits at the north end of the Yellow Road bridge over the Panther River. A third waits in the middle of the long Red Ring Road bridge across the Upper Niben at the southeast corner of Lake Rumare. A fourth can be found on the Gold Road north of Anvil at the turnoff for Lord Drad's Estate.

The two others stand a 50 percent chance of putting in an appearance—one in a rocky defile on the Gold Road east of Skingrad and the other near a nameless fort-style tower on the

Red Ring Road at the northeast corner of Lake Rumare—just down the hill from Fort Chalman.

You're smarter than you look.

Bandit Highwayman

HORSES

Imperial Legion Horse

Bay Horse

You're given a Paint Horse by Prior Maborel at Weynon Priory early in the Main Quest and pick up a great Black Horse with glowing eyes (Shadowmere) from Lucien Lachance as a reward midway through the Dark Brotherhood quests. But you can also procure horses from stables outside each of Cyrodiil's cities.

If you can afford the investment—horses start at 500 gold—it's a good idea. As mentioned elsewhere, horses are a fast, durable resource that provides a nice compromise between fast-travel and soldiering through the wilderness on foot. After a while, you may even develop a fondness of them.

The purchase is a very straightforward affair. Each stable boards several types of horses but sells only one—save for the Imperial City, which has a, uh, supply problem. The price is fixed—your Mercantile skills have no effect here—and is the same for each breed game-wide. As soon as the money changes hands, you'll find your horse—now named "My [horse type] Horse"—waiting beside the ostler outside the corral.

Which one should you buy? Well, any horse is better than none at all. But if money's no object, get a black one. It has speed and combat abilities superior to the other four breeds. (The White Horse, slightly cheaper, is the hardiest in the game, with 400 hit points.)

Anvil—Horse Whisperer Stables: Clesa will sell you a White Horse for 4,000 gold.

Bravil—Bay Roan Stables: Molag Bal worshipper Isabeau Bienne will sell you a Bay Horse for 1,000 gold.

Bruma—Wildeye Stables: Petrine will sell you a Paint Horse for 500 gold.

Cheydinhal—Black Waterside Stables: Tovas Selvani will sell you a Black Horse for 5,000 gold.

Chorrol—North Country Stables: Bongond will sell you a Chestnut Horse for 2,500 gold.

Imperial City—Chestnut Handy Stables: Some horses are being boarded here, but none are for sale. Talk to stable-hands Restita Statlilia and Brielus Gawey and stable owner Snak gra-Bura to get to the bottom of it. (Gra-Bura has been…eating them.)

Leyawiin—Five Riders Stable: Cat-Face will sell you a Paint Horse for 500 gold.

Skingrad—Grateful Pass Stables: Ugak gra-Mogakh does not eat her horses, or at least doesn't say so, and can sell you a Bay Horse for 1,000 gold.

Stealing corralled horses is okay, too. The drawback is that, while your own horse will remain on station forever when you dismount, a stolen horse will eventually find its way home. And it's an expensive addition to your bounty if you get caught.

Bay Horses can be found Bravil, Imperial City, Leyawiin, and Skingrad stables, and at the Roxey Inn on the Red Ring Road at the northeast corner of Lake Rumare.

Black Horses can be found at the Cheydinhal and Imperial City stables and in a corral at Brindle Home, a small settlement west of the Imperial City in the Great Forest.

They are also used by four couriers delivering the *Black Horse Courier* newspaper. (See that section under "Reading Materials" for details.)

Chestnut Horses can be found at the Chorrol and Imperial City stables and at the Brina Cross Inn on the Gold Road west of Kvatch.

Paint Horses can be found at the Cheydinhal, Imperial City, and Leyawiin stables, near the Bruma stables, and at Brindle Home.

Paint Horse

White Horses can be found at the Imperial City and Leyawiin stables and near the Anvil stables.

Non-standard horses: Those used by the 17 Imperial Legion troopers who patrol the wilderness are a hybrid, with Bay Horse speed but White Horse hit points. These wandering guards appear at the small settlement of Aleswell, north of the Imperial City along the Red Ring Road; near the Oblivion gate outside Anvil; on the Orange Road south of Bruma, southwest of the junction with the Silver Road; on the Orange Road, roughly at the midpoint between Bruma and the junction with the Silver Road; near the Cheydinhal stables; on the Orange Road northeast of Chorrol; southeast of the Odiil farm along the Black Road; west of the Imperial City on the Black Road near the junction with the Red Ring Road; on the Red Ring Road near Fort Virtue, southwest of the Imperial City; on the Red Ring Road south of the Imperial City, near the Ayleid ruin Sardavar Leed; southeast of the Imperial City at the junction of the Red Ring and Yellow Roads; at Wellspring Cave on the east shore of Lake Rumare; near the Roxey Inn, on the Red Ring Road at the northeast corner of Lake Rumare; at the Gold Road crossroads west of the Kvatch refugee camp; near the Gottshaw Inn on the Gold Road southwest of Kvatch; just north of Leyawiin on the west side of the Lower Niben; and on the Gold Road east of Skingrad.

And in the Main Quest, Martin and Blades chief Jauffre ride horses from Weynon Priory to Cloud Ruler Temple and from Cloud Ruler Temple to the Imperial City. These are both christened "Weynon Priory Horse," and don't quite match up with any of the standard breeds.

HOUSES

You can buy a house in every Cyrodiil city. The haunted house in Anvil's northeast corner can be purchased only in the Miscellaneous quest "Where Spirits Have Lease." It's a simpler affair in the other seven cities.

Most of the time, you'll need to contact the local ruler (who doubles as a real-estate agent), raise his or her Disposition, and inquire about "Buy a house in town." (The exceptions are the Imperial City and Skingrad. See those sections for details.)

Again, the price and terms are fixed. No haggling over the price, and no pre-purchase walkthrough. (Except for Velwyn Benirus in Anvil, no one tries to put anything over on you.) You pay your money and get the key and a referral to a local shop that sells house-related amenities.

These items are listed with the shop's books. See, you're not buying individual articles of furniture but bills for fixed sets of goods. It's like dealing with an interior decorator. Depending on the size of your house, these may include packages for the balcony area (Skingrad only), bedroom area, den area (Skingrad only), dining area, dressing area, hall area, kitchen area, reading area, servant quarters (Skingrad only), sitting area, storage area, study area, suite area (Chorrol only), rack assortment, and wall hangings—with some packages specific to certain floors of your home.

The offered packages will always be appropriate to the house you've purchased, so you needn't fear buying things you don't need. Once you've bought everything your house can hold, the "quest" ends. And it'll all be in place when you return to the house—now christened "My [your community's name here] House." (Exception: Chorrol, where it is called "Arborwatch: My House.")

Surprises? A couple—both in Skingrad.

BRAVIL

The small, dingy house is on the south side of the canal below Luciana Galena's place. You'll have to raise Count Regulus Terentius's Disposition to 50 for him to discuss it. "It's not much to look at," he says, "but the smell will soon make you forget how ugly it is." Price: 4,000 gold. Furniture reference: Nilawen at The Fair Deal—the second building to the east as you make your way south from the city gate.

BRUMA

The property in Bruma is a pleasant two-story log house that's just to the north when you enter Bruma via the East Gate. You'll have to raise Countess Narina Carvain's Disposition to 60 for her to discuss it. Price: 10,000 gold. Furniture reference: Suurootan at Novaroma—between the Jerall View inn and Nord Winds, one tier down from the castle.

Countess Narina Carvain

CHEYDINHAL

For sale is a pleasant two-story house near the town statue (and next to Willow Bank) in the southwest corner of town. You'll have to raise Count Andel Indarys's Disposition to 60 for him discuss the purchase. Price: 15,000 gold. Furniture reference: Borba gra-Uzgash at Borba's Goods and Stores, located on the main drag two doors east of the West Gate.

CHORROL

The spacious stone house called Arborwatch sits next to the Mages Guild on the central rotunda. You'll have to raise Countess Arriana Valga's Disposition to 70 for her to discuss the purchase, and you'll need a Fame of 13 or higher to complete it. Price: 20,000 gold. Furniture reference: Seed-Neeus at Northern Goods and Trade, just west of the South Gate.

IMPERIAL CITY

This hole-in-the-wall is in the slums on the west side of the Waterfront District's harbor wall—just west from the pirate ship. But it *is* in the Imperial City! As there's no local ruler, visit Vinicia Melissaeia at the Office of Imperial Commerce in the Market District. Price: 2,000 gold. Furniture reference: Sergius Verus at Three Brothers Trade Goods—located in the little strip mall southeast of the Commerce office.

LEYAWIIN

Leyawiin's property is a small but serviceable house near the center of town—just north of Rosentia Gallenus's house and across the street from Weebam-Na's. You'll have to coax Count Marius Caro's Disposition up to 60 to discuss the purchase. Price: 7,000 gold. Furniture reference: Gundalas at Best Goods and Guarantees, just to the north up the street.

Eyja

SKINGRAD

The purchase of the manor house Rosethorn Hall isn't just another acquisition. It also involves a pair of mini-quests.

Skingrad's Count Janus Hassildor, a Vampire, can't help you here. Instead, speak to court steward Hal-Liurz about buying the house and you'll be referred to a Shum gro-Yarug—the count's butler. Maybe he's not around. If you've already performed the Thieves Guild quest "Lost Histories" and opted for the solution that involved getting a job in the castle, you already know the Orc's routine: He heads down to the West Weald Inn in town a little after 10 a.m. and then heads for the

Colovian Traders at noon. If you haven't finished "Lost Histories," no one will expressly tell you where he is, but just follow your compass.

Gro-Yarug isn't easily impressed. You must raise his Disposition to 70 to discuss the matter and need a Fame of 15—not to mention 25,000 gold—to close the deal. (Also a chilly heart, as the purchase evicts current tenant Vandorallen Trebatius. He'll remove to a room at the Two Sisters Lodge when you buy the place.) Gro-Tarug supplies the key and a referral to Gunder at Colovian Traders on the main drag in Skingrad.

Helping Hands

This is where things get interesting. Gunder has an assistant named Eyja. She won't have much to say until you buy furnishings for the servants' quarters. And given that you may have blown your fortune on the house, and that furnishing this place in detail requires a whole separate fortune, that could take a while.

When you do get the servants' quarters package, try her again. She's heard about your purchase and wonders if you have anyone in mind for the servant job. "For 150 gold and a roof over my head, I'm yours," she says. "Well, to help around the house, I mean."

Agree, and she'll immediately take off for your new house, settle into quarters in the cellar, and slip right into her new duties. (She has a key and so can come and go as needs be.)

You now have three new topics. If you've installed kitchen furnishings, "Food" produces a helping of Eyja's homemade shepherd's pie and "Drink" brings forth a bottle of Rosethorn mead. The pie is a marvelous multi-function ingredient—with Dispel, Fortify Agility, Cure Disease, and Shield effects—and the mead will Fortify Endurance and Strength while at the same time Drain Intelligence and Willpower.

Finally, ask about "Eyja" for an account of her grim life to date. Happily, things have recently taken a turn for the better.

The Rosethorn Cache

In the top-floor bedroom, there's a little housing around the top of the stairs. On top of that housing, against the room's west wall, is a "Long Forgotten Note."

The trick is getting to it. A high-level acrobat should have no trouble jumping up beside the housing and grabbing the note on the fly, but a less skilled jumper will need to leap from the

bed (or the adjacent dresser, if the room has been furnished) to the fireplace mantel and then quickly atop the housing.

The note kicks off a second mini-quest. It reveals that treasure is hidden in the house and mentions a riddle as being the key.

"Two bodies have I, though both joined in one. The more I stand still, the quicker I run."

The answer: an hourglass. But you can skip the riddle and just search the cellar. One of the two pillars has four clusters of garlic hanging from it. Between the pillar, the ceiling, and a diagonal support on the pillar's east side, you'll find an hourglass. Inside the hourglass are five flawless diamonds, three flawless emeralds, two flawless sapphires, and the Ring of the Gray. Stealth characters take note: the ring is the real treasure of the cache, as it will Fortify Sneak, Marksman, Security, and Acrobatics as well as Resist Poison and Detect Life!

Long Forgotten Note

HUNTING

Now and then, you'll do a bit of hunting for wildlife in quests: Mountain Lions in the Fighters Guild quest "A Rat Problem" and Wolves and Bears in the Daedric quest "Hircine."

But you can also go hunting on your own, then sell the pelts and ingredients or use them yourself. Indeed, Huurwen at the Anvil Fighters Guild and Rasheda at Fire and Steel in Chorrol suggest this as a way of making your way in the world. And Honditar, who lives outside Chorrol, offers some advice: Poison your arrows to bring down the skittish Deer more quickly.

Mountain Lion

FREEFORM QUESTS

BEAR

You must be at Level 9 to hunt Black Bear and Level 16 for Brown; look in forest regions. The "best bets" locations are listed in the "Master Trainer Quests" chapter under "Destruction Training."

West Weald Brown Bear

BOAR

For Boar, you need to be Level 7 or higher. Look in forest regions. The same "best bets" as for Bears apply.

Boar

DEER

Any level will do. The best bets for either gender—the game has both does and the hardier bucks—are the region just north of Dagny's Camp, which is northeast of Kvatch and west-northwest of Skingrad; on the east shore of Niben Bay across

from Bravil and south-southeast of the Ayleid ruin Nenalata; and just east-northeast of Leyawiin right around the Yellow Road.

MOUNTAIN LION

To hunt Mountain Lions you need to be Level 12 or higher, and you want to look in plains regions. Your best bets are in the scrubby hills just southeast of Anvil; the area around Fort Variela, midway down the west bank of the Upper Niben; and the area just northwest of the Imperial City and south of

READING MATERIAL

BLACK HORSE COURIER

Sinkhole Cave.

Have you read all the issues of this Cyrodiil newspaper?

All told, there are 19 —six issues that are available at the beginning of the game and 13 new ones that become available only after you complete certain Daedric, Dark Brotherhood, Miscellaneous, and Thieves Guild quests.

The "back issues" are used mainly to clue the player to obscure quest lines and game elements. They are "Assassination!"; "A New Guild for Fighters?"; "New 'Doomstones' Series!"; "Gray Fox, Man or Myth?"; "Gray Fox Unmasked!"; and "Night Mother Rituals!"

The new issues, more in the nature of post-quest perks, are "Prank Spoils Society Gathering!" (available after the Daedric quest "Sanguine"); "Rain of Burning Dogs!" (available after the Daedric quest "Sheogorath"); "Tragic Accident! Baenlin Dead!" (available after the Dark Brotherhood quest "Accidents Happen"); "Adamus Phillida Slain!" (available after the Dark Brotherhood quest "Permanent Retirement"); "Anvil Tarts Thwarted!" (available after the Miscellaneous quest "The Siren's Deception"); "Cheydinhal Heir Saved!" (available after the Miscellaneous quest "The Wayward Knight"); "Greatest Painter Safe" (available after the Miscellaneous quest "A Brush with Death"); "Pale Pass Discovery" (available after the Miscellaneous quest "Lifting the Vale"); "Poor Burdened by Taxes!" (available after the Thieves Guild quest "Untaxing the Poor"); "Waterfront Raid Fails!" (available after the Thieves

Guild quest "Misdirection"); "New Watch Captain Named" (available after Thieves Guild quest "Taking Care of Lex"); "Vampire Nest in the City!" (available after the Thieves Guild quest "Boots of Springheel Jak"); and "Palace Break-In?" (available after the Thieves Guild quest "The Ultimate Heist").

Where to find them? The back issues are all over the place—"Assassinations!" appears in 26 locations—but you can find all six at the *Black Horse Courier*'s office in the Market District or five of the six by talking to four couriers found in the wilderness. The couriers, all generic Breton women on

horseback, can be found:

- On the Yellow Road just north of the Ayleid ruin Arpenia. She moves to a spot just southeast of the Yellow Road bridge over the Corbolo River.

- Just outside the Chorrol stables. She heads out the Black Road to a lake just south of the road.

- Near Leyawiin's East Gate. She makes for the same spot near the Corbolo crossing as the first.

- Outside Anvil's main gate. She moves northeast to a spot near the Brina Cross Inn.

The source for the quest-related issues depends on the type of quest that inspired the issue. The seven Thieves Guild-related issues—two back issues and five new—can be obtained from four Imperial City vendors daily between 8 a.m. and 6 p.m.: Tertius Favonius near the palace gate in the Elven Gardens District; Pennus Mallius on the west side of the central rotunda in the Temple District; Vlanarus Kvinchal in the Waterfront District near the southwest end of the bridge to the mainland; and Cicero Verus in the Market District just around the corner from Red Diamond Jewelry near the Arena gate.

The four issues that deal with Miscellaneous quests are available either from pub operators or from select people in the relevant community. "A Brush with Death" and "Lifting the Vale" flow from any Imperial pub operator, "Cheydinhal Heir Saved!" from Imperial male publicans in Cheydinhal, and "Anvil Tarts Thwarted!" from Imperial men in Anvil who aren't in the Imperial Legion or the Dark Brotherhood.

The two issues that deal with the Dark Brotherhood are available at the *Courier* offices and from the four couriers in the wilderness after you complete the respective missions. The Baenlin issue is also available through male Nords and Imperials until you kill Valen Dreth in the follow-up quest "Scheduled for Execution." And the Adamus Phillida issue is available from Imperial males in the Imperial Legion until you complete the follow-up quest "The Purification."

The two issues that deal with Daedric quests are available only in the immediate or nearest community. Look for the first—a run-down on the naked dinner party at Castle Leyawiin—in the castle's servants' quarters and dungeon and in Leyawiin proper at the Three Sisters Inn and Five Claws Lodge. The latter, covering the Sheogorath's shower of German shepherds in Border Watch, appears only in Bravil at the Fighters and Mages Guilds, the Lonely Suitor Lodge, and Silverhome-on-the-Water.

BACK PAGES

In addition, you can perform a pair of undocumented mini-adventures off information in back issues of the *Courier*.

One comes from "Gray Fox Unmasked!" This is a light-hearted story about the various confession(s) that were elicited from Vlanarus Kvinchal by the Imperial Watch in an aftermath of Kvinchal's skooma overdose.

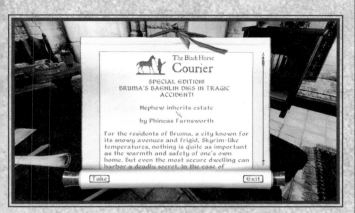

Vlanarus lives with his brother Kastav and sister Bronsila in a shack in the Waterfront District slums and works as a *Courier* vendor in the district. Talk to him. He won't seem insane at all. But you've stumbled on a triangle of hatred. Ask about "Imperial City" and Vlanarus complains bitterly about his good-for-nothing brother Kastav.

Kastav works at the western Imperial Trading Company Warehouse on the waterfront. He may express equal disdain for his "witch of a sister," Bronsila. (Note that this comment may appear randomly.)

And Bronsila, who works at the eastern warehouse, may say she is "so sick of Vlanarus, I could scream." Nothing comes of it all, but it's kind of funny!

The other mini-quest comes out of "Night Mother Rituals!"—a report on the rise in the performance of the dark ritual used to summon the Dark Brotherhood assassins guild.

The paper reports that one Claudius Arcadia, formerly of Talos Plaza, is now a guest of the state on precisely this charge. Sure enough, if you speak to the Imperial Prison jailor and ask to visit a prisoner, you can speak to Arcadia. He freely admits praying to the Night Mother. But he doesn't say who he wanted dead. Can you find out?

You can. It's slightly tricky. The info's in Arcadia's locked house, just south of the West Gate. The Imperial Legion has taken over the place and has a guard stationed there around the clock.

Assassination!

You can pickpocket the house key from Legion commander Adamus Phillida (not easy; he has a Sneak skill of 40) or kill him in the Dark Brotherhood quest "Permanent Retirement" and simply take it. Or you can wait until the guard goes to bed (a little after midnight) and then pick the four-tumbler lock on the front door and the one- to- five-tumbler one on the upstairs door.

Arcadia's journal is in a chest just opposite the door on the north side of the upstairs room. His intended victim: Rufio. (Check out the cellar for evidence of Arcadia's preparations for the ritual.) However, you can't sort out why Arcadia wants Rufio dead or warn Rufio that he's in danger.

In fact, *you're* the danger. Rufio will be your first victim (in the quest "A Knife in the Dark") if you join the Dark Brotherhood, and you'll use his enraged spirit to help you clear out the guild's Cheydinhal sanctuary in "The Purification."

Books

Excluding books referenced in quests and quest lines, volumes new to Oblivion include:

Guide to Cheydinhal

Advances in Lockpicking: A Security skill book found on the top level of Fingerbowl Cave (a Necromancer/undead lair just northeast of Aleswell north of the Imperial City) and Mach-Na's Books in Cheydinhal.

Ahzirr Traajijazeri: A Hand-to-Hand skill book found in two training rooms—one below J'Ghasta's house in Bruma and the other in the Dark Brotherhood Sanctuary in Cheydinhal.

The Amulet of Kings: The background on the singular artifact Uriel Septim VII gives you at the beginning of the game. You'll find this common book in chapels, castles, Mages Guilds, and the odd private home, but it's easiest to find in the library of the Chorrol guild and at First Edition in the Imperial City.

The Argonian Account, Books 1–4: Volumes 1 and 3 in this set are skill books (Athletics and Illusion). The first one appears only in loot and the other only at the Arcane University's Mystic Archives. Volumes 2 and 4 are far more common. You'll come across the latter in every city chapel, and the former is especially popular in Chorrol, where you'll find multiple copies at the Mages Guild, The Oak and Crosier inn, and Renoit's Books.

Battle of Sancre Tor: A Blade skill book found in a display case in Castle Bravil's Great Hall—the lock has four or five tumblers—or in loot.

Before the Ages of Man: A Mysticism skill book found on an enchanting station in the Arcane University's Chironasium.

Beggar: This Athletics skill book, the first volume in a four-book series, can be found in the Great Hall of Cloud Ruler Temple.

Beggar Prince: Standard (i.e., non-skill) book with information especially useful to a Thieves Guild member. Available from book vendors and in loot. You'll find numerous copies in the Arcane University's Mystic Archives, the libraries of the Chorrol and Skingrad Mages Guilds, and at the First Edition bookstore in the Imperial City's Market District.

The Black Arts on Trial: This Mysticism skill book can be found at the Mystic Emporium in the Imperial City's Market District.

Calcinator Treatise: An Alchemy skill book that can be found in leveled loot and in the Miscellaneous quest "Two Sides of the Coin."

Daughter of the Niben: An Alteration skill book found on a shelf in the living quarters for the Skingrad Mages Guild.

De Rerum Dirennis: An Alchemy skill book found on a shelf at All Things Alchemical in Skingrad.

The Doors of Oblivion: This Conjuration skill book can be found in the Anvil Mages Guild's library, on a table in the Great Hall of Cloud Ruler Temple, and on another in the tower above Fort Caractacus on the north side of Lake Rumare.

Dwemer History and Culture: This standard (but rare) book is the first chapter in a history of Dwarven histories—penned by Hasphat Antabolis, an old buddy from Morrowind. It turns up at book vendors; in loot; in Anvil's royal quarters; in Cheydinhal at the guard barracks and Oghash gra-Magul's house; the Chorrol Mages Guild's living quarters; Cloud Ruler Temple's library; in the Arcane University in the Arch-Mage's and mages quarters and the Mystic Archives; at First Edition in the Imperial City's Market District; in the palace library; on a bookshelf in Ahdarji's house in Leyawiin; and in the Temple of the Emperor Zero near Bravil.

The Exodus: This Restoration skill book can be found on a shelf in the dining room in the hall of Skingrad's Great Chapel of Julianos.

Father of the Niben: This Marksman skill book appears on a shelf in the north wing of Bravil Castle's private quarters.

Fighters Guild History, 1st ed. (a.k.a. **History of the Fighters Guild**): This Heavy Armor skill book can be found in a locked (four- or five-tumbler) display case in the Chorrol Fighters Guild, a three-tumbler case in the offices of the Anvil guild, and an unlocked case in the Arcane University's Mystic Archives.

Fire and Darkness: This Blade skill book can be found in a chest in the Imperial City sewers during the Thieves Guild quest "The Ultimate Heist."

Fundamentals of Alchemy: Basic alchemy textbook with useful info for beginners. A staple in Mages Guilds Cyrodiil-wide.

Glories and Laments: This rare book about a visit to Ceyatatar may be your introduction to Ayleid civilization. You'll find copies in the Great Hall of Cloud Ruler Temple, in the Imperial City homes of Ayleid experts Umbacano (Talos Plaza) and Herminia Cinna (Elven Gardens), and at

Rindir's Staffs in the Market District.

Gods and Worship: Common book on the influence of gods (or just god-like entities) on mortal life in Tamriel. Most readily found at First Edition in the Imperial City, Mach-Na's Books in Cheydinhal, Renoit's Books in Chorrol, and the Skingrad Mages Guild.

Phintias

Guide to [city]: You know all about Cyrodiil's cities. But read these eight guides anyway—if only for entertainment value. They're all written by Alessia Ottus (who lives with her husband, Hastrel, in the Imperial City's Temple District). She's a devout follower of the Nine Divines…and an evident racist who sees sin and iniquity everywhere—especially among people she doesn't like. (Bravil is "the dark grate of the sewer drain, where foul and appetizing debris collects.") The books are all over the place. If you can't find them, you're not playing *Oblivion*.

Heavy Armor Repair: This Armorer skill book is found only in Marauder and tomb loot.

Hiding with the Shadow: Though somewhat inaccurate—it asserts there is no Thieves Guild—this book at least clues you to the existence (though not the location) of a Nocturnal shrine and provides an early peek at the tale of the Gray Fox's age-old theft of Nocturnal's cowl. You'll find a copy in the outer portion of the Lake Arrius Caverns.

History of Lock Picking: Nice run-down on this science. Available most readily at First Edition—or, if you already have a talent for lockpicking, beside a crate in the small cellar of Astinia Atius's house in Talos Plaza.

Immortal Blood: This Hand-to-Hand skill book—a spooky tale of vampirism—can be found on shelves in the cellar of Seridur's house in the Imperial City's Temple District, in J'Ghasta's house in Bruma, and just inside a small tent at the Bandit camp outside the Ayleid ruin Vilverin—across the water from the exit from the Imperial Prison sewers.

King: This Blunt skill book, the final volume of the four-book series that begins with ***Beggar***, can be found on a shelf in Castle Anvil's royal quarters.

The Last King of the Ayleids: Nice account of the late Ayleid empire. Not required reading for the Miscellaneous quest "Secrets of the Ayleids," though it confirms what you'll learn from quest-giver Umbacano. Nine copies exist,

but one's on the fourth level of the Ayleid ruin Atatar, and most of the others are either well locked-up or inaccessible until you've made progress in one or another quest line. However, you can find a copy at First Edition in the Imperial City's Market District or pickpocket the copy carried by Orintur, who can be found at the Cheydinhal Mages Guild or Willow Bank.

Bugak gro-Bol

Legend of Krately House: This Sneak skill book, a scary stage play, can be found in the library at Cloud Ruler Temple.

The Legendary Sancre Tor: This Blunt skill book can be found on a shelf in Vilena Donton's quarters in her Chorrol home.

Light Armor Repair: The Armorer skill book can be found on a shelf in the Castle Bravil barracks.

Liminal Bridges: This Conjuration skill book is in a display case on the second floor of the Arcane University's Mystic Archives.

Mace Etiquette: This Blunt skill book can be found in loot.

The Lusty Argonian Maid

Magic from the Sky: Useful treatise on the Ayleid's celebrated magic. Copies can be found in the Anvil and Leyawiin Mages Guilds; the Great Hall of Bruma Castle; the Arcane University's Mystic Archives; Ra'jhan's house in the Elven Gardens section of the Imperial City; Alval Uvani's house in Leyawiin; and the Ayleid ruins Atatar and Vahtacen.

Mannimarco, King of Worms: This Alchemy skill book, an epic poem, can be found in the Arcane University's Mystic Archives.

Ceramic Urn

Manual of Armor: Common volume on armor basics. Found most readily at Slash 'N Smash in the Imperial City's Market District, Alval Uvani's house in Leyawiin, and the Mystic Archives at the Arcane University.

Manual of Arms: Common volume on the rules of weaponry. Useful for a beginning player. Found in quantity at First Edition in the Imperial City's Market District, the Arcane University's Mystic Archives, and The Archer Paradox in Bravil.

Manual of Spellcraft: There are two books by this name. One you'll steal in the Mages Guild quest "Bruma Recommendation." The other, minus the marginalia, can be found in vast numbers elsewhere in the game—the most readily accessible being the Chorrol Mages Guild's library.

More than Mortal: Volume 10 in Marobar Sul's Ancient Tales of the Dwemer series consists of a tale about an enterprising thief called "The Dowry." Pick it up at the Arcane University in the Arch-Mage's quarters and the Chironasium; at Ruslan's house in the Imperial City's Temple District; in the library of the Leyawiin Mages Guild, and in Newheim the Portly's house in Anvil.

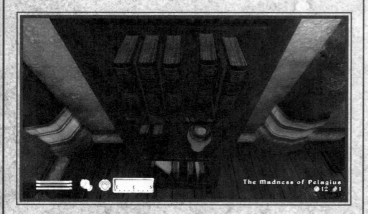

The Madness of Pelagius

Mysticism: A rare book that seeks to explain this most amorphous of the magical disciplines. Glarthir's house in Skingrad contains four of the 14 copies, and there are two more at the Chorrol Mages Guild.

Proper Lock Design: This Security skill book lies on a desk on the second floor of Dareloth's house in the Imperial City's Waterfront district. (You'll have to complete the Thieves Guild quest line for access to this structure.)

Purloined Shadows: This Sneak skill book can be found only in loot.

Reality and Other Falsehoods: This Alteration skill book sits on a shelf on the second floor of Southern Books in Leyawiin.

Brief History of the Empire, v 3

The Red Kitchen Reader: This Athletics skill book is on a desk in Baeralorn's bedroom in the private quarters of Castle Anvil.

The Refugees: This Light Armor skill book appears in Cloud Ruler Temple's Great Hall and at First Edition in the Imperial City's Market District.

Remanada: A fragment, found in the Cloud Ruler Temple library, that lays out the birth of the legendary Reman. (His father was King Hrol, his mother a "mound of mud.")

Report: Disaster at Ionith: Fascinating account of Uriel V's failed invasion of the continent of Akavir. Found predominantly in Fighters Guilds.

Response to Bero's Speech: Look for this Destruction skill book in the Arcane University's Mystic Archives.

Rislav the Righteous: This Light Armor skill book can be found only in Bandit and Vampire loot.

Sacred Witness: This Sneak skill book is in the antechamber complex through which you'll make your escape from the Lake Arrius Caverns in the "Dagon Shrine" segment of the Main Quest.

Song of Hrormir: This Blade skill book (an epic poem) can be found in Drels Theran's room in the east wing of Castle Bravil's private quarters and in the chest of the two would-be gladiators who practice on the Arena grounds.

Souls, Black and White: This Mysticism skill book lies on a bier in the northwest corner of the second level of Fort Cuptor and also appears in loot.

Ten Commands: Nine Divines: Basically, advice on how to stay on the good side of the empire's "official" gods. Lots of copies are floating around—in greatest profusion at the Mages Guilds (notably the Chorrol guild's library), the Arcane University's Mystic Archives, the Cloud Ruler Temple library, and the First Edition (Market District) and Southern Books (Leyawiin) shops.

Thief: This Acrobatics skill book, the second volume in the series that begins with Beggar, can be found in S'krivva's house in Bravil.

Thief of Virtue: This little tale—about a thief who left his mark's home with more than he'd bargained for—shows up in shops (notably, Mach-Na's Books in Cheydinhal), the Arcane University's Mystic Archives, loot, private homes, and a range of dungeons.

Trials of St. Alessia: The source of the apocalyptic verse about the failure of the Dragonfires, this standard tome can be found in greatest quantity in the library for the Chorrol Mages Guild, the First Edition bookstore in the Imperial City's Market District, and in Cyrodiil's chapels.

Varieties of Daedra: Nifty book by one of the dissident priests of Morrowind that explains what is understood of the workings of the Daedric world. It can be found in bookstores (including Renoit's in Chorrol and Southern Books in Leyawiin); in Mages Guilds (in Anvil, Brail, Bruma, and Leyawiin) and Fighters Guilds (in Bravil and Leyawiin); Cloud Ruler Temple's library; the Mystic Archives at the Arcane University; and a number of private homes, including Vilena Donton's house in Chorrol, Fathis Ules's place in the Imperial City's Elven Gardens District, Umbacano Manor in Talos Plaza, and Summitmist Manor in Skingrad.

The Warp in the West: This Block skill book on the Tamrielic equivalent of a nuclear event can be obtained from Brother Piner at Weynon Priory or found either in the Great Hall at Cloud Ruler Temple or in loot.

Warrior: This Block skill book—the third volume in the four-book set that starts with ***Beggar***—sits on a shelf in the royal bedroom at Castle Leyawiin.

Way of the Exposed Palm: This Hand-to-Hand skill book hides under a mushroom on the south side of the bottom level of Fieldhouse Cave.

OTHER SKILL BOOKS

Here's a list of skill books that have been imported from Morrowind:

The full 12-volume *2920* series: Nine of these titles—all but Volumes 3, 11, and 12—are skill books.

Volume 1, *Morningstar*, is a Blade skill book found on a shelf in Uleve Hlervu's room in the private quarters of

Castle Anvil and Tsavi's room in the private quarters of Castle Leyawiin. (It's also the reward in the Fighters Guild quest "The Wandering Scholar.")

Guide to Cheydinhal

Volume 2, *Sun's Dawn*, is a Mysticism skill book sitting on a desk in the Chapel Hall of Skingrad's Great Chapel of Julianos. Volume 4, *Rain's Hand*, is a Restoration skill book lying on a shelf in the Great Hall of Bravil's Great Chapel of Mara. Volume 5, *Second Seed*, is a Speechcraft skill book found on a bookshelf in Chancellor Ocato's quarters in the Imperial Palace.

Volume 6, *MidYear*, is a Heavy Armor skill book that is on a shelf at Fire and Steel in Chorrol. Volume 7, *Sun's Height*, is a Mercantile skill book sitting atop a desk at the *Black Horse Courier* offices in the Imperial City's Market District. Volume 8, *Last Seed*, is a Sneak skill book found atop a dresser in City-Swimmer's house in Bravil.

Volumes 9 and 10 are both Conjuration skill books. Volume 9, *Hearthfire*, is in the chapel of Bruma's Great Chapel of Talos, and Volume 10, *Frostfall*, is on a desk in the chapel hall of Anvil's Chapel of Dibella.

The full seven-volume *A Dance in Fire* series: All seven are skill books. Volumes 1 and 4, both devoted to Acrobatics, are found atop a dresser in Ganredhel's house in Cheydinhal and on a hall table in the Great Hall of Castle Kvatch. Volume 2, a Block skill book, is on a table on the ground floor of the Guard House in the northeast section of the Imperial City's Elven Gardens District.

Volume 3, an Athletics skill book, sits on a bookshelf on the top floor of Uuras the Shepherd's house in the southwest corner of Skingrad. Volume 5, a Marksman skill book, is on a writing table beside the fireplace in Regner's house in Bruma. And Volumes 6 and 7, both Mercantile skill books, can be found, respectively, on a shelf on the second floor of Casta Scribonia's house in Chorrol and either received as the reward in the Miscellaneous quest "Two Sides of the Coin" or found in boss-level Vampire and Bandit loot.

The Armorer's Challenge: Look for this Armorer skill book atop a shelf on the second floor of the Cheydinhal Fighters Guild, or purchase it from First Edition in the Imperial City's Market District. (You must read the book to get Gin-

Wulm to train you in the Master Trainer quest "Armorer Training.")

The Art of War Magic: This Destruction skill book lies on a shelf on the upper level of Leafrot Cave—northeast of the northeasternmost headwaters of the Panther River.

Before the Ages of the Man: This Mysticism skill book is in the Enchanting Center on the ground floor of the Arcane University's Chironasium.

Biography of the Wolf Queen: A Speechcraft skill book, this volume is found in a chest in Armand Christophe's house in the Waterfront District and is received as the reward in the Miscellaneous quest "Caught in the Hunt."

The Black Arrow: This is a two-volume set. The first volume, an Acrobatics skill book, is in a chest at the foot of a bed in Torbal the Sufficient's house at Brindle Home—a small settlement in the Great Forest well north of Skingrad. The second one, devoted to the Marksman discipline, can be found in Teinaava's chest in the Dark Brotherhood's Cheydinhal Sanctuary (under the Abandoned House) or in boss-level Vampire and Bandit loot, or received as a reward in the Miscellaneous quest "Two Sides of the Coin."

The Buying Game: This Mercantile skill book sits a low shelf on the second floor of Fathis Ules's house in the Imperial City's Elven Gardens District.

Cherim's Heart of Anequina: This Armorer skill book is on a desk on the second floor of the First Edition bookstore in the Imperial City's Market District.

Chimarvamidium: This Heavy Armor skill book can be found on a shelf in the barracks at the Imperial Legion Compound in the Imperial City.

Death Blow of Abernanit: A Block skill book, this volume lies in a chest atop a dresser in a bedroom off the dining hall in the Anvil Fighters Guild.

The Dragon Break: The Alteration skill book is on a shelf below a hall table on the second floor of Dovyn Aren's house in the Imperial City's Elven Garden District.

The Firsthold Revolt: Find this Mysticism skill book in a bookshelf in the cellar of the Cheydinhal Mages Guild.

The Gold Ribbon of Merit: A Marksman skill book, this tome is in a chest in the training room of the Dark Brotherhood's Cheydinhal Sanctuary.

Hallgerd's Tale: The Heavy Armor skill book is in a chest on the top level of the Chorrol Fighters Guild's tower.

The Horrors of Castle Xyr: It's a Destruction skill book and it's in a bookshelf on the top floor of the Bravil Mages Guild.

How Orsinium Passed to Orcs: The Heavy Armor skill book's on a desk at the center of the Lord's Manor in Castle Bruma.

Ice and Chitin: A Light Armor skill book, this volume lies in a chest at the foot of a bed on the second floor of the west wing of Ahdarji's house in Leyawiin.

The Importance of Where: This Blunt skill book's on a table in the first room of Castle Bravil's dungeon.

Incident in Neocrom: The Illusion skill book lies atop a dresser on the second floor of Willow Bank in Cheydinhal.

Last Scabbard of Akrash: An Armorer skill book, this volume can be found on a shelf on the second floor of A Fighting Chance in the Imperial City's Market District.

The Locked Room: The Security skill book appears in a chest in the Smuggler's Cave below Castle Anvil.

Lord Jornibret's Last Dance: Devoted to the Light Armor discipline, this one's found only on a table in Bleak Flats Cave—north-northwest of Skingrad.

The Lunar Lorkhan: The Alteration skill book can be found behind an overturned table at the starting location in Henantier's Dreamworld during the Miscellaneous quest "Through a Nightmare, Darkly"; is received as a reward in the Miscellaneous quest "Two Sides of the Coin"; and appears in boss-level Conjurer and Necromancer loot.

Master Zoaraym's Tale: The Hand-to-Hand skill book can be received as a reward in the Miscellaneous quest "Two Sides of the Coin" or the Settlement quest "Bear Season" and found in boss-level tomb creature and Marauder loot.

The Mirror: You'll find the Block skill book on a shelf in a storage room on the ground floor of the Leyawiin City Watch barracks.

The five-volume ***Mystery of Talara*** series: Only the first four are skill books. They're found largely in loot. Volumes

2, 3, and 4—Restoration, Destruction, and Illusion skill books—are in Jorundr's chest in the Miscellaneous quest "Two Sides of the Coin" and in boss-level Necromancer and Conjurer loot. (In addition, Volume 4 appears under a table in the tower above Fort Caractacus, which is on the north shore of Lake Rumare.) Volume 1, an Acrobatics book, also appears in "Two Sides" loot and in boss-level Bandit and Vampire loot.

Night Falls of Sentinel: The Blunt skill book is found only on a shelf on the top level of Goblin Jim's Cave north of Skingrad.

Notes of Racial Phylogeny: A Restoration book, this one's in an unlocked chest in the Chapel Hall of Chorrol's Chapel of Stendarr.

Palla: A two-volume set, but only Volume 1's a skill book. Specifically, it's an Illusion book, and it's found only on an end table in the final level ("Dearth Quarters") in Arkved's Tower, which is south of Lake Poppad.

The Ransom of Zarek: An Athletics skill book, it's in a cupboard against the outer wall of the Arena Bloodworks.

The Rear Guard: The Light Armor skill book's in a chest in the training room of the Dark Brotherhood's Cheydinhal Sanctuary—below the Abandoned House near the Great Chapel of Arkay.

Sithis: You'll find this Alteration skill book on a desk in the Chapel Hall of Leyawiin's Great Chapel of Zenithar.

Song of the Alchemists: Naturally, it's an Alchemy skill book, and, naturally, it's in the Arcane University's Lustratorium (a.k.a. the Alchemy Headquarters). It's in a bookshelf at the rear of the ground floor.

Surfeit of Thieves: This Security skill book appears in "Two Sides of the Coin" loot (Miscellaneous quest) and in boss-level Bandit and Vampire loot.

Vernaccus and Bourlor: The Marksman skill book is on the ground floor of Renoit's Books in Chorrol. (In a bookshelf, where all good books should be.)

The Warrior's Charge: Check Jorundr's chest in the Miscellaneous quest "Two Sides of the Coin" and in boss-level Necromancer and Conjurer loot for this Conjuration skill book.

Withershins: A Restoration skill book, it's found only in a corner bookshelf in the library of the Leyawiin Mages Guild.

The Wolf Queen series: Seven volumes of this eight-volume set (all save Volume 8) are skill books. Volume 1, a Security book, is on a shelf in Dro'Shanji's house in Bravil. The second volume, devoted to the Hand-to-Hand skill, is on a shelf in the Lord's Manor in Castle Skingrad. The third, an Illusion book, is on a desk in the basement of the Bruma Mages Guild. The fourth, a Mercantile book, is on the counter at the Office of Imperial Commerce in the Imperial City's Market District. Volumes 5 and 7, both Speechcraft books, are found on an end table on the ground floor of Hastrel Ottus's house in the Imperial City's Temple District and a bookshelf in the lord's quarters in Castle Cheydinhal. And, finally, Volume 7, a Sneak skill book, is in a bookshelf in the Dark Brotherhood's Cheydinhal Sanctuary.

Words and Philosophy: The Blade skill book's on a shelf in Modryn Oreyn's house in the southwest corner of Chorrol.

ROMANCE

A couple of folks in Cyrodiil play around on their spouses. You can play private detective and root out the infidelities, but you can't bring them to the attention of the wounded parties.

Elisa Pierrane

At a Disposition of 60, Roderic Pierrane (one of the gamblers from the Arena) will concede that he sees a lot of Irene Metrick and claims they're just good friends. But he asks you not to tell his wife, Elisa, as "she wouldn't understand."

No, she wouldn't. In fact, Pierrane and Metrick are *very* good friends. If you are persistent in your surveillance of Pierrane, who lives in the southeast quadrant of the Imperial City's Elven Gardens District, you'll discover that he sleeps with Metrick at her home in the district's southwest quadrant on Sundays from midnight to 4 a.m.

Elisa Pierrane

The only hint you'll get that something might be amiss with Heinrich Oaken-Hull and his little Bosmer wife is the general skepticism in Anvil about the efficacy of a human/Bosmer marriage. The lady, Hasathil, acknowledges the difficulties of her husband being "at sea nine months out of ten. But Anvil's a friendly town, and the Nine console me."

She is also "consoled" by Enilroth, who works at Morvayn's Peacemakers. Follow either one and you'll discover that the two Bosmers meet daily from 4 p.m. to 8 p.m. in the stable outside Anvil. If this isn't suspicious enough, a search of Oaken-Hull's house will turn up a love letter—behind the small table around the corner to the left as you enter the second floor.

...AND NOT QUITE ROMANCE

Mirabelle Monet

Have you met Mirabelle Monet? Elves, Orcs, and Nords in Anvil speak very highly of her, albeit with a nudge and a wink.

This medium Sneak trainer runs The Fo'c'sle (a rather contorted abbreviation of "forecastle")—an Anvil boarding house for sailors. She has nothing to offer you in the way of accommodations. "I reserve my beds for seamen," she says.

So we gathered. From midnight to 6 a.m., she ritually sleeps with her five lodgers. She exhibits a slight preference for the demented Wood Elf, Thurindil.

To the best of our knowledge, you can't get in on this action. Would you really want to?

Mirabelle Monet

TOO MUCH FIDELITY

At the edge of a pond just west of Fort Nikel (itself west of the Imperial City near the Red Ring Road), you'll see what appears at a distance to be the floating body of a headless Zombie.

Nath Dyer

Get closer and you'll see this Zombie has a name: Nath Dyer. On his body are three primrose leaves and a love letter—a unique variation on a love letter you'll find at other locations in the game. Dyer conceived a passion for a woman (whose name is not revealed anywhere), asked permission to court her, and used the primrose as one might use a rose in the real world to call attention to oneself in a crowded room. We're guessing he was unsuccessful.

Note that there are 25 copies of four other love letters floating around in the game. Most of them are used simply for color. (The exception is the one in Oaken-Hull's house.)

The game is fairly overflowing with semi- and wholly meaningless paper, ranging from handbills to shopping lists to business correspondence to directions and instructions.

RUNESTONES

Doomstones aren't the only standing stones in the wilderness. Alongside them are three varieties of Runestones —similar in their rough appearance to the Doomstones but for the green runic script that appears down the side of most.

The 24 Runestones are arranged in three types: Hestra, Reman, and Sidri-Ashak (all legendary rulers in Cyrodiil's past). These are distinguished from each other by the types of "bound" weapons and armor they provide when activated.

A bound item is a Daedric entity, summoned from Oblivion, that is doing service as an object. Once equipped, a bound item cannot be unequipped until the binding spell runs out. Which, in this case, means five minutes in real time.

The Hestra stones set you up with gauntlets and either a dagger or mace—depending upon whether your Blunt or Blade skill is higher. (A tie goes to the mace.) The Remans get you a cuirass and a longsword or axe, and the Sidri-Ashak ones provide a helmet and bow.

The 10 Hestra Runestones are located:

- Southeast of Bruma just east of the junction of the Orange and Silver Roads.

- A short distance to the north of that stone, just south of the point where the Silver Road turns west toward Bruma.

- Just northwest of Bruma itself.

- Northwest of Cheydinhal, southwest of the Lake Arrius Caverns.

- South-southeast of Cheydinhal and east-northeast of nearby Lake Poppad.

- Well south of Cheydinhal on the west bank of the Reed River—just north of the spot where it flows into the Corbolo.

- About halfway between Cheydinhal and Bruma, just east of Silvertooth Cave.

- On the Red Ring Road northeast of the Imperial City, just north of Fort Chalman.

- Above the north shore of Lake Rumare, between Fort Caractacus and Fort Empire.

- At the center of the large peninsula on the northwest corner of the large central island in Lake Rumare.

The nine Reman Runestones are:

- East of Kvatch and southwest of Fort Istirus, just above the Strid River.

- Just off the Gold Road east of Kvatch and southeast of the Ra'sava Camp.

- West of the Imperial City, southeast of Breakneck Cave.

- Northwest of Skingrad, southwest of Bleak Flats Cave.

- Well north-northeast of Kvatch, between the Ayleid ruins Talwinque (to the southeast) and Varondo (to the northwest).

- Just northwest of Kvatch.

- East of the north-south portion of the Silverfish River between the Ayleid ruin Ondo to the southwest and Arrowshaft Cavern to the northeast.

- South of the Yellow Road bridge across the Panther River—just northwest of the road after it turns southwest to detour around some hills.

- Just northeast of Leyawiin, between the Yellow Road and the Amelion Tomb.

The five Sidri-Ashak Runestones are:

- Just north of the Main Quest dungeon Sancre Tor.

- On the Orange Road southwest of Bruma, southeast of Underpall Cave.

- Northwest of Anvil.

- Just north of Azura's shrine in the Jerall Mountains.

- On the south shore of Lake Rumare, just off the Red Ring Road, across the lake to the southwest from Fatback Cave.

SIGIL STONES

As you venture into the Oblivion realms in the Main Quest and certain Miscellaneous quests ("The Wayward Knight" and "Attack on Fort Sutch") or to close random gates in the wilderness, you'll build up a library of Sigil Stones. Perhaps you've already tried out a few. Well, there are a lot more of them than is immediately apparent, and they have a lot of effects that can get up your enemy's nose and smooth your own path.

When you activate the stone at the top of a Daedric Citadel, you take it and keep it. (The one exception is the Great Sigil Stone in the Main Quest mission "Great Gate," which you have to supply to Martin on your return. You're compensated when the siege crawler blows up on the battlefield outside Bruma and a Sigil Stone drops from its front end.) When selected in your inventory, that stone can then be used to enchant an unenchanted item without the benefit of an enchanting station.

There are 150 types of Sigil Stones—30 varieties, with five levels of magical power within each. The variety of stone you'll receive in a given tower is chosen at random. Indeed, you could theoretically receive the same stone again and again, though each does have a fixed number of maximum uses. (The lowest is 18 and the highest 80, but given the wealth of possibilities, you're unlikely to bump up against any of these limits before the next *Elder Scrolls* game appears.)

Each stone carries a pair of mutually exclusive enchantments—one that affects an enemy or its abilities and another that acts directly on your own character. If you select a weapon, you'll be offered only the anti-enemy enchantment. It takes effect on a strike by that weapon. If you select clothing or armor, you'll be offered only the constant-effect character enchantment.

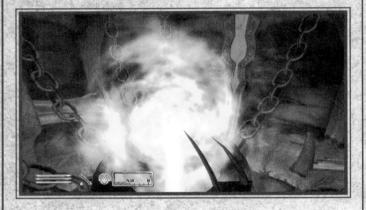

Once you complete the enchantment, the stone vanishes.

The power of those enchantments is adjusted to your character's current level. Hence, at Levels 1–4, you'll always get a Descendant Sigil Stone (the weakest); at Levels 5–8 a Subjacent stone; at Levels 9–12 a Latent stone; at Levels 13–15 an Ascendant stone; and at Levels 17 and up a Transcendent stone (the strongest).

SIGIL STONE ENCHANTMENTS

Enemy Effect	Character Effect
Absorb Agility	Fortify Agility
Absorb Endurance	Resist Disease
Absorb Fatigue	Fortify Fatigue
Absorb Health	Fortify Health
Absorb Intelligence	Fortify Intelligence
Absorb Magicka	Fortify Magicka
Absorb Speed	Fortify Speed
Absorb Strength	Fortify Strength
Burden	Feather
Damage Fatigue	Fortify Fatigue
Damage Health	Fortify Health
Damage Magicka	Fortify Magicka
Demoralize	Fortify Willpower
Disintegrate Armor	Shield
Dispel	Spell Absorption
Disintegrate Weapon	Fortify Blade skill
Disintegrate Weapon	Fortify Blunt skill
Fire Damage	Fire Shield
Fire Damage	Light
Fire Damage	Resist Fire
Frost Damage	Frost Shield
Frost Damage	Resist Frost
Frost Damage	Water Walking
Shock Damage	Night-Eye
Shock Damage	Resist Shock
Shock Damage	Shock Shield
Silence	Chameleon
Silence	Resist Magic
Soul Trap	Resist Magic
Turn Undead	Detect Life

TRAINING BY WATCHING

In a couple of spots, you can raise your skills free of charge by simply watching NPCs practicing combat.

One is a small pavilion north of the Arena, where would-be gladiators Branwen and Saliith practice hand-to-hand combat from 6 a.m. to 1 a.m. Get up close to the fighters for a minute or so. You'll soon get a message that you've picked up some tips and that your Hand-to-Hand skill has risen by 5 points.

The other location is the plaza outside Cloud Ruler Temple. Here the fighters are the Blades Pelagius and Fortis, the hours 5 a.m. to 8 p.m., and the skills gained Blade and Block (2 points in each case).

UNDERWATER

CHESTS

A number of chests lie hidden under the sea and in ponds. The most notable are located:

- Just south of the grate in Cheydinhal's south wall. This will contain gold, with a small chance of jewelry and a sizable chance of some clutter.

- In the middle of Niben Bay southeast of Bravil, you'll find a pair of chests near the entrance to the Wizard's Grotto (which you'll visit in the Thieves Guild quest "Arrow of Extrication"). Each contains gold, with a 15 percent chance of a lockpick and 10 percent chances of silver nuggets, a repair hammer, arrows, stealth-related potions, and a scroll.

The following are identical in contents to the most of those out in the surface wilderness. (See the "Wilderness Caches" section.) You'll find them:

- Just off the Anvil docks from the spot where Astia Inventius is painting.

- Two in a small lake in the great West Weald wilderness between Fort Black Boot and the Ayleid ruin Nornalhorst.

- In the southeastern headwaters of the White River.

- Below the dock on the small lake near the end of the Black Road west of Chorrol.

- Beside the central rock in a small pond north of Skingrad.

- Off the Gold Coast west of the Ayleid ruin Beldaburo.

- At the bottom of a waterfall southwest of the Ayleid ruin Ondo on the north-south stretch of the Silverfish River.

- Beside the dock southwest of Black Dog Camp on the Panther River.

- Near the southern tip of the southernmost headwaters of the Panther.

- At the east end of a small pond northeast of Walker Camp north-northeast of Cheydinhal.

- At the southeastern tip of a swamp southeast of Fort Doublecross, northeast of Cheydinhal at the west edge of a great swamp.

- In a swampy region east-southeast of Nocturnal's shrine—north-northeast of Leyawiin on the Yellow Road—and just northwest of a wayshrine to Mara.

- Below the Green Road bridge across a nameless inlet off the Lower Niben southeast of Bravil.

- On the bottom of Topal Bay, southeast of Tidewater Cave.

- Where Topal Bay meets the Lower Niben.

- On the north side of Lake Poppad.

- Beside a dock on the east shore of Lake Rumare northwest of the Wawnet Inn.

- Underwater beside a large rock in a swamp southeast of Fieldhouse Cave.

- Below a small dock on the north side of the headwaters of the Corbolo River.

- Underwater just east of a triangular island in the Lower Niben—southeast of Reedstand Cave and north-northeast of Fort Redman.

- At the bottom of a pond east of Shadow's Rest Cavern, with another below a waterfall to the north.

- West-northwest of Chorrol in the Colovian Highlands, at the bottom of a pond north of one of the inactive wayshrines.

CLAM DIVING

As in Morrowind, you can go clam diving. More than 300 clams dot the game world, and in each there's a 75 percent chance of finding a pearl.

Where? They're all over the place. However, you'll find them in clusters of three or more at only a handful of places.

There's just one spot with four—in Lake Rumare north-northeast of Sinkhole Cave, which is north of the Imperial City.

You'll find three-clam clusters in the lake just south of the four-clam cluster; near the north shore, north of the exit from the Imperial Prison sewers; just southeast of the dock near that same exit; north and northeast of the north exit from the Imperial City sewers; and southeast of the Imperial City, east of Fatback Cave.

Clams

Away from the lake, more clusters await in the Abecean Sea west of the Gold Coast ruin Crowhaven and in a pond south of Nisin Cave—in that broad expanse of depopulated wilderness along the Elsweyr border between Skingrad and Bravil.

UNDOCUMENTED QUESTS

UDERFRYKTE MATRON

A monster lurks in the high country in northeastern Cyrodiil.

You get wind of the creature in a couple of places. The more accessible is Aerin's Camp to the southwest. From the camp, make your way north-northeast behind the rocks and you'll soon find the body of Andre Labouche. On the body is a letter from Labouche's daughter that mentions in passing a creature known as the Horror of Dive Rock. (Also mentioned is the fact that Labouche is super-clumsy.)

Dive Rock is the pinnacle to the northeast. How do you get up there? There's no fixed path, but we've made it to the top by detouring south from the camp and then tacking back and forth across the mountain face in search of a foothold while executing a rapid series of small jumps. At the top, make your way north to a rock-strewn gully. Follow the gully southwest. Climb out the west side at first opportunity, follow slopes west, and Dive Rock will soon show up on your radar.

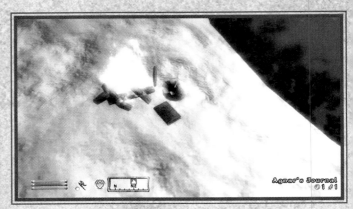

Agnar's Journal

Here, on an icy sliver of rock, you'll find an unoccupied campsite: a tent, supplies, and "Agnar's Journal"—an account of the writer's ascent to the top slot in the Nord tribe at Thirsk, his marriage to Svenja Snow-Song, and their quest to destroy "Uderfrykte Matron."

If you've played Morrowind's *Bloodmoon* expansion, these will be familiar names. On the island of Solstheim, the player can meet Svenja, kill a monster called the Udyrfrykte, and assume command of the Thirsk settlement. (Agnar the Unwavering writes that that hero moved on in search of new challenges.) That was the child of the creature you're about to face.

Agnar the Unwavering

Read the full journal. It contains useful advice for the battle to come. Udy's mom has definitely got it goin' on, with 500 hit points, Chameleon ability, and a 100 percent resistance to frost. But she is just as vulnerable to fire as she is immune to the cold, and fire magic plus an enchanted weapon or, best of all, a weapon enchanted with significant fire magic (à la Goldbrand from the Daedric quest "Boethia") will quickly be the death of her.

(While you're at the campsite, step up to the west edge of the overlook for a special benefit: a spectacular view of northeast Cyrodiil—to Cheydinhal and beyond—that writes to your map the locations of Kingscrest Cavern, the Ayleid ruin Fanacas, and Quickwater Cave.)

So where's this critter? Make your way back to the gully you used to reach Dive Rock and follow it southeast to a rock-strewn shelf. Here you'll find the body of the unfortunate Agnar and, nearby, the Matron herself. Agnar's carrying nothing exceptional, but Svenja (in pieces) is still making the monster's stomach rumble, and you can retrieve her Frostwyrm Bow (with a 15 point Frost Damage enchantment) and body parts.

A RING OF KEYS

A little quest can be found in Pale Pass—a hidden valley you'll explore in the Miscellaneous quest "Lifting the Vale." Concealed around the vale are four containers. Three contain keys—each of which unlocks the next container in the sequence. The fourth contains a potent magic ring.

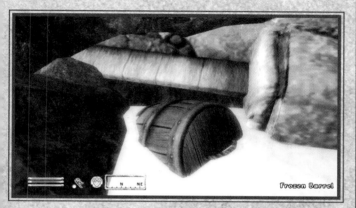

Frozen Barrel

From the tower that contains the entrance to the ruined Pale Pass fort, descend the path toward a frozen lake. Rather than following the path as it continues to the south, turn north. Climb over the rocks and walk around the debris of the destroyed fortress; up against the rocks, next to a big mushroom, you'll find a barrel containing a crumpled note and rusty key. The note is an account of the theft of a ring from a wizard, of the wizard's pursuit, and the concealment of the ring.

Do you see the second tower west of the one we've just visited, somewhat higher on the mountainside? Climb up and enter it. Now, see the bush below and just ahead of you? The chest is under it. It contains an "Old Key."

The next container is near the path. From the statues, follow the path up the hill to the southeast. Where the path turns straight south, you'll see, off to your left, a curving section of stone wall and some large gray rocks. The chest containing a "Forgotten Key" is behind the rocks.

The last one's tricky. It's high up in the mountains at the south end of the vale, and it's not near the path. Return to the door to the Serpent's Trail and head west. Initially, you'll find the slope too steep to climb, but farther west it becomes more gradual and you'll be able to make your way south to a great gray rock outcropping. The chest is half-buried in the ground in front of the outcropping. Inside, you'll find the Circlet of Omnipotence—a ring that boosts your Agility, Endurance, Speed, Strength, and Willpower by 3 points each!

UNIQUE ITEMS

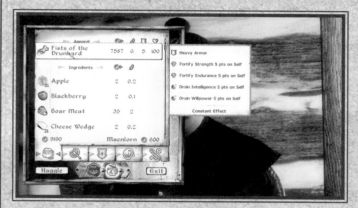

Many shops in Cyrodiil offer at least one item that can be found nowhere else in the game.

Yes, they are expensive.

ARMOR

Fists of the Drunkard, for sale at the Flowing Bowl in Anvil, are heavy gauntlets with attached 5-point boosts in the Strength and Endurance attributes that are paid for by identical drops in Intelligence and Willpower.

Gauntlets of Gluttony, available at the Hammer and Axe in Bruma, drain 30 points from your Health to add 15 to your Strength.

Dondoran's Juggernaut, available at Nord Winds in Bruma, is a heavy Dwarven cuirass that boosts your Strength and Endurance attributes by 10 points each, while taking it out of your Speed attribute and your Athletics skill.

Monkeypants, available at Novaroma in Bruma, is a set of light greaves that feeds 10-point increases in the Acrobatics and Athletics skills by draining 5 points from the Willpower attribute.

Rasheda's Special, available at Fire and Steel in Chorrol, is a pair of heavy gauntlets that boosts your Strength attribute and Armorer skill by 5 points each.

Boots of the Swift Merchant, available at Northern Goods and Trade in Chorrol, fortifies your Mercantile and Speechcraft skills by 10 points each and your Speed attribute by 5—while giving you 30 percent weaknesses to disease and poison.

The Aegis of the Apocalypse, available at The Best Defense

in the Imperial City's Market District, is a heavy cuirass that boosts your Blade, Blunt, and Heavy Armor skills by 5 points each—at the expense of your Health (which drops by 20 hit points) and Luck (which drops 5 points).

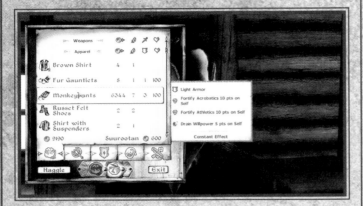

Quicksilver Boots, available at Divine Elegance in the Market District, boost the wearer's Agility and Speed attributes by 10 points each, at the expense of the Heavy and Light Armor skills, which drop by 5 points each.

The Birthright of Astalon, available at The Gilded Carafe in the Market District, is an Elven cuirass that boosts your Agility attribute by 5 points and your Magicka by 50.

The Hands of the Atronach, available at the Mystic Emporium, also in the Market District, are heavy ebony gauntlets with 20 percent fire, frost, and shock resistance enchantments.

The Tower of the Nine, available at Stonewall Shields in the same district, is a heavy Akaviri shield that casts a 5 percent Shield spell while fortifying your Block and Heavy Armor skills by 5 points each—and draining your Light Armor skill by 10 points.

The Helm of the Deep Delver, available at Three Brothers Trade Goods, also in the Market District, is a heavy Dwarven helmet that casts a Light spell out to 60 feet, gives you 30 percent resistance to disease and poison, and drains your Speed attribute by 5 points.

The Orcish Helm of Ferocity, available at Hammer and Tongs in Skingrad, drains the Intelligence, Personality, and Willpower attributes by 5 points each to feed commensurate increases in the Blade, Blunt, and Hand-to-Hand skills.

CLOTHING

Apron of the Master Artisan, available at Lelles' Quality Merchandise in Anvil, boots your Alchemy, Armorer, and Security skills by 5 points each.

Robe of Creativity, available at The Fair Deal in Bravil, boosts your Intelligence and Personality attributes by 5 points each at the expense of Willpower, which drops by 5.

Ring of Transmutation, available at A Warlock's Luck in Bravil, transmutes your Strength and Endurance attributes (which each drop 10 points) into Magicka (which rises by 50).

Councilor's Hood, available at Nord Winds in Bruma, boosts

your Speechcraft skill by 10 points and gives you a 25 percent resistance to poison.

Cowl of the Druid, available at Borba's Goods and Stores in Cheydinhal, has a 40-foot Detect Life effect and boosts your Alchemy and Marksman skills by 5 points each—all to the detriment of your Blade skill, which is drained of 10 points.

Imperial Breeches, available at The Copious Coinpurse in the Imperial City's Market District, boosts your Personality attribute and Mercantile and Speechcraft skills by 5 points each.

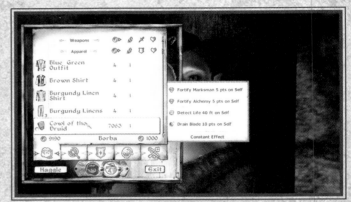

Veil of the Seer, available at Edgar's Discount Spells in the Imperial City's Market District, has a 60-foot Detect Life effect and fortifies Willpower by 5 points.

Mantle of the Woodsman, available at The Main Ingredient, also in the Market District, boosts your Speed attribute and Alchemy skill by 5 points, while draining your Strength and Endurance attributes by the same amount.

Spectre Ring, available at Red Diamond Jewelry, also in the Market District, has a 100 percent Feather (slow-fall) effect and a 25 percent Chameleon effect and boosts your Security and Sneak skills by 5 points. Downside: Your Strength drops 10 points and your Endurance drops 5.

Nistor's Boots, available at Best Goods and Guarantees in Leyawiin, boost your Speed attribute and Athletic skill by 5 points each—and also enable you to breathe underwater.

Ring of Wortcraft, available at All Things Alchemical in Skingrad, boosts your Endurance and Luck attributes and your Alchemy skill by 5 points while draining 10 from your Intelligence.

Vest of the Bard, available at Colovian Traders in Skingrad, increases your Personality attribute and Speechcraft skill for 5 points at the expense of your Willpower, which drops by 5.

WEAPONS

At Morvayn's Peacemakers in Anvil, you'll find the Truncheon of Submission, which boosts your Health 20 points by knocking your Fatigue down 50.

The Bow of Infliction, available at The Archer's Paradox in Bravil, knocks the target's Marksman skill down by 15 points for a minute and knocks five points for his Agility.

Captain Kordan's Saber, available at The March Rider in

Cheydinhal, enables you to absorb 10 points of its target's Agility and Endurance attributes and Blade skill for 30 seconds.

At Rindir's Staffs in the Imperial City's Market District, you'll find Apotheosis—a staff that simultaneously zaps its target with 33 points of fire, frost, and shock damage.

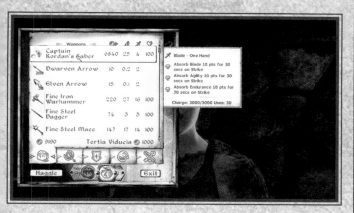

At Three Brothers Trade Goods in the same district, you can buy the Akaviri Sunderblade, with acid-like effects that disintegrate your enemy's armor and weapon.

At Jensine's "Good as New" Merchandise, also in the Market District, is the Akaviri Warblade, which damages the target's Health (15 points), Fatigue (30 points), and Magicka (30 points).

The Battleaxe of Hatred at A Fighting Chance in the same district takes 5 points off the target's Strength, Willpower, and Endurance.

Destarine's Cleaver, available at The Dividing Line in Leyawiin, chops 5 points off the target's Strength and Endurance.

SCROLLS

At Renoit's Books in Chorrol, you'll find the Stormrider Scroll, which casts a five-second, 100 percent Resist Shock spell on the caster while doing 100 points of shock damage to targets within a radius of 25 feet.

At Southern Books in Leyawiin, you'll find the Annal of the Fire Nexus, which works in a similar way with fire damage (out to 30 feet) and resistance.

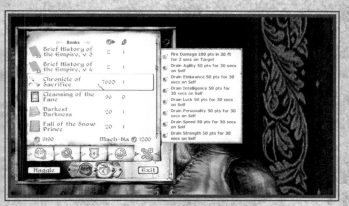

Chronicle of Sacrifice, found at Mach-Na's Books in Cheydinhal, isn't quite so nice. It drains all eight of your attributes by 50 points for 30 seconds while doing 100 points of fire damage to targets within 20 feet.

And the Document of Puerile Banter at First Edition in the Imperial City fortifies your Endurance and Willpower by 50 points for five minutes—but also drains your Personality attribute and Speechcraft skill by 50 points for two and a half minutes.

REPLICAS

In counterpoint to the useful unique items, there are also 22 types of unique but utterly useless weapon and armor replicas floating around in the game. Each of the 13 varieties of weapons and nine varieties of armor has a Damage and Health of 1.

What are these "ceremonial" items about? They are stowed in four- or five-tumbler display cases in the Fighters Guild branches, Castle Bravil, the Arch-Mage's Tower at the Imperial City's Arcane University, and Francois Motierre's house in Chorrol. Hence, you can see them through the glass and identify their apparent exoticism…and only realize their uselessness after you break in and get them.

Display Case @ Very Hard

The game does let a diligent adventurer know how useless they are. A few of these items are sitting out in the open for your easy inspection/appropriation: the Dwarven bow on the counter at The Archer Paradox in Bravil, the Elven longsword in a niche in the Ayleid ruin Kemen, and the Elven helmet on a bier in the Ayleid ruin Lipsand Tarn.

VAMPIRE HUNTING

We've covered the phenomenon of vampirism elsewhere in the book. The other side of coin is killing Vampires.

Did you complete the Miscellaneous quest "Order of the Virtuous Blood"? One upshot is a continuing bounty of 250 gold for each portion of Vampire dust you present to Roland Jenseric. You can make a small fortune as a freelance Vampire hunter.

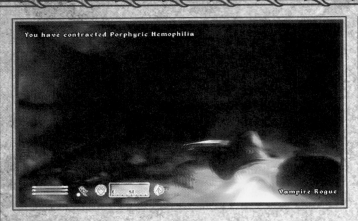
Vampire Rogue

You'll find them in the following locations: the Ayleid ruins Fanacas (north-northeast of Cheydinhal), Lipsand Tarn (north of Chorrol), Ninendava (east-northeast of the Main Quest dungeon Sancre Tor), and Nornalhorst (east-southeast of Skingrad); Barren Cave (west of Cheydinhal); Bloodcrust Cavern (from the Mages Guild quest "Information at a Price"); Crowhaven (from the Miscellaneous quest "Origins of the Gray Price"); forts Carmala (south of Chorrol), Hastrel (well north-northwest of Kvatch), Naso (beyond the Reed River south-southeast of Cheydinhal), Redman (on the west shore of the Lower Niben northwest of Fisherman's Rock), Redwater (from the Dark Brotherhood quest "A Matter of Honor"), and Vlastarus (east of Skingrad); Gutted Mine (from the Daedric quest "Azura"); the lair below Jakben Imbel's house in Talos Plaza (from the Thieves Guild quest "Boots of Springheel Jak"); Memorial Cave (from "Order of the Virtuous Blood"); and Redwater Slough (from the Miscellaneous quest "Vampire Cure").

Vampire Rogue

WAYSHRINES AND CHAPEL ALTARS

The wayshrines—circular Romanesque structures found in the wilderness—are a Nine Divines counterpart to the Daedric shrines. They don't offer quests (though an over-arching quest is hidden here), but give blessings. If you've raised your Fame since your last visit to any wayshrine, you'll receive a blessing when you activate it.

The blessings from god to god have a lot in common. Each will restore all eight of your attributes and 200 hit points, and cures any existing disease. However, each blessing also incorporates a unique component—typically a 10-point, 10-minute boost for one or two of your stats.

A secondary benefit: Once you've visited one of a deity's wayshrines, you can receive blessings (at half the magnitude and duration of the wayshrine blessing) from that same deity's altars, which you'll find along the periphery of any of Cyrodiil's eight major chapels.

However, note that the large central altars of the Nine in those chapels (and the four minor chapels) operate independently of the wayshrines and give you the same core benefits as the wayshrine blessings (but none of the unique ones). You can use them if you don't have a bounty and your Fame exceeds your Infamy.

And, finally, once you've activated one wayshrine for each of the nine gods, simply activate an altar of the Nine Divines to receive a new power: Pilgrim's Grace, which boosts all eight attributes by 10 points for five minutes.

THE WAYSHRINES

AKATOSH

The four wayshrines are: southeast of Skingrad and east of the Ayleid ruin Silorn; east of Anvil and just north of Fort Strand; south of Bruma, north of the Orange Road; and just outside the south wall of Cheydinhal. Blessing: Magicka and Speed.

ARKAY

The three wayshrines are: well southwest of Skingrad and south of the Ayleid ruin Silorn, near the Elsweyr border; north of Anvil, north of the Brina Cross Inn on the Gold Road and just southeast of Bleak Mine; and southwest of Skingrad, to the southeast of Fat Rat Camp. Blessing: Health.

DIBELLA

The three wayshrines are: just southwest of the Imperial City, on the Red Ring Road east of Fort Virtue; well northeast of Leyawiin, east of the Yellow Road and southeast of the Drunken Dragon Inn; and south of Chorrol and just northeast of Fort Carmala. Blessing: Personality.

JULIANOS

The four wayshrines are: south-southeast of Chorrol—roughly between the Weatherleah estate and the Rock Bottom Caverns to the west-northwest; northeast of Cheydinhal, north of Fort Farragut; south of the Imperial City, on the Yellow Road about halfway between its junction with the Red Ring Road and Cracked Wood Cave; and just west-northwest of the Imperial City on the great central island in Lake Rumare. Blessing: Intelligence and Magicka.

KYNARETH

The three wayshrines are: about equal distances northwest of Skingrad and southwest of Chorrol, north-northwest of Fort Dirich, east-southeast of the Ayleid ruin Nonugalo and southwest of Rock Bottom Caverns; in the Nibenay Basin, on the northeast shore of a nameless lake between the Yellow Road and the northern stretch of the Silverfish River; and just off the Gold Road east of Skingrad. (If you've completed the Main Quest segment "Dagon Shrine," the Skingrad Oblivion Gate will be nearby.) Blessing: Agility.

MARA

The three wayshrines are: west of Skingrad, roughly between the Cursed Mine and Meridia's shrine; northeast of Leyawiin, partly submerged in the swamp southwest of Fieldhouse Cave; and a short ways northwest of Anvil. (If you've completed the Main Quest segment "Dagon Shrine," the Anvil Oblivion Gate will be nearby.) Blessing: Willpower.

STENDARR

The three wayshrines are: well southwest of Chorrol, near the Hammerfell border, right on top of the "e" in "The Colovian Highlands"; southeast of Sheogorath's shrine, just west of the Green Road roughly halfway between Leyawiin and Bravil; and on the central peninsula on the east shore of Lake Rumare. Blessing: Endurance.

TIBER SEPTIM

The three wayshrines are: midway between Skingrad and Kvatch, just east of the Ayleid ruin Miscarcand; south of the Imperial City, on the Green Road just southeast of the Inn of Ill Omen; and south-southeast of the Imperial City, on the west side of the Upper Niben, between Hircine's shrine and Fort Variela. Blessing: Strength.

ZENITHAR

The three wayshrines are: along the Gold Road southwest of Kvatch and just southeast of the Gottshaw Inn; south of the Faregyl Inn just off the Green Road south of the Imperial City; and just north of the Flooded Mine, which is itself just north of Bravil. Blessing: Luck.

 There are a pair of ruined wayshrines—one east-northeast of Collapsed Mine in the Valus Mountains and the other on the Hammerfell border in the mountains west-northwest of Chorrol. You can't activate them…but each does have a chest with some modest loot.

There are dozens of chests out in the wilderness. Some are easy to find. They're often sited within surface ruins and near dungeon entrances, and we'll dispense with these here. Some are pure hell.

- At the northwest end of the bridge that stretches northwest across Lake Rumare between City Island and the mainland, a coffin contains a jewelry box and water-walking and healing potions. The box contains as many as three pieces of jewelry—with a 10 percent chance of a magic one—and a 10 percent chance of another potion.

- At the end of a dock north of the Ayleid ruin Vilverin, just across from the Imperial Sewers exit, sits an open crate. Inside the crate is a jewelry box. Inside the jewelry box, you'll find gold and quite possibly a silver nugget and a piece of jewelry.

- Way up in the Jeralls, east-southeast of Bruma, is a nameless campsite. In the chest nearby, you'll find gold and three pieces of "clutter."

- Southeast of Bravil and southwest of Fort Irony on the west side of the channel between Niben Bay and the Lower Niben, is a burned house. The ruins hold a torn sack of grain, a crate of clutter, and a chest containing gold, with a small chance of a lockpick and smaller ones of silver nuggets, a repair hammer, arrows, a stealth-related potion, and a scroll.

- On the west side of the Upper Niben, southwest of the Ayleid ruin Culotte, you'll find a disused dock/storage area. Most of the stuff here is of litttle use, but you'll find another chest like the one above.

- Did you find the shipwreck at the mouth of the Brena River, which separates Cyrodiil from Hammerfell? The wreck itself is inaccessible, but on the little island just to the west, you'll find another chest like the one described above and an open chest containing a silver urn and tankard.

- At the abandoned campsite west of the Ayleid ruin Anutwyll, which is north of Bravil, you'll find a chest with a restorative potion (possibly two).

- In the Colovian Highlands well southwest of Chorrol and just west and above the entrance to Infested Mine, you'll find a dead Goblin atop a chest. (On the evidence of the beer bottles, he drank himself to death.) The chest is a boss-level container. It will always contain gold, with 25 percent chances of extra gold, gems, poison potions, and lockpicks; 10 percent chances of jewelry, magic jewelry, a Goblin weapon and armor, and Soul Gems; and a 5 percent chance of a magic weapon.

- The Necromancers occupying Cadlew Chapel—on the north side of the mouth of the Silverfish River— evidently are having dead bodies delivered to them by ship. You'll find one coffin on the dock west of the chapel (which contains junk) and another on the shore, which contains gold, with a small chance of Necromancer ingredients, jewelry, and Soul Gems.

- In a burned building on the Red Ring Road east-southeast of Memorial Cave are two chests, a sack of gold, and a barrel of ingredients. (This turns out to be the original location of All Things Alchemical—now located in Skingrad.)

- Someone took a spill off a cliff along the Black Road northeast of Chorrol. Beside the skeleton, you'll find a pair of sacks containing a healing potion and food.

In addition, you'll find a standard wilderness chest that contains up to 55 pieces of gold (but usually much less), with a 75 percent chance of "clutter" that could include silver items, animal pelts, jewelry, iron arrows, or silver nuggets (along with some honest-to-goodness clutter), and a 15 percent chance of a lockpick. These can be found:

- Inside a fallen tree, south of Breakneck Cave, west of the Imperial City.

- The forest between Shadow's Rest Cavern, northeast of Chorrol and south of the Ayleid ruin Ninendava to the north-northeast (at least four chests of various descriptions).

- Near the Stendarr wayshrine that's west-northwest of Fort Ontus in the Colovian Highlands.

- On an island off the Gold Coast west-southwest of Crowhaven.

- In a patch of viper's bugloss plants southeast of Mongrel's Tooth Cave (north of Kvatch).

- On a ridge northwest of the Ayleid ruin Niryastare, above the Brena River.

- North of Malacath's shrine, above the Brena River.

- Behind the upper portion of a waterfall southwest of the Ayleid ruin Ondo on the north-south stretch of the Silverfish River.

- Way up in the Jeralls in the depopulated region east-northeast of the Ayleid ruin Hame—marked with four skulls impaled on spears (Hame is east of the Corbolo River headwaters).

- On a narrow slice of land enclosed by the hairpin curve on the Panther River.

- Below the bridge west of the Ayleid ruin Morahame (just north of the westernmost bend in the Panther River).

- Between two great rocks in the forest southeast of the Inn of Ill Omen (off the Green Road south of the Imperial City).

- Beside a rock at the first eastward bend in the Larsius River, which flows out of Elsweyr and empties into Niben Bay just north of Bravil.

- West-northwest of Bravil, in a cluster of Japanese honeysuckle plants in a clearing midway between Bloodmayne Cave and Fort Black Boot.

- In a patch of bog beacon plants south-southwest of Fort Blueblood (east-southeast of Leyawiin).

- In the forest southwest of Onyx Caverns (east-northeast of Leyawiin near the Black Marsh border).

- Under a piney bush along the Orange Road southwest of Bruma.

- Behind the bottom of the southern waterfall at a lake west-northwest of Barren Cave (along the Blue Road west-southwest of Cheydinhal).

- In the forest north of Cracked Wood Cave, on the Yellow Road southeast of the Imperial City.

- Under a euonymus bush up against the western exterior wall of the Arcane University.

- In a small, natural surface cave in a gully west of Bruma, northwest of Boreal Stone Cave and east of Echo Cave.

- On a mountain slope south of the Ayleid ruin Ninendava and east of the Main Quest dungeon Sancre Tor.

- Off the Orange Road southwest of Bruma and southeast of Underpall Cave.

- Behind the eastern of two waterfalls above the small lake located northwest of Black Rock Caverns, which is itself northwest of Chorrol.

- Just west-southwest of Chorrol, in a grove at the base of a slope southwest of the point where the Black Road turns northwest.

- West of Kvatch and north of the Gottshaw Inn—among small rocks southwest of a huge rocky overlook.

- East-southeast of Anvil north of the mouth of the Strid River, enclosed between three great rocks, with a second chest in a similar predicament just to the east-northeast.

- Behind a large rock on the Gold Road west-southwest of Kvatch and east of the Ayleid ruin Garlas Agea. (Beside the chest is a copy of the book *Myth or Menace?*) A second chest can be found among the rocks just to the southwest.

- On the east side of an island just south of the Anvil lighthouse.

- North-northeast of Crowhaven—well concealed by bushes in a cluster of rocks northwest of a large rock.

- South of a large rock at the end of the northern branch of the eastern headwaters of the Panther River.

- On an island where the western of the northern headwaters flows into the Panther.

- Beside a large rock at the southern tip of the Panther's southern headwaters.

- Atop a shoe-shaped rock high in the Valus Mountains southeast of Cheydinhal and northeast of Dark Fissure.

- In the Valus Mountains east-southeast of Cheydinhal— on the top level of a nameless surface ruin northeast of Fort Scinia.

- On a nameless grave in the Valus Mountains just south of Boethia's shrine.

- In the Valus foothills west of Boethia's shrine and northeast of Sercen Camp.

- Partly submerged beside a large rock on the west side of the Lower Niben between White Stallion Lodge and the hamlet of Water's Edge.

- On an island in the channel just south of Bravil.

- On a rocky shelf beside a waterfall west of a pond northeast of Fort Black Boot.

- On the western of two islands in Topal Bay southeast of Leyawiin.

- Partly submerged in Topal Bay, on the south side of a peninsula south of Leyawiin.

- Beside a rock in the forest west-northwest of Leyawiin and south of the Ayleid ruin Telepe.

- Partly buried under snow in the Jerall Mountains northeast of the Ayleid ruin Sedor and northwest of Gutted Mine.

- On a rock atop a small section of battlements in the Jerall Mountains northwest of Cloud Ruler Temple.

- Beside a large rock just southwest of the Ayleid ruin Anga, east of the Silver Road, southeast of Bruma.

Similar chests containing up to 55 pieces of gold, with small chances of lockpicks (15 percent), silver nuggets, a scroll, and a stealth-related potion (10 percent) can be found at three wilderness locations:

- In a small tower on the Red Ring Road northwest of Fort Alessia at the southeast corner of Lake Rumare. (You'll need to use the adjacent rocks to reach the inside of the tower.)

- In a nameless tower below a bridge north of Nonwyll Cavern (which is itself north of Chorrol).

- In a small tower on the Red Ring Road northeast of Fort Nikel (along with a sack). You'll find another chest in another small tower south of that same fort. As with other towers with no conventional entrance, you'll have to do some jumping to get inside.

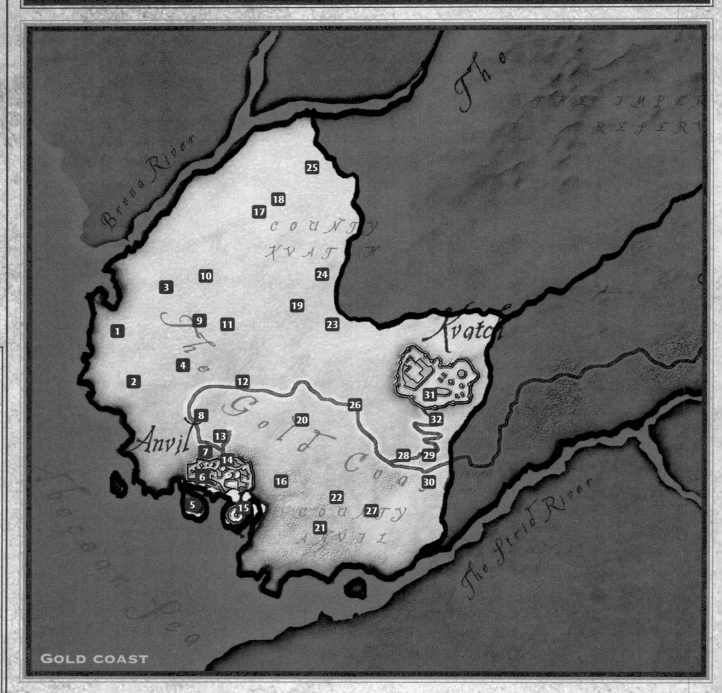

GOLD COAST

1. **Beldaburo:** Ayleid ruin used as a Conjurer lair. Two levels with leveled enemies—Conjurers, Daedra, undead—and gas and spike traps. Loot: fair—notably the Conjurer boss's chest on the second level.

2. **Crowhaven:** Ruined Imperial fort used as a Vampire lair. Two levels with Vampires (notably, Lord Lovidicus) and critters. Quest hooks: Lord Lovidicus's lair on the upper level is the objective of the Miscellaneous quest "Origin of the Gray Prince."

3. **Malacath's Shrine:** Surface shrine to Daedric god Malacath. Orc worshippers there include Shobob gro-Rugdush, who is the source for the Daedric quest "Malacath."

4. **Atrene Camp:** Abandoned surface encampment.

5. **Anvil Lighthouse**: Lighthouse keeper Ulfgar Fog-Eye is a contact in the Dark Brotherhood quest "Following a Lead."

6. **Anvil Dock Gate**: Well, there's no actual gate here, but this is indeed the quickest way for a fast-traveler to reach the Anvil docks.

7. **Horse Whisperer Stables**: They sell White horses here.

8. **Hrota Cave**: Bandit hideaway. One level has Bandits and rotten-plank, swinging-mace, and cave-in traps. Decent loot in the chests. Objective for Fighters Guild quests "Den of Thieves" and "Newheim's Flagon."

9. **Lord Drad's Estate**: Farm operated by prosperous Dark Elf who, with wife Lady Drad, is a contact in the Daedric quest "Malacath." Manor house is a potential target during the freelance/fencing phase of the player's Thieves Guild experience.

10. **Fort Sutch**: Ruined Imperial fort used as a mercenary stronghold. One level with numerous mercenaries. Loot: so-so. Objective for Dark Brotherhood quest "Bad Medicine." After you complete the "Dagon Shrine" segment of the Main Quest, you'll find on the surface northeast of the tower some Imperial troops who serve as the source for the Miscellaneous quest "Attack on Fort Sutch."

11. **Bleak Mine**: Silver mine owned by Lord Drad. One level with guard and Ogres. Loot includes a boss chest and silver-bearing rocks. Objective for Daedric quest "Malacath."

12. **Brina Cross Inn**: Initial objective for Mages Guild quest "Anvil Recommendation."

13. **Whitmond**: Lone resident Maeva the Buxom is the quest-giver for the Settlement quest "When the Vow Breaks."

14. **Anvil Main Gate**: The entrance to the residential portion of Anvil.

15. **Castle Anvil**: For now, we're just telling you where it is. See the "Anvil" map for details.

16. **Fort Strand**: Ruined Imperial fort taken over by Marauders. Two levels with swinging-mace and swinging-log traps. Decent loot. Objective for Settlement quest "When the Vow Breaks."

17. **Varus Camp**: Small Bandit camp. A couple of enemies but no real loot.

18. **Niryastare**: Ayleid ruin that has been taken over by the undead. A boss on the bottom level—and lots of gas traps and one spike trap. Decent loot—most of it in locked containers.

19. **Bodean Camp**: More or less a repeat of #17.

20. **Garlas Agea**: An Ayleid ruin that's been adopted by Necromancers. A single level with a Necromancer boss, and a mess of swinging-blade and gas traps. Fair loot. No quest hooks—but the Ayleid reference work you'll obtain in the Mages Guild quest "Vahtacen's Secret" will teach you the ruin's English name: Caverns of Lore.

21. **Gweden Farm**: Home of seductive women who lure innocent travelers inside to rob them. Objective of the Miscellaneous quest "The Siren's Deception."

22. **Smoke Hole Cave**: A huge tomb. Three levels (the top one is the hub for the other two) contain over two dozen enemies, mostly undead, and there's good loot on the lower two levels. No quest hooks, but Smoke Hole's a little adventure in itself.

23. **Fort Wariel**: A ruined Imperial fort taken over by Marauders. Enemies include a boss and a battlemage. Respectable loot.

24. **Brittlerock Cave**: Daedra in a Cyrodiil cave? It's been known to happen. You'll find plenty of them here—and one Slaughterfish. Decent loot. Objective for the Fighters Guild quest "The Wandering Scholar."

25. **Last Chance Camp**: The standard Bandit-camp setup from #17 and #19.

26. **Gottshaw Inn**

27. **Troll Candle Camp**: Not the standard Bandit-camp setup. Here you'll find Alawen—master trainer in the Marksman skill and the objective in the "Marksman" Master Trainer quest.

28. **Belletor's Folly**: A mine that has been taken over by Bandits. Three levels with leveled enemies, a few of which will be Bandits. The loot's okay. And note that dead Dark Elf treasure hunter on the bottom level, with a rusty shortsword stuck in his gut. In some dungeons, you'll find *live* treasure hunters. See the "Freeform Quests" chapter for details.

29. **Kvatch**: Kvatch itself, up the hill to the north, is pretty much a smoking hole in the ground. This refugee camp is what's left of the civilian population of Kvatch. Depending on how things play out, you may recover Martin here in "Breaking the Siege of Kvatch" in the Main Quest.

30. **Dasek Moor**: A mixed-use dungeon—with Marauders on the top and bottom levels and mostly undead creatures in between. The bottom level has swinging-mace traps, the Marauder boss, and his chest.

31. **Kvatch**: The Chapel of Akatosh is one of the two buildings still standing in the city; it is your final objective in "Breaking the Siege of Kvatch" in the Main Quest and the kickoff point for the follow-up Miscellaneous quest "The Battle for Castle Kvatch." (The castle, not marked, is just to the northwest.)

32. **The Barricades**: Savlian Matius, whom you'll meet here, is the quest-giver for "Breaking the Siege of Kvatch" in the Main Quest.

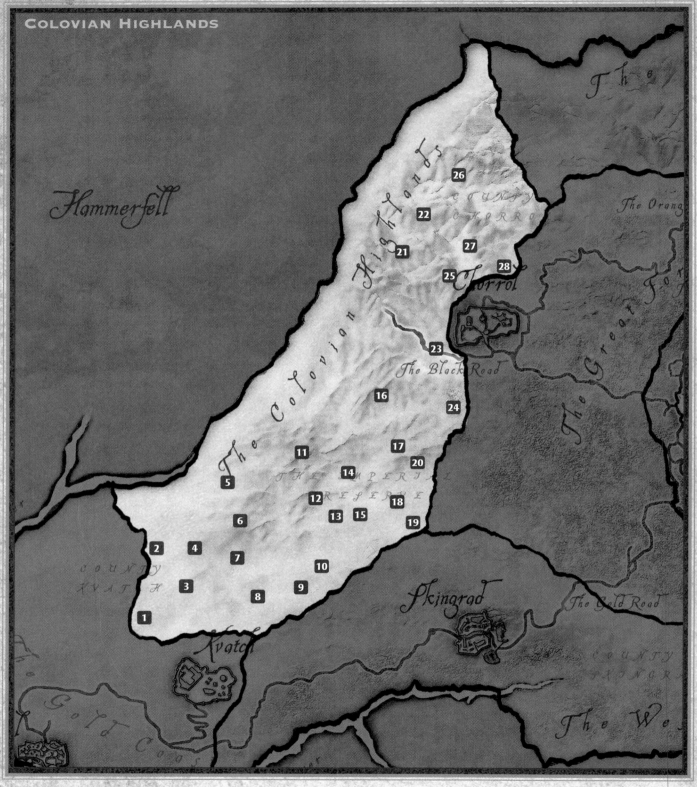

COLOVIAN HIGHLANDS

Hammerfell

The Colovian Highlands

The Black Road

The Great For...

Chorrol

COUNTY CHORROL

THE IMPERIAL RESERVE

COUNTY KVATCH

Kvatch

Skingrad

The Gold Road

COUNTY SKINGRAD

The Gold Coast

The We...

The Orang...

1. **Trumbe:** An Ayleid ruin turned undead lair. Good loot, including a boss's chest and Welkynd Stones, but a lot of the chests are locked.

2. **Fort Hastrel:** A Vampire lair in a former Imperial fort. Respectable loot when you take into account the strength-

fortifying Gauntlets of Potence and Magicka-damaging War Axe of Seduction between two statues atop a raised area on the west side of the bottom level. (Use the little shelves in the corners to help you jump to the top.)

3. **Shattered Mine:** A former mine turned Bandit hideaway. You'll find enemies spread over two levels, swinging-mace and swinging-log traps, and a fair amount of loot.

4. **Camp Ales:** Another of those little Bandit camps, with one Bandit (who could turn out to be a dog) and marginal loot.

5. **Infested Mine:** Infested with Marauders and five swinging-mace traps in the Spent Galleries.

6. **Varondo:** This Ayleid ruin has been taken over by Conjurers and their pet Daedra. Great loot, too—not just chests, but Welkynd and Varla Stones!

7. **Mongrel's Tooth Cave:** A cave inhabited by mythic enemies of varying type and number. Quality of the loot will vary.

8. **Fort Linchal:** This fort is mentioned in the Mages Guild quest "Necromancer's Moon," though you're not actually sent there. As you might expect, you'll be up against Necromancers, lots of 'em, in this three-level dungeon. Watch for dart traps on the top and bottom levels and the Necromancer boss on the bottom. Naturally, a Necromancer boss means a Necromancer boss chest!

9. **Dagny's Camp:** Like #4, with the chance of an extra Bandit.

10. **Talwinque:** Bandit base with an Ayleid motif across the three levels—including a boss on the third—and swinging-mace traps on the top two levels. Loot includes Welkynd Stones on the second level and a boss chest and a Varla Stone on the third level.

11. **Fort Ontu:** Peaceful mage stronghold (with some sinister trappings) that becomes accessible in the Mages Guild quest "The Necromancer's Amulet," in which this dungeon is the objective. (At the end of that quest, it'll turn hostile.) Mages spread over two levels, with decent loot (including a boss chest on the second level). Dart traps on the top level.

12. **Brotch Camp:** Slightly larger version of the standard Bandit camp, with two baddies.

13. **Echo Mine:** Bandit hideaway with numerous enemies and fair loot that includes a decent amount of silver. (Some of the loot is behind a breakaway wall.)

14. **Nonungalo:** An Ayleid ruin that has been taken over by mythic enemies— a leveled assembly of legendary critters that could consist of anything from Ogres on down to Imps, with a presiding boss. Watch for spike and swinging-blade traps.

15. **Valley View Camp:** #9 revisited.

16. **Broken Promises Cave:** A Bandit cave. A pretty fair amount of loot for a one-level cave—including a boss chest. Cave-in and swinging-mace traps.

17. **Wind Cave:** A three-level enemy lair with a heavily populated bottom level—including a boss and his boss chest.

18. **Fort Dirich:** Undead hangout that features a boss. Good loot, with two boss containers. Dart traps. Possible objective in Settlement quest "A Venerable Vintage."

19. **Sanguine Shrine:** Daedric shrine. Engorm is the quest-giver for the Daedric quest "Sanguine."

20. **Rock Bottom Caverns:** Goblin lair with a boss. Doubles as a display room for log (three) and swinging-mace (four) traps. Decent loot—including a boss chest.

21. **Fort Rayles:** A two-level Conjurer lair with Daedra and two bosses. Loot includes two boss chests and a Magicka-draining War Axe of Jolts (on an overpass above the second boss). Cave-in, dart, and pit traps.

22. **Cloud Top:** A surface ruin, high on a mountain shelf, where you'll find a charred corpse. Objective in the Mages Guild quest "Chorrol Recommendation."

23. **Pillaged Mine:** Two-level Goblin den with lots of enemies, modest loot, and log and swinging-mace traps.

24. **Wendir:** A particularly nasty tomb. On the top level, you'll find eight enemies—at least half of them undead. The bottom level features more, plus a boss. It's also a clearing house for traps: gas, Dark Welkynd Stone, pit, spike, and blade. Boss chest on each level. Location of an Ayleid statue needed for the Miscellaneous quest "The Collector."

25. **Black Rock Caverns:** Big Easter Egg. Starts out as a regular Bandit cave, with baddies and a modest amount of loot and a swinging log trap. See the "Freeform Quests" chapter for details.

26. **Lipsand Tarn:** A Vampire lair in an Ayleid ruin, with enemies spread over two levels. Spike traps. Lots of loot, including Welkynd Stones and a Varla Stone, an Elven Ceremonial Helmet up top, and a boss coffin down below. Possible objective in the Mages Guild quest "Chorrol Recommendation."

27. **Nonwyll Cavern:** High-end mythic enemy lair. It's light work up above, with Trolls and a single swinging-mace trap, but heavy lifting down below, with Trolls, Ogres, a Minotaur, and a cave-in trap. Objective in the Fighters Guild quest "The Master's Son."

28. **Hrotanda Vale:** Bandit hideaway...mainly. A couple undead share this two-level dungeon with Brigands, including a Bandit boss. Loot includes Welkynd and Varla Stones.

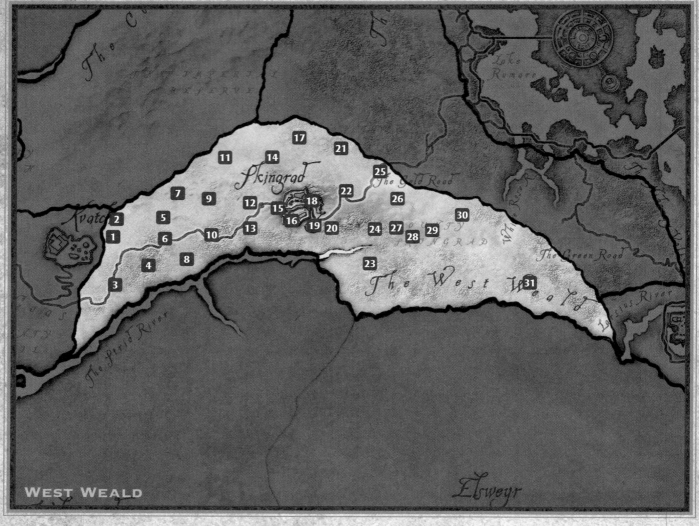

WEST WEALD

WORLD MAPS

1. **Shetcombe Farm:** Source for the Settlement quest "The Sunken One."

2. **Sandstone Cavern:** Critter lair with a blend of mythic enemies and real-world critters spread over two levels. Objective for the Settlement quest "The Sunken One."

3. **Mortal Camp:** A small Bandit camp.

4. **Gnoll's Meeting Camp:** More or less #3. (No actual Gnolls.)

5. **Miscarcand:** Nasty three-level Ayleid ruin and a battle-ground between the resident undead and the scavenging Bitterfish Goblins. Skirmishes occur throughout the dungeon, with a bunch of a boss-level enemies among the combatants. Good loot, including Welkynd Stones and a Varla Stone. Objective in the "Miscarcand" segment of the Main Quest.

6. **Ra'sava Camp:** A small Bandit camp.

7. **Shardrock:** Remote farm. Source for the Settlement quest "Bear Season."

8. **Fort Istirus:** Mentioned as a Necromancer lair in the Mages Guild quest "Necromancer's Moon," but not an actual quest destination. Numerous Necromancers, including a

boss, are spread over three levels. Watch for dart traps on the first and third.

9. **Meridia's Shrine:** Daedric shrine and source of the Daedric quest "Meridia."

10. **Fyrelight Cave:** Mythic enemies and a boss chest can be found on the second level—as can a key to the third.

11. **Fallen Rock Cave:** Principally an undead lair. Takes a while to live up to its name, but finally does in a dead-end passage in the northwest corner. Objective in the Fighters Guild quest "Unfinished Business."

12. **Cursed Mine:** Big Bandit hideaway, with enemies spread over three levels. Boss and boss chest on the bottom level. This is used as the reference point for a meeting with Skingrad's count in the Mages Guild quest "Ulterior Motives."

13. **Fat Rat Camp:** A small Bandit camp.

14. **Bleak Flats Cave:** Undead—and one scared NPC. Objective in Mages Guild quest "Skingrad Recommendation."

15. **Grateful Pass Stables:** They sell Bay horses here.

16. **Skingrad—West Gate**

17. **Goblin Jim's Cave**: Base for the White Skin Goblins—one of several tribes you can manipulate for fun and profit. See "Fun with Goblins" in the "Freeform Quests" chapter. Goblins and Goblin Jim (who isn't one) inhabit the third level.

18. **Skingrad—East Gate**

19. **Castle Skingrad**

20. **Bloodcrust Cavern**: Vampire lair and objective for the Mages Guild quest "Information at a Price." Before the quest goes live, you'll find just a few Vampires—but the number doubles when you're on the quest. Okay loot, including a boss chest.

21. **Shadeleaf Copse**: Three nirnroot plants surround a pond. One of your first objectives in the Miscellaneous quest "Seeking Your Roots."

22. **Derelict Mine**: Base for the Sharp Tooth Goblins. Plenty of Goblins, as well as two tribal totems—the Sharp Tooths' own (at the bottom) and that of their White Skin neighbors (on the second level).

23. **Silorn**: Necromancer base with lots of enemies. Loot includes Welkynd and Varla Stones. Objective in the Mages Guild quest "Ambush."

24. **Gro-Bak Camp**: A small Bandit camp, but with guaranteed enemies.

25. **Gray Rock Cave**: Mythic enemy lair with separate entrances for its two levels.

26. **Fort Vlastarus**: Vampire lair. Loot includes a boss chest. Possible objective for the Settlement quest "A Venerable Vintage."

27. **Howling Cave**: Critter and undead hangout, unless the Daedric quest "Meridia" is running, in which case it's also (on the bottom level) a Necromancer base. Respectable loot, including a boss container.

28. **Collarbone Camp**: A small Bandit Camp.

29. **Nornalhorst**: A Vampire lair, including a boss on each of the two levels; swinging-blade, chopping-blade, and gas traps; and Welkynd and Varla Stones.

30. **Nisin Cave**: Mythic enemy lair.

31. **Fort Black Boot**: Conjurer lair that includes a boss and decent loot, including a boss chest.

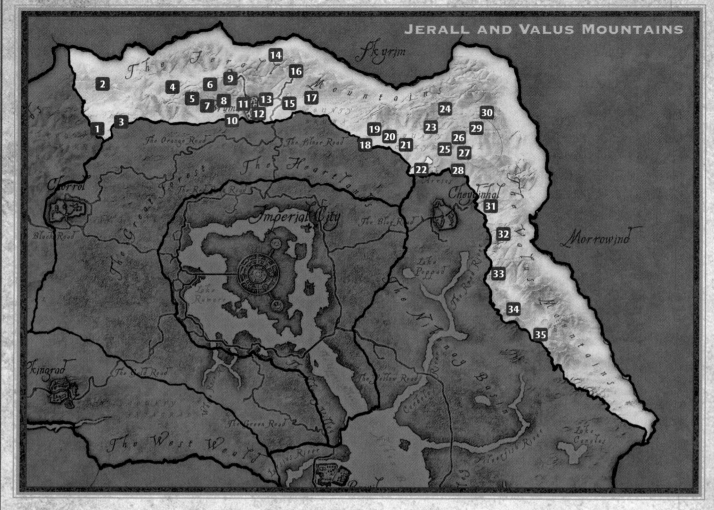

1. **Sancre Tor:** Giant dungeon from the "Blood of the Divines" segment of the Main Quest, inhabited by the ethereal side of the undead family tree (Ghosts and/or Wraiths). Lots of boss chests. Dart traps on the entry level.

2. **Hermaeus Mora's Shrine:** Daedric shrine and the source of the final Daedric quest, "Hermaeus Mora."

3. **Ninendava:** Vampires, Zombies, and other undead, oh my. One swinging-blade trap and one boss coffin. Location of an Ayleid statue needed for the Miscellaneous quest "The Collector."

4. **Echo Cave:** Three-level habitat for Necromancers and various and sundry undead that's used in the final Mages Guild quest, "Confront the King." A Necromancer boss—and the Necromancer boss-of-bosses, Mannimarco—can be found on the bottom level, surrounded by claw traps. Multiple boss chests throughout.

5. **Boreal Stone Cave:** Petite, nearly empty cave that is your final objective in the Miscellaneous quest "A Brotherhood Betrayed."

6. **Rielle:** Two-level Ayleid ruin/undead hangout with nice chest loot (plus the usual Welkynd Stones) and not-so-nice chopping-blade traps.

7. **Applewatch:** Remote farmhouse. Initial objective in the Dark Brotherhood quest "Next of Kin."

8. **Capstone Cave:** Bandit hideaway with a boss chest and a range of traps.

9. **Cloud Ruler Temple:** Mountain fortress that is your final destination in the "Weynon Priory" segment of the Main Quest and, thereafter, your base of operations until the Main Quest's conclusion.

10. **Bruma Caverns:** Mythic Dawn spies use this cave to sneak in and out of the city in the "Spies" segment of the Main Quest.

11. **Castle Bruma**

12. **Bruma—East Gate**

13. **Wildeye Stables:** They sell Paint horses here.

14. **Serpents Trail:** The only known entrance to the lost valley containing the ruins at Pale Pass. Used in the "Lifting the Vale" Miscellaneous quest.

15. **Plundered Mine:** Two-level base for the Three Feather Goblins. (See "Fun with Goblins" in the "Freeform Quests" chapter for details.) So-so loot—a bit of it behind a breakaway wall on the top level.

16. **Dragonclaw Rock:** The first milestone in the Miscellaneous quest "Lifting the Vale."

17. **Gnoll Mountain:** Objective in the Dark Brotherhood quest "The Coldest Sleep."

18. **Silvertooth Cave:** Two-level Goblin lair with a boss, a boss chest, and swing-mace and rotten-plank traps on the top level.

19. **Sedor:** Ayleid ruin occupied by Ogres. Objective in the Fighters Guild quest "The Stone of St. Alessia."

20. **Hidden Camp:** Small Bandit camp.

21. **Gutted Mine:** Vampire lair. Objective in the Daedric quest "Azura."

22. **Lake Arrius Caverns:** Mythic Dawn base you'll invade in the "Dagon Shrine" segment of the Main Quest.

23. **Azura's Shrine:** Daedric shrine, source of the Daedric quest "Azura."

24. **Temple of the Ancestor Moths:** Monastic compound. The four-level catacombs is the objective in the Thieves Guild quest "Turn a Blind Eye."

25. **Lord Rugdumph's Estate:** Initial objective in the Fighters Guild quest "The Noble's Daughter."

26. **Kingscrest Cavern:** Big (four-level) mythic enemy lair—notable for the many withered trees on its bottom level.

27. **Walker Camp:** All over western and central Cyrodiil, these camps have been more or less identical. This one isn't. The two guys here are Camonna Tong thugs who are delivering skooma to a dead-drop location outside nearby Kingscrest Cavern (#26). See "Drugs" in the "Freeform Quests" chapter for details.

28. **Fanacas:** A Vampire lair quartered in an Ayleid ruin. Location of an Ayleid statue needed for the Miscellaneous quest "The Collector."

29. **Aerin's Camp:** Another seeming Bandit camp that isn't. Tobern is the master of the Acrobatics skill, and he can train you to the highest level in the game. And on the body of Andre, which you'll find behind the rocks to the north-northeast, you'll find a letter that hints at some freeform gameplay farther up the mountains. (Hint: Andre fell.) See "The Udyfrykte Matron" in the "Undocumented Quests" chapter for details.

30. **Dive Rock:** Easter Egg. Not the highest spot in the game—the mountains farther east are higher—but Dive Rock has the best view in all Cyrodiil, and this has some nice consequences. The journal beside the fire contains clues useful in the freeform quest alluded to in #29.

31. **Kemen:** Two-level undead lair housed in an Ayleid ruin, with the usual Welkynd Stones and a couple of Varlas on the bottom level. Chopping-blade and gas traps on the bottom level.

32. **Fort Scinia:** Mixed-use undead and Marauder lair. Boss chest on the upper of the two levels. Swinging-mace traps. Objective in the Settlement quest "A Venerable Vintage."

33. **Doomed Mine:** Bandit hideaway with modest loot and swinging-mace traps.

34. **Boethia's Shrine:** Daedric shrine and the source of the Daedric quest "Boethia."

35. **Hame:** Three-level Necromancer lair with a lot of "work product" walking around. Boss chests on the top and bottom levels. Spike traps on the top.

1. **Weatherleah**: A country estate, taken over by Ogres, that is central to the Miscellaneous quest "Legacy Lost." (You'll also visit it in the follow-up, "Sins of the Father.")

2. **Hackdirt**: Strange, isolated village that is at the center of the Miscellaneous quest "Shadow Over Hackdirt."

3. **Elenglynn**: Ayleid ruin with more traps than enemies. The enemies consist of a Necromancer boss, a regular old Necromancer, and undead. The traps consist of Dark Welkynd Stones, swinging blades, and a set of spikes. The substantial loot includes non-dark Welkynd Stones, Soul Gems, and a boss chest.

4. **Chorrol—North Gate**

5. **Chorrol—South Gate**

6. **North Country Stables**: Chestnut horses can be bought here.

7. **Fort Carmala**: A Vampire lair. Loot's so-so, with a couple of Soul Gems and a couple of Fire Damage arrows. Possible objective in the Miscellaneous quest "A Venerable Vintage."

8. **Redguard Valley Cave**: The Ogres that looted Weatherleah (#1) are based here.

9. **Chorrol—Castle Chorrol**

10. **Crumbling Mine**: Bandit hideaway right under Chorrol's walls. You'd think the Bandits and their boss might run into trouble with the City Watch. But if you go all the way to the bottom of the mine, you'll see why they haven't: A break in the cave wall leads to Chorrol's sewer system. Chorrol

has a sewer system? Yes, but you can't squeeze through the crack, and even if you could, nothing of significance lies beyond.

11. **Weynon Priory:** A little monastery where the chief of the Blades holds court. It's your first stop on the Main Quest (when you deliver the Amulet of Kings to Jauffre) and your third (when you deliver the presumptive heir). And in the Miscellaneous quest "The Killing Field," you'll find the Odiil boys waiting on the road nearby.

12. **Serpent Hollow Cave:** Mundane two-level mythic enemy lair, with enemies on top and more (with the boss) on the bottom. Not much loot apart from a nice boss chest on the bottom level.

13. **Brindle Home:** Isolated hamlet that figures in the Daedric quest "Molag Bal."

14. **Odiil Farm:** Objective in the Miscellaneous quest "The Killing Fields."

15. **Molag Bal's Shrine:** Amazingly enough, the source of the Daedric quest "Molag Bal."

16. **Narfinsel:** An Ayleid ruin with a population of mythic enemies (Imps to Ogres) and a boss. Nice loot including Welkynd Stones and a boss chest.

17. **Shadow's Rest Cavern:** Another critter lair—a two-level cave with mythic enemies up top and more mythic and real-world critters down below. Fair loot.

18. **Gottlesfont Priory:** A sisterly counterpart to Weynon Priory. The two residents of this bosky cloister gather the healing lady's mantle leaves—in the chapel and the nearby house—which you're free to take.

19. **Fort Wooden Hand:** Marauder lair in a combination fort/cavern. Note that the bottom level consists of two separate sections—the smaller and eastern one, defended by a Marauder boss, contains the best loot.

20. **Fort Ash:** Two-level Goblin lair. The mace and dart traps on the top level are especially nasty, and the boss and boss chest are down on the bottom.

21. **Lindai:** Undead lair, with enemies spread over two levels. Nice loot, with boss chests on each level, Welkynd Stones, and Varla Stones. Lots of gas, swinging-blade, and spike traps on the top level. Objective in one variant of the Miscellaneous quest "Secrets of the Ayleids."

22. **Breakneck Cave:** Three-level mythic and real-world critter lair with lots of beasties.

23. **Green Mead Cave:** Another critter lair.

24. **Ceyatatar:** Conjurer's lair in an Ayleid ruin spread over three levels. Nice loot, with two boss chests, Welkynd Stones, and Soul Gems on the bottom level. Note that the left-hand stairs from the large room at the beginning of the first level descend to a passage where you'll find a view of a waterfall. You can get to the pool at the bottom of the falls (and the dead adventurer it contains) only from the second level. Referred to in the book *Glories and Laments*.

25. **Haynote Cave:** Three-level critter den with mythic and real-world enemies.

27. **Yellow Tick Cave:** A two-level Conjurer lair.

28. **Fort Coldcorn:** Critter lair with mythic enemies, including a boss. Respectable loot, including a boss chest.

29. **Moranda:** Three-level Ayleid ruin with mythic enemies on the top two levels and only gas traps on the third. Loot's okay, with a single Varla Stone on the third level and also a statue you'll collect in the Miscellaneous quest "The Collector."

30. **Clavicus Vile's Shrine:** Source for the Daedric quest "Clavicus Vile."

31. **Felgageldt Cave:** Two-level Bandit hideaway. Fair loot, including a boss chest, an iron claymore, and a pair of flawed gems.

32. **Underpall Cave:** A huge undead dungeon—plus a Necromancer boss—spread over five densely interwoven levels. Not much loot, considering its size. Loads of swinging-mace traps on a bridge across the South Keep level. The featured attractions are the giant underground lake on the bottom level (in which only one nondescript chest is concealed) and a big, bad Necromancer boss.

33. **Piukanda:** An undead dungeon quartered in an Ayleid ruin, which includes bosses on the second and third levels. Swinging-blade traps on the second level. Great loot, including Welkynd and Varla Stones and two boss chests.

34. **Outlaw Endre's Cave:** A two-level Bandit hideaway. Boss chest on the upper level. Entrance to the bottom is hidden by a pull-rope secret door.

35. **Fort Roebeck:** Two-level Conjurer lair.

36. **Nenyond Twyll:** Necromancer lair in an Ayleid ruin over two levels. Decent loot, with a boss chest and Varla Stones on the second level. Objective in the Mages Guild quest "Liberation or Apprehension?"

37. **Unmarked Cave:** Three-level mythic enemy and beast lair. Secret doors throughout and cave-in traps on initial and "Mazeway" levels. Boss chest on entry level.

38. **Faregyl:** The Faregyl Inn. Source of the Settlement quest "The Potato Snatcher."

39. **Pothole Caverns:** Necromancer lair. Two swinging-mace traps and a log trap—the latter set up for your own use. The cell key's in a chest at the north end of the dungeon.

40. **Horn Cave:** Mixed-use dungeon, with mostly Bandits up above and mythic enemies down below. Watch for swinging-mace traps on the top two levels and a cave-in trap on the third.

41. **Bleaker's Way:** A village where ordinarily-at-odds Nords and Dark Elves live together in peace—at least until you show up to perform the Daedric quest "Mephala."

42. **Inn of Ill Omen:** Destination in the Dark Brotherhood initiation quest "A Knife in the Dark."

43. **Toadstool Hollow:** Mainly an undead dungeon, but with a lot of critters mixed in over three levels. Little loot. Two cave-in traps on the entry level.

44. **Charcoal Cave:** A mixed-use dungeon, with mythic enemies on the two upper levels and Bandits on the first and the third (including a boss). All told, you'll find so-so loot (including a boss chest) and log traps (one on the entry level and three on the third).

45. **Wenyandawik:** An Ayleid ruin occupied by undead creatures (including a boss) spread over two levels. Excellent loot, including Welkynd and Varla Stones and a boss chest. Swinging-blade traps on the bottom level. Location of an Ayleid statue needed for the Miscellaneous quest "The Collector."

46. **Mingo Cave:** Nondescript cave with mythic enemies, a drop of chest loot (plus some modest equipment near the skeleton in the entry hall), and a cave-in trap.

47. **Anga:** Pitch-black Ayleid ruin. The only overtly hostile residents are two undead. You'll get the "Forgotten" here to kill off the invading priests in the Daedric quest "Namira." Good loot, including two boss chests.

48. **Hircine's Shrine:** Source of the Daedric quest "Hircine."

49. **Namira's Shrine:** Source of the Daedric quest "Namira."

50. **Robber's Glen Cave:** Imps and chests. Objective in the Fighters Guild quest "More Unfinished Business."

51. **Red Ruby Cave:** A mythic enemy lair with modest loot spread over two levels.

52. **Mephala's Shrine:** Source of the Daedric quest "Mephala."

53. **Frostfire Glade:** Isolated region reached only through Frostfire Cave. Guarded by a leveled Atronach. No loot. Objective in the Miscellaneous quest "Tears of the Savior."

54. **The Beast's Maw:** Mythic enemy and low-end critter lair.

55. **Fort Horunn:** Three-level mythic enemy lair with a boss and boss chest on the bottom level.

56. **Harm's Folly:** A farm in the Jerall foothills. Source of the Settlement quest "Revenge Served Cold."

57. **Desolate Mine:** A Goblin lair that is the objective in the early Fighters Guild quest "The Desolate Mine." Okay chest loot. Rolling-log and swinging-mace traps.

Heartlands

1. **Fort Nikel**: Marauder/Bandit base with a boss chest.

2. **Fort Empire**: Two-level mythic enemy lair with two bosses on the bottom level and a boss chest.

3. **Fanacasecul**: An Ayleid ruin inhabited by tomb creatures with an undead boss among them. Good loot, including Welkynd Stones and a boss chest.

4. **Fort Virtue**: More tomb creatures, with another boss and another boss chest. Also a bunch of swinging-mace and dart traps.

5. **Wawnet Inn:** Source for the Settlement quest "A Venerable Vintage."

6. **Weye:** Source for the Settlement quest "Go Fish."

7. **Vindasel:** All critters—until you find the warrior Umbra. (Or rather, the once-ordinary person possessed by the soul of the warrior Umbra.) Objective for the Daedric quest "Clavicus Vile," which yields one of the best swords in the game. In this Ayleid ruin, you'll also find Welkynd Stones, a boss chest, and spike and gas traps.

8. **Dzonot Cave:** Bandit lair. Two boss chests on the second of the two levels. Swinging-log trap.

9. **Aleswell:** Little farm community with an inn. Source for the Miscellaneous quest "Zero Visibility."

10. **Fingerbowl Cave:** A four-level, cavernous tomb. The third level has been staked out by a sizable group of Necromancers, which may explain the presence of so many undead creatures.

11. **Fort Caractacus:** The fort above the dungeon is the objective in the Miscellaneous quest "Zero Visibility." The dungeon below the fort is a small Conjurers' lair.

12. **Sinkhole Cave:** This two-level Bandit lair or the Ayleid ruin Vilverin (#36) is likely to be "baby's first dungeon." Pit-laden inner section. Ordinary loot, but you'll be happy to have it.

13. **Chestnut Handy Stables;** These are the only stables in the game where you cannot buy a horse. However, many Imperial citizens keep their horses here.

14. **Imperial City—Talos Plaza District**

15. **Imperial City—Waterfront**

16. **Old Bridge**

17. **Pell's Gate:** Imperial City suburb. Initial destination in the Daedric quest "Clavicus Vile."

18. **Fort Homestead:** A three-level Marauder lair. Lots of dart and swinging-mace traps. Boss chest on the bottom level.

19. **Imperial City—Temple District**

20. **Imperial City—Palace District**

21. **Imperial City—Elven Gardens District**

22. **Imperial City Sewers—North Exit**

23. **Imperial City—Market District:** It has the greatest variety of shops of any of the cities.

24. **Imperial City—Arena:** This is where you go fight in the Arena as a combatant, or to bet on fights.

25. **Imperial City—Arboretum**

26. **Imperial City—Arcane University:** The headquarters of the Mages Guild, and the only place in the game to make your own spells or enchant your own magical items.

27. **Sercen:** Bandit lair in an Ayleid ruin. Boss. Good loot, including Welkynd Stones and a boss chest. Swinging-mace trap.

28. **Imperial City—Prison**

29. **Fatback Cave:** Three-level Goblin lair. The Gobs are intermingled with nuisance beasts (Rats and Mudcrabs) on the top and bottom levels but are relatively thick on the second "Great Chamber" level. Many mace and log traps—especially on the third level, where you'll find the Goblin boss and the lion's share of the treasure.

30. **Sardavar Leed:** Two-level Conjurer lair in an Ayleid ruin. Loads of 'em and their pet Daedra on the top level, and just a few (including the Conjurer boss) on the bottom. Nice loot, including a boss chest. Mind yer P's and Q's on the bridges on the upper level. Location of an Ayleid statue needed for the Miscellaneous quest "The Collector."

31. **Imperial City Sewers—Southeast Exit**

32. **Sweetwater Camp:** Small Bandit camp.

33. **Imperial Prison Sewers Exit**

34. **Moss Rock Cavern:** A Necromancer lair, with the usual share of undead and nuisance beasts. Good loot, including a boss chest and gems. Objective in the Settlement quest "The Gravefinder's Repose."

35. **Roxey Inn:** Source of the Settlement quest "The Gravefinder's Repose" and possible source for the Miscellaneous quest "Zero Visibility." Hangout of the mercenaries who are your rivals in the Miscellaneous quest "Secrets of the Ayleids."

36. **Vilverin:** The other likely "baby's first dungeon." Mixed-use, four-level habitat for Bandits (top level), undead (the rest), and a single Necromancer (on the bottom level). This dungeon also incorporates a couple of small, non-quest stories. (You can learn about a trapped Bandit and get some backstory on the Necromancer.) Pretty fair loot throughout, including a boss chest on the bottom and lots of loose gear on the way down. Location of an Ayleid statue needed for the Miscellaneous quest "The Collector."

37. **Sideways Cave:** A lost Ayleid ruin concealed in a three-level mythic enemy lair. See the "Freeform Quests" chapter for details.

38. **Fort Alessia:** Two-level Marauder hideaway. Swinging-mace traps and a bridge trap. Fair loot, including a boss chest on the bottom level.

39. **Memorial Cave:** Vampire lair. Fair loot, including a boss coffin. Final objective in the Miscellaneous quest "Order of the Virtuous Blood."

40. **Fort Variela:** Two-level Necromancer base with a boss chest on the bottom level.

41. **Fort Urasek:** You're not the only visitor to this densely populated two-level Goblin lair. On the second level, in a small prison with a five-tumbler lock (the key's in a sack near the door), you'll find Marauders fighting Goblins. Wait 'em out and kill the winners. Dart, log, bridge, and swinging-mace traps. Middling loot, including a boss chest.

42. **Fort Chalman:** Undead dungeon with a boss, good loot (including a boss chest), and swinging-mace traps.

43. **Wellspring Cave**: Mages Guild facility, ordinarily empty, that links the mainland to a grove on the island just to the west. Objective in the Mages Guild quest "A Mage's Staff," when you'll find it's been invaded by Necromancers and their pets. The exit to the island can't be opened until the quest goes live.

44. **Fort Magia**: Three-level undead tomb. Lots of water, with a fair number of Slaughterfish. Undead boss and two boss chests on the bottom level. Possible destination for the Settlement quest "A Venerable Vintage."

45. **Shinbone Cave**: Two-level Goblin lair with all manner of traps.

46. **Flooded Mine**: Empty, save for Shaleez, whom you'll have to kill in the Dark Brotherhood quest "Final Justice." (Boss chest, too.)

47. **Veyond's Cave**: An *Argonian* tribal cave not dissimilar to certain of the Goblin lairs, with shaman and a chieftain boss. However, the Argonians don't have Goblin-style tribal names or totems, and this is the only cave of its type. (Not to be confused with the Ayleid ruin Veyond.) Water, water everywhere.

48. **Exhausted Mine**: Bunch of Goblins in a not-quite-tapped-out three-level mine. Objective in the Settlement quest "Revenge Served Cold."

49. **Roland Jenseric's Cabin**: A destination in the Miscellaneous quest "Order of the Virtuous Blood."

50. **Empty Mine**: Empty it ain't. You'll still find silver and Goblins on all three levels.

51. **Culotte**: Ayleid ruin with Zombies, a boss chest, and a bridge trap. Location of an Ayleid statue needed for the Miscellaneous quest "The Collector."

52. **Belda**: Conjurers and their Daedra have holed up in a two-level Ayleid ruin equipped with bridge and spike traps up top and excellent loot throughout—including a mother lode of Welkynd Stones, a Varla Stone, and some Soul Gems.

53. **Nagastani**: Two-level mythic enemy lair with a couple of Zombies. Nice loot, with lots of Welkynd Stones, one Varla Stone, and a boss chest. Lots of gas traps (and a few swinging blades) up top.

54. **Barren Cave**: Vampire lair with two bosses and a boss coffin.

NIBENAY

1. **Bloodmayne Cave:** Looks like a Bandit cave where the Bandits have gone for a walk and left the pets (mythic and real-world) in charge...unless the Fighters Guild quest "The Fugitives" is running. Swinging-mace, gas, and rolling-log traps on the upper level and a boss chest on the bottom.

2. **Anutwyll:** Two-level Ayleid ruin that's been taken over by mythic creatures. Gas traps and a Varla Stone up above, Welkynd Stones and a boss chest down below.

3. **Bay Roan Stables:** Bay horses can be purchased here.

4. **Bravil—North Gate**

5. **Castle Bravil**

6. **Fathis Aren's Tower (a.k.a. Temple of the Emperor Zero):** Surface tower that is inaccessible from the surface and can be reached only via hidden dungeons entered in the north wing of Castle Bravil. Objective in the Thieves Guild quest "Arrow of Extrication."

7. **Fort Sejanus:** Two-level Conjurer lair. You'll find loose potions in addition to the usual chest loot.

8. **Cracked Wood Cave:** Base of the Bloody Hand Goblins. Boss chest, Fire Damage arrows, and swinging-mace traps. One of two possible objectives in the Miscellaneous quest "Goblin Trouble."

9. **Cropsford:** Would-be settlement. The warring Goblin tribes from Cracked Wood Cave (#8) and Timberscar Hollow (#10) have overrun it. You can put things right in the Miscellaneous quest "Goblin Trouble."

10. **Timberscar Hollow:** Base of the Rock Biter Goblins. Boss chest. See #8 and #9.

11. **Bawnwatch Camp:** We'd say there's not a soul here— only there is a soul here. Your initial destination in the Miscellaneous quest "The Forlorn Watchman."

12. **Bawn:** Three-level Ayleid ruin borrowed by the undead. Boss on the third level. Boss chests on the second and third. Welkynd Stones on the first and third and a Varla Stone in between. Gas traps on the second and a spike trap on the third.

13. **Fort Irony:** Goblin lair. Objective in the Settlement quest "A Venerable Vintage." Swinging-mace traps.

14. **Fort Grief:** The "fort" part applies just to the surface ruin. The dungeon beneath is actually The Hunter's Run, which you'll visit in the Miscellaneous quest "Caught in the Hunt."

15. **Fort Aurus:** Conjurer lair. Possible destination in the Settlement quest "A Venerable Vintage."

16. **Newt Cave:** Three-level mythic critter dungeon. Trolls on the second level. Some loose equipment.

17. **Nornal:** Tricky four-level Marauder/undead lair. Loot includes Varla Stones on the "Varlasel" level and a boss chest on the "Ageasel" level. Home to the dead-drop location at which you'll find orders for the Dark Brotherhood quest "A Kiss Before Dying" and a possible destination also for the Miscellaneous quest "Vampire Cure."

18. **Arkved's Tower:** Not the biggest dungeon in the game by acreage, but by levels. *Seven* of 'em, occupied chiefly by Daedra until you reach Arkved himself in his "Death Quarters." Objective in the Daedric quest "Vaermina."

19. **Muck Valley Cavern:** Mainly a critter lair. One of the objectives in the Dark Brotherhood quest "Next of Kin."

20. **Vaermina's Shrine:** Daedric shrine, source of the Daedric quest "Vaermina."

21. **Wenderbek Cave:** Base of the Skull Breaker Goblins. See "Fun with Goblins" in the "Freeform Quests" chapter.

22. **Crestbridge Camp:** The would-be settlers who were chased away from Cropsford (#9) stopped running here. Source for the Miscellaneous quest "Goblin Trouble."

23. **Fort Cedrian:** Two-level Marauder base. Downstairs, you'll face a boss and find some nice loot—including a boss chest and a royal cuirass (with a Resist Poison enchantment).

24. **Cadlew Chapel:** Imagine the Weynon Priory chapel taken over by Necromancers.

25. **Nenalata:** A three-level Ayleid tomb. Boss chests on the first two levels and Varla and Welkynd Stones on the third. Final objective in the Miscellaneous quest "Secrets of the Ayleids."

26. **Bramblepoint Cave:** Three-level mythic creature lair. Boss and boss chest on third level. Destination in the Settlement quest "No Stone Unturned."

27. **The Mouth of the Panther:** You'll find the wreck of the *Emma May* and a bunch of sailor ghosts in the Miscellaneous quest "The Forlorn Watchman."

28. **Knights of the Thorn Lodge:** The clubhouse for a tough-talking but ineffectual chivalric order run by the Cheydinhal count's son. Complete the Miscellaneous quest "The Wayward Knight," and you'll become an honorary member.

29. **Black Waterside Stables:** Black horses can be bought here.

30. **Morahame:** Mythic creature dungeon with a boss chest, Welkynd Stones, loose equipment, and chopping-blade and Dark Welkynd Stone traps.

31. **Wind Range Camp:** Small Bandit camp.

32. **Quickwater Cave:** Two-level creature/critter lair, with mythic creatures up above and Slaughterfish down below.

33. **Castle Cheydinhal**

34. **Cheydinhal—West Gate**

35. **Harlun's Watch:** Small community. Destination in the Fighters Guild quest "Mystery at Harlun's Watch."

36. **Cheydinhal—East Gate**

37. **Vahtacen:** Ayleid ruin with a puzzle dividing its two levels. Nominal undead presence on the top, significant one on the bottom. Two boss chests on each. Lots of Dark Welkynd Stone and some swinging-blade traps down below. Destination in the Mages Guild quest "Vahtacen's Secret."

38. **Drakelowe:** Isolated house. Initial destination in the Miscellaneous quest "Vampire Cure."

39. **Squandered Mine:** Bandit lair. But the boss, behind a secret door on the third level, is undead! Swinging-mace and log traps. Some loot behind a breakaway wall on the top level. Possible destination in the Miscellaneous quest "Vampire Cure."

40. **Crayfish Cave:** Big mythic creature den. Fairly nondescript—save for the fact that the first level serves as a hub for the remaining four. Bosses and boss chests in the "Soggy Bottom" and "Vents" levels. As above, possible destination in the Miscellaneous quest "Vampire Cure."

41. **Trossan Camp:** Small Bandit camp.

42. **Mackamentain:** Three-level Necromancer lair in an Ayleid ruin. Boss and boss chest on the bottom level. Spike and gas traps. Location of an Ayleid statue needed for the Miscellaneous quest "The Collector."

43. **Sage Glen Hollow:** Two-level Conjurer lair with Conjurers (including a boss) up the wazoo. Boss chest, too.

44. **Imperial Bridge Inn:** Source of the Settlement quest "No Stone Unturned."

45. **Fort Flecia:** Goblin lair with a boss and rolling-log and swinging-log traps.

46. **Fort Farragut:** Base for Dark Brotherhood quest-giver Lucien Lachance. Dark Guardians that patrol the halls can be bypassed. Destination of the Dark Brotherhood mini-quest "Of Secret and Shadow" and the source of the Brotherhood quest "The Purification."

47. **Carbo's Camp:** Small Bandit camp.

48. **Swampy Cave:** Troll City. Destination in the Fighters Guild quest "Mystery at Harlun's Watch."

49. **Black Dog Camp:** Small Bandit camp.

50. **Rickety Mine:** Two-level Bandit lair. Boss and boss chest, with some loot hidden behind a breakaway wall. Swinging-log trap on the bottom level.

51. **Hero Hill:** Dead-drop location that contains your orders for the Dark Brotherhood quest "Affairs of a Wizard."

52. **Dark Fissure:** Three-level Necromancer lair. The area outside the front door is the destination in the Mages Guild quest "Necromancer's Moon." (You don't have to dip into the fissure itself.) If you do, you'll find a boss (and a boss coffin) on the third level.

53. **Fort Naso:** Vampire lair with boss and boss coffin. Dart and swinging-mace traps.

54. **Sercen Camp:** Small Bandit camp.

55. **Fort Facian:** Two-level undead lair with boss and boss chest.

56. **Deserted Mine:** Two-level Bandit hideaway. Some loose equipment. Rolling-log trap on the top level. Mythic-creature boss is behind a breakaway wall on the bottom level. (It has a plank leaning against it.)

57. **Fort Entius:** Two-level Conjurer lair. Boss, boss chest, loose equipment, and a couple of bridge traps on the top level.

58. **Ondo:** Mixed-use two-level Ayleid ruin, with mythic creatures mainly up top and undead mainly down below. Gas traps at the end of the top level and an especially nasty one at the beginning of the bottom. Mythic boss and boss chest on the bottom level.

59. **Peryite's Shrine:** Daedric shrine and source of the Daedric quest "Peryite."

60. **Bedrock Break:** Mythic and real-world critter lair. No cameos by Pebbles and Bam-Bam.

61. **Fort Gold-Throat:** Goblin lair, with boss, boss chest, and a fair amount of loose equipment. Swinging-mace traps.

62. **Wendelbek:** Big Necromancer lair. Welkynd and Varla Stones and Soul Gems are spread across all four levels, and boss chests are on the "Sel Aran Mathmedi" and "Silaseli" levels. (Only the "Silaseli" one comes with a boss.) Many traps are on the entry and "Sel Aran Mathmedi" levels. Location of an Ayleid statue needed for the Miscellaneous quest "The Collector." Mentioned in the Mages Guild quest "Necromancer's Moon," but not a quest destination.

63. **Kindred Cave:** On the topmost of the three levels, this is evenly divided between Necromancers and real-world critters. Below, it's all Necromancer.

64. **Collapsed Mine:** Two-level Bandit lair with swinging-log and mace traps.

65. **Arrowshaft Cavern:** A blend of mythic and real-world creatures in this three-level lair, with the mythic ones gaining ascendance the deeper you go. Mythic boss and chest on the third level.

66. **Lost Boy Cavern:** Like Black Rock Caverns and Sideways Cave, this four-level Necromancer lair has its own story. (See the "Freeform Quests" chapter for details.)

67. **Nayon Camp:** Small Bandit camp.

68. **Redwater Slough:** Vampire lair. You'll find a Shortsword of Numbing, with a Frost Damage enchantment, in a coffin high on the wall in the first big room. Destination in the Miscellaneous quest "Vampire Cure."

69. **Fort Redwater:** Two-level Vampire lair. Boss and boss coffin on the bottom level. Dart traps on both levels.

70. **Leafrot Cave:** Two-level undead dungeon. Loot includes Destruction skill book. Destination in the Dark Brotherhood quest "Affairs of a Wizard."

71. **Fort Cuptor:** Two-level Necromancer lair. Pit traps. In addition to the usual chest loot, you'll find a Mysticism skill book, Soul Gems, potions, a topaz, and some equipment.

72. **Garnet Camp:** Small Bandit camp.

73. **Malada:** Two-level Ayleid ruin. Mostly mythic and real-world creatures up top (but also an undead boss). Only undead on the lower level. Welkynd Stones and a Varla Stone. Gas and Dark Welkynd Stone traps upstairs and a spike trap downstairs. Destination in the Miscellaneous quest "Nothing You Can Possess."

74. **Abandoned Mine:** Two-level Bandit hideaway, with boss. Swinging-mace and rolling-log traps. Some loot behind a breakaway wall.

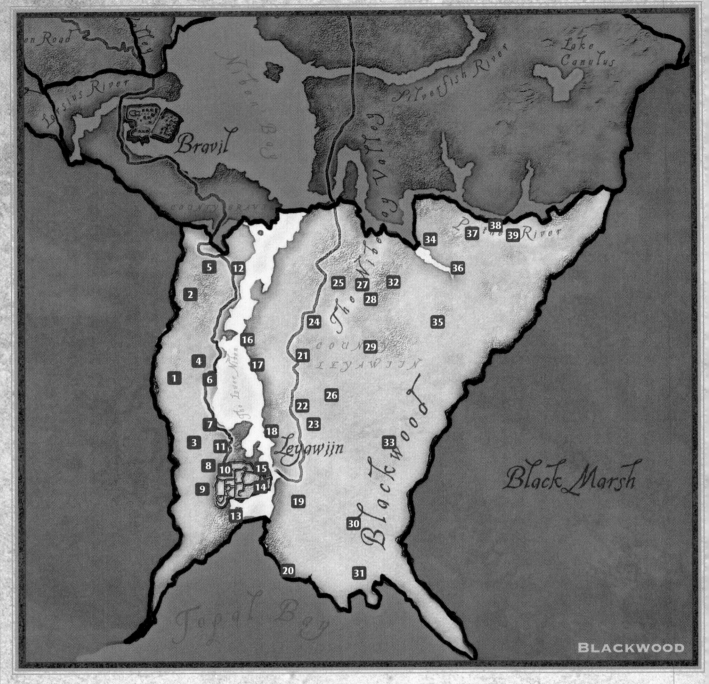

BLACKWOOD

1. **Border Watch**: Small Khajiit community. Destination in the Daedric quest "Sheogorath."

2. **Sheogorath's Shrine**: Daedric shrine and source of the Daedric quest "Sheogorath."

3. **Telepe**: Small Ayleid ruin. Destination in the Miscellaneous quest "Knights of the White Stallion."

4. **Rockmilk Cave**: A four-level Bandit hideaway, but, more particularly, a Black Bow Bandits hideaway. (They're mingled with plain old Bandits and Marauders who are having a dust-up.) Black Bow bosses on the second and third levels. (One of the bosses has a boss dog named Pumpkin in his tent.) Boss chests on the second and

bottom levels; loose gems on the bottom level. Swinging-mace, cave-in, and rolling-log traps. See "Fun with the Black Bow Bandits" in the "Freeform Quests" chapter.

5. **Fort Nomore**: Two-level mythic creature lair, with boss and boss chest on the second level.

6. **Water's Edge**: Small settlement. Destination in the Fighters Guild quests "Amelion's Debt" and "Infiltration."

7. **White Stallion Lodge**: You'll get the key if you complete the Miscellaneous quest "Knights of the White Stallion."

8. **Five Riders Stables**: They sell Paint horses here.

9. **Greyland:** Small house. Destination in the Settlement quest "Raid on Greyland."

10. **Leyawiin—West Gate**

11. **Undertow Cavern:** Two-level Bandit lair. Up top, generic Bandits, one Black Bow representative, and rolling-log and swinging-mace traps. On the bottom, two boss chests—both underwater.

12. **Reedstand Cave:** Two-level mythic and real-world creature lair. Boss and boss chest on the second level.

13. **Forsaken Mine:** Whole lotta dead folks on the upper level. Whole lotta Trolls on the bottom. Destination in the Fighters Guild quest "Trolls of Forsaken Mine."

14. **Castle Leyawiin**

15. **Leyawiin—Northeast Gate**

16. **Fort Redman:** Two-level Vampire lair, with the boss and boss chest on the second level. Dead-drop location for your orders for the Dark Brotherhood quest "A Matter of Honor."

17. **Fisherman's Rock:** Brigand camp. Destination in weird Miscellaneous quest "Mazoga the Orc."

18. **Amelion's Tomb:** Two-level crypt. Family tombs were all over the place in Morrowind, but we suppose Cyrodiilic customs are different. At any rate, apart from the mausoleum in the Imperial City's Palace district, this is the only one in the province. Boss and boss chest on the bottom level. Cave-in trap on the top. Possible destination in the Fighters Guild quest "Amelion's Debt."

19. **Darkfathom Cave:** Daedra cave! And without any Conjurers around to summon them. Destination in the Miscellaneous quest "Whom Gods Annoy."

20. **Tidewater Cave:** Critter lair. Destination in the Daedric quest "Nocturnal."

21. **Nocturnal's Shrine:** Daedric shrine, and the source of the Daedric quest "Nocturnal."

22. **Blankenmarch:** Small settlement. A "Blankenmarch contract" is alluded to in a Fighters Guild conversation, but there is no quest here.

23. **Veyond:** A four-level Ayleid ruin containing Trolls, Trolls, and more Trolls. Boss chests on the "Mathmalatu" and "Gandrasel" levels. Chopping-blade traps on "Gandrasel" and "Bangrara."

24. **Arpenia:** Nuisance critter lair that's like a display room for traps. Initial destination in the Fighters Guild quest "Azani Blackheart."

25. **Barren Mine:** Base for the Dust Eater Goblins. See "Fun with Goblins" in the "Freeform Quest" chapter for details.

26. **Fort Doublecross:** Three-level Necromancer lair. Boss chests on the "Caves" and "Battlemage Muster" levels. One of three anchors for an eastern search for the nirnroot plants needed for the Miscellaneous quest "Seeking Your Roots."

27. **Atatar:** Four-level Bandit hideaway in an Ayleid ruin supplied with all manner of traps. Boss chest on the "Loria" level. Final destination in the Fighters Guild quest "Azani Blackheart."

28. **Drunken Dragon Inn:** One of the destinations in the Dark Brotherhood quest "Next of Kin."

29. **Fieldhouse Cave:** Three-level Conjurer lair. Boss and boss chest on the bottom level. (Also a Hand-to-Hand skill book.) Rotten-plank and swinging-log traps on the second level. Another good anchor for a search for the nirnroot plants needed for the Miscellaneous quest "Seeking Your Roots."

30. **Fort Blueblood:** Two-level Marauder lair. Boss chest and lots of loose equipment. Swinging-mace traps. Destination in the Mages Guild quest "Leyawiin Recommendation" (which adds additional Marauders—including a boss—to the mix).

31. **Bogwater:** A small surface encampment. Destination in the Dark Brotherhood side quest "The Renegade Shadowscale."

32. **Haunted Mine:** Two-level Goblin lair, with swinging-mace traps and some loot hidden behind a breakaway wall.

33. **Onyx Caverns:** Two-level Bandit lair. Boss and boss chest on the bottom level. Swinging-mace traps upstairs and swinging-log and rolling-log traps downstairs.

34. **Welke:** Undead lair quartered in a three-level Ayleid ruin. Boss and boss chest on the bottom level. Welkynd Stones and a Varla Stone on the second and third levels. Gas and swing-blade traps on the top level. Location of an Ayleid statue needed for the Miscellaneous quest "The Collector."

35. **Fort Teleman:** Below the surface, a two-level Necromancer lair, with boss. On the surface, another good starting point for a search for the nirnroot plants needed for the Miscellaneous quest "Seeking Your Roots."

36. **Shattered Scales Cave:** Two-level mythic creature lair.

37. **Marsh-Punk Camp:** Small Bandit camp.

38. **Bloodrun Cave:** Necromancer lair, with boss and boss chest.

39. **Seran Camp:** Small Bandit camp.

CITY MAPS

IMPERIAL
LEGION

ELVEN
GARDENS

MARKET
DISTRICT

TALOS
PLAZA

PALACE
DISTRICT

ARENA
DISTRICT

TEMPLE
DISTRICT

ARBORETUM

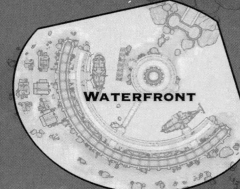

WATERFRONT

ARCANE
UNIVERSITY

IMPERIAL CITY DISTRICTS

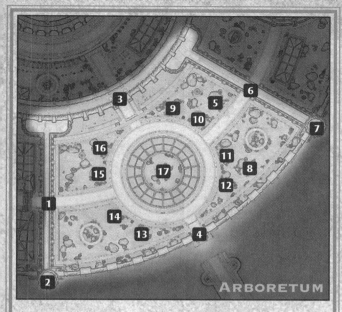

ARBORETUM

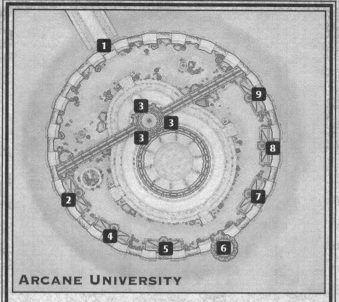

ARCANE UNIVERSITY

1. Exit to the Temple District.

2. **South Watchtower**

3. Exit to Green Emperor Way in the Palace District.

4. Exit to the bridge to Arcane University.

5. **South East Tunnels:** The sewers. You'll use this entrance to reach the Arena Sewers and, eventually, the "Old Way" into the Imperial Palace, in the Thieves Guild quest "The Ultimate Heist."

6. Exit to the Arena District.

7. **Southeast Watchtower**

8. **Beggar's Sleeping Mat:** After the Thieves Guild quest "Lost Histories," Larthjar moves here.

Statues of the Nine Divines

9. Julianos, God of Wisdom and Logic

10. Stendarr, God of Mercy

11. Mara, Mother-Goddess and Goddess of Love

12. Dibella, Goddess of Beauty

13. Arkay, God of the Cycle of Birth and Death

14. Akatosh, The Dragon God of Time

15. Kynareth, Goddess of Air

16. Zenithar, God of Work and Commerce

17. Tiber Septim, God of War and Governance

1. Exit to the bridge to the Arboretum.

2. **Lustratorium:** a.k.a. Alchemy Headquarters. Julienne Fanis buys and sells ingredients, alchemical equipment, and potions. She appears in the Arch-Mage's Tower (#3) during the Miscellaneous quest "Tears of the Savior."

3. **Arch-Mage's Tower:** Three-level tower, with the lobby on the first level, the Council Chambers on the second, and the Arch-Mage's quarters on the third. Raminus Polus in the lobby gives you the middle-tier Mages Guild quests, figures in the Miscellaneous quest "Vampire Cure," and sells spells. You'll meet Bothiel here in the Mages Guild quest "Necromancer's Moon," and Julienne Fanis in the Miscellaneous quest "Tears of the Savior"; you may also meet Tar-Meena in the Main Quest segment "The Path of Dawn." In the Council Chambers, you'll receive the later Mages Guild quests from Arch-Mage Hannibal Traven and meet Irlav Jarol in the Mages Guild quest "Vahtacen's Secret." In the Thieves Guild quest "Misdirection," you'll steal a staff from the Arch-Mage's quarters; once you complete the Mages Guild quest line, that room becomes your own.

4. **Chironasium:** a.k.a. Enchanting Center. You'll visit with Delmar here to arrange creation of your Mage's Staff in the Mages Guild quest "A Mage's Staff," and find Illusion master Martina Floria here in the Master Trainer quest "Illusion Training." Floria also recharges magic items.

5. **Practice Rooms:** Want to watch a spellcaster in action? A high-level Breton mage named Renald Viernis puts on a daily demonstration of Mysticism and Destruction spells here.

6. **Imperial Watchtower**

7. **Mage Quarters:** A source of one of the empty Grand Soul Gems needed in the Miscellaneous quest "Vampire Cure."

8. **Mystic Archives:** You may consult Tar-Meena here in the Main Quest segment "The Path of Dawn." You'll find the book *Necromancer's Moon* here in the Mages Guild quest of the same name. (It's also useful in the Daedric quest "Vaermina.") Another find is the *Modern Heretics* book, which gives you two topics that provide the locations of Daedric shrines. *The Cleansing of the Fane* provides you with the location of the Ayleid ruin Malada in the Miscellaneous quest "Nothing You Can Possess." Boderi Farano is a medium-level Mysticism trainer with a role in the Master Trainer quest "Mysticism Training."

9. **Praxographical Center:** a.k.a. Spellmaking Center. Borissean and Gaspar Stegine both sell spells. Outside, you can attend lectures about the Doomstones. (See the "Freeform Quests" chapter.)

5. **Spectator Box:** Once you've bet on a match, you may watch it play out from these box seats and, every so often, snatch something from one of your fellow spectators.

6. **Arena hopefuls' camp:** A pair of would-be combatants practice night and day in this little colonnade. If you watch them awhile, you'll get a surprise.

7. Exit to the Arboretum.

8. **Southeast Watchtower**

9. **Statue of Pit Fighter Morihaus:** Morihaus led St. Alessia's armies in the taking of White Gold Tower and the overthrow of the Ayleid Hegemonies.

10. **Statue of Queen Alessia:** First ruler of Cyrodiilic Empire and Founder of the Nine Divines.

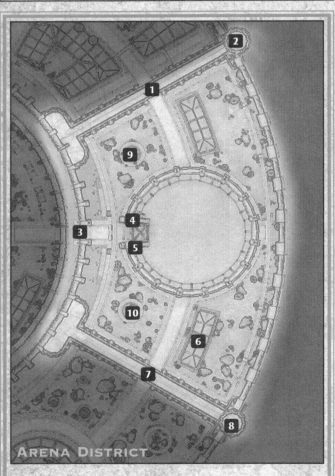

ARENA DISTRICT

1. Exit to the Market District.

2. **Northeast Watchtower**

3. Exit to Green Emperor Way in the Palace District.

4. **Bloodworks:** The underpinning of the Arena, where you'll sign up as a combatant and be assigned matches against the Yellow team and, at length, against the grand champion.

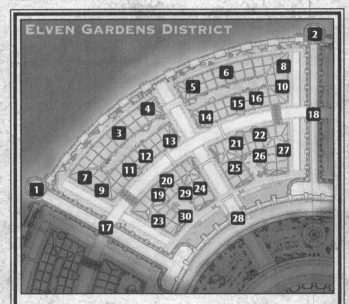

ELVEN GARDENS DISTRICT

1. **Northwest Watchtower**

2. **North Watchtower**

3. **Irene Metrick's House:** The master of the Blunt skill has a role in the Master Trainer quest "Blunt Training." (She also refers you to four other trainers.)

4. **Cyronin Sintav's House:** This is the fellow whom Helvo Atius in Talos Plaza accuses of starting the trouble between the Sintavs and Atiuses.

5. **Guard House**

6. **Tertius Favonius's House:** This lady's man has settled down with Romana Faleria. (Sure enough, you'll find receipts for new furniture on the desk in their bedroom…but she's the real source of interest here. Push her Disposition up to 50 and ask after "Imperial City," and she'll reveal that the City Watch is "so completely on my ass" that she has to lay low—and that she has some dosh set aside to tide her over. Where? Well, it's probably

a reference to a nice chest and a couple of jewelry boxes upstairs at Favonius's house.)

7. **Adrian Decanius's House**

8. **Othrelos's House:** A medium-level Sneak trainer, with a part in the Master Trainer quest "Sneak Training." Housemate Mandil is a midlevel Security trainer.

9. **Dul gro-Shug's House:** This low-level Light Armor trainer bumps you to a pair of additional Elven Gardens trainers.

10. **Marinus Catiotus's House**

11. **Lorkmir's House:** You can buttonhole skooma addict Faelian here in the Dark Brotherhood quest "The Lonely Wanderer" and kill him away from prying eyes.

12. **Iniel Sintav's House:** The patriarch of the Sintav clan. His family, which holds him in high regard, visits him in its entirety on Sunday mornings and stays for the day.

13. **The King and Queen Tavern:** Proprietor Ley Marillin offers bed (10 gold) and board. Lady-in-waiting Pista Marillin is an Arena gambler. In the Miscellaneous quest "Where Spirits Have Lease," you'll catch up to Velwyn Benirus here.

14. **Luther Broad's Boarding House:** Proprietor Broad offers bed (10 gold) and board. You'll have a reunion here with the Blade Baurus in the Main Quest segment "The Path of Dawn." And Mr. Broad can point you to the Daedric shrine to Mephala.

15. **Dovyn Aren's House:** A low-level Alteration trainer.

16. **Ida Vlinorman's House:** This low-level Acrobatics trainer claims to be a "chapel climber." You won't see her perform this sport, but you may nevertheless wonder if you can do it yourself. We think you can.

17. Exit to Talos Plaza.

18. Exit to the Market District.

19. **Wumeek's House:** Arena gambler and pal of Weebam-Na from Leyawiin. (He'll visit the latter on the 19th of each month.)

20. **Fathis Ules's House:** The fifth and last of the Thieves Guild fences, Ules buys and sells everything but spells. He conducts business from 7 p.m. to 5 a.m. from a stool in a leafy enclosure behind his house in the southwest part of the district—except when he's in Chorrol as the quest-giver in the Miscellaneous quest "Sins of the Father." Once the Thieves Guild quest line is complete, he effectively becomes your in-house fence, operating out of the unofficial guild offices in Dareloth's house in the Waterfront District.

21. **Roderic Pierrane's House:** An Arena gambler who also happens to be sleeping with Irene Metrick.

22. **Ra'jhan's House**

23. **Geem Jasiin's House**

24. **Jastia Sintav's House**

25. **Kastus Sintav's House**

26. **Entrance to the Elven Gardens Sewers:** You'll traverse this sewer with Baurus en route to your rendezvous with Mythic Dawn operatives in the Main Quest mission "The Path of Dawn." In the first discrete section of this sewers, you'll find entrances to the cellars of Irene Metrick (#3) and Othrelos (#8), and a Goblin dungeon called the Sewer Waterworks. This last entrance leads into a separate section of the Elven Gardens Sewers— through which you can reach a third cellar (that of Thieves Guild fence Fathis Ules at #20) and the entrance to the Sunken Sewers, where the meeting with the Mythic Dawn occurs. The Sunken Sewers hook up with the Talos Plaza Sewers.

27. **Herminia Cinna's House:** This Ayleid expert has a role in the Miscellaneous quest "Nothing You Can Possess."

28. Exit to Green Emperor Way in the Palace District.

29. **Fathis Ules's Chest:** Fathis sits on this chest during the day. As a Thieves Guild fence, he will conduct business from here.

30. **Beggar's Sleeping Mat:** Fralav the Faker sleeps here.

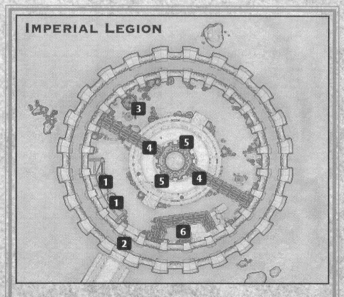

IMPERIAL LEGION

1. **Imperial Legion Offices:** In the Thieves Guild quest "Taking Care of Lex," you'll have to use the Legion seal that's locked up in this building. In the Dark Brotherhood quest "Permanent Retirement," you'll place Adamus Phillida's severed finger here.

2. Exit to the bridge to the Market District.

3. **J'Baana's Tent:** The Khajiit is the master of the Security skill. You'll locate him in the Master Trainer quest "Security Training." You'll have to talk to him at the gates that separate the public from the prison areas

(#4), steal a gate key, or pick the lock on the door in The Bastion.

4. Key-required gates that lead to the prison portion of the enclosure.

5. **The Bastion:** The Imperial City Prison. You'll begin your game in a cell in its bowels, escape by following in the wake of the doomed emperor, return in the Dark Brotherhood quest "Scheduled for Execution" to kill the fellow who taunted you mercilessly when you approached your cell, and, optionally, can visit prisoners here in the Miscellaneous quest "Imperial Corruption" and as a kind of prequel to the first Dark Brotherhood quest "A Knife in the Dark."

6. **Armory:** After you complete the Main Quest, you may think you're due some palpable reward. Here it is. If you speak to Chancellor Ocato, you'll find he now has a "Champion of Cyrodiil" topic. Use it. Ocato reports that he has ordered a suit of Imperial Dragon armor to be manufactured for you. It will appear two weeks later in this building. (You're not told this at the time, but you will get a journal entry and map marker when it's ready, and the door, usually equipped with a five-tumbler lock, will be unlocked.) There are light and heavy suits—you'll get the one for which your skill is higher—but the two types look the same and have identical enchantments: Resist Frost for the boots, Resist Magic for the cuirasses, Resist Poison for the gauntlets, Resist Fire for the greaves, and Resist Shock for the helmets.

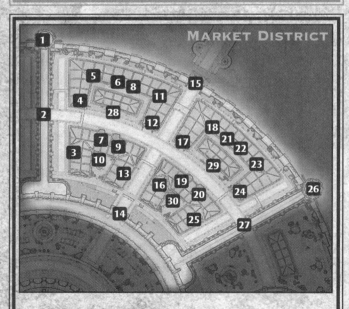

MARKET DISTRICT

1. **North Watchtower**

2. Exit to the Elven Gardens District.

3. **Stonewall Shields:** Proprietor Viator Accius buys and sells weapon, armor, torches, and miscellaneous items, and offers repair services from 8 a.m. to 8 p.m.

4. **Divine Elegance:** Proprietor Palonirya buys and sells clothing from 8 a.m. to 8 p.m. Palonirya is also the master of the Mercantile skill, and you'll be referred to her in the Master Trainer quest "Mercantile Training."

5. **Mystic Emporium:** Proprietor Calindil buys and sells weapons, armor, books, miscellaneous items, spells, and magic items from 8 a.m. to 8 p.m.

6. **Slash 'N Smash:** Proprietor Urbul gro-Orkulg buys and sells weapons, armor, torches, and miscellaneous items from 8 a.m. to 8 p.m. He also offers repair services and likes using the word "big."

7. **Edgar's Discount Spells:** Proprietor Edgar Vautrine buys and sells spells and magic items from 8 a.m. to 8 p.m.

8. **The Gilded Carafe:** Proprietor Claudette buys and sells ingredients, alchemical equipment, and potions from 8 a.m. to 8 p.m. Claudette Perrick is one of the merchants who complain about the practices of The Copious Coinpurse in the Miscellaneous quest "Unfriendly Competition."

9. **Rindir's Staffs:** Proprietor Rindir buys and sells weapons, armor, clothing, and magic items from 8 a.m. to 8 p.m.

10. **Entrance to the Market District Sewers:** A largish in-city dungeon. An enterprising thief will note the exits into the cellars of The Best Defense (#11) and The Main Ingredient (#25) shops. (Another connects to the "Under the Bloodworks" sewer and two to the North Tunnel, which leads to the sewer system's north exit.) Lots of loot and one especially nice chest at the south end of the northern of two central rectangular rooms.

11. **The Best Defense:** Jointly operated by Maro Rufus and Varnado. Both buy and sell weapons, armors, torches, and miscellaneous items from 8 a.m. to 8 p.m. Both men offer repair services, and Varnado is a midlevel trainer in Heavy Armor with a role in the Master Trainer quest "Heavy Armor Training." Gin-Wulm is ostensibly a smith at this shop, but it's really just a place to sleep, and you'll mainly find this master of the Armorer skill (whom you'll meet in the Master Trainer quest "Armorer Training") wandering the district and the neighboring Elven Gardens.

12. **Office of Imperial Commerce:** You'll need to see Vinicia Melissaeia to buy the House for Sale in the city's Waterfront District.

13. **The Copious Coinpurse:** Proprietor Thoronir buys and sells everything but spells from 8 a.m. to 8 p.m. You'll uncover the source of the cheap goods found here in the Miscellaneous quest "Unfriendly Competition."

14. Exit to Green Emperor Way in the Palace District.

15. Exit to the Imperial Legion Compound.

16. **First Edition**: Here you can acquire Book 3 of Mankar Camoran's *Commentaries on the Mysterium Xarxes* in the Main Quest; *The Armorer's Challenge* in the Master Trainer quest "Armorer Training"; *The Cleansing of the Fane* in the Miscellaneous quest "Nothing You Can Possess"; and *Knightfall* in the Miscellaneous quest "Tears of the Savior." And proprietor Phintias can also prove a useful resource in the Miscellaneous quest "Order of the Virtuous Blood." He buys and sells books, and only books, from 8 a.m. to 8 p.m.

17. *Black Horse Courier*: Cyrodiil's equivalent of the "free weekly." It's sponsored by the Imperial administration and written by freelancers. Six back issues are available at the start of the game, and 13 more appear after the completion of certain quests.

18. **Three Brothers Trade Goods**: The three brothers are Sergius, Tertullian, and Cicero Verus. But only the first two actually work here. (Cicero distributes the *Black Horse Courier*.) Each buys and sells everything but spells from 8 a.m. to 8 p.m. (Note that Sergius is absent on Sundays and Tertullian on Tuesdays and Thursdays.) Tertullian voices the complaint against The Copious Coinpurse in the Miscellaneous quest "Unfriendly Competition."

19. **The Merchants Inn**: Proprietor Velus Hosidius offers room (20 gold) and board. Like all inns and taverns, it's open around the clock. The inn is Thoronir's first stop when you follow him in the Miscellaneous quest "Unfriendly Competition."

20. **A Fighting Chance**: Proprietor Rohssan buys and sells weapons, armor, torches, and miscellaneous items, and offers repair services from 8 a.m. to 8 p.m. If you blow the first initiation quest for the Thieves Guild (in "May the Best Thief Win"), you can get a second that involves a sword from Rohssan's upstairs quarters. He's also a medium-level trainer in the Armorer skill and, as such, plays a part in the Master Trainer quest "Armorer Training."

21. **Jensine's "Good as New" Merchandise**: Proprietor Jensine buys and sells everything save for alchemical equipment and spells from 8 a.m. to 6 p.m. She has parts in the Miscellaneous quests "Unfriendly Competition" and "Imperial Corruption." If you follow Jensine after work on Tuesdays and Thursdays, you'll find she goes looking for Fathis Ules—a Thieves Guild fence just happens to be offering his fencing services at the same time.

22. **Warehouse**: General-purpose warehouse, with watchman (Gelephor).

23. **The Feed Bag**

24. **Red Diamond Jewelry**: Proprietor Hamlof Red-Tooth buys and sells clothing and miscellaneous and magic items from 8 a.m. to 8 p.m.

25. **The Main Ingredient**: Proprietor Ogier Georick sells ingredients, alchemical equipment, and potions from 8 a.m. to 8 p.m. He's another of the complainants against The Copious Coinpurse in the Miscellaneous quest "Unfriendly Competition." The shop's an easy source for the nightshade required in the Miscellaneous quest "Vampire Cure" and the Cyrodiilic brandy required for the Daedric quest "Sanguine."

26. **Northeast Watchtower**: Captain Audens Avidius has an office here. You will deal with him in the Miscellaneous quest "Imperial Corruption.".

27. **Exit to Arena District.**

28. **Statue of Uriel Septim III**: Commemorating Uriel III's victory in the War of the Red Diamond.

29. **Statue of Pelagius IV**: Son of Tiber Septim.

30. **Beggar's Sleeping Mat**: Simplicia the Slow sleeps here.

PALACE DISTRICT

1. Exit to the Elven Gardens District.

2. Exit to the Talos Plaza District.

3. Exit to the Temple District.

4. **Tomb of Prince Camarril**: In the Main Quest segment "The Path of Dawn," you'll activate this tomb at the appointed hour to learn the location of a Mythic Dawn hideaway.

5. **Palace**: The exterior door says the "Elder Council Chambers." However, that's just one of your destinations here. In the Main Quest, you'll visit the chambers in the final segment of the Main Quest—"Light the Dragonfires!"—to set in motion Martin's official selection as Tamriel's new emperor. You'll return twice in the final Thieves Guild quest, "The Ultimate Heist"—

once to activate a giant hourglass in the cellar ("crypt") and again via the sewers and attached dungeons to reach the Palace Guard barracks and the Palace Library.

6. Exit to the Market District.

7. **Trentius Family Mausoleum:** You'll visit this crypt in the Miscellaneous quest "Unfriendly Competition."

8. Exit to the Arena District.

9. Exit to the Arboretum.

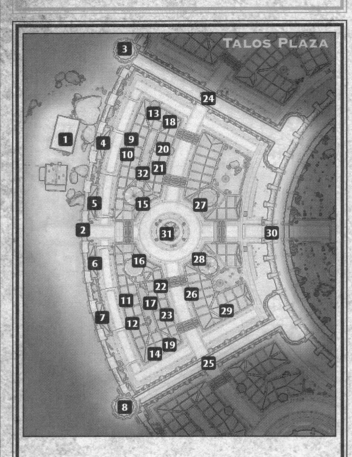

TALOS PLAZA

1. **Chestnut Handy Stables:** No horses for sale. But maybe you'd like a sandwich.

2. **West Gate:** To the bridge to the mainland.

3. **Northwest Watchtower:** Watch captain Itius Hayn has his office here. You must find him for the "Imperial Corruption" Miscellaneous quest.

4. **Usheeja's House:** Guard at Umbacano Manor.

5. **S'rathad's House**

6. **Claudius Arcadia's House:** Actually, it's an Imperial Legion clubhouse. Arcadia's in the Imperial City Prison for praying to the Dark Brotherhood's Night Mother.

7. **Ontus Vanin's House:** Vanin knows the locations of the three Daedric shrines: to Hircine, Mephala, and Vaermina. You'll also visit his home in the Thieves Guild quest "Misdirection."

8. **Southwest Watchtower**

9. **Soris Arenim's House:** Arenim and his wife, Erissare, figure in the Mages Guild quest "Bravil Recommendation."

10. **Astinia Atius's House:** She alludes to a bloody feud between the Sintav and Atius families. In this informal mini-quest, you'll have to speak other members of the two clans to learn what it's about.

11. **Agarmir's House:** Agarmir has a part in the Miscellaneous quest "Unfriendly Competition."

12. **Matthias Draconis's House:** Another Umbacano guard. You'll kill him, along with the rest of his family, in the Dark Brotherhood quest "Next of Kin."

13. **The Foaming Flask:** Proprietor Ernest Manis provides food only (no beds). The tavern's open around the clock.

14. **Samuel Bantien's House:** A low-level Security trainer.

15. **Ulen Athram's House:** Ulen and wife Dralora gamble at the Arena. Ulen's also a Mythic Dawn agent who'll come after you if you approach him after completing the "Dagon Shrine" mission in the Main Quest. The clue: You'll find Books 1 and 2 of the *Commentaries on the Mysterium Xarxes* in his top-floor study.

16. **Tiber Septim Hotel:** Proprietor Augusta Calidia provides bed (40 gold) and board. You can find Gwinas here in the Main Quest's "Path of Dawn" segment. You'll track Faelian to the hotel in the Dark Brotherhood quest "The Lonely Wanderer." If you allied with S'razirr in the Miscellaneous quest "Nothing You Can Possess," you can meet him here afterward to pay him off.

17. **Talos Plaza Sewers Entrance:** Depending how you get down here, you'll have one of two experiences. The southern section of the sewer reached through this manhole is a modest, square dungeon inhabited by nuisance beasts. This leads to the South West Tunnels through two exits on the south side of the square and the basement of Dinari Amnis on the northwestern spur. (The South West Tunnels serve simply to connect the Talos Plaza Sewers and Temple Sewers.) The northern portion can't be reached from here; you'll have to go through the Sunken Sewers under the Elven Gardens District. This is a little Goblin realm—including a boss and boss-level chest.

18. **Ra'jiradh's House:** The three Khajiit brothers who publish the *Black Horse Courier* live here.

19. **Angelie's House:** Her full name's Angelie Blakeley. She's the daughter of a sailor who was lost at sea.

20. **Thamriel's House:** Thamriel is said to hear voices. Her caregiver, Elragail, wonders if it's ghosts.

21. **Dynari Amnis's House:** You'll find Methredhel here in the Thieves Guild quest "Misdirection."

22. **Sevarius Atius's House**: See #10 and #23. Leader of the Atius clan, he reveals that the Imperial Watch has imposed a ceasefire between the feuding Atiuses and Sintavs.

23. **Helvo Atius's House**: Evidently this fellow has been blamed for starting the trouble between the Atiuses and Sintavs.

24. Exit to the Elven Gardens District.

25. Exit to the Temple District.

26. **Dorian's House**: Dorian won't like you. Ever. There's no explaining it by talking to other folks, and a search of his house won't turn up anything—except that he can be profitably burglarized as a penalty for not liking you. Which, we suppose, will make him like you less than ever.

27. **Umbacano Manor**: A rich collector of Ayleid artifacts, Umbacano provides a trio of Miscellaneous quests: "The Collector," "Nothing You Can Possess," and "Secrets of the Ayleids." He buys very specific items. His servant, Jollring, will come looking for you with a proposal should you sell one of the Ayleid statues found in certain ruins.

28. **Jakben Imbel's House**: You'll visit the house—and possibly the Vampire lair below—in the Thieves Guild quest "Boots of Springheel Jak."

29. **Areldil's House**: You'd swear from his extensive rep that this fellow would turn out to be a Security trainer. But he isn't!

30. Exit to Green Emperor Way in the Palace District.

31. **Statue of Akatosh**: The God of Time in his Dragon aspect.

32. **Beggar's Sleeping Mat**: No Coins Draninus sleeps here.

TEMPLE DISTRICT

1. Exit to Talos Plaza District.
2. **Southwest Watchtower**

3. **Gilen Norvalo's House**: Gilen and Ralsa Norvalo each have parts in the Miscellaneous quest "Order of the Virtuous Blood."

4. **The All-Saints Inn**: Proprietor Willet provides bed and board. He's ready for business when you are. Barter gold: 50. The bed's available for 15 gold. And he'll refer you, very obliquely, to the Miscellaneous quest "An Unexpected Voyage."

5. **Pennus Mallius's House**

6. **Surius Afranius's House**: Yet another guard in the employ of the Ayleid artifact collector Umbacano in the Talos Plaza District, Surius shares the place with brothers Ancus and Praxedes.

7. **Algot's House**: Full name: Algot the Northerner.

8. **Marana Rian's House**: You'll visit her in the Master Trainer quest "Sneak Training." (Rian's the master of that skill.)

9. **Hastrel Ottus's House**: An evangelist for Akatosh. Ida Ottus does the same for Mara. And Alessia is the author of all those religion-tinged city guide books.

10. **Graman gro-Marad's House**: You'll free gro-Marad—the bouncer at The Bloated Float inn in the Waterfront District—in the Miscellaneous quest "An Unexpected Voyage." And his wife, Umog, is a night guard for Umbacano—and the only one that can be bribed to look the other way should you decide to steal back the items you've procured for him.

11. **Trenus Duronius's House**: Skooma freak. When you need skooma in the Dark Brotherhood quest "The Lonely Wanderer," his home is the most convenient target for a burglary.

12. Exit to Green Emperor Way in the Palace District.

13. **Temple of the One**: Scene of the finale in the Main Quest. Tandilwe is the master of the Speechcraft skill. Jeelius first appears as an intended sacrificial victim in the Main quest mission "Dagon Shrine." If you free him, and he escapes, he'll reappear here. If he doesn't—or you sacrifice him yourself—he won't.

14. Exit to the bridge to the Waterfront District.

15. **Hagaer's House**: Hagaer is a book addict. He's got 51 of them upstairs. These include the rare *The Last King of the Ayleids* and *Hanging Gardens* and the useful *Varieties of Daedra*.

16. **Stantus Varrid's House**

17. **Ruslan's House**: One of two district residents who report a bad apple in the City Watch's barrel in the Miscellaneous quest "Imperial Corruption."

18. **J'mhad's House**

19. **Roland Jenseric's House**: Jenseric's accused of being a Vampire (and biting his girlfriend) in the Miscellaneous quest "Order of the Virtuous Blood." He'll go into

hiding in a cabin near the Blue Road out to Cheydinhal.

20. **Seridur's House**: Seridur's a member of the Order of the Virtuous Blood—and he's actually the Vampire.

21. **Grey-Throat's House**: Another member of the Order of the Virtuous Blood, from the Miscellaneous quest of the same name.

22. **Luronk gro-Glurzog's House**: With Ruslan (#17), gro-Glurzog makes a complaint against an Imperial Watch trooper in the Miscellaneous quest "Imperial Corruption."

23. Exit to the Arboretum.

24. **Amantius Allectus's House**: In the Thieves Guild quest "May the Best Thief Win," you'll have to steal this fellow's diary. (He claims to be in town working on a new edition of *Lives of the Saints*, but, to judge from the journal, much of his attention seems to have been

devoted to an attempt to create a Vampire plant!) The house is also notable as having the district's only entrance to the Temple Sewers. (The sewers can also be reached from the Talos Plaza Sewers via the South West Tunnel.) However, it admits you only to the southern part of the sewers. To reach the northern part, head northwest to the South West Tunnel and then make your way northeast to a second Temple Sewers entrance. This gives you access to the northern part of the sewer—another Goblin realm with a boss chest and lots of broken crates.

25. **Salomon Geonette's House**

26. **South Watchtower**: Hieronymus Lex has his office here. You will need to break into it for the Thieves Guild quest "Untaxing the Poor."

27. **Beggar's Sleeping Mat**: Ragbag Buntara sleeps here.

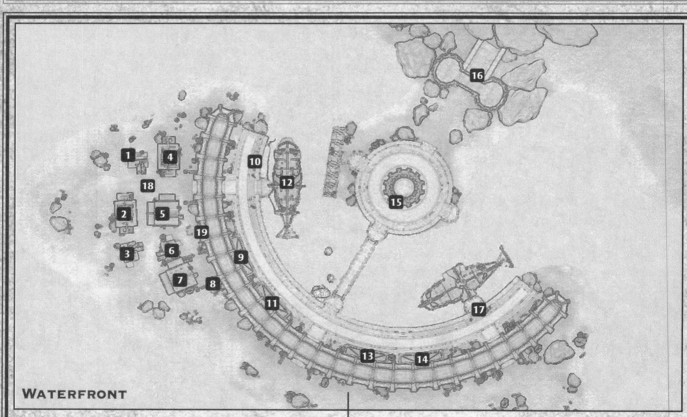

WATERFRONT

1. **Shack for Sale**: To buy this dump, you'll have to visit the Office of Imperial Commerce in the Market District.

2. **Jair's Shack**

3. **Kvinchals' Shack**: They may tell you, though they probably won't, but the three Kvinchals siblings don't get along.

4. **Armand Christophe's House**: Christophe is one of two Thieves Guild lieutenants. But he won't transact business at his home. See #8.

5. **Myvryna Arano's House**: Myvryna is the messenger who brings your invitation to join the Thieves Guild if you take the prison route into that organization. She's also the traitor who gets snatched up in the Thieves Guild quest "The Elven Maiden."

6. **Methredhel's House**: Methredhel is one of your competitors for admission to the Thieves Guild in "May the Best Thief Win." If she beats you to the required diary, you can steal it back from her home. She'll come looking for you in the Thieves Guild quest "The Elven

Maiden." You'll have to find her in "Misdirection." And in "Turn a Blind Eye," she'll come looking for you again with instructions for your rendezvous with the Gray Fox.

7. **Abandoned Shack**

8. Thieves Guild meeting place: Armand Christophe will give you the early guild quests here at midnight.

9. **Dareloth's House**: It's boarded up and inaccessible until you complete the Thieves Guild quest line and become guildmaster. At that point, it turns into a guild clubhouse.

10. An open crate: It allows you to board the *Marie Elena* quietly in the Dark Brotherhood quest "A Watery Grave."

11. **Imperial Trading Company Office**

12. *Marie Elena*: A pirate ship with nasty pirates who'll first warn you away from getting too close and then attack if you don't take the warning. You must kill the captain in the Dark Brotherhood quest "A Watery Grave." (See #10.)

13. **Imperial Trading Company Warehouse**: Has nothing of note inside.

14. A different **Imperial Trading Company Warehouse**: Armand Christophe hides out in this one during the Thieves Guild quest "The Elven Maiden."

15. **Lighthouse**: Operator Velan Andus concedes the lighthouse is for show. Only "an idiot" would try to navigate the Waterfront at night, he says. (It also incorporates a guard barracks.)

16. Tunnel to the Temple District.

17. **The Bloated Float**: Proprietor Ormil provides bed (10 gold) and board. Sleep at this floating inn to kick off the Miscellaneous quest "An Unexpected Voyage."

18. **Hieronymus Lex**: This is where Captain Lex can be found in the Thieves Guild quests "The Elven Maiden" and "Misdirection."

19. **Beggar's Sleeping Mat**: Puny Ancus sleeps here. You can also find Amusei here prior to the Thieves Guild quests starting.

CITY MAPS

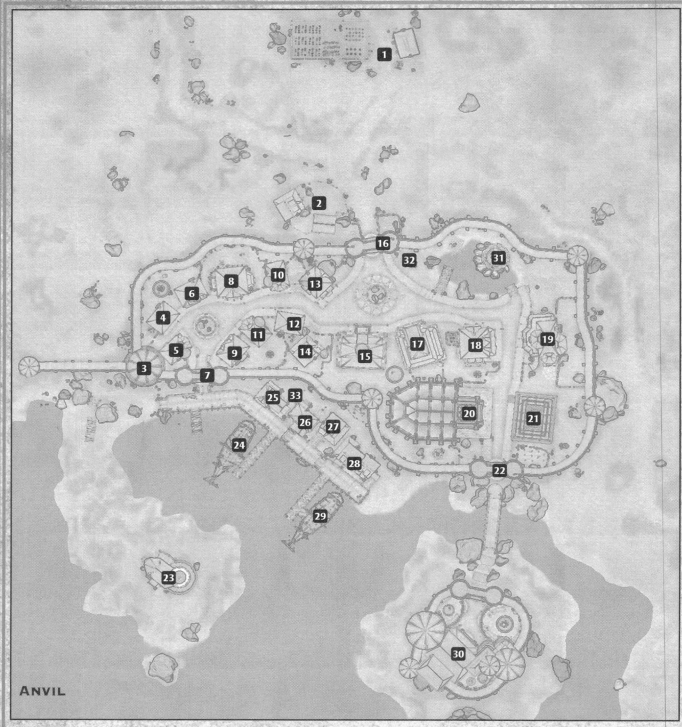

Anvil

1. **Whitmond:** Small farm that is the source of the Settlement quest "When the Bow Breaks."
2. **Horse Whisperer Stables:** Between 8 a.m. to 8 p.m., Clesa, the ostler, sells a White Horse for 4,000 gold.
3. **City Watch Barracks**
4. **Gogan's House:** This gentleman and his "wife," Maelona, play parts in the Miscellaneous quest "The Siren's Deception."
5. **Jesan Sextius's House**
6. **Quill-Weave's House:** This low-level Acrobatics trainer has a part in the early Fighters Guild quest "A Rat Problem."
7. Gate to the city docks.
8. **The Count's Arms:** Proprietor Wilbur offers room and board. The room's 25 gold. You'll meet Velwyn Benirus at this watering hole several times in the course of the Miscellaneous quest "Where Spirits Have Lease."

9. **Newheim the Portly's House**: You'll recover a stolen flagon for this fellow in a Fighters Guild side quest, "Newheim's Flagon."

10. **Arvena Thelas's House**: You'll look into what's killing this lady's pet Rats in the early Fighters Guild quest "A Rat Problem."

11. **Pinarus Inventius's House**: Pinarus, a hunter, will help you with "A Rat Problem." He's also a midlevel Marksman trainer with a role in the Master Trainer quest "Marksman Training."

12. **Silgor Bradus's House**: You'll visit Rusia Bradus in the Master Trainer quest "Athletics Training." (Silgor must be another Anvil-based sailor; he appears nowhere in the game.)

13. **Morvayn's Peacemakers**: Proprietor Varle Morvayn buys and sells weapons, armor, torches, and miscellaneous items, and offers repair services from 8 a.m. to 8 p.m. In the Dark Brotherhood quest "Following a Lead," you'll catch his apprentice, Enilroth, leaving fake orders at a "dead drop" location nearby. (Enilroth's not exactly a straight arrow. He's also messing around with Hasathil, a Wood Elf who's married to Heinrich Oaken-Hull.)

14. **Abandoned House**: But not uninhabited. Here you'll meet with "A Stranger" in the Thieves Guild quest "Taking Care of Lex."

15. **Mages Guild**: Carahil is the source of the Mages Guild quest "Anvil Recommendation." She's also a medium-level trainer in the Master Trainer quest "Illusion Training." In addition, Marc Gulitte is a medium-level trainer in the Master Trainer quest "Destruction Training." He also sells spells and recharges magical equipment. Thaurron sells spells and has a pet Imp named Sparky who follows him around the joint. Felen Relas sells ingredients, alchemical equipment, miscellaneous items, and potions from 8 a.m. to 8 p.m., and also serves as a low-level Alchemy trainer.

16. **Main Gate**: This leads out to the Gold Road.

17. **Fighters Guild**: You'll get a number of early guild quests from Azzan. He's also a midlevel trainer in the Blunt skill and so has a part in that Master Trainer quest. In addition, Rhano is a midlevel trainer in the Master Trainer quest "Blade Training." Huurwen is a low-level trainer in the Block skill, Vigdis in the Blunt skill, and Rufrius Vinicius in the Hand-to-Hand skill.

18. **Heinrich Oaken-Hull's House**: Heinrich's wife, Hasathil, has a thing going with fellow Bosmer Enilroth.

19. **Benirus Manor**: You'll buy this haunted mansion—and have to de-haunt it—in the Miscellaneous quest "Where Spirits Have Lease."

20. **Chapel of Dibella**: Trevaia buys and sell potions and spells.

21. Garden

22. Gate to Castle Anvil.

23. **Anvil Lighthouse**: You'll talk to lighthouse keeper Ulfgar Fog-Eye and visit the creepy basement apartment in the Dark Brotherhood quest "Following a Lead."

24. *Serpent's Wake*: You'll visit this ship in the Miscellaneous quest "The Ghost Ship of Anvil."

25. **Flowing Bowl**: Tavern only (no beds). It's operated by twins. Publican Maenlorn, who wears brown, buys and sells everything but spells. Caenlorn, who wears blue, doesn't sell a thing. Hirtel, who turns up here as a guest after your visit to Kvatch, is a recent import from the Kvatch refugee camp. The inn figures in the Miscellaneous quest "The Siren's Deception."

26. **Lelles's Quality Merchandise**: Proprietor Norbert Lelles buys and sells everything but spells from 8 a.m. to 8 p.m. In the Fighters Guild quest "The Unfortunate Shopkeeper," you'll have to prevent the shop from being burglarized.

27. **Harborside Warehouse**: Nothing special here. It's looked after by Wilhelm the Worm.

28. **The Fo'c'sle**: No vacancy. The proprietor of this sailors-only inn is Mirabelle Monet, who is a medium Sneak trainer with a part in the Master Trainer quest "Sneak Training." And one of her lodger/lovers is Hauls-Ropes-Faster—a medium Athletics trainer with a role in the Master Trainer quest "Athletics Training." Lodger Isolde is a Mythic Dawn agent who attacks you if you approach her after completing the "Dagon Shrine" segment of the Main Quest. (Clue: She's carrying a copy of *Commentaries on the Mysterium Xarxes*, Book 1.) And Thurindil is in Fight Club.

29. *The Sea Tub Clarabella*: Pirate ship with three decks for your plunderin' pleasure. Nice loot in a chest in the captain's cabin. And should you pickpocket Captain Baszone Patneim for the chest key, you'll also find a note from First Mate Filch that suggests the ship recently arrived from Leyawiin and that its cargo—the four sheep on the middle deck—ain't pirate-y enough for Filch's tastes.

30. **Castle Anvil**: You may visit the castle in the Main Quest's "Allies for Bruma" mission to secure additional troops for that city's defense in "Defense of Bruma." You'll also pop in during the Thieves Guild quest "Taking Care of Lex" and again for the finale to the last Thieves Guild quest, "The Ultimate Heist." Orrin in the blacksmith's quarters is the fourth in the line of Thieves Guild fences and buys and sells everything but spells.

31. **Statue—The Selkie of West Skerry**: This seal-maid's lover stole the selkie's seal skin, hoping to keep her from leaving him for the sea, but the lover's wife had secretly cut the skin in two, leaving one part so the selkie might find it. The selkie donned her partial skin, and discovered herself neither seal nor maid, but half-seal and half-maid. She fled the land but is said to guide lost mariners to land in the dense fogs of the Gold Coast.

32. **Beggar's Sleeping Mat**: Penniless Olvus sleeps here.

33. **Beggar's Sleeping Mat**: Imus the Dull sleeps here.

BRAVIL

1. **Bay Roan Stables**: From 8 a.m. to 8 p.m., the ostler, Isabeau Bienne, will sell you a Bay Horse for 1,000 gold.

2. **Great Chapel of Mara**: The medium-level trainer Marz has a hand in the Master Trainer quest "Restoration Training." Uravasa Othrelas is a low-level Speechcraft trainer.

3. **Mages Guild**: Delphine Jend sells spells and is a midlevel Destruction trainer. Ardaline is a medium-level Alchemy trainer who sells ingredients, alchemical equipment, miscellaneous items, and potions. You'll recover her stolen staff in the Mages Guild quest "Bravil Recommendation." Ita Rienus is a medium-level Mysticism trainer who sells spells and recharges magical items. You may also deal with each of the three trainers in the Master Trainer quests for their respective disciplines. In addition, you'll speak to Kud-Ei in the Mages Guild quest "Bravil Recommendation" and the Miscellaneous quest "Through a Nightmare, Darkly" and Aryarie in the Fighters Guild quest "More Unfinished Business."

4. **Lonely Suitor Lodge**: Proprietor Bogrum gro-Galash offers room (10 gold) and board. You'll meet Maglir and his intimidating Blackwood Company pal, Jee-Tah, at this inn in the Fighters Guild quest "More Unfinished Business" and usurer Kurdan gro-Dragol in the Miscellaneous quest "Caught in the Hunt."

5. **Varon Vamori's House**: This medium Speechcraft trainer plays parts in the Mages Guild quest "Bravil Recommendation" and the Master Trainer quest "Speechcraft Training."

6. **Henantier's House** (downstairs) and **Aleron Loche's House** (upstairs): You'll rescue both of these guys in Miscellaneous quests—the former in "Through a Nightmare, Darkly" and the latter (via his wife, Ursanne, who lives here as well) in "Caught in the Hunt."

7. **The Archer Paradox**: Proprietor Daenlin buys and sells weapons, armor, torches, and miscellaneous items, and offers repair services from 8 a.m. to 8 p.m. (He's closed on Sundays, when he goes hunting near Flooded Mine.)

8. **Ungolim's House** (downstairs) and **Ranaline's House** (upstairs): Ungolim's the target in the Dark Brotherhood quest "A Kiss Before Dying." And Ranaline, who works at the Lonely Suitor Lodge (#4), is one of Bravil's two Mythic Dawn agents. She'll go "live" when you complete the "Dagon Shrine" mission in the Main Quest and thereafter attack should you approach her. The cult connection is intimated by the presence of Book 2 of the *Commentaries on the Mysterium Xarxes* on her bed. (Not to mention Book 1 in her inventory.)

9. **Lucky Lady Statue**: Until you reach the end of the Dark Brotherhood quest line, activating this statue boosts your Luck. The Crypt of the Night Mother beneath the statue is the scene of the finale in the Dark Brotherhood quest line. And once you ascend to the top rank in the Brotherhood, you'll get instructions from the statue.

10. **Carandial's House** (downstairs) and **Skooma Den** (upstairs): No wonder Carandial spends much of her time exploring the Ayleid ruin Anutwyll just outside Bravil.

11. **A Warlock's Luck**: Proprietor Ungarion buys and sells books, clothing, alchemical equipment, spells, and magic items from 8 a.m. to 8 p.m.

12. **House for Sale** (downstairs) and **Luciana Galena's House** (upstairs): Galena is a Thieves Guild fence and medium-level trainer in the Light Armor discipline and may figure in the Fighters Guild quest "The Fugitives." She buys and sells everything but spells.

13. **S'krivva's House** (downstairs) and **City-Swimmer's House** (upstairs): S'krivva's a Thieves Guild quest-giver and doyen who also figures in the Master Trainer quest "Security Training" and may figure in the Fighters Guild quest "The Fugitives." (She's also a skooma trafficker.) City-Swimmer is a low-level Sneak trainer.

14. **Dro'shanji's House** (downstairs) and **Andragil's House** (upstairs): Medium trainer Dro'shanji figures in the Master Trainer quest "Security Training," and Andragil is master of the Block skill.

15. Gate to the Green Road.

16. **Silverhome-on-the-Water**: Proprietor Gilgondorin offers room (20 gold) and board. Gilgondorin may figure in the Miscellaneous quest "The Forlorn Watchman."

17. **The Fair Deal**: Proprietor Nilawen and assistant Nordinor (who's a drug dealer on the side) buy and sell everything but spells from 8 a.m. to 8 p.m.

18. **Fighters Guild**: Tadrose Helas buys and sells weapon, armor, torches, and miscellaneous items and offers repair services and low-level Armorer training. Nahsi is a low-level Hand-to-Hand trainer. The anonymous guild porter offers repair services.

19. **Castle Bravil**: The path to court mage Fathis Aren and his Temple of the Emperor Zero begins in his quarters in the castle's north wing in the Thieves Guild quest "Arrow of Extrication." (You can kill him in that quest, but note that Aren is also a low-level Conjuration trainer and thus useful if kept alive.) Castle smith Hans Black-Nail is a Mythic Dawn agent who goes "live" when you complete the "Dagon Shrine" mission in the Main Quest and attacks if you approach him. The giveaway: The two copies of *Commentaries on the Mysterium Xarxes*, Book 1 in his east wing quarters.

20. **Beggar's Sleeping Mat**: Wretched Aia Sleeps here.

21. **Beggar's Sleeping Mat**: Cosmus the Cheat sleeps here.

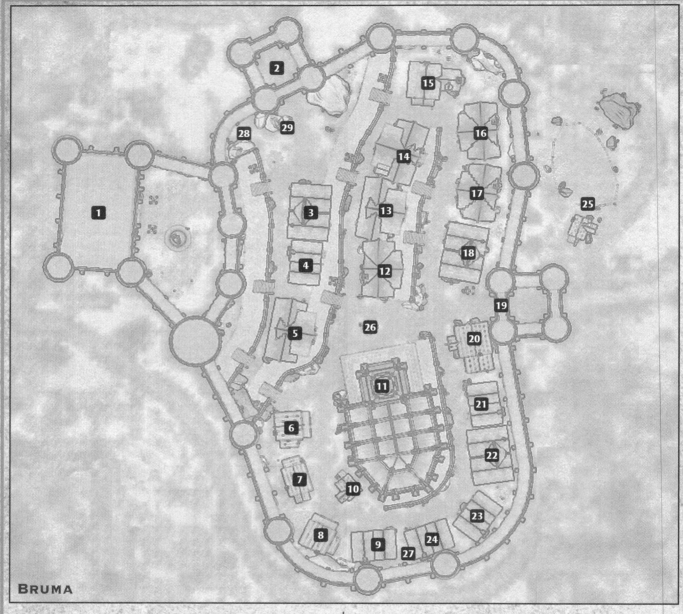

BRUMA

1. **Castle Bruma**: You'll visit the castle to speak to Captain Burd and Countess Narina Carvain in the respective "Spies" and "Defense of Bruma" segments of the Main Quest; Carvain again in the Miscellaneous quest "Lifting the Vale"; and the prisoner Jorundr in the Miscellaneous quest "Two Sides of the Coin."

2. **North Gate**: To Cloud Ruler Temple and points west.

3. **Nord Winds**: Jointly operated by Olfand and Skjorta. Olfand buys and sells weapons, armor, torches, and miscellaneous items from 8 a.m. to 8 p.m. (He also offers repair services and low-level Light Armor training.) Skjorta deals in clothing only—and has a habit of running around Bruma drunk in the middle of the night.

4. **Novaroma**: Proprietor Suurootan and assistant Karinnarre buy and sell everything but spells from 8 a.m. to 8 p.m.

5. **Jerall View**: Inn proprietor Hafid Hollowleg offers room and board. The room's 25 gold. He also has a part in the Miscellaneous quest "A Brotherhood Betrayed."

6. **Bradon Lirrian's House**: The late Lirrian is accused of being a Vampire in "A Brotherhood Betrayed."

7. **Istrius Brolus's House**: Jantus Brolus is a low-level Illusion trainer.

8. **Jearl's House**: Jearl and house guest Saveri Faram are Mythic Dawn spies whom you'll put down in the "Spies" segment of the Main Quest. The house's cellar is connected to Bruma Caverns southwest of town.

9. **Arnora's House:** Arnora's involved in the Miscellaneous quest "Two Sides of the Coin." And if you're in the Thieves Guild, she gives you info that provides a reason to search Jearl's home in the Main Quest mission "Spies."

10. **Ongar's House:** Again, if you're in the Thieves Guild, Ongar the World-Weary can help you in the "Spies" quest. He's also the first in a series of Thieves Guild fences. He'll buy and sell anything but spells. He does business from 6 p.m. to 6 a.m. at Olav's Tap and Tack.

11. **Great Chapel of Talos:** In "Defense of Bruma," the council of war between the Main Quest principals takes place in this chapel. Low-level Restoration trainer Cirroc figures in the Fighters Guild quest "The Stone of St. Alessia," and midlevel Conjuration trainer Arentus Falvius is part of the Master Trainer quest "Conjuration Training." Isa Raman buys and sells spells.

12. **Honmund's House:** Honmund's partner, Alga, is a low-level Speechcraft trainer.

13. **Fighters Guild:** Right-Wind is a low-level trainer in the Blade skill, Bumph gra-Gash in the Heavy Armor skill. The anonymous porter provides repair services.

14. **Mages Guild:** Jeanne Frasoric gives you the Mages Guild quest "Bruma Recommendation." After you complete it, J'skar can train you up to 40 in the Destruction skill. Volanaro sells spells and recharges magical items. Selena Orania sells ingredients, alchemical equipment, miscellaneous items, spells, and potions. But only for a while. You'll find the guild in ruins, and almost everybody dead, in the Mages Guild quest "A Plot Revealed."

15. **Hammer and Axe:** Proprietor Fjotreid buys and sells weapons, armor, torches, and miscellaneous items and offers repair services from 8 a.m. to 8 p.m.

16. **Lyra Rosentia's House**

17. **Baenlin's House:** Baenlin's your target in the Dark Brotherhood quest "Accidents Happen."

18. **House for Sale**

19. **East Gate:** The exit to the Silver Road and points south and east.

20. **Olav's Tap and Tack:** Proprietor Olav offers room and board. (The room's 10 gold.) He also lends a hand in the Miscellaneous quest "A Brotherhood Betrayed."

21. **Brotch Calus's House:** Calus is a medium-level trainer in Alchemy.

22. **J'Ghasta's House:** The Khajiit is your target in the Dark Brotherhood quest "Broken Vows."

23. **Helvius Cecia's House:** The "Hand-to-Hand Training" quest will lead you to master Hand-to-Hand trainer Cecia. And you'll meet the Gray Fox here to get instructions for the Thieves Guild quest "Turn a Blind Eye."

24. **Regner's House:** Edla Dark-Heart is a low-level Marksman trainer.

25. **Wildeye Stables:** From 8 a.m. to 8 p.m., the ostler, Petrine, will sell you a Paint Horse for 500 gold.

26. **Statue of Tiber Septim:** God of War and Governance, Emperor and Founder of the Septim dynasty.

27. **Beggar's Sleeping Mat:** Jorck the Outcast sleeps here.

28. **Beggar's Sleeping Mat:** Fetid Jofnhild sleeps here.

29. **Hero of Bruma Statue:** A statue erected by the good people of Bruma as a reward for your services. In order for this memorial to appear, you'll need to complete the Main Quest mission "Defense of Bruma." Then separate yourself from Martin, moving briefly to a different region, and return to him. When you return, the statue will be enabled. Activate the base to read the inscription. And note that it's not just a generic statue, but an exact duplicate of your character—right down to the equipment. The pose is always the same, but the armor and weapon are the best you have in inventory at the time you return to Martin. Hence, you can "edit" the statue to your liking by varying what's in your possession when this snapshot is taken.

CHEYDINHAL

1. **Knights of the Thorn Lodge**: You'll gain admittance to this clubhouse when you complete the Miscellaneous quest "The Wayward Knight."

2. **Black Waterside Stables**: From 8 a.m. to 8 p.m., the ostler, Tovas Selvani, will sell you a Black Horse for 5,000 gold.

3. **West Gate**: To the Blue Road and the Imperial City.

4. **Castle Cheydinhal**: You may visit the castle for the Miscellaneous quests "The Wayward Knight" and "Corruption and Conscience" and to secure troops after the completion of the former quest in the Main Quest segment "Allies for Bruma." Ra'qanar is a medium-level

trainer in the Hand-to-Hand skill. Naspia Cosma, the count's steward, is a low-level trainer in the Blade skill.

5. **Newlands Lodge**: Proprietor Dervera Romalen offers room (10 gold) and board. You'll visit this inn to seek out Guilbert Jemane in the Miscellaneous quest "Separated at Birth."

6. **Cheydinhal Bridge Inn**: Proprietor Mariana Ancharia offers room (40 gold) and board. You'll meet Garrus Darelliun here in the Miscellaneous quest "Corruption and Conscience."

7. **Mages Guild**: Falcar provides the Mages Guild quest "Bruma Recommendation" (which sends you down the

well in the backyard)—and Deetsan, a low-level Alteration trainer and future branch chief, helps you get through it. Uurwen recharges your magical items. Trayvond the Redguard sells spells.

8. **House for Sale**

9. **Borba's Goods and Stores**: Proprietor Borba gra-Uzgash and assistant Magra gro-Naybek buy and sell everything but spells from 8 a.m. to 8 p.m. Gra-Uzgash can also provide the location of Boethia's shrine and three non-quest dungeons.

10. **Mach-Na's Books**: Mr. Na buys and sells books from 8 a.m. to 8 p.m. You may put in here in search of books on a couple of occasions—notably for *The Cleansing of the Fane* in the Miscellaneous quest "Nothing You Can Possess"—or have occasion to poke the owner with a dagger in the Miscellaneous quest "Vampire Cure." He's also a low-level trainer in the Mercantile skill. And raise his Disposition to 50 and ask about "Cheydinhal" for a colorful take on the Dark Elves, Imperials, and the city generally.

11. **The March Rider**: Proprietor Tertia Viducia buys and sells weapons, armor, torches, and miscellaneous items from 8 a.m. to 8 p.m.

12. **Fighters Guild**: Burz gro-Khash is one of two initial Fighters Guild quest-givers. The anonymous guild porter, like all Fighters Guild porters, offers repair services.

13. **Rythe Lythandas's House**: You'll visit this house in the Miscellaneous quest "A Brush with Death."

14. **Willow Bank**

15. **Magrum gra-Orum's House**: Home also to her husband, the gangster Dulfish. (Is it any wonder the place is in his wife's name?) Ms. Orum can put you on to the locations of two ruined Imperial forts that have been taken over by the undead.

16. **Great Chapel of Arkay**: Ohtesse and Gruiand Garrana are midlevel trainers in Restoration and Speechcraft, respectively. Hil the Tall provides low-level Illusion training. You will go here for the Thieves Guild quest "The Elven Maiden."

17. **Aldos Othran's House**: The confiscation of this house by the City Watch is at the heart of the Miscellaneous quest "Corruption and Conscience." Aldos is now living in the streets.

18. **Llevana Nedaren's House**: Neighbor Nedaren also figures prominently in "Corruption and Conscience."

19. **Riverview**: Servants Tanasa Arano and Tolisi Girith are Mythic Dawn agents who go "live" and attack you if you approach them after you complete the "Dagon Shrine" segment of the Main Quest. How do you know? You'll find a copy of the *Commentaries on the Mysterium Xarxes*, Book 1 in their cellar quarters and Book 2 on Arano's person.

20. **Ohtimbar's House**

21. **Ganredhel's House**: You'll meet with the Gray Fox at this house to get your instructions for the Thieves Guild quest "Boots of Springheel Jak." As a medium trainer in Acrobatics, Ganredhel also figures in the Master Trainer quest "Acrobatics Training."

22. **Abandoned House**: In the cellar is a Dark Brotherhood Sanctuary—entered with the proper password either through the house or, later, through the well to the rear. It's the source of most of the early Brotherhood quests. Ocheeva is your first contact. Vampire Vicente Valtieri is a quest-giver and eventually offers to turn you into a Vampire as well. The Khajiit M'raaj-Dar buys and sells everything.

23. **Oghash gra-Magul's House**: Member of the Orum gang.

24. **Bazur gro-Gharz's House**: Member of the Orum gang.

25. **Northeast Gate**: To Fort Farragut—the hideaway of Dark Brotherhood recruiter Lucien Lachance.

26. **Statue of Galerion the Mystic**: Founder of the Mages Guild.

27. **Statue of Arkay**: God of the Cycle of Birth and Death.

28. **Beggar's Sleeping Mat**: Bruccius the Orphan sleeps here.

29. **Beggar's Sleeping Mat**: Luckless Lucina sleeps here.

30. **Wayshrine of Akatosh**: Confers a blessing of Magicka and Speed.

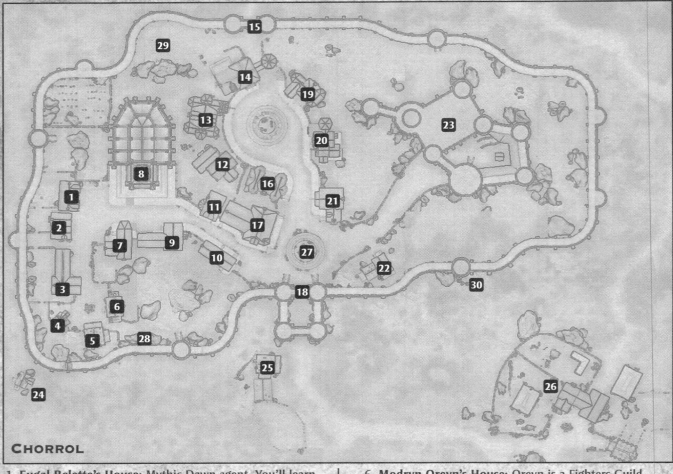

CHORROL

1. **Eugal Belette's House**: Mythic Dawn agent. You'll learn this if you approach him after completing the "Dagon Shrine" mission in the Main Quest (when Belette attacks you) or before then if you pickpocket him for the key to the key-locked cellar and room.

2. **Casta Scribonia's House**

3. **Reynald Jemane's House**: Jemane, who figures in a trio of Miscellaneous quests ("Separated at Birth," "Legacy Lost," and "Sins of the Father"), is more easily found at The Grey Mare inn.

4. **Malintus Ancrus's House**: Ancrus is a low-level Security trainer, and partner Glistel a low-level Sneak trainer. Glistel's references (via the "Chorrol" topic) to the two being "well-known in certain circles" is a reference to the Thieves Guild. Both are members, and you'll meet the Gray Fox here to receive instructions for the Thieves Guild quest "Arrow of Extrication."

5. **Valus Odiil's House**: Odiil, like his neighbor, is more readily found at The Grey Mare. He'll supply the Miscellaneous quest "The Killing Field." As a medium-level trainer in Heavy Armor, he also figures in the Master Trainer quest "Heavy Armor Training."

6. **Modryn Oreyn's House**: Oreyn is a Fighters Guild quest-giver, and for his later, off-the-books quests, you'll meet him here.

7. **Alberic Litte's House**: We're a little unclear on Litte's relationship with his wife, Carmen. She lives here alone. Litte hangs out mainly at the Mages Guild and sleeps there as well. But they occasionally get together for lunch at the house. No explanations in dialogue or gossip. A Conjuration widow?

8. **Chapel of Stendarr**: You'll revive Francois Motierre in the chapel's undercroft in the Dark Brotherhood quest "The Assassinated Man."

9. **Jirolin Doran's House**

10. **Northern Goods and Trade**: Proprietor Seed-Neeus sells everything but weapons, armor, and spells from 8 a.m. to 8 p.m. When her daughter, Dar-Ma, disappears on a business trip, she also gives you the Miscellaneous quest "Shadow over Hackdirt." Finally, she's a midlevel trainer in the Mercantile skill.

11. **Renoit's Books**: Proprietor Estelle Renoit buys and sells books from 8 a.m. to 8 p.m.

12. **Arborwatch**: This mansion is Chorrol's "House for Sale."

13. **Mages Guild**: Teekeeus is the source of the Mages Guild quest "Chorrol Recommendation" (a.k.a. "Fingers of the Mountain"). The guild is one of the ready sources for the nightshade (and two of the Grand Soul Gems) required in the Miscellaneous quest "Vampire Cure." Athragar and Alberic Litte (barter gold: 20) are medium-level trainers of Alteration and Conjuration, respectively. Both sell spells, and Alberic is also your source on the bad blood between Teekeeus and Earana in the Mages Guild quest "Chorrol Recommendation." Angalmo is a low-level Mysticism trainer who sells ingredients, alchemical equipment, miscellaneous items, and potions. Contumeliorus Florius recharges magic items. And many useful books can be found in the guild's expansive library, which contains well over 300 volumes.

14. **Fighters Guild**: You'll need to see Vilena Donton for admittance to the guild. Modryn Oreyn supplies you with periodic duties quests and, beginning with "Trolls of Forsaken Mine," a series of renegade missions that send you up against the competing Blackwood Company. Sabine Laul can put you onto the location of the Weatherleah estate in the Miscellaneous quest "Legacy Lost." She'll also buy and sell weapons, armor, torches, and miscellaneous items and offer repair services. (You can also get repair services from the generic guild porter.) Lum gro-Baroth is a medium-level Block trainer.

15. **North Gate**: To the Orange Road.

16. **Francois Motierre's House**: You'll "kill" this fellow here—and then resurrect him under the Chorrol chapel—in the Dark Brotherhood quest "The Assassinated Man."

17. **The Oak and Crosier**: Proprietor Talasma offers room and board. Given the perception in town that The Oak's an upscale establishment, the room's a surprisingly cheap 10 gold. Thieves Guild uber-fence Fathis Ules hangs out here for the Miscellaneous quest "Sins of the Father." (See the Imperial City—Elven Gardens District map for details on Ules.)

18. **South Gate**: You can enter the linked towers to the east and west. (They're mainly storage/break rooms.)

19. **Rimalus Bruiant's House**: Bruiant and his wife, Rena, are celebrated locally for their dogs, Kezune ("Kezu") and Bailey. They seem to be mainly Rena's dogs. They follow her all over town.

20. **Vilena Donton's House**: Home to the gun-shy head of the Fighters Guild and, more importantly, to her remaining son, Viranus. You'll accompany him in the Fighters Guild quest "The Master's Son" and find his body in "Trolls of Forsaken Mine."

21. **Fire and Steel**: Proprietor Rasheda buys and sells weapon, armor, torches, and miscellaneous items and offers repair services from 8 a.m. to 8 p.m. She's also a midlevel Armorer trainer.

22. **The Grey Mare**: Proprietor Emfrid supplies room and board. The room's 10 gold. She's also a good source of info on topics relevant to Chorrol and its environs. This low-end pub is also a home away from home to Earana, who plays a significant role in the Mages Guild quest "Chorrol Recommendation" (a.k.a. "Fingers of the Mountain"); a second home to Valus Odiil (quest-giver for the Miscellaneous quest "The Killing Field") and drunken Reynald Jemane (quest-giver for the Miscellaneous quest "Separated at Birth"); and a waypoint for his brother Guilbert (quest-giver for the companion Miscellaneous quest "Legacy Lost"). Regular Gaturn gro-Gonk is just an object lesson on what happens to Fighters Guild members who don't mind their Ps and Qs.

23. **Castle Chorrol**: You may see Countess Valga to secure additional troops in the "Allies for Bruma" segment of the Main Quest. She'll also provide the Miscellaneous quest "Canvas the Castle." One option in the Miscellaneous quest "Sins of the Father" is to return the Honorblade of Chorrol to castle steward Laythe Wavrick. Castle mage Chanel is a low-level Destruction trainer.

24. **Honditar's House**: This medium-level Athletics trainer can provide some dirt on Hackdirt in the Miscellaneous quest "Shadow over Hackdirt."

25. **North Country Stables**: From 8 a.m. to 8 p.m., the ostler, Bongond, will sell you a Chestnut Horse for 2,500 gold.

26. **Weynon Priory**: Your first stop in the Main Quest after your escape from the Imperial City Prison. See the Main Quest's map section for details.

27. **Statue—The Touch of the Healer's Hand**: Represents the Second Era healer, St. Osla, ministering to the fallen at the Sack of Sancre Tor.

28. **Beggar's Sleeping Mat**: Lazy Kaslowyn sleeps here.

29. **Beggar's Sleeping Mat**: Nemus the Mooch sleeps here.

30. **Crumbling Mine**: A Bandit lair that stretches beneath the city walls.

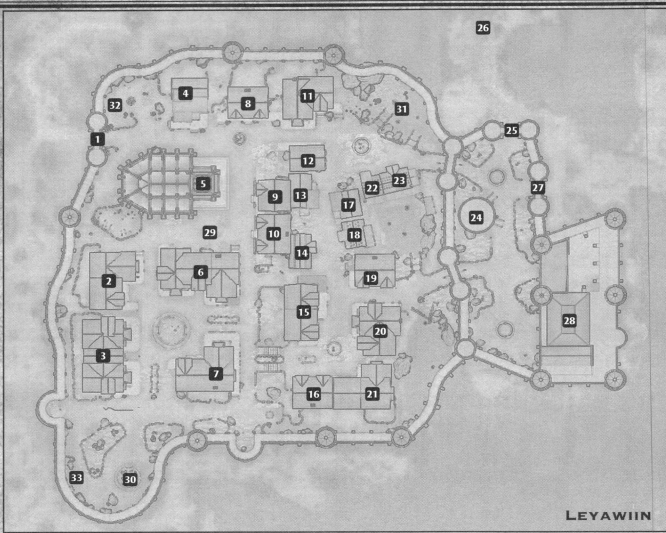

LEYAWIIN

City Maps

1. **West Gate:** To the Green Road and points north.

2. **Southern Books:** Proprietor Bugak gro-Bol buys and sells books from 8 a.m. to 8 p.m. He's also a trainer in the Blunt skill. ("Blunt" might be said to be gro-Bol's personal style; his greeting is "buy a goddam book.")

3. **Mages Guild:** Agata gives you the Mages Guild quest "Leyawiin Recommendation." S'drassa gives you the Miscellaneous quest "Tears of the Savior." Dagail is the master trainer in Mysticism. Alves Uvenim can give you the location of the shrine to the Daedra lord Nocturnal.

4. **Five Claws Lodge:** Proprietor Witseidutsei offers room and board. The room's 10 gold. You'll calm some anxious spirits here in the Fighters Guild quest "Drunk and Disorderly."

5. **Great Chapel of Zenithar:** Avrus Adas sells spells here.

6. **Fighters Guild:** Sherina is a midlevel Blade trainer. Brodras is a low-level trainer in the Heavy Armor skill. You'll meet Modryn Oreyn here in the Fighters Guild quest "Azani Blackheart."

7. **Blackwood Company Hall:** The home base of the Fighters Guild's nemesis. You'll visit the hall when you go undercover in the Fighters Guild quest "Infiltration" and again in that quest line's finale, "The Hist." Jeetum-Zee is your initial contact in "Infiltration." In "The Hist," you'll have to kill him, Ja'Fazir, and Ri'Zakar to get the cellar key and then kill mage attendants Sings-Like-Thunder and Hears-Voices-in-the-Air in the basement to destroy the Hist tree.

8. **The Dividing Line:** Proprietor Tun-Zeeus buys and sells weapons, armor, torches, and miscellaneous items, and offers repair services from 8 a.m. to 8 p.m.

9. **Margarte's House:** Margarte provides work for the downtrodden members of the local Fighters Guild in the quest "Drunk and Disorderly." She's also a medium-level trainer in the Mercantile skill. Husband Eitar works as a smith at The Dividing Line and provides repair services and low-level Armorer training.

10. **Three Sisters Inn:** The sisters are Shamada, Shomara, and Shuravi. We're guessing they're Khajiits. Shamada's the hostess, Shomara cooks, and Shuravi actually runs

CITY MAPS

the joint. She'll offer rooms at 40 gold a night as well as food and drink. Points of interest: This is one of the better locations for whacking Caelia Draconis in the Dark Brotherhood quest "Next of Kin." And Shamada also alludes to some trouble involving the Trans-Niben region that you won't hear much about elsewhere.

11. **Best Goods and Guarantees**: Proprietor Gundalas and assistant Elsynia buy and sell everything but spells from 8 a.m. to 8 p.m.

12. **Ra'Jahirr's House**

13. **Cingor's House**: He's Leyawiin's one-man Neighborhood Watch. But we suspect it's just a cover. He's also in the Mythic Dawn. No one tells you so. The only hint is the copy of the *Commentaries on the Mysterium Xarxes* Book 2, which you'll find on a bed. He's not set up to attack you, but you can enrage him into attacking by talking down his Disposition.

14. **House for Sale**

15. **Rosentia Gallenus's House**: Ms. Gallenus is having some trouble with a Daedric staff. You'll fix things for her in the Miscellaneous quest "Whom Gods Annoy."

16. **Mahei's House**: An informal mini-quest: Numeen is looking for her husband, the low-level Athletics trainer Mahei. If he's not home, you can go looking for him. (Usually, he's fairly close to his wife.) You'll learn from Mahei that he's hiding from her. And a curiosity: The couple is pals with Countess Alessia Caro. If Numeen's at home and the Thieves Guild quest "Ahdarji's Heirloom" isn't running, there's a 50 percent chance the lady will visit Numeen. The Argonians dine at the castle on Wednesdays and the countess at their home on Thursdays.

17. **Dar Jee's House**: This second in the line of Thieves Guild fences buys and sells everything save spells from 8 p.m. to 6 a.m. You'll find him right in front of his house during those hours.

18. **Weebam-Na's House**: The Rat hunter Weebam-Na and his partner, Bejeen, have a key part in the Daedric quest "Nocturnal," and Weebam has a small one in the Miscellaneous quest "Mazoga the Orc."

19. **Ahdarji's House**: You'll recover a lost ring for this lady in the Thieves Guild quest "Ahdarji's Heirloom." In addition, she's a midlevel trainer in Light Armor.

20. **J'Bari's House**: J'Bari is the master of Light Armor. You'll have to find him a new Elven cuirass in the Master Trainer quest "Light Armor Training." Housemate Tsrava is a medium trainer in Acrobatics.

21. **Alval Uvani's House**: You'll assassinate this traveling merchant in the Dark Brotherhood quest "A Matter of Honor." This is the best location for the bump-off, as Uvani lives alone. (Unfortunately, he's rarely here.) But whether you kill him here or not, search this rented house. On the second floor, enter the northern room and activate the picture over the head of the bed. You've just found the only safe in the game. Pick the five-tumbler lock—there's no key—and you'll find a copy of the Dark Brotherhood charter and the hood and robe of a member of the Brotherhood's governing Black Hand.

22. **Otumeel's House**: This fellow has an odd pastime. If you raise his Disposition to 50, he'll confess that he breaks into people's houses and doesn't steal things. He just rearranges them. (That said, we've never actually seen him do this.)

23. **Betto Plotius's House**

24. **City Watch Barracks**: One of your targets in the Dark Brotherhood quest "Next of Kin," Caelia Draconis, sleeps here. But trying to off her here with guards all around is effectively committing suicide. (After you kill Adamus Phillida in the Dark Brotherhood quest "Permanent Retirement," his bodyguard will commit actual suicide here.)

25. **North Gate**

26. **Coast Guard Station**: Your best bet for killing Adamus Phillida in the Dark Brotherhood quest "Permanent Retirement" comes when he leaves this station without his armor. After the Main Quest ends, Phillida pal Decentius Opsius spins a good yarn about Torral the Pilot.

27. **Northeast Gate**

28. **Castle Leyawiin**: You may visit the castle to secure additional troops in the "Allies for Bruma" segment of the Main Quest; to assist Mazoga the Orc in the Miscellaneous quest of the same name; to take on a "Knights of the White Stallion" Miscellaneous quest (which involves killing the leader of the Black Bow bandits); and to strip the countess and her dinner guests down to their skivvies in the Daedric quest "Sanguine."

29. **Statue of Zenithar**: God of Work and Commerce.

30. **Statue of Torval the Pilot**: The First Era High Elf explorer who charted the sea lanes around Tamriel and who discovered the River Niben.

31. **Pond**: This is where the Thieves Guild fence Dar Jee occasionally swims.

32. **Beggar's Sleeping Mat**: Deeh the Scalawag sleeps here.

33. **Beggar's Sleeping Mat**: Rancid Radirsha sleeps here.

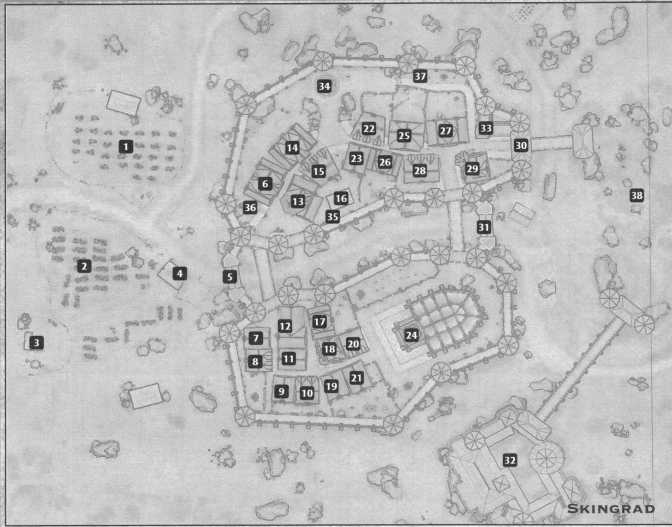

SKINGRAD

1. **Surilie Brothers Vineyards:** One of Skingrad's two competing wine-makers.

2. **Tamika Vineyards:** And the other. Even competitor Davide Surilie acknowledges that Tamika's wine is superior to his own!

3. **Sheep Shed:** Used by Uuras the Shepherd's small flock.

4. **Grateful Pass Stables:** From 8 a.m. to 8 p.m., ostler Ugak gra-Mogakh will sell you a Bay Horse for 1,000 gold.

5. **West Gate:** To Kvatch and Anvil.

6. **Fighters Guild:** Low-level Block trainer Fadus Calidius knows the locations of the Daedric shrine to Sanguine and Goblin Jim's Cave. Ah-Malz knows the location of Derelict Mine. The guild porter offers repair services.

7. **Reman Broder's House:** Vineyard worker Broder is a medium-level Marksman trainer.

8. **Ambroise Canne's House:** Canne's a midlevel trainer in the Block skill—meaning he plays a role in the Master Trainer quest "Block Training."

9. **Undena Orethi's House:** Undena has an unusual lifestyle: She's a self-proclaimed pilgrim in search of the perfect tomato. (Apparently it lies along the Gold Road east of the city. Every so often she'll head out that way and pause on a hillside—as if waiting for something.) Nords, Orcs, Khajiits, and Argonians like Orethi's own tomatoes just fine.

10. **Uuras the Shepherd's House:** His flock can be found west of town, and you'll find 20 samples of yarn in his house. But Uuras's real love is cheese (and Athletics, in which discipline he is a low-level trainer.)

11. **Salmo the Baker's House:** Skingrad is famous for his sweetrolls. It's an ingredient with three positive effects—Restore Fatigue (first), Resist Disease (second), Fortify Health (fourth)—and one adverse one (Damage Personality). However, he doesn't sell them himself, but delivers them to the neighboring Two Sisters Lodge and the West Weald Inn.

12. **Two Sisters Lodge:** Proprietor Mog gra-Mogakh offers room (10 gold) and board. The other sister, Ugak, runs the stables (#4) outside town. The four Vampire

hunters in the Mages Guild quest "Information at a Price" are staying here.

13. **West Weald Inn**: Proprietor Erina Jeranus provides room (20 gold) and board. The tenants are a colorful bunch. You'll meet Maglir, Oblivion's Designated Obnoxious Wood Elf, in the Fighters Guild quest "Unfinished Business." You can also run into Count Hassildor's butler, Shum gro-Yarug, in the Thieves Guild quest "Lost Histories." In the wine cellar, you'll find Sinderion, who's instrumental in the Miscellaneous quest "Seeking Your Roots" and, as master of the Alchemy skill, in the Master Trainer quest "Alchemy Training." (This renaissance man also sells ingredients, alchemical equipment, and potions.) And Else God-Hater, while not expressly hooked into a quest, will supply a fairly elaborate backstory for her name. This spellsword is also a Mythic Dawn agent who blows cover and attacks on your approach after you've completed the "Dagon Shrine" mission in the Main Quest. The giveaway: The presence of Book 2 of the *Commentaries on the Mysterium Xarxes* on a desk in her room upstairs.

14. **Mages Guild**: Adrienne Berene gives you the guild's "Skingrad Recommendation" quest. Druja can help you with it, and if you're a pretty bad guy, Sulinus Vassinus will actually do the quest for you. All three of them sell spells, and the last two offer low-level Mysticism and Conjuration training, respectively. Vigge the Cautious recharges magical items.

15. **Colovian Traders**: Proprietor Gunder buys and sells everything but spells. You can find Count Hassildor's butler, Shum gro-Yarug, here in the Thieves Guild quest "Lost Histories" or if you're buying a house in Skingrad. (If the latter, you can hire a servant here as well.) This is also the current residence of Eyja, the maid who can be hired to keep Rosethorn Hall clean.

16. The West Weald Inn's own disused stable.

17. **Surilie Brothers' House**: Gaston and Davide run the winery north of the Gold Road to the west of town. Davide is the third person you'll be directed by Glarthir to tail in the Miscellaneous quest "Paranoia."

18. **Glarthir's House**: Skingrad's resident eccentric, Glarthir thinks three townies are plotting against him and sends you out to watch them (with nasty consequences) in the Miscellaneous quest "Paranoia."

19. **Bernadette Peneles's House**: One source of Glarthir's paranoia is this vineyard worker, who has no designs whatsoever on her neighbor.

20. **Shameer's House**: Low-level trainers don't kick you up the line to their medium-level counterparts. This Marksman trainer is the exception: She refers you to medium Marksman trainer Reman Broder.

21. **Tamika's House**: Home of wine-maker Davide Surilie (see #2).

22. **Lazare Milvan's House**: This nobleman has a bad habit of challenging people to duels.

23. **All Things Alchemical**: Falanu Hlaalu buys and sells ingredients, alchemical equipment, and potions from 8 a.m. to 8 p.m. Hlaalu points you to the Daedric shrine to Sanguine. And, in the Miscellaneous quest "Seeking Your Roots," he is alone among Cyrodiil's alchemists in revealing that Sinderion is at the West Weald Inn. And we think he's up to something really nasty in the Graveyard, too.

24. **Great Chapel of Julianos**: Tumindil sells spells. Marie Palielle is a low-level Restoration trainer. The chapel undercroft is haunted.

25. **Nerastarel's House**: And so is this house! You'll find three leveled undead creatures downstairs and one to three upstairs. Are they guards or visitors themselves? In any case, they're wrecking the place. Nerastarel himself doesn't appear in the game, and no clue is offered as to his whereabouts.

26. **Hammer and Tongs**: Proprietor Agnete the Pickled buys and sells weapons, armor, torches, and miscellaneous items and offers repair services from 8 a.m. to 8 p.m. She has a reputation both for her armor-repair skills and the ferocity of her hangovers.

27. **Summitmist Manor**: You'll kill everyone here in the Dark Brotherhood quest "Whodunit?"

28. **Rosethorn Hall**: Skingrad's House for Sale is the most lavish and expensive in the game. It comes with a pair of attached Freeform mini-quests: "Helping Hands" and "The Rosethorn Cache."

29. **Toutius Sextius's House**: Target #2 of the paranoid Glarthir in the Miscellaneous quest "Paranoia."

30. **East Gate** (high)

31. **East Gate** (low)

32. **Castle Skingrad**: You can visit the castle to obtain a troop commitment in the Main Quest segment "Allies for Bruma," and you'll be back in the Mages Guild quests "Ulterior Motives" and "Information at a Price"; in the Thieves Guild quest "Lost Histories" and the Miscellaneous quest "Vampire Cure"; to pick up orders for the Dark Brotherhood quest "Broken Vows"; and possibly to collect some rare wine in the Master Trainer quest "Alchemy Training."

33. **Town Guard House**

34. **Statue of King Rislav Larich**: Rislav the Righteous on his horse with his hawk on his hand.

35. **Beggar's Sleeping Mat**: Foul Fagus sleeps here.

36. **Beggar's Sleeping Mat**: Nigidius the Needy sleeps here.

37. *Lost Histories of Tamriel*: Theranis hid this book here for the Thieves Guild quest "Lost Histories."

38. **Amusei's Meeting Place**: In the Thieves Guild quest "Lost Histories," you have to get Amusei to this spot before he will tell you where the book is hidden.

INDEX

INDEX

CREDITS

BETHESDA SOFTWORKS

Written By
Peter Olafson

Additional Writing
Erik Caponi
Brian Chapin
Jon Paul Duval
Kurt Kuhlmann
Al Nanes
Mark Nelson
Bruce Nesmith
Emil Pagliarulo
Ken Rolston

Additional Screenshots:
Matt Carofano
Tony Greco

Editor-in-Chief
Pete Hines

Production Coordinators
Ashley Cheng
Jeff Gardiner
Craig Lafferty

Additional Production Support
Erin Losi
Paris Nourmohammadi

Maps and Layout/Design work
Lindsay Muller
Mike Wagner

Oblivion **created by**
Bethesda Game Studios

Oblivion **Executive Producer**
Todd Howard

Special thanks to: Tim Lindsay, Mike Ryan, Tim Lamb, Kevin Kauffman, Mike Lipari and, of course, everyone else at Bethesda Softworks, Bethesda Game Studios, and ZeniMax Media, Inc.

PRIMA GAMES

Managing Editor
Jill Hinckley

Editors
Kate Abbott
Alaina Yee

Copyeditor
Deana Shields

Guide Design
Marc Riegel

Guide Layout
James Knight